Blue Notes

The author in rehearsal
(photo taken by Cris Hamilton)

Blue Notes

Profiles of Jazz Personalities

Robert P. Vande Kappelle

RESOURCE *Publications* • Eugene, Oregon

BLUE NOTES
Profiles of Jazz Personalities

Copyright © 2011 Robert P. Vande Kappelle . All rights reserved. Except for brief quotations in critical publications or reviews, no part of this book may be reproduced in any manner without prior written permission from the publisher. Write: Permissions, Wipf and Stock Publishers, 199 W. 8th Ave., Suite 3, Eugene, OR 97401.

Resource Publications
An Imprint of Wipf and Stock Publishers
199 W. 8th Ave., Suite 3
Eugene, OR 97401
www.wipfandstock.com

ISBN 13: 978-1-61097-283-3
Manufactured in the U.S.A.

To
John Bauerlein
Paul Nagy
Mike Sakash
[awesome trio of jazz mentors]

and

Tony Mowad
radio host of WDUQ FM's nightly jazz show,
whose signature sign-off reminds us to
"keep a bit of love in our heart
and a taste of jazz in our soul."

America's secret weapon is a blue note in a minor key.
—Felix Belair Jr.

The story of jazz is a miniature history of the modern mind . . . No jazz is an island. All jazz is part of the mainland of Western spiritual development.
—William Grossman

The reflection of life in all its complexity has no truer image than that found in jazz . . . In a century rife with the predictable, the dehumanizing, and the dispiriting, jazz affirmed the fresh, the human, the hopeful. It came to represent humanity at its best: striving for beauty, personal achievement, and perfection, and communicating a message that brings pleasure to the world.
—John Edward Hasse

Jazz is spontaneous, honest, and natural, and it is a celebration of life itself.
—Tony Bennett

Contents

Directory of Featured Artists   ix
Acknowledgments   xxi
Introduction   xxiii

1   January   1

2   February   36

3   March   69

4   April   105

5   May   140

6   June   177

7   July   212

8   August   248

9   September   284

10   October   318

11   November   353

12   December   387

Jazz Trivia Quiz   423
Appendix I: Entry Points for the Enjoyment of Jazz Music   431
Appendix II: Recommended Entry-level Recordings   432
Appendix III: Historical Overview (including Jazz Styles and Timeline)   433
Select Bibliography   445
Topical Index   447
Index of Names   449

Directory of Featured Artists

Jazz Notables	Page	DOB	DOD	Area of Renown
A				
Abrams, Muhal Richard	303	Sept. 19, 1930		pianist/composer
Adams, Pepper	325	Oct. 8, 1930	Sep. 10, 1986	bari saxophonist
Adderley, Cannonball	299	Sept. 15, 1928	Aug. 8, 1975	alto saxophonist
Ali, Rashied	212	July 1, 1935	Aug. 12, 2009	drummer
Allen, Harry	330	Oct. 12. 1966		tenor saxophonist
Allyson, Karrin	241	July 27, 1964		vocalist
Altschul, Barry	6	Jan. 6, 1943		drummer
Ammons, Gene	120	Apr. 14, 1925	Aug. 6, 1974	tenor saxophonist
Armstrong, Lil (Hardin)	38	Feb. 3, 1898?	Aug. 27, 1971	pianist/vocalist
Armstrong, Louis	215	Aug. 4, 1901	July 6, 1971	trumpeter/vocalist
Auld, Georgie	161	May 19, 1919	Jan. 8, 1990	tenor saxophonist
Ayers, Roy	294	Sept. 10, 1940		vibraphonist
Ayler, Albert	226	July 13, 1936	Nov. 1970	tenor saxophonist
B				
Bailey, Buster	232	July 19, 1902	Apr. 12, 1967	clarinetist/sop sax
Baker, Chet	411	Dec. 23, 1929	May 13, 1988	trumpet/vocalist
Barbarin, Paul	145	May 5, 1899	Feb 17, 1969	drummer
Barbieri, Gato	383	Nov. 28, 1934		tenor sax/composer
Barnet, Charlie	346	Oct. 26, 1913	Sept. 4, 1991	sax/leader
Basie, Count	271	Aug. 21, 1904	Apr. 26, 1984	leader/pianist
Bates, Django	319	Oct. 2, 1960		pianist/trumpet/comp
Bechet, Sidney	155	May 14, 1897	May 14, 1959	clarinetist/s sax
Beiderbecke, Bix	79	Mar. 10, 1903	Aug. 6, 1931	cornetist
Bellson, Louie	217	July 6, 1924	Feb. 14, 2009	drummer/leader
Bennett, Tony	250	Aug. 3, 1926		vocalist
Benson, George	93	Mar. 22, 1943		guitarist/vocalist
Berendt, Joachim-Ernst	233	July 20, 1922	Feb. 4, 2000	writer/producer
Berigan, Bunny	354	Nov. 2, 1908	June 2, 1942	trumpeter/leader
Bernstein, Artie	39	Feb. 4, 1909	Jan. 4, 1964	bassist

Directory of Featured Artists

Name	Page	Born	Died	Role
Berry, Chu	297	Sept. 13, 1908	Oct. 30, 1941	tenor saxophonist
Berton, Vic	216	July 5, 1896	Dec. 26, 1951	drummer
Bigard, Barney	71	Mar. 3, 1906	June 27, 1980	clarinetist
Blakey, Art	329	Oct. 11, 1919	Oct. 16, 1990	drummer/leader
Blanton, Jimmy	323	Oct. 1918	July 30, 1942	bassist
Blesh, Rudi	23	Jan. 21, 1899	Aug. 25, 1985	writer/producer
Bley, Paul	363	Nov. 10, 1932		pianist
Bolden, Buddy	290	Sept. 6, 1877	Nov. 4, 1931	cornetist
Bose, Sterling	60	Feb. 23, 1906	June 1958	trumpeter
Boswell, Connee	389	Dec. 3, 1907	Oct. 11, 1976	vocalist
Brackeen, JoAnne	240	July 26, 1938		pianist
Braxton, Anthony	180	June 4, 1945		alto sax/clarinetist
Brecker, Michael	101	Mar. 29, 1949	Jan. 3, 2007	tenor saxophonist
Breuker, Willem	356	Nov. 4, 1944	July 23, 2010	sax/clarinet/composer
Brown, Clifford	350	Oct. 30, 1930	June 26, 1956	trumpeter
Brown, Marion	292	Sept. 8, 1931	Oct. 10, 2010	alto saxophonist
Brubeck, Dave	392	Dec. 6, 1920		pianist/composer
Brunis, Georg	41	Feb. 6, 1902	Nov. 19, 1974	trombonist
Burns, Ralph	209	June 29, 1922	Nov. 21, 2001	arranger/composer
Burnside, Vi	125	Apr. 19, 1915	Nov. 19, 1964	tenor saxophonist
Burrell, Kenny	246	July 31, 1931		guitarist
Butterfield, Billy	15	Jan. 14, 1917	Mar. 18, 1988	trumpeter
Byrd, Donald	395	Dec. 9, 1932		trumpeter/educator
Byron, Don	361	Nov. 8, 1958		clarinetist

C

Name	Page	Born	Died	Role
Calloway, Cab	413	Dec. 25, 1907	Nov. 18, 1994	vocalist/leader
Carmichael, Hoagy	376	Nov. 22, 1899	Dec. 27, 1981	song writer/pianist
Carney, Harry	105	Apr. 1, 1910	Oct. 8, 1974	bari saxophonist
Carter, Benny	256	Aug. 8, 1907	July 12, 2003	a sax/trumpeter
Carter, James	3	Jan. 3, 1969		tenor saxophonist
Carter, Ron	143	May 4, 1937		bassist
Catlett, Sid	18	Jan. 17, 1910	Mar. 25, 1951	drummer
Charlap, Bill	333	Oct. 15, 1966		pianist
Cheatham, Doc	190	June 13, 1905	June 2, 1997	trumpeter
Cherry, Don	372	Nov. 18, 1936	Oct. 19, 1995	cornetist
Christian, Charlie	244	July 29, 1916	Mar. 2, 1942	guitarist
Christy, June	374	Nov. 20, 1925	June 21, 1990	vocalist

Directory of Featured Artists

Clark, Sonny	234	July 12, 1931	Jan. 13, 1963	pianist
Clarke, Kenny	2	Jan. 2, 1914	Jan. 26, 1985	drummer
Clayton, Buck	365	Nov. 12, 1911	Dec. 8, 1991	trumpeter
Cobb, Jimmy	23	Jan. 20, 1929		drummer
Cole, Cozy	335	Oct. 17, 1906	Jan. 29, 1981	drummer
Cole, Nat "King"	87	Mar. 17, 1917	Feb. 15, 1965	pianist/vocalist
Coleman, Ornette	78	Mar. 9, 1930		sax/composer
Coleman, Steve	305	Sept. 20, 1956		alto saxophonist
Coltrane, John	308	Sept. 23, 1926	July 17, 1967	t and s saxophonist
Colyer, Ken	124	Apr. 18, 1928	Mar. 8, 1988	trumpeter/guitarist
Connick, Harry, Jr.	295	Sept. 11, 1967		pianist/vocalist
Corea, Chick	189	June 12, 1941		pianist/composer
Coryell, Larry	106	Apr. 2, 1943		guitarist
Cox, Ida	62	Feb. 25, 1896	Nov. 10, 1967	vocalist
Crosby, Bing	141	May 2, 1904	Oct. 14, 1977	vocalist

D

Dameron, Tadd	58	Feb. 21, 1917	Mar. 8, 1965	comp/leader/pianist
Daniels, Eddie	338	Oct. 19, 1941		clarinetist/tenor sax
Davis, Eddie "Lockjaw"	70	Mar. 2, 1922	Nov. 3, 1986	tenor saxophonist
Davis, Miles	168	May 25, 1926	Sept. 28, 1991	trumpeter/leader
Davison, Wild Bill	5	Jan. 5, 1906	Nov. 14, 1989	cornetist
Dearie, Blossom	136	Apr. 28, 1926	Feb. 7, 2009	vocalist/pianist
DeFrancesco, Joey	115	Apr. 10, 1971		organist
DeFranco, Buddy	53	Feb. 17, 1923		clarinetist
DeJohnette, Jack	257	Aug. 9, 1942		drummer
Delaunay, Charles	19	Jan. 18, 1911	Feb. 16, 1988	writer/producer
De Paris, Wilbur	12	Jan. 11, 1900	Jan. 3, 1973	trombonist
Dixon, Bill	322	Oct. 5, 1925	June 16, 2010	trumpeter/composer
Dodds, Baby	412	Dec. 24, 1898	Feb. 14, 1959	drummer
Dolphy, Eric	198	June 20, 1928	June 29, 1964	a sax/b clarinet/flute
Domnérus, Arne	408	Dec. 20, 1924	Sept. 2, 2008	alto sax/clarinetist
Dorham, Kenny	281	Aug. 30, 1924	Dec. 5, 1972	trumpeter
Dorsey, Jimmy	67	Feb. 29, 1904	June 12, 1957	clarinet/sax/leader
Dorsey, Tommy	382	Nov. 27, 1905	Nov. 26, 1956	trombonist/leader
Drew Sr., Kenny	279	Aug. 28, 1928	Aug. 4, 1993	pianist

E

Eckstine, Billy	220	July 8, 1914	Mar. 8, 1993	vocalist/leader

Directory of Featured Artists

Eldridge, Roy	33	Jan. 30, 1911	Feb. 26, 1989	trumpeter/leader
Ellington, Duke	137	Apr. 29, 1899	May 24, 1974	comp/lead/pianist
Eubanks, Kevin	369	Nov. 15, 1957		guitarist/leader
Europe, James Reese	59	Feb. 22, 1881	May 10, 1919	leader
Evans, Bill	265	Aug. 16, 1929	Sept. 15, 1980	pianist
Evans, Gil	154	May 13, 1912	Mar. 20, 1988	arr/comp/pianist
Evans, Herschel	248	[Aug. 1] 1909	Feb. 9, 1939	tenor saxophonist

F

Favors, Malachi	272	Aug. 22, 1937	Jan. 29, 2004	bassist
Fitzgerald, Ella	132	Apr. 25, 1917	June 15, 1996	vocalist
Fontana, Carl	231	July 18, 1928	Oct. 10, 2003	trombonist
Fountain, Pete	214	July 3, 1930		clarinetist
Francis, Panama	409	Dec. 21, 1918	Nov. 11, 2001	drummer
Freeman, Bud	118	Apr. 13, 1906	Mar. 15, 1991	tenor saxophonist
Friesen, David	146	May 6, 1942		bassist

G

Gabler, Milt	162	May 20, 1911	July 20, 2001	producer
Gadd, Steve	114	Apr. 9, 1945		drummer
Garbarek, Jan	72	Mar. 4, 1947		tenor saxophonist
Garner, Erroll	192	June 15, 1921	Jan. 2, 1977	pianist
Gaslini, Giorgio	341	Oct. 22, 1929		pianist/composer
Getz, Stan	37	Feb. 2, 1927	June 6, 1991	tenor saxophonist
Giddins, Gary	91	Mar. 21, 1948		writer
Gilberto, Astrud	102	Mar. 30, 1940		vocalist
Gillespie, Dizzy	340	Oct. 2, 1917	Jan. 6, 1993	trumpeter/leader
Glenn, Tyree	378	Nov. 23, 1912	May 18, 1974	trombonist/vibes
Goldkette, Jean	88	Mar. 18, 1893	Mar. 24, 1962	pianist/leader
Gonella, Nat	76	Mar. 7, 1908	Aug. 7, 1998	trumpeter/voc/leader
Gonsalves, Paul	224	July 12, 1920	May 14, 1974	tenor saxophonist
Goodman, Benny	173	May 30, 1909	June 13, 1986	clarinetist/leader
Gordon, Dexter	65	Feb. 27, 1923	Apr. 25, 1990	tenor saxophonist
Grappelli, Stéphane	28	Jan. 26, 1908	Dec. 1, 1997	violinist
Gray, Glen	184	June 7, 1906	Aug. 23, 1963	a sax/leader
Gray, Wardell	49	Feb. 13, 1921	May 25, 1955	tenor saxophonist
Green, Benny	108	Apr. 4, 1963		pianist
Greer, Sonny	400	Dec. 13, 1895	Mar. 23, 1982	drummer
Grimes, Henry	355	Nov. 3, 1935		bassist
Gruntz, Georg	203	June 24, 1932		keys/comp/leader

Directory of Featured Artists

Guarnieri, Johnny	94	Mar. 23, 1917	Jan. 7, 1985	pianist/composer

H

Hackett, Bobby	34	Jan. 31, 1915	June 7, 1976	cornetist
Haden, Charlie	254	Aug. 6, 1937		bassist
Haig, Al	236	July 22, 1922	Nov. 16, 1982	pianist
Hall, Edmond	156	May 15, 1901	Feb. 11, 1967	clarinetist
Hamilton, Scott	296	Sept. 12, 1954		tenor saxophonist
Hammond, John	402	Dec. 15, 1910	July 10, 1987	producer
Hampton, Lionel	127	Apr. 20, 1908	Sept. 1, 2002	vibraphonist
Hancock, Herbie	117	Apr. 12, 1940		pianist/composer
Hardwick, Otto	175	May 31, 1904	Aug. 5, 1970	alto saxophonist
Hargrove, Roy	334	Oct. 16, 1969		trumpeter
Hasselgard, Stan	321	Oct. 4, 1922	Nov. 23, 1948	clarinetist
Hawkins, Coleman	375	Nov. 21, 1904	May 19, 1969	tenor saxophonist
Heath, Percy	138	Apr. 30, 1923	April 28, 2005	bassist
Hemphill, Julius	26	Jan. 24, 1938	Apr. 2, 1995	a sax/comp/leader
Henderson, Fletcher	406	Dec. 18, 1897	Dec. 29, 1952	leader/arr/pianist
Henderson, Joe	131	Apr. 24, 1937	June 30, 2001	tenor saxophonist
Hentoff, Nat	187	June 10, 1925		writer
Herman, Woody	157	May 16, 1913	Oct. 29, 1987	lead/clarinetist/voc
Hill, Teddy	393	Dec. 7, 1909	May 19, 1978	tenor sax/leader
Hines, Earl	417	Dec. 28, 1903	Apr. 22, 1983	pianist/leader
Hinton, Milt	202	June 23, 1910	Dec. 19, 2000	bassist
Hirt, Al	360	Nov. 7, 1922	Apr. 27, 1999	trumpeter
Hodes, Art	367	Nov. 14, 1904	Mar. 4, 1993	pianist/prod/writer
Hodges, Johnny	239	July 25, 1907	May 11, 1970	alto and soprano sax
Holiday, Billie	112	Apr. 7, 1915	July 17, 1959	vocalist
Holland, Dave	318	Oct. 1, 1946		bassist/comp
Horn, Shirley	140	May 1, 1934	Oct. 20, 2005	vocalist/piano
Horne, Lena	210	June 30, 1917	May 9, 2010	vocalist
Hyman, Dick	77	Mar. 8, 1927		keys/comp/arranger

I

Ingham, Keith	40	Feb. 5, 1942		pianist

J

Jamal, Ahmad	213	July 2, 1930		pianist
James, Harry	85	Mar. 15, 1916	July 5, 1983	trumpeter/leader
Jarman, Joseph	298	Sept. 14, 1937		reeds/composer
Jarreau, Al	81	Mar. 12, 1940		vocalist

Directory of Featured Artists

Jarrett, Keith	148	May 8, 1945		pianist/composer
Jefferson, Carter	385	Nov. 30, 1945	Dec. 9, 1993	tenor saxophonist
Jobim, Antonio Carlos	27	Jan. 25, 1927	Dec. 8, 1994	songwriter/guitar
Johnson, Bunk	415	Dec. 27, 1889	July 7, 1949	trumpeter
Johnson, J.J.	24	Jan. 22, 1924	Feb. 4, 2001	trombonist
Johnson, James P.	36	Feb. 1, 1894	Nov. 17, 1955	pianist/composer
Johnson, Lonnie	44	Feb. 8, 1889	June 16, 1970	guitarist/vocalist
Jones, Hank	282	Aug. 31, 1918	May 16, 2010	pianist
Jones, Jo	324	Oct. 7, 1911	Sept. 3, 1985	drummer
Jones, Philly Joe	228	July 15, 1923	Aug. 30, 1985	drummer
Jones, Quincy	84	Mar. 14, 1933		arr/comp/leader/prod

K

Kaminsky, Max	291	Sept. 7, 1908	Sept. 6, 1994	trumpeter
Kelly, Wynton	388	Dec. 2, 1931	Apr. 12, 1971	pianist
Kirby, John	420	Dec. 31, 1908	June 14, 1952	bassist/leader
Kirk, Andy	171	May 28, 1898	Dec. 11, 1992	leader/bassist
Kirk, Rahsaan Roland	255	Aug. 7, 1935	Dec. 5, 1977	t sax/flute/leader
Kirkland, Kenny	314	Sept. 28, 1955	Nov. 11, 1998	keyboardist
Krall, Diana	370	Nov. 16, 1964		vocalist/piano
Krupa, Gene	16	Jan. 15, 1909	Oct. 16, 1973	drummer/lead
Kuhn, Steve	95	Mar. 24, 1938		pianist/composer

L

Lacy, Steve	237	July 23, 1934	June 4, 2004	soprano sax/comp
LaFaro, Scott	107	Apr. 3, 1936	July 6, 1961	bassist
Laine, Cleo	348	Oct. 28, 1927		vocalist
Lambert, Dave	197	June 19, 1917	Oct. 3, 1966	vocalist/arranger
Lamond, Don	267	Aug. 18, 1920	Dec. 23, 2003	drummer
Land, Harold	55	Feb. 18, 1928	July 27, 2001	tenor saxophonist
Lang, Eddie	344	Oct. 25, 1902	Mar. 26, 1933	guitarist
LaRocca, Nick	116	Apr. 11, 1889	Feb. 22, 1961	cornetist
Lee, Jeanne	32	Jan. 29, 1939	Oct. 24, 2000	vocalist
Lee, Peggy	170	May 27, 1920	Jan. 21, 2002	vocalist
Levy, Lou	73	Mar. 5, 1928	Jan. 23, 2001	pianist
Lewis, George	227	July 14, 1952		trombonist/composer
Lewis, John	142	May 3, 1920	Mar. 29, 2001	pianist/composer
Lewis, Meade "Lux"	287	Sept. 4, 1905	June 7, 1964	pianist
Lewis, Mel	150	May 10, 1929	Feb. 2, 1990	drummer/leader
Lion, Alfred	128	Apr. 21, 1908	Feb. 2, 1987	producer

Directory of Featured Artists

Lockwood, Didier	47	Feb. 11, 1956		violinist
Lovano, Joe	418	Dec. 29, 1952		tenor saxophonist
Lunceford, Jimmie	182	June 6, 1902	July 12, 1947	leader

M

Machito	52	Feb. 16, 1908	Apr. 15, 1984	lead/voc/maracas
Mangelsdorff, Albert	288	Sept. 5, 1928	July 25, 2005	trombonist/leader
Mann, Herbie	122	Apr. 16, 1930	July 1, 2003	flutist/leader
Maria, Tania	149	May 9, 1948		pianist/vocalist
Marsalis, Wynton	337	Oct. 18, 1961		trumpeter/lead/comp
Marshall, Kaiser	188	June 11, 1899?	Jan. 3, 1948	drummer
Marshall, Wendell	343	Oct. 24, 1920	Feb. 6, 2002	bassist
Matlock, Matty	135	Apr. 27, 1907	June 14, 1978	clarinetist
Mazur, Marilyn	9	Jan. 8, 1955		drummer
McConnell, Rob	50	Feb. 14, 1935	May 1, 2010	trombonist/lead/arr
McCorkle, Susannah	1	Jan. 1, 1946	May 19, 2001	vocalist
McDuff, Brother Jack	301	Sept. 17, 1926	Jan. 23, 2001	organist
McFerrin, Bobby	80	Mar. 11, 1950		vocalist
McKinley, Ray	196	June 18, 1910	May 7, 1995	drummer/vocalist
McLaughlin, John	4	Jan. 4, 1942		guitarist
McLean, Jackie	158	May 17, 1931	Mar. 31, 2006	alto saxophonist
McPartland, Marian	90	Mar. 20, 1918		pianist
McRae, Carmen	113	Apr. 8, 1920	Nov. 10, 1994	vocalist
McShann, Jay	13	Jan. 12, 1916	Dec. 7, 2006	pianist/leader
Mengelberg, Misha	181	June 5, 1935		pianist/composer
Metcalf, Louis	66	Feb. 28, 1905	Oct. 27, 1981	trumpeter
Metheny, Pat	261	Aug. 12, 1954		guitarist/composer
Mezzrow, Mezz	362	Nov. 9, 1899	Aug. 5, 1972	clarinetist
Miller, Glenn	69	Mar. 1, 1904	Dec. 15, 1944	leader/trombonist
Miller, Marcus	191	June 14, 1959		bass guitarist
Mills, Irving	17	Jan. 16, 1894	Apr. 21, 1985	publisher/lyricist
Mingus, Charles	129	Apr. 22, 1922	Jan. 5, 1979	bassist/composer
Monk, Thelonious	328	Oct. 10, 1917	Feb. 17, 1982	pianist/composer
Montgomery, Wes	74	Mar. 6, 1923	June 15, 1968	guitarist
Moreira, Airto	252	Aug. 5, 1941		percussionist
Morello, Joe	230	July 17, 1928	Mar. 12, 2011	drummer
Morgan, Lee	222	July 10, 1938	Feb. 19, 1972	trumpeter
Morton, Jelly Roll	339	Oct. 20, 1890	July 10, 1941	comp/pianist
Moten, Bennie	366	Nov. 13, 1894	Apr. 2, 1935	pianist/leader

Directory of Featured Artists

Motian, Paul	96	Mar. 25, 1931		drummer
Mulligan, Gerry	110	Apr. 6, 1927	Jan. 19, 1996	b sax/arr/leader
Murphy, Turk	403	Dec. 16, 1915	May 30, 1987	trombonist
Murray, David	56	Feb. 16, 1955		tenor saxophonist

N

Nance, Ray	397	Dec. 10, 1913	Jan. 28, 1976	trumpet/violin/voc
Nash, Lewis	419	Dec. 30, 1958		drummer
Navarro, Fats	309	Sept. 24, 1923	July 7, 1950	trumpeter
Newborn Jr., Phineas	401	Dec. 14, 1931	May 26, 1989	pianist
Newman, David Fathead	61	Feb. 24, 1933	Jan. 20, 2009	tenor saxophonist
Niehaus, Lennie	177	June 1, 1929		alto sax/composer
Noble, Ray	404	Dec. 17, 1903	Apr. 2, 1978	leader/arr/composer
Noone, Jimmie	130	Apr. 23, 1895	Apr. 19, 1944	clarinetist
Norvo, Red	103	Mar. 31, 1908	Apr. 6, 1999	vibraphonist

O

Oliver, King	151	May 11, 1885	Apr. 8?, 1938	cornetist/leader

P

Page, Hot Lips	30	Jan. 27, 1908	Nov. 5, 1954	trumpeter/vocalist
Page, Walter	45	Feb. 9, 1900	Dec. 20, 1957	bassist/leader
Parker, Charlie	280	Aug. 29, 1920	Mar. 12, 1955	alto saxophonist
Parlan, Horace	21	Jan. 19, 1931		pianist
Pass, Joe	14	Jan. 13, 1929	May 23, 1994	guitarist
Pastorius, Jaco	387	Dec. 1, 1951	Sept. 12, 1987	bass guitarist
Patitucci, Frank	410	Dec. 22, 1959		bassist
Paul, Les	186	June 9, 1915	Aug. 13, 2009	guitarist
Payton, Nicholas	311	Sept. 26, 1973		trumpeter
Peacock, Gary	153	May 12, 1935		bassist
Pepper, Art	284	Sept. 1, 1925	June 15, 1982	alto saxophonist
Peterson, Oscar	264	Aug. 15, 1925	Dec. 23, 2007	pianist
Pettiford, Oscar	316	Sept. 30, 1922	Sept. 8, 1960	bassist
Phillips, Flip	97	Mar. 26, 1915	Aug. 17, 2001	tenor saxophonist
Pizzarelli, Bucky	10	Jan. 9, 1926		guitarist
Pollack, Ben	201	June 22, 1903	June 7, 1971	drummer/leader
Ponty, Jean-Luc	315	Sept. 29, 1942		violinist
Powell, Bud	312	Sept. 27, 1924	Aug. 1, 1966	pianist
Powell, Mel	48	Feb. 12, 1923	Apr. 24, 1998	pianist/arranger
Pozo, Chano	7	Jan. 7, 1915	Dec. 2, 1948	percussionist

Q

Directory of Featured Artists

Quebec, Ike	266	Aug. 17, 1918	Jan. 16, 1963	tenor saxophonist
R				
Raeburn, Boyd	347	Oct. 27, 1913	Aug. 2, 1966	leader/saxophonist
Rainey, Ma	133	Apr. 26, 1886	Dec. 22, 1939	vocalist
Reeves, Dianne	342	Oct. 23, 1956		vocalist
Reinhardt, Django	25	Jan. 23, 1910	May 16, 1953	guitarist
Remler, Emily	302	Sept. 18, 1957	May 4, 1990	guitarist
Rivers, Sam	310	Sept. 25, 1923		saxophonist/pianist
Roach, Max	11	Jan. 10, 1924	Aug. 16, 2007	drummer
Rollins, Sonny	293	Sept. 7?, 1930		tenor saxophonist
Roppolo, Leon	86	Mar. 16, 1902	Oct. 5, 1943	clarinetist
Rosolino, Frank	270	Aug. 20, 1926	Nov. 26, 1978	trombonist
Rowles, Jimmie	269	Aug. 19, 1918	May 28, 1996	pianist
Royal, Marshal	391	Dec. 5, 1912	May 8, 1995	alto sax/clarinetist
Rudd, Roswell	371	Nov. 17, 1935		trombonist
Rushing, Jimmy	276	Aug. 26, 1903?	June 8, 1972	vocalist
Russell, William	64	Feb. 26, 1905	Aug. 9, 1992	writer/producer
Russo, Bill	204	June 25, 1928	Jan. 11, 2003	composer/arranger
S				
St. Cyr, Johnny	123	Apr. 17, 1890	June 17, 1966	guitarist/banjoist
Sanborn, David	245	July 30, 1945		alto saxophonist
Sanchez, David	286	Sept. 3, 1968		saxophonist
Sandoval, Arturo	358	Nov. 6, 1949		trumpeter/pianist
Sbarbaro, Tony	206	June 27, 1897	Oct. 30, 1969	drummer
Schifrin, Lalo	199	June 21, 1932		composer/pianist
Schuller, Gunther	364	Nov 22?, 1925		composer/conductor
Scofield, John	414	Dec. 26, 1951		guitarist
Scott, Ronnie	31	Jan. 28, 1927	Dec. 23, 1996	tenor saxophonist
Scott, Tony	195	June 17, 1921	Mar. 28, 2007	clarinetist
Shaw, Artie	165	May 23, 1910	Dec. 30, 2004	clarinetist/leader
Shearing, George	262	Aug. 13, 1919	Feb. 14, 2011	pianist
Shepp, Archie	166	May 24, 1937		saxophonist/educator
Shorter, Wayne	275	Aug. 25, 1933		saxophonist/comp
Silver, Horace	285	Sept. 2, 1928		pianist/composer
Sims, Zoot	349	Oct. 29, 1925	Mar. 23, 1985	tenor saxophonist
Sinatra, Frank	399	Dec. 12, 1915	May 14, 1998	Vocalist
Smith, Bessie	121	Apr. 15, 1894	Sept. 26, 1937	Vocalist
Smith, Bill	307	Sept. 22, 1926		clarinetist/composer

Directory of Featured Artists

Smith, Buster	274	Aug. 24, 1904	Aug. 10, 1991	alto sax/clarinetist
Smith, Jimmy	394	Dec. 8, 1925	Feb. 8, 2005	Organist
Smith, Joe "Fox"	207	June 28, 1902	Dec. 2, 1937	Trumpeter
Smith, Mamie	169	May 26, 1883	Oct. 30, 1946	Vocalist
Smith, Willie "The Lion"	380	Nov. 25, 1897	Apr. 18, 1973	Pianist
Snow, Valaida	178	June 2, 1904	May 30, 1956	trumpeter/vocalist
Solal, Martial	273	Aug. 23, 1927		pianist/arranger
Stacy, Jess	259	Aug. 11, 1904	July 1, 1995	Pianist
Stańko, Tomasz	223	July 11, 1942		Trumpeter
Staton, Dakota	179	June 3, 1931	Apr. 10, 2007	Vocalist
Steward, Herbie	147	May 7, 1926		Saxophonist
Stewart, Slam	306	Sept. 21, 1914	Dec. 10, 1987	Bassist
Strayhorn, Billy	384	Nov. 29, 1915	May 31, 1967	composer/pianist
Sun Ra	164	May 22, 1914	May 30, 1993	comp/leader/keys
Sweatman, Wilbur	42	Mar. 8, 1936	Feb. 26, 1982	clarinetist/leader

T

Tatum, Art	331	Oct. 13, 1909	Nov. 5, 1956	Pianist
Taylor, Billy	238	July 24, 1921	Dec. 28, 2010	pianist/educator
Teschemacher, Frank	82	Mar. 13, 1906	Mar. 1, 1932	clarinetist/alto sax/
Thompson, Lucky	194	June 16, 1924	July 30, 2005	Saxophonist
Thornhill, Claude	258	Aug. 10, 1909	July 1, 1965	leader/composer
Threadgill, Henry	51	Feb. 15, 1944		alto sax/composer
Tjader, Cal	229	July 16, 1925	May 5, 1982	Vibraphonist
Tristano, Lennie	89	Mar. 19, 1919	Nov. 18, 1978	pianist/educator
Turner, Big Joe	159	May 18, 1911	Nov. 24, 1985	Vocalist
Turrentine, Stanley	109	Apr. 5, 1934	Sept. 12, 2000	tenor saxophonist
Tyner, McCoy	398	Dec. 11, 1938		pianist/composer

V

Van Gelder, Rudy	381	Nov. 2, 1924		recording engineer
Vasconcelos, Naná	249	Aug. 2, 1945		percussionist
Veal, Reginald	357	Nov. 5, 1963		bassist
Veasley, Gerald	242	July 28, 1955		bass guitarist
Venuti, Joe	300	Sept. 16, 1903	Aug. 14, 1978	violinist

W

Wallace, Sippie	353	Nov. 1, 1898	Nov. 1, 1986	vocalist/pianist
Waller, Fats	163	May 21, 1904	Dec. 15, 1943	pianist/composer
Washington, Kenny	172	May 29, 1958		drummer

Directory of Featured Artists

Watanabe, Kazumi	332	Oct. 14, 1953		guitarist
Waters, Ethel	351	Oct. 31, 1896	Sept. 1, 1977	vocalist
Watrous, Bill	185	June 8, 1939		trombonist
Watters, Lu	407	Dec. 19, 1911	Nov. 5, 1989	leader/trumpeter
Webb, Chick	46	Feb. 10, 1909	June 16, 1939	drummer/leader
Webster, Ben	98	Mar. 27, 1909	Sept. 20, 1973	tenor saxophonist
Webster, Freddie	263	Aug. [14], 1916	Apr. 1, 1947	trumpeter
Wein, George	320	Oct. 3, 1925		pianist/impresario
Welsh, Alex	221	July 9, 1929	June 25, 1982	trumpeter/vocalist
Werner, Kenny	373	Nov. 19, 1951		pianist
Whiteman, Paul	99	Mar. 28, 1890	Dec. 29, 1967	leader
Wiley, Lee	327	Oct. 9, 1908	Dec. 11, 1975	vocalist
Wilson, Cassandra	390	Dec. 4, 1955		vocalist
Wilson, Nanc	57	Feb. 20, 1937		vocalist
Wilson, Teddy	779	Nov. 24, 1912	July 31, 1986	pianist
Workman, Reggie	205	June 26, 1937		bassist

Y

Young, Lester	277	Aug. 27, 1909	Mar. 15, 1959	tenor saxophonist

Z

Zawinul, Joe	219	July 7, 1932	Sept. 11, 2007	keys/composer

Acknowledgments

Music has been an ongoing passion in my life and a lifelong avocation. My love of music ultimately goes back to the influence of my mother, whose missionary work in Latin America included organ and piano accompaniment for church activities, choir directing, and singing duets with my father. She was not a trained musician, but she generously offered her humble talents wherever they were needed. She was my first piano teacher, and I am grateful for the discipline she instilled in me and for her refusal to accept hackneyed excuses such as the possibility that my fingers might break from so much practicing. "I never heard of anyone breaking their fingers playing the piano," she replied matter-of-factly, and that ended the argument. She modeled the art of compromise by setting standards I could reach before going out to play. Remarkably, piano practice became a win-win situation. I owe my piano-playing skills to her gentle determination and to other instructors during my formative years, including Dick Foulkes, a professor of theology and a world-class pianist.

During my undergraduate years, I spent several summers traveling across North America as a pianist representing The King's College, accompanying vocal quartets. One professor at the college, Mary Nocera, enlarged my musical horizons and those of other students by purchasing two season tickets at the Metropolitan Opera in New York City. The second ticket was for a friend or a student. An evening at the opera often began with a trip to an art museum, and then dinner at a fine New York City restaurant. Every college student should have at least one professor like Miss Nocera.

In the early 1990s, while teaching religious studies at Washington and Jefferson College (W&J), I audited several music classes at the college, including a course on jazz taught by John Bauerlein. In addition to the history of jazz, that course involved extensive music listening. I fell in love with the subject matter, particularly with the saxophone and its role in jazz. Shortly thereafter I began taking lessons on saxophone, then on clarinet, with Bill Manfredi, a local wind instrumentalist who included jazz duet arrangements among his instructional techniques. Upon reaching an acceptable level of proficiency, I joined the Washington and Jefferson Wind Ensemble and played tenor saxophone for six years under the direction of Michael Sakash, a talented director, performer, and composer. For several years I took private lessons with this gifted musician, including during a January term, when I audited his class in jazz improvisation. I am grateful to each of these individuals for enabling me to appreciate good music and for enlarging my perspective through their talent and passion for music.

My gratitude also extends to other colleagues at the college, including Paul Nagy, whose conversations over lunch, particularly in his retirement years, helped keep the pas-

Acknowledgments

sion for jazz alive. It was Paul who introduced me to the Pittsburgh Jazz Society, to the jazz series at the Manchester Craftsmen's Guild, to jazz programs at Pittsburgh jazz station WDUQ FM, and to the godfather of jazz in western Pennsylvania, Tony Mowad. Tony's sponsorship of jazz and his intimacy with current performers helps keep Pittsburgh on the jazz map and nurtures the jazz scene in the region. His nightly radio program on WDUQ brings enjoyment to the lives of listeners everywhere and his invaluable work as president and founder of the Pittsburgh Jazz Society is widely appreciated.

Various individuals read drafts of the manuscript during the writing process, including music professors Mike Sakash and Kyle Simpson. I am grateful for their support and commendation. Fran Verri, an employee at Jerry's Records in Pittsburgh, Pennsylvania, and a musical savant, read the manuscript and offered suggestions. Jerry, the proprietor of Jerry's Records, was consistently helpful with his time and resources. His expertise and that of his staff greatly enhanced my purchasing ability and made it possible for me to gather a sizeable collection of jazz and classical LPs at an affordable price. Additional LPs came from the estate of Dr. "Abe" Abernathy, offered generously by his widow Janet Abernathy.

I remain indebted to numerous individuals at W&J College for assistance along the way, including Claudia Sweger of the Information and Technology Services Department, Robert Reid of the Communications Department, and Rachel Bolden, John Henderson, and Anna Mae Moore of the U. Grant Library.

Heartfelt thanks go to my wife Susan for her support of my musical passion. She reminds me that it was my piano-playing ability, in addition to my uncommon last name, that made me a suitable candidate for marriage. I remind her that musicians love an audience and that evenings of musical reverie also helped seal the deal on my end.

Introduction

LIFE IS FILLED WITH profound memories, some happy and exhilarating, others sad and even tragic, but apart from the experiences that cause such memories, life would be trivial and devoid of meaning. Most of us can remember in vivid terms the specific circumstances of our lives when we heard of certain historic events: the stock market crash in 1929; the attack on Pearl Harbor; the explosion of the first atomic bomb over Hiroshima; the first lunar landing; the assassinations of John F. Kennedy, Robert Kennedy, and Martin Luther King Jr.; and more recently, the terrorist attacks on September 11, 2001.

Of life's happy memories, one of the sweetest is surely that universal experience we call our "first love," a moment of emotional infatuation or physical intimacy we treasure forever. Many music lovers can recall with comparable vividness their discovery of certain musicians, a first hearing of a song or musical performance, or an introduction to a specific musical genre such as classical, rock, soul, or jazz. For me, such memories include the first hearing of Rachmaninoff's Third Piano Concerto, recorded live at New York City's Carnegie Hall in 1958 by the twenty-three-year-old pianist Van Cliburn shortly after his stunning victory at the First International Tchaikovsky Piano Competition in Moscow at the height of the Cold War; the clarinet glissando at the start of George Gershwin's "Rhapsody in Blue"; the arresting quality of voice exhibited by a youthful Barbra Streisand at the gripping climax to her rendition of "Happy Days are Here Again"; my first exposure to the Beatles when they appeared on the Ed Sullivan show in 1964; and attending a live performance by the Cuban-born Paquito D'Rivera, whose skill and energy on clarinet and alto sax galvanized my passion for jazz. Each of these unique musical experiences has combined to form my musical treasury of "first loves."

Ken Burns recalls that when he began his PBS television series on jazz, he had perhaps two jazz records in his fairly large music collection. "Today," he states, "I can't find all the others . . . I listen to jazz all the time . . . I play it day and night, in the car, as I go to bed, as I write now, its sophisticated rhythms and elegant lines simply medicine for me."[1]

My own experience with jazz was not all that different. Prior to my "discovery" of jazz some twenty years ago, when I purchased a single jazz album at a used-record sale, I knew very little about jazz, having only a few albums in my record collection that were related to jazz, including some bossa nova albums recorded by Stan Getz and one by Brazilian vocalist Astrud Gilberto. One cold Saturday morning I was among the first to line up outside the WQED studios of Pittsburgh, Pennsylvania's classical music station. The CD era had rendered phonograph players obsolete, so patrons of the classical station had donated their old LPs for purchase by nostalgic record collectors. Hoping to find

---

1. Ward and Burns, Jazz: A History, x.

Introduction

albums by popular groups from the 1950s to the 1970s, I felt fortunate to locate some records by the Beatles and Elton John. Later, after the number of customers had decreased significantly, I made my way to the jazz section, an area that had seen a great deal of traffic earlier in the day. Though the remaining albums were in poor condition, one album caught my attention, probably more for the modernistic painting by Joan Miró on its cover than for its musical content. Titled *Time Further Out*, the recording was by the Dave Brubeck Quartet.

That night I found myself enthralled as I listened to the album, particularly to those tracks written in odd time signatures. Having listened to music—classical, popular, sacred—all my life and having performed publicly on piano and guitar, I was nevertheless transfixed. That experience was an awakening, the start of a love affair with jazz that resulted in a musical collection that has grown to thousands of albums, tapes, and CDs. Eventually I enrolled in courses on jazz and began taking lessons on the clarinet and saxophone. The purchase of that old jazz album affected my musical tastes forever. Hardly a day has gone by since that I have not listened to jazz, talked with others about it, analyzed it, or done research on the subject.

My induction into the jazz fraternity, I've since discovered, has been replicated many times. Jimmy McPartland, a founding member of the group of Chicago youngsters known since the 1920s as the Austin High Gang, recalls how in 1922 he and a few of his schoolmates first became interested in jazz:

> Every day after school, Frank Teschemacher and Bud Freeman, Jim Lannigan, my brother Dick, myself, and a few others used to go to a little place called the Spoon and Straw. It was just an ice-cream parlor where you'd get a malted milk, soda, shakes, and all that stuff. But they had a Victrola there, and we used to sit around listening to the bunch of records laid on the table . . . This went along for two or three months; we'd go in there every day, and one day they had some new Gennett records on the table, and we put them on. They were by the New Orleans Rhythm Kings, and I believe the first tune we played was "Farewell Blues." Boy, when we heard that—I'll tell you we went out of our minds. Everybody flipped. It was wonderful . . . We stayed there from about three in the afternoon until eight at night, just listening to those records one after another, over and over again. Right then and there we decided we would get a band and try to play like these guys.[2]

Another such convert, jazz critic Gene Lees, recalled his discovery of jazz pianist Bill Evans, which occurred in 1959, shortly after he joined the jazz periodical *Down Beat*: "In the office, I noticed among a stack of records awaiting assignment for review a gold-covered Riverside album titled *Everybody Digs Bill Evans*, bearing the signed endorsements of Miles Davis, Cannonball Adderley, Ahmad Jamal, and others of like stature. I took the album home and, sometime after dinner, probably about nine o'clock, put it on the phonograph. At 4 A.M. I was still listening, though by now I had it memorized."[3]

Music—like romance—is the language of the soul. Music allows us to express ourselves, and in so doing makes us feel alive. Jazz music, the only art form created by

---

2. Shapiro and Hentoff, Hear Me Talkin', 118–19.
3. Gottlieb, Reading Jazz, 419.

Americans, reminds us that the genius of America is improvisation, that America's unique experiment is a profound intersection of freedom and creativity, for better and for worse. A good beat, a contagious rhythm, an emotional ballad, creative improvisation: jazz has it all. This book, like the stories above, is written for those who appreciate jazz, for those who treasure each day and are open to daily moments of discovery, awakening, and renewal, and for all who are ready to reconnect with musical "first loves."

As an enduring expression of America's promise and genius, jazz functions as a prism through which much of American history can be told—and felt. Tragic, bawdy, creative, and rhythmic, the story of jazz, like jazz music itself, is fascinating, compelling, and honest. It keeps things real, and so it necessarily becomes a story about race and prejudice and class conflict, suggesting in powerful ways that those who represent the underneathness of society might actually be at the center of history.

It is fair to say that no one can study American culture, whether religious or secular, without appreciating the role of jazz. Jazz has been described as "America's music," and though it is no longer exclusively so, its influence in American culture has been pervasive. Rock, funk, soul, rap, show music, movie scores, television shows, and modern concert music all contain elements drawn from jazz. Jazz has inspired creation in other art forms as well, including dance, choreography, literature, and painting. There is something so compelling about this music that it can be said to define the human being in the twentieth century. In the words of Quincy Jones, a central figure in jazz and popular music for the past half-century: "I can only hope that one day America will recognize what the rest of the world already has, that our indigenous music, jazz, is the heart and soul of all popular music."[4]

WHAT IS JAZZ?

The roots of jazz, its history, indeed its primal nature, display an inclusivity and openness that beckon performer and audience alike to participate in a ritual reminiscent of the call and response characteristic of the "holiness" worship traditions. There is a palpable spirituality to this music which reminds us that all music, when it addresses humanity's needs, hopes, and fears, is spiritual and hence, therapeutic. So what is this music that has had such a consistent commitment from its participants and such powerful initial responses on its hearers?[5]

There is no generally accepted definition of the word "jazz," nor is it known where the word came from or what it originally meant. To some extent, jazz likes to consider itself a mystery, so much so that when Louis Armstrong was asked what jazz was, he is said to have responded, "If you gotta ask, you'll never know." The story, though apocryphal, illustrates an attitude universal to jazz musicians and listeners alike, that at the heart

---

4. Hasse, Jazz: The First Century, iv.

5. Here I am primarily concerned with jazz as an aesthetic, with its evocative and spiritual qualities, and not so much with technical definitions of the term.

Introduction

of this music lies something inexplicable that can be felt but not explained.[6] This doesn't mean, however, that jazz cannot be analyzed or described, for jazz texts try to do just that.

In his popular *Jazz Styles*, James Gridley provides the following categorization:

1. For many people, music need only *be associated with the jazz tradition* to be called jazz. For example, music might be called jazz because it has a bluesy flavor, or because it uses instruments associated with jazz, such as saxophones or drums, or because it has "jazzy rhythms" or displays manipulations of pitch and tone quality that are associated with jazz, such as blue notes, scoops, or smears.

2. For others, a jazz performance is one that *projects a jazz swing feeling*. According to this view, jazz is a feeling more than anything else, a way of playing music more than the type of music being played.

3. A third group views jazz as a type of music that *requires improvisation* (this perspective, though essential to most jazz, fails to distinguish from other kinds of music that also employ improvisation, such as pop, rock, and the music of India and Africa).

4. The most common definition seems to be one that *requires both improvisation and swing* in the jazz sense.[7]

Dizzy Gillespie got to the heart of the matter when he described jazz in the following manner: "Improvisation is the meat of jazz. Rhythm is the bone." When a performance exhibits these qualities, in a manner deemed inspired, then you have jazz at its best.

Ultimately, jazz is more than mere music. For jazz would not exist apart from people: performers, composers, arrangers, producers, critics, authors, and finally, listeners. Jazz is the story of extraordinary human beings, "protean geniuses—black and white, male and female, addicts and orphans, prostitutes and pimps, sons of privilege and of despair—who . . . took enormous risks, shouldered unimaginable responsibility, and are able to do what the rest of us can only dream of: create art on the spot."[8]

CONTRIBUTIONS OF *BLUE NOTES* TO THE JAZZ GENRE

Blue Notes is written for a general audience, including jazz fans, students, performers, scholars, educators, radio show hosts, writers, nostalgia buffs, and a growing number of teenagers and discerning young adults. The readable entries should prove useful to music lovers in general, particularly those who are interested in biographical literature.

This book contains profiles of 365 jazz personalities, one for each calendar day of the year (including February 29; Louis Armstrong, jazz's most notable figure, is featured twice). Each profile contains a story, some heartwarming, others tragic, but all memorable. The first entry (January 1) tells a poignant story—a story of hopeful beginnings and tragic endings. And that, of course, is the account of everyone's life. For an alphabetical list of the 365 jazz artists featured in the entries, consult the Directory of Artists section at the front of the book.

6. Collier, The Making of Jazz, 4.
7. Gridley, Jazz Styles, 6-7. For an extended discussion of the topic, see pp. 1–10.
8. Ward and Burns, Jazz: A History, ix.

Introduction

Entries are subject to limitations of length—approximately one page—and subject matter—to a single person born on that date (the exceptions are July 4 [Louis Armstrong], for reasons given in that entry, August 1 [Herschel Evans] and 14 [Freddie Webster], October 6 [Jimmy Blanton], and November 26 [Rudy Van Gelder], when individuals whose date of birth is uncertain or unknown are used as substitutes for lesser known personalities). On some days of the year the pool of candidates is sizeable, requiring a difficult choice, while on other days the selection is obvious, due to the few available choices. In all cases, the candidate whose biography offers the most interesting or compelling story dictates my choice for each day. With few exceptions, entry dates are based upon the "Calendar of Jazz Births and Deaths" located in the second edition of the *New Grove Dictionary of Jazz*.[9]

Due to the limitations of length and subject matter noted above, some prominent jazz personalities could not be featured in the text. Most of these individuals, however, are discussed in one or more of the entries themselves, and their names are listed in the Index of Names. Despite its biographical presentation, this work can also be read as a primer on jazz, for the daily entries contain valuable information on jazz styles, jazz history, instruments and instrumentalists, and such related topics as racism and drug use. To access this information, readers are encouraged to consult the Topical Index.

By definition, profiles are sketches, and brevity is a hard taskmaster. When it claims its "pound of flesh," brevity requires a surgeon's skill, an editor's insight, and a comedian's wit. The following accounts provide memorable vignettes that can be read for benefit and enjoyment. Limited by space and perspective, each essay highlights facets of a jazz personality's life or career that might encourage interest, curiosity, or further investigation on the part of the reader.

Readers may approach this book in a number of ways:

- as an engaging introduction to the topic of jazz music;
- as a reference volume, noting interesting and sometimes hard to find facts about jazz personalities (including performers, composers, arrangers, lyricists, bandleaders, producers, critics, authors, educators, recording engineers, record producers, and publishers);
- as a daily reading about jazz that provides relevant information to that day of the year;
- as an inductive text that encourages serendipitous pursuits and helps connect jazz personalities with the larger history of jazz, its evolution, and its principal styles.

Modern readers, whether serious or merely curious about the topic of jazz, can benefit greatly from one or all of these approaches. Used inductively, this book may be appropriate as a companion text in academic settings where individual research and direct hands-on involvement with the subject matter are deemed essential.

Readers looking for background information or a brief overview of jazz music are encouraged to consult the appendix, where they will find:

---

9. See Appendix 2 of Kernfeld, New Grove Dictionary of Jazz, Vol. 3, 1082–1141.

Introduction

- a quiz on jazz trivia, with answers.
- entry points for the enjoyment of jazz
- recommended entry-level jazz recordings
- a historical timeline of jazz
- a summary of jazz styles and key personalities
- selected readings and jazz-related websites

The following entries contain numerous items of information, including (1) vital statistics (date and place of birth [b.] and death [d.]) (2) styles or genres with which artists are identified (3) instrumental category (or other contribution to jazz), (4) a listing of notable jazz personalities born or deceased on that day, and (5) biographical material.

Some entries tell a story that, while connected to the individual that is featured, addresses the larger story of jazz itself. And that's what makes this text different from other books on jazz. This work is synthetic in that it combines two essentially different approaches on jazz currently available to the consumer: jazz biography and jazz history. In addition to essential biographical information on specific artists, entries include references to collaborative work with other musicians and, where appropriate, to major musical recordings.

Chapter 1

January

JANUARY 1—SUSANNAH MCCORKLE (1946–2001)
b. Berkeley, CA; d. New York, NY
Vocalist
[Vocal Jazz; Traditional Pop; Standards]

Other jazz notables born on this day: Papa Celestin (1884); Al McKibbon (1919); Milt Jackson (1923); Chris Potter (1971)
Jazz notables deceased on this day: Alexis Korner (1984)

♪

During her thirty-year career Susannah McCorkle seemingly had everything go her way—talent, intelligence, good looks, and a successful career. An ambitious performer, she also wrote for the *New Yorker* and published a number of short stories. Known as one of the top interpreters of lyrics during the 1980s and '90s—with a clear, natural voice described as combining Billie Holiday inflections with an occasional hint of Marilyn Monroe—Susannah was at or near the top of her field when she took her life on May 19, 2001 by jumping from her New York apartment to the street below.

Her life and career reveal barely a glimmer into the circumstances that led to her tragic suicide. As the daughter of an anthropologist, she spent time during her formative years living in Mexico and Venezuela, in addition to the U.S. She studied Italian Literature at the University of California at Berkeley and upon graduation she traveled to Paris. There she discovered recordings by Holiday and soon became involved in jazz. Following a short stay in Rome, she moved to London, where she worked with Keith Ingham (to whom she was briefly married), among others, and performed with visiting Americans such as Dexter Gordon, Ben Webster, and Bobby Hackett (who called her "the best singer since Billie Holiday"). Throughout her career she recorded many "songbook" sets, dedicated to the music of particular composers or lyricists. The poignant titles of certain albums, including her Grammy-nominated collection, *The People That You Never Get to Love* (1981) and the more recent *From Broken Hearts to Blue Skies* (1998), hint at an inner melancholia.

The greatest irony is that this beloved singer took her life soon after compiling a collection of *Most Requested Songs* (2001). This final album, a parting gift to her fans, was made more wistful by reflections on the album sleeve. Perhaps, as she wrote in the liner notes for her reading of "If I Only Had a Heart," she was including herself among those individuals who "have trouble experiencing their own emotions and yearn to feel something, anything." Apparently, this disillusioned dreamer learned to sublimate her inner feelings, for whatever anguish she bore served as a catalyst for her artistry. Like Billie Holiday, who initially inspired her, Susannah was able to communicate a song because she lived with emotional pain. Rather than distort or alter the lyrics, she used her jazz sensibility to bring out their hidden beauty, thereby attracting devoted fans. Her personal tragedy should draw additional listeners to this lovesome flower, cut in her prime.

JANUARY 2—KENNY CLARKE (1914–1985)

b. Pittsburgh, PA; d. near Paris, France

Drummer; Bandleader

[Bop]

Other jazz notables born on this day: Nick Fatool (1915)
Jazz notables deceased on this day: Erroll Garner (1977); Eddie Heywood (1989); Nat Adderley (2000)

♪

Unless adopted or raised in strong foster homes, children who lack parental influence during their formative years often develop unwholesome patterns later in life. Rootless, they may wander through careers, marriages, and even homelands. Kenny Clarke was such a person. Lacking a proper start in life, but resilient and flexible, he spent much of his career searching—for a name, a home, an identity, even a certain birthdate (he may have been born on January 9). Abandoned by his father and left homeless with the passing of his mother, he was placed in the Coleman Industrial Home for Negro Boys (1919–26). Like Louis Armstrong, who six years earlier had been placed in a home for waifs, young Kenny's experience was mollified by the opportunity to learn music. After experimenting with various brass instruments, he eventually took up drums. He left school to become a musician, touring in a band that included another Pittsburgh native, trumpeter Roy Eldridge.

Up to this point he had worked as Kenny Spearman, but when he went to New York in 1935 he dropped his surname and became Kenny Clarke. Around 1940, some of the younger musicians who felt that swing had fallen into a rut began developing their own original styles. While a member of Teddy Hill's big band, Clarke and fellow sideman Dizzy Gillespie began experimenting with new rhythmic conceptions. The novel thing that Clarke added at this time was to shift the ground beat from the bass drum to the lighter sound of the cymbals, thereby freeing the bass drum for accent and surprises—"dropping bombs," as the practice came to be called. Listening to Clarke's offbeat rhythms, Hill inadvertently gave Clarke his nickname, "Klook," when he called the drummer's style "klook-mop stuff." Around 1941 Klook began leading the house band at Minton's

Playhouse, a bar in Harlem where young modernists gathered in a series of jam sessions that permanently altered the jazz world, creating a form of music known as bebop or "bop." In the process, he became the jazz world's first bop drummer.

In 1943 Clarke was drafted into the army, where misfortune struck again. While stationed in Alabama he married jazz singer Carmen McRae, but caught AWOL (absent without leave), he was shipped to the European war zone and remained in France until 1946. His marriage suffered during this period and after four years he and McRae separated. But he acquired a taste for Paris, a place to which he would return frequently. In search of a religious identity, Clarke became a Muslim after the war and briefly took the name Liaquat Ali Salaam. A decade later, after he had participated in numerous landmark events, including recording historic albums with Miles Davis's Birth of the Cool group and performing as a member of the groundbreaking Modern Jazz Quartet, Clarke finally moved to France permanently. Home at last, he co-led the influential Clarke-Boland Big Band and established himself as a major figure on the European jazz scene.

JANUARY 3—JAMES CARTER (1969–)

b. Detroit, MI

Saxophonist; Bass Clarinetist; Leader

[CONTEMPORARY JAZZ; HARD BOP; POST-BOP; AVANT-GARDE JAZZ; SOUL-JAZZ]

Other jazz notables born on this day:

Jazz notables deceased on this day: Kaiser Marshall (1948); Earl Swope (1968); Wilbur DeParis (1973)

♪

Born to a musical family in Detroit, Carter was fascinated early on by the appearance of the saxophone, and he began performing shortly after receiving his first instrument when he was eleven. He played jazz at the nearby Blue Lake Arts Camp and then toured Scandinavia with the Blue Lake Monster Ensemble in 1985. That year, while still in high school, he gigged with trumpeter Wynton Marsalis. In 1988 Carter played with Lester Bowie in New York and by 1988 he was touring with Julius Hemphill. He has since recorded and performed with some of today's top jazz artists, as well as leading his own highly versatile band.

Potentially the most exciting saxophonist to come to the fore during the 1990s, Carter caused a sensation with his recordings for the Japanese DIW label. When *JC On the Set* was issued in 1993, Carter's entrance on the first selection, a unique montage of pops, squeals, and split-tones, was sensational. The album was universally acclaimed as the finest debut by a saxophonist in decades.[1] On *Jurassic Classics*, recorded a few months later, he devised another stunning opening, this time for "Take the 'A' Train," its two-note train whistle, like the screeching of wheels, kicking off a breathless ride down the tracks. His initial album with Columbia later in 1994, *The Real Quiet Storm*, an album of ballads,

---

1. Bogdanov et al., *All Music Guide to Jazz*, 207.

received unequivocal praise from jazz critic Gary Giddins: "if jazz is to enjoy a genuine breakthrough beyond the nonimprovisatory kitsch that saddles the charts, here is music with rhythm in its feet, light in its eyes, and brains in its back alley soul."[2]

Carter is often compared to Rahsaan Roland Kirk, the largely self-taught saxophonist, inventor, and one-man reed section who, like the unclassifiable Carter, was a totally original performer. Beginning on saxophone a scant three years after Kirk's death in 1977, Carter embodies Kirk's scholastic understanding of the instrument's history, as well as his exuberant style and expansive spirit. The owner of sixty woodwind instruments, Carter performs skillfully on most reeds, and while the tenor sax is his main instrument, he also plays the soprano, alto, and baritone saxes, in addition to the clarinet, bass clarinet, oboe, and bass flute. His musical taste also runs the gamut, from straightahead to swing to free jazz. Carter often switches unexpectedly between styles, and the effect can be exhilarating or disorienting.

Though not everyone approves of Carter's intrepid playing style, all agree, however, that Carter is an astounding technician with unlimited potential for development. This unconventional musician may soon be considered one of the all-time greats in jazz.

JANUARY 4—JOHN MCLAUGHLIN (1942–)

b. Kirk Sandall, Yorkshire, England

Guitarist; Bandleader; Composer

[POST-BOP; FUSION; WORLD MUSIC]

Other jazz notables born on this day: Frankie Newton (1906); Joe Marsala (1907); Frank Wess (1922)

Jazz notables deceased on this day: Paul Chambers (1969); Eddie Barefield (1991); Leo Wright (1991); Les Brown (2001)

♪

If originality is the engine that drives improvisation, McLaughlin is the engineer. An innovative fusion guitarist in the early 1970s, he played a specially built electric guitar with two necks, one having six and the other twelve strings. Later he designed a guitar based on the Indian vina, a seven-string instrument with four playing strings and three accompanying strings. Equally adept on acoustic and electric guitar, McLaughlin is one of the most complete performers on his instrument, at home playing blues, bop, free jazz, fusion, Indian music, or in a classical setting.

A self-taught guitarist, McLaughlin learned blues and flamenco before turning to jazz. In the early 1960s he moved to London, where he played in R&B bands and with such formidable rock musicians as Jack Bruce, Ginger Baker, Mick Jagger, and Eric Clapton. The 1960s was a time of unprecedented social upheaval in the Western world, precipitated by conflicts in faraway places as well as on perennially peaceful college campuses, but it brought in its wake opportunities for self-discovery, growth, and renewal. Embracing this

---

2. Giddins, *Visions of Jazz*, 633–34.

restless ethos, McLaughlin became interested in Eastern philosophy, religion, and music and joined the Theosophical Society. By 1969 he was in New York, participating with fellow visionary Miles Davis in some of the latter's most influential albums, including *In a Silent Way*, and *Bitches Brew*, albums that virtually created the genre known as jazz-rock fusion.

In 1970 McLaughlin became a disciple of the guru Sri Chinmoy. Seeking inspiration through self-discipline and meditation, McLaughlin decided to abstain from alcohol and drugs, thereby participating in a growing trend towards clean living in the drug-ridden jazz scene. He sought to form a band as a vehicle for his growing spirituality, and at Sri Chinmoy's suggestion, named it Mahavishnu, meaning "divine compassion, power, and justice." After recording such masterpieces as *The Inner Mounting Flame* and *Birds of Fire* with his Mahavishnu Orchestra, possibly the greatest jazz-rock band of all time, McLaughlin surprised the music world by switching to acoustic guitar and playing Indian music with Shakti, a group that made a strong impact on the emerging world music scene during its brief tenure. In 1975 McLaughlin moved back to Europe, where he felt jazz was understood and respected more as an art form than for its commercial value.

Since then, McLaughlin has continued his experimental ways, leading the One Truth Band, playing with guitarists Al DiMeola and Paco DeLucia, and touring with organist Joey De Francesco. In the mid-1980s he participated in additional recordings with Miles Davis and then performed in a retrospective concert with Miles in Paris in 1991. Like Davis, McLaughlin did much to popularize jazz and move it forward; he serves as a reminder that boundless invention is an essential quality of jazz.

JANUARY 5—WILD BILL DAVISON (1906–1989)

b. Defiance, OH; d. Santa Barbara, CA

Cornetist; Leader

[DIXIELAND]

Other jazz notables born on this day: Shotaro Moriyasu (1924)
Jazz notables deceased on this day: Artie Whetsol (1940); Charles Mingus (1979)

♪

Wild Bill Davison, one of the great cornetists in the Dixieland tradition, had a colorful playing style that matched his strong personality. Despite a successful, sixty-year career, much of it spent as a member of the house band at Eddie Condon's nightclub in New York, he will forever be associated with one of the great tragedies in jazz history, the death of legendary Chicago clarinetist Frank Teschemacher. In 1932, while leading a big band with Teschemacher, Davison was at the wheel when his car was blindsided by a taxi, resulting in Teschemacher's death. Though the accident had not been Davison's fault, his jazz colleagues ostracized him. The resultant guilt and emotional pain forced him to spend the rest of the decade in relative obscurity, leading his own small groups in the jazz backwaters of Milwaukee. His playing began to attract attention after some recordings were issued in 1940, and by 1941 he relocated to New York, the jazz capital of the world.

His work there and with the Original Dixieland Jazz Band culminated in some brilliant recordings with Georg Brunis in 1943 that solidified his reputation. After a period in the army, he joined guitarist Eddie Condon, whom he had known in Chicago, beginning a lengthy stint at the latter's New York nightclub.

Condon, a fine rhythm guitarist whose music—hot jazz laced with elements of swing—had played a prominent role in the emergence of Chicago jazz in the late 1920s, was, by the mid-1940s earning a reputation as a jazz entrepreneur and media personality. From 1942 to 1946 Condon organized a series of racially integrated all-star concerts in New York, including one of the earliest jazz programs on television (April 1942). Riding the wave of the traditional-jazz revival after World War II, he founded his own nightclub in 1945. During the next fifteen years, Condon presented accomplished instrumentalists at his clubs, concerts and television shows.

Wild Bill figured prominently in many of these activities, including a series of important Columbia recordings from 1953 to 1957. His commanding presence and reliable cornet lead made him a perfect fit for the long nights and hard pace of Condon's club. His physical playing style—growls, rips, flares, shakes, and heart-on-sleeve Irish sentimentality on ballads—personified Condon's Chicago jazz image and led to Davison's emergence as a star in Dixieland circles. Davison used his image to good cause by introducing numerous African-Americans into Condon's band, most notably Edmond Hall and Walter Page. Other accomplishments included Davison's appearance with Condon at the inaugural Newport Jazz Festival in 1954.

Davison moved to the West Coast in 1960, touring internationally and recording constantly. His colorful life was filled with remarkable episodes, and he pursued his musical career until the end, visiting Japan only a few weeks before his death. *The Wildest One*, a 1996 biography by Hal Willard, contains many hilarious anecdotes and confirms how unique a life Wild Bill lived, and how he earned his reputation.

JANUARY 6—BARRY ALTSCHUL (1943–)

b. New York, NY

Drummer

[AVANT-GARDE JAZZ]

Other jazz notables born on this day: Louis De Vries (1905); Bobby Stark (1906); Vernon Brown (1907); Don Sickler (1944)
Jazz notables deceased on this day: Dizzy Gillespie (1993)

♪

During the 1950s, when most jazz fans had their eyes on the beboppers, a "new thing" was emerging in obscure nightclubs, rehearsal halls, and practice rooms across America. Like the pioneers of the bop movement, these new players were motivated by the same idea: to "free" jazz from what they saw as restrictions of ordinary harmony, chords, bar lines, and even the scale. This striving against musical barriers did not arise out of thin air, but was produced by a confluence of forces current in the 1950s and '60s, including the black civil rights movement, a broadening interest in left-wing thought, and the commitment to a philosophic idea then current, that everyone should be free to "do their own thing." The new forms of jazz that emerged during the 1960s and '70s were often grouped under umbrella terms such as "free jazz" or "avant-garde." Though the earliest avant-garde efforts in jazz can be dated to the experiments of Lennie Tristano and his disciples during the late 1940s and early '50s, avant-garde jazz emerged as a mature movement in 1964, when a series of six concerts billed as the "October Revolution in Jazz" was presented at New York's Cellar Café. Later that year an influential but short-lived collective, the Jazz Composers Guild, was formed to further the jazz avant-garde.

Largely self-taught until 1960, when he began to study with drummer Charlie Persip, Barry Altschul joined the jazz avant-garde in the early 1960s. From 1964 to 1970 he played regularly with pianist Paul Bley, who had participated in the famous October Revolution and helped organize the Jazz Composers Guild. Altschul joined the guild in 1964 and remained with the group until 1968, by which time it was called the Jazz Composer's Orchestra Association. In the early 1970s Altschul was the drummer for Circle, a band that with members Chick Corea, Dave Holland, and Anthony Braxton is considered the most technically adept free-jazz ensemble ever.[3] Thanks to a background in traditional jazz styles, which gave him a solid grounding on which to build his free playing, and an interest in African, Brazilian, Indian, and Caribbean music, Altschul's work with Circle was stylistically all-encompassing. Having started in the 1960s avant-garde, he eventually explored the entire spectrum of jazz history, including bop, hard bop, and even swing. Altschul recognized that avant-gardists are intrinsic to jazz, part of its ongoing nature. As he mentioned: "The avant-garde was a period that was necessary to extend the vocabulary of the musicians themselves . . . After a while the avant-gardists become the contemporary, then they become the mainstream."[4]

In the mid-1970s Altschul developed his ideas further by teaching drumming, publicizing his method through an instructional book on the subject. He continues to perform and record with trios and quartets while leading his own groups.

JANUARY 7—CHANO POZO (1915–1948)

b. Havana, Cuba; d. New York, NY

Percussionist; Vocalist; Dancer

[AFRO-CUBAN JAZZ; LATIN JAZZ; SALSA]

Other jazz notables born on this day: Henry "Red" Allen (1908); Sam Woodyard (1925); Kenny Davern (1935); Billy Harper (1943)
Jazz notables deceased on this day: Johnny Guarnieri (1985); Fred Hopkins (1999)

♪

---

3. Bogdanov et al., *All Music Guide to Jazz*, 29.
4. Gottlieb, *Reading Jazz*, 13.

Due to his incredibly brief career in North America, only the most discerning fans know Chano Pozo's name today, but in New York City in the late 1940s, he was a sensation. With Dizzy Gillespie, he played a major role in the founding and popularizing of Latin jazz, essentially a mixture of bebop and Cuban folk music.

In 1946, fresh from a contract with RCA, Gillespie organized an orchestra and, at the band's third session, recorded "Manteca," one of his greatest compositions. With justifiable immodesty, Gillespie likened the December 22, 1947 recording to "a nuclear weapon when it burst on the scene." The record, one of the most important ever made in the United States, served to consummate the marriage of Cuban music with American music. So important is that performance that the salsa movement of the 1970s can be traced back to it. Despite previous attempts by popular entertainers to blend the musical cultures, this was the first time an attempt had been made to fuse elements of jazz and Latin music at a serious artistic level.

The origin of "Manteca" goes back to 1939, when Gillespie, then with Cab Calloway's Orchestra, became interested in Cuban music. Another trumpeter, the Cuban-born Mario Bauzá, was in that band, and the two instrumentalists became friends. When Gillespie left Calloway to start his own big band, he asked Bauzá to recommend a Cuban percussionist. Bauzá introduced him to Chano Pozo, a recent immigrant already famous in Havana as an entertainer and composer. The two began collaborating immediately, and while on tour in California, Pozo came to Gillespie with a suggestion for a new piece. The result, "Manteca," was passed on to Gillespie's arranger Gil Fuller, for orchestration. The piece had its premiere at Carnegie Hall on September 1947, and was an immediate success.

Pozo was a rough customer, a brawler who carried a bullet lodged too near his spine to be removed. As an entertainer, Pozo performed show-stopping routines, often stripping to the waist to show off his oiled torso, singing, dancing, and playing simultaneously. During his brief career with Gillespie (1947–48), he provided the starting point for much popular music of the late 1940s and the 1950s. The collaboration between the two men supplied the initiative for North American musicians and some of the listening public to more fully appreciate the tradition of Latin music. Compositions like "Manteca" teamed Gillespie's blistering trumpet with Pozo's fiery conga improvisations. In works like Gillespie's "Algo Bueno" (also known as "Woody'n You") and George Russell's *Afro-Cuban Suite*, Pozo's contribution to the ensemble laid the foundation for the later jazz work of musicians such as Candido and Mongo Santamaria. A disgruntled cocaine dealer shot Chano to death in a Harlem bar a month shy of his thirty-fourth birthday, bringing his promising career to an abrupt halt.

JANUARY 8—MARILYN MAZUR (1955–)

b. New York, NY; grew up in Denmark

Drummer; Percussionist; Bandleader; Composer

[AVANT-GARDE; POST-BOP; FUSION]

Other jazz notables born on this day: Bill Goodwin (1942); Dave Weckl (1960)
Jazz notables deceased on this day: Ray Bauduc (1988); Georgie Auld (1990)

♪

While North America is the birthplace of jazz, it is by no means its only home. From its earliest days, jazz had a significant fan base in Europe, not just in England, France, and Germany, but also in Italy, Eastern Europe, and even Scandinavia, where visiting American jazz musicians toured regularly and where some lived for extended periods of time. And though jazz plays a larger role in American society than in Europe, the difference seems more a matter of quantity than quality, for Europe has produced dozens of first-rate players, and most young musician there, of all colors, nationalities, and of both sexes, seem either to play or want to play jazz.[5]

Scandinavia is home to a number of world-renown jazz musicians, including tenor saxophonist Jan Garbarek, trumpeter Palle Mikkelborg, double bassist Niels-Henning Orsted Pedersen, electric guitarist Terje Rypdal, violinist Svend Asmussen, bari saxophonist Lars Gullin, vocalist Karin Krog, and the subject of this profile, drummer Marilyn Mazur.

Born in New York of Danish and African-American parents, Mazur moved to Denmark with her family when she was six. She first studied classical piano and dance and by the age of fifteen was writing her own compositions. She took up drums and percussion a few years later while working with the group Zirenes (1973–78) and in 1979, after attending the Royal Danish Conservatory of Music, she formed the all-woman ten-piece ensemble the Primi Band. Her international breakthrough came in 1985, when she was hired by Miles Davis to record on his album *Aura*. She continued working with him intermittently through 1989, while also touring with Gil Evans (1986) and Wayne Shorter (1987). In 1989 she returned to Denmark to lead her own band Future Song and then Pulse Unit, an adventurous unit that featured many of her compositions and on which her husband Klavs Hovman played bass. In the 1990s she also worked with Orsted Pedersen and recorded regularly with Garbarek.

Mazur performs on a wide variety of exotic percussive instruments but, unlike many of her male counterparts, she uses a subtle drumming approach. Her style, likened to the lightness of a dancer, reflects not only her feminine artistic sensibility but also her biracial and multicultural milieu. Though female drummers like Mazur and others who emerged during the 1970s and '80s—Americans Cindy Blackman and Terri Lyne Carrington being the most distinguished—are still not commonplace in jazz, they are no longer the rarity they were in the 1930s, '40s, and beyond, when pioneers like hard-swinging drummer Pauline Braddy helped novelty groups such as The International Sweethearts of Rhythm succeed in a market dominated by all-male bands.

5. Kirchner, *Oxford Companion to Jazz*, 547.

BLUE NOTES

JANUARY 9—BUCKY PIZZARELLI (1926–)

b. Paterson, NJ

Guitarist

[SWING; STANDARDS]

Other jazz notables born on this day: Ed "Montudi" Garland (1885?); Kenny Clarke (1914 [or Jan 2]), Betty Roche (1920);

Jazz notables deceased this day: Vido Musso (1982)

♪

Among guitarists active in jazz from the 1920s to the 1960s, a select few—Eddie Lang, Django Reinhardt, Charlie Christian, and Wes Montgomery—are considered giants of their era, while other legends, among them Carl Kress, George Van Eps, George Barnes, and Bucky Pizzarelli, are less widely known or recognized, in part because they performed as studio artists throughout much of their career.

A superior guitarist much appreciated by musicians in the swing tradition, Bucky Pizzarelli has been a fixture in jazz and the studios since the early 1950s. Inspired by George Van Eps, who in the late 1930s pioneered a seven-string guitar (the extra bass string allowed him to play bass lines simultaneously with chords and lead solos), Pizzarelli acquired a reputation for exceptional solo performances, in addition to his proficiency as a classical guitarist.

Bucky began his professional career in 1943, when at the age of seventeen he toured with Vaughn Monroe's dance band. He rejoined the group from 1946 to 1952, following a stint in the military. In 1952 he entered the demanding world of studio work, joining the staff of NBC. He remained under contract with NBC until 1966, taking time out to tour with the Three Suns trio (1956–57) and intermittently with Monroe. In 1966 he switched to ABC, playing as a studio musician on the *Dick Cavett Show*. That same year he played with Benny Goodman, beginning an association that lasted until the bandleader's death in 1986 and included four European tours in the early 1970s. During this period, Pizzarelli's reputation began to blossom and his career as a jazz musician took off. He recorded duos with Zoot Sims, Bud Freeman, Stephane Grappelli, and for a number of years collaborated regularly with the older guitarist George Barnes. Their spectacular breakup after a quarrel was amusingly reported by Whitney Balliett in *New York Notes* (1972): "The guitarists' swan set at the tiny St. Regis room was played not on their instruments but on each other."[6] While maintaining a busy recording schedule, Pizzarelli has worked with many classicists, including Bob Wilber and Bobby Hackett, as well as with his own trio.

Since the early 1980s Bucky has played to great acclaim in duets with his son and pupil John, who also performs on a seven-string guitar. Father and son duos are relatively rare in jazz, but Bucky and John's numerous joint recordings show little evidence of a generation gap between them. Whether together or apart, the Pizzarellis are among a select few that have helped perpetuate the Van Eps legacy of an easygoing modern swing combined with the harmonically sophisticated lead style made possible by the seven-string guitar's extra bass string.

6. Carr et al., *Jazz: The Rough Guide*, 43.

JANUARY 10—MAX ROACH (1924–2007)

b. New Land, NC; d. New York, NY

Drummer; Composer

[BOP; HARD BOP; POST-BOP; AVANT-GARDE]

Other jazz notables born on this day: Haywood Henry (1913 [or Jan 7]); Allan Eager (1927); Waymon Reed (1940)

Jazz notables deceased this day: Ernie Caceres (1971); Eddie Safranski (1974); Joe Farrell (1986)

♪

Capable drummers, like the rudder on a ship, are indispensable to any jazz combo. When they possess creativity, they are even more invaluable. Add leadership qualities, and you have Max Roach, one of the most outstanding and innovative drummers of his time.

Roach started playing the drums at age ten and by the time he was eighteen he became associated with Charlie Parker, Dizzy Gillespie, and other emerging talents. As the house drummer at Monroe's Uptown House, he participated in jam sessions there and at Minton's Playhouse that led to the development of the bop style. During the 1940s he performed with many of jazz's leading figures and participated in some of the era's seminal moments, including Parker's first recording session as leader (1945), Miles Davis's *Birth of the Cool* recordings of 1949 and 1950, and the celebrated Massey Hall concert of 1953. In 1954 he formed the Brown/Roach Quintet with trumpeter Clifford Brown, a group that virtually defined the hard bop of the 1950s.

Throughout the 1960s Roach was a committed political crusader. An outspoken man heavily affected by the burgeoning civil rights movement and his relationship with activist singer Abbey Lincoln (to whom he was married from 1962 to 1970), Roach became a fervent supporter of racial equality, and that no doubt hurt his career at various junctures. In 1960 he recorded *We Insist! Freedom Now Suite*, a seven-part collaboration with Oscar Brown Jr., and soon thereafter he disrupted a Miles Davis/Gil Evans concert in Carnegie Hall by marching to the edge of the stage holding a "Freedom Now" placard, protesting the Africa Relief Foundation (for which the event was a benefit).

In a profession marred by early deaths—especially the bebop division—Max Roach was a shining survivor. He and Kenny Clarke instigated a revolution in jazz drumming that persists to this day when they shifted the fixed pulse from the bass drum of the hi-hat to the ride cymbal. The result was a lighter, far more flexible texture; it gave drummers more freedom to explore the possibilities of their drum kits while allowing bop virtuosos on the front lines to play at faster speeds. To this base Roach added qualities of his own—a ferocious drive, the ability to play a solo with a definite storyline, mixing up pitches and timbres, the deft use of silence, and the dexterity to use the brushes as brilliantly as the sticks. But Roach didn't stop there. A rare, unclassifiable breed, he maintained the curiosity and the willingness to grow as a musician, moving beyond bop into new compositional structures, unusual instrument lineups, unusual time signatures, atonality, even music for television, film, and the symphony hall.[7] Despite his collaboration with numerous composers/arrangers throughout his career, Roach wrote the greater part of the material performed by his groups in the last forty years. It is not an exaggeration to say that he composed every time he played the drums.

JANUARY 11—WILBUR DE PARIS (1900–1973)

b. Crawfordsville, IN; d. New York, NY

Trombonist; Bandleader

[DIXIELAND]

Other jazz notables born on this day: Tab Smith (1909); Jack Nimitz (1930); Johnny Varro (1930); Lee Ritenour (1952)

Jazz notables deceased this day: Kenny Clare (1985); Ram Ramirez (1994); Ike Isaacs (1996); Bill Russo (2003)

♪

Wilbur De Paris, an excellent ensemble player and an important bandleader in the Dixieland tradition, is credited with helping to keep alive New Orleans jazz in the 1950s. He began his career as an alto horn player around 1912, performing with his father's circus band and then on the Theater Owners' Booking Association (TOBA) circuit. During a visit to New Orleans in 1922 he played C-melody saxophone with Louis Armstrong and worked with A. J. Piron's famous orchestra before switching permanently to trombone.

TOBA had been established in 1921 by two white theater owners based in Tennessee, with the purpose of managing vaudeville bookings for African-American performers. By 1923 the association extended to eighty-five houses in most of the major cities of the South, Southwest, and Midwest. While it was notorious for its demanding schedules and low pay, the organization enabled comedy teams, specialty acts (jugglers, acrobats, dancers), singers, and others to appear before black audiences and created steady employment for performers such as Ma Rainey, Bessie Smith, and Ethel Waters. A number of early jazz musicians, including Bennie Moten and Count Basie, also started their careers on the circuit, but by 1932 a combination of factors, such as the Depression, competition from the film industry, and personal conflicts among theater owners, brought the association to an end, and nearly all its houses were converted to motion picture theaters.[8]

Canny, observant, and possessing a good business sense, De Paris pursued his dream to be a bandleader; he formed a short-lived band in Philadelphia in 1925 and then one at the Cinderella Ballroom in New York. Unable to keep his dream alive, he worked as a sideman for the next eighteen years, including three years as a member of Luis Russell's orchestra, which backed Louis Armstrong (1937–40). In 1943, after short stints with Ella Fitzgerald and Roy Eldridge's big band, he attempted to form yet another band, this time with brother Sidney, a talented trumpeter. The attempt was unsuccessful, though he was

---

7. Bogdanov et al., *All Music Guide to Jazz*, 1071.
8. Kernfeld, *New Grove Dictionary of Jazz*, Vol. 3, 739–40.

able to join Duke Ellington's prestigious orchestra (1945–47) as replacement for legendary Tricky Sam Nanton, Ellington's longtime "growl and plunger" technician.

In 1947 De Paris finally found success as a leader, forming a band that became one of the most consistently inventive Dixieland-oriented groups of the 1950s. The band, reminiscent of Jelly Roll Morton's Red Hot Peppers of the late 1920s, established an eleven-year residency at Jimmy Ryan's (1951–62), one of the most celebrated of all New York clubs, where it entertained audiences nightly with its energy and professionalism.

JANUARY 12—JAY MCSHANN (1916–2006)

b. Muskogee, OK; d. Kansas City, MO

Pianist; Vocalist; Bandleader

[SWING; PIANO BLUES; JUMP BLUES]

Other jazz notables born on this day: Trummy Young (1912); Ronald Shannon Jackson (1940); Olu Dara (1941); George Duke (1946); John Etheridge (1948), Jane Ira Bloom (1955)

Jazz notables deceased this day: Capt. John Handy (1971); Joe Albany (1988)

♪

During the 1920s and '30s there was a thriving jazz scene in Kansas City, Missouri. Numerous significant jazz musicians became associated with "Kansas City style jazz," a form of orchestral jazz developed by the territory bands of that region. Because the area had strong traditions of orchestral ragtime and rural blues, Kansas City jazz evolved along different lines from the urban jazz of New Orleans, Chicago, and New York. Avoiding complicated arrangements, Kansas City style bands preferred short musical phrases called riffs and simple head arrangements (created spontaneously during a performance, learned by ear, and kept in the heads of the players). These gave more freedom to the soloists and allowed the musicians to concentrate on the rhythmic drive for which the style is known. The most important early Kansas City group was that of Bennie Moten, which later served as the basis of the Count Basie Orchestra. Although no Kansas City swing musician could rival Count Basie as an innovative pianist and bandleader, in the early 1940s, as Basie's orchestra took up a somewhat more conservative approach than before (at least in the recording studio), it was Jay McShann's big band that most faithfully maintained the Kansas City style of loose-limbed arrangements based on riffs, solos, and swing rhythm.

McShann, known as "Hootie," had a long career as bandleader, pianist, and singer, but his most enduring claim to fame is his connection with young Charlie Parker. McShann played in Oklahoma and Arkansas before moving to Kansas City where, in 1937, he formed a sextet and, by 1939, his own big band. When he first heard Charlie Parker one night in 1937, he told the impressive seventeen-year old saxophonist that he sounded different from everyone else in Kansas City. Within a few years, Parker's sound would astound the rest of the world. In 1938, when the authorities began to clamp down on crime and corruption in Kansas City, Parker left for Chicago and then New York, where he gained notoriety. The following year, however, upon hearing of his father's death, he returned to Kansas City. Duke Ellington, passing through town with his band, offered the youngster a job, but Parker chose instead to go on the road with his old friend McShann. It was during this time that Parker acquired his unusual nickname. According to McShann, the band was on its way to a concert in Nebraska when one of the cars hit a stray chicken, a yardbird. Parker jumped out, cradled it in his arms, and took it to their destination, where he had it cooked for dinner. From that point on, Parker was known as "Yardbird" or "Bird" for short.

Parker remained with McShann for two and a half years and made his first recordings with the band, thereby laying the foundation for his legendary career. Though McShann went on to significant fame of his own, primarily as a pianist/vocalist, his band of 1939 to 1943 is undoubtedly his most enduring claim to fame.

JANUARY 13—JOE PASS (1929–1994)

b. New Brunswick, NJ; d. Los Angeles, CA

Guitarist; Leader

[BOP; HARD BOP]

Other jazz notables born on this day: Percy Humphrey (1905); Danny Barker (1909); Quentin Jackson (1909); Melba Liston (1926)
Jazz notables deceased this day: Sonny Clark (1963); Michael Brecker (2007)

♪

Norman Granz surely must have known what he was talking about when, in the late 1970s, he called Joe Pass "unquestionably the best jazz guitarist in the world." Granz, you might recall, was the jazz impresario and recording executive who began the concert series Jazz at the Philharmonic (JATP) in the 1940s and later established several successful record labels, including Verve and Pablo. However, it took Pass a long time to acquire his stellar reputation. In fact, it required a herculean personal effort, in addition to help from an important friend, for him to rise from the obscurity into which he had fallen during the 1950s.

Born Joseph Anthony Jacobi Passalaqua, Joe showed incredible promise as a youngster. He started playing at the age of nine, and four years later he performed in a group patterned after the groundbreaking Quintette du Hot Club de France. When he was fourteen, the prodigy spent the summer touring with Tony Pastor's swing band. He left school early to play professionally; by 1947 he was performing with Charlie Barnet's big band. The following year he went to New York, where he performed with Brew Moore, but upon being drafted he joined the navy. And that's when his promising career began to unravel, for after his release from the military he became addicted to heroin and spent the next decade in and out of prisons, hospitals, and halfway houses. In his darkest hour, he was offered a second chance, and this time he made the most of it.

In 1961, together with other jazz musicians in Synanon, a self-help organization for drug addicts, Pass made a recording that attracted some critical attention, particularly for his relaxed manner and astounding technical ability. For several years he worked in studios in Los Angeles, making a bit of a stir with his *For Django* set (1964) and several other recordings for Pacific Jazz and World Pacific. From 1965 to 1967 he toured with George Shearing's group and in 1973 with Benny Goodman, but he remained in relative obscurity until pianist Oscar Peterson recommended him to his manager, Norman Granz. In December 1973 he recorded his first solo album, *Virtuoso*, for Granz's Pablo label. The success of this album catapulted him to fame and immediately he began to dominate jazz popularity polls for his instrument. From that point on he was greatly in demand for concerts, festivals, and recording sessions, notably as an accompanist to Ella Fitzgerald and Sarah Vaughan, and as a member of Peterson's groups. By the 1980s he was probably the most widely recorded jazz guitarist, including albums as an unaccompanied soloist, in duos, and with such masters as Count Basie, Duke Ellington, and Dizzy Gillespie. Pass moved to Hamburg, Germany in 1989, where he married and remained active until his death from cancer in 1994. The newlywed dedicated his final album, *Songs for Ellen* (1992), to his bride.

JANUARY 14—BILLY BUTTERFIELD (1917–1988)

b. Middletown, OH; d. North Palm Beach, FL

Trumpeter and Flugelhorn Player

[SWING; DIXIELAND; TRADITIONAL POP]

Other jazz notables born on this day: Jimmy Crawford (1910); Joe Muranyi (1928); Kenny Wheeler (1930); Grady Tate (1932)
Jazz notables deceased this day: George Baquet (1949); Alton Purnell (1987)

♪

Billy Butterfield showed a lot of promise as a youngster. He was disciplined, creative, and possessed a beautiful tone on trumpet. But music was strictly an avocation, for Billy hoped to be a doctor. As a student at Transylvania College he played in campus bands, but times were tough during the Depression, so he took time off to play in the bands of Austin Wylie and Andy Anderson. Bob Crosby, brother of singer Bing Crosby, spotted Butterfield during his stint with Wylie. Bob had recently become leader of a band made up of former members of Ben Pollack's band, and he was still recruiting. Butterfield joined Crosby's group from 1937 to 1940 and became an instant star. A career in medicine was no match for stardom, and Butterfield never looked back. The orchestra's unique brand of big-band Dixieland jazz achieved international popularity during an era when swing was the thing, and Crosby's band helped lead the way to the eventual New Orleans revival during the 1940s. Crosby featured Butterfield's wide-range and huge-toned trumpet on numerous recordings with the big band and with the Bobcats, his widely acclaimed small group. Among the Crosby soloists that joined Butterfield in the Bobcats were trumpeter Yank

Lawson and bassist Bob Haggart, who later formed a band called the World's Greatest Jazz Band. As a vital member of that group from its inception in 1968 until 1972, Butterfield helped define the ensemble's sound.

In 1940 Butterfield joined Artie Shaw's band. During his six-month stay he participated in Shaw's famed small group, the Gramercy Five, and he took a classic solo on Shaw's rendition of "Stardust." After stints with Benny Goodman, Les Brown, and in the recording studios, where his skill as a sight-reader brought him many offers, Butterfield spent time in the military. Following the war he tried his hand at leading a big band, but the postwar period was a difficult time for big bands. After two trying years, Butterfield returned to the more profitable studio work. As a staff musician at ABC, he worked out an informal partnership with cornetist Bobby Hackett to guarantee that one or the other would be available for studio recordings if an opportunity for jazz work came up. The two musicians, the most artistic swing trumpeters in North America during the post-war period, created a strong musical legacy together and remained inextricably connected in jazz lore.

During the 1950s Butterfield produced inventive work with Jackie Gleason and Ray Conniff. At the end of that period, as studio work diminished in New York, Butterfield led small groups on tours of colleges while continuing his residency in the house bands at Nick's and Condon's, two of the city's most famous Dixieland-style clubs. In later years he continued playing in Dixieland settings both for records and concerts, until cancer finally immobilized him.

JANUARY 15—GENE KRUPA (1909–1973)

b. Chicago, IL; d. Yonkers, NY

Drummer; Bandleader

[SWING; DIXIELAND]

Other jazz notables born on this day:
Jazz notables deceased this day: Jack Teagarden (1964)

♪

Gene Krupa was the first drummer to be a superstar. Prior to Krupa, drum solos were a rarity and a drum set was thought of as merely a supportive instrument, but with his good looks and colorful playing, Krupa became a matinee idol, changing the image of drummers forever.[9] Building on the formative influences of Baby Dodds, Zutty Singleton, and later, the virtuoso drumming of Chick Webb, Krupa became the first major jazz soloist on his instrument. Although he developed into a superb craftsman, his playing was often marred by a tendency towards exhibitionism and vulgar technical display. Nevertheless, his commitment to jazz was genuine, as was reflected brilliantly in the bands he led. It is ironic that he is remembered more for his bombastic solo on Goodman's "Sing, Sing, Sing" than for the many tasteful recordings he made with his own groups in later years.

---

9. Bogdanov et al., *All Music Guide to Jazz*, 733.

A drummer from childhood, Krupa first attracted attention on recordings made in 1927 with the McKenzie-Condon Chicagoans. That year he made history as the first musician to use a full drum set on records. He continued to be part of the Chicago jazz scene until the early years of the Depression, when he moved to New York to work in studio and pit bands as a sideman to Red Nichols, Eddie Condon, and Bix Beiderbecke. In 1934 he joined Benny Goodman's new orchestra and for the next three years he was an important part of that pacesetting band, in addition to Goodman's trio and quartet. After he nearly stole the show at Goodman's 1938 Carnegie Hall Concert, Krupa left Goodman to form his own band. Fine players such as Vido Musso and the excellent singer Irene Daye were assets to his orchestra, but it wasn't until 1941, when he added singer Anita O'Day and trumpeter Roy Eldridge and learned to diminish the drum's overpowering role, that Krupa's big band really took off.

In 1943 Krupa, now an international star on record and in films, was arrested on a trumped-up charge of contributing to the delinquency of a minor (ostensibly for hiring an underage band boy). Unfortunately, the bad publicity from his arrest and short jail sentence (he won his case when it came to appeal) forced the breakup of his orchestra. Later that year he was back with Goodman for an emotional reunion. He worked briefly with Tommy Dorsey before putting together another big band in 1944. By the late 1940s the group had developed a superb ensemble sound and had become one of the finest big bands, with musicians such as Gerry Mulligan, Frank Rosolino, and Urbie Green among its sidemen. After breaking up his band in 1951, Krupa regularly worked with trios or quartets, toured with Jazz at the Philharmonic, ran a drum school with Cozy Cole, and had occasional reunions with Goodman. Despite gradually worsening health in the 1960s that forced him into semi-retirement, Krupa remained a major name up to his death. Sadly, a fire destroyed his houseful of memorabilia shortly before he died.

JANUARY 16—IRVING MILLS (1894–1985)

b. New York, NY; d. Palm Springs, CA

Impresario; Music Publisher; Lyricist; Vocalist

[CLASSIC JAZZ]

Other jazz notables born on this day: Vido Musso (1913)
Jazz notables deceased this day: Fate Marable (1947); Ike Quebec (1963); Jabbo Smith (1991); Gene Harris (2000)

♪

While Irving Mills's role in jazz was as an organizer rather than as a musician, his contributions are central to jazz history. A shrewd, tough businessman, he is most famous for his work as Duke Ellington's manager during 1926 to 1939, when he published his music and helped him gain his residency at the Cotton Club. In addition, he secured numerous recording sessions, film contracts, and other important engagements for his client. He also wrote the lyrics to some of Ellington's songs, including "It Don't Mean a Thing if It Ain't Got That Swing," "Mood Indigo," and "Sophisticated Lady." (Readers should note that Barney Bigard, Ellington's long-time clarinetist, composed "Moon Indigo" and "Sophisticated Lady," songs regularly attributed to Ellington.)

In 1919, with his brother Jack, Mills established a music publishing business that specialized in the work of African-American artists. He also worked as a talent scout, record producer, and band manager. In addition to Ellington, Mills helped promote the careers of Cab Calloway, Benny Carter, Fletcher Henderson, Jimmie Lunceford, and Don Redman, and appeared as a singer on many sessions. He put together all-star recording groups under such names as the Whoopee Makers and the Irving Mills's Hotsy Totsy Gang (featuring Bix Beiderbecke, Benny Goodman, Jack Teagarden, and Hoagy Carmichael), and in 1931 became the manager for an orchestra that he renamed the Mills Blue Rhythm Band. However, his name will forever remain linked with that of Ellington.

In 1923, when Ellington moved from his native Washington, DC to Harlem to see if he could succeed in what was then America's most glamorous atmosphere, he joined Elmer Snowden's six-piece outfit at the Hollywood Club, a rough club in the center of Times Square. When the band discovered that Snowden was pocketing more than his share of the take, they forced him out and made Ellington the leader. The band stayed at the club (later renamed the Kentucky Club) for four years, except during the summer, when heat forced it to close down. By 1924 Ellington's band had the hottest sound in town, but he needed help getting his music recorded and published.

In 1926 he hired Mills, a Kentucky Club regular, as manager and the following year he relocated to the Cotton Club, Harlem's most prestigious club. That became the turning point in Ellington's career. Though it came with a high price tag—Mills would receive 55 percent of the orchestra's earnings—Ellington never regretted the deal, for his move to the Cotton Club catapulted Duke to fame. Some members of the band objected, especially when Mills's name began appearing as the co-composer of songs Ellington alone had written. But Ellington never complained publicly about his arrangement, though it confined him to a modest lifestyle for much of his career.

JANUARY 17—BIG SID CATLETT (1910–1951)

b. Evansville, IN; d. Chicago, IL

Drummer

[SWING]

Other jazz notables born on this day: Terrence Holder (1897); Bob Zurke (1912); Cedar Walton (1934); Ted Dunbar (1937); Cyrus Chestnut (1963)
Jazz notables deceased this day: Charlie Ventura (1992)

♪

Big Sid Catlett packed a lot into his short life. A flashy showman but also a superb musician, he was every bit the equal of such better-known contemporaries as Jo Jones or Gene Krupa.[10] One of the outstanding drummers of the swing period, he had a bright, firm touch and absolute metrical precision in his right-hand ride patterns. He knew how to

---

10. Bogdanov et al., *All Music Guide to Jazz*, 212.

generate enormous intensity in big-band performances while providing expert accompaniment in small-group settings. Revealing a clear sense of logical development, he provided some of the most satisfying extended solos in pre-modern jazz drumming. Perhaps most remarkable was his individual way of adapting to all the jazz styles then available, which made him one of the most flexible drummers in the history of jazz.

Catlett grew up in Chicago, where he learned the rudiments of drumming. An easygoing, softhearted giant, often dressed in green chalk-striped suits and brightly flowered neckties, Catlett came to New York in 1930 to join Elmer Snowden's band. He quickly acquired the reputation as "a musician's drummer"; his spirit and great drive made him the center of attention wherever he went. Before long his musical skills and his flair for showmanship guaranteed work with the elite bands of the period, including with Benny Carter (1932), McKinney's Cotton Pickers (1934–35), Fletcher Henderson (1936), and Don Redman (1936–38). Catlett became Louis Armstrong's drummer of choice, working in the trumpeter's band from 1938 to 1942. "Though he was such a powerful fellow he could play very lightly and delicately without sounding weak," said Max Kaminsky, "and his generosity matched his size. He'd give you the shirt off his back if you needed it."[11] The 1940s bebop revolution clearly pinpointed Catlett's versatility. Where the conflicts of jazz fashion traumatized fellow drummer Dave Tough, the easygoing Catlett simply crossed Fifty-Second Street and sat in with Parker and Gillespie. In 1941 he played with a particularly excellent Benny Goodman big band that also included trumpeters Billy Butterfield and Cootie Williams. From 1942 to 1944 he worked with Teddy Wilson's small group, then led his own small bands in various cities and made recordings with Lester Young, Dizzy Gillespie, and Benny Carter.

Catlett played non-stop through the 1940s, seldom bothering to go to bed, and by the late '40s he was visibly ill. He worked again with Armstrong, playing Dixieland with his All-Stars from 1947 to 1949, until a heart attack forced him to retire from the demands of touring. He continued to play, however, working with Eddie Condon and John Kirby in New York and then as house drummer in a Chicago club. In 1950, while attending a Hot Lips Page benefit, he collapsed in the wings of the Chicago Opera House. The following year he contracted pneumonia and then died suddenly of a heart attack; he was only forty-one.

JANUARY 18—CHARLES DELAUNAY (1911–1988)

b. Paris, France; d. near Paris, France

Writer; Producer

[CLASSIC JAZZ; SWING; BOP]

Other jazz notables born on this day: Irene Kral (1932); Al Foster (1944); Steve Grossman (1951)

Jazz notables deceased this day: Al Hall (1988)

♪

---

11. Carr et al., *Jazz: The Rough Guide*, 128.

One of the myths accompanying European attitudes toward jazz almost from its inception is that Europeans have always been more sensitive and receptive to jazz than Americans. As with all myths, this one has some substance. Europeans, for instance, wrote about jazz earlier than Americans did, and they have often written about it better since. And whereas there has always existed a much larger market for jazz in the United States than in Europe (today there are more real jazz clubs in New York City alone than in all of Europe), on that continent jazz is treated as an art form and has a thriving audience.[12] By the late 1920s European musicians had been exposed, through touring American groups and especially through records, to a good deal of jazz. Though English musicians had a linguistic advantage, the pivotal event in European jazz occurred in Paris. This was the founding, in 1932, of the Hot Club de France, the most celebrated jazz club in history.

The club's initial impulse came from a few students who had little knowledge of jazz but wanted a place to take girls dancing. They asked Hugues Panassié, a young saxophonist who had already written about jazz, to be president, and the twenty-year old turned the group into a legitimate jazz organization. In 1933 Charles Delaunay, son of the celebrated painters Sonja and Robert Delaunay, became involved in the organization. He served as its general secretary and was particularly active in promoting concerts. Eventually a jazz band named the Quintett du Hot Club de France was formed, fronted by two outstanding musicians, violinist Stéphane Grappelli and the Gypsy guitarist Django Reinhardt. For the remainder of the 1930s much of the most important activity in the European jazz world revolved around this band.

In 1934, just four months after the first issue of the earliest American jazz magazine, *Down Beat*, Delaunay and Panassié established the journal, *Jazz Hot*, and two years later Swing, a record label in France devoted exclusively to jazz. With the outbreak of war the journal was discontinued but in 1946, after he and Panassié had reactivated *Jazz Hot*, Delaunay traveled to the U.S. to supervise recordings for the Swing label, where he encountered a revolutionary new form of jazz known as bebop. Europeans, isolated from America by the war, were shocked by their sudden encounter with bebop, but with a penchant for philosophic debate, they soon divided passionately into two camps: the traditionalists and the beboppers. So ferocious was the dispute that Delaunay and Panassié, colleagues for fifteen years, split, with Panassié in the New Orleans camp and Delaunay with the beboppers. Panassié took over the Hot Club, Delaunay the magazine *Jazz Hot*, and they never spoke again. Undaunted, Delaunay continued his progressive efforts on behalf of jazz, lecturing, writing, arranging recording sessions, and organizing concerts—most notably the Paris Jazz Festival of 1949. In 1969, after years of promoting jazz, he began his tenure as vice-president of the International Jazz Federation.

---

12. Collier, *Making of Jazz*, 314.

JANUARY 19—HORACE PARLAN (1931–)

b. Pittsburgh, PA

Pianist

[Hard Bop]

Other jazz notables born on this day: Israel Crosby (1919)
Jazz notables deceased this day: Alcide "Slow Drag" Pavageau (1969); Gerry Mulligan (1996)

♪

Horace Parlan, like Django Reinhardt and others who have overcome physical disabilities and thrived, has been a long-time inspiration to musicians and fans alike. At the age of five, Parlan's right hand was partly crippled by polio, and as a consequence the fourth and fifth fingers of his right hand were rendered useless. He studied piano from the age of twelve and compensated by developing a strong left-hand technique, in addition to inventive chord voicings. Parlan had a gift for relaxed, swinging music that gave his piano playing a central yet unassuming role. His style, like Reinhardt's, actually benefited from his disability.

Parlan began playing in R&B bands in the Pittsburgh area (1952–57) and briefly with Sonny Stitt in Washington, DC before he relocated to New York, where he had the distinction of being Charles Mingus's pianist (1957–59) during a period that saw the release of two of Mingus's finest recordings, *Blues and Roots* and *Mingus Ah Um*. One of the reasons for the richness of those recordings was Parlan's individualistic style, which combines highly rhythmic right-hand phrases with unusual chords in the left. As a soloist, however, he developed a style that Mingus found irresistible, using short melodic runs with the right hand that culminated in chunky percussive chords.[13] Using his physical disability to further advantage, Parlan avoided blues clichés yet managed to sound more blues-influenced than many other pianists of his generation.

Parlan's stint with Mingus proved to be a significant stimulus to his career, both through their recordings and the bandleader's influence. Parlan recorded frequently in the early 1960s, as leader and also as sideman. He played in a quartet with Booker Ervin (1960–61) and in a quintet led by Eddie "Lockjaw" Davis and Johnny Griffin (1961–62) before he joined the sensational Rahsaan Roland Kirk (1963–66).

Due to the scarcity of jazz work during the late 1960s and early '70s, Parlan moved to Copenhagen in 1973, where he performed steadily and gained international recognition for his distinctive style. Copenhagen, home to Scandinavia's foremost jazz club, the Montmartre Jazzhus, has engaged many outstanding musicians since it opened in 1959, when it hosted George Lewis and his band for two weeks. While many Danish musicians began their careers at Montmartre, a number of Americans established residencies there, including Stan Getz, Dexter Gordon, Kenny Drew, Idrees Sulieman, and Thad Jones, in addition to Parlan, all of whom settled for some time in or near Copenhagen. Among his many activities since taking up residence in Copenhagen, Parlan has toured Japan, co-led

---

13. Bogdanov et al., *All Music Guide to Jazz*, 981.

a quintet with Doug Raney, recorded outstanding albums with saxophonist Archie Shepp, and played with the tribute band Mingus Dynasty.

JANUARY 20—JIMMY COBB (1929–)

b. Washington, DC

Drummer

[Hard Bop]

Other jazz notables born on this day: Valery Ponomarev (1943); Andy Sheppard (1957); Jeff "Tain" Watts (1960)
Jazz notables deceased this day: David "Fathead" Newman (2009)

♪

In 1959 Miles Davis recorded one of the best-loved and most pivotal albums in modern jazz, *Kind of Blue*. Every track on the album was modal, and the playing was spare, controlled, and moody. This album, considered by many critics and observers as the most influential in jazz history, featured Davis, John Coltrane, Bill Evans, Cannonball Adderley, and Paul Chambers. With the exception of Davis, all were on their way to jazz stardom and each is now numbered among the most influential of all time on their instrument. By that time, of course, Davis was the dominant figure in jazz, and his rhythm sections were regarded as the best units of the period. The drummer on *Kind of Blue*, as well as on many other fine Davis sessions from 1958 to 1962, was Jimmy Cobb.

A superb drummer, Cobb's style is in the classic hard-bop tradition of Philly Joe Jones, Max Roach, and Art Blakey. Like Kenny Clarke, Cobb's strength lies in his solid time keeping. Largely self-taught, Cobb showed a great deal of talent early on, playing locally with Charlie Rouse, Leo Parker, Frank Wess, Benny Golson, Billie Holiday, and Pearl Bailey, before leaving Washington, DC at the age of twenty-one to join saxophonist Earl Bostic. Shortly thereafter he formed a trio with pianist Wynton Kelly that for three years accompanied his then wife Dinah Washington, for whom he also acted as musical director until 1955. Washington, the finest blues singer of her generation and one of jazz's most distinctive vocalists, had trouble maintaining relationships (Cobb is said to have been one of at least nine husbands during her thirty-nine-year lifespan), and she soon sent Cobb packing.

He joined Cannonball Adderley's quintet from 1956 until it disbanded in 1957, then played briefly with Stan Getz and Dizzy Gillespie before following Adderley into Davis's group, where he replaced Philly Joe Jones. During his nearly five year period with Davis, Cobb recorded with Davis sidemen Adderley, Coltrane, Chambers, and Kelly, as well as with Kenny Dorham, Wayne Shorter, Paul Gonsalves, Art Pepper, Bobby Timmons, Wes Montgomery, and others. He left Davis in 1962 to form a trio with Chambers and Kelly that performed successfully until Chambers's death in 1969. From 1970 to 1978, fifteen years after his work with Washington, Cobb accompanied yet another stellar vocalist, the incomparable Sarah Vaughan. He remained active into the twenty-first century, performing, recording, and teaching in a variety of contexts. Under the auspices of Duke University he spent three summers teaching at the "Charlie Parker College" in Italy. During the 1980s he taught at the New School for Social Research in New York and worked with the Joe Albany trio, in addition to extensive freelance outings and regular appearances with cornetist Nat Adderley's groups. In the late 1990s the indefatigable drummer recorded with Cobb's Mob, a small group of likeminded musicians whose members were drawn from the New School.

JANUARY 21—RUDI BLESH (1899–1985)

b. Guthrie, OK; d. Gilmanton, NH

Writer; Record Producer; Broadcaster

[NEW ORLEANS JAZZ; RAGTIME]

Other jazz notables born on this day: Steve Gilmore (1943)
Jazz notables deceased this day: Russell Procope (1981); Peggy Lee (2002)

♪

During the 1930s New Orleans jazz was in retreat in America. By 1933 bandleaders King Oliver and Jelly Roll Morton had virtually disappeared and cornetist Nick LaRocca, leader of the Original Dixieland Jazz Band, had become a building contractor. Trombonist Kid Ory, who had taken New Orleans jazz to California in 1919, went into chicken farming. Swing was in, and Dixieland music seemed irrelevant. The swing band movement's popularity during the 1930s caused a predictable reaction. In fact, there were two reactions, one looking backward and another looking forward. One group, consisting mainly of African-American beboppers, wanted something new, something distinct that could not be imitated by whites. Another group, consisting of jazz writers and older fans that saw the rise of the swing bands as a sellout to commercialism, considered only the New Orleans style as authentic jazz. Within this group was a contingent of young jazz musicians who had originally been swept up by imported New Orleans music in their native Chicago. Though they had not forgotten their mentors, most were now earning their living in dance bands. These talented musicians included jazz purists like Mezz Mezzrow, who spoke out against "commercial" bands and called for a return to "authentic" New Orleans—black New Orleans—music. Mezzrow's views had some effect on musicians in America and greatly influenced the pioneer French jazz writer Hugues Panassié. In his second history of jazz (*The Real Jazz*, 1942), Panassié pronounced the clarinet playing of Benny Goodman and Artie Shaw to be "like birds twittering in the trees," and urged for a return to "pure" New Orleans jazz. Mezzrow and Panassié seemed to agree that few white musicians could play "real" jazz.[14]

One of the movement's strongest advocates was Rudi Blesh, who during the early 1940s served as jazz critic for the *San Francisco Chronicle*. Like Mezzrow, he argued that only African-Americans, preferably those from New Orleans, could play jazz. In 1943, af-

---

14. Kirchner, *Oxford Companion to Jazz*, 307.

ter giving a series of lectures on jazz at the San Francisco Museum of Art, Blesh promoted concerts with veteran New Orleans musicians such as Bunk Johnson and Kid Ory. In 1944 he moved to New York and became jazz critic for the *New York Herald Tribune*. He threw himself wholeheartedly into the debate between adherents of traditional jazz (derided by opponents as "moldy figs") and the champions of bebop, but he later came to see both sides of the dispute and sponsored concerts contrasting the two styles. In 1946, with Harriet Janis, he founded Circle, a small but significant jazz record company that began reissuing classic New Orleans-style recordings. From 1947 to 1950 he hosted *This Is Jazz*, a radio program that promoted top New Orleans jazz artists. His history of jazz, *Shining Trumpets* (1946), was an informative though flawed volume because of its bias against 1930s swing music. In 1950, also with Janis, he wrote the first history of ragtime, *They All Played Ragtime*. In later years he taught jazz history at various colleges and helped rediscover traditional jazz musicians such as Eubie Blake.

JANUARY 22—J.J. JOHNSON (1924–2001)

b. Indianapolis, IN; d. Indianapolis, IN

Trombonist; Composer; Leader

[Bop; Hard Bop; Third Stream]

Other jazz notables born on this day: Juan Tizol (1900); André Hodeir (1921); Eberhard Weber (1940); Michal Urbaniak (1943)

Jazz notables deceased this day: Ed "Montudi" Garland (1980)

♪

As trombonist, J.J. Johnson was in a class by himself. Considered by some to be the finest trombonist of all time, he is clearly the most influential and important postwar jazz trombonist. During the 1940s he achieved a quantum leap on the trombone, managing to transfer the bebop innovations of Charlie Parker and Dizzy Gillespie to his unwieldy instrument and playing with such speed and deceptive ease that some listeners simply assumed he was playing valve (rather than slide) trombone.[15] While his earliest recorded solos reveal a thick tone and aggressive manner, he already displayed an impressive mobility by 1944, when he played at the first Jazz at the Philharmonic concert. During the late 1940s, as he worked to adapt bop patterns to the trombone, his solos suffered from an emphasis on speed and an over reliance on memorized formulas. By the late 1950s, relieved of the need to prove himself alongside the beboppers, his playing had improved significantly, making his instrument a more convincing vehicle for extended soloing than in the hands of almost anyone else.

James Louis Johnson (his nickname "J.J." arose from his manner of initialing compositions early in his career; later he made "J.J." his legal name) studied piano before taking up the trombone at the age of fourteen. After working with territory bands, he joined Benny Carter's band at the age of eighteen, staying from 1942 to 1945. He moved permanently

---

15. Bogdanov et al., *All Music Guide to Jazz*, 672–73.

to New York in 1946 and for the next few years played small-group jazz at various clubs with all the top bop musicians, including Bud Powell, Max Roach, Fats Navarro, Charlie Parker, the Dizzy Gillespie big band, and the Miles Davis Birth of the Cool nonet. J.J. also recorded with such sidemen as Powell, Sonny Rollins, and the Metronome All-Stars, and in 1952 toured with an all-star group that included Davis. His worsening financial situation forced him to retire from music temporarily in 1952, but in 1954 he formed a highly successful two-trombone quintet with Kai Winding that became known as Jay and Kai. This group remained intact until 1956, bringing Johnson's work to a larger audience and establishing his reputation as the leading jazz trombonist.

After disbanding the combo, J.J. began composing ambitious works that drew attention to his talents as a composer. He had a gift for melody that made him an effective composer, and from the 1950s, his jazz albums were filled with original compositions. In 1970 he moved to Los Angeles, where he successfully wrote television and film scores. Johnson was so famous in the jazz world at this time that he kept winning *Down Beat* polls, despite infrequent recordings and performances. In 1987 he returned to Indianapolis and withdrew again from jazz, as he helped to take care of his wife during a long terminal illness. After her death in 1992 he re-emerged as an active player once again, remaining at the top of his field during the 1990s. He fell ill with prostate cancer and took his own life on Feb. 4, 2001.

JANUARY 23—DJANGO REINHARDT (1910–1953)

b. Liverchies, near Luttre, Belgium; d. Fontainebleau, France

Guitarist

[SWING]

Other jazz notables born on this day: Benny Waters (1902); Michel Warlop (1911); Jack Kluger (1912); Teddy Napoleon (1914); Marty Paich (1925); Gary Burton (1943)
Jazz notables deceased this day: Kid Ory (1973); Babs Gonzales (1980); Lou Levy (2001); Brother Jack McDuff (2001)

♪

Mention the words "Gypsy guitarist," and any jazz fan will tell you they refer to Django Reinhardt, "the most creative jazz musician to originate anywhere outside the USA," according to Duke Ellington's son Mercer. Django was the first hugely influential jazz figure to emerge from Europe, and he remains one of the most influential Europeans to this day.[16] His harmonic concepts were startling for their time, as were his remarkable technique and trenchant rhythmic sense. He developed into a soloist of unique character, creating a deeply personal style based on his own cultural heritage.

The hero of jazz lovers under the Nazis and the personification of stubborn individualism, Django's life is as incredible as his music. Born in a shantytown to a traveling show entertainer known as "La Belle Laurence," the illegitimate Jean Baptiste was called

---

16. Bogdanov et al., *All Music Guide to Jazz*, 1060.

Django from the first. The musical prodigy grew up in a Gypsy camp near Paris, and by the age of fifteen he had traveled widely as a professional. A disastrous caravan fire in 1928 badly burned his left hand, depriving him of the use of the fourth and fifth fingers. Through sheer willpower he compensated for his paralysis by developing a revolutionary and spellbinding technique based on his limitations. Influenced by Louis Armstrong, Duke Ellington, and by the playing of the great American guitarist Eddie Lang, Django formed a quintet with violinist Stéphane Grappelli in 1934 and the band soon became associated with the Hot Club de France, a record society that occasionally put on concerts. The Hot Club's next presentation, starring Coleman Hawkins, also featured the Quintette du Hot Club de France and successfully launched Django's career.

Within a year the quintet began to acquire international fame and in the next five years recorded more than two hundred sides, most of them acknowledged classics. The group's hard-swinging music, influenced by the violin-guitar duo of Joe Venuti and Lang, caught on quickly throughout Europe. At the outbreak of war in 1939, Grappelli remained in London, where the group had been playing, and Django returned to France. During the war years, as an unintended result of the Nazi occupation, jazz became more popular than ever. In France, Django enjoyed the greatest acclaim of his career, and even in Germany there were clandestine groups of jazz fans that met to listen to records. Jazz, of course, was anathema to the Nazis, who considered it the product of an unholy alliance between Africans and Jews. But to those who hated the Nazis, jazz stood for democracy and freedom, and Django, the illiterate, freewheeling Gypsy, became the movement's reluctant poster boy. After the war ended, Django performed in the U.S. briefly with his idol Duke Ellington, resumed touring with his own quintet, and held several reunions with Grappelli before he died from a stroke in 1953, when he was only forty-three.

JANUARY 24—JULIUS HEMPHILL (1938–1995)

b. Fort Worth, TX; d. New York, NY

Alto Saxophonist; Composer; Leader

[AVANT-GARDE; FREE JAZZ]

Other jazz notables born on this day: Joe Albany (1924); Marcus Printup (1967)
Jazz notables deceased this day: Don Fagerquist (1974); Les Spann (1989); Walter Bishop Jr. (1998)

♪

John Coltrane's death in the summer of 1967 had a baleful impact on all of jazz. His personality and artistic pilgrimage somehow epitomized the enigmatic, restless 1960s, and his passing symbolized jazz's capitulation to rock. Record labels folded, clubs closed, and the future looked bleak for jazz. But jazz came roaring back in the mid-1970s with the return of mainstream artists such as Sonny Rollins and Dexter Gordon. Perhaps more surprisingly, it also saw an upturn in the fortunes of a group that until then had stood far outside the commercial mainstream—the avant-garde, whose practitioners had maintained their enthusiasm and sense of adventure despite a diminutive audience. The jazz avant-garde had lacked a forceful and charismatic leader since Coltrane's death, and it had been further demoralized in 1970 when free-jazz saxophonist Albert Ayler was found dead under mysterious circumstances at the age of thirty-four. But by the end of the 1970s the movement had been revitalized by an infusion of musical daring, thanks largely to the Art Ensemble of Chicago, formed in 1969, and the World Saxophone Quartet (WSQ), formed in 1976. By playing a form of jazz that mixed complex structures and free improvisation with a pleasing sound and showmanship, the WSQ (Hamiet Bluiett, Oliver Lake, David Murray, and Julius Hemphill) emerged as the closest thing to a mainstream success the jazz avant-garde had seen since Coltrane.

The members of the quartet all had ambitions of their own—Hemphill with his theatrical presentations and one-man audio dramas; Lake, alternating between solo sax recitals and his disco jump band; Bluiett and Murray organizing orchestras—but it was as a unit that the four musicians found their largest audience and arguably the most effective outlet for their compositions as well. Of the four, Hemphill had the deepest commitment to write for the quartet's unique instrumentation. He was so prolific that his sound came to embody the WSQ approach. By 1980 he was earning comparison with Benny Carter and Duke Ellington and other great orchestrators who had devised a trademark sound for saxophones. By this time, WSQ was one of the most prominent ensembles in jazz, concertizing everywhere and attaining a measure of critical consensus when Martin Williams added its 1981 recording of "Steppin'" to the revised edition of the *Smithsonian Collection of Classic Jazz*, the only selection recorded after 1966.

After the WSQ forced Hemphill out in 1990, he formed his own sextet and played until his death in 1995. The WSQ was only a part of what Hemphill achieved before his death, after years of illness—diabetes, heart disease, cancer—robbed him of a leg (he had a partial amputation in 1982) and of music making. As saxophonist Marty Ehrlich, one of Hemphill's most steadfast disciples, indicated: "He got lumped in with the avant-garde, but he was really his own academy."[17]

JANUARY 25—ANTONIO CARLOS JOBIM (1927–1994)

b. Rio de Janeiro, Brazil; d. New York, NY

Songwriter; Pianist; Guitarist; Vocalist

[BRAZILIAN JAZZ; BOSSA NOVA; WORLD FUSION]

Other jazz notables born on this day: Wellman Braud (1891); Benny Golson (1929)
Jazz notables deceased this day: Seldon Powell (1997); Roy Porter (1998)

♪

In 1959 the release of the film *Black Orpheus* introduced Brazil's musical bounty to the world. Exotic percussion instruments and call-and-response singing filled the soundtrack, interspersed with compositions by Antonio Carlos Jobim and Luiz Bonfa, young musi-

---

17. Giddins, *Visions of Jazz*, 549.

cians in Rio's artistic community. Their music fused the textures and rhythms of Brazil with elements from classical music, popular music, and American jazz to create the bossa nova, a style that would soon exert an enormous influence on jazz around the world.[18]

Jobim has been called the George Gershwin of Brazil—and rightly so, for both musicians contributed large bodies of songs to the jazz repertoire and both tend to symbolize their countries in the eyes of the rest of the world. Acknowledging the influence of Cole Porter as well as the French impressionist composer Claude Debussy, Jobim also gleaned a great deal from the recordings of Gerry Mulligan, Chet Baker, Barney Kessel, and other West Coast jazz musicians of the 1950s. The Brazilian samba gave his music a uniquely exotic rhythmic underpinning.

Born in Rio, Jobim originally pursued a career as an architect. But by the time he turned twenty, the lure of music was too powerful, so he started playing piano in nightclubs and working in recording studios. He first found fame in 1956 when he teamed with lyricist Vinícius de Moraes to provide part of the score for a play called *Orfeo do Carnaval* (later made into the film *Black Orpheus*). Over the years this songwriting duo composed such famous songs as "Chega de Saudade (No More Blues)," "A Felicidade," "The Girl from Ipanema," and "Insensatez." In 1958, as music director of Odeon Records, Jobim persuaded the company to record a then unknown Brazilian singer, Joao Gilberto, performing "Chega de Saudade." The recording was a great commercial success and launched the bossa nova craze. Jobim's breakthrough outside Brazil occurred in 1962 when Stan Getz and Charlie Byrd scored a surprise hit with his tune "Desafinado," and later that year he and several other Brazilian musicians were invited to participate with them and Dizzy Gillespie at a concert in Carnegie Hall. Fueled by Jobim's songs, the bossa nova became an international fad into the late 1960s.

Jobim preferred the recording studios to touring, and he made several outstanding albums of his music as a pianist, guitarist, and singer. When Brazilian music was in its American eclipse after the 1960s, Jobim retreated into the background, but in 1985, as the idea of world music and a second Brazilian wave gathered steam, Jobim began touring again. By the time of his final concerts in Brazil (1993) and at Carnegie Hall in New York (1994), Jobim was receiving the universal recognition he deserved, including a host of tribute albums and concerts that followed his sudden death of heart failure.

JANUARY 26—STÉPHANE GRAPPELLI (1908–1997)

b. Paris, France; d. Paris, France

Violinist

[Swing]

Other jazz notables born on this day: Alice Babs (1924); Dick Nash (1928)
Jazz notables deceased this day: Kenny Clarke (1985); Attila Zoller (1998)

♪

---

18. Kirchner, *Oxford Companion to Jazz*, 548.

Prior to the advent of bebop, there were three acknowledged masters of jazz violin: Joe Venuti, the most important violinist in early jazz; Stuff Smith, the most forceful swing fiddler in jazz history; and Stéphane Grappelli, the pioneering Frenchman whose longevity and enthusiastic playing helped establish the violin as a jazz instrument.

Grappelli's mother died when he was three years old, and due to his father's inability to care for him, he lived in orphanages and then on the street. When he was twelve he returned to his father, who purchased a violin for the budding musician. While studying at the Paris Conservatoire (1924–28), he played in movie theaters and dance bands and in 1927, when talking films arrived, he began to work with the Gregorians, playing piano in a big band led by a flamboyant French dancer named Gregor.

The next important step in Grappelli's development was the formation of the Quintette du Hot Club de France. In 1928, at the Croix du Sud club, Grappelli met Django Reinhardt, another young musician trying to come to terms with jazz. At this time Django was still an unknown musician laboring in obscure cafés and music halls, but one night in 1933, at the Hotel Claridge, their acquaintance turned into a musical partnership. With the addition of two more acoustic guitars and a bass, a pioneering jazz quintet was formed that produced a sensational series of recordings and performances. Much later, Grappelli joked: "We were the first rock 'n' roll band in the world. I don't know anybody who had three guitars before we did."[19]

The brilliant pair hit it off musically from the start even though their lifestyles were very different. The elegant and fastidious Grappelli contrasted almost completely with his illiterate, helter-skelter alter ego. Django was forever disappearing from hotel suites to spend a few days at Gypsy encampments, playing his guitar for nothing while engagements worth thousands of francs had to be canceled. In many respects Grappelli played the father to Django, chiding him for his behavior, taking care of his contracts, even signing his autographs for him on the sly. Django undoubtedly resented this aspect of their relationship.

As chance would have it, the quintet was in London at the outbreak of the war. Django and the others left for Paris, but Grappelli, who was single, stayed in England, effectively ending the group. In 1964 Grappelli and Reinhardt had the first of several reunions although they never worked together on a regular basis. During the 1950s and '60s Grappelli performed in clubs throughout Europe, but he remained somewhat obscure in the U.S. until his first visit in 1969, when he performed at the Newport Jazz Festival. Since that time he traveled regularly and won polls consistently, remaining open-minded without altering his swing style. Grappelli stayed at the top of his field until he was eighty-nine, his colossal technique, sculptured lines, and elegant repertoire remaining one of jazz's most graceful sounds.

---

19. Kirchner, *Oxford Companion to Jazz*, 540.

BLUE NOTES

JANUARY 27—HOT LIPS PAGE (1908–1954)
b. Dallas, TX; d. New York, NY
Trumpeter; Vocalist

[JAZZ BLUES; SWING; DIXIELAND]

Other jazz notables born on this day: Will Marion Cook (1869); Charlie Holmes (1910); Dick Meldonian (1930); Bobby Hutcherson (1941); Bob Mintzer (1953)
Jazz notables deceased this day: Don Abney (2000); Friedrich Gulda (2000)

♪

During the 1920s and '30s Kansas City was a hub of jazz activity. Once the notorious political boss Tom Pendergast took control of the city, the town was wide open for gambling, narcotics, and prostitution. Gangster-run saloons and cabarets proliferated at such a rate that Kansas City boasted the largest concentration in America. They provided work for a lot of musicians, and with so much happening, Kansas City musicians became addicted to after-hours jam sessions. Sessions sometimes ran from midnight until the following noon. Under this competitive pressure the city's musicians developed into powerful improvisers without losing sight of the main concern, the ability to swing.

Two bands stood above all others in Kansas City at this time: Walter Page's Blue Devils and the Bennie Moten Orchestra. In 1935 the best players from each organization came together under the leadership of Count Basie, a pianist who had played with both bands. One of the members of Basie's band was Hot Lips (Oran Thaddeus) Page, a talented blues vocalist and one of the great swing trumpeters of all time. Throughout his career Page built upon his formative Kansas City experience, thriving on the atmosphere of impromptu jam sessions, where his searing tone, dramatic phrasing, and improvised blues lyrics were a joy to his audience and an inspiration to his fellow musicians.

In 1936 Page was principal soloist with Count Basie's band but he left after Joe Glaser, Louis Armstrong's manager, signed him to a solo contract that many regard as having crippled his potentially illustrious career. Glaser, knowing that Armstrong was suffering with lip trouble and might be finished, signed Page as a possible replacement for his star trumpeter. But after Armstrong's lip recovered, Glaser rapidly lost sight of his second-string player, and Page had reason to see himself as an Armstrong wannabe. But by this time "The Trumpet King of the West," as he was billed, was building a storehouse of confidence, showmanship, and technique. When Basie left for Chicago with his new band, Page stayed behind to front his own band. Had he gone east with Basie, he probably would have acquired greater fame. Page eventually moved to New York, where he led his own bands before he joined Artie Shaw's band (1941–42), during which time he attracted much publicity. From 1943 to 1949 he freelanced in smaller groups, and in the 1950s he appeared mainly as a soloist. During this time he recorded with many all-star groups and was always welcomed at jam sessions.

Throughout his career, Page was often plagued by bad luck: his hit record of "St. James Infirmary" with Shaw came just as the group disbanded; a later best seller with

Pearl Bailey, "Baby, It's Cold Outside," launched Bailey but left Page unremembered; and his signing to a long contract by Glaser came just before his probable breakthrough into stardom with Count Basie. It is ironic that the first full-scale reissue of Page's material on LP came seventeen years after his death, the year that Armstrong died.

JANUARY 28—RONNIE SCOTT (1927–1996)

b. London, England; d. London, England

Tenor Saxophonist; Bandleader

[Bop; Post-Bop]

Other jazz notables born on this day: Bob Moses (1948); Henry Johnson (1954)
Jazz notables deceased this day: Ray Nance (1976); Jimmy Crawford (1980); Ray Biondi (1981)

♪

Because of the worldwide popularity of American jazz, nightclubs that present jazz can be found in almost every country. Of these countries, England has one of the longest and richest histories of jazz and one of the most famous jazz nightclubs in the world, Ronnie Scott's. This establishment, founded by tenor saxophonist Ronnie Scott in 1959, continues to operate as London's major center for modern jazz, despite Scott's tragic death in 1996. While the club originally specialized in presenting American jazz soloists, it also maintained a reputation for recording and promoting British musicians.

Ronnie Scott, originally a bebop specialist, developed a career remarkably similar to that of John Dankworth, another of England's best-known jazz musicians. Both were born in 1927, both worked in some of the same bands, and both played in transatlantic ship bands after World War II solely to hear the new jazz being played by such musicians as Dizzy Gillespie, Charlie Parker, and Bud Powell. The ship band experience was important for them because it brought them to New York frequently at the time when bebop was emerging. Both were barely out of their teens and still susceptible to new movements. They became committed to bop and pursued it through a number of lean years before it became profitable. Both developed sufficient reputations as jazz players to allow them to work in the U.S. on the strength of their names: Scott toured America in 1955 and Dankworth played at the Newport Jazz Festival and Birdland in 1959. That year, in partnership with businessman and former saxophonist Peter King, Scott opened the club in London that became one of the leading jazz venues in Europe. Dankworth also went on to fame, finding a different sort of partner—he married vocalist Cleo Laine in 1958—and establishing himself as one of Europe's most important jazz bandleaders.

After he formed his London club, Scott performed there with his own groups, leading a quartet from 1960 to 1967, an eight-piece band with John Surman and Kenny Wheeler (1968–69), and a trio from 1971 to 1975. As a member of the Clarke-Boland Big Band (1962–73), he recorded with John Dankworth's orchestra and continued to lead his own groups, including a big band that accompanied Ella Fitzgerald, Nancy Wilson, and other singers. In 1978 the club established its own record company and label, Ronnie Scott's Jazz House. Despite the worldwide fame of his club (he opened a second club in Birmingham in 1991) and his longstanding role as an effective figurehead of British jazz, Scott lacked self-confidence, caused in part by insecurity over his own musical abilities. Following a period of deepening depression, exacerbated by poor health and a dental problem that prevented him from playing, he took his own life on Dec. 23, 1996.

JANUARY 29—JEANNE LEE (1939–2000)

b. New York, NY; d. Tijuana, Mexico

Vocalist

[AVANT-GARDE; FREE JAZZ]

Other jazz notables born on this day: Ed Shaughnessy (1929); Derek Bailey (1932); Frank Assunto (1932)

Jazz notables deceased this day: Jack Hylton (1965); Sonny Payne (1979); Cozy Cole (1981); Malachi Favors (2004)

♪

Jeanne Lee is considered the most creative singer to have emerged from the avant-garde of the 1960s. Her haunting, highly expressive voice is better known in Europe than in America, in part because of her lengthy association with German vibraphonist Gunter Hampel, and also because many of her recordings were done for European labels, including Hampel's own Birth label. Critics have lauded her innovative vocal approach, which combines acrobatic vocal maneuvers with deep, emotive interpretations. Able to improvise dense, complex lines with the precision and flexibility of a great instrumentalist, she was equally at home in the simple idiom of a spiritual.

Born a child prodigy into a musical family (her father was a classically trained concert singer and her mother was a pianist), Lee won an amateur contest at the Apollo Theatre in Harlem but, unlike other singers who began their careers in this fashion, she moved into a classically influenced free-jazz style. She studied modern dance (rather than music) at New York's Bard College (1956–60), and while a student there she met pianist Ran Blake. They formed a duo and recorded together; her concerts and recordings with him were lauded by critics as demonstrating the first fresh approach to jazz singing since the emergence of Sarah Vaughan. In 1964 she moved to California, where she performed with Ian Underwood and David Hazelton, whom she later married.

While in Europe in 1967, Lee established a close musical association with Hampel, who became her second husband. She worked regularly with him into the mid-1990s, appearing with his Galaxie Dream Band and recording over twenty albums together. During the 1960s and '70s she also recorded with some of jazz's most distinguished avant-gardists, including Archie Shepp, Sunny Murray, Anthony Braxton, Enrico Rava, Andrew Cyrille, and Cecil Taylor. In the 1980s she concentrated on performing her own compositions, which unite her interests in song, dance, and poetry. In 1989 she recorded as a member of Reggie Workman's group at the Knitting Factory in New York, where her approach to improvisation met with a ready acceptance. In 1993, while teaching in New York, Boston, and elsewhere, she formed a duo with cellist David Eyges and recorded with soprano saxophonist Jane Bunnett. In 1995 she participated in a haunting remembrance of the fiftieth anniversary of the bombing of Hiroshima and Nagasaki with pianist Mal Waldron and flutist Toru Tenda in Japan. In 2000, after teaching in Europe, she faced colon cancer without medical insurance and died several months after undergoing surgery. To help the family with expenses, benefit concerts were held by a number of jazz musicians, including Hampel, Joseph Jarman, Rashied Ali, Hamiet Bluiett, and Abbey Lincoln, among others.

JANUARY 30—ROY ELDRIDGE (1911–1989)

b. Pittsburgh, PA; d. Valley Stream, NY

Trumpeter; Bandleader

[SWING; MAINSTREAM JAZZ]

Other jazz notables born on this day:
Jazz notables deceased this day: Fred Beckett (1917); Tiny Davis (1994); George James (1995); Bob Thiele (1996)

♪

One of the most exciting trumpeters to emerge during the swing era was Roy Eldridge, a hard-driven, diminutive player known as "Little Jazz." As one of the most competitive musicians in jazz history, Eldridge's combative approach, chance-taking style, and strong musicianship inspired the next musical generation, most notably Dizzy Gillespie.[20] Though he heard many great trumpeters during his formative years, in the end it was saxophonists Benny Carter and Coleman Hawkins whom Eldridge emulated. The saxophone model helped him to develop a technical edge over his competitors, and by the mid-1930s he was recognized as the most vital young trumpet player in New York.

Born in Pittsburgh, Eldridge was a gifted musician from the start. At fifteen he left home to play in carnival and circus bands. He moved to New York in 1931 and played in various dance bands in Harlem, including with Teddy Hill. His broadcasts from the Savoy Ballroom with Hill's band were heard widely and dazzled many listeners, including Gillespie, who considered them the transforming experience of his life.[21] In Hill's band he became a close friend with Chu Berry, and the two often went out on the town to take on challengers at cutting contests, thereby establishing a custom that Eldridge pursued throughout his career. His recorded solos with Hill in 1935 (backing Billie Holiday) and later with Fletcher Henderson brought Eldridge a great deal of attention. In 1936 he formed a successful band in Chicago, followed by a ten-piece unit at the Arcadia Ballroom in New York. By this point Eldridge was widely regarded as the outstanding jazz trumpet soloist of his time, and he began to receive attractive offers from white swing bands. When

---

20. Bogdanov et al., *All Music Guide to Jazz*, 370
21. Giddins, *Visions of Jazz*, 191–92.

he joined Gene Krupa's orchestra in 1941, he became one of the first black jazz musicians to be accepted as a permanent member of the brass section of a white big band. But the difficulties of traveling with a white band during a racist period caused the volatile trumpeter to suffer a nervous breakdown, and after a brief stint with Artie Shaw he vowed never to work again in the U.S. with a white band.

In the early 1940s Eldridge took a leading part in the jam sessions at Minton's Playhouse in New York that later crystallized in bop, but by the end of the decade he came to the realization that his playing was not as modern as the beboppers. He reached a point of crisis in 1950 while on tour with Benny Goodman and he decided to take a sabbatical in France. His stay during 1950 and 1951 restored his confidence as he realized that being original was more important than being modern. Eldridge recorded steadily after that. During the 1950s he was one of the stars of Jazz at the Philharmonic (where he battled Charlie Shavers and Gillespie), and by 1956 he often teamed with Hawkins in a quintet. The 1960s were tough for all jazz musicians, but from 1970 until 1980, when he was incapacitated by a stroke, he led a traditional jazz group at Jimmy Ryan's in New York, where he fueled his competitive spirit by taking on all comers.

JANUARY 31—BOBBY HACKETT (1915–1976)

b. Providence, RI; d. Chatham, MA

Cornetist; Bandleader

[SWING; DIXIELAND]

Other jazz notables born on this day: Benny Morton (1907)
Jazz notables deceased this day: Gregory Herbert (1978); Grant Green (1979); Si Zentner (2000)

♫

When Louis Armstrong switched from cornet to the more brilliant-sounding trumpet in the mid-1920s, he effectively ended the cornet's dominance in jazz. The only other pacesetting cornetist of the era, Bix Beiderbecke, died prematurely in 1931, after a career of only six years. The cornet, however, never entirely disappeared from jazz, as demonstrated by practitioners such as Joe Smith, Red Nichols, and Bobby Hackett.

Hackett was a supremely melodic jazz improviser whose cornet tone was glorious in all registers. When he first emerged he was known as "the new Bix" on account of the similarity of their approaches, but very soon he developed his own distinctive sound.[22] Because much of his life was spent playing in clubs with small bands, he was often typed as a Dixieland stylist, though his sophisticated phrasing and subtle use of harmonies enabled him to fit into many types of jazz ensemble. Originally a guitarist (on which he doubled until the mid-1940s), he initially specialized on cornet while working with Pee Wee Russell in 1933. He led his own band in 1936 and the following year moved to New York and played with Joe Marsala. He came to prominence after taking the role of

---

22. Bogdanov et al., *All Music Guide to Jazz*, 523.

Beiderbecke at Benny Goodman's famous 1938 Carnegie Hall concert (recreating Bix's solo on "I'm Coming Virginia"). He began a longstanding affiliation with Eddie Condon, and by 1939 had a short-lived big band at the Famous Door. After a brief stint with close friend Glenn Miller (1941–42), he took a job as staff musician at NBC. From 1944 to 1946 he was a member of Glen Gray's Casa Loma Orchestra and thereafter worked on the staff of ABC with Billy Butterfield, while performing regularly at Eddie Condon's and other clubs. By this time he had a severe drinking problem. Though he learned to control it, the habit helped induce the diabetes that eventually killed him. Hackett's gift for playing second cornetist made him a regular companion and recording colleague to Armstrong; in 1947 he was a principal figure in Armstrong's acclaimed Town Hall concert.

During the early 1950s Hackett's made his greatest recordings for Jackie Gleason's bestselling "mood music" albums, but that collaboration ended because Gleason paid him only slightly above union scale. Hackett produced masterpieces with Jack Teagarden (*Coast to Coast* is one of the greatest Dixieland albums ever) and by 1956 he led a band at the Henry Hudson hotel that sought to modernize Dixieland. When the group did not catch on, Hackett returned to studio work and to stints with Goodman. In 1965 he became official accompanist for Tony Bennett and remained active until his death. He co-led a well-recorded quintet with Vic Dickenson (1968–70) and participated in sessions with Mary Lou Williams, with the World's Greatest Jazz Band, and even with Dizzy Gillespie. Adored by singers (he was one of the few master accompanists on his instrument), Hackett was universally loved for his graceful music and for his congenial spirit.

Chapter 2

February

FEBRUARY 1—JAMES P. JOHNSON (1894–1955)
b. New Brunswick, NJ; d. New York, NY

Pianist; Composer

[Ragtime; Stride; Classic Jazz]

Other jazz notables born on this day: Tricky Sam Nanton (1904); Sadao Watanabe (1933); Joshua Redman (1969)
Jazz notables deceased on this day: Alex Hill (1937); Buddy Stewart (1950)

♫

In New York, jazz pianists of the early 1920s were called "ivory ticklers" or simply ticklers. Since jazz was part of the popular culture, audiences expected to hear the hit songs of the day, as personalized by their favorite players. The ticklers exploited the orchestral potential of the piano with right hand embellishments and a "striding" left hand that alternated bass notes with midrange chords. This combination led to the name "stride piano," the principal style of the 1920s. The top stride players were easterners centered in New York, particularly in Harlem. Of the stride pianists, the best and most influential was James P. Johnson.

Johnson's style, a balance of earthiness and sophistication, was due to his upbringing and to four years of classical training. He initially learned from his mother, a Virginian who loved country dances, and later admitted that a lot of his music was based on southern dance steps and rhythms. When his family moved to Jersey City, Johnson began lessons with a classical teacher named Bruto Giannini. Recognizing his pupil's talent and appreciating his uncommon bent, Giannini allowed Johnson to go on playing his stomps and rags, but also taught him harmony, counterpoint, and the classics of European keyboard literature. By 1912 Johnson was playing regularly in New York, performing at clubs in "Hell's Kitchen," a tough area between Sixtieth and Sixty-Third streets also known as the "Jungle," where workers from the South danced most of the night to the accompaniment of a solo piano. In this environment, where fighting and dancing competed with the sounds of the piano, Johnson developed an aggressive style that was both imaginative and strong. Intensely dedicated to his music, Johnson gained a feeling for the piano by practicing in the dark. He also played through a sheet to improve his dexterity, and by the start of World War I he was accepted as one of the leading pianists in his style. In 1917 he published the first of some two hundred songs and pieces, one of which, "Carolina Shout," became the signature composition of stride.

As the era's most sophisticated pianist, Johnson recorded with many blues singers, including Bessie Smith and Ethel Waters. He wrote Broadway musicals (one of his scores, "The Charleston," became America's most famous dance number) and collaborated with Fats Waller, his most famous pupil. During the Depression he turned his attention to the composition of large-scale works, but with the revival of traditional jazz in the late 1930s he began appearing again in clubs and at concerts. In 1940 he suffered the first of a series of eight strokes, which marked the slow decline in his health that led to his death in 1955. Despite critical neglect during his lifetime, the brilliance of his work often elicited the admiration of fellow pianists. As Duke Ellington once wrote: "It was me, or maybe Fats [Waller], who sat down to warm up the piano. After that, James took over. Then you got real invention—magic, sheer magic."[1]

FEBRUARY 2—STAN GETZ (1927–1991)

b. Philadelphia, PA; d. Malibu, CA

Tenor Saxophonist; Leader

[HARD BOP; WEST COAST JAZZ; COOL; BOSSA NOVA; POST-BOP]

Other jazz notables born on this day: Louis Keppard (1888); Sonny Stitt (1924); James "Blood" Ulmer (1942); Louis Sclavis (1953)

Jazz notables deceased on this day: Alfred Lion (1987); Mel Lewis (1990)

♫

Musicians like Stan Getz have a style that is hard to characterize because they don't fit comfortably into any particular niche. Because of his light tone and occasionally delicate approach, modeled after the incomparable Lester Young, Getz is often associated with the cool school, although his roots were in swing. In 1948, as a member of a famous Woody Herman reed section known as the Four Brothers, his eight-bar improvisation on a Ralph Burns's ballad, "Early Autumn" (1948), established him instantaneously as a major improviser in an advanced swing style. His celebrated performance, with its tender melody and delayed rhythm, captured the imagination of many young jazz musicians and helped to precipitate the "cool" reaction to bop in the years that followed.

One of the all-time great tenor saxophonists, Getz was known as "The Sound" because of his tone, one of the most beautiful ever heard.[2] He got his professional start with Jack Teagarden in 1943, when he was just sixteen, and this was followed by stints with Stan Kenton, Jimmy Dorsey, and Benny Goodman. After achieving fame with Herman's Second Herd (1947–49), he formed the first of many bands and remained a leader for the

---

1. Kirchner, *Oxford Companion to Jazz*, 167.
2. Bogdanov et al., *All Music Guide to Jazz*, 463.

rest of his life. Despite being out of circulation in 1954 due to drug problems, a recurring issue for Getz during the 1950s, he remained a constant poll winner. After a stint with Jazz at the Philharmonic (1957–58) and an extended stay in Europe (1958–61), Getz returned to the U.S. and recorded his personal favorite album, *Focus*, arguably the finest jazz-plus-strings album, with arranger Eddie Sauter's orchestra (1961). In 1962 he helped usher in the bossa nova era by recording *Jazz Samba* with Charlie Byrd; their rendition of "Desafinado" became a big hit. During the following year he recorded additional bossa nova flavored albums such as *Getz/Gilberto*, a 1964 collaboration with Antonio Carlos Jobim and Joao Gilberto that became his biggest seller, thanks in large part to "The Girl from Ipanema," one of the best-selling tracks in jazz history.

Despite the enormous popularity of his bossa nova albums, which made him a rich man and a household name, Getz's greatest acclaim came at the end of his life in recognition of the marvelous playing that characterized his final decade. In 1983 he recorded a deeply personal version of Billy Strayhorn's swan song, "Blood Count." Strayhorn had written it in the hospital a couple of months before his death in 1967, and Duke Ellington had included it in a Carnegie Hall concert and on a final album of Strayhorn compositions, *And His Mother Called Him Bill*. Ellington never played the song again. By the late 1980s Getz adapted it as his signature theme and played it on an almost nightly basis. "Blood Count," the composition that best embodies Getz's musical maturity, became the "Early Autumn" of his last years.[3]

FEBRUARY 3—LIL ARMSTRONG (1898 or 1902–1971)

b. Memphis, TN; d. Chicago, IL

Pianist; Leader; Vocalist; Composer

[New Orleans Jazz; Swing]

Other jazz notables born on this day: Kid Thomas Valentin (1896); Snooky Young (1919); Bobby Durham (1937)

Jazz notables deceased on this day: Andy Razaf (1973)

♪

On November 12, 1925, Louis Armstrong entered the OKeh studios in Chicago with a newly assembled band called Louis Armstrong and his Hot Five, and between that year and 1928 the Hot Five (later the Hot Seven) embarked on one of the most influential recording projects in jazz. With pianist Lil (Hardin) Armstrong, clarinetist Johnny Dodds, trombonist Kid Ory, and banjoist Johnny St. Cyr, Armstrong recorded a series of classics that are considered the height of New Orleans jazz.

In addition to her work with Armstrong's groundbreaking small-group recordings, Lil Armstrong will always be known for her influence in shaping Armstrong's career, though she had an important career of her own. After studying classical music at Nashville's Fisk University, Hardin moved to Chicago in 1917, where she worked as a song plugger, dem-

---

3. Giddins, *Visions of Jazz*, 409.

onstrating sheet music for $3 a week. As an ultra-modern jazz pianist, she soon graduated to orchestral work, getting a whopping $55 a week to accompany Sugar Johnny's Creole Orchestra. As her reputation grew, she moved on to Freddie Keppard's Original Creole Orchestra before joining King Oliver and Sidney Bechet at the Dreamland Café, where she also led her own band. In 1922, after touring the West Coast with Oliver, she joined his Creole Jazz Band. Oliver was well established at the Lincoln Gardens in 1922 when he sent a telegram to Louis, now the leading cornetist in New Orleans, asking him to play second cornet in what had become Chicago's hottest ensemble. Before long the teamwork between Armstrong and Oliver was the talk of Chicago, and it soon became obvious who was the better player.

On February 5, 1924, Louis and Lil married (she became the second of his four wives). Hoping to jumpstart her husband's career, particularly after Oliver let it be known that "as long as Louis is in my band, I'm still King," Lil persuaded her reluctant husband to break with his mentor, using as bait the discovery that the King had been withholding funds from his musicians. When Louis received an offer from the prominent New York bandleader Fletcher Henderson, Lil made sure he accepted it. A year later Louis was back in Chicago, playing at the Dreamland with Lil's band. Hardin kept a watchful eye on her husband's career, and before long he was ribbed because he worked for his wife. Tensions mounted, on and off the bandstand, and by 1931 they were separated. Despite their 1938 divorce, Lil continued to advertise herself as "Mrs. Louis Armstrong." After completing a postgraduate degree in music, she led several bands, among them an all-female group, and was house pianist for Decca. In 1940 she opened a restaurant in Chicago, and for the last thirty years of her life was a celebrated club pianist in the area. She recorded a talking record in 1959 on which she reminisced about her days with Louis, and ironically she died of a heart attack while taking part in a memorial concert for him, two months after his demise.

FEBRUARY 4—ARTIE BERNSTEIN (1909–1964)

b. New York, NY; d. Los Angeles, CA

Bassist

[CLASSIC JAZZ; SWING]

Other jazz notables born on this day: Papa Tio (1862); Tony Fruscella (1927); John Stubblefield (1945)

Jazz notables deceased on this day: Alphonse Picou (1961); Louis Jordan (1975); Junior Cook (1992); Joachim-Ernst Berendt (2000); J.J. Johnson (2001)

♪

On any given weekend, both in the United States and around the world, there are undoubtedly hundreds of doctors, lawyers, and members of other top professions who are performing as amateurs with jazz bands in clubs, auditoriums, and other such venues. Rarely, however, does a successful doctor or lawyer give up the practice for an uncertain career in jazz. Artie Bernstein was an exception to the rule. In the late 1920s, while he studied law at New York University, his passion was music. Though he graduated from law school and evidently passed his bar examinations, the lure of jazz could not be placated through avocational outlets, and he became a professional musician. It seems that he made the right choice, for he had a successful and rewarding career in jazz. His superb technique and his rhythmic drive made him a sought-after accompanist by leading vocalists and instrumentalists and by the film studios.

As a child Artie played the cello before switching to bass. In 1930, having decided on a musical profession, he began working with Ben Pollack and then Red Nichols, with whom he also recorded. After a stint with the Dorsey Brothers studio band (1932–32), he made a series of recordings with small groups, backing artists as varied as Jack Teagarden, the Boswell Sisters (1931–36) Connee Boswell, Lee Wiley, Red Norvo, Mildred Bailey, Adrian Rollini, and Frankie Trumbauer. In the mid-1930s he made a number of outstanding recordings with Billie Holiday and Teddy Wilson. From 1939 to 1941 he worked with Benny Goodman's big band and sextet, and while with Goodman he also recorded with Ziggy Elman, Ida Cox, Lionel Hampton, and Cootie Williams. In 1941 he moved to California to work in film studios. He was so highly regarded at this time that *Down Beat* named him "Best Double Bass Player" in 1943. After serving in the air force during World War II he again worked as a studio musician until his death in 1964, following a serious illness.

Despite his outstanding talent, which placed him regularly in the company of jazz's top performers, Bernstein is hardly known by fans. The reason is simple: except for a two-year stint with Goodman, Bernstein spent most of his time in the studios, out of the public eye. But it was there that his skills flourished, accompanying stars such as Fred Astaire, Count Basie, Bix Beiderbecke, Benny Carter, Charlie Christian, Bing Crosby, Tommy Dorsey, Billy Eckstein, Roy Eldridge, Dizzy Gillespie, Coleman Hawkins, Lena Horne, Frank Sinatra, Fats Waller, Ethel Waters, Chick Webb, Lee Wiley, and many others. His work is evident in numerous jazz anthologies and on countless recordings. Jazz would certainly have been impoverished if Bernstein had chosen to practice law instead of music.

FEBRUARY 5—KEITH INGHAM (1942–)

b. London, England

Pianist

[Swing; Dixieland Revival]

Other jazz notables born on this day: Bill Mays (1944); David Gilmore (1964)
Jazz notables deceased on this day: Doug Watkins (1962); Ake Persson

♪

Because of its special relationship with the United States, Great Britain often has difficulty determining whether or not it is part of Europe. According to Mike Zwerin, a British author who seemingly speaks from personal experience, "Great Britain is jazzistically rich but suffers from cultural schizophrenia." For this reason, he adds ironically, British jazz musicians "are well known for not being very well known anywhere else."[4] By this he

---

4. Kirchner, *Oxford Companion to Jazz*, 542.

means that British musicians often spend more time on the Continent or in the United States than in Britain, and those that remain in England often remain unknown elsewhere. British jazz pianists make a good case. The two best known, certainly in America, are George Shearing and Marian McPartland, both of whom left the United Kingdom for America in the mid-1940s. Of those remaining, perhaps the most famous is Gordon Beck, whose acclaim comes from his work with Phil Woods European Rhythm Machine during 1969 to 1972, when he became a virtual superstar in France. Then there is Keith Ingham, who performed with many of the best British mainstream musicians in the mid-1960s before he moved permanently to the United States in 1977.

Ingham began playing piano when he was ten and was mainly self-taught, though he must have received help and encouragement from his father, a church organist. He first played in nightclubs while on government service in Hong Kong, monitoring Chinese airfields during the Cold War. In 1966, after graduation from Oxford University, where he specialized in classical Chinese languages, he began playing the piano professionally in London. For the next ten years he worked with top British musicians while performing with visiting American musicians. From 1973 to 1983 he worked in New York and London as music director for singer Susannah McCorkle, with whom he recorded several albums. They were married for a while, but then divorced in the late 1970s.

In 1977 he settled in New York, where he played at Eddie Condon's club, with Benny Goodman, and with groups such as the World's Greatest Jazz Band, in addition to accompanying McCorkle and working as soloist in hotels, piano bars, and jazz festivals. In the mid-1980s he toured Britain with the Eddie Condon Memorial Band and collaborated with vocalist Maxine Sullivan (their album *Songs from The Cotton Club* was nominated for a Grammy). Since then he has continued performing solo (mostly in the U.S. but with occasional visits to England) and with small groups, often with likeminded musicians such as the acoustic guitarist Marty Grosz, singer Peggy Lee, and the swing tenor saxophonist Harry Allen. It seems he has found a home in New York, where he leads a number of all-star groups, including one called the New York Nine.

FEBRUARY 6—GEORG BRUNIS (1902–1974)

b. New Orleans, LA; d. Chicago, IL

Trombonist

[CLASSIC JAZZ; DIXIELAND]

Other jazz notables born on this day: Sammy Nestico (1924); Don Fagerquist (1927); Nelson Boyd (1928); Larry Grenadier (1966)
Jazz notables deceased on this day: Les Hite (1962); Vince Guaraldi (1976); Art Taylor (1995); Gus Johnson (2000); Wendell Marshall (2002)

♪

Around 1900 the slide trombone replaced the valve trombone in popularity because of its ability to play "slurs" (portamentos). The portamento became stylish about the time jazz was emerging, and as a consequence became part of the New Orleans style of jazz. Because its deeper notes could serve both contrapuntal and rhythmic purposes, the trombone forged an important link between the melody instruments (trumpet and clarinet) and the rhythm section. While less sophisticated trombonists focused on the instrument's syncopative role, others, including the more proficient Georg Brunis and Kid Ory, exploited the portamento and vibrato effects that are intrinsic to an approach known as the "tailgate" style. The name came from the common practice by early bands to advertise while playing on wagons, and it was supposed that the trombonist would occupy the wagon's "tailgate," where he would have adequate room to play.

Georg Brunis, the son of a baker who played violin and of a mother who was a pianist, was the best known of six musical New Orleans brothers. A superstitious person, he shortened his name (George Brunies) from thirteen letters to eleven on the advice of a numerologist. Brunis was entirely self-taught and never learned to read music. By the age of eight he was playing alto horn in a family trio and with Papa Jack Laine's Reliance Brass Band; he changed to trombone a few years later. About 1920 he went to Chicago, where he played in a band led by Paul Mares. After working with a Mississippi riverboat band he joined Mares's Friars Society Orchestra, remaining with the ensemble when it became known as the New Orleans Rhythm Kings. In 1924 he began a long association with clarinetist Ted Lewis, touring and recording extensively until 1934. That year he appeared at New York's Famous Door with another showman, Louis Prima, and from 1936 he began a long residency at Nick's club. He forged two classic partnerships during the Dixieland revival era, with Muggsy Spanier's Ragtimers in 1939 (he participated in sixteen excellent recordings) and with Wild Bill Davison in 1944. During this time he also played frequently with pianist Art Hodes and again with Lewis. After two years at Eddie Condon's club in New York (1947–49) he returned to Chicago, where he led his own band and held a residency at Club 1111 for nine years (1951–59). Despite illness in the late 1960s, Brunis remained busy for the last fifteen years of his life.

Though his programs often included cut-up routines, such as playing trombone with his foot or inviting customers to stand on his stomach during a performance, Brunis always played "like it was his last night on earth."[5] Notorious for his musical nonchalance—he never practiced and was known for his ability to play without warming up—throughout a long and busy career he defined the trombone role in a Dixieland ensemble, perfectly embodying the archetypal tailgate trombonist.

FEBRUARY 7—WILBUR SWEATMAN (1882–1961)

b. Brunswick, MO; d. New York, NY

Clarinetist; Bandleader; Composer

[RAGTIME; CLASSIC JAZZ; DIXIELAND]

Other jazz notables born on this day: Eubie Blake (1883)
Jazz notables deceased on this day: Red McKenzie (1948); Sonny Parker (1957); Peanuts Holland (1979); Bobby Troup (1999); Blossom Dearie (2009)

---

5. Carr et al., *Jazz: The Rough Guide*, 102.

February

♪

One of the pioneer jazz bandleaders, Wilbur Sweatman cut an album with his Jass Band in 1917, thereby becoming the first African-American musician to record under the name of jazz. By this time he was already a show business veteran, a clarinetist and composer whose work anticipated many jazz conventions.[6] While Sweatman is best remembered for closing his shows by performing "The Rosary" on three clarinets simultaneously, his enduring legacy comes from his role in the development and popularization of jazz. His long career in vaudeville took ragtime and jazz across the U.S. and his Columbia recordings of 1918 to 1920 are the first African-American jazz recordings to feature collective improvisation and embellishment. His bands functioned as a preparatory school for young jazz musicians, most notably Count Basie, Sidney Bechet, Wellman Braud, Duke Ellington, Jimmie Lunceford, and Coleman Hawkins.

Sweatman's professional work began with a vaudeville band around 1897, and by 1902 he was assistant leader of a circus concert band. Later that year he joined a minstrel band under the leadership of W.C. Handy, and by 1903 he had formed his own band in Minneapolis, presenting a mixture of ragtime, vaudeville, and early jazz. After a decade of touring he settled in New York in 1912, where he led bands and performed with some of the most prominent African-American musicians. During World War I he appeared in many benefits, and in 1919 he led a band that included the legendary cornetist Freddie Keppard. He continued to work in shows, music revues, and vaudeville through the 1920s, and in March 1923 he employed jazz hopefuls Duke Ellington, Sonny Greer, and Otto Hardwick with his act at the Lafayette Theatre in Harlem. In the 1920s Sweatman also ran his own booking agency, which handled both African-American and white musicians. He retired from performance in the early 1930s to concentrate on his agency while publishing music and managing musician's estates, most notably that of Scott Joplin. He played a few engagements during the 1940s and remained musically active into the early 1960s, despite injuries suffered in an incapacitating automobile accident.

Although the credit for the first jazz recording goes to five white New Orleans musicians known as the Original Dixieland Jazz Band, who on February 26, 1917, entered the Victor studios in New York City and recorded the novelty "Livery Stable Blues" (in which the horn players emulated barnyard animals) that established jazz as a national craze, the honor probably belongs to Sweatman's improvised solo recordings of his composition "Down Home Rag," made in December 1916, two months earlier. Of greater musical worth is the recording of "Joe Turner Blues" of April 1917, a jazz session in which Sweatman's clarinet playing is accompanied by five African-American saxophonists. This recording, on the Pathé label, is the earliest undisputed African-American jazz recording.[7]

---

6. Bogdanov et al., *All Music Guide to Jazz*, 1211.
7. Kernfeld, *New Grove Dictionary of Jazz*, Vol. 3, 696.

BLUE NOTES

FEBRUARY 8—LONNIE JOHNSON (1889–1970)

b. New Orleans, LA; d. Toronto, Canada

Guitarist; Vocalist

[Country Blues; Jazz Blues; Classic Jazz]

Other jazz notables born on this day: Pony Poindexter (1926); Gene Lees (1928); Eddie Locke (1930); Joe Maini (1930)

Jazz notables deceased on this day: Mercer Ellington (1996); Jimmy Smith (2005)

♫

Before amplification, the guitar had relatively little impact on jazz, with a dozen or so important exceptions. Although acoustic jazz guitar reached its apotheosis with the French Gypsy Django Reinhardt, the instrument's earliest pioneer was Lonnie Johnson, a true blues originator whose style influenced a host of subsequent blues immortals, including Robert Johnson, Elvis Presley, and Jerry Lee Lewis. Blues guitar simply would not have developed as it did without Johnson. He was there at the very beginning, helping to define the instrument's future within the genre; his melodic conception far surpassed most of his pre-World War I peers. Known in later years as a blues singer, Johnson's skill on guitar was greatly admired by the most advanced jazz musicians in the 1920s. Over his career he made some five hundred recordings, including an estimated 130 between 1925 and 1932 with emerging stars such as Duke Ellington and Louis Armstrong and a series of duets with white jazz guitarist Eddie Lang, who renamed himself Blind Willie Dunn to conceal interracial teamwork.

The son of a musician and a member of a large musical family, Johnson started playing guitar and violin professionally in cafés and theaters of the Storyville district of New Orleans while in his teens. He sailed to London in 1917 to work in a revue, and upon his return home two years later, he learned that most of his family had died in a flu epidemic. He began working on riverboat bands with Charlie Creath, Fate Marable, and others. In 1925 he won a blues contest sponsored by OKeh Records and he made his debut playing guitar, piano, violin, and kazoo. The label hired him and under the title of staff musician he enjoyed great success as a blues artist and recorded at an astonishing pace. In 1927 he participated in Louis Armstrong's pioneering Hot Five recordings. He played a key role on three pieces, including in a series of exchanges with the leader on "Hotter Than That," one of the most exuberant jazz performances on record. During this period he kept very busy, backing singers, accompanying Duke Ellington's orchestra, and recording groundbreaking duets with Lang's group in 1928 and 1929.

He struggled during the Depression, playing for radio and working day jobs in the Cleveland area, but after settling in Chicago in 1937 he began recording and leading small groups again. By the mid-1940s he appeared as a featured soloist on amplified guitar. He enjoyed one of the biggest hits of his long career with the mellow ballad "Tomorrow Night," the best selling R&B record of 1948. During the 1950s he worked as a janitor in Philadelphia before a local disk jockey started him on the comeback trail with an Ellington concert in New York. He gained a new, younger audience during the 1960s folk/blues revival, at which time he moved to Toronto, where he was a popular figure with local fans. His long, remarkable career came to an end in 1969, when a car struck him; he died the following year of related complications.

FEBRUARY 9—WALTER PAGE (1900–1957)

b. Gallatin, MS; d. New York, NY

Bassist; Bandleader

[SWING]

Other jazz notables born on this day: Peanuts Holland (1910); Bill Evans [saxophonist] (1958)

Jazz notables deceased on this day: Herschel Evans (1939); Charlie Fowlkes (1980)

♪

Walter Page, known as "Big-Un" for his size and for the sheer volume of sound with which he drove his bands, was one of the greatest bassists of the swing era. Jo Jones, who spent many years working closely with Page as a member of Count Basie's celebrated rhythm section, put Walter Page in perspective when he said: "The greatest band I ever heard in my life was Walter Page's Blue Devils band. Musically, Page was the father of Basie, [big band vocalist Jimmy] Rushing, Buster Smith . . . and me too, because without him I wouldn't have known how to play drums."[8] Count Basie had a similar initial experience with the Blue Devils when he first heard them in a Tulsa, Oklahoma hotel room. The music he heard that morning was so clear and so good that he thought it must be a new Louis Armstrong record. But it was Walter Page and his Blue Devils, playing from a truck bed in the street below, cruising around town advertising that night's show. Basie ran downstairs, overwhelmed by the powerful experience. "The Blue Devils . . . was the greatest thing I had ever heard," he later wrote. "I had never heard the blues played like that." Shortly thereafter he too was a member.

A longtime resident of Kansas City, Page worked occasionally with Bennie Moten's band in the early 1920s and in 1925 he founded his own band, the Original Blue Devils, in Oklahoma City. Formed at a time when bands all over the country were struggling to survive, Page's group was a cooperative band, its members sharing all things in common. As one of the most successful of the "territory bands" that roamed the Southwest in the late 1920s, it played so many dates one year that the men had just eight days off. Its ranks included some of the region's finest musicians—Hot Lips Page, Buster Smith, Count Basie, Jimmy Rushing, Lester Young, and Eddie Durham, in addition to Page himself. But after 1929, even the Blue Devils began to feel the sting of the Depression. The more successful Benny Moten Orchestra, based in Kansas City, lured away Basie, Rushing, Hot Lips, and—eventually—even Walter Page, with offers of better pay and easier times. The Blue Devils struggled, sometimes playing to audiences of three people, its membership varying from

---

8. Shapiro and Hentoff, *Hear Me Talkin'*, 289.

fourteen to as few as three or four. The band traveled as far south as Galveston, Texas and as far north as Minnesota in pursuit of gigs, and it was in Minneapolis one night in 1930 that they persuaded Lester Young to join the band, promising the future superstar better times ahead. There was, however, only so much success a touring band could extract from the depressed economy, and one day, as they toured Kentucky and West Virginia in 1933, they found themselves out of funds. The Blue Devils boarded a freight train bound for Kansas City, the era's feel-good capital and a mecca for jazz musicians. Page joined Moten's band and stayed on in 1935, when Basie took over, sublimating his own aspirations to those of his former pianist and thereby achieving jazz immortality.

FEBRUARY 10—CHICK WEBB (1909–1939)

b. Baltimore, MD; d. Baltimore, MD

Drummer; Bandleader

[SWING; BIG BAND]

Other jazz notables born on this day: Sir Roland Hanna (1932); Rufus Reid (1944)
Jazz notables deceased on this day: Buddy Tate (2001)

♪

Chick Webb, writes Richard S. Ginell, "represented the triumph of the human spirit in jazz and in life."[9] Hunchbacked and dwarf-like in stature, this inspirational giant fought off congenital tuberculosis of the spine in order to become the first great drummer of the swing era and one of the most competitive bandleaders of the big band era. Using a specially constructed drum set and a great variety of other percussion instruments, he created complex, thundering solos that paved the way for Buddy Rich and other admirers. Although his band did not become as influential as some of its contemporaries, it was feared in the battles of the bands in Harlem's Savoy Ballroom.

Chick (William Henry) Webb received his nickname as the result of his small size. The story that he was dropped and severely injured in infancy is undoubtedly apocryphal; the more likely account is that he became a diminutive hunchback after suffering tuberculosis, then a common inner-city disease.[10] He played homemade drums before he was able to acquire a proper set with his earnings as a newsboy. Around 1925 he moved to New York and the following year he established his first band, which included a youthful Johnny Hodges. Webb finally settled into the Savoy in 1931, where he quickly became a fixture. Constantly on the lookout for talent (he regularly exchanged musicians with Fletcher Henderson), he jealously defended his band's reputation at the Savoy, taking on all comers with a variety of specialty acts and tightly rehearsed newly commissioned arrangements. In 1933 Webb hired arranger Edgar Sampson and trumpeter Taft Jordan, and by then his group could hold off all opposition, with the possible exception of Duke Ellington, whose band defeated him in a famous March 1937 encounter. Webb's most

---

9. Bogdanov et al., *All Music Guide to Jazz*, 1314.
10. Kernfeld, *New Grove Dictionary of Jazz*, Vol. 3, 898.

celebrated battle came a few months later, when he took on Benny Goodman's band, then at its peak. According to Helen Oakley Dance, who covered the event, an estimated ten thousand people showed up, half of whom were turned away at the door, causing a traffic jam that lasted all night. Webb, sensing the gravity of the occasion, gave the band a last minute pep talk: "Tonight we got to make history. Our future depends on tonight." The verdict, rendered by fans and critics alike, was unanimously in Webb's favor.

In 1935 Webb hired a homeless eighteen-year-old singer named Ella Fitzgerald after she won a talent contest at the Apollo Theatre. He became her legal guardian and in 1938 she provided him with his biggest hit, "A-Tisket, A-Tasket." From that point on he built his show around her. As the band's fame grew, Webb's precarious health began to fail. After a fatal operation in Johns Hopkins Hospital in Baltimore, his final words were, "I'm sorry, I've got to go." He was just thirty years old. Fitzgerald, who fronted his band for the next three years, spoke for all who knew the "little giant" (as Gene Krupa called him) when she sang a moving rendition of "My Buddy" at his funeral.

FEBRUARY 11—DIDIER LOCKWOOD (1956–)

b. Calais, France

Violinist

[POST-BOP; FUSION]

Other jazz notables born on this day: Bob Casey (1909)
Jazz notables deceased on this day: Edmond Hall (1967); Jaki Byard (1999)

♪

Musicians create jazz in innumerable ways, at times manifesting their skills and developing their voices on instruments that have lost frontline prominence. Prior to the 1940s the violin played an integral role in jazz, and although its role has changed significantly over the years, it has continued to be viable in many styles of jazz, thanks to the work of four pioneering musicians who in the first half of the twentieth century established the instrument's reputation in jazz: Joe Venuti, Stéphane Grappelli, Stuff Smith, and Eddie South. Though not as central as it once was, the violin's position as a solo instrument in jazz continues, thanks to American players such as Ray Nance, Leroy Jenkins, Jerry Goodman, Billy Bang, Mark Feldman, and Regina Carter, who leads the youngest generation of jazz violinists. In Europe, where there has been a long established tradition of classical and folk violinists, significant contributors to jazz include—in addition to the pioneering work of Grappelli—Michel Warlop, Svend Asmussen, Jean-Luc Ponty, Michal Urbaniak, Zbigniew Seifert, and Didier Lockwood, who heads the youngest generation of players from the Continent. In the 1980s Lockwood was considered the next in a line of great French violinists after Grappelli and Ponty, but as of yet has not fulfilled those pacesetting expectations.

Lockwood has had a diverse career thus far, ranging from fusion to swing and advanced hard bop styles, and his latest work, including eclectic performances with Indian-born Raghunath Manet, suggests continued exploration. Lockwood's father, a violin teacher in Calais, got Didier started on violin by the age of six. Eventually the youngster went to Paris, where he studied at the Paris Conservatory. While there he heard Jimi Hendrix, Johnny Winter, and John Mayall, and soon he was playing rock and blues. At this time he also became interested in jazz, particularly after hearing Ponty's 1969 fusion album with Frank Zappa, *King Kong*. In 1972, at the age of sixteen, Didier stopped his formal training and soon joined the French rock group Magma, with which he recorded a live double album. A few years later he met Grappelli at the North Sea festival and soon he was playing standards and touring with him. At this time Lockwood formed a fusion group called Surya that included his brother Francis on keyboards. Following the work of Jerry Goodman, Michal Urbaniak, and Ponty, this band combined jazz and rock with classical overtones. By 1979 Lockwood had diversified even further and was playing with five or six fusion bands while touring with Grappelli and recording straight-ahead jazz with musicians such as Gordon Beck, Niels-Henning Orsted Pedersen, and Tony Williams. Lockwood performed in the U.S. on several occasions in the 1980s and recorded an acoustic album in 1986 with fellow violinists John Blake and Urbaniak. In the 1990s he recorded several all-star sessions as leader, playing in the tradition of the legendary Grappelli. In 1999 he dedicated an entire CD to the master, who had died just shy of his ninetieth birthday in 1997.

FEBRUARY 12—MEL POWELL (1923–1998)

b. New York, NY; d. Valencia, CA

Pianist; Arranger

[SWING]

Other jazz notables born on this day: Tex Beneke (1914); Bill Laswell (1955)
Jazz notables deceased on this day: Muggsy Spanier (1967); Eubie Blake (1983)

♪

In 1941 George T. Simon, editor-in-chief of *Metronome*, began plugging an eighteen-year-old pianist named Melvin Epstein: "I get more kicks out of Mel's playing than any other pianist in the business," he told bandleader Benny Goodman. Goodman agreed to give Powell an audition, and soon the youngster, who had recently changed his name to Mel Powell, was on the payroll. He performed and recorded as Goodman's pianist and arranger and formed a lifelong friendship with the leader.

A child prodigy, Powell began to play classical music at the age of four, but by his early teens, after hearing Teddy Wilson, he turned to jazz. A gifted athlete, Mel played baseball during his formative period, attaining a semi-professional level until he seriously injured his finger, which forced him to choose music over a career in sports. Possessing limitless ability and a versatile technique, he played intermission piano at Nick's club while still in his teens. Prior to joining Goodman, Powell was a busy New York musician; he worked with Bobby Hackett, Georg Brunis, and Zutty Singleton (1939), performed and recorded with Wingy Manone, acquired big-band experience in Muggsy Spanier's short-lived orchestra, and wrote arrangements for pianist Earl Hines. After his first stint with Goodman in 1941 and 1942 (he worked with the clarinetist from 1945 to 1948 and again between 1953 and 1955), he was briefly a member of the CBS orchestra under Raymond Scott. He spent 1943 to 1945 in the military, where he played with the Glenn Miller Army Air Force Band. During this time he also performed as an unaccompanied soloist and recorded in Paris with the Jazz Club American Hot Band, which included the legendary guitarist Django Reinhardt. Following his discharge from the service he rejoined Goodman's group (he participated in the filming of *A Song is Born* in 1948), recorded with Jazz at the Philharmonic, and worked in the Los Angeles film studios.

By 1950 everyone recognized Powell's talent; his reputation in jazz was stellar, and he seemed destined for stardom. However, after attending Yale University, where he studied composition with Paul Hindemith and piano with Nadia Reisenberg, he pursued a career as a classical composer. He taught music theory at Queens College and then composition at Yale, and in 1959 he was awarded a Guggenheim fellowship. Powell's advanced compositions soon became familiar items on American concert programs, and in 1969 he was appointed professor and founding Dean of Music at the California Institute for the Arts, where he worked for nearly thirty years. Since his graduation from Yale, Powell had occasional returns to jazz; he recorded classic albums with Ruby Braff and Paul Quinichette in the mid-1950s. In 1986 he emerged once again, playing for jazz cruises and recording a remarkable set with Benny Carter and others in 1987 at the Floating Jazz Festival. Powell continued to compose and perform, even after being diagnosed with muscular dystrophy, and was awarded a Pulitzer Prize in 1990.

FEBRUARY 13—WARDELL GRAY (1921–1955)

b. Oklahoma City, OK; d. Las Vegas, NV

Tenor Saxophonist

[SWING; BOP]

Other jazz notables born on this day: Wingy Manone (1900); Les Hite (1903); Helen Oakley Dance (1913); Keith Nichols (1945); Adam Cruz (1970)

Jazz notables deceased on this day: George T. Simon (2001)

♪

When the bebop revolution emerged from the underground in 1944, it burst forth with a fury. By 1948 virtually all of the young jazz players, with the exception of those participating in the Dixieland revival, were caught up in its vortex. Bop was new, it was exciting, and it was glamorous, and most of the young musicians wanted to be in on it. But it also sported a dark side. Bop players were heavily involved in drugs, and the movement was acquiring an overdose of tragic heroes.[11]

Bop's academy, where the earliest adherents to the new style were trained, was the big band of Earl Hines and the Billy Eckstine band that spun off it. In 1939 Eckstine be-

---

11. Collier, *Making of Jazz*, 397.

came the principal vocalist in Hines's big band where, as supporter of young avant-garde jazz musicians, he was instrumental in bringing to that band future stars such as Dizzy Gillespie, Charlie Parker, and Sarah Vaughan. In 1943 (unfortunately during a recording strike by musicians), this band became the first bebop orchestra. By the time the strike ended, Eckstine had left Hines and taken Gillespie, Parker, and Vaughan with him. However, school was still in session, and bop's influence continued to spread in ever-widening circles. Alumni of these two bands included a roster of performers who would make a mark on jazz for decades to come, including Fats Navarro, Sonny Stitt, Gene Ammons, Tadd Dameron, Lucky Thompson, Miles Davis, Dexter Gordon, and Wardell Gray.

Together with Dexter Gordon, his jamming and recording partner from 1947 to 1952, Wardell Gray was one of the top tenors to emerge during the bebop era. A transitional figure who gravitated towards bebop but was convincing in whatever style he played, his Lester Young-influenced tone made his playing attractive to swing musicians as well as younger modernists.[12] Gray grew up in Detroit, playing in local bands as a teenager. He performed with Earl Hines during 1943 to 1945 and then moved to Los Angeles, where he became a major part of the Central Avenue scene, having nightly tenor battles with Dexter Gordon, immortalized in the latter's famous recording, "The Chase" (1947). He also recorded with Charlie Parker in 1947 before joining Benny Goodman's small group, where he was an important figure in that leader's first experimentation with bop (1948). He moved to New York and worked at the Royal Roost, first with Count Basie, then with the resident band led by Dameron. After a period with Goodman's big band (1948–49) and various recording sessions, including with Basie's small group in 1950 to 1951 ("Little Pony" is a classic), he returned to freelance work on the West Coast and then to Las Vegas. Ironically Wardell Gray, who in the late 1940s was an inspiration to some younger musicians due to his opposition to drug use, himself became involved in drugs while working with the dancer (and heroin addict) Teddy Hale in Las Vegas. He died mysteriously after a hotel engagement, his body found along a road in the desert. One of bop's many tragic heroes, he was just thirty-four at the time of his death.

FEBRUARY 14—ROB MCCONNELL (1935–2010)

b. London, Ontario, Canada; d. Toronto, Ontario, Canada

Trombonist; Bandleader; Arranger; Composer

[SWING; BOP]

Other jazz notables born on this day: Herlin Riley (1957)
Jazz notables deceased on this day: Baby Dodds (1959); Bola Sete (1987); Charles Moffett (1997); Louie Bellson (2009); George Shearing (2011)

♪

Canadian-born Rob McConnell, a man of many talents, was a trombonist, a composer, an arranger, a music teacher, a clinician, and the leader of one of the best big bands in existence. An excellent soloist, he played valve trombone in Toronto for nearly four de-

---

12. Bogdanov et al., *All Music Guide to Jazz*, 500.

cades. Despite his playing ability, McConnell was primarily known as an arranger and bandleader who, with his Boss Brass, set new standards for jazz writing, including the use of complex unaccompanied passages played in close harmony section by section. The National Association of Jazz Educators voted him "Best Arranger" in tribute to the widespread use of his published arrangements by academic institutions across America. Since 1968 his main vehicle of jazz expression was his orchestra, a part time band that recorded annually. Comprising many of Toronto's top musicians, the band performed in Europe and South America as well as across Canada and the United States, including gigs with Mel Tormé, Joe Williams, The Hi-Lo's, and Oscar Peterson.

McConnell's account of his start on trombone is reminiscent of Benny Goodman's initiation on clarinet: "My older brother was a trumpet player and I knew every jazz trumpet player . . . [W]hen I was fifteen years old, I wanted to play trumpet, but by the time they got to me in the school band, they didn't have any. They said, 'All that's left is this slide trombone' . . ." Some years later, after three years of work in a brokerage house, he returned to music, playing with dance bands in Toronto before moving to New York, where he performed and recorded with the Canadian trumpeter Maynard Ferguson (1964). He returned to Toronto, where he played in a band called Nimmons' 'n' Nine Plus Six (led by Phil Nimmons) for several years and worked as a studio musician and arranger. In 1968 he formed the sixteen-piece Boss Brass as a studio band that emphasized commercial music, using his own charts of then popular tunes. The group originally consisted of brass instruments plus a rhythm section but in 1970, after reed player Moe Koffman organized a group of players to picket an establishment where the Brass were playing, with placards saying "Unfair to Woodwinds: We Want In," McConnell indicated that he favored the broader arranging possibilities offered by a saxophone section, and he agreed to expand the band. The group acquired an international reputation during the 1980s, owing in part to its excellent recordings, each distinguished by McConnell's brilliant arranging and by the superb technical abilities of his players. Throughout his career he received numerous awards for his outstanding accomplishments in music, including, as of 2003, fifteen Grammy nominations (with three wins) and eight Juno (Canadian Grammy) nominations; he won four times. In 1999 his government announced that he had been made an Officer of the Order of Canada, thereby enrolling him in the ranks of Boss Brass regulars who had preceded him in receiving the honor, including Ed Bickert, Guido Basso, and the pesky, prescient Moe Koffman.

FEBRUARY 15—HENRY THREADGILL (1944–)

b. Chicago, IL

Alto Saxophonist; Flutist; Composer; Bandleader

[AVANT-GARDE]

Other jazz notables born on this day: Taft Jordan (1914 or 1915); Nathan Davis (1937); Marty Morell (1944)

Jazz notables deceased on this day: Nat King Cole (1965); Pee Wee Russell (1969); Zbigniew Siefert (1979); Al Cohn (1988); Betty Roche (1999)

BLUE NOTES

♪

Henry Threadgill is one of the musical masterminds of the past four decades. As one of the avant-garde's great composers, his unique musical art embraces the world of music in its entirety, fusing calypso-flavored rhythms, rags, circus marches, reggae and Latin beats, a range of folk and ethnic forms, even carnival music, with classical motifs.

Born in Chicago, Threadgill began playing music when he was five. He picked up the saxophone in high school, where his teacher was John Hauser, who had played with Charlie Parker. Threadgill continued his formal musical education at Wilson Junior College, whose atmosphere he likened to that of Fifty-Second Street in New York during the first years of bebop (musicians like Anthony Braxton, Muhal Richard Abrams, and Joseph Jarman, who later pushed the frontiers of music, were there) or to the Harlem Renaissance. Threadgill also attended the American Conservatory of Music, where he majored in flute, piano, and composition and studied with Stella Roberts, who influenced him enormously: "I'd bring her my compositions, and if she found something that didn't work, she'd go to the window, point out a building, and discuss its architecture."

In 1969, after service in Vietnam, he returned to Chicago and joined the Association for the Advancement of Creative Musicians, where he formed the trio Air, one of the most influential bands of the 1970s and early '80s. Threadgill moved to New York City in 1975 and quickly became an integral and influential member of creative circles flourishing in lower Manhattan's lofts and clubs. Following the disbanding of Air in 1985, Threadgill formed a number of unique ensembles, each one using different instrumentation, including X75 (with four bassists), Sextett (actually seven members, with two drummers and a cellist), and Very Very Circus (adding tubas, trombones, and two guitarists to create a musical impression of two circus rings). Inspired by creative individuals in all walks of life, Threadgill finds musical ideas everywhere, but particularly in unusual situations.

FEBRUARY 16—MACHITO (1908–1984)

b. Tampa, FL; grew up in Havana, Cuba; d. London, England

Bandleader; Vocalist; Maracas Player

[CUBAN JAZZ; AFRO-CUBAN JAZZ; LATIN JAZZ]

Other jazz notables born on this day: Bill Doggett (1916); Charlie Fowlkes (1916); Howard Riley (1943); Pete Christlieb (1945); Jeff Clayton (1955)

Jazz notables deceased on this day: Bob Zurke (1944); Gene Schroeder (1975); Charles Delaunay (1988); Jimmie Powell (1994)

♪

Latin musicians have been a constant factor in jazz since 1929, when Puerto Rican trombonist Juan Tizol joined Duke Ellington's orchestra, becoming an indispensable member of that distinguished ensemble for fifteen years. Another groundbreaking figure, perhaps the most significant early on, was Cuba's Mario Bauzá, a bass clarinetist in the Havana Symphony before he immigrated to Harlem in 1930, where he became Chick Webb's lead trumpeter and, later, musical director. In 1937 he wrote his brother-in-law Frank Raúl Grillo, inviting him to "come and starve with me." Grillo, known as Machito, followed Bauzá to New York, and the duo founded the Afro-Cubans, a seminal band that overcame musical and racial barriers by mingling Cuban, Puerto Rican, and North American musicians. Machito played a huge role in the history of Latin jazz, for his bands of the 1940s were probably the first to achieve a fusion of powerful Afro-Cuban rhythms and jazz improvisation. Machito was the frontman, singing, conducting, and shaking maracas, while Bauzá was the innovator, enlarging the band and hiring jazz-oriented arrangers. The result was a blend that included the Cuban repertoire and rhythm section with a trumpet and sax frontline more typical of the African-American bands.

Though Machito claimed he was born in 1908, other dates appear in the sources, including 1912, the date on his social security card. The son of a cigar manufacturer, Grillo received his nickname Macho (male) as the first son born after three daughters; one of his older siblings, Graciela, later sang in his bands. Though born in Florida, Machito grew up in Havana, where he became a professional musician before his return to the U.S. in 1937. He worked with several Latin artists and orchestras in the late 1930s and recorded with the then dominant Latin bandleader Xavier Cugat. After an aborted attempt to launch a band with Bauzá, Machito founded the Afro-Cubans in 1940; he hired Bauzá the following year as music director, where he remained for thirty-five years. In 1943, while Machito served in the army, Graciela (Bauzá's wife) led the band until his discharge as a result of a leg injury. The Afro-Cubans began to catch on after the war; between 1947 and 1949 they performed at concerts with Stan Kenton's big band and recorded or played with several of the leading bop musicians, including Charlie Parker, Flip Phillips, Milt Jackson, Howard McGhee, Brew Moore, and Armando Peraza. Later Cannonball Adderley, Herbie Mann, Johnny Griffin, and other jazz stars recorded with the Afro-Cubans. Playing regularly at New York's Palladium, the "Temple of Mambo" on Broadway and Fifty-Third Street, Machito's band often performed for high-voltage fans such as Dizzy Gillespie, Marlene Dietrich, Jackson Pollock, Allen Ginsberg, and Marlon Brando, who appeared for the club's dance contests. Machito's band reached its peak of popularity during the mambo craze of the 1950s; it survived the upheavals of the 1960s and continued into the 1970s and early '80s. The band was playing at Ronnie Scott's club in London in 1984 when Machito suffered a fatal stroke.

FEBRUARY 17—BUDDY DEFRANCO (1923–)

b. Camden, NJ

Clarinetist; Bandleader

[Bop]

Other jazz notables born on this day: Charlie Spivak (1907)
Jazz notables deceased on this day: A.J. Piron (1943); Paul Barbarin (1969); Thelonious Monk (1982)

Despite the clarinet's central role in early jazz—it remained the main woodwind instrument until the 1930s—by 1945, especially with the advent of bop, the instrument experienced a decline in use. Younger reed players, enthralled with the saxophone's expressive qualities, began finding fault with the clarinet. Criticizing its thinner, less expressive tone and associating it with the older styles they were rejecting, many of them regarded the clarinet simply as a stage in their development as saxophonists. In spite of its waning importance, a few younger players in the 1940s and '50s adopted the clarinet. Some were uninterested in bop and simply wished to continue the swing tradition of Artie Shaw and Benny Goodman, but a few modernists, influenced by Charlie Parker's alto playing, did emerge. The dominant figure was Buddy DeFranco, one of the great clarinetists of all time and, until the rise of Eddie Daniels, the top clarinetist to emerge since 1940.[13] Among the few clarinetists to transfer Parker's language to the clarinet, DeFranco made the clarinet a respectable bop instrument.

When he was fourteen Boniface (Buddy) DeFranco won an amateur swing contest in Philadelphia sponsored by Tommy Dorsey. After working with several name bands on alto saxophone, including those of Gene Krupa (1941–42) and Charlie Barnet (1943–44), he performed with Dorsey's orchestra on and off from 1944 to 1948, when he was featured on clarinet. After several failed attempts to lead his own big band, he mainly performed in smaller groups, including George Shearing's quartet (1948) and Count Basie's octet (1950–51). At this time he participated in the making of a short film, but due to segregation, was not seen with the otherwise all-black cast (he was replaced on screen by Marshal Royal). During the 1950s and early '60s DeFranco was primarily a bandleader, though he recorded frequently (his sidemen included drummer Art Blakey and pianists Kenny Drew and Sonny Clark) and participated in some of Norman Granz's Verve jam sessions, including a 1954 tour with Jazz at the Philharmonic. He settled on the West Coast, where he led a new quartet (1961–64), and then replaced Ray McKinley as leader of the Glenn Miller ghost band (1966–74). Performances in London in 1980 marked the beginning of a long association with vibraphonist Terry Gibbs, with whom he co-led a quintet into the 1990s.

Due to the apparent incompatibility of his instrument and his preferred style, bop, DeFranco was frequently obliged to perform under circumstances that failed to challenge his abilities. Unfortunately, this led to the same criticism of technique without taste that was leveled against equally gifted stars such as Oscar Peterson and Buddy Rich. A talented improviser with a liquid tone and a consummate mechanical technique, it was DeFranco's misfortune to be the best (he won the *Down Beat* poll nineteen times) on an instrument that after the swing era dropped drastically in popularity.

---

13. Bogdanov et al., *All Music Guide to Jazz*, 323.

FEBRUARY 18—HAROLD LAND (1928–2001)

b. Houston, TX; d. Los Angeles, CA

Tenor Saxophonist

[Hard Bop]

Other jazz notables born on this day:
Jazz notables deceased on this day: Henry Ragas (1919); Yank Lawson (1995)

♪

During the 1950s and '60s African-Americans began to build on a paradigm shift in consciousness that emerged after World War II; they started thinking differently about themselves, their place in American society, and the methods for bringing about change. "Black is beautiful" emerged as a powerful slogan, soul food became popular, and Afros were in style. But more importantly, African-Americans assumed leadership of the emerging civil rights movement. Blacks, of course, saw jazz as their contribution to American culture. If black was beautiful, why not play jazz in a black way? By way of response, a number of jazz styles emerged during the 1950s, though the majority, including some of the "cool" styles that persisted, differed only slightly from bebop. The underlying difference, however, was the conscious attempt by these players to build upon the African-American folk music tradition out of which jazz had grown. It was to their roots, primarily the gospel churches and the blues, that this second generation of bop players went in search of inspiration. As this new music developed, it came to be called "funk" or "soul" music, but a third term, "hard bop," seemed the most technically accurate.

The year 1954, considered to be hard bop's pivotal year, was a period of great promise for the future of modern jazz. Several sessions that year, taken together, may be regarded as constituting the birth of hard bop. In February, pianist Horace Silver played with a quintet led by drummer Art Blakey at the Birdland jazz club; the trumpeter for that session was Clifford Brown, who in the next two years would become the most distinguished trumpeter in the hard bop style. Six months later, Brown was in a recording studio with drummer Max Roach to begin one of the most potent collaborations in modern jazz. Between 1954 and 1956, the Clifford Brown-Max Roach Quintet, which included pianist Richie Powell, bassist George Morrow, and tenor saxophonist Harold Land, "laid down some of the most breathtaking small-group jazz ever recorded." [14]

Harold Land, whose birth date appears incorrectly as December 18 in several sources, was raised by an aunt after his birth and grew up in San Diego. After gaining experience with local bands, he moved in 1954 to Los Angeles, where he joined the quintet led by Brown and Roach. Land toured widely and recorded with this groundbreaking group for eighteen months. In late 1955 he left the quintet so that he could be with his family in Los Angeles. From 1955 he worked with Curtis Counce (1956–58) and with Gerald Wilson's big band. He also led his own groups, co-led bands with Bobby Hutcherson (1967–71) and Blue Mitchell (1975–78), and continued performing on the West Coast, occasionally

---

14. Kirchner, *Oxford Companion to Jazz*, 378.

with his son Harold Land Jr. on piano. Land's decision to settle on the West Coast, a region of the United States not often associated with hard bop, kept him underrated, but it made him a winner with his family.

FEBRUARY 19—DAVID MURRAY (1955–)

b. Oakland, CA

Tenor Saxophonist; Leader

[AVANT-GARDE; FREE JAZZ; M-BASE; POST-BOP]

Other jazz notables born on this day:
Jazz notables deceased on this day: Lee Morgan (1972); Shorty Sherock (1980); Claude Hopkins (1984); Fred Norman (1993)

♪

Around the mid-1970s a new generation of avant-garde musicians overturned many assumptions generated by their predecessors. Armed with a broad agenda, these younger musicians interpreted the idea of freedom as "the capacity to choose between all the realms of jazz, mixing and matching them not only with each other but with old and new pop, R&B and rock, classical music and world music."[15] Perhaps the most resourceful of these younger players was David Murray, who by the age of twenty identified himself with the avant-garde tradition.

Because these musicians had honed their music in places like Chicago, St. Louis, and Los Angeles and not in New York, where much of the press and the record industry resides, the jazz world was caught by surprise in 1975 when wave after wave of avant-garde musicians began relocating to New York, settling into deserted industrial spaces and other undervalued segments of urban real estate below Fourteenth Street. Seemingly overnight, new jazz venues appeared, many of them in apartments or lofts. In September of that year two musicians from California, the writer Stanley Crouch and twenty-year old David Murray, joined the migration, opening a loft space of their own called Studio Infinity.

A giant of the avant-garde and one of the most recorded, Murray has long displayed the willingness to play most styles of jazz, from completely free improvisations to bop. Brought up in the gospel tradition—by the age of nine he accompanied his mother and other members of his family's band at a Pentecostal congregation in Berkeley, California—he was introduced to jazz while a student in the Berkeley school system, and by the age of thirteen he was one of the leaders of a soul group. He attended Pomona College in Los Angeles, where he studied and played with Crouch, Bobby Bradford (a former Ornette Coleman sideman), James Newton, and Arthur Blythe, who introduced him to free jazz (1973–75). He moved to New York and made his first recordings in 1976, the same year that he became a founding member of the World Saxophone Quartet, one of the era's most prominent jazz ensembles. The members of the quartet all had separate careers, most notably Murray, who blossomed into one of the most distinctive (and prolific) jazz musi-

---

15. Ward and Burns, *Jazz: A History*, 365.

cians of the 1980s and '90s. During those decades, his recording activity reached nearly absurd levels—probably no contemporary jazz musician led more dates on more labels. Not content to play with one group at a time, Murray often led several bands simultaneously, including quartets, his widely celebrated octet, and a big band, in addition to duos, trios, and solo work. In the late 1990s alone Murray played with jazz musicians of every inclination, as well as rock, hip-hop, gospel, European, and African musicians. A gifted composer, arranger, and a performer of outstanding plasticity and passion, Murray was awarded the prestigious Danish Jazzpar prize in 1991.

FEBRUARY 20—NANCY WILSON (1937–)

b. Chillicothe, OH

Vocalist

[VOCAL JAZZ; TRADITIONAL POP; STANDARDS; BALLADS]

Other jazz notables born on this day: Jimmy Yancey (1898); Oscar Alemán (1909); Frank Isola (1925); Lew Soloff (1944); Anthony Davis (1951)
Jazz notables deceased on this day: Zachary Breaux (1997)

♪

Debates about what constitutes jazz singing and which vocalists should be included or excluded from the jazz community, have raged for decades. During the 1920s and '30s such definitions were of less consequence, for during that era American music flourished in numerous overlapping styles—folk, blues, gospel, jazz, musical theater, Tin Pan Alley ballads and novelties, and swing.

Because the current jazz mainstream is so close to its popular past, the line between jazz and pop remains difficult to discern and makes the task of defining jazz singers even more frustrating. Vocalists, it seems, have always been a part of the popular music scene. From Louis Armstrong to Billie Holiday, Ella Fitzgerald, Sarah Vaughan, Anita O'Day, Dinah Washington, and Mel Tormé, every major jazz vocalist, without exception, has had at least one foot in pop. Nancy Wilson, a remarkably versatile interpreter of popular music, perfectly illustrates the point. While she regularly crossed over into the pop and R&B markets—between 1962 and 1971 she had ten Hot 100 singles and twenty-nine chart LPs—she remains best known as a jazz performer. Her singing, with its wide range of musical and emotional intensity, reflects the influence of Dinah Washington, one of the most controversial singers of the mid-twentieth century. Despite Washington's popularity, her cardinal sin, at least with the critics, was to cultivate a distinctive vocal style that was at home in all kinds of music, from jazz to pop.

Virtually every major singer to emerge before 1960 came out of the big band experience, and Nancy was no exception. After gaining early experience in nightclubs and on television shows in Columbus, Ohio—at the age of fifteen she won her own television series as part of a talent competition—she toured the Midwest and Canada with the blues-driven Rusty Bryant band (1956–58). In 1959 she sang in Columbus with the quintet of Cannonball Adderley, who encouraged her to go to New York. She took his advice and quickly obtained a recording contract with Capitol. Hailed as a major new artist, she received national recognition with albums such as *Like in Love* and *Nancy Wilson with Billy May's Orchestra*. Her sessions with George Shearing, including 1960s *The Swingin's Mutual*, and her subsequent work with Adderley—arguably her finest recordings—further cemented her growing reputation.

In the years to follow she concentrated on a career in popular music, touring extensively and hosting her own Emmy-winning variety series for NBC, *The Nancy Wilson Show*. Unlike Dinah Washington, who was accused of selling out to commerce, in the 1980s Wilson returned to jazz, her first love. During the 1990s she also began hosting the *Jazz Profiles* series on National Public Radio, a weekly one-hour documentary program that brings to life the history of jazz. A performer who long ago could have rested on her laurels, Wilson released her sixtieth recording, *If I Had My Way*, on her sixtieth birthday.

FEBRUARY 21—TADD DAMERON (1917–1965)

b. Cleveland, OH; d. New York, NY

Composer; Arranger; Bandleader; Pianist

[BOP]

Other jazz notables born on this day: Al Sears (1917); Nina Simone (1933); Warren Vaché (1951)

Jazz notables deceased on this day: Frank Horrox (1972)

♪

Somewhere around 1940 a new sound emerged in the jazz world. Its presence became so definitive that all pre-1940 styles came to be known as "classic jazz" and all styles since 1940 became classified as "modern jazz." The name given to the first modern jazz style is bebop, and the first modern jazz musicians were alto saxophonist Charlie Parker, pianist Thelonious Monk, and trumpeter Dizzy Gillespie. In 1943 Billy Eckstine, a vocalist with the Earl Hines big band, assembled the first bebop band, an orchestra that comprised a who's who of bop members: Gillespie and Fats Navarro on trumpet, Gene Ammons and Dexter Gordon on sax, Tommy Potter on bass, Art Blakey on drums, Sarah Vaughan on vocals, and Tadd Dameron as arranger. Of this elite corps, Dameron is the least known. The reason is simple: bop musicians, placing less emphasis on arrangements and more on solo improvisation, achieved immortality as soloists, and Dameron was a pianist of mediocre talent. His fame, therefore, was not achieved as a performer, but as bop's consummate arranger/composer. Undervalued during his lifetime, except by fellow musicians, Dameron was a unique contributor at the crossroads between swing and bop, particularly in compositions like "Good Bait" and "Hot House."

Tadd Dameron was born Tadley Ewing Peake, the son of Isaiah and Ruth Peake. When his mother later married a restaurant owner named Adolphus Dameron, Tad and his brother, Caesar, legally changed their names to Dameron. Tad got his start in the swing era, when he toured and contributed modern arrangements for a variety of bands; by the mid-1940s he was writing charts for such bands as Jimmy Lunceford, Count Basie, Eckstine, and Gillespie. His most famous composition, "Hot House," was written at this time (1945) and was recorded by both Gillespie and Parker. Though Dameron was always modest about his own piano playing, he performed occasionally with Gillespie (1945), as a member of Babs Gonzales's group Three Bips and a Bop (1946–47) and later with his distinguished sextet, a group that featured Fats Navarro and Miles Davis successively. In 1949 he led a group with Davis at the Paris Jazz Festival and he wrote for Artie Shaw's final orchestra; in 1953 he led a nonet that featured Clifford Brown and Philly Joe Jones. Earlier, at the suggestion of a numerologist, Tad had added an extra "d" to his name for good luck, but by 1953, Tadd needed more than luck. His drug addiction interfered with his career, causing him a run of misfortune that culminated in imprisonment, the loss of rare master tapes from recording sessions, and ultimately, his premature death. In 1958 he was arrested for possession of narcotics and spent much of 1959 to 1961 in jail. After his release he worked through several heart attacks until his death from cancer at the age of forty-six. Many of his orchestrations were re-created for the 1980s group Dameronia, a nonet led by longtime associate Philly Joe Jones.

FEBRUARY 22—JAMES REESE EUROPE (1881–1919)

b. Mobile, AL; d. Boston, MA

Bandmaster; Songwriter

[DANCE BANDS; RAGTIME]

Other jazz notables born on this day: Rex Steward (1907); Buddy Tate (1912); Harvey Mason (1947); Joe LaBarbera (1948)

Jazz notables deceased on this day: Nick La Rocca (1961); Derek Humble (1971)

♫

America entered the Great War on April 6, 1917, and on New Year's Day of the following year French servicemen and civilians witnessed an unusual sight as the two thousand men of the Fifteenth New York Regiment landed on the coast of Brittany. The officers were white, as had been the case with all previous American soldiers who had come to France, but the enlisted men were all African-Americans, including the members of the unit's large regimental band. The French onlookers were even more puzzled as the band began its distinctive version of the "Marsellaise," for these Americans played with such rhythmic drive and zest that it took the native listeners several bars before they recognized the piece as their own national anthem. The band's director was Lieutenant James Reese Europe, who had been a prominent dance bandleader in New York before America entered the war, the man who, as musical director for the dancers Vernon and Irene Castle, had introduced the country to the fox-trot.[16]

---

16. Ward and Burns, *Jazz: A History*, 59, 66.

Born in Alabama and raised in Washington, DC, Reese was recruited as musical director for all-black revues on Broadway and saw it as his duty to reveal to the world "the musical proficiency of the African race." Because the New York local of the American Federation of Musicians barred blacks from membership, Europe created a rival organization in 1910, the Clef Club. He formed a 105-piece Clef Club Symphony Orchestra and organized a pioneering concert of African-American music at Carnegie Hall. The concert was a success, as indicated by a review in the *New York Evening-Journal*: "The Negroes have given us the only music of our own that is American—national, original and real." Europe's was the first African-American ensemble to make recordings (1913), playing music by African-American composers.

During World War I Europe's U.S. army band played with a rhythmic excitement no other concert band could match. Their music was not jazz—it was still orchestrated ragtime—but it was filled with jazz elements. The supreme moment was a wildly successful concert in Paris (1918), when the band performed with some of the greatest bands in the world and gained the adulation of the huge crowd, numbered at fifty thousand. The British, French, and Italian bandmasters were impressed as well, and asked to examine the instruments Europe's men had used; they couldn't believe ordinary instruments were capable of producing such sounds. After his discharge Europe had big plans, including a National Negro Symphony Orchestra, a new Broadway musical, and locating new outlets for jazz. He was barely thirty-nine when he took his band on a triumphant tour of the nation. On May 8, during intermission at a Boston concert, Europe was accused of unfair treatment by one of his musicians, a man named Herbert Wright. Without warning the high-strung drummer plunged a penknife into Europe's neck. The wound did not seem serious at first, but it proved to be fatal, for Jim Europe bled to death later that night.

FEBRUARY 23—STERLING BOSE (1906–1958)

b. Florence, AL; d. St. Petersburg, FL

Trumpeter and Cornetist

[CLASSIC JAZZ; SWING]

Other jazz notables born on this day: Johnny Carisi (1922)
Jazz notables deceased on this day: Billy Kyle (1966); Alan Dawson (1966); Tony Williams (1997); Stanley Dance (1999)

♪

Sterling Bose was not the musical equivalent of Bix Beiderbecke, but their careers, lifestyles, and even manner of death bear an uncanny resemblance. Let's start with Bix's story. In 1924 bandleader Jean Goldkette recruited Beiderbecke for his prestigious orchestra, resident at the Graystone Ballroom in Detroit. Goldkette was a shrewd businessman as well as a competent musician, and when he discovered that Bix was unable to read music, he was forced to fire him. In 1925 Beiderbecke joined up with Frankie Trumbauer ("Tram") to play at the Arcadia Ballroom in St. Louis. The two men became close friends, even though they were opposites in many ways: Tram was debonair and businesslike, while Bix was a confirmed alcoholic and somewhat drunk all the time. In 1926, when Tram became musical director of Goldkette's premier band, he brought Bix with him, and for a year he and Bix were costars in the all-star orchestra. For Beiderbecke, at the peak of his powers, this was a triumphant return after his first-time failure, and these were golden days for the Goldkette ensemble. The following year Goldkette temporarily disbanded his ensemble and within weeks the two friends were members of Paul Whiteman's orchestra, the best-known, highest-paid band in America. Bix was productive through 1928 but by the following year, he was drinking suicidally. Suffering from pneumonia and acute alcoholism, he died in pain and horror in a New York boardinghouse in 1931 (for additional information on Beiderbecke, examine the entries for March 10 and 18). Ian Carr explains Bix's early demise: "He was a person of enormous talent but meager character or self-discipline, and his creative despair . . . made him take refuge in alcohol."[17]

Strangely enough, the same could be said of Sterling Bose. Certainly Sterling "Bozo" Bose's credentials were stellar. A good early cornetist influenced by Beiderbecke, he moved to St. Louis in 1923. There he played and recorded with the Arcadian Serenaders, performing opposite Bix and Tram's band at the Arcadian Ballroom. Bose joined Goldkette's Orchestra in Detroit during 1927 and 1928 (the period after Bix's departure), and after his stint in Detroit he worked with many successful musicians, including Ben Pollack (1930–33) Joe Haymes (1934–35), Benny Goodman (where his Beiderbecke style did not fit in), Glenn Miller (1937), Bob Crosby (1937–39), and Bobby Hackett (1939). The stories about Bose during this period seem remarkably similar to those of Bix a bit earlier: "The only anecdotes we have of the pre-war Bose seem to be drunken ones—he was once dragged out of the sea near death from trying to play his trumpet to the fishes, and as a 1930s Decca house musician he was part of an alcoholic quintet known as the Falling-Down Five."[18] Bose's musical reputation seemed to have vanished after the war, a sad echo of his earlier promise. He settled in Florida in 1948 and committed suicide at the age of fifty-two, following a period of illness.

FEBRUARY 24—DAVID "FATHEAD" NEWMAN (1933–2009)

b. Corsicana, TX; d. Kingston, NY

Tenor Saxophonist

[Hard Bop; Soul-Jazz]

Other jazz notables born on this day: Michel Legrand (1932)
Jazz notables deceased on this day: Teddy Brannon (1989)

♪

Despite the jazz influence of fellow Texan tenors Arnett Cobb, Illinois Jacquet, and Buddy Tate, David Newman played and recorded with a variety of non-jazz artists. An exceptional accompanist, his subtle sound graced the albums of dozens of singers, including

---

17. Carr et al., *Jazz: The Rough Guide*, 56.
18. Ibid., 81.

Roberta Flack and Aretha Franklin. Though his best work appears in relaxed, blues-based sessions with altoist Hank Crawford or fellow tenor Stanley Turrentine, it was his earthy improvisations with pianist/singer Ray Charles from 1954 to 1964 that remain his most characteristic work. He appeared with Charles on such landmark recordings as "I Got a Woman," "What'd I Say," and "Lonely Avenue."

Shortly after his birth Newman moved with his family to Dallas, where he took up alto saxophone. While in high school he played with fellow students Cedar Walton and James Clay, and it was at this time that he received his nickname. One day, while the band was rehearsing a John Philip Sousa march, Newman's music instructor, J. K. Miller, saw the sheet music upside down on David's music stand. Thumping him on the head for memorizing the music instead of sight-reading it, he labeled him "Fathead." His band mates made quite a fuss over the name and it stuck. Newman accepted the teasing graciously and turned the nickname into his trademark.

After two years of studying religion at Jarvis Christian College, Newman decided on a career in music and began playing professionally with Buster Smith, who had mentored Charlie Parker in 1937. On one of his tours Newman met Ray Charles, and the two musicians bonded immediately. In 1954 Newman began a ten-year association with the blind pianist, starting out on baritone saxophone and eventually becoming the band's star tenor soloist. Charles, sensing that Newman's nickname might be degrading, began calling him "Brains," but Newman's colleagues and friends refused to accept the change. While with Charles, Newman met Crawford, and the two began a lifelong friendship. In 1964 Newman returned to Dallas, but after two years he moved to New York, where he recorded under King Curtis and Eddie Harris and also appeared on a number of Atlantic albums, playing commercial and soul dates. Newman returned to Charles briefly in 1970 and 1971 and then played with Red Garland and with Herbie Mann's Family of Mann band (1972–74). During the 1970s, '80s, and '90s he maintained a fairly successful recording career, appearing as ace accompanist in a series of heavily orchestrated, pop-oriented sessions (including on Natalie Cole's best-selling album, *Unforgettable,* 1990). During this time he performed the role of Buster Smith and played on the soundtrack for the Robert Altman film *Kansas City* (1996). Newman toured internationally with his own band and sometimes as a member of the Statesmen of Jazz with distinguished luminaries such as Clark Terry, Bucky Pizzarelli, and Kenny Davern. His 2005 release, *I Remember Brother Ray*, became the top Jazz CD of the year.

FEBRUARY 25—IDA COX (1896–1967)

b. Toccoa, GA; d. Knoxville, TN

Vocalist

[Classic Female Blues]

Other jazz notables born on this day: Tommy Newsom (1929); Ake Persson (1932)
Jazz notables deceased on this day: Frank Assunto (1974)

February

♪

Ida Cox was a leading interpreter of the blues during the 1920s, during which time she and Ma Rainey were among Bessie Smith's greatest competitors. Born Ida Prather, Cox began her career at the age of fourteen, traveling with minstrel shows and touring the South in tent shows, where she performed both as a singer and a comedienne. By the early 1920s she was a star of the Theater Owners' Booking Association (TOBA) circuit, at which time she also performed with pianist Jelly Roll Morton. In 1923 she signed a contract with Paramount Records, which billed her as the Uncrowned Queen of the Blues. She recorded with the label in Chicago until 1929, often in the company of pianist Lovie Smith and trumpeter Tommy Ladnier. During this period she also toured extensively in vaudeville and cut tracks for competing labels, using pseudonyms like Velma Bradley, Kate Lewis, and Julia Powers. Like Smith and Rainey, Cox symbolized the liberated spirit of certain African American blues singers. A feminist before the word even existed, she targeted her songs directly to the black women in her audience. Her compositions often conveyed specific social messages: "Wild Women Don't Have the Blues" alludes to sexual freedom; "Pink Slip Blues" dealt with unemployment, and "Last Mile Blues" is a song about capital punishment. A stylish and wise businesswoman, she very much controlled her career. She hired all of her musicians, produced her own stage shows, and managed her own touring company.

By the 1930s, as people's taste in music changed, Cox lost some of her popularity. Although she recorded very little during those Depression years, she toured the South with her longtime accompanist, husband Jesse Crump, and the Northeast theater circuits, including Harlem's Apollo, where she was billed as "the Sepia Mae West." John Hammond brought her to New York City in 1939 to sing at Café Society, a Greenwich Village nightclub that had opened a year earlier with his help, and to appear at the second of his epoch-making *Spirituals to Swing* concerts at Carnegie Hall, where she was accompanied by an all-star band that included James P. Johnston, Lester Young, and Count Basie's outstanding rhythm section. The concert increased her visibility, particularly in jazz circles, for following the concert she recorded with a number of jazz artists, including Charlie Christian, Lionel Hampton, Fletcher Henderson, and Hot Lips Page. She made additional recordings and toured with shows until a 1944 stroke forced her into retirement. She emerged from retirement in 1961 to record a final session with jazz superstars Coleman Hawkins, Roy Eldridge, and Sammy Price. The album, highlighted by her signature song, "Wild Women Don't Have the Blues," proved to be one of the finest of her career. Having outlived her rivals Smith and Rainey by nearly thirty years, the sixty-five-year-old "Uncrowned Queen of the Blues" was still very much in control, her reign secure.

BLUE NOTES

FEBRUARY 26—WILLIAM RUSSELL (1905–1992)

b. Canton, MO; d. New Orleans, LA

Jazz Historian; Record Producer; Composer

[NEW ORLEANS JAZZ; DIXIELAND]

Other jazz notables born on this day: Chauncey Haughton (1909); Dave Pell (1925); Trevor Watts (1939)

Jazz notables deceased on this day: Gabor Szabo (1982); Roy Eldridge (1989); Slim Gaillard (1991)

♪

Although it was not yet apparent, the swing style was on its way out by the end of World War II. In the U.S. a group of jazz writers and some of the older fans had maintained that the rise of the swing bands was a sellout of the music. Rudi Blesh, an outspoken jazz critic, argued during the 1930s that only African-Americans, primarily those from New Orleans, could play authentic jazz. This feeling manifested itself through articles in the jazz press and in the first formal American books on jazz, particularly in the influential *Jazzmen: The Story of Hot Jazz Told in the Lives of the Men Who Created It* (1939), edited by Frederick Ramsey Jr. and Charles Edward Smith. Stimulated by this retrospective movement (known as the New Orleans, or Dixieland revival), a handful of record companies emerged, including Commodore and Blue Note, dedicated to recording this "pure" jazz. By 1940 jazz entrepreneurs, encouraged by the growing number of people interested in the older music, sought venues to promote it. Soon clubs opened in New York and elsewhere, and before long a white guitarist from Chicago named Eddie Condon organized a series of popular jam sessions at New York's Town Hall, which were broadcast over the air. The music they were playing, however, was not strictly New Orleans music. Writers and fans began to demand something purer.

In 1939 William Russell, doing research for his chapter on New Orleans for the book, *Jazzmen*, played an important role in the rediscovery of the sixty-year-old jazz pioneer Bunk Johnson, who had withdrawn to a small town near New Orleans, where he was employed as a common laborer. Russell persuaded the trumpeter to emerge from retirement, and in 1942 he made the first of a number of influential recordings for Russell's American Music label. Johnson, a genuine relic of the past, became a smash success, and the New Orleans revival was on its way, thanks in large measure to Russell's role.

William Russell, born Russell William Wagner, played violin from the age of ten, and later studied music in Chicago and New York, where he took up composition. Around 1930 he dropped his surname, to avoid comparisons with the famous classical composer by that name. While touring with a theatrical group, he became interested in early jazz records, which he collected and later resold through a record exchange he operated. From 1944 to 1957 he undertook a historic series of recordings for his label, including such musicians as Johnson, Baby Dodds, and George Lewis. In 1958 he became curator of the jazz archive at Tulane University in New Orleans and in that position he interviewed scores of veteran musicians for its oral history project. In 1992 the Historic New Orleans Collection acquired his vast collection of archival material and memorabilia, the result of nearly sixty years of collecting and writing. The William Russell Jazz Collection is now housed at Tulane's Williams Research Center.

FEBRUARY 27—DEXTER GORDON (1923–1990)

b. Los Angeles, CA; d. Philadelphia, PA

Tenor Saxophonist

[BOP; HARD BOP]

Other jazz notables born on this day: Freddie Keppard (1890); Mildred Bailey (1907); Hugues Panassié (1912); Abe Most (1920); Joey Calderazzo (1965)

Jazz notables deceased on this day: Horace Tapscott (1999)

♪

Dexter Gordon, the top tenor saxophonist to emerge during the bop era, grew up in the late 1930s, during the period when Lester Young had burst forth from Kansas City with an entirely new sound on tenor saxophone. The sole model for saxophonists up to that time was Coleman Hawkins, but Young changed all that. Gordon began imitating his style slavishly, but as the years passed and Charlie Parker's work started to dominate the jazz scene, Gordon perceptively picked up on that new style as well. Acquiring a distinctive sound, Gordon became the first musician to successfully transfer the characteristics of bop to the tenor, and the first tenor to adapt Young's style to bop.

No one in jazz worked harder, risked more, or fell harder than Gordon. Born a competitor, he was obsessed with the need to stay on top. His colorful life—with numerous comebacks—would easily have made a great Hollywood movie. Ironically, he received a nomination for an Academy Award in 1986 as the star in the feature film *Round Midnight*, but it was for a role inspired by the lives of jazz musicians Bud Powell and Lester Young. The son of a Los Angeles doctor, Dexter was so tall and handsome as a youngster that he drew a crowd wherever he went. At the age of seventeen, he quit school and joined a local band, and soon thereafter he began a three-year engagement with Lionel Hampton's touring band. After brief stints with Fletcher Henderson and then with Louis Armstrong's big band, his 1944 recordings with Billy Eckstine, Dizzy Gillespie, and Fats Navarro soon made him a primary figure in the bop movement. In 1946 he returned to Los Angeles, where he became involved with Wardell Gray and others in a sensational series of "saxophone duels."

As the 1950s began, Gordon seemed on the brink of still greater success. But like so many gifted musicians in jazz at the time, he had developed an addiction to heroin. Following the example set by Parker, whose genius every aspiring musician envied, Gordon's career was curtailed by his $200-a day habit (he was sentenced to jail from 1952 to 1954 and from 1956 to 1960). By the time he was back on the street, Gordon found work harder and harder to get. American culture had changed while he was in prison.

African Americans were now listening to rhythm and blues, white kids were hooked on rock music, and older people were staying home and watching television. In 1962 Gordon settled in Copenhagen; he remained on the continent for the next fifteen years, with only brief returns to the U.S. Huge acclaim for his visit (1976–77) prompted him to move back permanently. Gordon was named "musician of the year" by *Down Beat* magazine in 1978 and 1980 and he remained a popular figure until his gradually worsening health made him semi-active by the early 1980s. His final resurgence occurred when he was picked to star in the Bertrand Tavernier film *Round Midnight*; though his acting was realistic, his playing days by then were mostly behind him.

FEBRUARY 28—LOUIS METCALF (1905–1981)

b. Webster Groves, MO; d. New York, NY

Trumpeter; Leader

[CLASSIC JAZZ]

Other jazz notables born on this day: Lee Castle (1915); Svend Asmussen (1916); Marty Grosz (1930); Willie Bobo (1934); Pierre Dorge (1946)
Jazz notables deceased on this day: Billy Moore (1989)

♪

The year 1924 was formative in the development of jazz bands. On a snowy afternoon in February, Paul Whiteman, America's best-known bandleader, brought jazz to the concert stage for the first time. The concert, a "symphonic" form of jazz, ended with a newly commissioned composition by George Gershwin called "Rhapsody in Blue." The concert was a huge success and soon musicians everywhere were being drawn to the new music. That summer, another event of importance occurred when bandleader Fletcher Henderson took a position at the Roseland Ballroom, using the famous ballroom as a springboard to national fame. In September, Henderson persuaded Louis Armstrong to leave King Oliver's group in Chicago and join him in New York. Armstrong was a jazz specialist, and it was his arrival in 1924 that helped turn the Henderson band toward jazz. His style was rapidly maturing and his playing, with its propulsive swing and melodic invention, entranced other New York musicians. Although Armstrong was not the only jazz influence on New York musicians at this time, he was the most significant one.

In 1924 another trumpeter moved to this jazz-happy city. His name was Louis Metcalf, and he came to prominence as accompanist to a variety of classic blues singers. Despite his obvious talent, his ideas were somewhat harsh and disjointed by comparison with those of Armstrong. For two years he honed his skills, working with some of the city's best jazz musicians, including Willie "The Lion" Smith and Sidney Bechet. In 1926 he began the most important association of his career, recording with Duke Ellington and then joining Ellington's Cotton Club Orchestra during 1927 and 1928, where his solo style was a contrast to Bubber Miley's growling trumpet style. He can be heard on a classic 1927 rendition of Ellington's signature piece, "East St. Louis Toodle-Oo," and an unusual version of "Birmingham Breakdown," unique because of something that never occurs again on an Ellington record—a dual improvisation, in this case by Miley and Metcalf. When Metcalf left Ellington in 1928, perhaps due to the dominating presence of Miley, Duke's childhood friend, Arthur Whetsol, replaced him.

After his departure from the Cotton Club, Metcalf performed with Jelly Roll Morton and with the Luis Russell Orchestra and then recorded with Bessie Smith (1931). During the Depression he led his own band in Montreal, Canada, but by 1936 he was back in New York, where he formed a band that included Lester Young, Hot Lips Page, Clarence Holiday, and twenty-one-year-old vocalist Billie Holiday. That brief two-month engagement with Metcalf at the Renaissance Casino in New York marked the only time that Clarence performed in a band with his daughter. Throughout her career Billie contracted with many guitarists for her sessions, but she always avoided the father who had abandoned her soon after her birth. Metcalf spend the remainder of his career in relative obscurity; he led a band in Montreal from 1946 to 1952 and then returned to New York to perform in clubs.

FEBRUARY 29—JIMMY DORSEY (1904–1957)

b. Shenandoah, PA; d. New York, NY

Alto Saxophonist; Bandleader; Clarinetist

[SWING; BIG BAND]

Other jazz notables born on this day: Richie Cole (1948)
Jazz notables deceased on this day: Charlie Green (February, 1936—exact date unknown)

♪

There is no genetic law that says two brothers should be alike. Quite often they are, but sometimes they are very different, and such was the case with the Dorsey brothers, Jimmy and Tommy. Tommy was the extrovert, the forceful and domineering brother despite being twenty months younger than Jimmy. Jimmy, the milder of the two, was almost shy. The brothers did have several traits in common, however, including proficiency on their instruments, exceptional musical taste, and a good jazz sense. Tommy gained greater notoriety as a bandleader, but Jimmy was the superior jazz player.

Jimmy's father was a music teacher and marching band director. By the age of seven, the gifted youngster was playing cornet in his father's band; shortly thereafter he switched to reeds, alternating on alto saxophone and clarinet. Tommy took up trombone, and the two formed a unit in 1920. The brothers moved to New York in 1924, where they worked with top ensembles such as the California Ramblers, the Jean Goldkette Orchestra (1925), and Paul Whiteman's orchestra (1926). During this time Jimmy began recording extensively with leading Midwestern white jazz pioneers, including Bix Beiderbecke and Red Nichols. His performance with Nichols's popular group the Five Pennies established him as a leading jazz reed player. Beginning in 1927, Jimmy and Tommy organized studio-only ensembles, and then a permanent touring band in 1934. The following year, shortly after scoring a hit with "Lullaby of Broadway," the brothers had a falling-out over the tempo for a popular song and Tommy left to form his own group. By squabbling, the Dorseys lost crucial momentum in their careers. While they sorted themselves out, Benny Goodman emerged and was crowned King of Swing. Tommy quickly put together a commercial band and gave Goodman serious competition. Jimmy changed the group's billing to Jimmy Dorsey and His Orchestra and signed on to accompany host Bing Crosby on the weekly radio series *Kraft Music Hall*, remaining with the show until 1937. After leaving the show his band appeared in a number of films and recorded many hit songs, figuring among the era's most successful bands.

Despite their differences, the brothers formed a joint publishing company and in 1944 established a club in California. Jimmy continued to lead bands and appeared in a fictionalized film, *The Fabulous Dorseys* (1947). In 1953 he accepted an offer from his brother to join the Tommy Dorsey Orchestra as a featured player; soon thereafter the band began to be billed once again as the Dorsey Brothers Orchestra. From 1954 to 1956 the brothers hosted the live television series *Stage Show*, on which Elvis Presley made his national television debut in January 1956. Later that year Jimmy was diagnosed with throat cancer and in November his brother died suddenly, forcing Jimmy to take over the band until his own hospitalization in March. The reconciled brothers died six and a half months apart, at which time the orchestra was split into two memorial bands.

Chapter 3

March

MARCH 1—GLENN MILLER (1904–1944)
b. Clarinda, IA; d. between London and Paris

Bandleader; Trombonist

[Swing; Big Band]

Other jazz notables born on this day: Frank Teschemacher 1906); Ralph J. Gleason (1917); Bob Hardaway (1928); Ralph Towner (1940)

Jazz notables deceased on this day: Frank Teschemacher (1932); Clarence Holiday (1937); Bobby Timmons (1974); Charlie Spivak (1982); Freddie Green (1987)

♪

Benny Goodman's cross-country tour to California in the summer of 1935 is generally considered to have initiated the "swing era." By 1937 there were dozens of successful swing bands, including those of Tommy and Jimmy Dorsey and Glenn Miller, and by 1939 there were hundreds. Swing's impact on the American economy after 1935 was staggering. People who had never listened to jazz began filling ballrooms all over the country, and within a few years big bands became a hundred-million-dollar industry. And what made it all happen was the radio. Radio had only recently become a standard item in American homes, and it was listened to avidly. The big bands entered into a symbiotic relationship with the radio stations. For radio, bands playing in restaurants and dance halls were a source of free programming; for the bands, radio meant free publicity.

Glenn Miller lived in various locations in the Midwest while he was growing up; by 1918 his family had moved to Colorado. After a year of college he moved to Los Angeles, where he joined Ben Pollack's new band, contributing arrangements and taking a few trombone solos. A mediocre trombonist, he quit after talented Jack Teagarden was signed. In 1928 he moved to New York and by 1934 he was with the Dorsey Brothers Orchestra, remaining as trombonist and arranger for almost a year. His first big break as leader came with a 1939 summer engagement at the Glen Island Casino in New Rochelle, NY, a teenage center and major swing venue, which led to another important engagement at the Meadowbrook Ballroom in New Jersey. Both places offered frequent radio broadcasts, and by midsummer the Miller orchestra had developed a nationwide following.

Miller's reign as the most popular bandleader in the U.S. came relatively late in his career and was rather brief, but between 1939 and 1942 he utterly dominated popular music. He developed a distinctive sound in which a high-pitched clarinet carried the melody, doubled by a saxophone section playing an octave lower, and he used that sound to produce a series of hits that remain definitive examples of swing music.[1] He was the first artist to be credited with a million-selling disk for "Chattanooga Choo Choo," and he went on to become the toast of American popular music during World War II, producing a series of hits including "String of Pearls," "Moonlight Serenade" (Miller's theme), "Little Brown Jug," and "In the Mood."

In 1942 Miller, a staunch patriot, decided to enlist in the army. He organized the finest military jazz band ever heard, his Army Air Force Band, which in 1944 sailed for England. The band's weekly feature, *Strings with Wings*, was highly admired by the jazz world. On December 15, 1944, Miller left for Paris to arrange for his band's appearance, but his plane disappeared in bad weather over the English Channel. Miller was mourned internationally and a year later was awarded a posthumous Bronze Star.

MARCH 2—EDDIE "LOCKJAW" DAVIS (1922–1986)

b. New York, NY; d. Culver City, CA

Tenor Saxophonist

[HARD BOP; LATIN JAZZ; SOUL-JAZZ; SWING; BOP]

Other jazz notables born on this day: Orrin Keepnews (1923); Doug Watkins (1934); Buell Neidlinger (1936); Larry Carlton (1948)

Jazz notables deceased on this day: Charlie Christian (1942)

♫

Eddie Davis loved jazz, and he played it with exuberance. A competitive musician with an explosive, screaming style, he could hold his own in a saxophone battle with anyone. He taught himself to play tenor in the late 1930s, and within a year he was displaying his tough and assertive sound at Monroe's Uptown House, one of New York's early bebop shrines. However, his apprenticeship with larger ensembles in the 1940s, including those of Cootie Williams (1942–44), Andy Kirk (1945–46) and Louis Armstrong, led him towards rhythm and blues and away from bop. He began forming his own groups in 1946; one title from his first recording session, "Lockjaw," gave him his nickname, which is sometimes shortened to "Jaws" (he was also known as "The Fox," on account of his quick mind). Davis directed jam sessions at Minton's from 1947 to 1952, and remained a leader for most of his career, except for a tour with George Shearing in 1951 and spells with Count Basie's band during the 1950s and then again from 1964 to 1973. In the late 1950s he made his greatest impact in an organ-tenor trio with Shirley Scott, and from 1960 to 1962 he played in a quintet with fellow tenor Johnny Griffin, whose combative style matched his own.

---

1. Bogdanov et al., *All Music Guide to Jazz*, 868.

March

In 1962 the bottom fell out of the jazz market. The astonishing global popularity of the Beatles and other British rock groups at this time resulted in a deep decline in public enthusiasm for jazz. Desperate jazz musicians took jobs wherever they could find them. Discouraged by financial difficulties, Davis retired temporarily to become a booking agent. By 1964, when Davis rejoined Basie as saxophonist and road manager for the band, many of jazz's familiar landmarks were gone, including the Lincoln Gardens on Chicago's South Side, where Armstrong had played with King Oliver; the Cotton Club in Manhattan, where Duke Ellington had first broadcast his "jungle music"; and Harlem's Savoy Ballroom, where Chick Webb's band ignited the passion of countless fans during the 1930s and where Ella Fitzgerald first became a star. Even Birdland, the club named for Charlie Parker, abandoned jazz in 1965 for rhythm and blues. In 1968 the last club on Fifty-Second Street, the symbolic center of the jazz world, finally closed its doors.

There were many reasons, of course, for the near demise of straightahead jazz at this time. Davis blamed the jazz avant-garde, indicating that modern jazz players had abandoned the joy and light-hearted atmosphere that once prevailed in jazz. Davis managed to uphold his audience-pleasing style during the final decade of his career, when he settled in Las Vegas and teamed up with other swing-era stylists like Roy Eldridge (1974) and Harry "Sweets" Edison (1975–82). He remained a busy soloist until his death in 1986.

MARCH 3—BARNEY BIGARD (1906–1980)

b. New Orleans, LA; d. Culver City, CA

Clarinetist; Composer

[NEW ORLEANS JAZZ; SWING]

Other jazz notables born on this day: Pierre Michelot (1928); Jimmy Garrison (1934)
Jazz notables deceased on this day: Joe Marsala (1978); Sal Nistico (1991)

♪

Duke Ellington's contributions as bandleader were legendary. In addition to leading one of the earliest jazz-oriented big bands, his groups proved to be among the most stable and durable in jazz history. Some of his musicians remained with him for twenty or thirty years at a stretch. Despite their individual talents, Duke's musicians never had significant careers on their own. It was Ellington who discovered what they could do and then made them do it, and his ability to do this was crucial to his accomplishment. Over the years there were five standout players with Duke Ellington's bands: Cootie Williams, Johnny Hodges, Rex Stewart, Harry Carney, and Barney Bigard.

In an era of dazzling clarinetists, Bigard was a standout, using the outmoded Albert system of fingering to produce a larger sound than those around him. His contribution to the popularization of the clarinet is perhaps best summarized in the words of drummer Jo Jones: "Barney made the clarinet famous. This was *before* Benny Goodman."[2]

---

2. Carr et al., *Jazz: The Rough Guide*, 67.

Bigard learned clarinet from Lorenzo Tio Jr., the finest teacher in New Orleans, and he became perhaps the greatest Tio pupil of all. While still a clarinet student, he bought a new "novelty instrument," a tenor saxophone, and before long he was making a reputation on that instrument. In fact, during the mid-1920s his reputation on tenor may have been second only to that of Coleman Hawkins. In 1924 he moved to Chicago to join King Oliver's band, where he occasionally played clarinet. When Oliver found himself short of work in 1927, Bigard freelanced and then joined Duke Ellington in New York for his first Cotton Club season, where Johnny Hodges, the finest alto saxophonist in jazz before Charlie Parker, soon joined him; the two played side by side for the next fourteen years. During this period, the high watermark of his career, Bigard achieved a highly individual clarinet style, characterized by sweeping chromatic runs and long, continuous glissandos. Bigard tended to be showy and sometimes lacked direction as a soloist and therefore, like so many of his band mates, he needed Ellington's discipline in order to flourish. Duke adored Bigard's warm, woody tone but also appreciated his creative imagination, which was utilized on numerous Ellington compositions. In his early days with the band, Bigard wrote "Moon Indigo," a composition that epitomizes jazz for many people. He later sold the tune to Ellington for $25.

Worn down by the rigors of touring, Bigard quit the band in 1942 and settled in Los Angeles, where he formed his own small bands and worked in the film studios. His appearance with Louis Armstrong in the 1946 film *New Orleans* led to an important association as clarinetist with Armstrong's All Stars (1947–55 and 1960–61), with which he toured the world and participated in many outstanding recording sessions. Despite his success with the All Stars, Bigard's swing style, refined during his years under Ellington, sometimes seemed out of place with Armstrong's freewheeling individualists.

MARCH 4—JAN GARBAREK (1947–)

b. Mysen, Norway

Tenor Saxophonist

[Post-Bop]

Other jazz notables born on this day: Barney Wilen (1937); Bobby Shew (1941)
Jazz notables deceased on this day: Bobby Jaspar (1963); Tiny Grimes (1989); Art Hodes (1993); Teddy McRae (1999)

♪

Often associated with the birth of a "Nordic" sound in jazz, Jan Garbarek is one of Norway's most outstanding musicians. Composer George Russell described the tenor saxophonist as "just about the most uniquely talented jazz musician Europe has produced since Django Reinhardt." Clearly one of the most original individualists on saxophone to have emerged since the 1970s, his playing is characterized by a clear, pure tone and a strong impressionistic expression. "There is no rhetoric" in his playing, writes Ian Carr, "only poetry."[3] Rooted in the notion that all music is rooted in song, Garbarek's style is devoted to melody and to the clear articulation of melodious lines. Garbarek is also a fine composer, whose writing, as his playing, has been described as "the most beautiful sound next to silence." Inspired by mystery, nature and song, his long tones and liberal use of space have long been perfect for ECM; as one of the first artists to record for the German record label, Garbarek helped to create the renowned "ECM sound."

Born to a Norwegian mother and a Polish father, Garbarek taught himself to play saxophone at the age of fifteen, after hearing John Coltrane on the radio. The following year he won a competition for amateur jazz players, which led to his first professional work. An encounter with George Russell at a jazz festival in 1965 resulted in Garbarek's fascination with Russell's "Lydian Chromatic Concept of Tonal Organization," a modal approach to harmony that had been popularized in recordings such as Dizzy Gillespie's "CubanaBe/CubanaBop" (1947) and Miles Davis's *Kind of Blue* album (1959). Russell worked in Scandinavia in the late 1960s, and Garbarek became an important soloist in Russell's sextet and big band, performing with these groups during 1967 to 1973 and helping to establish the composer's works.

In 1970 Garbarek began a permanent affiliation with ECM and has since appeared on over thirty albums for the label, both as a leader and as a sideman. In the mid 1970s he formed a band that became pianist Keith Jarrett's European quartet, and it was this association that brought Garbarek greatest acclaim. His work on classic Jarrett recordings such as *My Song* and *Belonging* established him as one of the major saxophonists of the post-Coltrane period. In the later 1980s and '90s Garbarek explored a variety of contexts, recording with Nordic singers, Eastern musicians, and with the Hilliard Ensemble (a vocal quartet singing medieval and Renaissance liturgical music). His critical reputation has grown steadily over time, as has his international audience, and he has become one of the most successful jazz musicians in Europe.

MARCH 5—LOU LEVY (1928–2001)

b. Chicago, IL; d. San Clemente, CA

Pianist

[WEST COAST JAZZ; COOL; BOP]

Other jazz notables born on this day: Carol Sloane (1937)
Jazz notables deceased on this day: Bob Shoeffner (1983); Herb Hall (1996)

♫

Though it's not possible to please everyone all of the time, Lou Levy came close to being an exception. A superior bop-based pianist who played with widely diverse jazz artists over a long career, Levy managed to please and impress almost every musician with whom he worked. Even his one dismissal, at the hands of stern bandleader Tommy Dorsey, was accompanied by the mystifying words: "Kid, you play real good, but not for my band." Levy's

---

3. Carr et al., *Jazz: The Rough Guide*, 268.

ability to stick with a song's melody, even during improvisations, made him a valuable accompanist for soloists, instrumental and vocal alike.

As a twelve-year old learning to play the piano, Levy's jazz tastes were cultivated by listening to the recordings of Charlie Parker and Lester Young. In the late 1940s and early '50s he gained professional experience with a succession of big bands, including a successful two-year stay with Woody Herman's Second Herd (1948–49)—which contained some of the era's most brilliant white musicians—and a brief three-month stint with Dorsey in 1950, where his contributions went largely unappreciated. An important early collaboration came in his hometown of Chicago in 1947, when he accompanied vocalist Sarah Vaughan. Sarah was beginning her solo career at the time, having just recorded with Parker, and Levy was still a teenager. Sarah's gig happened to be near his home, so she would pick him up each night and bring him back home after the show. Vaughan taught Levy a great deal about accompaniment during their brief partnership, and from that point on he began to acquire a reputation as an outstanding accompanist to singers, including June Christy, Peggy Lee, Ella Fitzgerald (1957–62), Anita O'Day, Nancy Wilson, and Frank Sinatra. Listening when Peggy Lee performed (he was her accompanist for eighteen years, beginning in 1955), he learned about the importance of the lyrics, as opposed to the purely musical part. Emulating Lester Young, Bill Evans, Miles Davis, Parker and other great players who emphasized the lyrics of a piece, Levy made it a point to follow the lyrics whenever he was playing and always to think of the melody. "No matter how far into improvising I am," he noted in an interview, "the lyric is going through my head. That makes a great difference in how you play."

Following a three year hiatus from music in 1951, when Levy worked for his in-laws in a family publishing business in Minneapolis, he joined saxophonist Stan Getz, an old friend and colleague from the Woody Herman days. They worked together effectively in various quartet settings over the next quarter of a century. What made him effective in this and other small-group roles were techniques he picked up from vocalists like Vaughan and Lee: "When I accompany Stan Getz I'm accompanying a voice, a very fine voice, and it's just as important to know what to do for a guy with a horn in his mouth as it is for somebody who opens his mouth and sings lyrics."

MARCH 6—WES MONTGOMERY (1925–1968)

b. Indianapolis, IN; d. Indianapolis, IN

Electric Guitarist; Leader

[CROSSOVER JAZZ; HARD BOP]

Other jazz notables born on this day: Red Callender (1916); Howard McGhee (1918); Peter Brotzmann (1941); Palle Mikkelborg (1941); Flora Purim (1942); Charles Tolliver (1942).

Jazz notables deceased on this day: Eddie Durham (1987)

♪

Critics generally rank Wes Mongomery as the most important and influential jazz guitarist after Charlie Christian. Like Christian, whose recorded solos he memorized in his youth, Montgomery invented phrases with tremendous rhythmic drive. But he also took advantage of recent developments in jazz harmony and melody, as well as improvements in the construction of electric guitars, to create a unique style. Wes played with a deep, soulful swing that gave his melodies unusual propulsion, and he was the first guitarist to improvise in octaves, a startling technique that made his listeners think he was overdubbing his solos. Taking advantage of recent developments in jazz harmony and melody as well as improvements in the construction of electric guitars, Montgomery created a unique style using his thumb instead of a plectrum, thereby achieving a softer attack and a more mellow sound than anyone except possibly Jim Hall. His use of the thumb also freed his fingers for the playing of octaves, chordal passages, and for various kinds of strumming. His mastery of these techniques created a sensation among younger guitarists, and the playing of octaves, in particular, became a trademark.

It took John Leslie "Wes" Montgomery a long time to become a success. He was brought up in Columbus, Ohio, where around 1935 he received a four-string guitar from his brother Monk, but it wasn't until 1943, after the family had returned to Indianapolis, that he took up the instrument seriously. Inspired by Charlie Christian, Wes taught himself to play a six-string electric guitar, and he was soon playing with local bands. He toured and recorded with Lionel Hampton (1948–50) before returning to Indianapolis, where he remained in obscurity during much of the 1950s, working a day job and playing at clubs most nights. He formed a trio with his brothers, vibraphonist Buddy and electric bassist Monk (1957–59), and before long his virtuosity resulted in an extraordinarily successful solo career, best represented by *The Incredible Jazz Guitar of Wes Montgomery* (1960), the album that made him famous in the jazz world. This and other Riverside albums represent Montgomery at his peak, accompanied by the finest rhythm sections available, and he soon began to dominate the jazz polls.

With the collapse of Riverside, Montgomery moved to Verve, where during 1964 to 1966 he recorded a series of mostly orchestral and big band dates. These albums, though unrepresentative of his talents, considerably broadened his audience. His rendition of "Goin' out of my Head" (1965) won a Grammy Award, and the album *A Day in the Life*, recorded for the A&M label, was the best-selling jazz LP of 1967.

Montgomery continued to appear in small groups during this period, notably with the Wynton Kelly Trio and in a quintet that included his brothers. A little-known fact about Montgomery was that he often performed for free in local bars for the less affluent of his fans at the same time he played concert dates for pay. He died of a heart attack in 1968; he was only forty-three and at the height of his popularity.

MARCH 7—NAT GONELLA (1908–1998)

b. London, England; d. Gosport, England

Trumpeter; Vocalist; Bandleader

[DIXIELAND]

Other jazz notables born on this day: Alcide "Slow Drag" Pavageau (1888); Lee Young (1917)
Jazz notables deceased on this day: Willie Smith (1967); Al Klink (1991)

♪

Nat Gonella was one of the great characters in British jazz. He was also one of the few European to survive the dance bands of the 1920s and '30s and perform his brand of music in the post-bebop era. He still played at clubs and packed the house in the 1980s. Inspired by Louis Armstrong (he played in a similar style, between Dixieland and swing, and even resembled him physically), Nat Gonella was an excellent trumpeter and a spirited singer.

Gonella was born in a London slum and, like Armstrong, he spent time in an orphanage, where he played cornet in the boys' band. He became intrigued by jazz upon hearing Armstrong's "Wild Man Blues" (1927) in a record shop while on tour with Archie Pitt's Busby Boys. His first solos on record were with Billy Cotton's band in 1930; one of those cuts, "Bessie Couldn't Help It," became the first recorded example of "scat" singing by a British vocalist. After a year with the Roy Fox Band, he remained with the group when Lew Stone took over (1932–35). While with Stone he formed the Georgians, a band-within-a-band named after his popular signature song, "Georgia on My Mind." The Georgians packed theaters, broadcast regularly, and appeared in films up to 1939, at which time Gonella visited the U.S. and recorded four excellent tracks with John Kirby's orchestra.

Upon returning to London he re-formed his New Georgians (1940–41), but was soon conscripted into military service. This period saw a drastic change in Gonella's fortunes, not the least of which involved serving with the Pioneer Corps, whose tasks included constructing latrines. Upon his discharge he found himself in a drastically different musical climate. The supremacy of the big dance bands was under attack from two opposite camps, the traditionalists and the beboppers. Mistakenly, Gonella jumped on the bebop bandwagon, pursuing a brief and unsuccessful flirtation with jazz fashion. The result was a financial disaster. In that bitterly divided period, those who recalled Gonella's Armstrong-inspired trumpet were appalled at his betrayal, while the followers of bebop were distrustful of his apparent conversion. For a while Gonella became something of a lost figure in jazz.

He relaunched his jazz career in 1959 with the sixteen-piece Armstrong-style New Georgia Jazz Band, which recorded frequently during the next three years, though the arrival of the Beatles and the collapse of the traditional-jazz boom in England curtailed his newfound success. In the early 1970s he gave up playing trumpet and moved to Gosport, in the south of England, where he sang in the jazz club and became a beloved figure. He remained active and popular throughout his life, appearing to full houses as late as 1998, just before his ninetieth birthday. At his funeral, ten thousand lined the streets of Gosport to pay their respects to Nat Gonella, Britain's longest-lived and most eminent jazz figure.[4]

MARCH 8—DICK HYMAN (1927–)

b. New York, NY

Keyboardist; Composer; Arranger; Leader

[CLASSIC JAZZ; STRIDE; SWING]

Other jazz notables born on this day: George Mitchell (1899); George Coleman (1935); Gabor Szabo (1936)

Jazz notables deceased on this day: Tadd Dameron (1965); Ken Colyer (1988); Red Callender (1992); Billy Eckstine (1993)

♫

If Art Tatum was the greatest creative artist in jazz, Dick Hyman is the outstanding re-creative pianist and composer. Described as "the ultimate musical chameleon," Hyman is a world-class musician with a Tatum-like mastery of the piano. His amazing eclectic ability as a pianist enables him to reproduce every style of piano jazz, from ragtime to contemporary. He once recorded an album on which he played "A Child is Born" in the style of eleven different jazz pianists. While developing a masterful ability to improvise in his own piano style, Hyman has researched and recorded the earliest periods of jazz, including the piano music of Scott Joplin, Jelly Roll Morton, Eubie Blake, and Fats Waller, which he often features in his recitals. Other solo recordings include the music of Irving Berlin, Harold Arlen, Cole Porter, George Gershwin, and Duke Ellington. His versatility has resulted in well over one hundred albums under his own name or under pseudonyms such as Knuckles O'Toole, one of his ragtime piano aliases. Hyman's concerts feature encyclopedic surveys of piano styles that range from Joplin to Cecil Taylor and that include valuable historical commentary, a feature formalized in *Dick Hyman's Century of Jazz Piano*, a CD-ROM (1998) based on his recitals. Hyman's fame for his ability to perform any musical style on virtually any keyboard instrument has overshadowed his accomplishments as an outstanding arranger, composer, and jazz historian.

Hyman studied classical music at an early age and while attending Columbia University he won twelve lessons from Teddy Wilson in a radio contest. He played with Charlie Parker, Dizzy Gillespie, Lester Young, Red Norvo, Benny Goodman, and other jazz greats early in his career, but he claims his best musical education came in the 1950s, when as a studio musician on radio and television, he had to shift from one style to another on an almost daily basis and where exceptional sight-reading and impromptu compositional skills were essential to his survival. His prolific career in New York studios won

---

4. Carr et al., *Jazz: The Rough Guide*, 288.

him seven Most Valuable Player awards from the National Academy of Recording Arts and Sciences.

After a stint as the musical director of *The Arthur Godfrey Show* (1959–62), he collaborated with Leonard Feather on some *History of Jazz* concerts (doubling on clarinet) and even performed rock and free jazz. In the 1970s he re-examined classic jazz with the New York Jazz Repertory Company and the Perfect Jazz Repertory Quintet (1976), and started writing soundtracks for Woody Allen films. In the 1980s his duets with cornetist Ruby Braff matched gems created by Earl Hines and Louis Armstrong in the late 1920s, a period of classic jazz Hyman regularly revisits. Based in Florida since the 1990s, Hyman maintains a busy schedule.

MARCH 9—ORNETTE COLEMAN (1930–)

b. Fort Worth, TX

Saxophonist; Composer

[AVANT-GARDE JAZZ; FREE FUNK; FREE JAZZ]

Other jazz notables born on this day: Herschel Evans? [DOB uncertain]
Jazz notables deceased on this day: Monty Budwig (1992); Bob Crosby (1993)

♫

One of the most important innovators of the jazz avant-garde and the most controversial musician in the history of jazz, Ornette Coleman gained both loyal followers and detractors when he burst on the scene in the 1950s. In November 1959 he arrived in New York for a two-week engagement at the Five Spot, a favorite hangout for abstract painters and other freethinking individuals. Coleman's arrival was a signal that a radical transformation of jazz was underway. Icons like Armstrong and Ellington, Parker and Gillespie, Monk and Davis, had made their individual statements while working within agreed-upon rhythm, harmony, and chord sequences. Coleman challenged all that. Jazz, he said, must be "free." Coleman's audience at the Five Spot was filled with curious musicians who labeled him either a genius (Leonard Bernstein among them) or a fraud, but as a result of his extended stay, free jazz became an established fact.

As a primitive artist, Coleman's attempts to play in an original style were consistently met with hostility both by audiences and fellow musicians. His distinctive sound—raw, atonal, and seemingly incoherent—evidently developed early, and he stubbornly stuck to it, even after a gang of toughs who disliked his music beat him up and smashed his saxophone. Coleman moved to Los Angeles in the early 1950s, where he worked as an elevator operator. While studying theory and harmony textbooks he developed his "Harmolodics" approach (which emphasized the equal importance of harmony, melody, and rhythm). This concept was so unorthodox that most musicians simply ignored him. At one point tenor star Dexter Gordon ordered him off the stage rather than let him sit in. Coleman not only looked out of tune (with a beard, uncut hair, and distinctive clothes made by his wife), he also sounded out of tune. In 1958, with the assistance of bassist Red Mitchell,

Coleman eventually landed a recording contract; two albums for Contemporary Records introduced the radical new talent to the jazz world.

During 1959 to 1961 Coleman recorded a series of classic albums for the Atlantic label, creating music that would affect many of the advanced improvisers of the 1960s, including John Coltrane and Eric Dolphy. In 1960 he released one of the most important recordings in the avant-garde movement, a thirty-eight-minute jam called *Free Jazz*, performed by an ensemble he called a double quartet. The piece lacked tempo, bar lines, chords, and even a strict pitch.

A few years later Coleman surprised the jazz world by going into temporary retirement, seeking fulfillment in composition. He found some success in this area and made lasting contributions to the jazz repertoire with compositions such as "Congeniality," "Peace," and the haunting "Lonely Woman," pieces that rank among the finest in jazz. Though he mellowed with time, Coleman has remained true to his highly original vision throughout his career. While not technically a virtuoso, he is a gigantic figure in jazz.

MARCH 10—BIX BEIDERBECKE (1903–1931)

b. Davenport, IA; d. New York, NY

Cornetist; Composer

[Classic Jazz]

Other jazz notables born on this day: Mino Cinélu (1957); Jeanie Bryson (1958)
Jazz notables deceased on this day: Allan Jaffe (1987)

♪

Leon "Bix" Beiderbecke, "the first great white jazz musician," reached adulthood during the Prohibition period, when many Americans found drinking to be something of a sport. But for Bix it became an obsession; by 1925 he was a confirmed alcoholic. Though musically an immortal, Bix was under-appreciated during his brief lifetime. Some years after his death, Dorothy Baker's novel, *Young Man with a Horn* (1938), began the process that was to make him a symbol of the Roaring Twenties. Possessor of a beautiful, distinctive tone and a strikingly original improvising style, Bix was jazz's first great lyricist. His interest in impressionistic harmonic language, together with his unique timbre (achieved through his unorthodox fingering), gave his work an introspective quality and set his playing apart from others. His originality made him the first white musician to be admired and imitated by black and white jazz performers alike.

Bix, who inherited the nickname from an older brother, began picking out tunes on the piano when he was three. The Beiderbeckes, a strict moral family, brought Bix up to pursue a significant and successful career, such as a doctor, lawyer, merchant, or minister. His parents introduced him to music early on, knowing that music was an attribute of a cultivated life. Bix loved music, but he resisted instruction. As a boy he had a few piano lessons, but he was self-taught on cornet and developed an unorthodox technique by playing along with recordings. At an early age he found in music something that was his own, an escape from parental control. His first contact with jazz came through the recordings of the Original Dixieland Jazz Band, and he was smitten by this new music, especially the cornet sound of Nick LaRocca.

His family disapproved of his interest in jazz and sent him to Lake Forest Military Academy near Chicago, a boarding school run along military lines. It was a mistake to place him so close to Chicago (the center of jazz at the time), for soon he and some friends began sneaking into town at night to hear, and occasionally play with, the New Orleans Rhythm Kings, the area's most important white band. Bix began drinking heavily; he was nineteen and he yearned for a life in jazz. He was expelled from the academy before his first academic year was over. The following year he helped form a band called the Wolverines, patterned after the Rhythm Kings, and by the age of twenty-one he was becoming a recognized figure among jazz musicians.

In 1924 he joined the impressive band led by Jean Goldkette, where he rose to prominence (see March 18 entry). Within three years he reached the pinnacle of his career as the featured soloist with Paul Whiteman's prosperous orchestra, the most popular band of the 1920s. But his alcoholism forced him to take a leave of absence in 1929, and he never returned. He spent his final year in a tiny one-room apartment outside of New York City, physically drained and financially depleted. His death in 1931, at the age of twenty-eight, was caused by pneumonia and acute alcoholism. The Jazz Age's quintessential legend died as he lived, a rebel.

MARCH 11—BOBBY MCFERRIN (1950–)

b. New York, NY

Vocalist

[Vocal Jazz; Neo-Bop]

Other jazz notables born on this day: Miff Mole (1898); Chauncey Morehouse (1902); Mercer Ellington (1919)
Jazz notables deceased on this day: Frankie Newton (1954); Hugh Lawson (1997)

♫

"Unconventional" may be the best way to describe Bobby McFerrin, the master of *a cappella* singing who, with his voice, performs polyphonic songs, imitates instruments, and produces rhythms against which he improvises. A ten-time Grammy Award winner, he is one of the world's best-known vocal innovators and improvisers. With a four-octave range and a vast array of vocal techniques, he has been described as "music's last true Renaissance man." Equally adept in jazz, pop, and classical settings, McFerrin ranks among the most distinctive singers in contemporary music; his octave-jumping trademark style and sudden shifts from falsetto to deep bass often sound like the work of several singers at once. His quick wit and wide knowledge of musical styles make his solo performances hugely entertaining.

Born to opera singers in New York, where his father was the first African-American male soloist at the Metropolitan Opera, McFerrin moved to Hollywood in 1955, when his father was hired to be the singing voice for Sidney Poitier in the movie *Porgy and Bess*. McFerrin's first love was the clarinet, but he switched to the piano around the time that braces became a necessity. For a while he considered becoming a priest, but that initial calling could not ultimately compete with his love of music. In 1977, after touring with the Ice Follies and performing with a series of cabaret acts, he decided to become a singer. In San Francisco he met legendary comedian Bill Cosby, who arranged for him to appear at the 1980 Playboy Jazz Festival. The following year he made a sensational appearance at the Kool Jazz Festival in New York, winning critical acclaim. After a tour with his own band and gigs with established jazz figures such as George Benson, Herbie Hancock, and Wynton Marsalis, he decided to perform as a soloist.

Inspired by the completely improvised solo concerts of pianist Keith Jarrett, McFerrin began working toward a similar goal. In 1983 he accomplished his goal, touring Europe without accompaniment and performing without prepared material. Audiences were bewildered at first, then amazed. Tapes of those concerts were made into *The Voice*, a 1984 release that remains his finest recording. This was the first time a jazz singer had recorded an entire album solo, without accompaniment or overdubbing, for a major label. In 1988 he had a worldwide hit with the easy listening album *Simple Pleasures*, his homage to the music of the 1960s. It contained "Don't Worry, Be Happy," a tune he created on the spot in the recording studio. The song won two Grammys and became one of the most popular songs of the late twentieth century. While at the brink of pop superstardom, McFerrin suddenly switched gears to begin a serious study of conducting. In 1990, on his fortieth birthday, he conducted the San Francisco Symphony Orchestra. Since that time he has managed to balance his disparate musical loves through a dual career as conductor and solo improviser.

MARCH 12—AL JARREAU (1940–)

b. Milwaukee, WI

Vocalist

[Contemporary Jazz; Soft Rock; Pop]

Other jazz notables born on this day:
Jazz notables deceased on this day: Charlie Parker (1955); Joe Morello (2011)

♪

Described as "a towering musical talent" by *Entertainment Weekly* magazine, Al Jarreau is a multi-faceted and charismatic performer. His innovative vocal style made him one of the most exciting and critically acclaimed performers of our time, with five Grammy Awards and scores of international awards. The only singer in history to win Grammy Awards in three different categories (Jazz, Pop, and R&B), Jarreau developed his style from the bop school of John Hendricks and Dave Lambert, which he refined and adapted to a fusion of jazz and soul music. Using superb intonation and no vibrato, he utilizes a large repertory of expressive sounds such as groans, tongue-clicks, and gasps. Although his recordings often reveal a commercial bent, his live performances, such as "Take Five" on the album *Look to the Rainbow*, place him with Bobby McFerrin among the foremost jazz and scat singers of his generation.[5]

The son of a minister, Jarreau began singing at the age of four, harmonizing with his brothers in church. In high school and college he excelled in sports, but he sang occasionally with a vocal group called The Indigos. In the mid-1960s, ten years before he began to receive attention, he sat in with some friends and recorded *1965*, an excellent debut album and his only strictly "pure jazz" recording to date. Though he was never really happy with the release, the album shows the kind of promising jazz singer Jarreau could have been had he pursued jazz over more commercial pursuits. After earning undergraduate and graduate degrees in psychology, he moved to San Francisco to begin a career as a social worker. He achieved success singing in local clubs and decided to pursue music full time.

He relocated to Los Angeles, where he played in small clubs and hoped for a breakthrough. Eventually he traveled to New York, and there he gained network television exposure on programs hosted by Johnny Carson, Merv Griffin, and Mike Douglas. In 1975 he finally got the break he needed when he signed to a recording contract with Warner Brothers. His first release, *We Got By*, won acclaim for its sophisticated brand of vocalese and earned Jarreau comparison to Billy Eckstine and Johnny Mathis. The album was well received internationally and led to a German Grammy for Best New International Soloist. The next two decades produced a run of successful albums, including the two-disc *Look to the Rainbow* (1977) and *All Fly Home* (1978), which earned Jarreau back-to-back Grammys for Best Jazz Vocal Performance. The early 1980s brought the platinum-selling *Breakin' Away*, which gained him two more Grammy awards (a third for Jazz Vocal and his first for Best Male Pop Vocalist), followed some years later by the smash hit "Moonlighting." During the mid-1980s Jarreau continued recording R&B and pop hits, which led to another Grammy for *Heaven and Earth* (1992), this time for best R&B Vocal Performance. Jarreau's mainstream pop success waned during the 1990s, and in 2000 he switched to the GRP/Verve label, where his contemporary jazz music found success with adult audiences.

MARCH 13—FRANK TESCHEMACHER (1906–1932)

b. Kansas City, MO; d. Chicago, IL

Clarinetist; Alto Saxophonist; Violinist

[CLASSIC JAZZ]

Other jazz notables born on this day: Bob Haggart (1914); Roy Haynes (1925); Blue Mitchell (1930); Terence Blanchard (1962); Stephen Scott (1969)
Jazz notables deceased on this day: Jimmy McPartland (1991)

---

5. Kernfeld, *New Grove Dictionary of Jazz*, Vol. 2, 358.

March

♪

In 1922, when Louis Armstrong started playing with King Oliver's Creole Jazz Band, the hot ensemble was a fixture at Lincoln Gardens. This section of Chicago's South Side was somewhat like New Orleans' famous Storyville, its clubs providing illegal pleasures of every sort. This was Al Capone's turf, and most of the clubs were owned or protected by bootlegging mobsters. From the start, Armstrong's talent was obvious to everyone. Shortly after his arrival, the first ten rows at the Gardens were filled with musicians, many of them young and white. These included Bix Beiderbecke, Eddie Condon, Benny Goodman (then barely a teenager), and members of the Austin High Gang.

The Austin High Gang, named for the high school most of the group attended on Chicago's West Side, was led by Frank Teschemacher, a shy violin student and saxophonist who would soon shift his allegiance to clarinet. He was able to convince four of his high school friends that they could successfully imitate the New Orleans Rhythm Kings, a popular white jazz group originally from New Orleans. In 1922 the Gang formed what may have been the first garage band: Jim Lanigan on piano, Jimmy McPartland on cornet, his brother Dick on guitar and banjo, Bud Freeman on C-melody sax, and Teschemacher on alto. They began hanging around the Friar's Inn to hear the Rhythm Kings in person and started getting pickup jobs around town. One day, while playing at a fraternity party on the South Side, they were invited to hear Oliver and Armstrong at the Lincoln Gardens. They became hypnotized by the band's novel sound, and from that moment on they followed Armstrong and Oliver all over town.

Teschemacher was born to an affluent family in Kansas City. He studied violin and banjo as a boy and knew the fundamentals of music by the time his family moved to Chicago. An original member of the Austin High School Gang, he took up the clarinet in 1925 and two years later was making definitive "Chicago-style" recordings with a variety of pickup groups. In 1928 he went to New York with Jimmy McPartland and other of his Chicago friends, but by the end of the year, having played with excellent musicians like Ben Pollack, Sam Lanin, and Red Nichols, he returned to Chicago, where he freelanced with like-minded performers such as cornetist Max Kaminsky. Though Teschemacher is believed to have been the equal of Goodman at this point, his recordings were never as remarkable as his live performances. Teschemacher seemed to have had a phobia about making records, for he was regularly drunk when he reached the recording studio. He never reached his potential, for in 1932 the twenty-five-year-old died in an automobile collision. One wonders how this excellent musician, one of the central figures in the Chicago jazz scene at the time, would have fared had he lived longer.

BLUE NOTES

MARCH 14—QUINCY JONES (1933–)

b. Chicago, IL

Arranger; Composer; Bandleader; Trumpeter; Pianist; Record Producer

[Bop; Swing; Crossover Jazz; Pop; Big Band]

Other jazz notables born on this day: Les Brown (1912); Mark Murphy (1932); Shirley Scott (1934)

Jazz notables deceased on this day:

♫

Quincy Jones is an inspiration to everyone he meets. Growing up during the Depression in Chicago and Seattle, he ran with a rough crowd. That is, until the night he and some friends broke into a recreation center. In one of the rooms he saw a piano. He had touched a piano before, but he had never thought about a career in music. Playing that piano lit a fire in him and changed the course of his life.

Jones went on to unparalleled success in a career that brought him accolades as composer, arranger, conductor, producer, and record company executive. In the process, he became the most nominated Grammy artist of all time, receiving seventy-six Grammy nominations and twenty-six awards. His achievements include composing scores for thirty-three major motion pictures and themes for numerous television shows. In 1980 he produced Michael Jackson's *Thriller* (1982), the best-selling album in the history of the recording industry. He also produced and conducted the historic recording "We Are the World," the best-selling single of all time, as a means to raise money for Ethiopian famine relief. Recalling his own roots and realizing that not all children find hope for their lives, in 1991 he started Listen Up Foundation to help the world's youth. The foundation's projects are as diverse as the music Jones has made throughout his fifty-year career.

While barely in his teens, Jones befriended Ray Charles, a local musician three years his elder. The two formed a combo and frequently stayed up late into the night writing arrangements to Dizzy Gillespie songs and other bebop compositions. Something about composing and arranging fascinated Quincy, and he knew that was what he wanted to do for the rest of his life. At eighteen he won a scholarship to Berklee College in Boston, but he dropped out abruptly to travel with bandleader Lionel Hampton (1951–53). During this period he began to work as a freelance arranger and became quite successful, providing charts for Clifford Brown, Tommy Dorsey, and Count Basie, among others. By 1956 he was traveling the world, performing as a trumpeter and music director with the Dizzy Gillespie band.

The following year he signed a contract with Mercury Records and relocated to Paris, where he studied composition and worked as a music director. In 1960, while touring Europe, he formed a big band of his own, but concert earnings left him deeply in debt. Mercury Records provided him with a loan, and he went to New York as music director for the label. In 1964 he was named Mercury's vice-president, thereby becoming the first African-American to hold a position in a major white-owned record company. He took a brief break from these activities to write arrangements for Frank Sinatra's recordings and concerts with Count Basie, including a memorable version of "Fly Me to the Moon," but thereafter he began writing for films and television. Despite a varied and successful career, Quincy never abandoned his love or appreciation for jazz; as he states: "jazz is the heart and soul of all popular music."

MARCH 15—HARRY JAMES (1916–1983)

b. Albany, GA; d. Las Vegas, NV

Trumpeter; Bandleader

[TRADITIONAL POP; SWING; BIG BAND]

Other jazz notables born on this day: Chippie Hill (1905); Jimmy McPartland (1907); Bob Wilber (1928); Cecil Taylor (1929); Charles Lloyd (1938)

Jazz notables deceased on this day: Pine Top Smith (1929); Lester Young (1959); Tommy Potter (1988); Bud Freeman (1991)

♪

In addition to being one of the most prominent instrumentalists of the swing era, James was also one of the most successful bandleaders during the first half of the 1940s (his big band was the most popular in the world from 1942 to 1946, after Glenn Miller went in the army), and he continued to lead a band until just before his death, forty years later.[6] Noted for his wide range and impressive technique, James gained a popularity that tended to obscure the fact that he was a very fine jazz improviser.

Growing up in the circus (his father was the bandleader and trumpet player and his mother an aerialist), James became a performer at the age of four, when he began working as a contortionist. At twelve he took over leadership of a circus band, and two years later, after winning a Texas music contest as a trumpeter, he turned professional. His first job with a national band came in 1935, when he joined Ben Pollack's band. Only nineteen, the handsome teenager was already a trumpet master. Jam session colleagues such as Teddy Wilson, Buster Bailey, and Johnny Hodges and New York's studio world quickly accepted him. In 1935 he married singer Louise Tobin, whom he divorced in 1943 to marry movie heartthrob Betty Grable (they divorced in 1965). In 1937 James joined Benny Goodman, and in two brief years he made his reputation as Goodman's most brilliant trumpet soloist ever.

In 1939, with Goodman's blessing, he formed his own big band and he remained a leader from then on. That spring he heard Frank Sinatra, an unknown singer, on a radio broadcast and hired him, though Sinatra left at the end of 1939 to join the more successful bandleader Tommy Dorsey. James began parading his limitless trumpet technique in virtuosic pieces such as "Carnival of Venice" and "Flight of the Bumble Bee," but it was a romantic feature from 1941, "You Made Me Love You," that established him as the most commercially successful jazz musician of the 1940s. James became a pop music idol

---

6. Bogdanov et al., *All Music Guide to Jazz*, 654.

during the war years (he was ineligible for military service due to a back injury), during which time he toured and broadcast constantly, in addition to making a number of films. One of his hits, "I Had the Craziest Dream," with vocals by Helen Forrest, was featured in *Springtime in the Rockies* (1942), a film memorable for having starred Betty Grable. By 1944 James's band featured Forrest, with whom he reportedly had a long affair. The declining popularity of the big bands led to the breakup of many by 1946, James's orchestra among them. The bandleader appeared in several films during the late 1940s and '50s, including playing himself in the film biography *The Benny Goodman Story* (1955). In 1957 he began touring with a re-formed big band and from then on he remained a popular attraction into the early 1980s, leading a band until a few days before his death.

MARCH 16—LEON ROPPOLO (1902–1943)

b. Lutcher, LA; d. New Orleans, LA

Clarinetist; Composer

[NEW ORLEANS JAZZ]

Other jazz notables born on this day: Ruby Braff (1927); Tommy Flanagan (1930)
Jazz notables deceased on this day: Ernie Royal (1983); Dannie Richmond

♪

In 1921 eight white musicians who called themselves the New Orleans Rhythm Kings began a seventeen-month run at a small cellar cabaret called the Friar's Inn, on Chicago's North Side. Mobsters like Dion O'Banion and young Al Capone, who would soon order O'Banion's death and take over as boss of the North Side, frequented the club, described by one customer as "funky, run-down, sinister and dusty." The key members of the Rhythm Kings—cornetist Paul Mares, trombonist Georg Brunis, and clarinetist Leon Roppolo—were childhood friends from New Orleans. Of all the white New Orleans-style bands, they created the most polished, relaxed style. Their 1922 recordings, highlighted by Roppolo's poised and coherent breaks, quickly established them as the finest jazz group on record and Roppolo as the first significant jazz soloist on records. Their authentic sound took the jazz world by storm, inspiring white players such as Bix Beiderbecke to play like them. When the group's records first appeared, members of the Austin High Gang learned to play jazz by memorizing lines one note at a time.

Despite a short career, Roppolo (his name is often misspelled Rappolo) was one of the most influential jazz clarinetists of all time. In addition to his work with the New Orleans Rhythm Kings, where he was a superb ensemble player, he was a highly imaginative soloist. His use of subtle tonal inflections and his ability to achieve a dynamic contrast between the clarinet's high and low registers lent his playing an emotional quality that set him apart from his contemporaries. Also a composer, he wrote such standards as "Farewell Blues," "Milenburg Joys (Golden Leaf Strut)," "Sugar Babe," and "Tin Roof Blues."

A handsome, high-powered young man, Roppolo learned to play the clarinet from his father, a saloon owner. Leon heard jazz from visiting bands and took informal lessons from Eddie Shields (the piano-playing brother of clarinetist Larry) while working in his band. He was also a friend with the Brunies family, with whom he toured. Around 1921, after playing on Mississippi riverboats, he traveled to Chicago with Brunis and Mares to form a band at the Friars Inn, soon to be known as the New Orleans Rhythm Kings. There he played the clarinet with a clear, singing sound all his own, experimentally bouncing the sound off the floors and pillars of his cramped quarters, often pausing to jot phrases and themes on his shirt sleeve. Roppolo went with Mares to New York in 1923 and the following year he worked in Texas, after which he returned to New Orleans. He joined Abbie Brunies's Halfway House Orchestra and played with Mares's re-formed Rhythm Kings in 1925. By now he was drinking and smoking marijuana, but he kept working until he suffered a mental breakdown later that year. He spent most of his remaining years in a mental institution, where he organized a band and continued to play, mainly on tenor saxophone.

MARCH 17—NAT "KING" COLE (1917–1965)

b. Montgomery, AL; d. Santa Monica, CA

Pianist; Vocalist; Leader

[VOCAL JAZZ; TRADITIONAL POP; JUMP BLUES; SWING; BALLADS]

Other jazz notables born on this day: Grover Mitchell (1930)
Jazz notables deceased on this day: Carl Perkins (1958); Gigi Gryce (1983)

♪

The 1950s were a period of unprecedented growth in the American economy. During that period the nation's gross national product grew by over one third as Americans achieved the highest standard of living in the history of the world. As America expanded economically, the hopes of African Americans grew as well, and they began to push for racial justice. On May 17, 1954, the United States Supreme Court ruled that in the field of education the doctrine of "separate but equal" had no place. White southerners responded with fury. The Ku Klux Klan experienced a rebirth and many others pledged to maintain segregation at all costs. On April 10, 1956, Nat King Cole, one of the most popular vocalists in the nation, was to perform in Birmingham, Alabama with the Ted Heath Orchestra. There were to be two shows that evening, an early show for white fans and a later one for black fans. As Cole emerged into the spotlight for the first show, five white men leaped onto the stage and began attacking the entertainer. Lee Young, Cole's drummer, shouted to Ted Heath to strike up the national anthem, hoping to curb the violence, but Heath was English and launched into "God Save the Queen" instead. Cole's assailants were eventually subdued and taken to jail. Cole limped back onstage, following an apology from the mayor and shouts of regret from white fans, but he refused to sing again until the black crowd waiting outside was ushered in.

No other performer in history had two such profoundly different public personalities as Cole: the hip leader of a black jazz combo in the 1940s and the eminent crooner of the 1950s and '60s with a predominantly white following. Though it was as pianist that he left his greatest influence—he was one of the truly great swing pianists, playing in a light style, with spare lines and brief, syncopated bursts of chords—his superb pop singing, relaxed and subtly syncopated, was also infused with jazz.

Cole grew up in Chicago, and by the time he was twelve he was playing organ and singing in the church where his father was pastor. In 1936 he moved to Los Angeles, where he formed a trio that settled into a long residency in Hollywood. The trio's piano/guitar/bass format inspired jazz performers such as Art Tatum, Oscar Peterson, and Ahmad Jamal to form similar combos. Nat recorded a great deal of exciting jazz during the 1940s, but his career changed permanently in early 1950 with the vocal recording of "Mona Lisa." Suddenly Cole was famous to the nonjazz public as a singer. Cole's white following was so large at this time that an attempt was made to secure him a weekly television show during 1956 and 1957, but due to the racism of the period he had difficulty finding a sponsor. When a Revlon executive claimed that a Negro could not sell cosmetics, Cole's response was classic: "Madison Avenue is afraid of the dark." His popularity continued until 1965, when he died from lung cancer at the age of forty-seven. In 1991 Natalie Cole accomplished a technological miracle when she sang a duet with him; the song, "Unforgettable," aptly summarized her father's career.

MARCH 18—JEAN GOLDKETTE (1893–1962)

b. Patras, Greece; d. Santa Barbara, CA

Orchestra Leader; Pianist; Entrepreneur

[CLASSIC JAZZ]

Other jazz notables born on this day: Bill Frisell (1951); Joe Locke (1959); Courtney Pine (1964)
Jazz notables deceased on this day: Billy Butterfield (1988)

♪

In the early 1920s, when jazz experienced a large influx of whites, African Americans and whites were isolated to a degree now unthinkable. As late as 1930 few white people in the United States had ever sat down to a meal with a black or even held a conversation with one as a social equal. African-Americans were not allowed into white restaurants or nightclubs, nor could they appear on the same bandstand with one another. Though racial relations would improve significantly over the next fifty years, a great deal of ignorance continued to be perpetuated. As a consequence, it was possible for one veteran white player to say, as late as the 1970s: "Jazz wasn't invented by those colored guys, it was invented by Bix Beiderbecke and the guys in the Jean Goldkette band."[7]

Goldkette, a classically trained concert pianist who immigrated to the U.S. in 1911, never played jazz music. His importance to jazz came from a chain of ballrooms he ran and his role as agent and organizer for some twenty different dance orchestras during the

---

7. Collier, *Making of Jazz*, 124.

1920s, including one of the leading black bands of the era, McKinney's Cotton Pickers, and a white group called the Casa Loma Orchestra, which in the early 1930s helped shape the course of the swing era. His most celebrated orchestra was the Victor Recording Orchestra, which operated from the Graystone Ballroom in Detroit and toured as the Jean Goldkette Orchestra.

In September 1924 Goldkette recruited Bix Beiderbecke, already making headlines with the Wolverines, to join Jimmy and Tommy Dorsey, Joe Venuti, and other members of his impressive band, only to fire him a few weeks later when he discovered that Bix was unable to read music. In 1926, however, when Goldkette hired Frank "Tram" Trumbauer as music director of his flagship orchestra, he agreed to include Beiderbecke as well. For Bix, now at the peak of his ability, this was a triumphant return, and his problems with music reading were quickly overcome. His ability to play odd notes like sixths, ninths, and seconds provided an explosive quality to the band's overall sound. Bix soon became the orchestra's top soloist, joining jazz notables such as Trumbauer, Venuti, Don Murray, Eddie Lang, Steve Brown, and arranger Bill Challis in the band's impressive lineup. In October 1926, after a successful tour of New England, the band was invited to play at Roseland, Manhattan's most prestigious ballroom, where they defeated Fletcher Henderson's orchestra, America's premier dance ensemble, at a musical contest. Henderson's band included some of the best musicians in the country, but that night they could not match Trumbauer, Beiderbecke, and the arrangements by Challis. In 1927 Goldkette was forced to disband his orchestra for financial reasons. Bix and Tram soon joined Paul Whiteman, the best-known, highest-paying bandleader in America. Goldkette's formative role in jazz ended in the early 1930s, when he dropped out of the jazz business to concentrate on his work as a booking agent and to perform as a classical piano soloist with the Detroit Symphony.

MARCH 19—LENNIE TRISTANO (1919–1978)

b. Chicago, IL; d. New York, NY

Pianist; Teacher; Leader

[AVANT-GARDE JAZZ; COOL; BOP]

Other jazz notables born on this day: Curly Russell (1917); Eliane Elias (1960)
Jazz notables deceased on this day: Clyde Hart (1945)

♪

Lennie Tristano, a uniquely complex individual, had an intellectual and experimental streak that ran deep. Born during an influenza epidemic, which affected his eyesight, he became totally blind by the age of nine. He played a variety of instruments as a youth and began working professionally at the age of twelve. He continued his musical education and eventually earned a master's degree in composition in 1943. Though he composed in the European classical forms at the conservatory, he pursued jazz privately, and by the time of his graduation he was an accomplished pianist who sounded like an amalgam of Earl Hines and Art Tatum. He possessed a thorough grounding in theory and composition, a prodigious piano technique, and some advanced ideas of his own, and by the mid-1940s he was one of the most thoroughly schooled musicians in jazz.

Like Stan Kenton, George Gershwin, and others before him, Tristano consciously attempted to weld jazz and classical music. He developed a personal philosophy of improvisation and began attracting gifted students, who were expected to memorize classic solo improvisations by Louis Armstrong, Lester Young, and other outstanding jazz performers, as well as improvise on compositions by J. S. Bach. Tristano moved to New York in 1946 and quickly earned a reputation as an eccentric genius with unusual ideas about music. The influential critic Barry Ulanov championed his work and in 1947 he was named *Metronome*'s Musician of the Year. His knowledge of instruments and his broadminded approach led to the founding of a school of jazz in New York in 1951, the first of its kind. Its faculty consisted of many of his most prominent students, including Lee Konitz, Billy Bauer, Warne Marsh, and pianist Sal Mosca.

In 1949 Tristano's sextet recorded the groundbreaking album, *Crosscurrents*, for the Capitol label. At the conclusion of the session, Tristano told the engineers to leave the mike open. He and his musicians began playing spontaneously, but in such an incomprehensible manner—without any predetermined reference to time, tonality, or melody—that the label refused to issue the take for some time. When it finally came out, under the title "Intuition"—musicians were as puzzled as the recording executives had been. What Tristano and his group had been playing was collectively improvised "free jazz"; their work anticipated by almost a decade the experiments of Ornette Coleman, Cecil Taylor, Charles Mingus, and others in the late 1950s. Tristano's experiments in multitrack recording and overdubbing, which began in 1951 with "Ju-Ju" and continued in 1955 with "Turkish Mambo" and "Requiem" (a piece he composed for Charlie Parker's funeral), inspired similar performances by Bill Evans and others in the 1960s. Although Tristano worked along lines others would follow, he was never in the main line of the development of jazz. Few musicians either understood or liked his music, but the relatively few who did remained committed to his uncompromising ideals.

MARCH 20—MARIAN MCPARTLAND (1920–)

b. Windsor, England

Pianist; Leader

[POST-BOP; SWING; BOP]

Other jazz notables born on this day: Harold Mabern (1936)
Jazz notables deceased on this day: Michel Warlop (1947); Irving Fazola (1949); Gil Evans (1988)

♪

One of the first female instrumentalists to make a major impact in her field, Marian McPartland has become famous for showcasing the world's top musicians on her *Piano Jazz* radio program on National Public Radio. Since 1978 Marian and her guests have teamed up for an hour of weekly jam sessions, reminiscences, and straight talk about influences and style. Described as "the reigning queen of jazz piano," McPartland has won *Down Beat* magazine's Lifetime Achievement Award and journalism's prestigious Peabody Award for her work as host of *Piano Jazz*. In addition to hosting her show, Marian maintains a busy schedule that includes recording, touring, lecturing, writing, composing, and teaching. She maintains her commitment to music education in the country's public schools by teaching jazz to schoolchildren at clinics and workshops around the country. Her books include *The Artistry of Marian McPartland*, a collection of transcriptions, and her classic book of jazz profiles, *All in Good Time*. Marian has become a conduit for the spreading and channeling of a wide range of jazz piano styles, and this is perhaps her strongest contribution to the field.

Born Margaret Marian Turner, she played piano by ear from an early age, performing Chopin waltzes in this manner when she was only three years old. She later pursued classical training at London's Guildhall School of Music. About this time she began listening to jazz recordings and attempted to copy pianists whose playing she enjoyed. During World War II she joined a four-piano vaudeville act that entertained Allied troops in Europe. In 1944, while on tour in Belgium, she met and began to play with her future husband, cornetist Jimmy McPartland, an original member of the Austin High Gang in the 1920s and one of the most influential figures in the history of jazz in Chicago. In 1946 Marian moved with her husband to the U.S., settling permanently in America while retaining her English citizenship. After the war she performed briefly with her husband's Dixieland quintet in Chicago before forming her own trio to follow the allure of bebop and other more modern musical styles.

It didn't take her long to overcome the resistance of local jazz musicians to her nationality and sex. In 1952 she landed a two-week stint at the renowned Hickory House in New York, where her ability to swing and her command of jazz styles resulted in a ten-year residency. The club became a gathering place for jazz colleagues such as Oscar Peterson, Benny Goodman, and Duke Ellington. In 1955 her trio, with drummer Joe Morello and bassist Bill Crow (Morello long-associated with the Dave Brubeck Quartet and Crow with Gerry Mulligan groups), was named Small Group of the Year by *Metronome* magazine. Over the years Marian has recorded for various labels, including on her imprint, Halcyon Records. Although she eventually divorced Jimmy, they remained close friends. Marian took care of Jimmy in his years of terminal illness and they remarried just weeks before his death in 1991.

MARCH 21—GARY GIDDINS (1948–)

b. New York, NY

Writer

Other jazz notables born on this day: Mike Westbrook (1936); Amina Claudine Myers (1942); Tiger Okoshi (1950)

Jazz notables deceased on this day: King Pleasure (1981)

BLUE NOTES

♪

In the United States, the home of jazz, those who wrote about this form of music contributed to the making of a fresh and distinct form of journalism known as "jazz criticism." Jazz criticism helps define and explain jazz's evolving styles and plays a controversial role as liaison between performer and listener. Prior to 1930, most writing about jazz was negative, for it blamed syncopated dance music with threatening the mores of American youth. A truly critical journalism for jazz did not begin until the 1930s, when the jazz critic emerged as both a studious listener and an irritant to musicians and fans. Many of these early writers hesitated to call themselves "critics," for they were opinionated college graduates, often Ivy Leaguers, who collected records, patronized nightclubs, and wrote for specialized and sophisticated magazines about what was still considered a popular and novel music. Jazz critics, some of them musically illiterate, often wrote insensitive material, prompting bandleader Benny Carter to respond in a 1937 *Metronome* article: "They sing not, neither do they play, hence forget them or forgive them . . . for they do not what they know."[8]

Thankfully, today's jazz critics are more knowledgeable and less brash than those youthful predecessors of the 1930s. Gary Giddins, the preeminent jazz writer of his generation and one of the most thoughtful, covers the world of jazz for the *Village Voice*. Founded in 1955 as the nation's first alternative newsweekly, the *Voice* introduced free, passionate journalism into the public discourse. Giddins, a columnist with the paper since 1973, began his professional career as a contributing editor to *Down Beat* and he remained with the jazz magazine until 1974. During the 1970s Giddins also held an appointment as a Smithsonian fellow (1974–75) and was a disc jockey at New York City radio station WBAI (1975–80), as well as a regular contributor to *Hi-Fi Stereo Buyer's Guide* and *New York Magazine*. From 1977 he taught at the School for Continuing Education at New York University and elsewhere. In 1985, with pianist/composer John Lewis, Giddins founded the American Jazz Orchestra, an ensemble dedicated to the performance of music from the past as well as newly commissioned works. The ensemble's extensive board of trustees included such jazz notables as Benny Goodman, Benny Carter, Thad Jones, and Muhal Richard Abrams. Giddins served as the orchestra's artistic director until 1992, when it ceased operation.

Giddins's lifelong devotion to jazz is exhibited in his numerous books, all written to critical acclaim. They include biographies on Louis Armstrong, Charlie Parker, and Bing Crosby, and volumes such as *Riding on a Blue Note*, *Rhythm-a-ning*, *Faces in the Crowd*, and the masterful *Visions of Jazz*, winner of the 1998 National Critics Circle Award and numerous other prizes. Called "the best jazz writer in America today" (*Esquire*), Giddins's eclectic range and meticulous attention to detail is astonishing. His writing, like the music he loves, is unconventional, infectious, and uplifting.

---

8. Kirchner, *Oxford Companion to Jazz*, 749.

March

MARCH 22—GEORGE BENSON (1943–)

b. Pittsburgh, PA

Electric Guitarist; Vocalist

[SMOOTH JAZZ; CROSSOVER JAZZ; CONTEMPORARY JAZZ; JAZZ-POP; HARD BOP]

Other jazz notables born on this day: Masahiko Togashi (1940)
Jazz notables deceased on this day: Sam Donahue (1974)

♫

During the 1950s and '60s baby boomers became increasingly disenchanted with all forms of jazz. This was partly due to the emergence of rock and roll, but also to the fault of a jazz tradition that had become increasingly inaccessible to a generation in search of rhythm and romance. In the 1950s, as jazz became increasingly abstract, young people began gravitating to musical forms outside jazz, first to rhythm-and-blues, then to forms that evolved from it. By the end of the 1960s, many of the remaining jazz fans despaired for the death of jazz music. However, progressive musicians such as jazz icon Miles Davis joined the rock revolution and created jazz-rock or "fusion" music. In 1968 Davis released the first of his albums to incorporate electric guitar, *Miles in the Sky*; it featured guest guitarist George Benson on one of its numbers. Benson, a John Hammond discovery, had recorded several highly regarded albums for Columbia by this time and was sought after as a sideman owing to his speed and agility on the guitar. An amazingly versatile musician, Benson is considered one of the greatest guitarists in jazz history. He can play in just about any style with supreme taste and a marvelous improvisational logic. He also sings, and it is his voice that has proved to be more marketable to the public than his guitar.

Benson started out professionally as a singer; he began performing in nightclubs at the age of eight and he recorded three years later. Exposure to records by Charlie Christian, Wes Montgomery, and Charlie Parker got him interested in jazz, and by 1962 the teenager was playing with organist Brother Jack McDuff's band. Benson formed his own quartet in 1965 and soon gained a solid jazz reputation on John Hammond-produced Columbia albums. He switched to the Verve label in 1967 and by 1968, shortly after the death of Verve star Wes Montgomery, producer Creed Taylor began promoting Benson as Montgomery's successor.

With the gradual decline of rock music (from an artistic standpoint) during the 1970s, fusion began to become more predictable. However, since electric jazz sold records, producers and some musicians searched for economic success in new combinations. Numerous forms of "crossover" music were tried during the 1980s and '90s, of varying worth from a jazz point of view, but many of them proved valuable in increasing the jazz audience. In the 1970s Benson began emphasizing vocals with his playing, particularly after signing with Warner Bros. in 1976. His first album for WB was the record-breaking *Breezin'*, which reached Number One on the Top Ten pop charts on the strength of its sole vocal track, "This Masquerade." This led to a string of hit albums in an R&B-flavored pop mode, culminating with the popular Quincy Jones-produced *Give Me the Night*. As the 1980s progressed, Benson's albums became increasingly more commercially oriented, though he continued to play conventional jazz occasionally, including with the Basie band in 1990. His move to the GRP label in 1996 catapulted him to the top of the contemporary jazz charts.

MARCH 23—JOHNNY GUARNIERI (1917–1985)

b. New York, NY; d. Livingston, NJ

Pianist; Harpsichordist; Composer

[STRIDE; SWING]

Other jazz notables born on this day: Dave Frishberg (1933); Gerry Hemmingway (1955)

Jazz notables deceased on this day: Pete Johnson (1967); Sonny Greer (1982); Zoot Sims (1985); Al Sears (1990)

♪

The period between 1940 and 1960 saw jazz piano styles undergo an amazing transformation. In 1940 there were three undisputed masters: Earl "Fatha" Hines, Teddy Wilson, and Art Tatum. Hines, who revolutionized jazz piano in the 1920s, is considered to be the source of most "modern" jazz piano. Wilson, a Hines disciple, was the Swing Era's most popular and imitated pianist. Tatum was simply the most brilliant and possibly the greatest jazz pianist of all time. In the 1940s, during the innovations of bebop, there were a number of lesser-known pianists who functioned mainly as sidemen with the era's big bands or preeminent instrumentalists. One of the most in-demand was Johnny Guarnieri. His attractive swing-based style creatively blended Hines, Wilson, Fats Waller, and Count Basie. He was also a master of stride piano, which he played at supersonic speed. Featured with both the Benny Goodman and Artie Shaw bands, he later became a mainstay in the radio studios. But between 1943 and 1947 he made countless jazz recordings with many of the greatest horn players, including classic sessions with Lester Young. Later in his career he cleverly recast much of his repertoire in 5/4 time, playing even "Maple Leaf Rag" in that unusual meter.

Guarnieri began classical studies on piano at the age of ten and switched to jazz after meeting Tatum and Willie "The Lion" Smith. Despite having small hands (Smith counseled him against a career as a jazz pianist for this reason), Guarnieri turned professional at the age of seventeen. In 1939 he succeeded Fletcher Henderson as pianist in Goodman's sextet and orchestra. Six months later, when Goodman disbanded, Guarnieri joined Artie Shaw's orchestra and gained fame playing harpsichord on Shaw's popular Gramercy Five recordings. He rejoined Goodman in 1941 and during this period recorded with Goodman's small group that featured Charlie Christian. His versatility and imagination guaranteed him non-stop work, including stints with Jimmy Dorsey's Orchestra and with Raymond Scott's CBS radio orchestra. While with Scott he worked in the evenings with Cozy Cole's trio at the Onyx Club; the group also accompanied Billie Holiday. In 1944 he joined Slam Stewart's trio at the Three Deuces and sat in with many other groups at clubs on Fifty-Second Street. During this period he slept in a CBS lounge so that he could accept recording dates as well as impromptu invitations to perform. He had important sessions with Young, Roy Eldridge, Coleman Hawkins, Louis Armstrong, and others, and also recorded frequently as leader. He joined the staff of NBC in New York and appeared on various television shows before moving to California in 1962, where he often played solo piano, toured occasionally, and taught. He was so effective and selfless as a teacher that his pupils financed a label to record him. He remained active until 1985, when he died suddenly while playing with Dick Sudhalter in New York.

MARCH 24—STEVE KUHN (1938–)

b. Brooklyn, NY

Pianist; Composer; Leader

[Post-Bop]

Other jazz notables born on this day: King Pleasure (1922); Renee Rosnes (1962)
Jazz notables deceased on this day: Jean Goldkette (1962); Arnett Cobb (1989)

♪

During the spring of 1959 John Coltrane was involved in what became two of the most famous jazz albums ever made: Miles Davis's *Kind of Blue* and his own *Giant Steps*. The latter was his first album as a leader for Atlantic and the first album over which he had control. Coltrane had for some time wanted to lead his own group—he did so periodically while with Davis—and in April 1960 he quit working for Davis and led a group at a Town Hall concert. Shortly thereafter he began a two-month engagement at the Jazz Gallery. He had wanted to hire McCoy Tyner on piano, but he was not available, so he opened with Steve Kuhn on piano, thereby making the Harvard-trained musician the original (and only white) pianist in his quartet. Many have wondered how Kuhn landed such a prestigious position. It turns out that Kuhn simply had the audacity to call Coltrane and ask for an audition when he heard the saxophonist was striking out on his own.

A prolific composer and an accomplished player steeped in the entire jazz piano tradition, Kuhn has worked in many types of settings over the years. His career seemingly started in his infancy, when his father began buying jazz records for him. The precocious toddler showed a remarkable affinity for jazz, arising by 6 a.m. to listen to records. Using his photographic memory, the boy could identify any record his father played. In 1943 his musical recall was written up in a book called *Low Man on the Totem Pole* (a book of oddities akin to Ripley's *Believe It or Not*).

Kuhn began classical piano lessons when he was five, under the guidance of the famous Boston piano teacher Madame Margaret Chaloff (Margaret Chaloff was the mother of Serge Chaloff, the talented baritone saxophonist in the Woody Herman band of the late 1940s). By the time he was fourteen he accompanied Serge professionally. In 1959 after his graduation from Harvard, Kuhn moved to New York, where he worked with Kenny

Dorham (1959–60), and then in Coltrane's quartet. From 1961 to 1964 he was a member of Stan Getz's quartet; it was during this period that Getz fashioned his popular fusion of jazz and bossa nova. In 1967, after stints with Charles Lloyd and Art Blakey and an extended stay with Art Farmer's quartet (1964–66), Kuhn moved to Stockholm, Sweden, where jobs were more plentiful, and he remained in Europe until his return to the U.S. in 1971. During the 1970s he recorded for the ECM label. Two albums of that period, *Trance* and *Ecstasy*, represent Kuhn's versatility. *Trance* is performed by a hard-driving quartet, whereas *Ecstasy*, recorded a few days later, is a pensive and impressionistic solo album. In the latter part of the 1970s Kuhn co-led a group with singer Sheila Jordan; their album *Playground* became his best-selling work. For a while he played commercial music, though he returned to his musical preference in the mid-1980s, when he formed an acoustic trio, and he has remained with jazz ever since.

MARCH 25—PAUL MOTIAN (1931–)

b. Philadelphia, PA

Drummer; Composer

[AVANT-GARDE JAZZ; POST-BOP]

Other jazz notables born on this day: Pete Johnson (1904)
Jazz notables deceased on this day: Sid Catlett (1951)

♪

In 1959 pianist Bill Evans formed a trio with bassist Scott LaFaro and drummer Paul Motian that produced a series of Riverside albums lauded as "one of the most significant bodies of work in the history of jazz."[9] Originally a guitarist, Motian developed into one of the most tasteful and sensitive of drummers. As a member of Evans's most famous trio, Motian helped define the role of the modern drummer in that type of intimate setting. In this group he created "a highly interactive style of playing in which his phrasing became less closely related to the meter of the composition than to the phrasing implied by the other group members; he also made effective use of varied textures and tone colors as elements of musical interest in themselves."[10] Armenian by background, Motian had since childhood been steeped in a music of complex time figures and was able to feed his companions polyrhythmic patterns that delighted them both. His subtle, groundbreaking work in the Bill Evans trio "originally followed the example of Philly Joe Jones, but went much farther in fragmenting the beat and interacting with the other members of the group. This ability lent itself extremely well to situations involving more avant-garde situations, and Motian developed to the point of playing authoritatively in all manner of contexts."[11]

---

9. Gottlieb, *Reading Jazz*, 421.
10. Kernfeld, *New Grove Dictionary of Jazz*, Vol. 2, 837.
11. Carr et al., *Jazz: The Rough Guide*, 547.

Paul Motian grew up in Providence, Rhode Island, and began playing drums at the age of twelve. He was in the navy during the Korean War and he studied at the Navy School of Music in Washington before being stationed in Brooklyn in 1953. After his discharge in 1954 he furthered his education at the Manhattan School of Music. In 1955 he began playing with many top jazz musicians from a wide variety of styles including Tony Scott, Gil Evans, Art Farmer, Lee Konitz, George Russell, Stan Getz, Lennie Tristano, Thelonious Monk, Coleman Hawkins, and Roy Eldridge. He remained with Evans after LaFaro's tragic automotive death in 1961, thereby providing continuity for the pianist during one of the most painful transitions of his career.

Motian joined Paul Bley's trio in 1963 and later formed a lasting musical partnership with Charlie Haden in Keith Jarrett's trios and quartets (1966–77), recording with Haden's Liberation Music Orchestra in 1969 and again in the 1980s and '90s. Motian recorded with blues-based Mose Allison in 1965, but his freelance work during the remainder of the decade concentrated on free jazz. Through his association with Carla Bley in the late 1960s he participated in the activities of the Jazz Composers Guild and the Jazz Composer's Orchestra Association, which included contributions to Bley's *Escalator over the Hill* (1968–71), one of the longest jazz-generated works in existence. In 1977 Motian began to lead his own groups. He also formed a long-standing trio with Joe Lovano and Bill Frissell (who became major jazz artists in the course of their association with the drummer) and a group called the Electric Bebop Band in the 1990s with tenor saxophonist Joshua Redman.

MARCH 26—FLIP PHILLIPS (1915–2001)

b. New York, NY; d. Fort Lauderdale, FL

Tenor Saxophonist

[East Coast Blues; Jump Blues; Swing; Bop]

Other jazz notables born on this day: Brew Moore 1924); James Moody (1925); Lew Tabackin (1940)
Jazz notables deceased on this day: Eddie Lang (1933)

♪

The jam session is as old as jazz itself. But it had always been a private rite among musicians, not a public manner of entertainment. That pattern was altered on July 2, 1944, when jazz entrepreneur Norman Granz staged a benefit concert at Philharmonic Hall in Los Angeles. For two years Grantz had been organizing small jam sessions for a circuit of Los Angeles clubs. His experiment proved so successful that he decided to apply his concept to the concert hall. The July 2 concert was followed by a for-profit concert on July 30, and before the year ended Jazz at the Philharmonic (JATP) concerts were monthly events. The following year Grantz applied the name Jazz at the Philharmonic to concerts that took place in various cities, and for the next two decades he led integrated ensembles across the nation and overseas.

His goals were twofold: to broaden the audience for jazz and to do so without compromising equal treatment for his musicians. Grantz handpicked the musicians for these concerts, and they were the cream-of-the-crop. By 1949 the format for the shows consisted of two parts, the first half being an all-star jam session while the second half featured individual sets by jazz superstars. At the completion of this segment the whole troupe joined together for a rousing finale. Sometimes there were informal "battles" between trumpeters and between tenor saxophonists, which appealed greatly to the audiences. Eventually the JATP troupes included organized groups (such as the Modern Jazz Quartet, the Miles Davis Quintet, and Duke Ellington's big band), but the "all-star jam" still occurred at every concert.

Over the years Grantz relied upon a select group of musicians to showcase his musical extravaganza; the regulars included Ella Fitzgerald, Oscar Peterson, Roy Eldridge, Ray Brown, and tenor saxophonist Flip Phillips, whom Granz introduced as "the exciting one." Phillips had earned his reputation during the mid-1940s, when he became a star with Woody Herman's First Herd (1944–46). With JATP, Flip's primary role was to arouse the audience with his energetic playing—most notably on "Perdido," the one jam-session centerpiece of every concert—and he relished his role. Always intensely rhythmic, he took the shouting and honking southwestern style common to both Ben Webster and Lester Young and in the late 1940s was the JATP crowd-pleaser. He toured regularly with JATP during 1946 to 1957, holding his own against heavy competition (including Charlie Parker and Young). Though these performances were exhibitionist and therefore popular with audiences, they were tasteless compared to his sumptuous ballad playing and the many swinging, melodic solos he recorded over the years.

During the 1960s and early '70s Phillips settled in Florida, working a day job and leading his own quartet. By 1975 he was back in music full-time, exhibiting the control, imagination, and warmth that characterized his mature style. Even in his eighties, Phillips never lost his ability to inspire.

MARCH 27—BEN WEBSTER (1909–1973)

b. Kansas City, MO; d. Amsterdam, Holland

Tenor Saxophonist

[SWING; TRADITIONAL POP]

Other jazz notables born on this day: Pee Wee Russell (1906); Sarah Vaughan (1924); Harold Ashby (1925)
Jazz notables deceased on this day: Sharkey Bonano (1972); Clifford Jordan (1993)

♪

During the 1930s Duke Ellington led a variety of outstanding bands, but in the early 1940s Victor Records billed Ellington's current band as the greatest of them all. This publicity translated into commercial as well as critical success, for between 1939 and 1941 his records outsold all other popular bands. With few exceptions, his every recording session in the early 1940s produced one or more classics. Ellington's achievement was in large part due to the personalities in his band, including two recent additions: Jimmy Blanton, a twenty-one-year-old bassist who would die of tuberculosis within three years (though that was enough time for him to revolutionize bass playing), and Ben Webster, who joined in January 1940 as Ellington's first tenor saxophone star. No one in the Ellington orchestra ever played more beautifully—or caused more trouble.

Webster excelled at conjuring a wide range of spellbinding sounds; he had a tough, raspy tone on stomps, yet on ballads he would play with unusual warmth and sentiment. His rich, creamy tone developed into one of the glories of the saxophone. With his breathy, sensual timbre, Webster spun out eloquent solos on ballads such as "Stardust" and "All Too Soon" (both 1940), whereas on up-tempo tunes such as "Cotton Tail" (which became a trademark during his three-year stay with Ellington) he roared "as few other saxophonists have ever roared."[12] These opposing musical styles led to the aptly titled 1989 biographical documentary film, *The Brute and the Beautiful.*

Polarities also characterized Webster's personal life. A former pianist (Webster learned to play rudimentary blues on the piano with help from his famous neighbor Pete Johnson) who got his start on saxophone playing alongside Lester Young in the Young Family troupe, he was a native of Kansas City and a hard-drinking veteran of the all-night tenor battles that characterized musical life there. One of his nicknames was "the Brute." When he was at home, he was the perfect son, but if he had a few drinks in him, he became a swaggering bully. The twin sides of his turbulent personality found expression through his horn, which both invigorated and inspired Ellington's saxophone section. Webster—sometimes charming and other times curt and rude to his employer—stayed with Ellington for three years. He left Ellington after an altercation caused by his arrogance while playing piano with the band. When he stayed at the keyboard too long, Ellington took offence, and Webster retaliated by cutting into shreds one of Ellington's prized suits.

In 1964, conscious of the changing tides of jazz fashion, he moved permanently to Copenhagen, touring Europe regularly during his final decade. At this time his unpredictability created a legendary persona second only to that of violinist Joe Venuti. Webster's personality now regularly veered between his two extremes: friendly and well-behaved when sober, but terrifying and unpredictable when drunk. Musically, however, he remained consistent, maintaining his passion and intensity to the end.

MARCH 28—PAUL WHITEMAN (1890–1967)

b. Denver, CO; d. Doylestown, PA

Bandleader

[CLASSIC JAZZ; POP]

Other jazz notables born on this day: Thad Jones (1923)
Jazz notables deceased on this day: W. C. Handy (1958); Tony Scott (2007)

---

12. Ward and Burns, *Jazz: A History*, 288.

BLUE NOTES

♪

A dance boom hit America shortly before the start of World War I, causing the recording industry to explode. Whereas in 1914 about twenty-seven million records were sold, by 1921 the figure was one hundred million. This upsurge in the record business created a demand for musicians as well as for a new fad in music that was called "jazz." Though what the public heard was merely dance music and arrangements of popular tunes dressed up with some jazz inflections, this commercial music had a bouncy beat and utilized occasional slurred notes suggested by the blue notes. By playing this kind of music, a number of musicians became famous and, in a few cases, rich. The best-known dance bandleader in America during the 1920s, and the most successful financially, was Paul Whiteman.

Born in Colorado, Whiteman was trained as a symphonic violinist and worked with both the Denver and San Francisco symphony orchestras. The first time he heard jazz being played by New Orleans musicians in San Francisco in 1915 was like an epiphany: "It was like coming out of blackness into bright lights ... My head was dizzy, but my feet seemed to understand ... I wanted to whoop. I wanted to dance. I wanted to sing. I did them all. Raucous? Yes. Crude—undoubtedly. Unmusical—as sure as you live! But rhythmic, catching as the small pox, and spirit-lifting."[13] Three years later, after leading a forty-piece navy band, he joined a dance band—only to be fired two days later for not being able to play "jazz," namely, to improvise on the spot. Humiliated but still drawn to the music, Whiteman determined to find a way to orchestrate jazz while rendering it as precise as symphonic music. His father, superintendent of music for the Denver public schools, was scornful of jazz, which may account for Whiteman's self-appointed mission to "make a lady of jazz."

In 1919 he took over leadership of a dance band with which he played, and within two or three years he made it the most popular band in the country. Whiteman matched his imposing presence on the bandstand—he was tall and heavily built—with mastery of self-promotion, and before long he became known as "The King of Jazz." Though he was no jazz player, he had a good ear for the music, and at one time or another most of the best white jazz musicians of the period worked in his band. The music he featured was heavy, overly-orchestrated, and almost entirely lacking in jazz feel, but by the early 1920s his lush style was widely copied at home and abroad. Early in 1924 Whiteman commissioned George Gershwin to write *Rhapsody in Blue*, and on February 12 jazz found itself on the concert stage for the first time. It was a distinctive kind of jazz, to be sure, but it helped fuel the jazz craze. It wasn't until 1927, when he acquired jazz musicians such as Bix Beiderbecke and Frank Trumbauer, that jazz could be associated appropriately with the name of Whiteman. African-American musicians may have resented the celebrity and riches Whiteman had gained by playing music they pioneered, but no one could deny the beneficial results of his efforts, which helped to make jazz an indelible part of American culture.

---

13. Ward and Burns, *Jazz: A History*, 99.

MARCH 29—MICHAEL BRECKER (1949–2007)

b. Philadelphia, PA; d. New York, NY

Tenor Saxophonist; Leader

[CROSSOVER JAZZ; CONTEMPORARY JAZZ; FUSION]

Other jazz notables born on this day: Pearl Bailey (1918)
Jazz notables deceased on this day: Floyd Smith (1982); Sid Weiss (1994); Luca Flores (1995); John Lewis (2001)

♪

Since the early years of jazz, Philadelphia has played an important role in the development of the genre, producing innovators and legends such as John Coltrane, Philly Joe Jones, Red Garland, Grover Washington Jr., Jimmy Smith, McCoy Tyner, Jerry Mulligan, Sun Ra, Benny Golson, Kenny Barron, Pat Martino, Jimmy Bruno, the Heath brothers, and the Brecker brothers. Known as a breakout town in the recording business, record companies often publicized records in Philadelphia first to find out if there was a market in the rest of the country. Performers like Cannonball Adderley and Horace Silver regularly tried their material in Philadelphia before they would record it. The theory was that if Philly liked it, the rest of the world would like it as well. During the late 1950s and early '60s the city's jazz, rock, and R&B scene was a great breeding ground for musicians, helping to create an open mind in music; many original players emerged from this vibrant environment. Randy and Michael Brecker, influenced by their diverse surroundings as well as by their father, a semi-professional jazz musician, went on to create a pioneering style of fusion jazz in the 1970s.

Michael, younger brother of trumpeter Randy, grew up in the culturally diverse Philadelphia music scene. He began his musical studies on drums, then on clarinet and alto sax, before switching to tenor while in high school, where he came under the influence of Coltrane's musical genius. He spent one year at Indiana University (1968–69), and then moved to New York, where he worked with several R&B bands before he formed the pioneering jazz-rock band Dreams with Randy and drummer Billy Cobham. In 1974, after a year in Horace Silver's quintet, Michael and Randy formed the Brecker Brothers, one of the most innovative and successful jazz-funk fusion bands of the decade. During this time they also operated the popular downtown Manhattan jazz club Seventh Avenue South. Michael also worked in the late 1970s band Steps (which later became Steps Ahead), but in due course he began to focus more on fronting his own groups.

Michael developed into possibly the most comprehensive saxophone talent of the 1970s and '80s. The most recorded saxophonist since 1975, he appeared on some five hundred studio sessions during the '70s and '80s (including with James Taylor, John Lennon, and Paul Simon). Brecker's jazz debut as leader, a quintet session recorded in 1986 with Pat Metheny, Kenny Kirkland, Charlie Haden, and Jack DeJohnette, was released to great acclaim and voted Jazz Album of the Year in *Down Beat* and *Jazziz* magazines. A remarkable technician known for his stylistic and harmonic innovations, the thirteen-time Grammy winner is one of the most studied instrumentalists in music schools throughout the world today. *Jazziz* magazine said it best: "You'll find no better example of stylistic evolution than Michael Brecker, arguably the most influential tenor stylist of the last 25 years."

MARCH 30—ASTRUD GILBERTO (1940–)

b. Bahia, Brazil

Vocalist

[BRAZILIAN JAZZ; VOCAL POP; BOSSA NOVA]

Other jazz notables born on this day: Ted Heath (1900); Karl Berger (1935)
Jazz notables deceased on this day: Larry Young (1978); Joe Williams (1999)

♪

During the early 1960s a Brazilian synthesis of cool jazz and the samba known as bossa nova became extremely popular in the U.S. The groundbreaking album was the commercially successful *Jazz Samba* (1962), a collaboration between jazz guitarist Charlie Byrd and tenor saxophonist Stan Getz. Byrd's tour of South America in 1961 had proved to be a revelation, for it was in Brazil where Byrd discovered the emerging bossa nova movement. The tour had been sponsored by the U.S. State Department, which in the mid-1950s perceived jazz as a potent symbol of democracy in action and began sending musicians around the world. Upon his return to the U.S., Byrd played some bossa nova tapes to Getz, who then convinced the Verve label to record the new music. The saxophonist's breezy, floating improvisations on *Jazz Samba* fit the gentle underlying rhythms perfectly. This album, on the strength of the single "Desafinado," launched the bossa nova craze in North America.

Before long Getz was recording with the Brazilian innovators themselves, notably guitarists Antonio Carlos Jobim and Joao Gilberto. On a 1963 session, Getz persuaded Gilberto's wife, Astrud, to sing the English lyrics to "The Girl from Ipanema," even though she was a housewife and had a delicate, untrained voice. Producer Creed Taylor wanted a few English vocals for maximum crossover potential, and Astrud was the only Brazilian present with any grasp of English. After her husband laid down his Portuguese vocals for the first verse of "The Girl from Ipanema," Astrud provided a hesitant, heavily accented second verse in English. Her cool-toned voice fit the song perfectly. Despite receiving no credits on the resulting LP, *Getz/Gilberto*, Astrud unwittingly became a celebrity a year later, when the album became the best-selling jazz album to that point and she became a star in America.[14]

A limited but strangely memorable singer, Astrud parlayed her unscheduled appearance into a lengthy career that resulted in nearly a dozen albums for Verve and a performing career that lasted into the 1990s. She went on to define the style of bossa nova singing as it was adopted in the U.S., employing a cool, breathy timbre, and singing at a moderate

---

14. Bogdanov et al., *All Music Guide to Jazz*, 469.

dynamic level with an even, flowing pulse.[15] Before the end of 1963 Verve capitalized on her success with the release of *Getz Au Go Go*, featuring a Getz live date with Astrud's vocals added later. Her first actual solo album, *The Astrud Gilberto Album*, was released in 1965 and barely missed the Top 40, its blend of Brazilian classics and ballad standards proving quite infectious with easy-listening audiences. Though she never returned to the pop charts in America, Verve paired her with ace arranger Gil Evans for 1966's *Look to the Rainbow* and Brazilian organist-arranger Walter Wanderley for *A Certain Smile, A Certain Sadness*, released later that year. She remained a pop star in Brazil but gradually disappeared in America after her final album for Verve in 1969.

MARCH 31—RED NORVO (1908–1999)

b. Beardstown, IL; d. Santa Monica, CA

Xylophonist; Vibraphonist; Leader

[SWING; COOL]

Other jazz notables born on this day: Freddie Green (1911)
Jazz notables deceased on this day: John Carter (1991); Jackie McLean (2006)

♪

"What Coleman Hawkins did for the tenor saxophone, Red Norvo did for the xylophone: took it out of vaudeville and put it firmly in the realm of jazz."[16] Born Kenneth Norville, he began on piano at the age of eight, but at an early point he became so skilled at playing by ear that lessons were discontinued. He taught himself to play marimba when he was fourteen and soon switched to xylophone. Active as a tap dancer in vaudeville in the late 1920s, Norvo joined Paul Whiteman's Orchestra in 1931, where he met Mildred Bailey, the band's outstanding vocalist.

Acknowledged as one of the finest jazz singers to emerge during the 1930s and as the first prominent female band singer, Bailey is said to have initiated that role on September 15, 1931, when Jack Kapp of Decca Records recorded her with the Casa Loma Orchestra. At a 1932 session she recorded "Rockin' Chair," a Hoagy Carmichael song, with some of Whiteman's sidemen, including Norvo, who backed her on vibes. The release became one of the year's major records and established the role of band vocalist for all time. The best thing that ever happened to Bailey was meeting Norvo, her third and last husband and her most important collaborator. The plump singer and her diminutive partner were married in 1933, and though they made an odd couple, the mismatched pair, known as "Mr. and Mrs. Swing," became a successful musical team.

With Whiteman's orchestra, Norvo played xylophone, marimba, and the vibraphone, a newly emerging instrument. He used the latter instrument as a novelty at this point, in part because a damper pedal for the instrument had not yet been developed, rendering it impractical for the fast and intricate mallet lines he favored. In 1936 Norvo and Bailey

---

15. Kernfeld, *New Grove Dictionary of Jazz*, Vol. 2, 35.
16. Hasse, *Jazz: First Century*, 79.

teamed with the young arranger Eddie Sauter to create three years' worth of "the most beautiful vocal records ever produced, each a . . . minor classic of shading and dynamics that would have a profound influence on many singers, including Frank Sinatra."[17]

Unfortunately, Mr. and Mrs. Swing did not get along as well personally as they did musically. Their band broke up in 1939 and their marriage followed early in 1940. Norvo continued leading his own bands until 1944, when he switched to vibes and joined Goodman's sextet. Keeping abreast of jazz developments, Norvo was responsible for a 1945 all-star record session that introduced many listeners to Charlie Parker and Dizzy Gillespie. After a year with Woody Herman's First Herd in 1946, Norvo settled on the West Coast, where he put together an unusual trio with guitarist Tal Farlow and bassist Charles Mingus. This group not only demonstrated the influence of bebop but also was the first of the "chamber jazz" bands that proliferated during the 1950s. Norvo was forced into a lower profile after a serious ear operation in 1961. From the mid-1970s to the mid-'80s he made several excellent recordings and toured Europe with Farlow. However, his hearing deteriorated and a serious stroke in 1986 led to a final retirement, after fifty-five years of music.

17. Gottlieb, *Reading Jazz*, 964.

Chapter 4

April

APRIL 1—HARRY CARNEY (1910-1974)

b. Boston, MA; d. New York, NY

Baritone Saxophonist

[Swing]

Other jazz notables born on this day: Duke Jordan (1922)
Jazz notables deceased on this day: Freddie Webster (1947); Eddie Miller (1991); Jesse Stone (1999)

♪

The history of the Duke Ellington band involves an astonishing array of musicians, most of whom were unknown until Ellington hired them, gauged their abilities, and tailored his writing to emphasize their best features. In 1926 he raided Elmer Snowden's band for Joe "Tricky Sam" Nanton, one of Ellington's most expressive voices over the next twenty years. Also in 1926 bassist Wellman Braud and clarinetist Rudy Jackson were recruited from a stage band. The New Orleans clarinetist Barney Bigard, who stayed for fifteen years, soon replaced Jackson. The most durable recruit of 1926 (or any other year) was Harry Carney, who was sixteen when he was hired for a one-nighter and stayed until his death forty-seven years later. Only Count Basie's guitarist Freddie Green matched Carney in the duration of his service to one leader.

The quality that most immediately distinguishes the Ellington sound is the baritone sax voice lead. A light must have glowed in Ellington's head when he heard Carney play, for he lost little time before making him the heart of the orchestra. "If he wasn't in Duke's band," Miles Davis said, "the band wouldn't be Duke."[1] A modest, unassuming man, Carney was for many years (until the arrival of Gerry Mulligan) the only important jazz soloist on that instrument. As a member of Duke Ellington's Orchestra, he achieved his goal of making the instrument indispensable in a big band. With a definitive tone and a style that was ideally sonorous in every range of the horn, his contribution to Ellington was immeasurable. His huge sound, which shouldered and sometimes led the saxophone section, was, with that of Johnny Hodges, the most irreplaceable of his leader's woodwind

---

1. Giddins, *Visions of Jazz*, 112.

voices. His use in later years of the technique of circular breathing allowed him to sustain the flow of sound indefinitely, further showcasing his rich tone as an essential element in the orchestral sound.

Carney began playing piano, clarinet, and alto saxophone in Boston, a few doors away from Johnny Hodges and Charlie Holmes. He was performing professionally in Boston when Ellington engaged him in June 1926 for a local job. Ellington persuaded Carney's parents to let their son join him on the road, with the understanding that Ellington serve as the young man's guardian. Carney played clarinet and alto at first, but after Otto Hardwick rejoined the band, he turned his attention to the big baritone saxophone, intent on impressing everyone with its necessity. Ellington fell for Carney's huge sound, and apart from adding bass clarinet in later years and traditionally taking the clarinet solo on "Rockin' in Rhythm," Carney played only baritone for his leader until 1974. A cultured, knowledgeable and good-natured person, he became Ellington's closest associate in later years. After Ellington died in 1974, Carney admitted that he no longer had anything to live for and he passed away only four months later.

APRIL 2—LARRY CORYELL (1943–)

b. Galveston, TX

Guitarist; Bandleader

[POST-BOP; FUSION]

Other jazz notables born on this day: Booker Little (1938)

Jazz notables deceased on this day: Bennie Moten (1935); Ray Noble (1978); Buddy Rich (1987); Julius Hemphill (1995)

♪

Although fusion music was not the first hybrid form in the history of jazz, it was the most notorious. This heterogeneous amalgamation brought together the seemingly disparate worlds of rock and jazz into a precarious bond that was condemned by older jazz purists (who referred to it as "con-fusion") but revered by a younger generation that related to its high energy.[2] As one of the pioneers of jazz-rock, Larry Coryell (dubbed "the Godfather of Fusion" by his disciple Al Di Meola) deserves a special place in the history of jazz. Although he cannot be identified consistently with any particular jazz style, he is one of the most original improvisers on guitar to have emerged during the 1960s and '70s. A true eclectic, Coryell has had difficulty unifying the opposing facets of his enormous talent: "the brash, loud, electrified rock-and-roller, the urbane jazz soloist, the sensitive acoustic guitarist, [and] the classical performer ... [I]n a sense, his dilemma is the dilemma of jazz today."[3]

While Miles Davis's *Bitches Brew* (1969) is generally cited as the galvanizing statement in fusion, it was not the first recording to combine jazz with rock. That notion

---

2. Kirchner, *Oxford Companion to Jazz*, 502.
3. Carr et al., *Jazz: The Rough Guide*, 166.

had been percolating since 1965, when jazz-trained hippies in Greenwich Village began blending both aesthetics at nearby nightclubs. As Coryell put it: "We were in the middle of a world cultural revolution. Everyone was dropping acid and the prevailing attitude was, 'Let's do something different.' We loved Wes [Montgomery] but we also loved Bob Dylan. We loved Coltrane but we also dug the Beatles. We loved Miles but we also loved the Rolling Stones."[4]

Coryell came to New York from Seattle, abandoning journalism studies at the University of Washington in order to try his luck as a musician. He began alternating between two bands to satisfy separate musical urges. His jazzier side was displayed with the Chico Hamilton Quartet, while his more experimental side was channeled through Free Spirits. In 1966 he recorded *The Dealer* with Hamilton, blending the blues with rock. That same year Free Spirits released *Out of Sight and Sound*, the first seminal jazz-rock recording. Coryell continued blazing the fusion trail with vibraphonist Gary Burton, whose album *Duster* (1967) blended rock with country music.

In 1969, after a brief stint with Herbie Mann, with whom he recorded *Memphis Underground*, one of the seminal albums of the period, Coryell formed his own group Foreplay. By 1973 this became the core of the jazz-rock band Eleventh House, one of the better groups that worked in fusion. After 1975 Coryell concentrated on acoustic guitar, recording as a soloist as well as in small groups and duos. In the early 1980s he took time off to deal with alcohol and drug-related problems. Thereafter he became a participant in the bop revival, though he occasionally incorporated elements of twentieth-century art music into his repertoire, including music by Stravinsky and Rimsky-Korsakov.

APRIL 3—SCOTT LAFARO (1936–1961)

b. Newark, NJ; d. Geneva, NY

Bassist

[POST-BOP]

Other jazz notables born on this day: Bubber Miley (1903); Bill Finegan (1917); Jimmy McGriff (1936); Eric Kloss (1949)
Jazz notables deceased on this day: Gene Sedric (1963); Sarah Vaughan (1990)

♪

By the early 1960s pianist Bill Evans was at the apex of his profession. Having recently worked with Miles Davis and contributed to the classic *Kind of Blue* album, jazz musicians and fans everywhere were beginning to acknowledge him as the most influential pianist in jazz. After his stay with Davis, Evans began to record and perform on a regular basis with an outstanding trio, gathering an ever-larger audience. His fame came in part from the presence in his trio of a brilliant young bassist, Scott LaFaro, a melodically oriented bass player with a gorgeous tone and a seemingly endless supply of fresh ideas. LaFaro had developed an almost guitarlike facility on the bass, in part by lowering the bridge,

---

4. Kirchner, *Oxford Companion to Jazz*, 503.

which brought the strings closer to the neck of the instrument. In his solo work with the Bill Evans trio, he expanded the role of the bass far beyond the established norm, thereby achieving a kind of parity with the pianist. With the addition of drummer Paul Motian, Evans brought together two talented individuals who were musically compatible as well as dedicated to the goal of developing a trio committed to the concept of simultaneous improvisation. For a brief period, as it turned out, the members formed one of the most cohesive and subtly inventive groups ever to perform, for the sound they created was the manifestation of a true artistic unison. The interplay between the three musicians (with an almost equal role by each) was highly influential and nearly telepathic.[5]

During 1961 the Bill Evans Trio spent a good deal of time at the Village Vanguard, a basement club in New York's Greenwich Village that was becoming a center for live jazz. The Vanguard's policy at this time was to schedule a matinee as well as an evening performance on Sundays, and those afternoon sessions became a mecca for the most discerning jazz audience in the city. On June 25 the trio performed five sets—two in the afternoon and three in the evening. Two albums resulted from that live recording: *Sunday at the Village Vanguard* and *Waltz for Debby*. The group's sensitive sound and instant rapport on those recordings created a legacy that has been called Bill Evans's finest hour. Working as a close-knit team, Evans, LaFaro, and Motian produced an intermeshed music in which each responded to the other. It was this group, and that day's recorded performance, which made Evans famous. Tragically, ten days later, while Scott LaFaro was driving back to his parents' home in upstate New York, his car veered off an unlit rural road into a tree and he was killed instantly. He was only twenty-five years old.

The shock of LaFaro's death stayed with Evans for years. He felt that because of his heroin habit he made made insufficient use of the time he and Scott had together. LaFaro had seen Evans sinking into addiction and tried repeatedly to dissuade him from his habit. According to Gene Lees: "After LaFaro's death, Bill was like a man with a lost love, always looking to find its replacement."[6]

APRIL 4—BENNY GREEN (1963–)

b. New York, NY; grew up in Berkeley, CA

Pianist

[Neo-Bop]

Other jazz notables born on this day: Gene Ramey (1913); Jake Hanna (1931); Hugh Masekela (1939); Gary Smulyan (1956)

Jazz notables deceased on this day: Tiny Parham (1943); Bob Short (1976)

♫

In 1993 jazz pianist Oscar Peterson received the Glenn Gould Prize, a prestigious lifetime achievement award given by a Canadian organization formed to perpetuate the ideas and

---

5. Bogdanov et al., *All Music Guide to Jazz*, 3rd ed., 352.
6. Gottlieb, *Reading Jazz*, 423.

accomplishments of Glenn Gould. So far the prize has been awarded six times. Starting with 1993, the winner of the prize is asked to name a promising young musician as protégé. Peterson's choice was Benny Green. Although not yet an innovator, Green had by this time revealed a knack for the blues, combining the piano styles of Bobby Timmons, Wynton Kelly, and Gene Harris with Peterson's speed, dexterity, and ability to swing.

Benny's interest in jazz came through his father, an amateur saxophonist who exposed Benny to such jazz giants as Bud Powell and Thelonious Monk. He studied classical piano at an early age and then jazz piano privately. As a teenager he played in the Bay Area with Joe Henderson and Woody Shaw. After moving to New York in 1983 he met two musicians who would have a profound formative influence on his playing style and career: vocalist Betty Carter and drummer Art Blakey. One evening in 1983, as the twenty-year-old sat in with Blakey's group, Carter stopped by to check him out. She was impressed, and within a week he had won a spot in her band.

Inspired initially by Billie Holiday and especially by Sarah Vaughan, Carter sang in a way that was instrumentally conceived. Her highly personalized improvisations, combined with her husky, saxophone-like voice quality, influenced a whole generation of younger singers. In various ways Carter was a singer's parallel to Blakey, engaging young musicians and regularly helping to launch their careers. In 1987 Green left Carter to join Blakey. He had followed Blakey closely since his California days, and playing with Blakey's Jazz Messengers was a dream come true. Blakey was a master teacher, a leader who inspired leadership in others.

In 1989 Green left the band to prove himself. He worked with Freddie Hubbard until 1992, when he joined Ray Brown, through whom he picked up an appreciation for Peterson. In 1996 Green took part in a New York Town Hall tribute concert to Peterson and then participated in a piano duet recording with his mentor.

APRIL 5—STANLEY TURRENTINE (1934–2000)

b. Pittsburgh, PA; d. New York, NY

Tenor Saxophonist

[Hard Bop; Fusion; Soul-Jazz]

Other jazz notables born on this day: Stan Levey (1926)
Jazz notables deceased on this day: Alan Shorter (1988); Louis Nelson (1990)

♪

Throughout his career Stanley Turrentine was an original performer, a tenor saxophonist who defied neat categorization. While highly regarded in soul-jazz circles, he was one of the finest tenor saxophonists of his time, in any style. With a sound described by Oscar Peterson as "the true tenor sound," Turrentine's highly expressive solos made him one of the most distinctive tenor stylists of his era. His early 1960s recording partnership with organist Jimmy Smith on such landmark sessions as *Midnight Special* and *Back at the Chicken Shack* provided some of the finest funk music of all time. Influenced by Don Byas,

Coleman Hawkins, and Sonny Rollins, his earthy blues style made him a natural in the role of the "Gene Ammons of the 1970s." Known for his big, warm, sound, "Mr. T" turned the blues into a highly successful career with four Grammy nominations. He played certain standards in his repertoire, including Marvin Gaye's "Don't Mess with Mr. T," Freddie Hubbard's "Gibraltar," and Michel Legrand's "Pieces of a Dream," like he owned them, and no one could play his composition, "Sugar," more soulfully.

Born in Pittsburgh, a city that has produced such jazz masters as Art Blakey, Earl Hines, and George Benson, Turrentine grew up in a musical family. His father, who had played tenor with the Savoy Sultans in the late 1930s, was a big influence, as was his piano-playing mother and his older brother, trumpeter Tommy Turrentine. As a child Stanley played piano by ear, and then took up tenor at the age of eleven. One of his earliest influences on sax was Illinois Jacquet, who once encouraged the twelve-year old to sit in with him. At seventeen he toured with Lowell Fulson's blues band (1950–51), whose featured pianist was Ray Charles. When he left Fulson, Turrentine moved to Cleveland, where he gigged with Tadd Dameron and his brother, Tommy. From 1953 to 1954 he worked with Earl Bostic (one of the greatest rhythm-and-blues sax players of all time) as John Coltrane's replacement. After three years in the army he joined Tommy in the Max Roach quintet (1959–60), where he cut his first albums and gained international exposure.

Turrentine started recording as a leader on Blue Note in 1959, then began a decade-long professional association with organist Shirley Scott, to whom he was married until 1971. When he moved to Philadelphia, Turrentine became acquainted with organ legend Jimmy Smith, and he quickly immersed himself in Smith's soulful sound. The organ-centered soul-jazz that Smith and Scott developed provided Turrentine the perfect move into pop territory. His first foray into this customer-friendly music began in 1969, when he signed with Creed Taylor's successful CTI label. His debut album for the label, *Sugar* (1970), became the first of a number of crossover albums that appeared on the charts throughout the 1970s. He returned to straightahead and soul jazz in the 1980s, cutting albums for Fantasy and Elektra before re-signing with Blue Note in 1984, when the label was revived. He remained on the ever-changing landscape of jazz until his untimely death in September 2000, caused by a massive stroke.

APRIL 6—GERRY MULLIGAN (1927–1996)

b. New York, NY; d. Darien, CT

Baritone Saxophonist; Arranger; Leader

[WEST COAST JAZZ; COOL]

Other jazz notables born on this day: Charlie Rouse (1924); Randy Weston (1926); André Previn (1929); Art Taylor (1929); Horace Tapscott (1934); Manfred Schoof (1936); Gerry Niewood (1943); John Pizzarelli (1960)
Jazz notables deceased on this day: Dick Cary (1994); Red Norvo (1999)

The most famous jazz baritonist of all time, Gerry Mulligan is one of modern jazz's most versatile figures. Though a confirmed modernist credited with spreading the cool idiom, he was equally at home in a big band, bop, or even a Dixieland context. Able to produce a lighter and sunnier sound on the baritone sax than anyone before him, he played his potentially awkward horn with the speed and dexterity of an altoist. These abilities brought him great popularity and domination in jazz polls on his instrument.

Mulligan was one of the icons of his generation, his lanky, red-haired image as familiar as the silhouette of Dizzy and his upturned trumpet. Born to a peripatetic Irish Catholic family, Mulligan settled in Philadelphia in 1944, where he wrote arrangements for the radio bands and played reed instruments professionally. After moving to New York in 1946, he became involved with the emerging cool-jazz movement, contributing scores and arranging for Claude Thornhill's big band. In the winter of 1947 to 1948, Mulligan became part of a steady stream of creative musicians who visited the basement home of Gil Evans, formerly an arranger for the Thornhill orchestra, and this led to his association with Miles Davis in the groundbreaking recording sessions (1949–50) known as the *Birth of the Cool*. His first notable recorded work on baritone was with this group, although his compositions and arrangements were more significant than his short solos—he contributed seven of the album's twelve pieces (including the definitive version of "Rocker" and the memorable "Jeru").

In 1950 he hitchhiked to Los Angeles to take a job with Stan Kenton's orchestra, though he returned to New York to record with his own tentet, which was modeled on Davis's ensemble. In 1952 he settled in Los Angeles and formed his first "pianoless" quartet, with Chet Baker on trumpet. The group quickly rose to fame, launching both Mulligan and Baker into stardom. As cool jazz became increasingly associated with the West Coast, Mulligan was seen as the standard by which West Coast jazz was defined.

A drug bust temporarily put him out of action and ended the quartet, but upon his release from jail in 1954, he began a new musical partnership with valve trombonist Bob Brookmeyer that was just as successful. Mulligan led a new tentet and various versions of his quartet in the mid-1950s and soon began dominating jazz polls on his instrument. During 1960 to 1964 he formed his thirteen-piece Concert Jazz Band, for which he composed, played baritone, and occasionally doubled on piano. After the big band broke up he toured extensively with the Dave Brubeck Quartet (1968–72) before forming a new big band. When he died in 1996 after a long illness, Mulligan was remembered, predictably, for his work in the 1950s. During his latter years he strongly resented that association. What he really always wanted to do, he claimed, was lead a big band.

BLUE NOTES

APRIL 7—BILLIE HOLIDAY (1915–1959)

b. Baltimore, MD; d. New York, NY

Vocalist

[VOCAL JAZZ; SWING; BALLADS; CLASSIC FEMALE BLUES]

Other jazz notables born on this day: Peanuts Hucko (1918); Mongo Santamaria (1922); Freddie Hubbard (1938); Alex Schippenbach (1938)

Jazz notables deceased on this day: Jimmy Garrison (1976); Maxine Sullivan (1987)

♪

A true jazz genius, Billie Holiday was clearly the most significant vocalist of the swing era; some observers consider her to be the greatest jazz singer who ever lived. She is the singer most frequently cited by jazz musicians when asked what music they would take to a desert island. "Lady Day" (as she was named by Lester Young) had a light, untrained voice and a limited range, but she had a natural ear and a voice that carried a wounded poignancy, hauntingly so when one realizes that the words were often autobiographical.

Holiday's early life is shrouded in legend, but it is fair to say that it was quite harsh. Her father, Clarence Holiday, a young jazz guitarist, abandoned Billie's mother, Sadie Fagan, while his daughter was still a baby. A teenager herself, Sadie often left her daughter with uncaring relatives. Billie dropped out of school after fifth grade and eventually joined her mother in New York. Before long she was supporting her mom and herself by working as a prostitute. One day Billie discovered her musical talent, and soon she was singing for tips in clubs. In 1933 talent scout John Hammond wandered into Monette's, a Harlem club where she was singing, and was immediately impressed. He brought one of his protégés, Benny Goodman, to a performance and shortly thereafter Holiday was in a recording studio with the clarinetist. After that came many fruitful sessions with pickup bands, which produced some of her best work and some of the best jazz recorded during the 1930s. At a studio session Hammond arranged in 1937, Holiday recorded with Lester Young, Count Basie's great saxophonist. Their styles matched perfectly, as did their personalities. For a while Lester even moved in with Holiday and her mom, though according to all accounts, their relationship was strictly platonic. These were some of the happiest days for both of them, prior to Holiday's heroin addiction and the subsequent rounds of jail sentences and harassment that led to her death in 1959.

Having grown up alone and unloved, Billie developed a lifelong inferiority complex that led to self-destructive behavior. Her progress through a series of nightclubs was accompanied by drinking problems and a desperate search for a father figure. With a strong sexual appetite and plenty of money to spare, the childlike singer was easy prey for a succession of men who came, used her, and left; she became helplessly dependent on each in turn. Though her artistry was at its peak in the mid 1940s, it was during this period that she became a heroin addict, and she spent much of 1947 in jail. Her story from then on is a gradual downhill slide. By 1958 she was living alone near New York's Central Park, feeding a pet Chihuahua from a baby's bottle (she had recently been refused permission to adopt a child). On May 31, 1959, she collapsed and was taken to the hospital. She died six weeks later, at the age of forty-four. The 1972 film, *Lady Sings the Blues*, featured Diana Ross struggling to overcome the conflicting myths and tragedies of Holiday's life. While the film underscored her tragic life, it also introduced many fans.

APRIL 8—CARMEN MCRAE (1920–1994)
b. New York, NY; d. Beverly Hills, CA
Vocalist

[VOCAL JAZZ; TRADITIONAL POP; STANDARDS; BOP; BALLADS]

Other jazz notables born on this day: Phil Schaap (1951)
Jazz notables deceased on this day: King Oliver (1938) [or April 10]

♪

Jazz writer Ralph J. Gleason once heard a waitress in a jazz club break into tears when Carmen McRae sang. "How can she know so much?" the girl sobbed. The question portrays McRae's ability to bring such a high degree of artistic reality to her performances. According to Gleason, that "melding of words and music and performance into one searing moment of truth" happens only occasionally in jazz. It happened with Bessie Smith, Ma Rainey, Billie Holiday, and also with Carmen McRae.

Championed in the 1950s by Gleason, McRae was an important figure among singers that were directly influenced by the emergence of bop. Her early and enduring influence was Holiday, though in the late 1940s and early '50s she also came under the influence of Sarah Vaughan. She was especially inventive as a scat singer, but it was her instinctive behind-the-beat phrasing and ironic interpretations of lyrics that made her most memorable.[7] McRae was a matchless ballad interpreter. She had a way of lingering, touching the emotions behind the lyrics, and bringing them to life. Her exquisite diction and her command of the harmonic possibilities of a song distinguished her style. Among her most interesting recording projects were an album of live duets with Betty Carter and brilliant tributes to Holiday, Thelonious Monk, and Vaughan. Her first Holiday tribute album (1961), with Eddie "Lockjaw" Davis filling the role of Holiday's instrumental partner Lester Young, was notable for the extent to which it did not imitate Holiday's manner. Her second tribute, *To Lady Day* (recorded in 1983 but released posthumously), featured Zoot Sims as tenor soloist. Her finest work, *Carmen Sings Monk* (1988), demonstrates how well Monk's blunt, quirky instrumental themes melded with her own conception of jazz melody.[8]

McRea studied classical piano at an early age and had her first important job in 1944, singing with Benny Carter's big band, though it would be another decade before her career really took off. She married drummer Kenny Clarke in 1944 and that year sang briefly in big bands led by Earl Hines and Count Basie. From 1946 to 1948 she performed and

---

7. Bogdanov et al, *All Music Guide to Jazz*, 850.
8. Kernfeld, *New Grove Dictionary of Jazz*, Vol. 2, 678.

recorded as a member of Mercer Ellington's orchestra. When Ellington's group disbanded in Chicago, she remained there for several years as a solo singer and pianist. During this time she separated from Clarke and began to develop her own distinctive style, under the tutelage of Vaughan. Around 1954 she returned to New York to work as an intermission singer and pianist at Minton's Playhouse. That year she made her first recordings as a leader and was named "best new female singer" by *Down Beat*. From that point on she pursued an active career as a solo vocalist. In 1956 she divorced Clarke and married bassist Ike Isaacs, who led her backup trio for two years. Isaacs and McRae later divorced and in 1967 she settled in the Los Angeles area. Because she refused to quit smoking, McRae was forced to retire in 1991 due to emphysema. She remained bedridden until a stroke ended her life in 1994.

APRIL 9—STEVE GADD (1945–)

b. Rochester, NY

Drummer

[FUNK; POST-BOP; CROSSOVER JAZZ; FUSION]

Other jazz notables born on this day: Sharkey Bonano (1902)
Jazz notables deceased on this day: Eddie Edwards (1963); Bob Casey (1986); Tom Cora (1998)

♪

In 1972 the conservatory-trained drummer Steve Gadd formed a rock band in Rochester, New York and headed to New York City with the hopes of achieving musical success. He found success, but not in the manner he expected, for when his band fizzled out, he became a busy studio musician. Despite a heavy schedule of studio work, he performed and recorded occasionally with Chick Corea's Return to Forever band, one of the most original and popular groups of the decade. In 1976 he joined the group Stuff, and in 1979 he was a founding member of Steps. By the end of the 1970s he was the most in-demand and probably the most imitated drummer in the world. In Japan, transcriptions of his solos were on sale, and all of the leading Japanese drummers were imitating him. Corea, one of the notable jazz figures of the 1970s, stated his reasons for Gadd's success: "Every drummer wants to play like Gadd because he plays perfect[ly] . . . He has brought orchestral and compositional thinking to the drum kit while at the same time having a great imagination and a great ability to swing."[9] A versatile and unclassifiable crossover artist, Gadd has recorded with artists of all styles and genres, though his best jazz recordings are those he made with Corea.

Encouraged by an uncle, a drummer in the army, Gadd started playing drums at the age of three and started formal lessons four years later. He and his brother tap-danced at a small club, where he played with local musicians and bands that passed through Rochester. At the age of eleven he demonstrated his skills by sitting in with Dizzy

---

9. Carr et al., *Jazz: The Rough Guide*, 264.

Gillespie. He attended the Manhattan School of Music for two years and then he transferred to Eastman School of Music in Rochester. At school he played in a wind ensemble and concert band, but after hours he played in a nearby club with performers such as Corea, Chuck Mangione, and Gap Mangione. After college he was drafted into the army and spent three years in a military band. Following his discharge he performed with Gap Mangione (1971–72) and played in Europe with Chuck Mangione. From 1972, his work in New York studios included sessions with Chet Baker, Corea (1975–81), Jim Hall, Carla Bley, George Benson, and Quincy Jones, among others. He also performed with many popular groups and singers, including James Brown, Aretha Franklin, Paul Simon, Stevie Wonder, and Steely Dan. In the early 1980s he toured with various jazz players, including Al Di Meola, Richard Tee, Sadao Watanabe, Eddie Gomez, and Corea. He also worked intermittently in the all-star Manhattan Jazz Quintet (1984–90) while leading his own impressive jazz-funk band (the Gadd Gang), which included Jon Faddis, Ronnie Cuber, Gomez, Tee, and others. Gadd finally tired of the New York studio scene and returned to Rochester, though he continued to record and tour internationally with major artists, notably Di Meola, Paul Simon, Al Jarreau, and Eric Clapton. In 1992 he reunited with Corea and toured as a member of Corea's quartet.

APRIL 10—JOEY DEFRANCESCO (1971–)

b. Springfield, PA

Organist; Leader

[Hard Bop; Soul Jazz]

Other jazz notables born on this day: Barry Ulanov (1918); Claude Bolling (1930)
Jazz notables deceased on this day: King Oliver (1938) [or April 8]; Dakota Staton (2007)

♫

In the 1950s the Philadelphia organist Jimmy Smith revolutionized, popularized, and defined the still standard approach to jazz organ, showing that the Hammond B-3 could be used creatively in a jazz context. Taking the organ/guitar/drum format (with optional saxophone) established by Wild Bill Davis and Milt Buckner, he replaced their big band-inspired chording and substituted fast-moving bebop lines. His shrill but punchy sound, punctuated with a distinct blues phrasing, helped define the "soul jazz" that emerged in the late 1950s. In his highly influential Blue Note sessions from 1956 to 1963, he turned a fusion of influences and styles (R&B, blues, gospel, bebop) into an attractive sound that many imitated. During the 1970s, under the influence of jazz-rock and with the growing popularity of electric pianos and synthesizers, younger players largely abandoned the B-3. However, in the 1990s players like Dan Wall, Larry Goldings, John Medeski, Barbara Dennerlein, and Joey DeFrancesco managed to renew the organ's presence and sought innovative uses for the B-3 in modern jazz settings.

BLUE NOTES

The comeback of the organ in the late 1980s was due in large measure to the rise of Joey DeFrancesco, a brilliant and energetic player heavily influenced by Jimmy Smith. Raised in the Philadelphia area, generally considered the most fertile club scene in the world for organ-centered jazz, Joey is the son of "Papa" John DeFrancesco, himself a fierce Hammond B-3 organ player. Joey got an early start on piano when he was five, and though he continued on that instrument, within a year he had switched to the organ. His father began taking him to clubs at an early age, and by ten he was playing for money on weekends. By the time he entered high school he was working steadily around town. During those years his trio was named Best High School Combo at MusicFest USA, a student competition; he was also the first winner of the Philadelphia Jazz Society's McCoy Tyner Scholarship. In 1987, at the age of sixteen, he was a finalist in the first Thelonious Monk International Jazz Piano Competition. By the time he left high school, the seventeen-year-old wunderkind was playing with Miles Davis (inspired by Davis, the versatile DeFrancesco took up trumpet, on which he sounded much like Davis) and had a recording contract with Columbia, though it was his work—particularly his international live performances—with guitarist John McLaughlin's Free Spirits trio in the mid-1990s that really brought him to prominence in the jazz world. DeFrancesco established particularly close musical relationships with other guitarists as well, including Paul Bollenback, Jimmy Bruno, and Dave Stryker. He also recorded with notable saxophonists such as Houston Person, Kenny Garrett, and Eric Alexander, but it is his own recordings, generally rousing affairs, that underline his significance as a leading figure of contemporary organ jazz.

APRIL 11—NICK LAROCCA (1889–1961)

b. New Orleans, LA; New Orleans, LA

Cornetist

[NEW ORLEANS JAZZ; CLASSIC JAZZ]

Other jazz notables born on this day: Emil Mangelsdorf (1925)
Jazz notables deceased on this day: Scott Joplin (1917)

♫

On December 1915 a representative of the Victor Talking Machine Company heard cornetist Freddie Keppard and his Original Creole Orchestra playing in a New York theatre and offered to record the group. Fearing that his competitors might steal his ideas, Keppard passed up the opportunity to be the first jazz musician to make a recording. Instead, that distinction went to a group known as the Original Dixieland Jazz Band. According to jazz historian James Lincoln Collier, "[o]n February 26, 1917, five white New Orleans musicians went into the Victor studios in New York City and made the first jazz record. It was the single most significant event in the history of jazz. Before this record was issued, jazz was an obscure folk music played mainly by a few hundred blacks and a handful of whites in New Orleans, and rarely heard elsewhere. Within weeks after this record was issued on

March 7, 'jazz' was a national craze and the five white musicians were famous."[10] Although the band's style seems very primitive today, the group was light years ahead of all the other bands that had previously recorded. Earlier, on January 30, Columbia had recorded the band playing two tunes, but the results were unacceptable and the recording was shelved. The Victor recording included the group playing the novelty "Livery Stable Blues" (in which the horn players emulated barnyard animals) and the "Dixie Jass Band One Step" (notice an early spelling of the word "jazz") and quickly released the music; "Livery Stable Blues" was the hit that really launched the jazz age. The band's visit to London during 1919 and 1920 helped introduce jazz to Europe, causing another sensation overseas.

The founder and leader of the Original Dixieland Jazz Band was Nick LaRocca, a cornetist from New Orleans. Raised in the tough Irish Channel section of the city, LaRocca was the son of a shoemaker from Sicily. As an Italian-American, Nick had always felt himself something of an outsider in his own hometown, a fact that may help account both for his enormous drive to succeed and for his unwillingness to acknowledge that African-Americans could have had anything to do with creating the music he would later claim to have helped originate. Had Nick's father had his way, his son would never have been a jazz musician. Considering professional musicians to be "bums," he insisted that his son study to become a doctor. When Nick proudly performed for his parents at about the age of nine, his father tore the horn from his son's hands and smashed it with an axe. Soon thereafter, when his father died, LaRocca abandoned all thought of a medical career and began playing music whenever he could. By the time he left New Orleans in 1916 to join Johnny Stein in Chicago, he had worked in at least fifteen bands. Less than three months later he broke away and formed, with trombonist Eddie Edwards, the group that became known as the Original Dixieland Jazz Band. The band included clarinetist Larry Shields, pianist Henry Ragas, and drummer Tony Sbarbaro. The band became quite popular in Chicago and then caused a sensation when they opened in New York in 1917.

APRIL 12—HERBIE HANCOCK (1940–)

b. Chicago, IL

Pianist; Composer; Leader

[POST-BOP; FUSION; MODAL MUSIC; HARD BOP; FUNK]

Other jazz notables born on this day: Johnny Dodds (1892)
Jazz notables deceased on this day: Herbie Nichols (1963); Buster Bailey (1967); Wynton Kelly (1971); Ted Buckner (1976)

♪

Having studied engineering and professing a love for gadgets, Herbie Hancock was perfectly suited for the electronic age. Despite his proficiency on the acoustic piano, he was one of the earliest champions of the Rhodes electric piano and Hohner clavinet and a collector of synthesizers and computers. Though he never gave up on acoustic jazz, his

---

10. Collier, *Making of Jazz*, 72.

curiosity, versatility, and capacity for growth seemed to find its main satisfaction pioneering new electronic music.

Born to a musical family, Hancock took up the piano at the age of seven and progressed so rapidly that four years later, in a young people's concert, he performed a solo with the Chicago Symphony Orchestra. He began his studies at Grinnell College as an electrical engineering major, but after two years he switched to music composition. Hancock left Grinnell one course shy of graduation and went to New York, where he made an immediate impact. His first album as leader, *Takin' Off* (1962), was an instant success. One of its tracks, "Watermelon Man," became a hit single and ultimately a jazz standard. In 1963 Hancock joined the Miles Davis quintet, where he became an integral member of one of the era's most legendary small-group units. Hancock stayed with Davis for five years, greatly influencing Miles's evolving direction. His stint with Davis established him internationally as one of the most important pianists of the period (he appeared on more recording dates during the 1960s than any other jazz pianist) as well as a composer of distinction (he created more jazz standards than any other member of his generation). In 1968 Hancock formed a sextet that evolved into one of the most exciting, forward-looking jazz-rock groups of the era. Now deeply immersed in electronics, his music sounded spacier and included extensive use of synthesizers.

The jazz scene, however, was in a perilous state at that time. Despite his status as one of the leading forces in the music, Hancock was unable to keep his groups together. Due to financial pressures and out of a desire to reach larger audiences, he embarked on a string of popular styles that were less jazz-like and more in touch with what younger audiences of the period wanted. Coming to the realization that he would never be a genius in a class with Parker or Coltrane, he decided to stop trying to write the great American masterpiece and merely concentrate on making people happy.[11] Ironically, it was this decision that led him to form a terrific funk band whose first recording, *Headhunters*, finally produced Hancock's masterpiece. That album became the best-selling album in the history of jazz, in part because of its hit single "Chameleon," and it turned him into an international superstar. In the late 1970s his music became more pop-oriented, a move that further heightened his popularity. Hancock continued to break new ground in the popular electronic funky medium. His 1983 hit "Rockit" helped make the album *Future Shock* a best seller. It was in this medium, as fusion innovator and pioneer of new electronic music, that Hancock's creativity seemed at its best.

APRIL 13—BUD FREEMAN (1906–1991)

b. Chicago, IL; d. Chicago, IL

Tenor Saxophonist; Leader

[SWING; DIXIELAND]

Other jazz notables born on this day: Teddy Charles (1928)
Jazz notables deceased on this day: Dorothy Ashby (1986)

11. Carr et al., *Jazz: The Rough Guide*, 320.

Bud Freeman was one of a number of white high school boys who turned out regularly to hear Louis Armstrong perform with King Oliver at the Lincoln Gardens, one of the most famous nightclubs along Chicago's South Side "Stroll." The Stroll's recreational attractions ran twenty-four hours a day, but what drew audiences and musicians alike was a concentration of musical talent that would be unrivaled until the ascendancy of New York's Fifty-Second Street in the 1930s. Night after night the youngsters made the trip to the South Side, and neither the fact that the club was "by and for Negroes," nor the presence of a 350-pound bouncer who teased them about coming to the Stroll for their "music lessons," could dissuade them from returning.

Bud learned more than music from his visits to the South Side. "In those days," he wrote, "we were brainwashed into believing that blacks were inferior to us." In the South Side he encountered African-Americans who were economically and politically deprived but who had a wonderful freedom of spirit. "They were not allowed to come into our shops and cinemas, but we whites were allowed to go out to their community, where they treated us beautifully. I found their way of life equally as important as their music. It was not just their music that moved me but the whole picture of an oppressed people who appeared to be much happier than we whites who had everything. It was on the strength of this that I developed a love for them and became a jazz musician."[12]

An original member of Chicago's Austin High School Gang, a group of high school students who got together in the autumn of 1922 in a West Side neighborhood called Austin, Freeman took up the C-melody sax in 1923, two years before he switched to tenor. Considered the first white saxophonist to acquire a distinctive jazz timbre, during the late 1920s and early '30s Freeman was the only strong alternative on tenor to the harder-toned style of Coleman Hawkins. As such, he exerted (together with Frank Trumbauer) a significant influence upon the legendary Lester Young. His playing was still quite primitive in 1927, when he made his recording debut with the McKenzie-Condon Chicagoans.

He moved to New York later that year and worked with Ben Pollack, Red Nichols, Joe Venuti, Eddie Condon, and others. He was featured on Condon's memorable 1933 recording "The Eel," a piece of saxophone wizardry that became his specialty. During the late 1930s Freeman was a star with Tommy Dorsey's Orchestra and Clambake Seven (1936–38) before a short stint with Benny Goodman (1938). He led the short-lived but legendary Summa Cum Laude Orchestra (1939–40) before he entered the military (where he led service bands). From 1945 he alternated between being a bandleader and working with Condon's freewheeling Chicago-style jazz groups. He traveled around the world and made scores of fine recordings. In the late 1970s he returned to Chicago, where he continued to play into his eighties. He died in 1991, only a few days after his old friend and Austin High colleague Jimmy McPartland.

---

12. Ward and Burns, *Jazz: A History*, 91.

BLUE NOTES

APRIL 14—GENE AMMONS (1925–1974)

b. Chicago, IL; d. Chicago, IL

Tenor Saxophonist; Leader

[Hard Bop; Soul-Jazz; Bop]

Other jazz notables born on this day: Shorty Rogers (1924); Eliot Zigmund (1945)
Jazz notables deceased on this day: Pony Poindexter (1988); Sammy Price (1992); Danny Turner (1995)

♪

Son of the great boogie-woogie pianist Albert Ammons, Gene came to fame in 1944 when he joined Billy Eckstine's groundbreaking band as its principal bop soloist, playing with leading modernists such as Dizzy Gillespie, Charlie Parker, Sarah Vaughan, Art Blakey, and Dexter Gordon. He is said to have acquired his nickname Jug when he failed to find a straw hat large enough to fit, and Eckstine said, "You've got a head like a jug."[13] In 1947, after Eckstine disbanded, Ammons returned to Chicago, where he performed with Sonny Stitt, recorded with his father, and began leading small groups. After playing briefly with Woody Herman's Third Herd in 1949, as replacement for Stan Getz, he worked at Birdland and other New York clubs, forming a partnership with Stitt that continued intermittently until 1955. Ammons worked mainly as a single after that, when he became a leading exponent of soul-jazz.

One of the astonishing things about performers that emerged during the bebop era was their heavy involvement with drugs. Drugs such as marijuana and even cocaine had always been a part of jazz. However, during the bop movement, heroin seemed to have been the drug of choice. The reasons are debated. Some blame organized crime, which may have targeted jazz musicians because they occasionally possessed a lot of cash. Many of the younger musicians considered the first fix to be an initiation; until you had experienced drugs, you were an outsider. And of course there was the mystique of Parker, and the belief that drugs actually enhanced one's ability to play. According to James Collier, "it is probable that 50 to 75 percent of the bop players had some experience with hard drugs, that a quarter to a third were seriously addicted, and that perhaps as many as 20 percent were killed by it."[14] Since the 1940s many of the most gifted musicians in jazz, including Ammons, were addicted. Drug problems kept him in prison (where he was allowed to continue playing) from 1958 to 1960 and 1962 to 1969, but after his release his style of playing, coupled with the commercial rise of soul music, led to an even greater increase in his popularity.

Known as one of the founders of the Chicago-centered "tough tenor" style of playing, a style that combines the technical intricacies of bop with the passion of blues and gospel music, Jug played bebop with the best (he consistently battled his friend Sonny Stitt to a draw), yet he was an influence on the rhythm-and-blues scene. Though he was

---

13. Kernfeld et al., *New Grove Dictionary of Jazz*, Vol. 1, 50.
14. Collier, *Making of Jazz*, 407.

known for his sweet ballad playing, it was his big sound and driving beat that established him as a giant of the modern jazz saxophone. Ammons worked steadily until 1974, when he was hospitalized with terminal cancer. It is ironic that on his final recording session, the last piece he played was a song titled "Goodbye."

APRIL 15—BESSIE SMITH (1895–1937)

b. Chattanooga, TN; d. Clarksdale, MS

Vocalist

[CLASSIC JAZZ; CLASSIC FEMALE BLUES]

Other jazz notables born on this day: Herb Pomeroy (1930)
Jazz notables deceased on this day: Machito (1984); Cleo Brown (1995)

♪

Bessie Smith was not the first woman to record the blues; Mamie Smith beat her to it in 1920. And there were other popular vocalists, including Ma Rainey, Ida Cox, Clara Smith, Chippie Hill, Sippie Wallace, and Alberta Hunter. But by 1923, when she recorded "Downhearted Blues," Bessie was the undisputed "Empress of the Blues." At a time when the blues were in vogue and most vaudeville vocalists were being dubbed "blues singers," Smith simply had no competition. She made almost two hundred recordings, of which her remarkable duets with Louis Armstrong are among her best. Cornetist Joe Smith was her preferred accompanist, but possibly her finest recording was "Back Water Blues," with James P. Johnson.

Known for her unconventional lifestyle, Smith was a prototype for wild women who sing the blues, right down to Janis Joplin, who lived in her hard-drinking, hard-loving, bisexual image.[15] From 1923 to 1929 she lived a stormy relationship with her no-good husband Jack Gee. The two fought—with words and fists—and during those tumultuous years she took a host of lovers, both men and women. Known for her hot temper, she could stand no rivals and sometimes refused to appear on the bill with singers who were more attractive or lighter skinned than she. Nobody, white or black, messed with her. One night, while she was performing under a tent in North Carolina, she stood up to half a dozen hooded Klansmen who were about to collapse the tent and forced them to flee with curses and threats.

A protégé of Ma Rainey, Smith sang in Rainey's minstrel show and by 1913—when she was eighteen, strikingly beautiful, and with a voice so powerful that it could be heard over the sound of a band—was stopping shows all around the South. By 1920 she had her own show in Atlantic City, and in 1923 she made the big career move to New York. Bessie worked and recorded steadily throughout the decade, using top musicians as her sidemen. Her summer tent show *Harlem Frolics* was a big success during 1925 to 1927—one thousand people were turned away from a performance in Kansas City—and Smith became the highest salaried black star in the world.

---

15. Carr et al., *Jazz: The Rough Guide*, 712.

Although by 1930 public interest in Smith began to wane, through her great gift of communication and her ability to reshape any given song to her own special vocal style, she set the standard for all future singing of the blues. Smith was cited as one of two major influences by Billie Holiday, whose recording debut by ironic coincidence took place only three days after Smith's final session, in the very same studio. In 1931 she was dropped by Columbia, although she was still at the peak of her powers and had literally saved Columbia Records from bankruptcy. By 1936 she was performing in shows and clubs again, but the following year she was involved in a fatal car crash in Mississippi. Seven thousand people attended her funeral, yet her grave went unmarked until 1970, when Janis Joplin and Juanita Green (once Smith's maid) helped finance a headstone. "The greatest blues singer in the world," it read, "will never stop singing."

APRIL 16—HERBIE MANN (1930–2003)

b. Brooklyn, NY; d. Santa Fe, NM

Flutist; Leader; Record Producer

[CROSSOVER JAZZ; AFRO-CUBAN JAZZ; JAZZ-POP; SOUL-JAZZ; JAZZ-FUNK]

Other jazz notables born on this day: Ray Ventura (1908); Alton Purnell (1911); Bennie Green (1923)

Jazz notables deceased on this day: Ove Lind (1991)

♪

Not many musicians have created single-handedly the style of music for which they are famous. Among the select few is Herbie Mann, a seminal figure in the American jazz scene of the 1960s and '70s. Largely on the strength of his talent for improvisation and willingness to experiment, Mann constructed a jazz style for the flute, raising to the rank of lead an instrument that prior to his arrival had been limited to a minor role in jazz. In the process, he attained a reputation as one of the most eclectic figures in the music world, readily mixing a wide range of styles to create music that crossed boundaries of every sort. Although his experiments did not always resonate with jazz critics, the result was a musical style that was accessible to the average listener. Due to his popularity with consumers, from 1957 to 1970 he won the *Down Beat* readers' poll each year. In the period 1962 to 1979, twenty-five of his recordings placed on the Top 200 pop charts; in 1970 alone, five of the twenty top-selling jazz albums bore his name on the cover—an unprecedented success for a jazz artist.

Born Herbert Solomon, Herbie was musically inclined from an early age. His first concerts took the form of raucous banging on kitchen pots and pans. His parents, driven to distraction, decided that their son's energies would be channeled more appropriately through exposure to popular music. In 1939 his mother took him to see the then reigning master of swing, Benny Goodman. Excited by the concert, Herbie soon exchanged his drumming for a clarinet. A few years later he switched to the tenor saxophone, an instrument that came to dominate post-World War II jazz. Like so many other tenor players of that time, Mann's style was based upon Lester Young's cool, highly melodic approach.

After serving overseas with a U.S. army band (1948–52), Mann heard that a group forming to record with an unknown singer named Carmen McRae needed a jazz flute player. Though he knew very little about jazz flute playing—the style had virtually no precedents in the American music scene up to that point—Mann quickly improvised a distinctive playing style. During the 1950s he passed through a succession of groups, recording extensively as a sideman while enlarging his creative mastery of the flute. In 1959 he formed his Afro-Cuban sextet, a group that combined four percussionists and vibes with the leader's flute. By now the most popular flutist in jazz, Mann toured Africa and Brazil and became one of the first North Americans to explore bossa nova and to record with Brazilian musicians. From the early 1960s on he explored a wide variety of musical styles, grafting elements of Middle Eastern, pop, rock, R&B, reggae, soul, and disco music onto jazz to reach a wide audience. In 1997 Mann crossed yet another boundary when he was diagnosed with inoperable prostate cancer. Out of this experience he formed a nonprofit foundation, using performances and recordings to help spread awareness about the deadly disease and its easy detection and prevention.

APRIL 17—JOHNNY ST. CYR (1890–1966)

b. New Orleans, LA; d. Los Angeles, CA

Guitarist; Banjoist

[NEW ORLEANS JAZZ]

Other jazz notables born on this day: Chris Barber (1930); Sam Noto (1930); Han Bennink (1942); Buster Williams (1942); Jan Hammer (1948)
Jazz notables deceased on this day: Henry "Red" Allen (1967); Teddy Kotick (1986)

♪

On November 25, 1925, Louis Armstrong entered the OKeh studio in Chicago and embarked on what many consider to be the most influential recording project in jazz, perhaps even in American music. Over the next three years he produced sixty-five sides with studio pickup bands known as the Hot Five and the Hot Seven. By 1928 Armstrong possessed an extraordinarily rich melodic imagination and the finest technique of any trumpeter in jazz. According to jazz critic Gary Giddins, even if Armstrong had never played after the final December 12, 1928 session, "he would still be the most eminent figure in jazz history." [16] The recordings provide an astonishing record of Armstrong's rapid climb to artistic maturity. In addition to Armstrong, the Hot Five recordings included Lil (Hardin) Armstrong, Johnny Dodds, Kid Ory, and the banjoist Johnny St. Cyr. The earliest sessions featured Armstrong on cornet, while the Hot Seven sessions featured him on trumpet and added drums (Baby Dodds) and tuba (Peter Briggs).

---

16. Giddins, *Visions of Jazz*, 94.

The OKeh label, founded in 1916, originally recorded white musicians, but in 1920 it broke the color line in recording Mamie Smith. When the company was besieged with orders from African-Americans, it started a subsidiary, OKeh Race, which became a leading provider of jazz, blues, and gospel recordings over the next decade. After the initial Hot Five session, Armstrong's OKehs were snatched up by musicians and were avidly collected by young white fans, even though the target audience was African-American. The loyalty of the so-called race market encouraged OKeh to record Armstrong as frequently as possible.

When St. Cyr recorded with Armstrong (1925–27), he was considered the era's preeminent banjoist, and therefore was the New Orleans player most in demand in Chicago recording sessions. He had taught himself to play on a homemade guitar, and from 1905 to 1908 he led a trio at lawn parties and fish fries. After that he played with many of New Orleans' finest bands, including Kid Ory's orchestra (1914–17), when King Oliver was the cornetist. He joined Fate Marable's riverboat band in 1918 and in 1923 went to Chicago, where he recorded with Oliver, Armstrong, and Jelly Roll Morton. During this period he played on a six-string "guitar banjo" that he constructed from a banjo head and a guitar neck and fingerboard. In his later years he played a regular guitar, and in the 1940s he also used an electric guitar. The unusual sound St. Cyr obtained from his hybrid instrument may be heard on Armstrong's "Gut Bucket Blues," where he plays a low single-string solo with a few accompanying chords. St. Cyr is best remembered for his role with Armstrong, though he also distinguished himself while working with Morton for Doc Cooke's Dreamland Orchestra in Chicago (1924–29). In 1930 he returned to New Orleans and made a living outside of music. Years later (1955) he moved to Los Angeles, where he led a band at Disneyland during his final decade.

APRIL 18—KEN COLYER (1928–1988)

b. Great Yarmouth, Norfolk, England; d. near Nice, France

Cornetist; Trumpeter; Guitarist

[TRAD JAZZ; NEW ORLEANS JAZZ; SKIFFLE]

Other jazz notables born on this day: Leo Parker (1925); Hal Galper (1938); Danny Gottlieb (1953)

Jazz notables deceased on this day: Willie "The Lion" Smith (1973)

♪

Before World War II European jazz players were, virtually without exception, swing players. They knew little about New Orleans music, and throughout the war, swing remained at the center of European jazz. But by the end of the war, the swing style was finished, not only in England, where swing bands and orchestras had been formed for morale purposes, but throughout the jazz world as well. In the U.S. bebop helped push swing out of the mainstream, whereas in Europe swing was replaced by a tidal wave of trad (traditional) jazz. Because of the generally higher tradition of musicality in Europe, the best of the European trad bands played more accurately and with better intonation than many of the American bands.

As one of England's leading trad jazz exponents, Ken Colyer made it clear very early in his career that his allegiance lay with traditional New Orleans jazz, not revivalist Dixieland jazz. Colyer helped organize a New Orleans-styled band called the Crane River Jazz Band in 1949. He left this group in 1951 and joined the Merchant Marines with the intention of shipping out to New Orleans. He deserted in Mobile, Alabama, and went to New Orleans, where he jammed with local legends such as clarinetist George Lewis and recorded with Emile Barnes and others. In 1953 he was deported from the U.S., and upon his return to England he led a group called the Jazzmen, which included Chris Barber and Monty Sunshine. As in the Crane River group, Colyer's performances included a segment that attempted to educate audiences about the roots of jazz. With his "band within a band" he played a guitar-based, highly rhythmic mutation of American folk music that became known as skiffle. In 1954, when he left the Jazzmen, the group coalesced around Barber and its banjo player, Lonnie Donegan and went on to have a hit skiffle record "Rock Island Line" that caught the imagination of a Liverpool youngster named John Lennon, who went on to international stardom with the Beatles. The Beatles, whose earliest gigs in the now famous Liverpool dance halls were as intermission players to trad bands, started as a skiffle band.

Beginning in 1954 Colyer split his time between leading trad jazz groups as a trumpeter and skiffle groups as a guitarist. His jazz band of the mid-1950s, based on the bands of Lewis and Bunk Johnson, rivaled Barber's group as the decade's leading British trad band. The collapse of the trad boom in 1962 had a minimal effect upon Colyer, for his aims had little to do with commercial appeal. After a bout with stomach cancer he was forced to retire temporarily, but by the end of the 1970s he was back to full power. In the 1980s, with his All-Star Jazzmen, he achieved near-legendary status in England before succumbing to recurrent illness. By 1987 he was living in a caravan in France and no longer playing. An autobiography, *When Dreams Are in the Dust*, speaks of his occasional dismay concerning the current state of jazz.

APRIL 19—VI BURNSIDE (1915–1964)

b. Lancaster, PA d. Washington, DC

Tenor Saxophonist; Leader

[SWING]

Other jazz notables born on this day: Alexis Korner (1928)
Jazz notables deceased on this day: Jimmie Noone (1944)

♪

By 1934 a new Chicago-based publication named *Down Beat* began to focus a regular spotlight on jazz, bringing news of its artists and their activities to the American public. Helen Oakley Dance became one of the magazine's earliest contributors, and the magazine began to bring attention to female performers. But its coverage also reflected current chauvinistic attitudes toward women in the field, and on some notable occasions, questioned the place of women in jazz. In February 1938 *Down Beat* printed an unsigned article titled "Why Woman Musicians Are Inferior." "Why is it," the author asked, "that outside of a few sepia females the woman musician never was born capable of sending anyone further than the nearest exit?"[17] The writer supported his prejudice with conventional arguments and reiterated the notion that only piano and strings were appropriate to the temperaments of women.

Since those words were written, much has changed. Even during those backward years, women such as Lil Armstrong, Blanche Calloway, Anna Mae Winburn, Mary Lou Williams, Valaida Snow, Ernestine "Tiny" Davis, Pauline Braddy Williams, Melba Liston, Marian Turner McPartland, and Vi Burnside arose to demonstrate that they could compose, arrange, lead a band, and perform on any instrument as competently as men. In 1943 Burnside joined the most famous of the women's bands, the International Sweethearts of Rhythm. Despite its humble origins at the Piney Woods School in Mississippi, a boarding school for poor and orphaned children, the eighteen-member swing band became quite popular in the 1940s, touring widely and appearing frequently on radio broadcasts. Unfortunately, few white people ever saw the Sweethearts, for they played at theaters that catered to African-Americans. Known to their audiences as the finest all-girl jazz band in the country, the Sweethearts attained a reputation equal to that of the great male bands of the period. Despite detractors, musical director Maurice King promoted his group enthusiastically: "You could put those girls behind a curtain and people would be convinced it was men playing." The group was often likened to the Lunceford band, and Lunceford himself had high praise for the women.[18]

A high school classmate of future tenor great Sonny Rollins, Burnside was quickly recognized as a musician with outstanding potential and became a major talent when she began playing professionally. Before being recruited to the Sweethearts as star soloist, Burnside played with all-female bands such as the Dixie Rhythm Girls and the Harlem Playgirls (1938–40). With her vigorous, swinging, melodic style in the tradition of tenor saxophonists Ben Webster, Coleman Hawkins, and Don Byas, she was held in high regard by her male peers and participated in battles with them, notably with Gene Ammons in Chicago in 1948. The following year, after the Sweethearts disbanded, she formed her own band, billed as the All Stars. In an age when men regarded women as inferior, Vi Burnside and a host of other musicians proved them wrong.

---

17. Ward and Burns, *Jazz: A History*, 268.
18. Gottlieb, *Reading Jazz*, 640.

APRIL 20—LIONEL HAMPTON (1908–2002)

b. Louisville, KY; New York, NY

Vibraphonist; Drummer; Bandleader

[NEW YORK BLUES; SWING; BIG BAND]

Other jazz notables born on this day: Tito Puente (1923); Henri Renaud (1925); Ran Blake (1935)

Jazz notables deceased on this day: Perry Bradford (1970); Ronnie Boykins (1980)

♪

Lionel Hampton's career, spanning three quarters of a century, was one of the monumental achievements of jazz. Though he was not the first jazz musician to take up the vibraphone (Red Norvo had preceded him in the late 1920s), it was he who gave it an identity in jazz. Like Louis Armstrong, Hampton was an extroverted performer, a showman who sang, danced, and played with an infectious drive matched by few players in the history of jazz.

As a youngster growing up in Chicago, Lionel (he often went by Hamp) was sent to a parochial school in Wisconsin, where a Dominican nun taught him snare drum techniques. When the academy was relocated, he returned to Chicago, where he frequented the Vendome Theatre to watch his idol and occasional teacher, percussionist Jimmy Bertrand (who also played xylophone), perform with the Erskine Tate band as it accompanied the silent films. Hamp began his career playing drums with Les Hite and other local bandleaders, and in 1927 he accepted Hite's invitation to go to the Los Angeles area. After working with a variety of bands, Hamp joined Hite to back Louis Armstrong at the Los Angeles Cotton Club. At a recording session in 1930 a vibraphone happened to be in the studio, and Armstrong asked Hampton to play some notes behind him. Lionel did so on "Memories of You," thereby becoming the first jazz improviser to record on vibes. At the Cotton Club, Hampton met dancer Gladys Riddle, who became his wife and a partner of uncommon business ability. She bought him a set of vibes, encouraged him to practice, and then sent him to study theory at the University of Southern California. After leaving Hite, Hampton formed his own band, pursuing that means as an effective way to feature his remarkable improvisatory gift.

In 1936 he was offered a residency at the Paradise Café, a sailors' hangout in Los Angeles. His nine-piece band was an immediate hit, and one night Benny Goodman came by and sat in. The following night Goodman brought Teddy Wilson and Gene Krupa, the other members of his trio, and soon all four were on stage playing together. Six weeks later Hamp was featured artist with Goodman's quartet. Due to his enthusiasm and his exciting solo work, he became an instant favorite and one of the stars of Goodman's organization. In 1937 RCA offered Hampton a recording contract with specially assembled all-star groups. The ninety resulting sides are among the best records of the swing era at its zenith, and feature practically every star of the period. In 1940 Hamp formed his own highly successful big band, and two years later his orchestra had a huge hit with "Flying Home."

The piece "clearly established the Hampton formula: high energy, screaming brass, and rhythms that could drive an audience to near-hysterical excitement."[19] Hampton's popularity allowed him to continue leading big bands off and on throughout his lengthy career until his death in 2002.

APRIL 21—ALFRED LION (1908–1987)

b. Berlin, Germany; d. San Diego, CA

Record Producer

[HARD BOP; SOUL-JAZZ; BOP; AVANT-GARDE; DIXIELAND; CLASSIC JAZZ]

Other jazz notables born on this day: Lorenzo Tio Jr. (1893); Mundell Lowe (1922); Sonny Berman (1925); Slide Hampton (1932); Ian Carr (1933)

Jazz notables deceased on this day: Eddie Sauter (1981); Irving Mills (1985); Helen Ward (1998); Nina Simone (2003)

♫

The relationship between jazz and sound recording is of paramount importance. Despite the ongoing debate over the question of what constitutes jazz, most observers agree that jazz's creativity is marked by the act of improvisation—a form of spontaneous composition. As a result, recordings of jazz act as snapshots, "freezing a single creative moment which can never be repeated without subconscious change. Because it is impossible for such a performance to be repeated exactly, each recording acquires a unique value, and it is this that has made the recording of jazz so vitally important."[20] In 1916 two leading companies, Columbia and Victor, became interested in recording jazz. The following year, both labels recorded the same group, a white band that called itself the Original Dixieland Jazz Band. The development of jazz through recording began to be fostered not only by the major recording companies but also by numerous independent labels. During the Great Depression, however, the music business came close to collapsing. American record companies, which had sold over one hundred million discs a year in the mid-1920s, were soon selling just six million a year. Independents such as OKeh, Gennett, and Paramount Records all went out of business. Victor stopped making record players for a time and sold radios instead.

With the emergence of swing music in the mid-1930s a new mood began to sweep America, and people who had never listened to jazz began filling ballrooms across the nation. Big band swing became a hundred-million-dollar industry. Thousands found work playing, managing, booking, and promoting swing music after 1935. Swing also rescued the recording industry. By 1939 fifty million records were sold in the U.S.[21] Of course, not everyone was intoxicated with big band swing. By the late 1930s a growing group of jazz writers and fans emerged, convinced that big swing bands were too regimented and com-

---

19. Carr et al., *Jazz: The Rough Guide*, 318.
20. Kernfeld, *New Grove Dictionary of Jazz*, Vol. 3, 371.
21. Ward and Burns, *Jazz: A History*, 240.

mercial and therefore a sellout to the spirit of jazz. A handful of small record companies arose, dedicated to recording the older, "purer" style of jazz. The most important of these were Commodore, founded by Milton Gabler, and Blue Note, the best known and longest lasting of the independents, created by two refugees from Nazi Germany, Alfred Lion and Francis Wolff. Lion emigrated to the U.S. in 1938 and helped inaugurate Blue Note the following year.

At first Blue Note concentrated on small-group swing and Dixieland, but in 1946 the label changed its focus to bebop and signed Thelonious Monk and Bud Powell. During 1955 to 1967, Blue Note's prime, the company recorded hard bop extensively. Decline set in after 1966, when the label was sold to Liberty. Lion retired in 1967, although he lived to see the relaunch of the company in 1985. The revived label has been tremendously successful; in addition to its many current stars, the company continues to reissue historic Blue Note material on CD.

APRIL 22—CHARLES MINGUS (1922–1979)

b. Nogales, AZ; d. Cuernavaca, Mexico

Bassist; Pianist; Bandleader; Composer

[BOP; AVANT-GARDE; POST-BOP]

Other jazz notables born on this day: Tommy Turrentine (1928); Paul Chambers (1935); Don Menza (1936); Barry Guy (1947)
Jazz notables deceased on this day: Earl Hines (1983); Don Pullen (1995)

♪

Charles Mingus, one of the most interesting and controversial figures of his era, created a legacy that grows with the passing of time. As a bassist he knew few peers, but had he been only a string player, few would know his name today.

Mingus grew up in the Watts district of Los Angeles, where the first music he heard was that of the church—the only music his stepmother allowed around the house. By the time he reached high school he was a serious student of music, receiving instruction from a swing bassist and studying five years under a former New York Philharmonic bassist. In 1943 the bass prodigy went on the road with Louis Armstrong and from that point on he played with some of the finest jazz figures of his age, including Charles Parker, Dizzy Gillespie, and his idol Ellington, who fired the irascible individualist after a brief appearance.

Mingus's greatest influence was felt from the mid-1950s to the early '60s. As the leading bass player in jazz, he was respected by musicians and critics alike, but it was his compositional experiments that attracted greater attention, making his compositions, rather than his playing, his major contribution to jazz. In 1955 he began leading his own ensembles, known as the Charles Mingus Jazz Workshop, and by the following year, with the release of "Pithecanthropus Erectus" (a musical attempt to describe the pride of the first human ancestor to stand erect), Mingus had emerged as a composer and leader.

Along the way he made a lot of enemies, sometimes causing violent confrontations on the bandstand. A big man physically, he used his size as a weapon of intimidation, and he was not above halting concerts to scold inattentive audiences or errant sidemen. At one of his concerts—a memorial to a dead colleague—he broke up the show by slamming down the piano lid, nearly smashing his pianist's hands. In 1962, during a rehearsal two days before a disastrous concert in New York's Town Hall, he got into an argument with Jimmy Knepper, a longtime colleague. Striking Knepper's face, Mingus broke his sideman's tooth, ruining the trombonist's embouchure. Three months later the mercurial leader rebounded with his masterful *The Black Saint and the Sinner Lady* (the only jazz album with liner notes by the artist's psychiatrist). Mingus was undoubtedly a musical genius, but his bullying personality and hot temper often became outlets for personal frustrations and anger over racial prejudice.

In the mid-1960s Mingus found himself in financial straits. Desperate after being evicted from his New York apartment, he went to the mental ward of Bellevue hospital and insisted that he be admitted. His fortunes improved during his final decade, due in part to the publication of his remarkable autobiography, *Beneath the Underdog* (1971), and to a Guggenheim grant. He traveled extensively until 1977, when he fell seriously ill from an incurable degenerative illness known as "Lou Gehrig's disease."

APRIL 23—JIMMIE NOONE (1895-1944)

b. Cut Off (near New Orleans), LA; Los Angeles, CA

Clarinetist; Leader

[NEW ORLEANS JAZZ]

Other jazz notables born on this day: Alan Broadbent (1947)
Jazz notables deceased on this day: Krzysztof Komeda (1969); Red Garland (1984): Juan Tizol (1984); Melba Liston (1999)

♪

In the spring of 1926 Louis Armstrong joined a band fronted by violinist Carroll Dickerson at the Sunset Café, one of the most successful clubs in Chicago. The café stood at the corner of Thirty-Fifth and Calumet, just off the South Side Stroll. This was a tough neighborhood, but customers packed the place every night to hear the band's star perform his magic. Armstrong wasn't the only master teacher working that neighborhood. Joe Oliver was playing at the Plantation Café just across the street, and next door to him was Jimmie Noone, at a famous club called the Nest. Customers like Eddie Condon often headed for the Nest in the early morning hours, after the Sunset and the Plantation had closed, and there, he wrote, we "listened to Jimmie Noone do things with a clarinet which no one had considered even probable."[22] Considered one of the three top New Orleans clarinetists of the 1920s (with Johnny Dodds and Sidney Bechet), Noone became a vital link between the older New Orleans style of clarinet playing and Chicago swing. His smooth style and

---

22. Ward and Burns, *Jazz: A History*, 159.

expressive use of blue notes influenced numerous clarinetists, including Buster Bailey, Barney Bigard, Joe Marsala, and particularly Benny Goodman.

By the age of fifteen Noone had made the trip to nearby New Orleans, where he took clarinet lessons from Lorenzo Tio Jr. and Bechet (the latter was only thirteen). A jolly, overweight man, Noone was soon friends with Freddie Keppard, in whose band he substituted for and later replaced Bechet. He also worked with New Orleans stars such as Buddy Petit and Kid Ory (whose trumpet player was Joe Oliver). In 1917 he went to Chicago to join Keppard's Creole Band at the Royal Gardens, and a year later he was with Oliver, remaining with him until 1920. For the next six years he was a member of Doc Cook's Dreamland Orchestra, one of Chicago's premiere bands. Although Noone recorded with Cook, it was when he started leading a band at the Apex Club (known as the Nest until 1926) that he hit his stride. By 1928 his quintet included Earl Hines and Joe Poston, but Noone was its star; soon he was recognized as the most influential clarinetist in Chicago. Visitors from Goodman to Marsala came to hear Noone "holding the horn over that great belly of his and playing like it was nothing";[23] so did Maurice Ravel, who showed up one night with the first clarinetist of the Chicago Symphony.

Noone's preeminent position in clarinet history has been somewhat obscured because he never settled in New York, the jazz capital. He mostly remained in Chicago, playing a form of small group jazz that by the late 1930s was temporarily out of fashion. By 1944 he was living on the West Coast, working on radio broadcasts with Kid Ory. He seemed on the brink of greater fame when he died unexpectedly from high blood pressure caused by overeating. According to Jimmie Noone Jr., his father "ate himself to death ... He didn't drink or smoke but he couldn't leave food alone."

APRIL 24—JOE HENDERSON (1937–2001)

b. Lima, OH; d. San Francisco, CA

Tenor Saxophonist

[HARD BOP; POST-BOP]

Other jazz notables born on this day: Johnny Griffin (1928); Frank Strazzeri (1930); Collin Walcott (1945)

Jazz notables deceased on this day: Lennie Hayton (1971); Mel Powell (1998)

♪

Joe Henderson was one of the last of the great saxophone innovators. Exposed to a great variety of music during his formative years, his distinctive sound and style incorporated elements from bebop, R&B, abstraction, rock, and ethnic music. Buoyed by his extraordinary melodic gift, his vision and playing sharpened and deepened over the years. When he arrived in New York in the early 1960s he joined a host of East Coast players who were carving out what is called "hard bop" or the Blue Note style. His early recordings with the Blue Note label began his successful career and he emerged, along with Frank Shorter and

---

23. Carr et al., *Jazz: The Rough Guide*, 570.

Booker Ervin, as one of the most original mainstreamers on tenor sax. Ervin died young and Shorter detoured into fusion, but Henderson kept plugging. The composer of such enticing riddles as "Isotope" and "The Bead Game," he contributed immeasurably to two of the most durable jazz hits of the 1960s, Horace Silver's "Song for My Father" and Lee Morgan's "The Sidewinder."

By the age of fifteen Henderson showed remarkable compositional skills when he wrote "Recordame," his first and one of his most enduring tunes. While studying flute and string bass at Wayne University—his classmates included Yusef Lateef, Hugh Lawson, and Donald Byrd—he learned theory and harmony with Larry Teal at the Teal School of Music, where he specialized in saxophone. In 1960, as a member of an army band at Fort Benning, Georgia, he won first place in an army talent show, and while in the military he toured around the world to entertain troops. After his discharge he played briefly with Jack McDuff and then gained recognition for his work with Kenny Dorham (1962–63), a veteran bop trumpeter who championed him and helped him get a Blue Note contract.

Henderson appeared on many Blue Note sessions both as a leader and as a sideman before joining Horace Silver's quintet (1964–66). He co-led the Jazz Communicators with Freddie Hubbard (1967–68) and then joined the Herbie Hancock sextet (1969–70). In 1971 he spent four months with the rock group Blood, Sweat and Tears. He formed his own band before moving to San Francisco, where he performed regularly and became active in music education. In 1985 he participated in the televised concert *One Night with Blue Note*, celebrating the relaunching of the label with which he was once so closely associated. In 1992 he returned to international attention when he signed with Verve and he led a series of critically acclaimed small-group sessions that included his 1992 Grammy-winning "Lush Life." With that recording, the second most popular jazz album of the year, "Henderson became the most prominent veteran participant in the ongoing bop revival."[24] His Verve recordings—tributes to Billy Strayhorn, Miles Davis, and Antonio Carlos Jobim—had marketable themes, and as a result he became a celebrity and a regular poll winner.

APRIL 25—ELLA FITZGERALD (1917–1996)

b. Newport News, VA; d. Beverly Hills, CA

Vocalist

[Vocal Jazz; Traditional Pop; Swing; Bop; Classic Female Blues; Ballads]

Other jazz notables born on this day: Earl Bostic (1913); Willis "Gator" Jackson (1928); Carl Allen (1961)
Jazz notables deceased on this day: Eddie South (1962); Dexter Gordon (1990)

♪

Known as "the First Lady of Song," Ella Fitzgerald was arguably the finest female jazz singer of all time.[25] Despite having a small and somewhat girlish voice, she offset those

---

24. Kernfeld, *New Grove Dictionary of Jazz*, Vol. 2, 219.
25. Bogdanov et al., *All Music Guide to Jazz*, 417.

qualities by near-perfect elocution and an extremely wide range (of three octaves) that she commanded with a remarkable agility and an unfailing sense of swing. Her mastery of swing eighth notes and perfect timing of syncopations enabled her to give performances that rivaled those of the best jazz instrumentalists in their virtuosity, particularly in her improvised scat solos, for which she was justly famous.

One would never guess from her joyous singing that her early days were as bleak as those of Billie Holiday. Her parents never married, and her stepfather abused her. Around 1921 she moved to Yonkers, New York with her mother and stepfather. When her mother died in 1932, she dropped out of high school, and two years later she was living on the streets of Harlem. On November 21, 1934, she got her big break. Overweight, awkward, and dressed in secondhand clothes, she decided to compete in an amateur show at the Apollo Theater in Harlem. Singing two songs in the style of her idol, Connee Boswell, she won the contest. She returned to the streets, entered other amateur events, and won again at a Harlem Opera House concert.

Meanwhile, bandleader Chick Webb was looking for a female vocalist that could help him reach the huge white audience that Benny Goodman and others now commanded. When his male singer, Charles Linton, brought Fitzgerald, Webb was appalled by her appearance. But it soon became apparent that she had an extraordinary voice, so Webb decided to give her a chance. It was the best decision he ever made. Starting in 1935, Ella began recording with Webb's orchestra, and by 1937 the majority of the band's selections featured her voice. That year she won first place as the best female vocalist poll in the country's leading jazz magazines. The following spring she and Webb recorded an old nursery rhyme, "A-Tisket, A-Tasket," which became Webb's biggest hit. After Webb died in 1939 Ella fronted the orchestra until 1941, when she disbanded the group and went solo. Her subsequent recordings for Decca produced numerous hits.

Around 1946, while she toured with Dizzy Gillespie's big band, she adopted bop as part of her style and started including exciting scat-filled romps in her sets. In 1955 she signed with Norman Grantz's Verve label and over the next few years she recorded her seminal "songbook" albums, dedicated to the works of George Gershwin, Harold Arlen, Johnny Mercer, Jerome Kern, Cole Porter, Irving Berlin, and Duke Ellington. Although those were not her most jazz-oriented projects, the prestigious projects did a great deal for her career and established Fitzgerald among the supreme interpreters of the popular song repertory. By the time of her death she was a household name and one of the world's undisputed musical treasures.

APRIL 26—MA RAINEY (1886–1939)

b. Columbus, GA; d. Rome, GA

Vocalist

[CLASSIC FEMALE BLUES]

Other jazz notables born on this day: Dave Tough (1907); Jimmy Giuffre (1921); Teddy Edwards (1924)
Jazz notables deceased on this day: Count Basie (1984)

BLUE NOTES

♪

From roughly 1920 to 1933, when the depths of the Depression brought everything to a halt, the blues reigned in the marketplace of African-American music, and the women who sang the blues ruled with it. In an era of musical queens and empresses, when women were the marquee names in blues, Ma Rainey was once the most celebrated of all. Though not the first blues singer to make records, by all rights she should have been, for she had been singing the music for over twenty years before her recording debut in 1923. With the advent of blues records, she became even more influential, immortalizing such songs as "See See Rider," "Bo-Weavil Blues," and the humorous showstopper, "Ma Rainey's Black Bottom."

When Rainey, the first of the great female blues singers, took up the blues around the turn of the century, she began the mass popularization of this black folk idiom that lies at the heart of jazz. Deep South in her identity, she sang, and in many cases wrote, blues songs that were rooted in the southern black experience. Southern blacks considered her a racial heroine because she understood her mostly rural, poor audience perfectly and played her role, with its possibilities for escape into glamour, to the hilt.

Ma (Gertrude Pridgett) Rainey's career began in a talent show in Columbus, Georgia when she was twelve, and soon afterwards she appeared as a cabaret singer. She married Will "Pa" Rainey in 1904 and then toured the South with him as Rainey and Rainey, Assassinators of the Blues. Their act consisted of comedy, singing, and dancing, but Madame Rainey—affectionately known as "Ma"—was the featured player. By the early 1920s she had become a headliner on the Theater Owners' Booking Association circuit. Her recording career came relatively late in her life. When the blues craze started in 1920, she was already thirty-four years old, and it wasn't until 1923 that she signed a contract with Paramount Records. Although her contract lasted only six years—in 1928 Paramount declined to resign her, even though she was the company's biggest selling star during the 1920s—she recorded over one hundred songs, and many of them became genuine blues classics. During these sessions, some of the most talented blues and jazz musicians of her era backed her, including Louis Armstrong, Fletcher Henderson, and Coleman Hawkins.

Although she was not a good-looking woman, she was a consummate entertainer. As a stage personality—with her elaborate gowns, twenty-dollar-gold-piece necklace, and her gold and diamond teeth—she knew what her audience wanted, and she always delivered. Rainey's career faded away in the early 1930s and she settled down in her hometown of Columbus. Although she had been out of show business only four years, when she died of a heart attack in 1939 her death certificate listed her occupation as "housekeeper." Yet she left an immense legacy, influencing successive generations of blues, country, and rock-and-roll musicians.

APRIL 27—MATTY MATLOCK (1907–1978)

b. Paducah, KY; d. Los Angeles, CA

Clarinetist; Arranger

[SWING; DIXIELAND]

Other jazz notables born on this day: Denzil Best (1917); Connie Kay (1927); Sal Mosca (1927)

Jazz notables deceased on this day: Al Hirt (1999)

♪

On February 7, 1928, federal agents raided a dozen of Chicago's leading North Side nightspots, took the names of hundreds of patrons caught with liquor, and padlocked the doors. Vice raids had already closed several of the South Side cabarets and Chicago, famous for its hot music and torrid nightlife, began to shut down. It got tough for musicians as well. By May, some two hundred of them had lost their jobs. As business slumped, Al Capone and his rivals began to war openly over the shrinking profits. When bombs gutted the Plantation Club, where Joe Oliver had been playing, musicians began a mass exodus. Most headed for New York, among them Oliver, Eddie Condon, Dave Tough, Gene Krupa, Max Kaminsky, and Ben Pollack.

Pollack's band had led the way in February, playing at the Million Dollar Pier in Atlantic City before appearing at New York's elegant Park Central Hotel. At this time the orchestra was loaded with young white talent. Chicagoans Benny Goodman, Jimmy McPartland, and Bud Freeman were members. Jack Teagarden, a musician who would reinvent the way the trombone was played, had recently replaced Glenn Miller. Pollack's band was moderately successful, but the talented youngsters he had rounded up were impatient with his traditional music and old-fashioned ways. In October 1929, when Goodman resigned, Pollack replaced him with Matty Matlock, a traditionalist who doubled as arranger.

Matlock grew up in Nashville, where he learned to play clarinet at the age of twelve. After early experience in a variety of lesser-known bands, he remained with Pollack until 1934, when a dispute forced Pollack to disband. In 1935 Matlock joined several musicians that appointed singer Bob Crosby as leader. Crosby's unique brand of big-band Dixieland jazz achieved great popularity during the late 1930s as he toured, held lengthy engagements in Chicago, and broadcast over the radio. Star soloists such as Eddie Miller, Yank Lawson, Billy Butterfield, Irving Fazola, Bob Haggart, and Matlock also played in Crosby's widely acclaimed small group called the Bobcats.

In 1936 all of this interest in the New Orleans style inspired Nick Rongetti, a former law student, to open a club named Nick's in Greenwich Village that featured Dixieland jazz. Soon other clubs opened in New York and elsewhere and the popularity of New Orleans-style jazz became a national sensation. Following the disbanding of Crosby's groups in 1942, Matlock moved to the West Coast, where he became a studio musician and continued as a sideman. He formed his own groups and continued writing excellent arrangements in the Dixieland tradition, including for Bing Crosby's radio shows and for bandleaders such as Paul Weston, Billy May, and Harry James. He also led a small group on radio and television that created the series *Pete Kelly's Blues*, which in 1955 became a feature film. Matlock was, with Fazola, the prototypical clarinetist in the Dixieland style. He perfected the sound of "arranged white Dixieland" as we know it today.[26]

APRIL 28—BLOSSOM DEARIE (1926–2009)

b. East Durham, NY; d. New York, NY

Vocalist; Pianist

[Vocal Jazz; Standards; Bop]

Other jazz notables born on this day: George E. Lee (1896); Mario Bauzá (1911); John Tchicai (1936); Steve Khan (1947)

Jazz notables deceased on this day: Murray McEachern (1982); Percy Heath (2005)

♪

Blossom Dearie had one of the most unusual styles to be heard in jazz and cabaret music. Her unique, high-pitched voice, quirky lyrics, and muscular piano playing singled her out as a true original. Despite a small, fragile-sounding voice, Dearie sang with intelligence, clarity, and originality, and her performances were enhanced by the way she stroked and caressed certain words and attacks others, while also making use of blues effects.[27] She gained a place in many jazz lovers' affections with her delivery and choice of material, including many of her own songs.

Actually born with the name Blossom Dearie, she began playing piano at an early age and studied classical music before making the switch to jazz while in high school. After graduation she moved to New York City and began appearing with vocal groups like the Blue Flames (a group within Woody Herman's orchestra) and the Blue Reys (a similar group in Alvino Rey's band). She also played cocktail piano around the city, and then moved to Paris in 1952 to form her own group, the Blue Stars, which subsequently evolved into the Swingle Singers. Dearie also appeared in a nightclub act with Annie Ross and made a short, uncredited appearance on King Pleasure's vocalese classic, "Moody's Mood for Love." In 1954 the Blue Stars hit the American national charts with a French version of "Lullaby of Birdland." After hearing her perform in Paris in 1956, Norman Granz signed her to his Verve label. Having recently married flutist Bobby Jaspar, she returned to the U.S. by the end of the year, where she started a solo career and led her own trio.

She established her reputation on record with a string of excellent albums for Verve during the 1950s, beginning with *Blossom Dearie* (1956); her sidemen on that album included jazz greats Herb Ellis, Ray Brown, and Jo Jones. Blossom became a fixture as a solo singer-pianist in intimate clubs in New York and Los Angeles, and by the 1960s had

---

26. Carr et al., *Jazz: The Rough Guide*, 497.
27. Kernfeld, *New Grove Dictionary of Jazz*, Vol. 1, 586.

gained international attention through such hits as her versions of two Dave Frishberg songs, "Peel Me a Grape" and "I'm Hip," and two original compositions dedicated to pop stars, "Sweet Georgie Fame" and "Hey John" (for John Lennon). Around this time she began performing annually in England, often at Ronnie Scott's club. After a recording break in the early 1960s, Dearie signed to Capitol for one album but then, on account of her unusual style, she recorded sparingly during the rest of the decade. In the early 1970s she formed Daffodil Records in order to release her work.

In 1985 she became the first recipient of the Mabel Mercer Foundation Award. Like Mercer, the doyenne of women salon stylists, Blossom attracted a devoted fan base, one that appreciates her commitment to musical excellence and her refusal to compromise. Dearie continued to perform during the 1980s and '90s, singing at the Ballroom in New York and traveling regularly to London, where she remained a popular attraction.

APRIL 29—DUKE ELLINGTON (1899–1974)

b. Washington, DC; d. New York, NY

Composer; Bandleader; Pianist

[Orchestral Jazz; Swing; Progressive Big Band]

Other jazz notables born on this day: Toots Thielemans (1922); Ray Barretto (1929); Andy Simpkins (1932); Dave Valentin (1952); Ira Coleman (1956)
Jazz notables deceased on this day: Miff Mole (1961); Cat Anderson (1981)

♪

For many musicians and listeners Ellington stands at the very top of musical achievement in the United States. He is without doubt one of the most significant figures in jazz history, not only as a performer or even as musician, but as consummate artist. There is simply no explanation for his musical genius. Born to a middle-class family, he grew up in a secure and happy home and from the start was a natural leader. As a boy Ellington was interested in painting, but as he grew up he began to realize that there were social advantages to playing the piano, not to mention financial benefits. Like many other aspiring pianists of his generation, Ellington listened to the ragtime and barrelhouse piano players of the era, teaching himself to play by slowing down the roll on the family pianola and placing his fingers on the depressed keys. By his late teens he was playing professionally, sometimes with bands of his own. When it came time to go to college, he passed up an art fellowship and chose a music career instead.

Ellington's first visit to New York came in 1922, where he worked briefly with Wilbur Sweatman, whose claim to fame came from playing three clarinets at once. A year later he returned to New York, this time as part of the Washingtonians, a five-piece group that included Sonny Greer, who would be Ellington's drummer for thirty years. As an aspiring composer, Ellington sought out Will Marion Cook, a renowned composer and conductor, hoping to match his success. One summer day, as they rode home together in a taxi, Cook urged Ellington to acquire a formal education at a conservatory. Ellington balked, replying that the academies were not teaching what he wanted to learn. In that case, Cook told him, "First . . . find the logical way, and when you find it, avoid it, and let your inner self break through and guide you. Don't try to be anybody else but yourself."[28] Ellington followed that advice throughout his career.

In 1927 Ellington began a three-year engagement as bandleader at Harlem's Cotton Club. With its glamorous revues and erotic dancing shows, no nightspot offered more thrills. Ellington fully understood the absurdity of much that went on at the Cotton Club. But the club also provided him with a priceless training ground, teaching him how to produce on deadline and how to showcase talented people. And while the "jungle music" tag would follow him for a time, neither distant Africa nor the perverse version of it that helped lure whites to Harlem was ever his source of inspiration. For that, he would always draw upon what he called "the everyday life and customs of the Negro." Unlike most other bandleaders, "Ellington wasn't interested primarily in establishing a good beat for dancing; he wanted to explore his musical imagination. Memories, sound colors, moods, emotions—these were his focal points . . . With musical insight and sensitivity, Ellington composed pieces with his players in mind . . . and in so doing, lifted individuality within his band to an artistic zenith."[29]

APRIL 30—PERCY HEATH (1923–2005)

b. Wilmington, NC; d. Southampton, NY

Bassist

[Hard Bop; Cool; Bop]

Other jazz notables born on this day: Lawrence Duhé (1887); Bob Shoffner (1900); Sid Weiss (1914); Mabel Scott (1915); Dick Twardzik (1931)

Jazz notables deceased on this day: Frank Socolow (1981); Jonah Jones (2000); Barry Ulanov (2000); Teddy Edwards (2003)

♪

The oldest of three distinguished musician brothers, Percy Heath grew up in Philadelphia in a musical family. But unlike saxophonist-composer Jimmy Heath and drummer Albert "Tootie" Heath, who performed professionally while still in their teens, Percy had no plans to enter a career in music. Only after his discharge from the air force, where he had trained as a fighter pilot during World War II (1943–45), did he take up music seriously. Having played violin as a child and sung in his family's gospel quartet, he switched to bass and enrolled in the Granoff School of Music, and within several months the versatile musician was performing in local bands; before long he was a member of the house trio at the Down Beat Club, where he accompanied such visiting musicians as Howard McGhee, the trumpeter who helped many young musicians during the 1940s. In 1947 Percy joined

---

28. Ward and Burns, *Jazz: A History*, 99.
29. Hasse, *Jazz: The First Century*, 62.

his brother Jimmy in McGhee's sextet and the following year they appeared at the first Festival International de Jazz in Paris.

In 1950 Dizzy Gillespie invited both brothers to join his newly-formed sextet (which included vibraphonist Milt Jackson and a young section player named John Coltrane) and within two years Percy was performing or recording with many of New York's most important bop musicians, including Miles Davis, Stan Getz, Fats Navarro, Sonny Rollins, J.J. Johnson, Charlie Parker, Thelonious Monk, Clifford Brown, and Horace Silver. Despite his relative inexperience, Percy quickly became one of the hottest bassists in New York.

In 1951 Percy's biggest break came when he was asked to replace Ray Brown in the Milt Jackson Quartet, which in 1952 became the Modern Jazz Quartet (MJQ). Brown, one of the era's most prominent and reliable bassists, had married Ella Fitzgerald and was working almost exclusively with her. In 1955, when Connie Kay replaced drummer Kenny Clarke, the personnel of the MJQ was finalized. But they needed the support of a strong record label. The following year brought them a contract with Atlantic, a young company that had found success in the rhythm-and-blues market. Atlantic had recorded some jazz sides as early as 1949, but when producer Ahmet Ertegun's older brother, Nesuhi, joined—Nesuhi had the distinction of teaching the first accredited jazz course at a university (UCLA)—the label began to concentrate on modern sounds. The MJQ, described by Martin Williams as "perhaps the best small ensemble in jazz history," was on its way to unbounded success.[30] For the next twenty years the band toured and recorded constantly, though Heath recorded with other groups when he was able. After the quartet's temporary breakup in 1974 Percy joined Jimmy and Tootie in the Heath Brothers Band (1975–82); he returned to the MJQ when it was reorganized in the early 1980s. In 1997 the remarkable forty-five-year-old quartet came to an end, and when Percy died in 2005, he was the last surviving member of the MJQ.

---

30. Giddins, *Visions of Jazz*, 388.

Chapter 5

May

MAY 1—SHIRLEY HORN (1934–2005)

b. Washington, DC; d. Cheverly, MD

Vocalist; Pianist; Leader

[Vocal Jazz; Ballads]

Other jazz notables born on this day: Ira Sullivan (1931)
Jazz notables deceased on this day: Raymond Fol (1979); Rob McConnell (2010)

♪

Unlike their predecessors in the band era, the leading singers who came to prominence in the 1950s and beyond tended to be introverted. Concentrating on feeling rather than technique, musicians such as Chet Baker, Blossom Dearie, and Shirley Horn all employed a minimalist technique and fundamentally small vocal instruments.

Widely regarded as the premiere singing pianist in jazz since Nat King Cole, Shirley Horn did not set out to be a singer. What she remembers first in her life is playing the piano. When she was four years old, she went to her grandmother home. The house had a parlor that was closed off with French doors, for it was only for company. But it contained a large piano. Shirley wasn't interested in playing outdoors with her cousins and the other children who gathered there. All she wanted to do was go into the parlor and sit on the piano stool. After several years of this her grandmother convinced Shirley's mother to let her take lessons. As a teenager, Shirley attended Howard University's Junior School of Music, where she concentrated on classical piano. But she eventually awakened to jazz and began listening to pianists like Oscar Peterson and Ahmad Jamal.

Soon thereafter she began playing piano gigs at local clubs and restaurants. Horn discovered the allure of her singing one night in December when a gentleman came for dinner in a restaurant where she was performing, holding a large teddy bear. He promised to give her the bear if she would sing "Melancholy Baby" for him, and that began her career as a vocalist. Audiences began asking her to sing and soon she realized how much she loved the role. She recorded her first release, *Embers and Ashes*, in 1960. The record found its way to trumpeter Miles Davis, who invited her to open for him at New York's Village Vanguard. Notoriously disdainful of singers, Davis was captivated by Horn's vocal approach (her entrancingly slow phrasing never fails to hypnotize an audience), an aesthetic much like his own. Producer Richard Seidel underscored the similarity in a 2003 segment of *Jazz Profiles* (National Public Radio) when he remarked: "[Shirley Horn] was how Miles Davis would sound if he could sing."

Shirley started dazzling audiences, and before long she was catapulted into a limelight she never sought. After the early 1960s she and Miles diverged musically, but in 1991 they collaborated on the title track of her critically acclaimed *You Won't Forget Me*. After recording several additional albums, she returned to Washington, choosing to play locally and raise a family. In 1987 she recorded a breakthrough album, *I Thought About You*, with the Verve label and thereby commenced an association that established her as a superior ballad singer and a talented pianist. Throughout her career, Horn never compromised her music or her personal life in pursuit of fame. She took her time with success in the same way she controls a slow and shifting tempo on her ballads, and it is this ability and quality, more than any other, that brought her accolades, awards and, ultimately, legendary status.

MAY 2—BING CROSBY (1903–1977)

b. Tacoma, WA; d. Madrid, Spain

Vocalist

[TRADITIONAL POP; STANDARDS; SWING; VOCAL JAZZ; AMERICAN POPULAR SONG]

Other jazz notables born on this day: Groove Holmes (1931)
Jazz notables deceased on this day: Leo Watson (1950)

♪

Bing Crosby, the most popular and influential media star of the first half of the twentieth century, dominated the entertainment world from the Depression until the mid-1950s. The undisputed best-selling artist until well into the rock era (with over half a billion records in circulation), he was the most popular radio star of all time and the biggest box-office draw of the 1940s. Despite a wide repertoire covering show tunes, country and western songs, religious hymns, patriotic songs, and ethnic ballads, Crosby's musical knowledge and sense of laidback swing was learned from early jazz music.[1]

Harry Crosby ("Bing" was a childhood nickname from one of this favorite comic strips) was born to a poor family that loved to sing. He received a few vocal lessons but soon grew tired of classical training. Bing sang in a high school band, and when he began attending nearby Gonzaga College (to become a lawyer), he was introduced to a local bandleader named Al Rinker (the brother of Mildred Bailey), who invited him to join his group, the Musicaladers, as vocalist and drummer. When the group broke up after his graduation in 1925, Crosby and Rinker headed for California, where they were hired by Paul Whiteman, then leader of the most popular band in the country and known as "The King of Jazz." With Barry Harris, a pianist and arranger, Crosby and Rinker sang as the

---

1. Bogdanov et al., *All Music Guide to Jazz*, 287.

Rhythm Boys in Whiteman's shows, and soon the trio became a popular attraction. When Whiteman's orchestra resumed touring in 1930, the Rhythm Boys, now quite popular on their own, stayed behind.

By 1931, the year of his big breakout into mainstream success, Crosby began recording with Brunswick Records, and by year's end had recorded several huge hits. Crosby's vocal work during this period is outstanding, particularly his jazz recordings with Bix Beiderbecke, the Rhythm Boys, and Whiteman-based small groups, where he is backed by the likes of Frankie Trumbauer, the preeminent white saxophonist of the era, and jazz guitarist Eddie Lang. With the advent of American involvement in World War II, Crosby entered the peak of his career, including starring in the first of his popular *Road* movies with Bob Hope and Dorothy Lamour. Additional popular success followed in 1941 with the introduction of Bing's biggest hit and the best-selling single of all time, "White Christmas."

Crosby's most relaxed and humorous work seemed to come with the jazz musicians he loved. While he was never primarily a jazz singer, he retained his interest in jazz and is best remembered in this context for his collaborations with Louis Armstrong. On records and in radio shows with jazz musicians such as Red Nichols and Connee Boswell, there were countless confirmations of his claim, "When all's done, my favorite music is Dixieland." Even jazz fans who find most of his later material too bland will notice the warmth in his voice on sessions with Bob Scobey, Eddie Condon, Matty Matlock, Louis Jordan, and best of all, on duets with Armstrong.[2] Crosby died of a heart attack while golfing in Spain.

MAY 3—JOHN LEWIS (1920–2001)

b. LaGrange, IL; d. New York, NY

Pianist; Composer

[THIRD STREAM; COOL; BOP]

Other jazz notables born on this day: Yank Lawson (1911)
Jazz notables deceased on this day: Billy Higgins (2001)

♪

As musical director of the Modern Jazz Quartet (MJQ), a jazz chamber group that flourished over four decades, John Lewis "found the perfect outlet for his interest in bop, blues, and Bach."[3] A representative of the "cool" piano style (characterized by a light touch and understated approach), he and the MJQ long helped make small-group jazz look respectable to the classical music community.

Lewis grew up in Albuquerque, New Mexico. Like Fletcher Henderson and Duke Ellington, he came from the middle class. He studied both music and anthropology at the University of New Mexico and then was drafted into the army, where he met drummer

---

2. Carr et al., *Jazz: The Rough Guide*, 173.
3. Bogdanov et al., *All Music Guide to Jazz*, 764.

Kenny Clarke, a unique and attractive stylist. In 1946 Clarke brought Lewis to Gillespie, who hired him as arranger, then pianist, for his big band. Gillespie's rhythm section now included Lewis, Clarke, bassist Ray Brown, and vibraphone virtuoso Milt Jackson. With Lewis on piano, Gillespie realized he had an ensemble within an ensemble.

Ever since 1935, bandleaders had introduced smaller units as a sort of entr'acte, mostly to give brass members a breather. Benny Goodman, Duke Ellington, Woody Herman, Artie Shaw, and others began recording those combos, thereby securing acceptance for what became known as "chamber jazz." Gillespie's intermission unit became quite popular, with audiences and musicians alike. When the Gillespie band broke up in 1950, the rhythm section considered continuing as a quartet. In 1952 they formed the Milt Jackson Quartet—the "MJQ." After several personnel changes, they agreed to form a cooperative renamed the Modern Jazz Quartet, thereby retaining the initials by which they were becoming known. When Connie Kay replaced Clarke, who moved to Europe in 1955, Lewis became the quartet's musical director, composing or arranging all its material. During this time Lewis also studied at the Manhattan School of Music, one of the country's leading conservatories. He was, by the early 1950s, a thoroughly schooled musician familiar with European music, especially the music of the Renaissance and the Baroque period, in which he took a particular interest. The group produced a delicate sound that was so polished and dignified that listeners likened it to classical chamber music. Not since Jelly Roll Morton's Red Hot Peppers thirty years earlier had a jazz group achieved such an exquisite balance between written and improvised passages, and between the soloist and the ensemble. The members often appeared in tuxedos and preferred to play in concert rather than in nightclubs, and this may explain why the band was first lauded in Europe. The influence of the MJQ grew rapidly.

Late in the 1950s Lewis organized jazz summer music schools in Lenox, Massachusetts (headquarters of the "third stream" movement, which combines jazz with classical styles), and from 1958 to 1982 he was musical director of the Monterey Jazz Festival in California. The quartet members played together regularly until 1974 and then regrouped occasionally thereafter for tours and recordings.

MAY 4—RON CARTER (1937–)

b. Ferndale, MI

Bassist; Leader

[HARD BOP; POST-BOP]

Other jazz notables born on this day: Sonny Payne (1926); Maynard Ferguson (1928); Lars Gullin (1928); Ron Carter (1937)
Jazz notables deceased on this day: Emily Remler (1990) [orAfter May 3]

During the latter half of the 1950s Miles Davis became the dominant figure in jazz. His rhythm sections were regarded as the best units of the period, and his quintet and sextet were generally recognized as the leading groups of the time. The start of the 1960s, however, was a difficult period for Miles, both personally and professionally. His spectacular quintet of the 1950s had dissolved shortly after the departure of John Coltrane in 1961. Without these musicians, Davis was having difficulty expressing his musical ideas. For the first time, he was beginning to look passé. But by 1963 things started to change. Miles began assembling a new quartet, one that would stay together for five years and would equal the quintet of the 1950s in popularity and innovation. The first to join was bassist Ron Carter, who had recently completed a master's degree in music. Next came drum prodigy Tony Williams, then only seventeen years old. Herbie Hancock, the brilliant and creative twenty-three-year-old pianist, rounded out the rhythm section. Together they catapulted Miles back to the forefront of jazz.

The epitome of class and elegance and one of the great accompanists of all time, Carter has been a world-class bassist and cellist since the 1960s. Nearly as accomplished in classical music as jazz, Carter began playing cello at ten, but when his family moved to Detroit, he ran into problems with racial stereotypes regarding the cello and switched to bass. He played in the Eastman School's Philharmonic Orchestra and gained his music degree in 1959. He moved to New York and enrolled at the Manhattan School of Music, where he earned a master's degree in 1961. During this period he also played in Chico Hamilton's quintet with Eric Dolphy.

By the early 1960s musicians were recognizing Carter's outstanding qualities—"his perfectly poised sense of time, brilliant technique, and a sound so resonant that in ballads it seemed as if the notes were being artificially sustained"[4]—though it wasn't until he joined Miles that he came to prominence. In March 1963 Carter joined Art Farmer's band, only to leave a week later to embark upon his most important association. As a member of Davis's quintet (1963–68), he formed with Hancock and Williams perhaps the smoothest rhythm section ever. The band's legendary greatness was due not only to the group's great rapport but also to the remarkable abilities of the individual players. Each member of the rhythm section displayed stunning technical ability for each had been conservatory trained. By the mid-1960s all three were the dominant influence on their respective instruments.

By 1968, when he left Davis, Carter was one of the most sought-after studio bass players, and in the decades that followed he participated on over one thousand albums with jazz, soul, and pop artists. Examples of his best work may be found in his recordings with Davis, with all-star groups such as V.S.O.P. (1976–77 and 1980s), and particularly in Herbie Hancock's 1965 album, *Maiden Voyage*.

---

4. Carr et al., *Jazz: The Rough Guide*, 123.

MAY 5—PAUL BARBARIN (1899-1969)

b. New Orleans, LA; d. New Orleans, LA

Drummer

[NEW ORLEANS JAZZ]

Other jazz notables born on this day: Pete Daily (1911); Sonny Parker (1925); Stanley Cowell (1941); Jack Walrath (1946)

Jazz notables deceased on this day: Hal McIntyre (1959); Cal Tjader (1982)

♪

Paul Barbarin, one of New Orleans' most famous drummers, grew up as part of a large musical family. His father Isadore played with several brass bands and three of his brothers were musicians, including Louis, who was also a drummer. During his career he played with some of early jazz's greatest figures, including Freddie Keppard, Jimmie Noone, Sidney Bechet, King Oliver, Louis Armstrong, and Luis Russell. Russell, perhaps the least known of these musicians today, led one of the great early big bands, an orchestra that during 1929 to 1931 could hold its own with nearly all competitors.[5]

Born in Panama, Russell moved to New Orleans in 1919, where as a trained pianist he was able to find ample work. Through his New Orleans contacts he eventually got a job with Oliver in Chicago, and he was with Oliver when the cornetist relocated to New York in 1927. Russell left Oliver to take over the leadership of a band that by 1929 boasted four major soloists in trumpeter Henry "Red" Allen (second only to Armstrong at the time), trombonist J. C. Higgenbotham, alto saxophonist Charlie Holmes, and clarinetist Albert Nicholas. As pianist, Russell joined guitarist Will Johnson, bassist Pops Foster, and the gifted Barbarin as a member of one of the top rhythm sections of the era. During the next couple of years this band backed Armstrong on a few of his early orchestra recordings and later (1935-43) functioned primarily as backdrop for Armstrong's singing and trumpet playing.

As a child Barbarin drummed on homemade instruments, and at one point he was arrested for drumming too loudly on his neighbor's steps. He showed such skill at a demonstration in court that the judge paid him his first income from music and dismissed the case.[6] Barbarin eventually saved up enough money to buy a set of drums, and by his teens he was a familiar figure in the Young Olympia Brass Band. In 1917 he struck out for Chicago to work its clubs and cabarets with, among others, Keppard and Noone, who became his brother-in-law. From 1923 to 1924 he returned to New Orleans to perform with the Onward and Excelsior bands before moving back to Chicago in late 1924 to join Oliver (1925-27).

He relocated to New York in 1928, where he joined Russell's notable band, remaining until 1932 and anchoring one of the top jazz groups of the era. He freelanced before rejoining Russell in 1935, and he stayed with the pianist when the orchestra became

---

5. Bogdanov et al., *All Music Guide to Jazz*, 1101.
6. Kernfeld, *New Grove Dictionary of Jazz*, Vol. 1, 132.

Armstrong's backup band. In 1938 he joined Red Allen's sextet that spent a period in Chicago and traveled to the West Coast (1942–43). Other than a period with Bechet in 1944 and some work with Art Hodes in Chicago (1953), Barbarin remained based in New Orleans, where he led his own bands, including his own Onward Brass Band, which he formed in 1955. It became his mission to see one of his bands march in the whites-only Proteus procession that precedes Mardi Gras. The year he finally accomplished his goal (1969) he collapsed on parade and died.[7]

MAY 6—DAVID FRIESEN (1942–)

b. Tacoma, WA

Bassist

[POST-BOP]

Other jazz notables born on this day:
Jazz notables deceased on this day: Wayman Carver (1967); Kai Winding (1983)

♪

David Friesen has been called "a well-known unknown," meaning that despite having a strong track record, he is hardly recognized by the general public. In 2002 Maurice Bottomley reviewed Friesen's album *Grace*, a recent release with pianist Jeff Gardner, and became an instant admirer, calling it "one of the year's most engaging jazz albums." Jazz critic Nat Hentoff's assessment of Friesen is also laced with superlatives: "Once in a great while, a musician emerges with such authority and such seemingly effortless originality that his place in the front ranks of his instrument is unquestioned. So it is with David Friesen . . . [He] is a phenomenon." Friesen's vast musical range testifies to his versatility in performing serene world music, heady acoustic jazz, and bop, as well as various amalgamations of these styles.[8]

In 1961, while stationed with the army in Germany, Friesen taught himself the bass and sat in with players such as Johnny Griffin and Art Taylor. Back in the U.S. he began jamming in Seattle with local musicians like Larry Coryell and even sat in with visiting giants such as Miles Davis, John Coltrane, and Bill Evans. After a period of touring, in 1973 he moved to Portland, Oregon, where he opened a coffee house. Following short stints with John Handy and Marian McPartland, Friesen worked with Joe Henderson for two years, followed by a summer tour of Europe with the Billy Harper Quintet (1975). In Europe he met trumpeter Ted Curson, who showcased Friesen's solo work. At the 1977 Monterey Jazz Festival, Friesen captured the audience of over seven thousand as he opened the festival with a bass solo. Later that year he toured the West Coast with guitarist John Stowell. In 1983 his association with flutist Paul Horn resulted in a historic four-week tour of the Soviet Union.

7. Carr et al., *Jazz: The Rough Guide*, 38.
8. Kernfeld, *New Grove Dictionary of Jazz*, Vol. 1, 856.

He has since led numerous successful tours worldwide, including to Europe, South America, Japan, and Australia. During the 1980s and '90s Friesen occasionally played an Oregon bass (an electrified acoustic bass); he currently plays the Homage bass, an instrument that sounds like a normal double bass, but with a lighter feel. Friesen continues to nurture his identity through solo concerts (he is one of two or three bassists worldwide that can play a solo concert and keep an audience riveted), duo projects (with such varied artists as alto saxophonist Bud Shank, German guitarist Uwe Kropinski, and violinist Ulli Dinter), trios (his work with Randy Porter and Alan Jones has been likened to the quintessential jazz trios of Bill Evans and Keith Jarrett), and with other small groups. His original music is imbued with elements of jazz, folk, classical, and Jewish music. Based in the Pacific Northwest, where he is a legend, Friesen is acquiring a fan base in Europe, Japan, and across the rest of America.

MAY 7—HERBIE STEWARD (1926–)

b. Los Angeles, CA

Tenor and Alto Saxophonist

[SWING; BOP; BIG BAND]

Other jazz notables born on this day: Edward Inge (1906); Teddy Bunn (1910); Michael Formanek (1958); Dwayne Dolphin (1963)
Jazz notables deceased on this day: Chippie Hill (1950); Ray McKinley (1995)

♫

In September 1947 bandleader Woody Herman formed an orchestra known as the Second Herd. The band, distinguished by an impressive four-man saxophone section, came to be called the Four Brothers, a nickname it got from an early hit by that name. Prior to their stint with Herman, three of the four—Herbie Steward, Zoot Sims, and Stan Getz—played tenor saxophones together, first in a pickup band in Los Angeles and then with Gene Roland. Arranger Jimmy Giuffre, a fourth saxophonist and composer of the "Four Brothers" tune, made up the last of the original foursome. Having disbanded the previous winter, Herman assembled his new reed section from this group, replacing Giuffre (who was unavailable at the time) with Serge Chaloff on baritone. Stewart, best known for his role with the Four Brothers, did not stay very long. He left the band on December 31, 1947, before the Four Brothers album became a hit, and thus it was his replacement, Al Cohn, who came to be better known to the general public as one of the Four Brothers. In January 1949, after Sims left, Giuffre finally joined the band on tenor. A year later, when Herman formed what became known as the Third Herd, he reduced the size of his reed section and used the three-tenors-and-baritone sound extensively.

Stewart, a saxophonist renowned for his versatility, cool tone, and exceptional sight-reading, began playing professionally in his early teens. In 1947, after work in the bands of Artie Shaw (1944–46) and Alvino Rey (1946), he joined Getz, Sims, and Giuffre as an original member of Herman's Four Brothers band, though he left shortly thereafter to play as a freelance. He worked briefly with the orchestras of Shaw, Tommy Dorsey, Elliot Lawrence, and Claude Thornhill and then joined Harry James's big band (1951–54). By now, most of the musicians who had participated at one time or another in the Four Brothers experiment had scattered. For a time, Steward and Cohn worked together again with Shaw. Later, while Steward played with James, Cohn became of one New York's busiest freelance arrangers and instrumentalists. Sims toured with the Benny Goodman sextet and with Stan Kenton's band before joining Gerry Mulligan's groups. Chaloff, plagued by ill health and an addiction to heroin, stayed in Boston much of the time.

On February 11, 1957, four of the Brothers were reunited in New York for a studio recreation of the original sound. Sims and Cohn were already in town, Steward was flown in from the West Coast, and Chaloff—seated in a wheelchair as a result of spinal paralysis—took a plane from Boston. In his liner notes to their recording, titled *The Four Brothers . . . Together Again!* Leonard Feather emphasized that every quality that gave the "Brothers" phase its importance in the story of jazz can be discerned on these sides. In his estimation, the album "offers swinging testimony that nostalgia, sometimes a merely narcissistic emotion, can indeed be a wonderfully vital factor in the creation and preservation of great music."

MAY 8—KEITH JARRETT (1945–)

b. Allentown, PA

Pianist; Composer; Leader

[Avant-Garde Jazz; Contemporary Jazz; Post-Bop; Fusion]

Other jazz notables born on this day: Red Nichols (1905); Mary Lou Williams (1910)
Jazz notables deceased on this day: Joe Maini (1964); Marshal Royal (1995)

♪

During the 1970s Keith Jarrett was "the enfant terrible of jazz piano." He commanded the highest fees ever for solo performances, many of which were staged at opera houses and classical concert halls. Playing the role of prima donna to the hilt, he interrupted his concerts with quasi-philosophical pronouncements and with irksome mannerisms while at the piano. Nevertheless, "Jarrett made the piano sing a new song, and nearly everyone loved it. No one did more to stimulate interest in jazz piano among a broad audience than [he] did in his decade of prominence,"[9] and by the mid-1980s he was considered the most influential living jazz pianist.

A child prodigy, Jarrett began studying the piano at the age of three. He turned professional during his elementary school years and toured extensively, performing solo recitals of classical music in addition to his own compositions. In 1963 he moved to New York, where Art Blakey heard him and immediately hired him. His stay with Blakey's Jazz Messengers lasted only four months, but during this time he gained critical attention. In 1966 he left Blakey to join the Charles Lloyd Quartet, an important trail-blazing group.

---

9. Len Lyons, *The Great Jazz Pianists* (New York: DA Capo Press, 1983), 295.

With Lloyd he toured Europe six times, the Far East once, and the USSR once—the first time a group of modern jazz musicians had played there. From 1969 to 1971 he worked with Miles Davis, first on electric organ while Chick Corea was playing electric piano and then on both instruments after Corea's departure.

Throughout the 1970s and '80s Jarrett recorded many albums and performed regularly as solo pianist. His solo concerts were unique in that they were totally improvised. These marathon sessions caused a sensation wherever he went. During that period he also recorded and played in several highly acclaimed quartets. In 1983 he formed a Standards trio with Gary Peacock and Jack DeJohnette that over the years produced a host of brilliant interpretations of standard tunes. Jarrett continued his solo work as well, and spent 1984 performing and composing exclusively classical music. In 1985 the tension between the demands of the classical world and his need to improvise reached a crisis point. Finding himself in a state of shock, he temporarily withdrew from musical activity altogether. His recovery came at home, where, in a state of inspiration that lasted several weeks, he used ordinary cassette recorders to tape about thirty pieces of improvised "ethnic" music, a feat he accomplished at home through overdubbing and by playing all the accompanying instruments himself. Twenty-six of the pieces were later released on a double LP called *Spirits*. This experience became a defining moment in Jarrett's life.[10] In 1996, while at the height of his powers, he was stricken with chronic fatigue syndrome, which forced him to cancel all concert dates. He is currently in a state of recovery.

MAY 9—TANIA MARIA (1948–)

b. Sao Luís, Brazil

Pianist; Vocalist; Leader

[BRAZILIAN JAZZ; JAZZ-POP; POST-BOP; LATIN JAZZ]

Other jazz notables born on this day: George T. Simon (1912); Dick Morissey (1920); Dennis Chambers (1959)

Jazz notables deceased on this day: Eddie Jefferson (1979); Woody Shaw (1989); Jimmy Raney (1995); Harry "the Hipster" Gibson (1991); Lena Horne (2010)

♪

One of the original crossover artists, Brazilian-born Tania Maria has been popular in the U.S. and internationally ever since she began recording for the Concord label in 1980. Self-styled as the "Queen of Brazilian Jazz," Tania's passionate, instantly recognizable sound is a blend of jazz, funk, and the popular music of Brazil. This eclectic fusion appeals to a great variety of audiences around the world. Her untrained voice, described as "strangely attractive" by Brian Priestly,[11] is best appreciated in a live setting, though her exhilarating stage presence is sometimes overdone. On records, her rhythmic piano play-

---

10. Carr et al., *Jazz: The Rough Guide*, 385.
11. Ibid., 486.

ing is regularly upstaged by her vocals, which are frequently scat sung in unison with her instrument, in the manner of George Benson.

Born in northern Brazil, Tania became fascinated by the rhythms of Brazilian music at an early age. Encouraged by her father, a metal worker and gifted amateur musician, she began her musical training at the age of seven, studying classical piano in order to accompany him on his weekend jam sessions. An interest in her nation's popular music developed into a fascination for jazz, and by the age of thirteen she began fronting a band of professional musicians. Tania's four sisters also had musical ability, but encouraged by their mother to rise above their impoverished roots, they pursued other professions. Tania also acquiesced. She studied law and started a family, but she set aside all of that in the early 1970s so that she could pursue music, her true love. Influenced by artists as diverse as Oscar Peterson, Bill Evans, Sarah Vaughan, Anita O'Day, Antonio Carlos Jobim, and Milton Nascimiento, she developed her own fusion of Brazilian rhythms and jazz, first in the clubs of Sao Paolo, then in Paris, where she relocated in 1974.

A recording artist since 1971, Tania came to the attention of Concord Records in the late 1970s, when guitarist Charlie Byrd recommended her to the label. Byrd's visit to Brazil in the early '60s and subsequent recording with Stan Getz (*Jazz Samba*, 1962) had made him one of the first popularizers of the bossa nova in the U.S. Tania's first album with the Concord label, *Piquant* (1980), turned heads and impressed critic Leonard Feather, who gave it his prestigious Golden Feather award. By 1982 Tania's music embraced funk and pop elements and her crossover album, *Come with Me*, was nominated for a Grammy. The title track became a huge international hit and is still heard in soul and jazz clubs across Europe, Japan, and America. The album marked her breakthrough from a Brazilian jazz-pop musician to the status of an international artist. At that time Tania was based in New York, where she recorded and toured extensively. She has since settled in France once again, where her unique sound remains in vogue. For all her travel, Tania remains a Brazilian musician at heart.

MAY 10—MEL LEWIS (1929–1990)

b. Buffalo, NY; d. New York, NY

Drummer; Leader

[Post-Bop; Bop]

Other jazz notables born on this day: Pee Wee Hunt (1907)
Jazz notables deceased on this day: James Reese Europe (1919)

♪

During the swing era, big bands were so closely associated with dancing that their revival in the 1950s required higher standards of musical proficiency. A purely musical big band—no dancers, no singers, no hits, and no nostalgia—was a risky proposition back then, despite the growing number of innovative jazz composers and arrangers. Of the few bands that did survive the swing era, only those led by Woody Herman and Stan Kenton dared show their disdain for dancers. From 1960 to 1964 famed baritone saxophonist Gerry Mulligan, a veteran arranger for postwar big bands led by Gene Krupa, Claude Thornhill, Elliot Lawrence, and Kenton and a leader of the cool-jazz movement, led a thirteen-piece concert ensemble called the Concert Jazz Band (CJB). Using new voicings, a wider span of instruments, and longer melody lines, the band debuted to critical acclaim and lasted long enough to spur a big band restoration. Mulligan hired the best musicians available and turned them over to outstanding writers such as valve trombonist Bob Brookmeyer. The band didn't have a pianist per se—Mulligan and Brookmeyer filled in when necessary—but it had a reliable rhythm section in bassist Bill Crow and the understated drummer Mel Lewis, a master of the big band idiom. Shortly after the demise of the CJB, Lewis joined forces with Thad Jones, long-time trumpeter with Count Basie's Orchestra (1954–63), taking Mulligan's gambit another step by creating a long-standing Monday night orchestra at the Village Vanguard.

Lewis's father was a drummer in the Buffalo area, and due to the scarcity of players during World War II, Mel followed in his father's footsteps. He began working professionally by the age of thirteen and he performed with several dance bands after that, including one led by Ray Anthony (1949–1950 and 1953–1954). At this time he changed his name from Sokoloff to Lewis, for Anthony did not want it to be known that he had hired a Jew.[12] During the mid-1950s Lewis gained recognition in the jazz world for his work with Kenton (1954–57), helping to generate the large ensemble's swing. In 1957 he settled in Los Angeles, where he worked as a studio drummer and in the big bands of Terry Gibbs, Gerald Wilson, and Mulligan. By 1965 Lewis had settled in New York, where he and Jones formed their orchestra, an eighteen-piece rehearsal band of leading studio jazz musicians that grew to be one of the top big bands in jazz.

In 1979, when Jones surprised everyone by his sudden departure for Europe, Lewis became the orchestra's sole leader. He continued the Monday night tradition at the Vanguard until his death in 1990; Brookmeyer, an original member of the ensemble, assumed Jones's role as music director. Some of the band's outstanding members during this period were Tom Harrell, Steve Coleman, Kenny Garrett, Bob Mintzer, Joe Lovano, Ted Nash, Gary Smulyan, Kenny Werner, Rufus Reid, and Marc Johnson. Lewis was diagnosed with cancer in 1985, but he continued working until a few weeks before his death. The ensemble continued after his death, when it became known as the Vanguard Jazz Orchestra.

MAY 11—KING OLIVER (1885–1938)

b. New Orleans, LA; d. Savannah, GA

Cornetist; Bandleader

[NEW ORLEANS JAZZ; CLASSIC JAZZ]

Other jazz notables born on this day: J. C. Higginbotham (1906); Carla Bley (1938)
Jazz notables deceased on this day: Johnny Hodges (1970)

---

12. Kernfeld, *New Grove Dictionary of Jazz*, Vol. 2, 586.

"I loved Joe Oliver," Louis Armstrong once said; "[h]e did more for young musicians . . . than anyone I know of." But no one messed with the King. A strict disciplinarian, he kept a brick near him on the bandstand to bang on the floor if his men didn't heed the stomping foot with which he started and stopped each number. According to one eyewitness, Oliver was appearing at a cabaret called the Abadie when he snatched the crown as New Orleans' finest cornetist from Freddie Keppard, Buddy Bolden's heir. For days, Oliver was annoyed that Keppard was drawing large crowds to another club just down the street. One day he went outside, lifted his horn to his mouth, and blew a sound so powerful and compelling that people poured forth from other spots along the street to witness its source. But in the end, it was neither Oliver's volume nor his competitiveness that won him his audience. It was his technique. An expert with mutes, he was able to create most any sound with his horn. According to Mutt Carey, who imitated Oliver, "Joe did most of his playing with cups, glasses, buckets and mutes . . . He could make his horn sound like a holy roller meeting!"[13]

Joe "King" Oliver is generally considered one of the most important musicians in the New Orleans style. Although originally a trombonist, by 1905 he was playing cornet regularly with various New Orleans bands. At this point he was still a restricted player, but around 1914 he improved to the point where he and his band were causing a stir, and by 1917 he was being billed as "King" by bandleader Kid Ory. As an ambitious businessman, he knew that jazz was moving upstream to Chicago, and that back home a new prodigy—Louis Armstrong—was ready to overthrow every other king in the city. So in 1919 he joined bassist Bill Johnson and clarinetist Lawrence Duhé at the Dreamland Ballroom in Chicago. By 1920 he became leader of the band and took his new team to California. After an unsuccessful year (Mutt Carey had arrived there first, with Kid Ory, and audiences saw Oliver as an imitator rather than the originator of Carey's muted tricks), Oliver returned to Chicago and opened up at the Lincoln Gardens with his Creole Jazz Band. He sent for his protégé, Louis Armstrong, and with Johnny Dodds, Honoré Dutrey, Lil Harden, and drummer Baby Dodds as a core, Oliver fashioned a remarkable band. Night after night the Gardens was packed with dancers and musicians listening to what George Wettling called "the hottest band ever to sit on a bandstand."

The great band broke up in 1924, after the Dodds brothers discovered that Oliver was withholding money from his sidemen's salaries. In 1927 he took a new package to New York, but his music was now behind the times. His last ten years paint a sad picture of a man overtaken by jazz fashion. By 1936 he was working as a janitor in a Savannah poolroom, stranded there after unsuccessful tours in the South. "He died in Savannah and was buried in the Bronx: a sad way to get back to New York."[14]

---

13. Carr et al., *Jazz: The Rough Guide*, 574.
14. Ibid.

MAY 12—GARY PEACOCK (1935–)

b. Burley, ID

Bassist

[AVANT-GARDE JAZZ; FREE JAZZ; POST-BOP]

Other jazz notables born on this day: Gerry Wiggins (1922)
Jazz notables deceased on this day: Victor Feldman (1987)

♪

As noted earlier (May 8), pianist Keith Jarrett's impassioned jazz ranks him among the leading keyboard artists and bandleaders of the late twentieth century. He deserves to be considered one of the major American musicians of his era for the astonishing variety and quality of his work. He also deserves credit for helping return younger jazz musicians to acoustic music, by showing there was an audience for it. His introspective solo concerts earned him a huge international following, which probably helped explain the unusually large audience (by jazz standards) garnered by his long-running trio with bassist Gary Peacock and drummer Jack DeJohnette. Following his more experimental efforts, undertaken by two groups during the 1970s that came to be called the American and European quartets, in the 1980s he led his Standards trio with Peacock and DeJohnette. Jarrett's apparent goal was to explore standard tunes in a freewheeling manner similar to that of the Bill Evans trios of the 1960s. Over the years this trio, true to its name, produced a host of brilliant interpretations of classic songs.

Peacock grew up in the Pacific Northwest and played piano and drums early on. When he was seventeen he went to Los Angeles to study drums and vibraphone. He joined the army in 1954, and while stationed in Germany he played with a military band and as a pianist in his own jazz band. In 1956, when his bass player was released, he switched to the bass, remaining in Germany after his discharge to play briefly with Albert Mangelsdorff, Hans Koller, Attila Zoller, and others. A subtle but adventurous bassist, Peacock's flexibility and consistent creativity became an asset to various important bands. Upon his return to Los Angeles he toured with Terry Gibbs and then performed locally with important jazzmen such as Harold Land, Art Pepper, Dexter Gordon, Bud Shank, Barney Kessel, Don Ellis, and Paul Bley, among others.

After moving to New York in 1962 Peacock worked with a variety of progressive musicians including Bill Evans (1962–63), Paul Bley, Jimmy Giuffre, Rahsaan Roland Kirk, and George Russell. In 1964, after a brief stint with Miles Davis, Peacock started an association with Albert Ayler, preferring free jazz to straightahead jazz. His adventurous recordings and tour of Europe that year in a quartet with Don Cherry and Sunny Murray established him as one of the most accomplished double bass players in jazz. But he suffered a perforated ulcer before that tour and soon afterwards largely withdrew from music. He studied Eastern philosophy and medicine and in 1969 moved to Japan, where he recorded with Sadao Watanabe, Masabumi Kikuchi, and several visiting Americans. He returned to the U.S. in 1972 and studied biology at the University of Washington

(1972–76). In 1977, after a tour of Japan with Bley and Barry Altschul, he made several recordings (and wrote a number of compositions) for the ECM label as a leader, notably an album that year with Jarrett and DeJohnette. From 1983 the group worked under Jarrett's name, becoming one of the most popular groups in jazz over the next dozen years.

MAY 13—GIL EVANS (1912–1988)

b. Toronto, Canada; d. Cuernavaca, Mexico

Arranger; Composer; Pianist; Bandleader

[MODERN BIG BAND; POST-BOP; FUSION; COOL]

Other jazz notables born on this day: Red Garland (1923)
Jazz notables deceased on this day: Chet Baker (1988); Tommy Turrentine (1997)

♪

In the winter of 1947 and 1948 a steady stream of musicians filed in and out of an apartment building on East Fifty-Fifth Street in Manhattan. The apartment was close to Fifty-Second Street, three blocks from the row of clubs on the West Side that since the mid-1930s constituted the living heart of jazz in New York City. Musicians would drop by Evans's one-room cellar home before or after work to socialize and have intellectual discussions. Regulars included pianist John Lewis (founding member of the Modern Jazz Quartet), drummers Max Roach and Kenny Clarke, composer George Russell, saxophonist Lee Konitz, arranger/baritone sax player Gerry Mulligan, trombonist J.J. Johnson, and eventually trumpeter Miles Davis. Evans and Davis hit it off immediately, for their ideas about music were very close.

The result was the formation of a landmark, though short-lived, nine-piece group that played live for two weeks at the Royal Roost in September 1948. In addition to the usual bop quintet instrumentation, the nonet featured an unusual horn section, consisting of French horn, tuba, trombone, and baritone sax. The group's urbane sound, the subtle, innovative scoring, and the calm, unhurried solos, seemed to be a reaction against the frenetic excesses of bop and ushered in what became known as the cool style of jazz. The band was a failure as a working unit, but recorded twelve sides between January 1949 and March 1950 that sold as singles and were finally collected on a 1957 album titled *Birth of the Cool*, which has since become recognized as a classic.

Born in Canada of Australian parents, Evans was raised in the American West and learned to love jazz by listening to Louis Armstrong and Duke Ellington over the radio. A self-taught musician, he led a band in California that in 1938 was taken over by singer Skinnay Ennis; Evans stayed on as arranger. In 1941 he joined Claude Thornhill's new group in the same capacity. Thornhill's orchestra was a distinctly unorthodox dance band that featured impressionistic, slow-moving arrangements with instrumentation then unusual in jazz: French horns, tuba, flute and piccolo. Emphasizing ensemble over improvised solo, Evans's scores for Thornhill produced a rich, dark-textured, "cool" orchestral sound foreshadowed in the works of Ellington. Later, in his work with Davis's nonet,

Evans captured the essential sound and texture of the Thornhill big band, using the smallest instrumentation possible. Oddly, critics and jazz audiences alike ignored Evans's work for both Davis and Thornhill.

In 1957, almost a decade after the *Birth of the Cool* sessions, Evans renewed his association with Davis. This time they put together three orchestral masterpieces: *Miles Ahead* (1957), *Porgy and Bess* (1959), and *Sketches of Spain* (1960). In these seminal albums, which adapted the classical concerto form to jazz, Davis was the only soloist, backed by a stellar nineteen-piece orchestra. The highly imaginative arrangements, combined with the soulful playing of Davis, refined and expanded the cool approach he and Davis spearheaded in the 1940s. With Davis's *Kind of Blue* (1959), these recordings remain among the all-time favorite albums in jazz.

MAY 14—SIDNEY BECHET (1887–1941)

b. New Orleans, LA; d. Paris, France

Clarinetist; Soprano Saxophonist

[NEW ORLEANS JAZZ; CLASSIC JAZZ; DIXIELAND]

Other jazz notables born on this day: Zutty Singleton (1898)
Jazz notables deceased on this day: Sidney Bechet (1959); George Treadwell (1967); Elmer Snowden (1973); Paul Gonsalves (1974); Frank Sinatra (1998)

♪

Sidney Bechet, one of classical jazz's greatest talents, was also one of jazz's most legendary figures. Known for his prima donna attitude, he attempted to dominate every musical situation he was in, and usually succeeded. Because of his combative nature, he became involved in numerous feuds. He was once deported from London for getting into a fight with a prostitute, and he spent eleven months in a French prison for a gunfight with another musician on a busy street in Paris. Prickly and troublesome, he also responded to the world with passion—he had a brief but tumultuous love affair with the great blues singer Bessie Smith—and this warmth is evident in his music. This barely controlled passion was one of the hallmarks of his style. During the 1920s Bechet traveled regularly to Europe, playing to admirers such as the Prince of Wales and the king of England. In 1949 he settled permanently in France, where he became a major celebrity and a national hero.

Bechet grew up in a musical family in New Orleans; his older brother, later a dentist, played clarinet. Sidney admitted he learned to play the clarinet by sneaking his brother's instrument out of its case and practicing it on the sly. Late one afternoon in 1907, a band led by cornetist Freddie Keppard was scheduled to play at the Bechet home. The clarinetist was late for the engagement and the band started to play without him. Suddenly, from inside the house, a clarinet joined in. It was Sidney, atop his brother's dentist chair, playing as loudly as he could. The boy was just nine years old and entirely self-taught. Despite parental opposition, by the time he was eleven or twelve he was playing regularly around

New Orleans, sitting in with some of the best bands in town. In New Orleans brass bands, the cornetist was considered the lead. But being second best was not good enough for Bechet, who began playing the clarinet with such power that he routinely overshadowed cornetists. In addition to his prowess as a musician, Bechet acquired a reputation for drunkenness and forgetfulness. One night, when he showed up for a job drunk and without his clarinet, someone lent him an E-flat instrument (instead of the standard B-flat). He played the whole night with it, transposing everything as he went along.

Bechet went to Chicago in 1917 and then joined Will Marion Cook's concert band, with which he traveled to New York and then to Europe, where he introduced jazz improvisation to amazed audiences everywhere. While in London, he ran across a straight soprano saxophone in a junk shop, liked it, and began to feature it onstage, making headlines. Though he was an extraordinary clarinetist, his genius was conveyed most effectively on the soprano saxophone, which became his primary instrument for the rest of his life. Bechet mastered the soprano to such an extent that few other jazz musicians were willing or able to challenge him, and until John Coltrane revived the instrument's popularity in the 1960s, he had the field virtually to himself.

MAY 15—EDMOND HALL (1901–1967)

b. New Orleans, LA; d. Boston, MA

Clarinetist

[NEW ORLEANS JAZZ; SWING]

Other jazz notables born on this day: Karin Krog (1937)
Jazz notables deceased on this day: Adrian Rollini (1956)

♪

In 1936, when Nick Rongetti opened the first Dixieland jazz club in Greenwich Village, he asked Bobby Hackett to lead the house band. Hackett hired Eddie Condon, a relatively unimportant guitarist from Chicago, who quickly became the central figure of a group of white Midwestern players that included Bud Freeman, Miff Mole, Jimmy McPartland, Pee Wee Russell, Max Kaminsky, and a few African-Americans such as Sidney Bechet and clarinetist Edmond Hall. The music these men played in the late 1930s and early '40s was not, in a strict sense, New Orleans music, nor was it the same thing they had pioneered in the 1920s. As the players matured, the music evolved, and soon other clubs in the Dixieland tradition opened in New York and elsewhere. In the early 1940s Condon organized a series of jam session at New York's Town Hall that were broadcast over the radio, and these helped widen the audience for the music. In 1945 Condon opened his own club, which was immediately successful.

Edmond Hall was an anomaly. He was one of the few blacks to make a career playing in the Dixieland style—although he disliked the music—and he was also the last African-American clarinetist to make a name in jazz. Considered one of the finest Dixieland clarinetists of his generation, Hall used a sharp attack and one of the fastest and broadest vibratos in the business, which gave his work a driving quality ideally suited to the

Dixieland style. Though it had taken him a long time to establish his own musical individuality, by the early 1940s he had a distinctive and gritty sound on the clarinet that was immediately recognizable.[15]

Raised as one of four clarinet-playing sons of the early clarinetist Edward Hall, Edmond worked in many bands in New Orleans and throughout the South before going to New York in 1928. There he became a featured soloist with the Claude Hopkins Orchestra, and despite the appalling touring conditions suffered by black musicians during the 1930s, he remained with Hopkins until 1935. With the exception of a short stint in 1937 with Lucky Millinder's big band, he concentrated on small groups for the rest of his life, most of which played in the Dixieland style. Possibly at the urging of John Hammond, Hall became a regular fixture at Café Society, starting in 1939, and over the next seven years he worked at the downtown and uptown locations of the club with Joe Sullivan, Henry "Red" Allen, and as a member of Teddy Wilson's sextet (1941–44). In 1942 he turned down the opportunity to join Duke Ellington's orchestra and began working with Condon (including appearances on his *Town Hall Concert* radio series). After four years as a bandleader in Boston (1946–50), he joined the newly formed house band at Condon's New York club. In the mid-1950s he toured the world as a member of Louis Armstrong's All-Stars (1955–58), and then resumed working with Condon and with his own quartet before making his final recording at Hammond's 1967 *Spirituals to Swing* concert. Much loved by all who knew him, Hall died suddenly from a heart attack after shoveling snow from his driveway.

MAY 16—WOODY HERMAN (1913–1987)

b. Milwaukee, WI; d. Los Angeles, CA

Bandleader; Clarinetist; Alto Saxophonist; Vocalist

[SWING; COOL; BIG BAND]

Other jazz notables born on this day: Dud Bascomb (1916); Betty Carter (1929); Friedrich Gulda (1930); Billy Cobham (1944)
Jazz notables deceased on this day: Django Reinhardt (1953); Hank Jones (2010)

♪

A fine swing clarinetist, an altoist influenced by Johnny Hodges, and a spirited blues vocalist, Woodrow "Woody" Herman's greatest significance to jazz was as the leader of a long line of big bands.[16] His openness to the desires of his soloists, coupled with his knack for hiring talented section players, enabled him to maintain continuity between his different bands while keeping his repertoire quite modern. His rare ability to assemble and sustain bands notable for the quality of their musicians became evident in the late years of World War II, when his group consisted of brilliant improvisers whose ensemble playing was vigorous and expansive. Igor Stravinsky was so impressed by its sound that in 1945 he composed his "Ebony Concerto" for the band.

---

15. Bogdanov et al., *All Music Guide to Jazz*, 528.
16. Ibid., 586.

As a child Herman sang in vaudeville. He started playing saxophone when he was eleven and four years later he was a professional musician. After picking up early experience with various big bands, he joined the Isham Jones orchestra in 1934. Two years later, when the veteran bandleader decided to disband, the members elected Herman as leader. The great majority of the early Herman recordings feature the bandleader as a ballad vocalist, but it was his instrumentals that caught on, and the ensemble became known as "The Band That Plays the Blues." His first band and his down-to-earth clarinet playing (as opposed to that of Goodman and Shaw) did much to live up to that reputation and in 1939 he had his first hit with the band's theme song, "At the Woodchopper's Ball." By 1943 the orchestra took its first steps toward becoming the Herd, and by the end of that year Woody had what was essentially a brand new orchestra. The band, later renamed the First Herd, became internationally famous for the force and originality of its music.

Herman disbanded late in 1946 to help his wife overcome her alcohol addiction, but by mid-1947 he had a new orchestra, the Second Herd, known thereafter as the Four Brothers band for its impressive saxophone section. Despite such popular numbers as "Four Brothers," "The Goof and I," and "Early Autumn," the band struggled financially. After its demise, Herman continued to lead other bands, and their high level of musicianship assured his ongoing reputation.

By the 1970s, as one of only several surviving jazz-oriented bandleaders from the swing era (along with Duke Ellington, Count Basie, Benny Goodman, and Stan Kenton) still touring the world with a big band, Herman returned to straightahead jazz, but by then he was under fire from the IRS due to an incompetent manager from the 1960s who had failed to pay thousands of dollars of taxes out of the sidemen's salaries. The IRS seized all his assets, including his home, which he rented back from the government. Falling inexorably into poverty, Herman was forced to continue touring and working into his old age. Despite deteriorating health, he celebrated his fiftieth anniversary as a bandleader with the formation of a new orchestra in 1986, a year before his death.

MAY 17—JACKIE MCLEAN (1932–2006)

b. New York, NY; d. Hartford, CT

Alto Saxophonist

[POST-BOP; HARD BOP]

Other jazz notables born on this day: Paul Quinichette (1916); Dewey Redman (1931); David Izenzon (1932)

Jazz notables deceased on this day: Lars Gullin (1976)

♪

"Jazz was born in a whiskey barrel," wrote Artie Shaw, "grew up on marijuana, and is about to expire on heroin." Alcohol had always been part of the jazz world, and marijuana had been part of it since the 1920s. But heroin was different—"drastic stuff," according to Louis Armstrong—and in the late 1940s it seemed to be everywhere. After World War II "[h]eroin came on the scene like a tidal wave," Jackie McLean remembered. He would be engulfed by it and would remain addicted for eighteen years.[17] For a time many of the most gifted musicians in jazz were on narcotics, including Art Blakey, Chet Baker, John Coltrane, Tadd Dameron, Dexter Gordon, Billie Holiday, Gerry Mulligan, Fats Navarro, Charlie Parker, Max Roach, Red Rodney, Sonny Rollins, and Sonny Stitt. Tenor saxophonist Stan Getz once tried to support his habit by holding up a drugstore, for which he spent six months in jail, only to return to drugs and alcohol as soon as he got out. "Heroin was our badge," Rodney recalled, "the thing that made us different from the rest of the world . . . It was the thing that gave us membership in a unique club, and for this membership we gave up everything else in the world. Every ambition. Every desire. Everything. It ruined most of the people." And it helped ruin Jackie McLean as well.

McLean long had his own sound, playing in a raw, urgent style that was grounded in bop but also deeply affected by free jazz; his unique sound is instantly recognizable. He was one of the few bop-oriented players of the early 1950s to explore free jazz in the '60s, drawing from the new music those qualities that fit his musical personality. Jackie was a close friend of Charlie Parker, and although they never recorded together, his style is an oblique reflection of Parker's. His tart sound and forceful lines have influenced an entire generation of altoists.

The son of guitarist John McLean, Jackie started on alto when he was fifteen. As a teenager he was friends with such neighbors as Bud Powell, Thelonious Monk, and Rollins. Powell recommended him to Miles Davis, with whom McLean worked in 1951 and 1952 and made his first recordings. These sessions were followed by performances with such jazz notables as Paul Bley, George Wallington, Charles Mingus, and, from 1956 to 1958, as a member of Blakey's Jazz Messengers. As a consequence of his addiction, McLean's cabaret card was rescinded in New York, meaning he was banned from playing in clubs. He recorded a classic series of twenty-one Blue Note albums between 1959 and 1967, some of them quite original and intense. After touring Japan in 1965 and Scandinavia in 1966, he began part-time teaching while counseling users of narcotics. He joined the faculty of the Hartt School of Music (Hartford, Connecticut) in 1968 and became less active as a player during the 1970s. In the late 1980s he returned to a more active playing schedule, recording with the passion of his earlier days.

MAY 18—BIG JOE TURNER (1911–1985)

b. Kansas City, MO; d. Inglewood, CA

Vocalist

[Jump Blues; Swing; Rock & Roll; R&B; Urban Blues]

Other jazz notables born on this day: Pops Foster (1892); Kai Winding (1922); Mike Zwerin (1930); Jim McNeely (1949)
Jazz notables deceased on this day: Tyree Glenn (1974); Vernon Brown (1979)

---

17. Ward and Burns, *Jazz, A History*, 358.

BLUE NOTES

♪

When the notorious Tom Pendergast began running Kansas City in 1926, the town became the wildest place in America. "If you want to see some sin, forget about Paris," said an editorialist for the Omaha *Herald*, "go to Kansas City." There had been nothing like it in America since Storyville. Clubs, cabarets, dance halls and brothels flourished in this prodigal's paradise, with names like the Pla-Mor Ballroom, the Reno Club (where for two dollars a trip, taxi dancers and their clients climbed constantly up and down a staircase that led to bedrooms on the second floor); the Hey-Hay (where customers sat on bales of hay); Dante's Inferno (where waitresses wore devil costumes); and the Chesterfield (where the waitresses wore nothing at all). Fast and gaudy, sensual and brassy, Kansas City was Prohibition's Vanity Fair. Musicians, scrambling for work in the rest of the country, had no trouble finding it in Kansas City. And what they found there was a distinct way of dealing with the blues. As Albert Murray has written: "The special drive of Kansas City music is . . . a device for herding or even stampeding the blues away." Kansas City musicians did not so much play the blues as *stomp* them, and singers did not so much sing the blues as *shout* them.[18]

The premier blues shouter of the postwar era was Big Joe Turner, a resilient figure in the history of blues who effortlessly spanned boogie-woogie, jump blues, even the first wave of rock and roll, enjoying great success in each genre.[19] Called "the Boss of the Blues," Turner's powerful physique (six feet two and weighing 250 lbs.) certainly matched his vocal might. A product of the wide-open Kansas City scene, by the age of fourteen he was working as a barman and cook at the Kingfisher Club, where he became known as "the singing bartender," for he simultaneously tended bar and sang the blues. In this role he attracted the attention of such bandleaders as Bennie Moten, Andy Kirk, and Count Basie, with whom he subsequently toured.

At the Kingfisher he met boogie piano master Pete Johnson, and the two formed a partnership that lasted throughout the 1940s including as co-owners of the Blue Room, a club in Los Angeles. In 1936 the pair traveled to New York under the sponsorship of John Hammond, where they appeared on the fabled *From Spirituals to Swing* concert (1938), kicking off a boogie-woogie craze that landed them a long-running slot at Café Society (along with piano giants Meade Lux Lewis and Albert Ammons). At that time they recorded the thunderous "Roll 'Em Pete," with spectacular piano playing by Johnson and a forceful, half-shouting vocal style by Turner. Throughout the 1940s and '50s Turner toured extensively and recorded many popular hits, including "Shake, Rattle and Roll" (1954), which precipitated a revolution in popular music. For a time it looked like he might become a rock star, though in the 1950s he returned to his jazz roots, proving with albums such as the classic *Boss of the Blues* (1956) that he was a jazzman at heart.

---

18. Ward and Burns, *Jazz: A History*, 196–97.
19. Bogdanov, *All Music Guide to Jazz*, 1260.

MAY 19—GEORGIE AULD (1919–1990)

b. Toronto, Canada; d. Palm Springs, CA

Tenor Saxophonist; Bandleader

[SWING; BOP]

Other jazz notables born on this day: Cecil McBee (1935)
Jazz notables deceased on this day: Elmo Hope (1967); Coleman Hawkins (1969); Teddy Hill (1978); Susannah McCorkle (2001)

♪

Artie Shaw, a much admired bandleader, formed eight or nine completely different musical ensembles before quitting music altogether in 1955. In 1938 he inaugurated his first successful big band and immediately began recording huge hits. His style, described by Gary Giddins as "evocative, sensuous, [and] seductively serious," was contagious. Of all the Shaw orchestras, this was by far the most popular. In addition to Shaw's superb clarinet playing, the band featured two tenor saxophonists, Georgie Auld and Tony Pastor, in addition to the powerful drumming of Buddy Rich and vocals by Helen Forrest. During 1938 to 1939 this ensemble was way ahead of the competition, dethroning Benny Goodman's orchestra and riding a crest of popularity until the moody Shaw quit briefly in 1939, making one of his many sojourns away from the music business. When he returned six months later, he formed a new and innovative band, but for the first three months of that interim, Auld maintained the band and its legacy as Shaw's replacement.

John Altwerger (Georgie Auld) had a long and varied career, adapting his tenor sound to many different musical situations. He moved from Canada to the U.S. in the late 1920s and switched from alto to tenor after hearing a Coleman Hawkins recording.[20] Following a brief stint with his own band, he came to prominence with Bunny Berigan (1937–38), in whose band he sounded much like Charlie Barnet, a popular saxophonist/bandleader. After spending a year with Shaw (1938–39), he played with Benny Goodman's orchestra and sextet, where he jammed with a group that included Goodman, Cootie Williams, Charlie Christian, and occasionally Count Basie on piano. After another spell with Shaw in 1942, Auld formed his own big band (1943–46), an excellent transitional unit between swing and bop that at various times included such modernists as Dizzy Gillespie, Erroll Garner, and Sarah Vaughan, with arrangements by the modernistic Tadd Dameron.

During the late 1940s Auld aligned himself firmly with the bebop movement, playing modern jazz at the Three Deuces and running his own club on Fifty-Second Street before joining Billy Eckstine's big band. In 1949 he formed a ten-piece band that performed in a bop-influenced style. After playing with Count Basie's octet (1950) and his own small band, he worked for ten years as a freelance. On account of lung problems he moved to the sunnier climate of California, where he opened his own nightclub, the Melody Room. Like Shaw, Auld formed yet another band, featuring swing-style arrangements written by Billy May. In the 1960s and '70s he worked mainly in popular music, playing in

20. Bogdanov, *All Music Guide to Jazz*, 49.

bands in Las Vegas and in Los Angeles studios. He occasionally formed bands that toured frequently in Japan, where he achieved great success. For a half-century Auld kept pace with stylistic developments without losing his musical identity. Yet unlike Artie Shaw, he never quit.

MAY 20—MILT GABLER (1911–2001)

b. New York, NY; d. New York, NY

Record Producer

[CLASSIC JAZZ]

Other jazz notables born on this day: Victor Lewis (1950)
Jazz notables deceased on this day: Bubber Miley (1932)

♪

By the end of the 1930s there was resentment in the jazz world against the swing bands and a corresponding desire to see the older jazz revived. A major effect was an interest in jazz record collecting. Readers should realize that during the 1930s all the early jazz records were out of print. Towards the end of the decade this gap began to be filled by reissues, at first by private labels, then gradually by the big three record labels, Victor, Decca, and Columbia, who had bought out the smaller labels in the early days of the Depression and had the old records in their vaults. Around this time a handful of small record companies started up, dedicated to recording the pure jazz. The earliest and most important of these was Commodore, founded by Milton Gabler.

On January 17, 1938, the day after Benny Goodman's triumphant concert at Carnegie Hall, jazz history of another sort was made in Gabler's small recording studio in Manhattan. Goodman's pianist Jess Stacy was there, and with him were five veterans of the early days of jazz in Chicago—the guitarist Eddie Condon, drummer George Wettling, trombonist Georg Brunis, saxophonist Bud Freeman, and clarinetist Pee Wee Russell—and two veterans of the small-group jazz they had known as youths, bassist Artie Shapiro and the cornetist Bobby Hackett. The five sides cut that day were true to the spirit of the 1920s; and they were superbly recorded. This was the first recording session for Commodore, and Gabler had gone to extraordinary lengths to get it right. Since the music he was recording was collectively improvised, he wanted to be able to hear each instrument clearly all of the time. New Orleans may have been "the cradle of jazz," Gabler said, but he wanted Commodore to be its "iron lung."[21]

During the Depression years college kids and professional record collectors had begun hunting for rare copies of older recordings. In 1930 Milt started the Commodore Music Shop in his father's radio store in New York, the first record shop to specialize in jazz, and in 1935 he began reissuing and selling a series of out-of-print jazz records on his United Hot Clubs of America label. His music shop was just nine feet wide, but it was a jazz mecca for collectors from all over the country. Gabler sold every kind of jazz

---

21. Ward and Burns, *Jazz: A History*, 263.

to his customers, but he preferred freewheeling small-group jazz. From 1938 until 1950 he supervised almost ninety Commodore sessions involving more than one hundred and fifty musicians, among them Eddie Condon's groups, Billie Holiday ("Strange Fruit" was recorded by Commodore when Columbia shied away from the controversial song), Coleman Hawkins, Lester Young, Jelly Roll Morton, and many other stars of swing and New Orleans jazz. In addition to Commodore, Gabler was quite active as a producer for Decca until 1973. He later spent several years remastering the Commodore catalogue for its eventual reissue by Mosaic in the late 1980s (totaling sixty-seven LPs). The sort of small-group jazz Gabler and his independent Commodore label recorded in the shadow of the big bands proved to be some of the era's most exciting music.

MAY 21—FATS WALLER (1904–1943)

b. New York, NY; d. Kansas City, MO

Pianist; Organist; Vocalist; Bandleader; Composer

[STRIDE; CLASSIC JAZZ; JIVE; SWING]

Other jazz notables born on this day: Christian McBride (1972)
Jazz notables deceased on this day: Blue Mitchell (1979); Eddie Moore (1990)

♪

One of the century's most irresistible entertainers, Thomas "Fats" Waller was a singer, composer, and comedian of great charm and ability. He was also one of the greatest pianists ever known to jazz. A pupil of James P. Johnson, he turned professional at the age of fifteen and became one of the greatest of the Harlem stride pianists. From 1934 until his death in 1943 he was one of the hottest entertainment properties in the country. A bon vivant, whose popularity for a time rivaled that of Louis Armstrong, he could party and jam all night. By his mid-twenties he was an alcoholic, drinking almost constantly. He was famous for showing up at a recording session with a hangover and without the required original music. Then he would sit down at the piano and compose musical gems. He wrote hundreds of enduring tunes, including "Ain't Misbehavin'" and "Honeysuckle Rose," some of them conjured up spontaneously, literally within minutes.

But there was another, more private side, to Waller. He was the favorite child of a mother whose early death he never accepted and the son of a devout lay preacher whom he permanently alienated when he chose to play what his father viewed as "the devil's music." Because his father wanted him to follow a religious career, he first played organ in his father's church, calling the instrument the "God box." Fats pioneered the use of the pipe organ and the Hammond organ in jazz, and despite his later pianistic acclaim, he always loved the organ best. He was one of the few keyboardists to play successful jazz on that instrument, writing the first jazz piece in three-quarter time for it, the "Jitterbug Waltz." During his teens, when he played the organ for silent movies at the Lincoln Theatre in Harlem, he gave lessons and encouragement to a young fan who came from New Jersey to hear him, Bill (later called "Count") Basie.

One of his few opportunities to play the organ for a wide audience came during a year he spent on the staff of a Cincinnati radio station in the early 1930s. Following his popular late night program there, where he sang and clowned and played the driving stride piano that was his specialty, the station offered a program of quiet organ music. The organist, unknown to his audience, was Fats Waller, playing with rare contentment. Ashton Stevens, a Chicago critic, once observed that the organ was the instrument of Waller's heart, the piano of his stomach.

In 1932 Waller hired a manager with a broad show business background and his new exposure turned him into a popular entertainer, with appearances in Hollywood films such as the all-black film *Stormy Weather* (1943). His attempts to balance an extensive touring schedule with film appearances and a recording schedule were short lived, however, for the demanding routine, coupled with heavy eating, drinking, alimony squabbles, and personal frustrations (such as not being taken more seriously as a musician) finally wore him down. He became ill while in Hollywood and died of pneumonia while riding the train back to New York. Despite the success of his public persona, Fats died a disappointed man.

MAY 22—SUN RA (1914–1993)

b. Birmingham, AL; d. Birmingham, AL

Composer; Bandleader; Keyboardist

[EXPERIMENTAL BIG BAND; AVANT-GARDE JAZZ; FREE JAZZ]

Other jazz notables born on this day: Eddie Edwards (1891)
Jazz notables deceased on this day: Hampton Hawes (1977); Lorez Alexandria (2001)

♪

A number of stylistically related African-American musicians from Chicago began to gain attention during the late 1950s and early '60s and finally received wide critical recognition during the late 1970s. The music of these players helped define avant-garde jazz for the 1960s and '70s. This stream of musicians can be considered under three headings: performers associated with bandleader Sun Ra; the Art Ensemble of Chicago (formed in 1969); and the World Saxophone Quartet (formed in 1976).

The first popular expression of this avant-garde movement in Chicago can be found in the work of Sun Ra (Herman Blount), an immensely creative pianist, composer, and arranger who had been active as a professional musician since the 1930s. Among jazz musicians he was one of the most controversial, for his music appeared to exist as an adjunct to a complicated religion. His concerts evolved into spectacular stage shows with outlandish costumes, all inspired by science fiction and Egyptian mythology.[22] Whenever he was asked about his background, he generally responded with explanations that he was part of an angel race, sent from another planet to rescue the planet Earth. A pioneer of avant-garde jazz and free improvisation, Sun Ra was one of the first jazz musicians to

---

22. Bogdanov, *All Music Guide to Jazz*, 1045.

experiment heavily with synthesizers, African rhythms, and modal improvisation. His concerts were multimedia events, involving singing, dancing, costumes, and unusual lighting. Toward the end of his career he even featured plate twirlers and fire-eaters in his colorful shows. A documentary film, *Sun Ra: A Joyful Noise*, was produced in 1980 to expose a larger audience to the band's musical and philosophical concepts.

Born with a remarkable ear for music, Herman Blount taught himself to read music and play the piano by the age of ten. While in high school, he toured in bands that traveled as far north as Chicago, where he settled in 1946. He began working at the Club DeLisa as a pianist and arranger for Fletcher Henderson's band (1946–47), and then continued his association with the club over the next five years, writing arrangements for Cotton Club-type stage shows that became the basis for his band's costumed theatrics. In 1951, after a period immersed in Egyptian studies, he joined a secret society "whose members studied the occult, advocated a form of Black Nationalism, and frequently preached about outer space."[23] He renamed himself Le Sony'r Ra (Sun Ra became his stage name) and formed a big band (which he called the Arkestra) that became significant in Chicago's avant-garde jazz movement. By 1960, when he moved to New York, he had attracted a considerable following, particularly among European jazz enthusiasts. Along with Cecil Taylor and Ornette Coleman, Sun Ra significantly influenced the new jazz styles of the 1960s. In 1968 he relocated to Philadelphia and reached large audiences through tours and by television appearances. While underrated by some listeners, others hold him in awe, including many who understand "that an outlandish, pseudo-galactic world was from his perspective less absurd than racist America."[24]

MAY 23—ARTIE SHAW (1910–2004)

b. New York, NY; d. Newbury Park, CA

Clarinetist; Bandleader; Composer; Arranger

[SWING]

Other jazz notables born on this day: Humphrey Lyttelton (1921); Rosemary Clooney (1928); Daniel Humair (1938); Marvin Stamm (1939); Don Moye (1946); Ken Peplowski (1959)

Jazz notables deceased on this day: Joe Pass (1994)

♪

Together with Benny Goodman, Shaw was the leading clarinetist and one of the most successful bandleaders of the swing era. Because he achieved his first major success two years after Goodman and his musical career was intermittent, his contribution is often considered secondary to that of his rival, but many jazz musicians find a warmth and creativity in Shaw's work that they miss in Goodman's, and many of his 1940s recordings,

---

23. Kernfeld, *New Grove Dictionary of Jazz*, Vol. 3, 684.
24. Ibid., 685.

including his classic rendition of "Star Dust," stand alongside the best jazz ever recorded.[25] Like Goodman, Shaw was an energetic spokesman for racial equality in jazz, hiring and recording black musicians such as Billie Holiday, Hot Lips Page, and Roy Eldridge. He was brave to hire Holiday, primarily because she was the first well-known black female singer ever to front a popular white band. Racism was certainly more blatant back then, but Shaw was ready to encounter it because he admired Holiday's talent and also because, as a Jew, he had suffered his own share of discrimination. As a leading musician of the swing period and a public figure, Shaw's handsome features, eight marriages (including to actress Lana Turner), and frequent disappearances, made him a darling of gossip columnists.[26]

Shaw (born Arthur Jacob Arshawsky) emerged as an entertainer in 1936, when he appeared with a string quartet at a jazz band competition. A short while later he formed a conventional swing band, and at a July 1938 session that inaugurated his new band and a contract with RCA he produced three smashing cuts, including "Any Old Time" (considered an instant classic by musicians, primarily for the alluring vocal chorus by Billie Holiday) and an arrangement of Cole Porter's exotic "Begin the Beguine," which became an immediate hit and changed Shaw's life. The surprise success of this recording made Shaw the rival of Goodman, transforming the clarinetist into a superstar and his orchestra into one of the most popular bands worldwide.[27] Shaw disbanded in November 1939 and went to Mexico for two months, a move that only served to provoke the publicity he sought to avoid. By 1950 he had taken up the Spanish guitar as a second instrument and gone into psychoanalysis; in 1955 he permanently gave up the clarinet to pursue his dreams of being a writer.

An overview of Shaw's paradoxical life necessarily ends on a questioning note: if you do something better than almost anyone else alive, how do you walk away from it? Shaw has been asked that question many times, but the fact that he invariably came up with different explanations helps keep the mystery alive. Over the years he received plenty of publicity for his many marriages and for leading and disbanding five orchestras, all of them distinctive and memorable, but the outspoken Artie Shaw deserves to be best remembered as one of the truly great clarinetists in jazz history.

MAY 24 ARCHIE SHEPP (1937–)

b. Fort Lauderdale, FL

Saxophonist; Playwright; Teacher

[AVANT-GARDE JAZZ; FREE JAZZ; HARD BOP]

Other jazz notables born on this day: Charles Earland (1941)
Jazz notables deceased on this day: Denzil Best (1965); Duke Ellington (1974)

---

25. Carr et al., *Jazz: The Rough Guide*, 693.
26. Kernfeld, *New Grove Dictionary of Jazz*, Vol. 3, 555.
27. Bogdanov, *All Music Guide to Jazz*, 1136.

By 1965 free jazz was firmly entrenched in the jazz world. It did not take over entirely, as bebop had done. Its audience was far too limited for that, and while college students sometimes booked some of the free-jazz players out of curiosity, rock was the chief musical interest of youth during that period. But the new music was being played in public and it was attracting the interest of many young jazz players. By the mid-1960s there were a number of younger players at home in the new style, among them saxophonists Albert Ayler, Steve Lacy, John Tchicai, and Archie Shepp. The one who had the widest following after free-jazz pioneers Cecil Taylor and Ornette Coleman was Shepp. A college graduate with a special interest in literature, during the 1960s he was closely associated with the avant-garde movement and with its manifestations as an expression of black solidarity. At that time he was viewed as perhaps the most articulate and disturbing member of the free generation, a feared firebrand willing to speak on the record in explicit fashion about social injustice and the rage he felt.[28]

As a youngster growing up in Philadelphia, Shepp began on piano, clarinet, and alto saxophone. In 1959 he graduated from Goddard College with a degree in dramatic literature. He played alto in dance bands and sought theatrical work in New York. At this time he switched to tenor and played in several free-jazz bands. In 1959 he worked briefly with Cecil Taylor and then co-led a group with trumpeter Bill Dixon. In 1963 he joined the New York Contemporary Five, an avant-garde group with Tchicai and Don Cherry.

By this point John Coltrane had taken an interest in him, helping him get a recording contract. Shepp expressed his thanks with an album of four Coltrane tunes. The album, titled *Four for Trane* (1964), proved to be Shepp's most important record, and it established him as a figure in the avant-garde. In 1965 Shepp played occasionally with Coltrane, working with him in various clubs and participating on Coltrane's classic avant-garde recording, *Ascension*. Shepp's appearance at the Newport Jazz Festival that year and the endorsement of his abilities by Coltrane were enormously helpful in establishing him nationally and internationally. Shepp's music had almost always been less abstract than that of the other avant-gardists, and his 1965 Newport concert revealed him to be a highly original composer, as well as a distinctive new voice on tenor. His music featured rock rhythms, jazz swing, harmonic structures, and occasional texts spoken by Shepp, including poetry readings and quotes from James Baldwin and Malcolm X.

Over the next few years he was the subject of a number of interviews, particularly in *Jazz*, a journal strongly supportive of the experimental musicians and the ideology of black rebellion. Shepp was literate, intelligent, and outspoken, and his statements made him a figure of contention in jazz. Starting in the late 1960s, around the time he became an academic, Shepp toned down his rhetoric and his music became more accessible.

---

28. Bogdanov et al., *All Music Guide to Jazz*, 1145.

BLUE NOTES

MAY 25—MILES DAVIS (1926–1991)
b. Alton, IL; d. Santa Monica, CA
Trumpeter; Flugelhorn Player; Bandleader
[Jazz-Rock; Modal Music; Hard Bop; Fusion; Cool; Bop]

Other jazz notables born on this day: Bill Robinson (1878); Jimmy Hamilton (1917); Marshall Allen (1924); Wallace Roney (1960)

Jazz notables deceased on this day: Wardell Gray (1955); Paul Quinichette (1983)

♪

The history of jazz is weighted with tragic individuals such as Bix Beiderbecke and Bud Powell, who failed to make the most of their vast potential. Miles Davis represents the reverse, for he possessed only a relatively modest natural ability. Yet he was able, by reason of intelligence and force of personality, to make himself one of the major figures in jazz.[29] Each time changes in music threatened to drive him from the forefront of jazz, he found a way to regain his place. From the mid-1950s into the 1970s he ruled jazz. Not even Louis Armstrong stood at the top for so long.

To examine Davis's career is to examine the history of jazz from the mid-1940s to the early 1990s, since he was at the center of almost every important innovation and stylistic development in the music during that period, including pioneering the "cool jazz" sound of the late 1940s, "modal jazz" during the late 1950s, and jazz-rock fusion styles in the late 1960s. And when he was not leading those changes, he was choosing sidemen and collaborators who forged the new directions. As a bandleader he was a brilliant talent scout, able to recognize potential in its formative stage and bring out the best in his sidemen. It can be argued that jazz stopped evolving when Davis wasn't there to push it forward.

Son of a dental surgeon and of a mother who was a music teacher, Miles grew up in a wealthy middle-class environment. When he graduated from high school in 1944 he insisted on going to New York to become a musician. To placate his father he agreed to enroll at the famous Juilliard School of Music. However, he soon dropped out in order to perform in the small clubs on Fifty-Second Street. Meanwhile, he located his idol, Charlie Parker, who happened to be in need of a place to stay, and Miles cleverly invited him to stay at his apartment. His aggressiveness paid off. He began working with Parker and by the age of nineteen he was a member of the quintet that in 1945 recorded some of the earliest bop tracks. The sessions established Miles as a unique stylist.

Davis is one of the most interesting yet paradoxical personalities in jazz. Tall, slim, handsome, and haughty, he epitomized the bon vivant: driving fast cars, escorting beautiful women, and always dressing to the hilt. He didn't need a last name, for every-one knew who Miles was. By the age of thirty-one Miles had become the representative African-American artist. People wanted to hear what he had to say on almost any topic. He was featured in fashion magazines and was the first subject of a *Playboy* interview. People who didn't even buy jazz records bought albums by Miles. According to Gary Giddins, Miles

---

29. Collier, *Making of Jazz*, 426.

"defined the era's stance and tone, its beat irreverence, high life, wounded introversion, and causeless belligerence. When [Louis] Armstrong attacked Eisenhower and segregation in 1957, he was harassed by a columnist who demanded a boycott as well as scrutiny from the FBI. When Davis stood up to the cops who bloodied him in front of Birdland a few years later, he was a symbol of the Civil Rights era."[30]

MAY 26—MAMIE SMITH (1883–1946)

b. Cincinnati, OH; d. New York, NY

Vocalist; Entertainer

[CLASSIC FEMALE BLUES]

Other jazz notables born on this day: Shorty Baker (1914); Ziggy Elman (1914)

Jazz notables deceased on this day: J. C. Higginbotham (1973); Phineas Newborn (1989); George Morrow (1992); Gil Fuller (1994); Sonny Sharrock (1994)

♪

In 1919 Mary Straine recorded a vaudeville routine with the legendary Bert Williams and became the first black woman ever to make a record. But no African-American woman had yet been recorded singing the blues. In 1920, after many efforts on the part of the African-American community to have a black female vocalist record the blues, a persistent black promoter named Perry Bradford finally persuaded OKeh Records to do so. Despite letters from pressure groups across the country threatening to boycott OKeh products if the company recorded black female vocalists, in 1920 the blues finally put African-American music on the map.

Though a rather obscure vaudeville singer and technically not a blues performer, Mamie Smith notched her place in jazz history as the first black female singer to record a vocal blues. Her initial recording date actually came about by accident when Sophie Tucker, a white singer, fell ill at the last minute and was unable to record. Bradford convinced OKeh to let Smith replace her, and the two relatively undistinguished numbers she recorded that day—with a white band accompanying her—did well enough that six months later she was back in the studio with a black band singing the blues. Using Willie "The Lion" Smith as her pianist, she recorded the phenomenally successful "Crazy Blues." The album sold thousands of copies in its first week, nearly a million in the next six months, and made record labels aware of the huge potential market for "race records," thus paving the way for Bessie Smith and other blues and jazz performers. "Crazy Blues" brought Smith instant stardom and great wealth.

Seizing the opportunity, the ambitious entertainer formed the Jazz Hounds, a band of top black musicians with whom she appeared in New York and around the South, where her shows had crowds lined up for blocks. Her superb taste in musicians—her Jazz Hounds featured such notables as Coleman Hawkins, Bubber Miley, and Johnny

---

30. Giddins, *Visions of Jazz*, 348.

Dunn—made her the envy of bandleaders like Fletcher Henderson, who raided her band and took musicians like Hawkins in order to create his own superb orchestra.

By the mid-1920s Smith had more money than she knew what to do with. For her stage appearances she wore $3000 feathered gowns, and she owned several palatial New York homes, each with luxury furnishings and a brand new electric player piano in every room. An attractive and lively stage personality, she remained a high-class entertainer, and her penetrating feminine voice exerted a powerful influence on audiences and singers everywhere. Although she performed regularly through the 1930s and early '40s, public interest in the blues was declining and she was suffering from a progressive arthritic condition. When her illness worsened, her manager (who later acquired the proceeds from her estate) provided no financial help. She died penniless in a Harlem hospital, following a long illness, and was buried in an unmarked grave on Staten Island.

MAY 27—PEGGY LEE (1920–2002)

b. Jamestown, ND; d. Bel Air, CA

Vocalist; Composer

[VOCAL JAZZ; TRADITIONAL POP; SWING]

Other jazz notables born on this day: Albert Nicholas (1900); Bud Shank (1926); Ramsey Lewis (1935); Niels-Henning Orsted Pedersen; Dee Dee Bridgewater (1950); Gonzalo Rubalcaba (1963)

Jazz notables deceased on this day: George Mitchell (1972); Sy Oliver (1988); Red Rodney (1994); Helen Oakley Dance (2001)

♪

By the early 1940s the first generation of jazz singers had largely run its course. World War II hastened the collapse of big bands, the training ground for so many vocalists. Dizzy Gillespie, Charlie Parker, Thelonious Monk, and Kenny Clarke were developing a new music that by 1945 would redefine jazz. Sarah Vaughan absorbed their bebop inventions, challenging swing band singers Ella Fitzgerald and Anita O'Day to update their own styles. Bing Crosby increasingly devoted his energies to Hollywood, leaving Frank Sinatra, Billy Eckstine, and a host of others to extend and refine his innovations. Dinah Washington and Kay Starr returned to blues and gospel roots and left Peggy Lee, a twenty-five-year-old from Jamestown, North Dakota, to fuse the contributions of her musical ancestors in a style that foreshadowed the "cool" vocalists (June Christy, Chris Connor, Helen Merrill, Julie London) of the 1950s.[31]

Like Sinatra and Fitzgerald, Peggy Lee started out as a big band vocalist but found her greatest success as a solo artist. Her alluring tone, distinctive delivery, breadth of material, and ability to compose many of her own songs made her one of the most captivating artists of the vocal era.[32] Despite a small voice and only a minimal use of improvisation, her

---

31. Kirchner, *Oxford Companion to Jazz*, 234.
32. Bogdanov et al., *All Music Guide to Jazz*, 757.

singing often crossed over into jazz. She repeatedly battled injury and ill health, including heart trouble and diabetes (she was often troubled by weight and glandular problems), in order to maintain a career that brought her a Grammy (in 1969 for "Is That All There Is?"), an Oscar nomination (in 1956 for *Pete Kelly's Blues*), and sold-out houses worldwide. Jazz critic Leonard Feather once remarked, "If you don't feel a thrill when Peggy Lee sings, you're dead, Jack."

Born Norma Engstrom, Lee's career began after a troubled childhood (her mother died when she was four and she was mistreated by her stepmother after her father remarried). Gaining her sense of swing by listening to Count Basie on the radio, she taught herself to sing and made her radio debut at the age of fourteen. She was employed by a radio station in Fargo (where she renamed herself Peggy Lee) and then twice traveled to Hollywood to make her fortune, though she returned home unsuccessfully. She finally got her break in 1941, when a vocal group she joined began appearing at a club in Chicago. Benny Goodman spotted here there and hired her as replacement for vocalist Helen Forrest, who was about to leave his band. Lee established herself as an outstanding blues singer with Goodman (1941–43), but she left the band in 1943, after marrying Goodman's guitarist, Dave Barbour. A year later she returned to music as a recording artist, and over the next fifteen years she recorded numerous hits for Capitol and Decca, including songs influenced by Latin, cabaret, pop, and the blues.

MAY 28—ANDY KIRK (1898–1992)

b. Newport, KY; d. New York, NY

Bandleader; Bassist; Tuba Player

[Swing; Big Band]

Other jazz notables born on this day: Tommy Ladnier (1900); T-Bone Walker (1910); Dave Barbour (1912); Claudio Roditi (1946)
Jazz notables deceased on this day: Mary Lou Williams (1981); Jimmie Rowles (1996)

♪

By the mid-1920s more than one hundred dance bands regularly crisscrossed the wide-open spaces between St. Louis and Denver, Texas and Minnesota, playing one-nighters. They were called "territory bands," and people regularly traveled hundreds of miles to dance with their favorite groups. No one worked harder or traveled more during the lean Depression years than Andy Kirk and his Clouds of Joy. Looking back over his twenty years playing one-nighters, Kirk disagreed with those who only remembered the bleak side of life during segregation: "If it hadn't been for one-nighters," he wrote, "I wouldn't have met Mrs. Mary McLeod Bethune and Dr. George Washington Carver. We couldn't stay in the white hotels . . . I'm glad now we couldn't. We'd have missed out on a whole country full of folks who put us up in their homes, cooked dinners and breakfasts for us, told us how to get along in Alabama and Mississippi, helped us out in trouble and became our friends for life. If it hadn't been for one-nighters, I wouldn't have known there were other people but rednecks in the South. I wouldn't have found out that not all white southerners wanted to put their foot on me. I wouldn't have found out there were Whites in the South I could talk to person to person, man to man."[33]

Kirk could have been an angry, embittered man all of his life. But he wasn't. Despite the tragedies of his early life—his mother died during his infancy and his father abandoned him shortly thereafter—he took an optimistic approach to life, choosing to be happy. Relatives in Denver, where he studied piano and singing, reared him. In 1918 he began playing bass saxophone and tuba in an ensemble led by the violinist George Morrison. With this group he visited New York in 1920, where he briefly worked with Jelly Roll Morton in the rhythm section. After playing with obscure groups, Kirk went to Dallas around 1927 to join Terrence Holder's Dark Clouds of Joy.

In 1929 he took leadership of the band (which was renamed Andy Kirk's Twelve Clouds of Joy), and moved to Kansas City. The orchestra included saxophonist John Williams and his talented wife Mary Lou Williams, who in 1931 became Kirk's arranger and pianist. The band became so popular that for a while it rivaled Moten's band, the Southwest territory's best band. The success of "Until the Real Thing Comes Along" (1936), featuring the singer Pha Terrell, established the band's lasting popularity. By this time Kirk was playing mostly in New York, often at large venues such as the Savoy and the Cotton Club. He continued leading successful bands until 1948, when he was forced to disband. Over the years, Kirk's ensembles featured a succession of outstanding tenor saxophonists (Ben Webster, Lester Young, Buddy Tate, Dick Wilson, Don Byas, Al Sears, Eddie "Lockjaw" Davis) and trumpeters (Harold "Shorty" Baker, Howard McGhee, Fats Navarro), but the group's preeminent musician was Mary Lou Williams, who at one time was billed—accurately—as "The Lady Who Swings the Band."

MAY 29—KENNY WASHINGTON (1958–)

b. Brooklyn, NY

Drummer

[Neo-Bop]

Other jazz notables born on this day: Gene Wright (1923); Dick Hafer (1927); Hilton Ruiz (1952)

Jazz notables deceased on this day: Ted Dunbar (1998)

♪

Devoted to jazz from childhood, Kenny Washington is one of the world's great authorities on the history of recorded jazz. Among the top straightahead drummers on the contemporary scene, he has developed a successful career as a freelance drummer. Brother of electric bass guitarist Reggie Washington, Kenny performed at an early age with his brother in a group called the Washington Brothers. Later, at his father's prompting, Kenny took lessons from former Dizzy Gillespie drummer Rudy Collins before studying per-

---

33. Ward and Burns, *Jazz: A History*, 251.

cussion at the High School of Music and Art. Already an expert drummer in his teens, Washington is one of a relatively small number of drummers on the contemporary scene whose playing is both interesting and thought provoking. Joining players such as Peter Erskine, Terry Clarke, Jeff Hamilton, Cindy Blackman, Adam Nussbaum, Joey Baron, Danny Gottlieb, Lewis Nash, Dennis Chambers, Marvin "Smitty" Smith, and Jeff "Tain" Watts, an elite crop of drummers who emerged during the 1970s and '80s, Washington proved to be the most historically informed of the younger drummers.

Beginning in 1977 he gigged with the Lee Konitz nonet before working with Betty Carter (1978–79) and Johnny Griffin. He then freelanced with top musicians such as Kenny Burrell, Milt Jackson, George Coleman, Tommy Flanagan, Jay McShann, and Benny Goodman, and twice replaced Dannie Richmond in Mingus Dynasty. From 1980 into the 1990s he performed with Griffin, and from the late 1980s he also played with Benny Carter, Clark Terry, Dizzy Gillespie, and the Carnegie Hall Jazz Band. Although he does some touring, Washington prefers to stay in the New York City area, where from the mid-1980s to the late '90s he was a house drummer for the Criss Cross label. During that period he also made a number of recordings for other labels, including performing in the April 1994 concert that celebrated the Verve label's fiftieth anniversary.

A hard-bop revivalist who is comfortable working in any setting, from delicate trio to swing-style big band, Washington has combined the best elements from the work of earlier drummers to form his own style, which is tasteful and unobtrusive. An expert in the history of jazz, Washington taught drumming at the New School in New York City. In 1997 he joined pianist Bill Charlap and bassist Peter Washington (no relation) in a trio patterned after the distinctive Ahmad Jamal Trio of the late 1950s. Building on similar perspectives to small-group playing, Charlap's lineup had its major label breakthrough in 2000 with the highly acclaimed Blue Note recording *Written in the Stars*, a fresh and distinctive approach to the Great American Songbook. Having inherited his father's passion for record collecting and jazz history, Kenny developed a second career as a disc jockey at jazz station WBGO in Newark, New Jersey, where he worked as an announcer for a program of big-band music.

MAY 30—BENNY GOODMAN (1909–1986)

b. Chicago, IL; d. New York, NY

Clarinetist; Composer; Bandleader

[SWING; BIG BAND]

Other jazz notables born on this day: Frankie Trumbauer (1901); Sidney De Paris (1905); Pee Wee Erwin (1913); Dave McKenna (1930)

Jazz notables deceased on this day: Valaida Snow (1956); Paul Desmond (1977); Hank Mobley (1986); Turk Murphy (1987); Sun Ra (1993); Tex Beneke (2000)

At the height of the Depression Benny Goodman had the perfect credentials to entertain a struggling nation. One of twelve siblings born to penniless Russian immigrants in Chicago, he received his first clarinet at the age of ten, and three years later he possessed his union card. Already as a teenager he was a meticulous and polished player, due in part to his professional training as a student of Franz Schoepp, a highly reputable Chicago clarinet teacher. Apart from Frank Teschemacher, who lacked Goodman's steely nerves, there was no clarinetist in Chicago to challenge his potential, and by 1925, when he was sixteen, he traveled west to join the Ben Pollack band in California. Though Goodman was a featured soloist, he left Pollack's group in 1929, determined to form his own band. For five years he was a very busy studio musician in New York, using the money he earned to support his mother and his siblings after his father had been killed in a taxi accident. He also worked in pit bands for Broadway shows alongside Red Nichols (one of the best known white trumpet players of the period), Glenn Miller, and Gene Krupa, a drummer much adored by fans for his good looks and energetic playing.

Goodman put his first band together in 1933 with the help of jazz patron John Hammond. Using arrangements of popular tunes made by Fletcher Henderson, Goodman's well-rehearsed ensemble showed that it was possible to play both jazz and dance music simultaneously. Late in 1934 he formed a band to play "hot music" on the late-night radio show, Let's Dance, which featured a Latin band, a sweet band, and a hot band, the latter slot going to Goodman. The show folded after six months, but it provided enough national exposure that, in the summer of 1935, Hammond and Goodman put together a cross-country tour of one-nighters winding up in California, a tour that is now considered to have initiated the "swing era."

After some major disasters (such as in Denver, where he was nearly fired for playing waltzes and comedy numbers), the band was well received at a Monday night performance in Oakland, and then on August 21 audiences nearly caused a riot at the Palomar Ballroom in Hollywood, the most famous dance floor on the West Coast. Chastened by his experience in Denver, Goodman decided to open with predictable material. He continued in that vein for an hour with little response, so by the second set he decided that if he were doomed to failure, he would go down on his own terms. He called for the Henderson charts and began playing "Sugar Foot Stomp." The crowd roared with approval and the band stayed at the Palomar for two months, performing national broadcasts from that location. Thus began the swing band boom. As the first white bandleader to adopt and popularize an uncompromising jazz style, Goodman brought a new audience and a new level of recognition to jazz, and for that reason he became the first "King of Swing."

MAY 31—OTTO HARDWICK (1904–1970)

b. Washington, DC; d. Washington, DC

Alto Saxophonist

[SWING; BIG BAND]

Other jazz notables born on this day: Albert "Tootie" Heath (1935); Paulinho Da Costa (948); Marty Ehrlich (1955)

Jazz notables deceased on this day: Billy Strayhorn (1967); Tito Puente (2000)

♪

In 1904, when Otto Hardwick was born in Washington, DC, the nation's capital had approximately one hundred thousand African-Americans, making this the largest black population of any city in the U.S. Black Washingtonians, proud of Howard University, ethnic schools, orchestras, choral societies, and a conservatory of music, had "a higher standard of culture among people of color than obtains in any other city."[34] Duke Ellington was born there in 1899, living just a few blocks from the White House during his formative years. He would never forget the lessons he learned from his junior high school principal, Miss Boston: "She taught us that proper speech and good manners were our first obligations, because as representatives of the Negro race we were to command respect for our people. This being an all-colored school, Negro history was crammed into the curriculum, so that we would know our people all the way back. They had pride there, the greatest race pride."[35] With just four months to go before graduation from high school, Ellington passed up a scholarship from the NAACP in painting and dropped out of school to become a musician. By this time he was taking occasional professional jobs as leader of a five-piece combo that included Hardwick and trumpeter Arthur Whetsol. When Ellington discovered that the big society bands advertised in the Yellow Pages, he took out an advertisement larger than all the rest, and it brought him work. In 1920 he recruited drummer Sonny Greer, trombonist Juan Tizol, and banjoist Elmer Snowden, who doubled as business manager. Snowden briefly took control of the group and left for New York in 1923. Ellington, tired of playing bland dance music, rejoined the group later that year, poised to make his mark.

Otto "Toby" Hardwick (often misspelled Hardwicke), a childhood friend of Ellington, remained with the bandleader until 1928. He was a great saxophonist, with a sweet tone on alto and a fluid style, but he had a habit of disappearing at inconvenient moments in Ellington's early band-building career. By 1930 he had his own band in Harlem, which featured an innovative five-man saxophone section. His band once bested Ellington's in a famous battle, and that may have pushed the more famous leader to enlarge his saxophone section. Two years later, when Hardwick rejoined his friend, he found Johnny Hodges leading the section and the band more regimented than it had been earlier.

---

34. Ward and Burns, *Jazz: A History*, 50.
35. Ibid., 52.

Over the years Hardwick composed pieces such as "Sophisticated Lady" with Ellington and he also invented some of jazz's most memorable nicknames, including "Tricky Sam" (Joe Nanton), "Little Jazz" (Roy Eldridge), "Floorshow" (Ray Nance), and "Swee' Pea" (Billy Strayhorn). Personal differences, as well as increased drinking and the demands of travel, resulted in Hardwick's departure from the band in 1946. He retired from music soon thereafter to work in hotel management and to run his own farm.

Chapter 6

June

JUNE 1—LENNIE NIEHAUS (1929–)

b. St. Louis, MO

Alto Saxophonist; Composer; Arranger

[Film Music; Cool; Bop]

Other jazz notables born on this day: Nelson Riddle (1921); Hal McKusick (1924)
Jazz notables deceased on this day: Papa Jack Laine (1966)

♪

In the 1950s Lennie Niehaus was an acclaimed alto saxophonist, playing, composing, and arranging for Stan Kenton's big bands. With Bud Shank and Art Pepper, the most prominent West Coast altoists of the period, he combined the influence of Charlie Parker with the style of Benny Carter. Since then, he is best known for his work as a leading Hollywood film composer, specifically for his collaboration with Clint Eastwood as musical director and composer of the 1987 film *Bird*, based on the life of Parker. In addition, Niehaus has been a prolific clinician for concert bands, orchestras, and small ensembles, and has written several texts on saxophone pedagogy. His playable style of writing has made his saxophone books among the most popular jazz books in the world today.

As a youngster growing up in Los Angeles, Niehaus was destined for musical greatness. His sister was a concert pianist and his father an expert violinist who started Lennie on violin at age seven. From violin he went to oboe and bassoon before taking up alto and clarinet at thirteen. Hearing his sister and father play advanced music got him interested in composition, and by his early teenage years he was writing music. In the late 1940s, while studying music at Los Angeles colleges, he began playing alongside such reedmen as Herb Geller, Herbie Steward, and Teddy Edwards. Following graduation, Niehaus joined Kenton's orchestra (1951–52), playing alto and occasionally writing for a band that was loaded with talent, featuring such soloists as trumpeter Conte Candoli, trombonist Frank Rosolino, and altoist Lee Konitz. In 1952 he was drafted into the army and assigned to the band at Fort Ord, California, where he met Clint Eastwood. Eastwood, a jazz fan from way back, left the army base whenever possible to hear jazz artists such as

Gerry Mulligan and Chet Baker perform. The two men had much in common. Upon his discharge, Niehaus returned to Kenton's band and worked there for the rest of the decade. During this period he also led his own groups and played alto on six albums, in a cool tone somewhat reminiscent of Konitz.

By the 1960s he abandoned playing and started orchestrating for the great film composer Jerry Fielding. Since Fielding's death, Niehaus has been a leading film composer in his own right. Although he largely left jazz in the 1960s, his work on *Play Misty for Me* and particularly the technically demanding music for the film *Bird*, allowed fans the opportunity to admire his jazz writing once again.[1] Since 1984 he has written scores for several other Eastwood films, including *Tight Rope, City Heat, Pale Rider*, and *The Bridges of Madison County*. Niehaus finally picked up the horn again when he taught twenty-six-year-old actor Forrest Whitaker, who played Parker in the movie *Bird*, how to play sax. He began to record again and perform in public, often with Kenton alumni, playing jazz alto as formidably as ever.

JUNE 2—VALAIDA SNOW (1904–1956)

b. Chattanooga, TN; d. New York, NY

Trumpeter; Vocalist; Dancer

[SWING]

Other jazz notables born on this day: Ernie Royal (1921)
Jazz notables deceased on this day: Bunny Berigan (1942); Doc Cheatham (1997); Andy Simpkins (1999)

♪

Despite the success of all-woman bands during the 1920s and early '30s and bands formed and led by female artists, the idea of a woman as musician remained practically nonexistent. Valaida Snow, one of the most popular attractions of the 1930s, was an outstanding exception. With a bit of luck, she might well have counted among the greatest entertainers of the early twentieth century. Instead, the gifted vocalist, dancer, arranger, and multi-instrumentalist remains little known outside of an avid cult following.

Snow was the product of a musical family. Her mother, a music teacher, taught Valaida and her sisters Lavaida, Hattie, and Alvaida to play a wide variety of instruments. The girls also sang and danced, but when Valaida turned professional at the age of fifteen, she focused on vocals and trumpet, and by 1924 she was already a featured performer in the Broadway musical, *The Chocolate Dandies*. For the rest of the 1920s she toured constantly, appearing throughout the U.S. and performing in London and Paris in the musical *Blackbirds*. In 1926 she toured the Far East, and in 1928 she headlined at Chicago's Sunset Café, where her energetic performances won the admiration of Louis Armstrong as well as Earl Hines, who soon became her lover. A striking woman who loved life, she kept on the move, touring Europe, the Middle East, and Russia. In 1933 she was back in

---

1. Bogdanov et al., *All Music Guide to Jazz*, 948.

Chicago with Hines, producing and starring in shows at the Grand Terrace Ballroom. She featured a number of tap dance routines, including an act where she used seven different pairs of shoes—everything from tap shoes to Russian boots—and often danced herself into near insensibility.[2] Her reputation helped bring her to Hollywood, where alongside then-husband Ananais Berry she appeared in a number of films.

By all rights Snow should have been a major superstar, but as a black performer she was subject to considerable racism and as a woman, was an outsider even within the jazz community. Her perfect pitch, gift for arranging, and brilliant trumpeting only made her that much more of a curiosity. Snow traveled back to Europe for more film work and live dates during the late 1930s. She was a sensation in Paris and Scandinavia, where her chauffeur drove her in a purple Mercedes, accompanied by a pet monkey dressed in a purple jacket and cap. In 1941, while in Nazi-occupied Copenhagen, she was captured by German forces and interned in a concentration camp. All of her belongings were confiscated and, like the other prisoners, she received fifteen lashes each week. Ill health reduced her weight to sixty-eight pounds. Eighteen months later she was freed as an exchange prisoner and allowed to return to New York, but she never fully recovered from the ordeal, physically or psychologically. When Hines saw her again in 1943, he reportedly did not even recognize her. She continued to work despite her personal suffering, but the spark was clearly gone. She died of a massive cerebral hemorrhage on May 30, 1956, at the age of fifty-one.

JUNE 3—DAKOTA STATON (1931–2007)

b. Pittsburgh, PA; d. New York, NY

Vocalist

[VOCAL JAZZ; TRADITIONAL POP; STANDARDS]

Other jazz notables born on this day: Ted Curson (1935); Grachan Moncur III (1937)
Jazz notables deceased on this day: Ralph J. Gleason (1975)

♪

During the late 1940s and early '50s, when Dakota Staton came of age as a vocalist, one of the most beloved yet most controversial singers was Dinah Washington. Beloved to her fans and fellow singers, Washington was controversial to critics, who accused her of selling out her art to commerce and bad taste. Her principal sin, apparently, was to cultivate a distinctive vocal style that was at home in all kinds of music, including R&B, blues, jazz, and pop.[3] Despite her early death—she died of an accidental overdose of diet pills mixed with alcohol at the tragically early age of thirty-nine—Washington had a huge influence on R&B and jazz singers such as Aretha Franklin, Esther Phillips, Nancy Wilson, Diane Schuur, and Staton.

---

2. Carr et al., *Jazz; The Rough Guide*, 722.
3. Bogdanov et al., *All Music Guide to Jazz*, 1302.

Known for her sassy brand of jazz blues, Staton has been called a stylistic link between the earthiness of Washington and the pop-funk iconoclasm of Chaka Khan. Staton gained a strong reputation as a soulful jazz singer early in her career, though she never broke through to become a major name. Born Aliyah Rabia, Dakota sang from early childhood and was an accomplished dancer by the age of five. As a teenager she took classical singing lessons, but after hearing Washington she chose to concentrate on a blues style and joined the cast of an African-American revue based in Pittsburgh. She moved to Detroit in 1950, and after performing in clubs in the U.S. and Canada, she appeared at a jam session in Harlem that led to a contract with Capitol in 1954 and to *Down Beat*'s New Star award the following year.

Although at this point she demonstrated enough of an R&B tinge to merit inclusion, along with the likes of Big Joe Turner and Fats Domino, in fabled disc jockey Alan Freed's first New York area Rock 'n' Roll party stage shows, she was evolving into a dynamic, jazz-based stylist. She achieved critical success and popular acclaim for her album *The Late, Late Show* (1957), on which she performed standards and scat solos accompanied by a swing sextet that included Jonah Jones and Hank Jones. She recorded steadily for Capitol through 1961, including with George Shearing in 1957. She also performed at Town Hall in New York (1959), toured with Benny Goodman (c. 1960), and recorded at the Newport Jazz Festival (1963). In 1965 she moved to England, and after her return to the U.S. in the early 1970s, she recorded two albums oriented towards soul jazz and gospel. She remained active through the 1980s and '90s, appearing at clubs and festivals. After a long absence from the studios, she made several recordings that were well received, including *Dakota Staton* (1990), with Huston Person on tenor sax.

A superb jazz-oriented singer, she concentrated on making albums and never enjoyed a hit single. This, coupled with the fact that she arrived on the scene after the rock and roll revolution had altered popular music forever, robbed Dakota of the widespread fame she may otherwise have enjoyed.

JUNE 4—ANTHONY BRAXTON (1945–)

b. Chicago, IL

Alto Saxophonist; Clarinetist; Pianist; Flutist; Composer; Leader

[AVANT-GARDE; FREE JAZZ; EXPERIMENTAL BIG BAND]

Other jazz notables born on this day: Britt Woodman (1920); Oliver Nelson (1932); Paquito D'Rivera (1948)

Jazz notables deceased on this day: Tommy Ladnier (1939); Allan Reuss (1988); Earle Warren (1994); Johnny "Hammond" Smith (1997); Steve Lacy (2004)

♪

Throughout jazz history, musical styles have been associated with geographical locations, such as New Orleans and Chicago Dixieland, West Coast jazz, and East Coast hard bop. In the late 1960s a group of free-jazz players coalesced around the Chicago-based

Association for the Advancement of Creative Musicians (AACM), a nonprofit organization founded by Muhal Richard Abrams in 1965 to promote the interests and needs of African-American avant-garde jazz musicians. Expected to maintain high moral standards, its members were required to contribute original compositions and give occasional recitals. In addition, their music was almost exclusively nonelectronic and separate from jazz-rock. The personnel for the AACM included prominent players of new music, foremost among them Anthony Braxton, one of the preeminent free-jazz saxophonists.

Braxton studied harmony and composition at Chicago School of Music (1959–63) and philosophy at Roosevelt University. After serving in the military from 1964 to 1966 he returned to Chicago, where he joined the AACM. In 1968 he made his recording debut, creating a milestone in jazz history with his double LP of solo alto saxophone (not released until 1971). The release of *For Alto*, the first album for unaccompanied saxophone ever recorded, brought him high praise and encouraged the fashion for solo instrumental performances. Although alto was his main instrument, Braxton eventually mastered virtually every reed instrument, from the clarinet and sopranino to the contrabass clarinet and bass sax.

He went to France for a period in 1969, but had little success. Upon his return he went to New York at Ornette Coleman's invitation, living in the latter's house for a while. For a year Braxton gave up music altogether and worked as a chess hustler in Washington Square Park. In 1970 he began an informal association with Chick Corea, after which he joined the mostly free unit Circle, with Corea, Dave Holland, and Barry Altschul. When Corea decided to quit the group, Braxton kept it going, adding trumpeter Kenny Wheeler to his quartet. Since the mid-1980s Braxton has toured and recorded frequently, in addition to his academic work as a professor of music at Mills College (1985–88) and Wesleyan University (early 1990s).

Of all the current leaders of the avant-garde, Braxton is probably the least accepted by the mainstream establishment. Some detractors (like Wynton Marsalis) have denied that his music is even jazz (particularly on account of its lack of swing), but since it contains a large amount of improvisation and the feeling of the blues, it certainly qualifies. Though his work is difficult to categorize, there is no denying its passion, sophistication, and originality. According to Chris Kelsey, Braxton's best work is on a level with any art music of the late twentieth century, jazz or classical."[4]

JUNE 5—MISHA MENGELBERG (1935–)

b. Kiev, Ukraine

Pianist; Composer

[AVANT-GARDE JAZZ; POST-BOP]

Other jazz notables born on this day: Pete Jolly (1932); Jerry Gonzalez (1949); Peter Erskine (1954)

Jazz notables deceased on this day: Mel Tormé (1999)

---

4. Bogdanov et al., *All Music Guide to Jazz*, 142.

BLUE NOTES

♪

One of Europe's top jazz pianists, Misha Mengelberg immigrated to the Netherlands with his family during his youth. The respected leader of the Instant Composers Pool (ICP) Orchestra, one of the consistently best creative jazz orchestras in the world, he is equally known for his integral role in the development of the jazz-influenced creative music that sprang up in the Netherlands during the 1960s. Most often found in lineups with the drummer Han Bennink, Mengelberg has been mixing composition and improvisation since the 1960s, when he helped establish the ICP (which sponsors performances by the Dutch avant-garde). Over the years, Mengelberg has collaborated with many of the best and best-known players in European avant-garde and American free jazz. Despite his long and full career, he remains a household name only among avant-garde jazz fans.

Mengelberg was born in Kiev to musical parents—his mother was a harpist, and his father was a composer and conductor. Willem Mengelberg, his great uncle, was the well-known conductor of the Amsterdam Goncertgebouw. Misha's father, Karel, worked on films in Kiev until around 1938, when the political climate in Ukraine became hostile, at which point Misha and his activist parents immigrated to Amsterdam. Misha wrote his first piece for piano at the age of four and has been composing ever since. As a young musician searching for his own voice, Mengelberg was attracted to dissonance. Crucial early influences include jazz pianists Thelonious Monk and Herbie Nichols, the composer John Cage, and the absurd-art movement Fluxus, with which he was involved in the 1960s. He studied piano and composition in Darmstadt in 1958 and continued his studies of music at the Royal Conservatory in The Hague (1958–64), concentrating on composition and classical music. At this time he came into contact with Cage and his music, and this further opened his mind to a more experimental approach to composition.

During the 1960s Mengelberg played in various settings with the like-minded Bennink, including in a quartet that recorded with Eric Dolphy on the legendary saxophonist's historic *Last Date* (1964). In 1967, with Bennink and the saxophonist Willem Breuker, he co-founded the ICP collective. The three iconoclastic musicians gave birth to Dutch "music theatre," which combines heavy doses of absurdity with musical and theatrical improvisation. In the 1970s Mengelberg became involved with European ensembles such as the Berlin Contemporary Jazz Orchestra and the ICP Orchestra, as well as playing with sympathetic American players like Lee Konitz and Roswell Rudd. Mengelberg continues to lead the ICP Orchestra, a band that serves as a forum for his composition, improvisation, and musical theater.

JUNE 6—JIMMIE LUNCEFORD (1902–1947)

b. Fulton, MO; d. Seaside, OR

Bandleader

[SWING; SWEET BANDS]

Other jazz notables born on this day: Al Grey (1925); Monty Alexander (1944); Zbigniew Seifert (1946); Paul Lovens (1949)

Jazz notables deceased on this day: George Wettling (1968); Stan Getz (1991)

♪

From 1925 to 1935 the big band movement had to accomplish two tasks. The first was to develop players who could sight-read difficult arrangements, and that occurred over time, through practice and experience. The second and related task was for big bands to find a way to play their arrangements with jazz feeling, that is, to make them swing. The solution was to create a leader for each section of the band, who would rehearse the section and achieve precision. As the swing bands took form, lead players came to be highly valued, for it was they, and not the hot soloists, who made the band work.

Jimmie Lunceford's band was one of the first to be distinguished by its quality of swing and well-disciplined musicianship. Though it was known for its exciting soloists and had perhaps the best saxophone section of any band, it was the band's showmanship, its astonishing ensemble precision, and the irresistible arrangements of Sy Oliver that brought dancers to their feet wherever it played.[5]

After studying music at Fisk University in Nashville, Lunceford accepted a job teaching music in Memphis, where he organized the Chickasaw Syncopators, a student jazz band that came to include old colleagues from Fisk such as Willie Smith, Ed Wilcox, and Henry Wells. From the start the band was dedicated to discipline and precision; no mistake was overlooked. The band eventually left the South and barely survived four tough years on the road. In 1933 the formerly cooperative band was reorganized as the Jimmie Lunceford Orchestra, with Lunceford and his manager, Harold F. Oxley, as sole owners. The band's breakthrough came in 1934, during a six-month engagement at the Cotton Club in Harlem, where they attracted a great deal of attention. More touring and a recording contract with Decca turned the young band into a hot commodity, and by 1935 the group had achieved a national reputation. Their tight ensembles and colorful shows made them one of the era's greatest attractions. The group's novelty numbers and regimented routines—such as trumpeters throwing their horns into the air and catching them in unison, or the musicians singing as a glee club—brought forth some detractors, who called Lunceford's sidemen "trained seals," but despite being showy, the ensemble was musically perfect.

Over the years the band maintained a hectic schedule of one-nighters, and by 1942 it was showing a good profit. Unfortunately, Lunceford underpaid his sidemen, not thinking to reward them for the lean years, and several crucial players left, including Oliver (who was lured to a better paying job by Tommy Dorsey) and Smith, the band's longtime lead saxophonist. Lunceford began treating his sidemen more fairly after that, claiming his band manager had misled him over wages, but the band never returned to its earlier form. Lunceford died a few years later, having collapsed while signing autographs at a music shop in Oregon. It seems he was poisoned by a racist restaurant owner who was angry about having to feed his band.

---

5. Bogdanov et al., *All Music Guide to Jazz*, 241.

JUNE 7—GLEN GRAY (1906–1963)

b. Roanoke, IL; d. Plymouth, MA

Alto Saxophonist; Bandleader

[SWING]

Other jazz notables born on this day: Tal Farlow (1921)
Jazz notables deceased on this day: Meade "Lux" Lewis (1964); Ben Pollack (1971); Bobby Hackett (1976)

♪

During the 1920s popular music had been part of a broad rebellion in art, morality, and social thought, and it is no accident that the period came to be called the Jazz Age. Associated with it were certain dance forms, modes of dress, and a private language. A similar amalgamation of diverse social forces occurred in the 1960s, when rock music provided the catalyst for a group of ideas centered on the notion of uninhibited freedom for all. Between the jazz boom of the 1920s and the rock boom of the 1960s, there occurred a similar movement—the swing era. It too had its modes of dress, its dance forms, and its slang. In an effort to revolt against middle-class propriety, this generation was ready for an art form that was frank, openly expressive, and even sexual.

On December 5, 1933, the repeal of the Twentieth Amendment brought Prohibition to an end. The cabarets that had supported the jazz bands began to die off. To get back their customers, clubs needed to offer new excitement. And they found it in hot dance bands that were playing a form of music that became known as "swing." Earlier that year, when Benny Goodman was forming a band in New York City with a jazz orientation, a number of bands were already playing the kind of music he had in mind, but only two of them were white: one was led by the talented but quarrelsome Dorsey brothers, and the other was the Casa Loma Orchestra, then broadcasting weekly over the CBS network from the Glen Island Casino in nearby New Rochelle.

Alto saxophonist Glen Gray formed the orchestra as a cooperative band from an ensemble contracted to dance band agent Jean Goldkette (called the Orange Blossoms). Gray had played in Detroit with Goldkette from 1924 to 1928 and from 1927 led the Orange Blossoms, to which several of Goldkette's sidemen belonged. In 1929 the group became known as the Casa Loma Orchestra, named after a Toronto ballroom that never opened. It was highly disciplined and played fairly stiff arrangements of popular tunes, but it could swing on occasion, and it contained several excellent soloists. In 1929 the band was booked into New York's Roseland Ballroom and received a recording contract. The group became a sensation from 1931 to 1935, and with cornermen such as clarinetist Clarence Hutchenrider, trombonist/singer Pee Wee Hunt, high-note trumpeter Sonny Dunham, and singer Kenny Sargent, it produced a string of records and became the first swing band to have its own commercially sponsored radio program (beating Goodman by nearly two years). In the 1940s key performers left and the draft took others, but Gray replaced them with young talent such as guitarist Herb Ellis and with veterans like cornetists Red Nichols and Bobby Hackett. Gray retired from touring in 1950 but continued to record with the band until his death in 1963. Although the later versions of the orchestra were better known, the big band was an early pacesetter during the late 1920s and early '30s, when there were few competitors.

JUNE 8—BILL WATROUS (1939–)

b. Middletown, CT

Trombonist

[Bop]

Other jazz notables born on this day:
Jazz notables deceased on this day: Jimmy Rushing (1972)

♪

During the 1940s J.J. Johnson accomplished the biggest breakthrough on the trombone when he essentially proved that anything Dizzy Gillespie could do on the trumpet he could match on the trombone. Regarded as the founder of the modern school of jazz trombone, Johnson spawned a host of followers, foremost among them Jimmy Cleveland, the Danish-born Kai Winding (with whom J.J. teamed up in a highly successful trombone duo in the 1950s), the Swedish trombonist Ake Persson, and younger players like Frank Rosolino, Urbie Green, and Jimmy Knepper. All were spectacular technicians, expanding the range of the trombone to the trumpet's upper register and playing things that a few years earlier could only have been played on other instruments.

Among present-day trombonists who continue the legacy of Johnson and his immediate successors, one of the most versatile is Bill Watrous, possibly the finest bop-oriented trombonist of the past thirty years.[6] Possessor of a beautiful tone and remarkable technique, Watrous was voted top jazz trombonist seven years in a row by *Down Beat* and has won the magazine critic's award twice. He has maintained a lower profile since moving to the West Coast in the late 1970s, where he has remained quite active.

His father, trombonist Ralph Watrous, first introduced him to music. He gained early experience playing in local Dixieland bands and big bands, and while in the military, stationed in Brooklyn, he found opportunity to study with Herbie Nichols, an influential jazz pianist and composer. Having grown up in the radio era, when swing music and big bands were in vogue, Watrous began to carve out an impressive career in music, making his professional debut with trumpeter Billy Butterfield and later performing with some of jazz's greatest bandleaders, including Woody Herman and Count Basie. From 1962 to 1967 he was a member of Kai Winding's various groups, which included from two to five trombones. At the same time he worked as a freelance musician with studio groups, including playing in the television band for Merv Griffin's show (1965–68) and working as a staff musician at CBS. After playing with the jazz-rock group Ten Wheel Drive in 1971,

---

6. Bogdanov et al., *All Music Guide to Jazz*, 1308.

Watrous came to prominence as the leader of Manhattan Wildlife Refuge (1973–77), a big band that recorded two superb albums for Columbia.

In 1977, while touring Texas, he was given an opportunity to play with the Chicago Cubs minor league baseball organization, but when he found out his band was scheduled for a trip to England that summer, he declined the offer. After moving to Los Angeles, he led a big band occasionally and worked in the studios, recording with prominent jazz musicians such as Frank Sinatra, Ray Charles, Ella Fitzgerald, and Sarah Vaughn, to name a few. His prodigious technique and musical ability have made him one of the leading trombonists of his generation, and he frequently travels across the country performing in schools and colleges, sharing his expertise with the next generation of potential jazz musicians.

JUNE 9—LES PAUL (1915–2009)

b. Waukesha, WI; d. White Plains, NY

Guitarist

[TRADITIONAL POP; SWING]

Other jazz notables born on this day: Kenny Barron (1943)
Jazz notables deceased on this day: Abe Lincoln (2000)

♫

Les Paul, a unique blend of musician and inventor, had such an enormous influence over the way American popular music sounds today that many tend to overlook his impact upon the jazz world. Considered the greatest jazz guitarist of his generation, Paul's early use of the electric guitar and pioneering experiments with multi-track recording, guitar design, and electronic effects have influenced countless jazz musicians, including George Benson, Al DiMeola, Stanley Jordan, Pat Martino, and Bucky Pizzarelli. As an inventor, he designed the Gibson Les Paul solid-body electric guitar to be the instrument of preference for jazz and country musicians. However, his guitar only achieved its true popularity when it began to be played loudly with mammoth distortion by rockers and bluesmen, making the sound of rock and roll possible. His many recording innovations, including sound-on-sound, overdubbing, reverb effects, and multi-tracking, greatly accelerated the advancement of studio recording. Ironically, the genre that Paul's guitar would come to dominate—rock and roll—put his own recording career into a slump for much of the 1960s and early '70s.

Born Lester Polfus, Les's interest in music began when he took up the harmonica at age eight. After a fling with the banjo, he took up the guitar and began playing professionally in Chicago under the stage name Rhubarb Red. By 1937 he had formed a trio and the following year he moved to New York, where he landed a featured spot with Fred Waring's Pennsylvanians, which gave Les nationwide exposure through its broadcasts. That job ended in 1941, shortly after he received a severe electric shock from his microphone stand during a jam session in his Queens basement. After a long recovery period and more radio jobs, Paul moved to Hollywood in 1943, where he formed a new trio. As a last-minute substitute for Oscar Moore, Paul played in the inaugural Jazz at the Philharmonic concert in Los Angeles on July 2, 1944. Later that year he hooked up with Bing Crosby, who featured Paul's trio on his radio show.

A serious automobile accident in 1948 shattered his right arm in three places. As an alternative to amputation, his arm was set at a permanent right angle, thumb pointed in, so he could play his instrument. After his recovery he teamed up with a young country singer named Colleen Summers, whom he married and renamed Mary Ford, and together they released a long string of spectacular overdubbed pop discs that he recorded in his home studio, using an 8-track tape deck he designed and built himself. Paul was a perfectionist, and his recordings sounded better than almost anything coming from major studios of the same period. The hits ran out in 1955, and after a bitter divorce from Ford in 1964, Paul went into semiretirement. In 1975 he re-emerged with a concert at New York's Carnegie Hall and two years later he released a Grammy Award-winning record with Chet Atkins. In 1984 Paul began a regular series of Monday night appearances in New York City jazz clubs, attended by visiting celebrities and fans that considered him an icon.

JUNE 10—NAT HENTOFF (1925–)

b. Boston, MA

Writer

Other jazz notables born on this day: Dicky Wells (1907)
Jazz notables deceased on this day: Lorenzo Tio Sr. (1908); Carl Kress (1965); Hubert Rostaing (1990); Nat Pierce (1992)

♪

Nat Hentoff has spent much of his life writing about civil rights and criminal justice. He expressed his stance on the rights of Americans to write and speak freely in his weekly column for the *Village Voice* in New York, as well as in his syndicated column for the *Washington Post* titled "Sweet Land of Liberty." An expert on the Bill of Rights, the Supreme Court, student rights, and education, he is considered a foremost authority in the area of First Amendment defense. In addition to these accomplishments, Hentoff is a leading expert on jazz music and the author of numerous pioneering works on the subject, including *The Jazz Makers* (1957), *The Jazz Life* (1961) and, more recently, *Listen to the Stories* (1995). His contributions on music can also be found in the *Wall Street Journal*.

When asked about prime influences in his career, Hentoff typically cites the Bill of Rights, a Jewish upbringing, and jazz. A self-described Jewish atheist and a civil libertarian, Hentoff's activist stance is clearly rooted in his childhood experiences in Boston, where "[g]angs of feral Catholic youth came roaring regularly into our ghetto, smashing heads and windows." Incidents such as these were offset by early encounters with jazz, on recordings as well as at jazz clubs like the Savoy, "just across the tracks that separated the Negro section [of Boston] from the white." His first live experience with jazz came at the age of twelve, when he evaded the bouncer's eye at a nightclub in order to hear Sidney Bechet play in person. Inspired by jazz, the following year he went to see a Count Basie show on the afternoon of one of the Jewish holidays, failing to make it to the synagogue. As he wrote in *The Jazz Life*: "Neither God nor my father struck me dead, though the latter thundered for weeks. In any case, my record collection continued to grow."

Hentoff started his career in journalism as the associate editor for *Down Beat* magazine (1953–57), and in that capacity he befriended several jazz legends, including Duke Ellington, Dizzy Gillespie, and Charles Mingus. In 1955, with Nat Shapiro, he published *Hear Me Talkin' to Ya*, the first history of jazz told by the musicians themselves. In 1957 he helped gather an extraordinary group of musicians for a live program called "The Sound of Jazz." Nothing like it had ever been tried before on American television. The all-star assemblage included Lester Young and Billie Holiday, reunited for the last time. They had made their first recordings twenty years earlier and had subsequently grown apart. But as Young got up, Hentoff remembered, "he played the purest blues I have ever heard, and [he and Holiday] were looking at each other . . . as if they were both remembering what had been . . . And in the control room we were all crying.[7] In 1960 Hentoff founded and ran the short-lived Candid label, producing important sessions by Mingus, Phil Woods, Abbey Lincoln, and other jazz artists. Since that time he has focused on social issues, though he has continued writing articles and books on jazz and penned numerous liner notes for jazz musicians.

JUNE 11—KAISER MARSHALL (1899 or 1902–1948)

b. Savannah or Augusta, GA; d. New York, NY

Drummer

[CLASSIC JAZZ; SWING]

Other jazz notables born on this day: Shelly Manne (1920)
Jazz notables deceased on this day: Frankie Trumbauer (1956)

♪

During the 1920s Kaiser Marshall rode the crest of a wave known as the Roaring Twenties. This was a rebellious and fun-loving period, and Marshall was the backbone of the first great jazz big band, an ensemble led by Fletcher Henderson, a masterful arranger, composer, and talent scout. Brought up in Boston, where he studied with George L. Stone, one of the era's most important drum teachers, Marshall moved to New York in the early 1920s. After playing briefly with the violinist Ralph "Shrimp" Jones, he joined Henderson and other former members of Jones's group in the house band at the Club Alabam, just off Broadway. The band already included at least three musicians who would become important jazz soloists—Coleman Hawkins, cornetist Joe Smith, and trombonist Big Charlie Green. This was not yet a jazz band but a popular dance orchestra specializing in light music tinted with jazz. Marshall remained with the band during its formative period and

---

7. Ward and Burns, *Jazz: A History*, 405.

continued with Henderson when he moved to the Roseland Ballroom in Times Square (1924).

When Smith left for a better-paying job, Henderson resolved to bring more fire to his band. Recordings by King Oliver and other New Orleans masters had begun to sell successfully in New York, so Henderson was overjoyed when Louis Armstrong accepted his offer to join him at the Roseland. The band gained a lot from Armstrong, for in addition to his electrifying tone, his superb technique, and his hot intensity, he had swing. No one knew what swing was till Armstrong came along. Marshall thrived with Henderson's stellar cast of musicians. This was "the Jazz Age," a time of plenty. But the lean years were close behind.

After the stock market crash of 1929 people were no longer misbehaving; they couldn't afford it. Jobs disappeared by the thousands, banks failed, and a drought turned the farmlands of the western Great Plains into the Dust Bowl. Many jazz musicians also found themselves out of work. Marshall scraped by during the Great Depression, forming short-lived bands and filling temporary musical vacancies, but finding nothing permanent. "Life is difficult," M. Scott Peck cautions at the start of his classic work, *The Road Less Traveled*, thus encouraging readers to consider tough times as the norm rather than the exception. This maxim might have seemed optimistic, even naive to Marshall as he toured Europe with Bobby Martin in 1938, when his entire library of music, which he had incorporated into Martin's band, was destroyed in a fire that ended their residency at the Mephisto nightclub in Rotterdam. Not one to quit, Marshall returned to the U.S., filling in where he could.

Opportunities improved during World War II with the revival of New Orleans jazz, and soon he found himself busy again, working with Dixieland musicians such as Wild Bill Davison, Bunk Johnson, Sidney Bechet, and Mezz Mezzrow. The future looked promising for Marshall as he recorded with the Mezzrow-Bechet band in December 1947, but in a final twist of fate, he died unexpectedly two weeks later, of complications arising from a simple case of food poisoning.

JUNE 12—CHICK COREA (1941–)

b. Chelsea, MA

Pianist; Composer; Leader

[FREE JAZZ; POST-BOP; FUSION]

Other jazz notables born on this day: Marcus Belgrave (1936); Geri Allen (1957)
Jazz notables deceased on this day: Jimmy Dorsey (1957); Bob Scobey (1963)

♫

In 1968 Chick Corea followed Herbie Hancock as pianist with the Miles Davis quintet. His work with Davis propelled him into joining the ranks of Hancock, Bill Evans, McCoy Tyner, and Keith Jarrett as the most prominent and most imitated contemporary pianists in jazz. A sensitive player with a singing tone and crisp technique, Corea successfully adapted to the electric piano and synthesizers, using them in a way that preserves his jazz feeling and personal voice. He probably did more to expand the role of alternative keyboards in jazz than any other pianist. His style, which originated with Bud Powell and Horace Silver, also includes such diverse influences as Latin American music and modern classical composers Paul Hindenmith and Bela Bartok.

Corea began on piano when he was four years old and on drums by the age of eight. His father, a professional musician, taught him the fundamentals of music, but his love of jazz came from listening to recordings of Dizzy Gillespie, Charlie Parker, and Billy Eckstine. At an early age he began transcribing the tunes and improvised solos of the hard bop pianist Horace Silver. His first important professional engagements came in 1962, with the Latin band of Mongo Santamaria, and that love of Latin music continued throughout his career. In 1967 he recorded with Stan Getz and also began fronting his own groups. His classic album, *Now He Sings, Now He Sobs* (1968), with bassist Miroslav Vitous and drummer Roy Haynes, hints at his growing interest in the freer and more European aspects of the contemporary avant-garde. The album features all original compositions and reveals the pianist's formidable compositional abilities. This recording inspired hundreds of pianists and became a staple in the collections of modern jazz musicians.

From 1968 to 1970 Corea worked with Miles, touring internationally, appearing at major festivals, and playing on some of Davis's most influential albums, including *Filles de Kilimanjaro, In a Silent Way, Bitches Brew,* and *Live-Evil*. The exposure with Davis made Corea an international jazz star and established him as one of the leading performers on electric keyboards. Corea's involvement with Davis marked the beginning of an extensive exploration of free improvisation. His desire to develop a more individual approach to free jazz prompted his departure from Davis in 1970, together with bassist Dave Holland. Corea and Holland formed a trio with Barry Altschul on drums, and then a quartet with Anthony Braxton on reeds. This group, called Circle, was very influential on the avant-garde scene, although toward the end of 1971, Corea left the group suddenly, feeling the need to establish a more accessible context for his music. Around this time Corea began the study of Scientology, which profoundly affected his subsequent work. From 1972 he attracted a wider audience with several versions of a band called Return to Forever, an electronic jazz-rock group with a strong Latin flavor, effective melodies, and romantic vocal lines.

JUNE 13—DOC CHEATHAM (1905–1997)

b. Nashville, TN; d. Washington, DC

Trumpeter; Leader

[SWING; DIXIELAND]

Other jazz notables born on this day: Si Zentner (1917); Attila Zoller (1927); Frank Strozier (1937)

Jazz notables deceased on this day: Benny Goodman (1986); Makanda Ken McIntyre (2001)

♪

Most trumpeters fade while in their sixties due to the physical difficulty of their instrument, but Doc Cheatham did not truly find his solo niche until he was nearly seventy. Most of his best recordings actually date from the later stages of his career, and no brass player his age has every played with such power and melodic creativity. On *Doc Cheatham and Nicholas Payton* (1994), a recording released in 1997, Cheatham (ninety-one years old) proved he could hold his own with the twenty-three-year-old Payton. On an earlier classic, *The Eighty-Seven Years of Doc Cheatham* (1992), the octogenarian dominates the music, despite the presence of a strong rhythm section. Throughout his career, Cheatham possessed an admirable technique, and his articulation and clarity of tone were striking. Though he played in big bands, he was at his best in small-group settings, where he could display his flexibility and his magnificent high register.

Doc (Adolphus Anthony) Cheatham's career dates back to the early 1920s, when he played saxophone in vaudeville theaters, backing such traveling singers as Bessie Smith and Clara Smith. He moved to Chicago in 1926, where he came under the influence of Louis Armstrong and Freddie Keppard; soon thereafter he recorded with Ma Rainey (on soprano sax as well as on trumpet). In Chicago he played with Albert Wynn, led his own group, and even subbed for Armstrong. He worked in Philadelphia with Wilbur DeParis (1927–28) and played briefly with Chick Webb before traveling to Europe with Sam Wooding (where he shared trumpet solos with his friend Tommy Ladnier). Due to his wide range and pretty tone, he played first trumpet with McKinney's Cotton Pickers and Cab Calloway throughout the 1930s. In the 1940s he joined Teddy Wilson, then Eddie Heywood (backing Billie Holiday on some recordings), both of whom used his delicate style to great advantage.

In 1945, when bebop came into vogue, he took a job with the post office and opened a New York teaching studio. He made a comeback in the 1950s, alternating between Dixieland (with Wilbur DeParis and Eddie Condon) and Latin bands, including those of Machito and Perez Prado. He played briefly with Benny Goodman during 1966 and 1967 but it wasn't until the mid-1970s that he felt truly comfortable as a soloist, when he built an international reputation through records and on tour. Cheatham was also an effective singer, whose half-spoken, half-sung vocals complemented his chance-taking trumpet flights. Over his final twenty years, Cheatham appeared worldwide in jazz clubs, at concerts, and at festivals. Considered the greatest ninety-year-old trumpeter of all time, he remained active until his death in 1997, following a performance with Payton at Blues Alley in Washington, DC.

JUNE 14—MARCUS MILLER (1959–)

b. New York, NY

Electric Bass Guitarist; Record Producer

[Crossover Jazz; Contemporary Jazz; Post-Bop; Fusion; Jazz-Funk; R&B]

Other jazz notables born on this day: Nappy Lamare (1905); Kenny Drew Jr. (1958)
Jazz notables deceased on this day: John Kirby (1952); Matty Matlock (1978); Herman Autrey (1980)

BLUE NOTES

♪

When one thinks of great jazz fusion bass players, two names come to mind: the late Jaco Pastorius and Marcus Miller. Among active eclectic bass players, none is better right now than Miller. In addition to bass guitar, he also plays other instruments, including bass clarinet, soprano saxophone, keyboards, guitar, and drums. A veteran studio player who has played on over five hundred recordings, Miller has also spent much of his career as a rhythm-and-blues producer. His most important work was with Miles Davis, contributing to the trumpeter's comeback in the early 1980s. Later in the decade he collaborated closely with Davis, composing, arranging, and often playing on the superb albums *Tutu*, *Siesta*, and *Amandla*. In addition, he produced many of David Sanborn's albums, as well as albums by Dizzy Gillespie, George Benson, the Brecker Brothers, Dave Liebman, and Kenny Garrett, to name a few. Known as the "Superman of Soul," Miller has also worked with many pop artists, including Frank Sinatra, Aretha Franklin, Elton John, the Bee Gees, and Luther Vandross. Using equal portions of soul, R&B, hip-hop, and contemporary jazz, Miller attempts to communicate a unified black music, transcendent of genre and time.

Born in Brooklyn and raised in Jamaica, New York, Miller played clarinet as a child, later adding piano and electric bass guitar. Introduced to jazz by drummer Kenny Washington, Miller soon became attracted to the work of Miles Davis, whose band once included Marcus's cousin, Wynton Kelly. Working professionally by the age of fifteen, a year later he was playing with flutist Bobbi Humphrey and keyboardist Lonnie Liston Smith. Marcus spent the next few years as a studio musician in New York, working with Bob James, Grover Washington Jr., and soul singers Roberta Flack and Aretha Franklin, among others. In 1979 he played in the house band for the television show *Saturday Night Live* and recorded as a sideman with Urszula Dudziak, whose recording "Roxanna" on the album *Future Talk* preserves a spectacular example of Miller's melodic solo playing. Miller joined Davis's band in 1980, spending two years with the fabled jazzman. During the same period he collaborated with Sanborn and recorded the first of his albums as a leader, which was highly influenced by pop and soul music. After Davis's death in 1991, Marcus formed his own band, performing in the style of Davis's later band.

JUNE 15—ERROLL GARNER (1921–1977)

b. Pittsburgh, PA; d. Los Angeles, CA

Pianist; Composer; Leader

[SWING; BOP]

Other jazz notables born on this day: Paul Mares (1900); Allan Reuss (1915); Jaki Byard (1922); Tony Oxley (1938)

Jazz notables deceased on this day: Wes Montgomery (1968); Art Pepper (1982); Ella Fitzgerald (1996)

♪

During the 1940s and '50s four outstanding pianists became household names beyond the jazz audience: Erroll Garner, George Shearing, Dave Brubeck, and Oscar Peterson. The most distinctive of these, perhaps the most unique of all pianists, was Garner, who proved that it was possible to be a sophisticated player without knowing how to read music.[8] A brilliant virtuoso who sounded unlike anyone else, Garner was successful in attracting a wide audience, and by the late 1950s he was one of the most popular musicians working in jazz. His song "Misty," written during this period, became a big hit, and has since become a jazz standard. A maverick, whose individualistic style actually stood outside the jazz tradition, Garner had neither obvious forerunners nor competent imitators. Yet at an amateur level, more players attempted to imitate his style than that of any other jazz pianist.

Having played piano from childhood, Erroll was a local celebrity by the age of ten, when he appeared on radio with a kids show, and by the age of sixteen he was working professionally with Leroy Brown's quartet and orchestra, where he acquired a swing style. Around this time, Pittsburgh-reared pianist Mary Lou Williams was traveling through town with Andy Kirk's band when she went to hear Garner. Impressed by his originality, she arranged to meet him and later even tried to teach him how to read music, but the youngster couldn't be bothered. That was fine with Williams, who realized immediately that the diminutive player "was born with more than most musicians could accomplish in a lifetime."[9]

Garner moved to New York in 1944, where he began performing in the clubs along Fifty-Second Street. By 1947, when he backed Charlie Parker on the famous "Cool Blues" session, the pianist was already in his groove. His unclassifiable style had an orchestral approach straight from the swing era but was open to the innovations of bop. He left jazz during the 1950s and from that point on Garner's accessible style became very popular. He rarely took a day off until illness forced his retirement in 1975. Able to sit at the piano without prior planning and record three albums in one day (all remarkable first takes), Garner made many records throughout his career. His prolific recording saga included an undisputable masterpiece—the live 1955 *Concert by the Sea*.

In liner notes for *Easy to Love*, a 1988 collection of previously unreleased cuts recorded in the early 1960s, actor (and pianist) Dudley Moore identified the unique element in Garner's playing as "sensuality," a quality engendered by the ability to maintain the beat with his left hand (like a rhythm guitar) while his right played chords slightly behind the beat: "Passion . . . that's what he had . . . A sprinkling of the demonic, a yearning for the tender, and a straight line to joy."[10]

---

8. Bogdanov et al., *All Music Guide to Jazz*, 456.
9. Gottlieb, *Reading Jazz*, 108.
10. Ibid., 924.

JUNE 16—LUCKY THOMPSON (1924–2005)

b. Columbia, SC; d. Seattle, WA

Tenor and Soprano Saxophonist

[Hard Bop; Bop]

Other jazz notables born on this day: Tom Harrell (1946)
Jazz notables deceased on this day: Chick Webb (1939); Lonnie Johnson (1970); Kid Thomas Valentine (1987); Bill Dixon (2010)

♪

Eli "Lucky" Thompson was one of the great tenors to emerge during the 1940s and one of the first "modern" soprano saxophonists (he took up the instrument prior to John Coltrane and around the same time as Steve Lacy), but he forever remained in the shadow of more spectacular players.[11] For a period of about twelve years, from 1944 to 1956, Lucky's career was propelled by a series of fortunate breaks, when he recorded with some of bebop's greatest stars, but after 1956 his opportunities in jazz were plagued by a streak of bad luck that marginalized his career and culminated in his embittered retirement from the jazz scene in 1974.

Raised in Detroit, Thompson acquired his first saxophone at the age of fifteen. After local gigs with players such as Hank Jones and Sonny Stitt, he moved to New York in the early 1940s, where he performed briefly with Lionel Hampton and Don Redman in 1943. During the summer of 1944 he was a member, with Charlie Parker and Dizzy Gillespie, of a new band led by Billy Eckstine. It was a fantastic band, its drummer Art Blakey recalled, a nurturing ground for bebop. But it only made a few instrumental records, due to a ban imposed by the recording industry, and those records were a pale reflection of what the men could do in person. "I can truthfully say . . . without any type of conceit," Eckstine remembered, "there was no band that ever swung like that band . . . but we never could get anywhere because [nobody could] hear it."[12] By winter Parker and Gillespie had left Eckstine, as did Thompson, who spent a year with Count Basie's orchestra. After leaving Basie he settled in Los Angeles, where he became a celebrated studio musician, recording more than one hundred recordings in a two-year span. In 1946 he participated in sessions with Charlie Parker and Dizzy Gillespie, as well as with Boyd Raeburn and the short-lived Stars of Swing. Lucky moved to Detroit in 1947 and the following year returned to New York, where he led his own band at the Savoy (1951–53) before contributing to the famous Miles Davis session, *Walkin'* (1954), which helped revive the trumpeter's career.

In 1956 Lucky was a top soloist with Stan Kenton; he toured Europe with Kenton, and then moved to France, where he lived during two periods (1957–62 and 1968–71). According to one account, his opportunities for a career in America declined after 1956 because he was blacklisted by Joe Glaser, Louis Armstrong's manager, following an argument during an airplane flight in which he refused to allow Glaser's star to leave the

---

11. Bogdanov et al, *All Music Guide to Jazz*, 1239.
12. Ward and Burns, *Jazz: A History*, 319.

aircraft first.[13] After his return to the U.S. and between periods of relative inactivity, Lucky taught at Dartmouth and Yale (1973–74), and then retired altogether from the music business. He moved to an island off the coast of Savannah, Georgia, where he gave his instruments to a dentist in exchange for dental work. Later, while living in Atlanta, he was badly beaten. During the 1990s the unlucky Thompson became a hermit and then lived homeless in Seattle.

JUNE 17—TONY SCOTT (1921–2007)

b. Morristown, NJ; d. Rome, Italy

Clarinetist

[Folk-Jazz; Post-Bop; Cool]

Other jazz notables born on this day: Sam Wooding (1895)
Jazz notables deceased on this day: Johnny St. Cyr (1966)

♫

Though originally perfectly at home with mainstream and bebop musicians, Tony Scott's concept and style were, even at an early point, unclassifiable. Dubbed "the biggest sound in the world," Scott played the clarinet with immense power and expressiveness, the whole jazz tradition evident in his work. A musical adventurer in a long and fascinating career, he anticipated several major new developments in jazz, including free jazz, Indo-jazz fusions, the gradual absorption by jazz of elements from ethnic music, and the progress towards the idea of "world music."[14] During the 1950s his career became entwined with that of the up-and-coming pianist, Bill Evans. Scott always claimed to have discovered Evans, and was able to offer the pianist regular club work for several years. In 1959 Scott was responsible for bringing together for the first time the trio of Evans, Paul Motian, and Scott LaFaro, who went on to jazz immortality.

After studying at Juilliard (1940–42), Scott (Anthony Sciacca) took part in jam sessions at Minton's Playhouse in 1941 and became one of the few clarinetists to play in the emerging bop style. It was there that he heard Parker: "The first time was when I was sitting in with Don Byas. Bird came in and started playing 'Cherokee.' Now Byas could play fast, but Bird! My mouth dropped. And I was supposed to blow right after him." The converging influences of Webster and Parker formed Scott's distinctive style; his huge but controlled tone stood out from hard-driving players such as Buddy DeFranco, Scott's counterpart in the early bebop movement. From 1942 to 1945 he served with the military in New York, playing alto saxophone in big bands, tenor in Dixieland bands, and clarinet and piano in small swing groups. After his discharge, Scott worked as a sideman with a wide variety of artists, including Webster, Duke Ellington, Billie Holiday, Sarah Vaughan, and Harry Belafonte.

---

13. Kernfeld, *New Grove Dictionary of Jazz*, Vol. 3, 752.
14. Carr et al, *The Rough Guide*, 687.

From 1953 he led his own groups, winning polls as a clarinetist and establishing himself as an important new voice on the instrument. Unfortunately the clarinet was not as popular in the 1950s as it had been during the swing era, and Scott was little known outside of jazz circles. By the mid-1950s he became despondent, feeling he could not make it as a jazz clarinet player. For a while conditions improved and he was quite popular, winning the *Down Beat* critics poll in 1958 and 1959—that year he fronted a quartet with Bill Evans, who had just left Miles Davis's sextet—but by this point Scott was convinced there was no future for him in America. New York seemed like a big cemetery, for all the people he cared about—Parker, Holiday, Lester Young—were dying. Lamenting the decline of his instrument in jazz—"The clarinet died, and I hate funerals"—he began a global pilgrimage, exploring the folk music of other countries. After six years of traveling in the Far East he settled in Rome. The journey of pianist Bill Evans, however, though more limited geographically, would shape profoundly the course of Western musical history.

JUNE 18—RAY MCKINLEY (1910–1995)

b. Fort Worth, TX; d. Largo, FL

Drummer; Vocalist

[SWING]

Other jazz notables born on this day: Bennie Payne (1907); Ray Bauduc (1909); Babe Russin (1911)

Jazz notables deceased on this day:

♪

From 1939 to 1942 Glenn Miller led the most popular band in the world and the most beloved of all the swing-era orchestras. His reign as the most popular bandleader in the U.S. came relatively late in his career and was rather brief, but during that period he utterly dominated popular music. Over time he has proven the most enduring figure of the swing era, with reissues of his recordings achieving gold record status forty years after his death.[15] There have been many Glenn Miller ghost orchestras since Miller's military plane was lost while flying in bad weather across the English Channel (December 1944), including one led by Peanuts Hucko and another by British bandleader Syd Lawrence, but most have been stuck in the role of recreating the past, including note-for-note duplications of the recorded solos. The oddest case is tenor saxophonist/vocalist Tex Beneke, who spent fifty years essentially performing the same routine he had done with Miller from 1938 to 1942. In 1956 the Miller estate hired Ray McKinley, a former drummer with the Miller band, to organize a new ghost band, and this official ensemble continued to record and perform under various leaders from then on. "Ray McKinley always was an amazing drummer," wrote critic George T. Simon. "He provided a swinging beat . . . that inspired

---

15. Bogdanov et al, *All Music Guide to Jazz*, 868.

musicians to play better. [And] he spent more time on getting just the right sound out of his drums than any other drummer I can recall."[16]

A top drummer during the swing era and a personable vocalist, McKinley started his career playing in territory bands, after which he joined the Dorsey Brothers Orchestra (1934). Following the brothers' acrimonious split in 1935, McKinley remained with the band under the leadership of Jimmy Dorsey. In 1939 he left to form a band with Will Bradley, where his vocals and the boogie-woogie piano playing of Freddie Slack made the band a hit. When the group broke up, McKinley led a short-lived big band and then joined the military, playing in Europe with Glenn Miller's Army Air Force Orchestra and a small group that included Peanuts Hucko and Mel Powell. After Miller's death in 1944, McKinley briefly shared the leadership of the band with Jerry Gray. In 1946 McKinley put together his own orchestra, which initially featured some very modern arrangements by Eddie Sauter.

Following a period of work as a freelance, McKinley toured the world for a decade (1956–66) with the new Glenn Miller Orchestra, performing much of the original repertory. Thereafter he led his own big band (1966–68) and a small group that performed in New York. In 1973 he fronted Tex Beneke's big band devoted to Miller's music, remaining with the ensemble until 1978, when he opted for semi-retirement. His love of music and the musical life led him to form yet another group in the mid-1980s, with which he made two tours of Australia. Thereafter he frequently led bands at Disney World and Disneyland.

JUNE 19—DAVE LAMBERT (1917–1966)

b. Boston, MA; d. Westport, CT

Vocalist; Arranger

[VOCALESE; BOP]

Other jazz notables born on this day:
Jazz notables deceased on this day: Al Lucas (1983); Thurman Green (1997)

♪

In the *Down Beat* readers' polls, a category for vocal groups first appeared in 1944. The Pied Pipers won for the first six years, then the Mills Brothers for three years, and after that the Four Freshmen and the Hi-Los. According to this poll, the top jazz vocal group in the world from 1958 through 1963 was Lambert, Hendricks, and Ross (LH&R). The three bop singers developed to a high degree the art of taking instrumental jazz records and setting lyrics to just about everything on them—not just the tunes themselves but also the styles and improvised material of specific soloists—a technique labeled vocalese. In the late 1950s this seminal vocal trio provided the perfect combination of elements necessary to establish the standard for both the jazz vocal group and the vocalese genre. Arranger Dave Lambert came out of the big band tradition and helped to create the vocal lines

---

16. Carr et al, *Jazz: The Rough Guide*, 508.

that made the trio sound so hip and swinging. Jon Hendricks, steeped in both bebop and blues, wrote clever lyrics. Annie Ross shared all of these backgrounds and also brought the group the theatrical flair it needed.[17] Injecting healthy doses of humor while interacting wonderfully with the accompanists, the three vocalists approximated the intimacy and high-flying interplay of the small groups that dominated jazz during the 1950s and early '60s.

Dave Lambert was already a veteran singer when LH&R was formed in 1957. Originally a drummer, he sang with Johnny Lang's big band before joining Gene Krupa's Orchestra (1944–45), and when he sang "What's This" with Buddy Stewart, it was considered the first vocal version of a bop line. Lambert led a group of singers during the late 1940s and '50s and appeared with bebop pioneer Charlie Parker on several occasions. In 1955 he teamed up with Hendricks to record "Four Brothers." The two vocalists then assembled a group of singers to rehearse vocalese versions of Count Basie arrangements, but when they had difficulty coming up with enough talented singers to fill in for all of the horns, they brought in Annie Ross (already an established singer) as vocal coach. However, once they discovered Ross, it was decided to use just the three of them and overdub the parts (a comparatively early example of the technique); the result was the classic 1957 album, *Sing a Song of Basie*. The recording caused a sensation and launched LH&R as a top act that regularly broke attendance records at clubs in New York, Chicago, and on the West Coast.

During the next few years they recorded several notable albums, including an actual collaboration with Basie and a collection of Duke Ellington songs. Bad health caused Ross to drop out of the group in 1962 and the group disbanded in 1964, though their influence continued in the vocal quartet, Manhattan Transfer, and in nearly every jazz vocal group formed after that. In 1964 Lambert returned to studio work in New York; his final recording was a scat-filled version of "Donna Lee" performed at a 1965 Charlie Parker memorial concert. Lambert died tragically in 1966, struck by a tractor-trailer while changing a tire on the Connecticut Turnpike.

JUNE 20—ERIC DOLPHY (1928–1964)

b. Los Angeles, CA; d. Berlin, Germany

Alto Saxophonist; Bass Clarinetist; Flutist; Leader

[AVANT-GARDE JAZZ; FREE JAZZ; POST BOP]

Other jazz notables born on this day:
Jazz notables deceased on this day: Pee Wee Erwin (1981); Sadik Hakim (1983)

♪

In the early 1960s, when John Coltrane formed his own quartet and chose to begin experimenting with free jazz, he hired a remarkable musician as an occasional fifth member. Coltrane had known Eric Dolphy since 1954, and over the years they had many conversa-

---

17. Kirchner, *Oxford Companion to Jazz*, 481–82.

tions on both music and eastern philosophy. Dolphy was as close a friend as Coltrane had, so in 1961, when Coltrane decided to add a second horn to his ensemble, he began using Dolphy as a part-time member of the group. Dolphy was a highly versatile musician, the first to influence the course of jazz on three different instruments: flute, alto saxophone, and bass clarinet. Although alto was his main horn, Dolphy is remembered for his contributions on flute, the most progressive to that time, and particularly for his exploration of the bass clarinet as a medium for jazz improvisation, perhaps his greatest contribution, for he virtually introduced that instrument to the mainstream. Dolphy mastered the complete range of every instrument he played, and he capitalized on almost every sound it could produce. His style perfectly fit the avant-garde mold. From 1960 to 1964, including while he played with Coltrane, Dolphy collaborated with Charles Mingus, recording some of the most outstanding jazz recordings of this period.

Dolphy's professional career began in 1948, when he recorded in Los Angeles with the bebop-influenced Roy Porter big band. After two years in the army he played in obscurity until he joined the Chico Hamilton quintet in 1958. The following year he settled in New York and soon became a member of Mingus's quartet. By 1960 he was recording regularly as a leader, though throughout his career he had difficulty gaining steady work due to his advanced style. During 1960 and 1961 he did freelance work with Ornette Coleman (he participated on Coleman's revolutionary 1960 album, *Free Jazz*) before joining the Coltrane quintet. A 1961 engagement at the Village Vanguard with Coltrane caused conservative critics to brand their style as "anti-jazz," due to the lengthy and extremely free solos. In 1964 Dolphy traveled to Europe with Mingus's sextet, arguably the bassist's most exciting band. Choosing to remain in Europe, Dolphy died shortly thereafter of a diabetic coma. He was barely thirty-six years old: another tragic example of an untimely death in a disproportionately long list of jazz geniuses.

Despite a mere six years on the U.S. jazz scene, Dolphy's influence as a skilled multi-instrumentalist gained him as much influence and respect as other prematurely deceased jazz giants, including Bix Beiderbecke, Jimmy Blanton, Charlie Christian, and Fats Navarro. Virtually all previous musicians were identified with one main instrument, to which others were clearly secondary. But Dolphy was equally adept on each of his three main instruments, and the tendency of players since his time (particularly reed players) to make a virtue of versatility stems mostly from him.[18]

JUNE 21—LALO SCHIFRIN (1932–)

b. Buenos Aires, Argentina

Composer; Pianist

[FILM MUSIC; BOP]

Other jazz notables born on this day:
Jazz notables deceased on this day: June Christy (1990)

---

18. Carr et al., *Jazz: The Rough Guide*, 208.

♪

During the second half of the twentieth century trumpeter Dizzy Gillespie was clearly the central figure in the effort to import Latin music into the developing jazz mainstream. In 1956 he formed a big band and played several long tours sponsored by the U.S. State Department, including extensive trips to the Middle East and South America; the band survived until 1958. This was the first time that the government had used jazz music as its cultural representative, and as the tours were immensely successful, jazz continued to be used in this capacity. During the 1970s and '80s Dizzy remained a world traveler, inspiring younger players wherever he went. In 1956, while on tour in Argentina, he met Lalo Schifrin, a classically trained pianist/composer who had recently formed Latin America's first jazz orchestra, a sixteen-piece band that was associated with a popular variety show on Buenos Aires television. Schifrin offered to compose an extended work for Gillespie's big band, and in 1958 he completed the five-movement *Gillespiana* suite, the same year he won Argentina's Academy award for his score to the film *El Jefe*.

A child prodigy, Schifrin was born in Buenos Aires to a musical household. His father, a symphonic violinist, was concertmaster of Argentina's foremost orchestra. At the age of six Lalo began a six-year course of study on piano with Enrique Barenboim, father of pianist/conductor Daniel Barenboim. In 1952 he enrolled at the Paris Conservatoire, where he attended Oliver Messiaen's classes and studied with Charles Koechlin, a heralded disciple of Maurice Ravel. At night, he earned his living playing jazz in the Paris clubs. In 1955, shortly before returning to Argentina, he represented his country in the International Jazz Festival in Paris. Three years later, after meeting Gillespie in Argentina, Schifrin moved to New York, where he gained prominence as pianist in Dizzy's quintet (1960–62). The *Gillespiana* suite was recorded in 1960 and received acclaim from critics and jazz fans alike. For the next two years Schifrin also served as Gillespie's musical director, and he recorded frequently with the bandleader. Schifrin provided Gillespie with yet another brilliant suite in 1962, *The New Continent*, before leaving the trumpeter's successful organization.

In 1964 Schifrin moved to Hollywood, where he composed distinctive scores for films and television shows, notably the theme for the *Mission Impossible* series. Schifrin has since become one of the most prolific film composers in Hollywood. The best of his film scores often employed elements of jazz and were most effectively set to action thrillers such as *Bullitt* (1968), *Cool Hand Luke* (1968), *Dirty Harry* (1971), and *Enter the Dragon* (1973). A true renaissance artist, Schifrin has contributed significantly to the musical vocabulary of the twentieth century. In addition to scores for more than one hundred films and televisions programs, he has had historic impact in jazz, popular, and classical music (including a project he calls *Jazz Meets the Symphony*), and is especially noted for experimental pieces like his *Jazz Suite on the Mass Texts* (1965), which fuse jazz to religion.

JUNE 22—BEN POLLACK (1903–1971)

b. Chicago, IL; d. Palm Springs, CA

Drummer; Bandleader

[CLASSIC JAZZ; SWING; DIXIELAND]

Other jazz notables born on this day: Hermeto Pascoal (1936)
Jazz notables deceased on this day: Pee Wee Hunt (1979); Emmett Berry (1993)

♪

A talented drummer and a superior bandleader, Ben Pollack was one of the forefathers of the big-band era. A kindly but deeply ambitious man, cursed with a large capacity for envy, Pollack had a great ear for talent but lacked the capacity to hang on to his discoveries. His Dixieland-oriented jazz bands of the late 1920s and early '30s became a storehouse of young white talent; Glenn Miller, Benny Goodman, Jack Teagarden, Jimmy McPartland, Harry James, Bud Freeman, Charlie Spivak, Yank Lawson, and Muggsy Spanier were among his young stars. Yet to his everlasting chagrin, he was unable to reap the rewards of his protégés.

After playing drums in various Chicago professional bands in his teens, Pollack joined the New Orleans Rhythm Kings in the early 1920s, where he established himself as the leading drummer in the early Chicago style of white jazz. After giving some thought to the idea of returning to his family's fur business, he formed the first of his own bands in 1926. Working mostly in Chicago and New York City, Pollack's bands became moderately successful, but the hot young talent that Pollack rounded up became impatient with his old-fashioned singing and commercially oriented shows. They resented it when he drove in a chauffeured limousine while they bounced around in a rented bus, and were appalled when he abandoned the drums in order to stay in the spotlight as conductor and crooner. Although Pollack was never a tyrant, his protégés played practical jokes, took record dates without him, and stood up to his views on and off the stand. Animosity finally exploded during a theater engagement in Brooklyn. Between shows, Goodman and McPartland liked to go up to the roof and play handball. One evening they badly scuffed their white band shoes, then wore them onstage. Disgusted when Pollack fired McPartland over the incident, Goodman promptly handed in his resignation.

Pollack resurfaced with another group of young stars, including Lawson, Matty Matlock, and Eddie Miller. But in December 1934, after making a more serious error of judgment—he allegedly gave favored treatment to his current girlfriend, singer Doris Robbins—this band broke up and then regrouped under the leadership of Bob Crosby. Pollack was deeply aggrieved over the walkout, particularly as he watched the Crosby band, Goodman, Glenn Miller, and others achieve a commercial success that he could only dream about. In 1936 Pollack's latest discovery, Harry James, also left unceremoniously to achieve fame and fortune. Over the next two years Pollack sought recompense through a $5 million lawsuit against Goodman, Victor Records, Paramount Pictures, and Camel Cigarettes for what he felt were lost earnings, a desperate move that died in the courts. During the 1940s and '50s he occasionally organized groups in California, but by the early 1960s he was running a restaurant in Palm Springs. On June 7, 1971, the still-embittered bandleader, weighed down by a developing heart condition and his acrimonious past, ended his life by hanging himself in his Palm Springs bathroom.

JUNE 23—MILT "THE JUDGE" HINTON (1910–2000)

b. Vicksburg, MS; d. New York, NY

Bassist

[SWING]

Other jazz notables born on this day: Helen Humes (1909); Eddie Miller (1911); George Russell (1923)
Jazz notables deceased on this day: Jerome Richardson (2000)

♪

By 1940 a new club called Minton's Playhouse on 118th Street in Harlem had begun to attract some of the most adventurous musicians in jazz. The venue was cramped and dingy, but it was managed by the former bandleader Teddy Hill, who had come up with the idea of making Monday evenings an open house, with free food and drink for any musician willing to play. Soon the all-night sessions attracted some of the best musicians in jazz, as many as thirty at a time, competing with one another for technical and artistic supremacy. Dizzy Gillespie, currently a trumpeter with Cab Calloway's orchestra, had performed with Teddy Hill's band in the late 1930s, and he lived for the jam sessions at Minton's, where he was free to experiment with fast tempos, fresh harmonies, and unfamiliar keys. While with Calloway, Dizzy found a kindred spirit in bassist Milt Hinton, also a regular at Minton's. During intermission, the two practiced together, trying different chords and progressions. Sometimes, such as during the band's residency at the Cotton Club, Hinton carried his bass up the fire escape so the two could conduct their musical experiments in private. Those harmonic experiments with Gillespie made Hinton a forerunner of modern jazz bass players.[19]

Considered the best bassist before the rise of Jimmy Blanton in 1939, Hinton probably appeared on more records than any other musician in the world.[20] In a career that spanned seventy years, he performed with virtually every luminary of the jazz and popular music world from Calloway, Gillespie, Louis Armstrong, and John Coltrane to Bing Crosby, Frank Sinatra, Bobby Darin, Barbra Streisand, and Paul McCartney. In addition to his expansive discography, Hinton also documented his career with a camera, and his collection of personal photographs has been the subject of two books and numerous gallery exhibitions around the world.

Having grown up in a musical family, Hinton moved to Chicago in 1919, where he gained valuable experience working alongside Benny Goodman in the Hull House band,

---

19. Kernfeld, *New Grove Dictionary of Jazz*, Vol. 2, 245.
20. Bogdanov et al., *All Music Guide to Jazz*, 599.

an organization that provided serious professional training to exceptional students from indigent families. Hinton began on violin, studying classical music, and by his senior year in high school he had taken up double bass. He began working professionally with legendary figures such as violinist Eddie South and trumpeters Jabbo Smith, Guy Kelly, and Freddie Keppard before joining Calloway's orchestra in 1936, where he became a mainstay for fifteen years. In 1951, when Calloway fired the entire band, Hinton moved into the New York club scene. In 1954 he became a staff musician at CBS, and he appeared on a countless number of recordings during the next fifteen years. Hinton spent his final decades as a senior jazz ambassador worldwide, appearing at jazz parties and international festivals and traveling widely as a jazz educator. He remained a vital figure in jazz until his death at the age of ninety.

JUNE 24—GEORGE GRUNTZ (1932–)

b. Basel, Switzerland

Keyboardist; Composer; Bandleader

[Post-Bop; Progressive Big Band]

Other jazz notables born on this day: Capt. John Handy (1900); Jeff Beck (1944); Clint Houston (1946); Marvin "Smitty" Smith (1961)

Jazz notables deceased on this day: Jimmy O'Bryant (1928); Massimo Urbani (1993)

♪

In 1989, during a meeting of a jazz club in Warsaw, Poland, delegates from several Eastern European countries gathered to discuss the implications of accommodating jazz with socialism. A Hungarian musician named Janos stepped to the microphone and announced the end of an era when he said, "I am not a Communist. I am not a socialist. I am a saxophonist." His declaration was also a challenge to America's jazz hegemony, for though the U.S. invented jazz and remained the music's only superpower, its days of sole dominion were over. By the mid-1980s between seven hundred and one thousand festivals of international importance were taking place annually around the globe, in places as far apart as Boston, Tokyo, and Nice. Since then, festivals have continued to grow in both size and number (there are some 250 jazz festivals a year in France alone), with international audiences numbering in the millions annually. In Japan, individual jazz concerts regularly attract up to four thousand fans, and the annual festival in Montreux, Switzerland draws audiences in excess of two hundred thousand. By the end of the twentieth century, jazz had become "the true world music," influencing almost every other music.[21]

Though he is little known in North America, the Swiss pianist George Gruntz long ago emerged as one of jazz's great bandleaders. Best known as a prolific composer and arranger, his work always displays an adventurous approach to jazz and has consistently pushed against accepted boundaries. His multinational Concert Jazz Band has long ranked among the greatest of all jazz big bands.

---

21. Kirchner, *Oxford Companion to Jazz*, 545.

Gruntz played locally in Switzerland and first attracted attention at the 1958 Newport Jazz Festival, where he appeared with the Marshall Brown International Youth Band. In the 1960s his trio in Europe accompanied touring American musicians such as Dexter Gordon, Chet Baker, and Rahsaan Roland Kirk, and formed the rhythm section of Phil Woods's European Rhythm Machine (1968–69). In 1970 Gruntz was appointed musical director of the Zurich State Theatre, a post he held until 1984, and from 1972 to 1994 he was artistic director of the Berlin Jazz Festival. In 1972 he co-founded the Concert Jazz Band, which over the years has included the cream of modern jazz musicians. Over the years Gruntz has recorded in many different settings, including with the Swiss All-Stars (a four-flute septet) and the Piano Conclave (comprising a rhythm section and six leading European pianists playing twenty keyboard instruments, from harpsichord to synthesizer), with which he has appeared at major festivals all over Europe. In 1991 members of the Gil Evans Orchestra joined Gruntz and his band at the Montreux festival, and under Quincy Jones's direction the huge international ensemble backed jazz icon Miles Davis (two months before the trumpeter's death), recreating some of Evans's famous orchestral arrangements from the late 1950s.

JUNE 25—BILL RUSSO (1928–2003)

b. Chicago, IL; d. Chicago, IL

Composer; Arranger; Trombonist

[COOL; PROGRESSIVE BIG BAND]

Other jazz notables born on this day: Johnny Smith (1922); Joe Chambers (1942); Bobby Naughton (1944)
Jazz notables deceased on this day: Johnny Mercer (1976); Alex Welsh (1982)

♪

Along with the bebop movement developed during the 1940s, the 1950s ushered in a lighter, more romantic style of jazz called "cool," a form of music that combined the melodic and swinging aspects of the earlier swing era with the harmonic and rhythmic developments of bebop. Big bands held over from the swing era, including the Woody Herman and Stan Kenton orchestras, incorporated elements of the bebop and cool styles into their music. The roots of cool jazz can be traced to various earlier styles, such as the laid back melodic approach of tenor saxophonist Lester Young, whose light airy tone offered cool musicians new directions to explore other than those of the hard driving bebop style. The cool movement also incorporated influences from classical music. Pianist Lennie Tristano cited J. S. Bach and Bela Bartók as major influences. By the mid- to late 1950s cool jazz would create a serious link between the worlds of jazz and classical music with a style called "Third Stream."

Bill Russo, one of a handful of arrangers with an ear for the textural potential of the large jazz orchestra, was a key element in the Stan Kenton orchestras of the 1950s. He contributed scores of sensitivity and depth to the fashionable bandleader, particularly during the early 1950s, when the orchestra was at its most creative. Born in Chicago, Russo attended school with the saxophonist Lee Konitz. Like Konitz, Russo studied music in the mid-1940s with Tristano, the influential guru of the restrained, chamber-jazz cool style. During this period Russo also played trombone in several dance bands, and from 1947 to 1950 he led an exploratory rehearsal band, Experiments in Jazz. This venture revealed Russo's interest in approaching jazz from unfamiliar angles—partly drawn from twentieth century classical developments—but he was not yet committed to a career in jazz. He was studying to be a lawyer.

However, when the invitation came in 1950 to join Kenton's high-profile Innovations Orchestra as trombonist, composer, and arranger, the temptation was too great (though he continued studying composition privately and later completed a degree in English literature). When Russo left Kenton, he did so to form his own band. In 1958 he won a grant from the Koussevitzky Foundation and he moved to New York, where he formed and conducted the Russo Orchestra, a large jazz ensemble. From 1957 to 1960 he taught at the Lenox School of Jazz (the center of the "third stream" movement) in Massachusetts, as well as at the Manhattan School of Music (1959–61). Two years later, after traveling to Rome, he settled in London, where he conducted the London Jazz Orchestra and worked for the BBC. In 1965 he returned to Chicago to direct the Center for New Music at Columbia College. Over his career, in addition to his own compositional activity, Russo has written several pioneering texts on jazz composition. In 1991 he founded the Chicago Jazz Ensemble, a retrospective group that mixed spontaneity with memorized material (much of it rare) from jazz soloists of the past.

JUNE 26—REGGIE WORKMAN (1937–)

b. Philadelphia, PA

Bassist

[AVANT-GARDE JAZZ; HARD BOP]

Other jazz notables born on this day: Don Lamphere (1928); Dave Grusin (1934); Joey Baron (1955); Bill Cunliffe (1956)

Jazz notables deceased on this day: Clifford Brown (1956); Richie Powell (1956); Ziggy Elman (1968)

♪

When "the New Thing," as avant-garde jazz was called, emerged around 1960, few knew what to make of it. Established concepts such as time, meter, rhythm, melody, and harmony were reconstructed or obliterated in order to fashion a music that was emotionally cathartic and intellectually challenging. Due in large part to the conservatism in the recording industry and radio, the style was at best a peripheral phenomenon. Though the passage of time has done little to ameliorate matters, a good many players continue to produce music that is startlingly fresh and decidedly off the beaten track. Bassist Reggie Workman is a prime example.

One of several outstanding double bass players who came to prominence in the 1960s, Workman has long been one of the most technically gifted of all bassists. As a youngster he played piano, tuba, and euphonium before taking up bass with rhythm-and-blues groups in 1955. Around this time he formed a trio in Philadelphia (with pianist McCoy Tyner and drummer Eddie Campbell) that accompanied such guest soloists as John Coltrane, Benny Golson, and Jackie McLean. As the house bass player at a local club he also worked with Phineas Newborn, Aretha Franklin, Yusef Lateef, Lee Morgan, and others.

When he relocated to New York in 1957, he worked with Red Garland and Roy Haynes and was a member of Coltrane's band for much of 1961, participating in several important recordings (including *Live at the Village Vanguard* and *Africa/Brass*) and touring internationally with Coltrane's small groups. After Jimmy Garrison took his place with Coltrane, Workman joined Art Blakey's Jazz Messengers (1962–64) and was in the groups of Lateef (1964–65), Herbie Mann, and Thelonious Monk (1967). He recorded frequently in the 1960s, including on Archie Shepp's classic album *Four for Trane* (1964), after which he became active in music education. Around 1984 he began collaborating with Maya Milanovic in theatrical performances, marrying the dancer/choreographer in 1986. In 1987 he joined the faculty of the New School for Social Research in New York, where he was later appointed professor of music. There he implemented and conducted classes such as the Coltrane Ensemble, Futuristic Music, Bass Ensembles, and the Art Blakey Ensemble. His close associations with John and Alice Coltrane led to various moving tributes to the saxophonist, including the production in 1987 of "The Coltrane Legacy" at New York City's Cathedral of St. John the Divine. Workman continues his dedication to programs that underlie the legacy of musicians such as Art Blakey and Charlie Parker, as well as to original contributions by other noted African-Americans.

JUNE 27—TONY SBARBARO (1897–1969)

b. New Orleans; d. New York, NY

Drummer

[CLASSIC JAZZ; DIXIELAND]

Other jazz notables born on this day: Shad Collins (1909 or 1910); Elmo Hope (1923); James Lincoln Collier (1928)
Jazz notables deceased on this day: Barney Bigard (1980); Chico O'Farrill (2001)

♫

Tony Sbarbaro is remembered primarily for his work with the Original Dixieland Jazz Band (ODJB), the ensemble that in 1917 became the first jazz band ever to record. On February 26 the Victor Company brought five white New Orleans musicians into a New York studio to record two tunes: "Dixieland Jazz Band One Step" and "Livery Stable Blues." The emphasis was on comedy. Nick LaRocca made his cornet whinny, Larry Shields crowed like a rooster on his clarinet, and Daddy Edwards made his trombone moo. No one improvised, yet the music was hotter and livelier than anything that had ever been recorded before. Released on March 7, that first jazz record sold over a million copies—more than any single record by Enrico Caruso or John Phillip Sousa—and before long the band was back in the recording studio. One moment jazz was unknown, the next it had become a serious national pastime. Back in New Orleans, musicians were swept up in the excitement caused by the ODJB's success. Dance-band violinists across town began losing their jobs because the ODJB did not happen to have one. Along with the rest of the country, Louis Armstrong listened to the ODJB's records. He liked the sound of Nick LaRocca's cornet but he loved Larry Shields's clarinet solo on "Clarinet Marmalade" and was soon reproducing it flawlessly on his horn. [22]

Sbarbaro, the ODJB's drummer, began playing in New Orleans with the Frayle Brothers' Band (1911) and later with Papa Jack Laine's Reliance Band. In 1916 he moved to Chicago to join the ODJB. While the band was playing at the Casino Gardens, the vaudeville star Al Jolson dropped by and would later claim that he was largely responsible for procuring the New York engagement at the Paradise Ballroom, part of the new Reisenweber Restaurant complex, that catapulted the combo to fame. At first, Manhattan dancers fled the dance floor when the band began to play its raucous music, but before long the new music was being hailed as a sensation. Reisenweber's ran advertisements proclaiming jazz as the latest fad, and put up a neon sign that read: THE ORIGINAL DIXIELAND JAZZ BAND—THE CREATORS OF JAZZ (the spelling had been changed from "Jass," LaRocca remembered, after children were seen scratching the letter "J" off the street posters). After a successful visit to London, the band returned to find New York filled with noisy imitators. The ODJB continued to do well for a time, but too much drinking and too many one-nighters eventually wore its members down. One by one they left. In 1925, when LaRocca suffered a nervous breakdown, the group disbanded. While other members occasionally returned to playing, only Sbarbaro (later known as Tony Spargo) had a full-time music career. He remained in New York, where he led a band and was a sideman with many Dixieland musicians. In the late 1950s he recorded with Connee Boswell and made further appearances at Dixieland clubs in New York, complementing his drumming with spirited kazoo playing.

JUNE 28—JOE "FOX" SMITH (1902–1937)

b. Ripley, OH; d. New York, NY

Trumpeter

[CLASSIC JAZZ; BLUES]

Other jazz notables born on this day: Adrian Rollini (1903); Pete Candoli (1923); John Medeski (1965)

Jazz notables deceased on this day: Red Nichols (1965)

---

22. Ward and Burns, *Jazz: A History*, 64.

During the mid-1920s the most prominent and versatile of the black New York bands was clearly that of Fletcher Henderson. From its 1923 debut, Henderson's band set a standard for contemporary arrangements and came quickly to include several individuals who would develop into first-rate jazz players, among them tenor saxophonist Coleman Hawkins and cornetist Joe Smith. The band was not yet a jazz band. The group thought of itself as a dance band, playing mostly waltzes and fox trots, with an occasional blues number. Smith, who was in and out of the band, possessed a beautiful tone and one of the most lyrical styles around, but his phrasing was stiff and lacked much jazz feeling. But the band began to gather a following and it recorded often.

In 1924 Henderson was offered a position at the Roseland, New York's largest and most opulent ballroom. Just days after the engagement began, however, Smith left for a better-paying job as musical director for *The Chocolate Dandies*, a revue by Noble Sissle and Eubie Blake. When he appeared on stage at the end of the show to play for the departing audience, his gentle, voice-like tone (played into a coconut-shell mute) froze the people in their tracks, causing the doorways to become jammed. Smith's sensational new style was quickly noted by Henderson, with whom he worked again from 1925 to 1928, a period during which he also recorded classics with Bessie Smith and became her favorite accompanist.[23] For a brief period in the 1920s Smith was considered the chief rival of Armstrong, who, like Smith, had also played as a soloist with Henderson (1924–25). However, the style of the two was entirely different. Smith's work had considerable period charm but little of Armstrong's invention, versatility, and durability.

Smith grew up in a musical family (his father led a brass band in Cincinnati and his six brothers all played trumpet). In 1919, after working locally, Smith left home to perform professionally. He toured the Midwest and East Coast and he appeared in Pittsburgh for a short time, where he impressed a young pianist named Earl Hines, who later cited his blues playing as an early influence: "I followed Joe everywhere in the world he went. I just couldn't believe [his style], and I wanted to play what he played. It gave me a lot of new ideas."[24] By 1922 Smith began accompanying vocalist Ethel Waters. After a stint with Mamie Smith's Jazz Hounds (1922–23), Smith worked as a freelance, recording with Henderson and with many of the era's top female vocalists. From 1929 he worked with McKinney's Cotton Pickers, where he became close friends with singer George "Fathead" Thomas. Smith's personality, wild and unpredictable, was the antithesis of his subtle and mellow musical style. One autumn night in 1930, when he and Thomas were drunk, he drove his friend into a fatal car accident: Thomas was killed and Smith never fully recovered from the shock. He returned to New York, where he died in a sanitarium after several years of mental decline.

---

23. Carr et al., *Jazz: The Rough Guide*, 716
24. Collier, *Making of Jazz*, 211.

JUNE 29—RALPH BURNS (1929–2001)

b. Newton, MA; d. Los Angeles, CA

Arranger; Composer; Pianist

[SWING; BOP; TRADITIONAL POP]

Other jazz notables born on this day: Alexander, Mousey (1922); Ove Lind (1926); Julian Priester (1935)

Jazz notables deceased on this day: Eric Dolphy (1964); Groove Holmes (1991)

♪

Despite a successful career as composer-arranger of film soundtracks, including Woody Allen's *Bananas* (1971), Bob Fosse's *Sweet Charity* (1969), *Cabaret* (1972), and *Lenny*, and Martin Scorsese's *New York, New York* (1977), Ralph Burns will always be remembered in the jazz world for his work with Woody Herman's first two Herds, and indirectly, as composer of "Early Autumn," the piece that ushered saxophonist Stan Getz to fame in 1949. Herman, a bandleader since 1936, began remaking his band in 1943, bringing together a remarkable group of musicians that included Burns as pianist-arranger, trumpeter Pete Candoli, trombonist Bill Harris, tenor saxophonist Flip Phillips, and a rhythm section driven by drummer Dave Tough and bassist Chubby Jackson. This First Herd, a wild, good-time band, was considered the era's most exciting new big band. Herman reached an audience essential to the band's success by getting around a recording ban currently imposed by the American Federation of Musicians. Months before the ban ended, Herman made V-discs, recordings distributed only to the troops. When the soldiers returned home in 1945, they demanded more great music and the Herd provided it, achieving a level of success never to be repeated by any postwar big band.

Family troubles caused Herman to break up the band at the height of its success in late 1946, but by mid-1947 he formed a new orchestra, the Second Herd, which came to be known as the Four Brothers band. With its three cool-toned tenors—Stan Getz, Zoot Sims, and Herbie Steward (later replaced by Al Cohn)—and baritonist Serge Chaloff forming the nucleus, this band had a different sound than its more extroverted predecessor. Though it did not capture the public's imagination in the way the First Herd did, the orchestra (called "the best white band that ever played music" by composer-arranger Johnny Mandel) will forever be associated with "Early Autumn," one of several requests Herman answered nightly over the next forty years. The composition's origins, as told by Gary Giddins, are worth recalling.[25]

In 1946 Ralph Burns, now devoted to composition, presented Herman with a three-part suite called "Summer Sequence." The leader recorded the suite with the First Herd, using the band's chief saxophonist, Flip Phillips. Columbia sat on the recording for a year, insisting that a fourth movement be added in order to release the entire work on two 78s. In 1947, with a new band, Herman recorded "Summer Sequence (Part IV)," complete with an eight-bar solo by Stan Getz and a closing melody that promised more than was

---

25. Giddins, *Visions of Jazz*, 407.

realized in that arrangement. One year later the band was back in the studio, this time for Capitol, playing a new piece by Ralph Burns called "Early Autumn," built entirely on that elusive closing melody. Once again, Getz was delegated an eight-bar solo, and this time it propelled him to stardom.

JUNE 30—LENA HORNE (1917–2010)

b. New York, NY; d. New York, NY

Vocalist

[VOCAL JAZZ; TRADITIONAL POP; SWING; SHOW TUNES]

Other jazz notables born on this day: Stanley Clarke (1951)
Jazz notables deceased on this day: Joe Henderson (2001)

♪

Although considered by many as a superior pop vocalist, Lena Horne was closely associated with many jazz artists, and the unique quality of her singing made hers a true jazz voice. An ageless beauty with an appealing personality, her talent and middle class upbringing helped her to crack the race barrier in Hollywood. In 1981, after a devastating twelve-month period when her father, husband, and son died, she appeared on the Broadway stage with a triumphant one-person show, *Lena Horne: The Lady and Her Music*, which ran for fourteen months and earned her a special Tony Award. She reached that pinnacle via a road that started in Harlem and was accompanied by stormy weather. Often regarded as a pioneer among African American performers, she spent much of her life battling racial and social injustice.

Born in Brooklyn, Horne became one of the most popular African American performers of the 1940s and '50s. Pushed by an ambitious mother into the chorus line of the Cotton Club when she was sixteen, she was the first African American signed to a long-term Hollywood studio contract. While at the Cotton Club she was introduced to the growing community of jazz performers, including Billie Holiday, Cab Calloway, and Duke Ellington. For the next five years she sang in New York nightclubs and performed on Broadway. After that she sang with Noble Sissle's Orchestra (1935–36) and recorded with Teddy Wilson. As vocalist with Charlie Barnet's primarily white swing band (1940–41), Horne was one of the first black women to work successfully on both sides of the color line. Her success came with a price, however, for on account of her race she was regularly denied room and service at the very hotels where she sang. Her breakthrough as a singer came in 1941 at Café Society, the first interracial club to be established in the U.S., where she earned great popularity singing with Wilson's combo.

From the early 1940s Horne's talent and striking looks took her into a string of films, including two memorable black musicals: *Cabin in the Sky* (with Ethel Waters, Duke Ellington, and Louis Armstrong) and *Stormy Weather*, with Calloway and Fats Waller. MGM sent her out on a tour of its theaters and as a result she became one of the top nightclub and theater box office attractions. By the mid-1940s she was the highest paid black actor in the country. In 1947 she married arranger-pianist Lennie Hayton; her marriage was not announced for three years because Hayton was white, which offended both blacks and whites to the extent that the couple received hate mail and threats of violence. During the 1950s she found herself blacklisted for her civil rights activism, and therefore unable to perform on television or in the movies. For seven years she worked as a singer, appearing in nightclubs and making some of her best recordings. By the 1960s she was once again a major cultural figure. Though much has changed since her debut at the Cotton Club, she never lost her ability to break hearts with her shimmering voice.

Chapter 7

July

JULY 1—RASHIED ALI (1935–2009)

b. Philadelphia, PA; d. New York, NY

Drummer

[AVANT-GARDE JAZZ; FREE JAZZ]

Other jazz notables born on this day: Earle Warren (1914)
Jazz notables deceased on this day: Claude Thornhill (1965); Lonnie Hillyer (1985); Chauncey Haughton (1989); Jess Stacy (1995); Herbie Mann (2003)

♪

When John Coltrane died in the summer of 1967, thousands of people around the world despaired, for Coltrane epitomized the spirit of jazz. Given Coltrane's determination to stamp himself with greatness, it was inevitable that he became interested in free jazz, for he could not allow a revolutionary current to pass without comment. In 1965 the saxophonist invited seven avant-gardists to join his quartet in the studio to record *Ascension*, a thirty-eight-minute collective improvisation that signaled Coltrane's total identification with the avant-garde.

Later that year Coltrane decided to use a two-drummer format for a gig at the Village Gate, hiring Rashied Ali to complement Elvin Jones, his legendary drummer. The pairing resulted in turmoil. McCoy Tyner, Coltrane's longtime pianist, quit in disgust, claiming all he could hear was noise; Jones left the band soon thereafter. The task of following Jones as drummer with Coltrane would have been a daunting one for any jazz drummer, particularly in the mid-1960s, when most listeners would have assumed that Elvin was the only drummer alive who possessed the requisite drive, imagination, and powerful sense of swing necessary to drive Coltrane's passions. As it turned out, even Jones had limitations, and since Coltrane was all about transcending limitations, the addition of Ali's asymmetrical flexibility helped propel the saxophonist further into the unknown. "Indeed, it was with the addition of Ali to his group that Coltrane's free jazz period truly began."[1]

---

1. Bogdanov et all, *All Music Guide to Jazz*, 3rd ed., 18.

Born Robert Patterson Jr., the drummer changed his name to Rashied Ali when his father became a Muslim. Earlier his family had been active in a Baptist church and his mother sang with Jimmie Lunceford's orchestra. Ali took up conga drumming at the age of nine, but it wasn't until he enlisted in the army (1952–55) that he received training as a percussionist. Upon his discharge he continued his studies at Philadelphia's Granoff School of Music. After working with various musicians locally, including Tyner, Lee Morgan, and Jimmy Smith, in 1963 Ali moved to New York, where he became involved in the free jazz scene. He performed with such musical free spirits as Pharoah Sanders, Don Cherry, Paul Bley, Bill Dixon, Sun Ra, Albert Ayler, and Archie Shepp before beginning his important association in 1965 with Coltrane, which ended with the latter's death.

Ali then left for Europe, working as a freelance before his eventual return to the U.S., where he resumed his place at the forefront of New York's music scene. In response to the decaying jazz scene in the early 1970s, Ali helped to organize the New York Jazz Musicians' Festival (1972), an attempt by jazz musicians to be economically self-sufficient. Later that year he formed Survival Records, and then in 1973 he opened Ali's Alley, a loft space that presented free-jazz performances. Although the Alley closed in 1979, its legacy continues in the New York jazz scene. Since that time Ali continued to refine his music and encourage a host of younger musicians.

JULY 2—AHMAD JAMAL (1930–)

b. Pittsburgh, PA

Pianist, Leader

[POST-BOP; COOL]

Other jazz notables born on this day: Jack Hylton (1892); Harlan Leonard (1905)
Jazz notables deceased on this day: Eddie "Cleanhead" Vinson (1988); Errol Parker (1998)

♪

While Ahmad Jamad never attained the level of celebrity that Errol Garner, Oscar Peterson, or Dave Brubeck did, for a short period in the late 1950s his trio reached a large audience. Unlike so many pianists of that era who imitated Bud Powell, Jamal's light touch and carefully planned trio arrangements showed the power that could be achieved with only a few well-placed notes. With his crisp, precise attack, he built solos dramatically, as few other pianists could, using the same, spare ingredients. His bouncy left-hand voicings and tantalizing right were a streamlined version of fellow Pittsburgher Garner.

Jamal's penchant for understatement greatly influenced many musicians, among them Miles Davis, who instructed his pianist Red Garland to try to sound like him. Davis admired Jamal's lean style, use of space, and simple embellishments, which became stylistic features of his own recordings.[2] Furthermore, Davis went on to cover much of Jamal's repertoire, thereby expanding Jamal's sphere of influence. Given Davis's great influence on other musicians, not only later pianists with Miles (Wynton Kelly and Herbie Hancock in particular) but also those who imitated them reflect the work of Jamal to some extent.

2. Kernfeld, *New Grove Dictionary of Jazz*, Vol. 2, 351.

Jamal began playing professionally in Pittsburgh when he was fourteen. Upon graduation from high school in 1948 he toured with an orchestra led by the trumpeter George Hudson. In 1950 he converted to Islam and changed not only his spiritual orientation but also his birth name (Fritz Jones). The following year he formed his first trio, the Three Strings, a group with guitarist Ray Crawford and bassist Eddie Calhoun (Israel Crosby took Calhoun's place in 1955), and he gained recognition while performing in an extended engagement at the Blue Note in Chicago. He achieved an early hit with his arrangement of the folk song "Billy Boy," which Garland popularized in 1956, following Jamal's conception faithfully. That year Jamal switched to a piano/bass/drums trio. By 1958, with Vernell Fournier on drums and Crosby on bass, he recorded his most popular and influential album, titled *Ahmad Jamal at the Pershing*. Jamal is best known for his treatments of "Poinciana" (his signature piece), "But Not for Me," and his own composition, "Ahmad's Rhumba," recorded in a big band version by Miles Davis and Gil Evans (1956).

In 1959 Jamal disbanded his trio in order to make a pilgrimage to the holy places of Islam. Shortly after his return to the U.S. he opened a supper club in Chicago, the Alhambra, which offered Middle Eastern food and no alcohol, but the club failed seven months later. Dissatisfied with the musician's erratic lifestyle, Jamal disbanded his trio in 1962 and virtually retired from music until 1965. He eventually formed a new trio and continued to perform in nightclubs, where his playing evolved progressively, ensuring his status as one of the most distinctive pianists in jazz.

JULY 3—PETE FOUNTAIN (1930–)

b. New Orleans, LA

Clarinetist

[Dixieland]

Other jazz notables born on this day: Johnny Coles (1926); John Klemmer (1946)
Jazz notables deceased on this day: Lee Collins (1960); Curly Russell (1986)

♪

"No matter how far upstream jazz may have come from New Orleans," writes Bill Coss, "there exists a nostalgia, in some cases a reverence, in most minds, for that early cradle of American music. And as a general rule, New Orleans musicians help to perpetuate that nostalgia and reverence." Pete Fountain is a classic example. Despite some touring and a brief hiatus in the late 1950s, he has lived his life in New Orleans, and when he has left town, he has done so reluctantly. "Do You Know What It Means to Miss New Orleans" is a song with a title of more than ordinary significance for Fountain, for throughout his lengthy career, no musician has epitomized New Orleans more than he. A quintessential New Orleans jazz clarinetist, Fountain has done much to secure recognition—and an aura of respectability—for jazz. Jazz was always supported by the hometown masses, but during the 1950s and '60s, Fountain succeeded in winning over the city's social, cultural, and business leaders as well. A Pete Fountain Day was eventually proclaimed in New Orleans, and in 1968 the city staged its first full-scale Jazz and Heritage Festival. Thanks largely to Fountain, jazz has returned home.

Pierre Dewey La Fontaine Jr. was born in the Crescent City in 1930; needing a more concise name, he eventually became Pete Fountain. His father played several instruments as an avocation, and he encouraged his son's interest in music. Pete began playing clarinet at the age of nine and soon demonstrated superior natural instinct and aptitude for the instrument. In the time-honored way, he developed his style and technique by jamming with bands in the city's French Quarter. His first professional gig came at a strip joint when he was sixteen, replacing his idol, clarinetist Irving Fazola (another musician who didn't like to leave home), who had just died. "I had to lie about my age to get that job," he confessed. "After a while the management found out and fired me, so I started gigging around the city, anywhere I could work." By 1950 his reputation was growing, and after touring the U.S. with the Junior Dixieland Band, he helped form the Basin Street Six. He next joined the Dukes of Dixieland and traveled to Chicago for a time, returning home when the group embarked on a national tour.

In 1956 Fountain scored a huge success at the Shrine Auditorium in Los Angeles, which led to an invitation from Lawrence Welk to make guest appearances on his popular television show. The two-week offer turned into a two-year engagement. The response of home viewers was phenomenal, but eventually the urge to return home and play his own style became too strong. "I guess champagne and bourbon just don't mix," he said. Back in New Orleans, he purchased a club on Bourbon Street, where he remained until 1978. He then relocated to the New Orleans Hilton Riverside, where he continued performing his brand of Dixieland music to a full house. For Pete Fountain, there's no place like home.

JULY 4—LOUIS ARMSTRONG [Part One] (1901–1971)[3]

b. New Orleans, LA; d. New York, NY

Trumpeter; Vocalist; Bandleader

[NEW ORLEANS JAZZ; CLASSIC JAZZ;
VOCAL JAZZ; SWING; DIXIELAND; TRADITIONAL POP]

Other jazz notables born on this day: Leonard Davis (1905); Aaron Sachs (1923); Mike Mainieri (1938)

Jazz notables deceased on this day: Buddy Petit (1931); Joe Newman (1992)

♪

Louis Armstrong was born on August 4, 1901, but until his birth certificate was found in the late 1980s, most everyone accepted his claim to have been born on July 4, 1900. Throughout his life Louis proudly celebrated his birthday on America's Independence Day, and did not knowingly misrepresent his age in 1918 when he was hired to play in Kid Ory's popular band. Though he was only seventeen, his honest mistake came in handy, for as an eighteen-year-old he was now old enough to work in a cabaret.

---

3. Due to Armstrong's preeminent position in jazz and his legendary role in jazz lore, two entries are assigned to him in this volume: July 4 and August 4. This entry covers material from his formative years.

A brief look at Armstrong's background and upbringing indicates that he overcame great odds. His father, William Armstrong, was a factory worker who abandoned the family soon after the boy's birth. Armstrong's mother Mayann, only fifteen at the time of his birth, went to work in a nearby red-light district, leaving Louis in the care of his paternal grandmother. (It should be remembered that in the New Orleans subculture in which Louis lived, prostitution was looked upon as an almost normal way of making a living; Armstrong's first wife, Daisy, was a prostitute). Once in school, Armstrong joined his mother, taking whatever odd jobs he could find in the Crescent City's poorest neighborhood, a violent and vice-ridden district known as "the Battlefield." Louis wore little more than rags and ate the cheapest of food, occasionally scavenging in garbage cans.

His mother, loving but irresponsible, frequently left Louis and his younger sister to the kindness of strangers for days at a time. Around the age of seven he became acquainted with an immigrant Jewish family from Russia named Karnofsky, who fed him, taught him songs, put him to work, and provided him with his first instrument, a tin horn. Because of that kindness, Armstrong retained a special affection for Jews, wearing a Star of David all his life. Despite the kindness of the Karnofskys, Louis dropped out of school at the age of eleven and joined a street-corner quartet, singing for pennies. Music fascinated him, but it couldn't keep him out of trouble.

The pivotal event of his formative years occurred in the early hours of New Year's Day, 1913, when he joined the revelry by firing six blanks from a gun one of his "stepfathers" had left in a trunk beneath Mayann's bed. The youngster was arrested and sentenced to the Home for Colored Waifs, a type of juvenile hall. The move proved fortuitous, for within months he was the leader of his school band. Four years later he was cornetist with the leading jazz band in New Orleans, and by his twenty-first birthday, his peers acknowledged him to be the best jazz musician alive.

JULY 5—VIC BERTON (1896–1951)

b. Chicago, IL; d. Hollywood, CA

Drummer; Percussionist

[CLASSIC JAZZ; BIG BAND]

Other jazz notables born on this day: Arthur Blythe (1940)
Jazz notables deceased on this day: Harry James (1983)

♪

By the 1920s, as jazz moved upriver from New Orleans to Chicago, major changes began to take place in the evolution of America's popular music. It was in Chicago that big bands became popular, and it was here that performers such as Vic Berton and Gene Krupa revolutionized drum playing. With the advent of the bigger ensembles, new techniques had to be developed. During the 1920s the drum solo came into being, and by the late '20s the extended solo became common. Because of this, the technical demand on the drummer was much greater. Drummers now began playing the bass drum on all four beats and playing what is now referred to as the jazz pattern (ding-ding-da-ding) on the cymbal. As drummers became famous for their technical prowess, major changes in the drum set started to occur, including the invention of the first hi-hat pedal cymbals around 1927. An inveterate inventor, Berton patented a precursor of the modern hi-hat cymbal in 1926, and by the 1930s his cymbal pattern had become commonplace.

The phrase "child prodigy" seems an understatement when describing Vic Cohen (Berton), who played percussion professionally in the pit orchestra of Milwaukee's Alhambra Theater by the time he was eight. He studied tympani at an early age and by the age of sixteen he was performing with the symphony orchestras of both Milwaukee and Chicago. During World War I he played for John Philip Sousa's navy band, and after the war he returned to Chicago and performed with several of the area's top dance bands before leading his own band at the Merry Gardens club. During this period he co-wrote the song "Sobbin' Blues," which became a standard among hot bands of the time. In 1924 he formed a friendship with Bix Beiderbecke and started managing and occasionally playing drums with Bix's current band, the Wolverines. Berton moved to New York in the mid-1920s, where his work with Red Nichols and his Five Pennies and his recordings with the commercial bands of Roger Wolfe Kahn and the Paul Whiteman Orchestra made him the best-remembered white jazz drummer of the 1920s. By 1930 he had moved to the West Coast, where he found work in the film industry, in addition to forming his own band and playing with the Los Angeles Philharmonic Orchestra.

A cocksure businessman with a fast-talking line, Berton's larger-than-life reputation grew after 1931, when he was arrested in Culver City for smoking marijuana with Louis Armstrong.[4] Berton had been sitting in with Armstrong's band at the New Cotton Club—he was so good that the band's young drummer, Lionel Hampton, had given him his seat the minute he walked into the club—and at the intermission the two old friends had walked outside to light up. At that point two policemen closed in, confiscated the evidence, and took them both into custody. Facing up to six months in jail and a thousand-dollar fine, the popular musicians were released after nine days with only a suspended sentence.[5] Berton spent his remaining years in Hollywood as a music director and percussionist for Paramount and 20th Century-Fox. He died in 1951 of lung cancer.

JULY 6—LOUIE BELLSON (1924–2009)

b. Rock Falls, IL; d. Los Angeles, CA

Drummer; Bandleader; Composer

[SWING; BOP]

Other jazz notables born on this day:
Jazz notables deceased on this day: Scott LaFaro (1961); Louis Armstrong (1971)

---

4. Carr et al, Jazz: *The Rough Guide*, 65.
5. Ward and Burns, *Jazz: A History*, 184.

BLUE NOTES

♪

Jazz musicians have pursued a variety of paths to reach their career goals, but few embarked on their journey in a manner as stunning as Louie Bellson, who in 1940 outplayed forty thousand other drummers to win the Slingerland National Gene Krupa drumming contest. In his long career he performed with such greats as Duke Ellington, Count Basie, Benny Goodman, Tommy Dorsey, Harry James, Ella Fitzgerald, Louis Armstrong, and many more. Voted into the halls of fame of both *Modern Drummer* magazine and the Percussive Arts Society, Bellson can be seen on videos and heard on nearly two hundred albums, for which he was a four-time Grammy Award nominee. In addition to his playing, he wrote more than three hundred compositions, as well as over a dozen books on drums and percussion. As an internationally acclaimed artist, he performed in most of the major capitals around the world and was second only to Bob Hope in the number of appearances at the White House. One of the great drummers of all time, Bellson's excellent, precise technique and flamboyant solo style placed him, with Buddy Rich, among the foremost big band drummers of the post-swing period.[6]

Described by critic Leonard Feather as "one of the most phenomenal drummers in history," Luigi Balassoni (Bellson) demonstrated his musical genius at an early age. He started on drums at the age of three, and when he was fifteen he pioneered using two bass drums simultaneously. After tap dancing at a local nightclub act and teaching at his father's music store in Moline, Illinois, he played professionally with Goodman when he was only eighteen (1942–43), including an appearance in 1942's *The Power Girl*, the first of his many film credits. Following military service with an army band, Bellson played with a succession of big bands, including those of Goodman (1946–47), Dorsey (1947–49) and James (1950–51), before replacing Sonny Greer in the Duke Ellington Orchestra. A talented writer, Bellson contributed "Skin Deep" and "The Hawk Talks" to Duke's permanent repertoire. Bellson left Ellington early in 1953, shortly after marrying Pearl Bailey, with whom he worked thereafter as music director and accompanist. He also toured with Jazz at the Philharmonic (1954–55), recorded many dates in the 1950s for Verve, and was with the Dorsey Brothers (1955–56) and Basie (1962) before rejoining Ellington (1965–66) and Harry James (1966).

Bellson led his own highly successful orchestra almost steadily since 1967. On his video, *Louie Bellson and His Big Band*, the drummer shares the stage with eighteen superb musicians, exploring contemporary sounds while maintaining the big-band tradition. Whether with a small or big band, Bellson maintained a tight schedule of clinics and performances at colleges, clubs, and concert halls. His Big Band Explosion, true to its name, exuded humor, fervor, and zest. One of his former employers, the distinguished Duke Ellington, named Bellson "the world's greatest drummer."

---

6. Kernfeld, *New Grove Dictionary of Jazz*, Vol. 1, 185.

JULY 7—JOE ZAWINUL (1932–2007)

b. Vienna, Austria; d. Vienna, Austria

Keyboardist; Composer; Bandleader

[Hard Bop; Fusion; Soul-Jazz; World Fusion]

Other jazz notables born on this day: Tiny Grimes (1916); Doc Severinsen (1927); Hank Mobley (1930

Jazz notables deceased on this day: Bunk Johnson (1949); Fats Navarro (1950)

♫

On August 16, 1969, four hundred thousand young people gathered in a pasture near Woodstock, New York, enduring hours of rain and mud to be together in the presence of their rock idols. Three days later, Miles Davis made his bid to become one of those idols when he entered a recording studio to cut the curious mélange of jazz and rock he called *Bitches Brew*. The pioneering album was a commercial success; it sold more copies in its first year (four hundred thousand) that any of his records had sold before. Fusion—the hybrid music Davis had helped to launch—was setting out to rebuild the following that jazz had lost to rock since the late 1950s. Early fusion yielded some memorable music, much of it made by bands formed by musicians who had played with one of Davis's groups. Perhaps the most widely admired fusion group was Weather Report, established in 1970 by two of the men who had played on the *Bitches Brew* album, saxophonist Wayne Shorter and Austrian keyboardist Joe Zawinul. Under their leadership, Weather Report rapidly established itself as one of the most creative and influential units in jazz history. The group achieved enormous popularity worldwide, appealing to audiences beyond jazz and progressive rock.[7]

A European from the heartland of the classical music tradition (Vienna), Zawinul's curiosity and openness to all kinds of sounds made him one of the driving forces behind the electronic jazz-rock revolution of the late 1960s and '70s.[8] At the age of six he was given an accordion, which he played by ear for about a year. Studies in classical piano and composition at the Vienna Conservatory followed soon thereafter, though he was unable to practice at home because his family had no piano. In 1944 he and other gifted students were evacuated to a private country estate in Czechoslovakia; there he was required to practice every day. Back in Vienna after the war he became interested in jazz, and when the film *Stormy Weather* arrived, he saw it twenty-four times. From then on he wanted to play with black musicians.[9]

In 1959 he won a scholarship to the Berklee School in Boston, but a week later he left to join Maynard Ferguson's band. After working as accompanist for blues and jazz singer Dinah Washington (1959–61), he joined Cannonball Adderley's quintet, staying until 1970. Zawinul's writing (his composition "Mercy, Mercy, Mercy" became a hit and won a Grammy award for the best instrumental performance) and bluesy soloing on piano were

---

7. Ward and Burns, *Jazz: A History*, 444–448.
8. Bogdanov et al., *All Music Guide to Jazz*, 1368.
9. Carr et al., *Jazz: The Rough Guide*, 856.

largely responsible for the Adderley quintet's popularity during the 1960s. While with Adderley, Zawinul evolved from a hard bop acoustic pianist to a jazz-rock pioneer on the electric piano. Davis took an interest in adding the electric piano to his band after hearing Zawinul play it with the Adderley band, and between 1969 and 1971 Zawinul played an important role as both player and composer on four seminal Miles Davis albums. This exposure with Davis brought Zawinul to the attention of a worldwide audience.

JULY 8—BILLY ECKSTINE (1914–1993)

b. Pittsburgh, PA; d. Pittsburgh, PA

Vocalist; Bandleader

[VOCAL JAZZ; TRADITIONAL POP; STANDARDS; BOP]

Other jazz notables born on this day: Louis Jordan (1908)
Jazz notables deceased on this day: Charlie Shavers (1971)

♫

An influential ballad singer with an appealing baritone voice, Billy Eckstine made a significant contribution to jazz during the 1940s, when he led the first bebop big band and was the era's most imitated vocalist. Though white bands of the era featured males singing ballads, the music industry forced black bands to stick to novelty or blues vocals, until the advent of Eckstine. Acknowledged as the first romantic black male in popular music, he became very successful with both black and white audiences, and his recordings for MGM from 1947 to 1957 made him a superstar.

Eckstine grew up in Washington, DC and studied at Howard University before embarking on a career as a singer in Buffalo and Detroit. Possessing impeccable diction, he found fame with the Earl Hines band (1939–43) in Chicago. In addition to novelty hits like "Jelly, Jelly" and "The Jitney Man," he introduced new songs such as "Skylark" over network radio, being the first black singer allowed to do so. As supporter of young avant-garde jazz musicians, he was instrumental in bringing to Hines's band future stars such as Dizzy Gillespie, Charlie Parker, and Sarah Vaughan. In the spring of 1944, after he and Gillespie left the band due to tensions between the older swing players and the young modernists, Eckstine began conversations with Dizzy that led to the formation of a new band. The orchestra was brilliant, its short life a who's who of bebop: Gillespie and Fats Navarro on trumpet; Gene Ammons and Dexter Gordon on sax; Tommy Potter on bass; Art Blakey on drums; Tadd Dameron on piano; and Sarah Vaughan, the young vocalist who was doing for jazz singing what the rest were doing instrumentally. Eckstine appointed Gillespie musical director, giving Dizzy's new musical ideas free rein in a big-band context. With the addition of Parker, the band was unlike any other in the world, far ahead of its time.

In the summer of 1944 the band embarked on a grueling tour of black venues across the South and Midwest. When the orchestra arrived in St. Louis and the third trumpet fell ill, Miles Davis got a chance to sit in for a week. He was a good sight-reader, but he could barely concentrate on playing, so mesmerizing was the sound around him. The thrill of first hearing that band lasted him a lifetime, and he spent the rest of his career trying, but never quite managing, to recapture the impression. "The band changed my life" he acknowledged. "I decided right then and there that I had to leave St. Louis and live in New York where all these bad musicians were."[10]

Unfortunately the band made very few recordings in 1944, due to a ban imposed by the recording industry. By winter Parker and Gillespie had left Eckstine (Parker's unreliability did not suit the rigors of touring, and he prevailed upon Gillespie to join him). In 1947, after disbanding for financial reasons, Eckstine returned to a career as a solo singer, temporarily becoming the country's most popular vocalist (1949–50). He then developed a nightclub routine, in which he sang ballads, undertook impersonations, and even played trumpet. But he never lost his love—or feeling—for jazz.

JULY 9—ALEX WELSH (1929–1982)

b. Edinburgh, Scotland; d. London, England

Trumpeter; Vocalist; Bandleader

[TRAD JAZZ; DIXIELAND]

Other jazz notables born this day: Joe Darensbourg (1906); Irv Kluger (1921); Colin Bailey (1934)

Jazz notables deceased on this day: Wingy Manone (1982)

♪

The revival of New Orleans-style jazz in America during the late 1930s and '40s sparked similar movements overseas. By 1941 Australian Graeme Bell organized a band that held an influential engagement playing Dixieland. Another early group was formed in France by the clarinetist Claude Abadie. Started in 1942 as an oddly assorted group including violins, the ensemble quickly grew into a New Orleans revival band. Shortly thereafter similar bands emerged in England, Holland, and elsewhere throughout Europe, including Russia and the countries under its influence. The music, known in Europe as the trad movement, really blossomed there after World War II. By the 1950s the explosion turned into a cultural phenomenon.

Perhaps the best known of the European trad bands were those of Alex Welsh, Humphrey Lyttelton, Ken Colyer, and Chris Barber in England; the bands of Abadie and Claude Luter in France; the Roman New Orleans Jazz Band (an Italian band formed in Rome in 1949 and given its name by Louis Armstrong); and the Dutch Swing College, under clarinetist Peter Schilperoort. The movement was particularly strong in England, where it reached its height between the mid-1950s and the early '60s. What impelled an artistic-philosophic current like trad is difficult to pin down. But what is surprising is how it seemed to appear all around the world at once. Almost at the same moment, traditional bands began to form in London, Paris, Melbourne, Stockholm, Rome, and San Francisco. Young jazz enthusiasts, for the most part students, started them, although in England

---

10. Ward and Burns, *Jazz: A History*, 374.

there was a mixture of young working men, who had concluded that the swing style was a decadent, or commercialized, form of the true jazz, which was the New Orleans style.[11]

The Alex Welsh band is remembered with more affection than almost any other British band, not only because it was one of the best small bands of its kind in the world, but because its members formed a tight "jazz family" unit.[12] Welsh, one of the first Scottish musicians to make a name for himself in a genre far removed from bagpipes, loved jazz since his high school days. Beginning his career as cornetist, he moved to London in 1954 and quickly formed a band that established a reputation for its dedication to the Dixieland style and the excellence of its playing. Ensuring that every position in the band was filled with an expert, exciting player, from the start Welsh placed the music's integrity above commercial success. Modeling his band after the best Chicago-style Dixielanders, Welsh gained a large following among trad jazz listeners as well as respect from top American players (in 1957 he declined an offer to join American trombonist Jack Teagarden). In the 1960s and '70s he toured frequently, including trips to the U.S. and regular appearances on television; in 1968 the band played to great acclaim at the Newport Jazz Festival. Known for his highlander range, Welsh continued reaching for his instrument's highest notes until shortly before his death.

JULY 10—LEE MORGAN (1938–1972)

b. Philadelphia, PA; d. New York, NY

Trumpeter

[Hard Bop]

Other jazz notables born this day: Noble Sissle (1889); Ivie Anderson (1905); Cootie Williams (1911); Milt Buckner (1915); Major Holley (1924)
Jazz notables deceased on this day: Jelly Roll Morton (1941); John Hammond (1987)

♪

The preeminence of hard bop in jazz from the late 1950s to the mid-1960s was such that it was a staple of just about every major record label in the music. But if hard bop had a home base, it was clearly Blue Note Records, founded in 1939 by German expatriate Alfred Lion. The label's golden age—1955 to 1967—coincided roughly with hard bop's own heyday. Almost every artist associated with hard bop recorded for Blue Note at that time; even such major figures of the period as Miles Davis, Sonny Rollins, and John Coltrane were nourished by hard bop's elemental synthesis of blues, swing, and bop.[13]

If there was a prototypical Blue Note artist during this fertile period, it may have been Lee Morgan, one of the great jazz trumpeters of the 1960s and the natural successor to Clifford Brown. In 1964 one of his compositions, "The Sidewinder," was a huge hit and the album by that name became one of Blue Note's best sellers. Morgan's instantly recognizable sound and style grew out of his main influences, Brown, Dizzy Gillespie,

---

11. Collier, *Making of Jazz*, 331.
12. Carr et al., *Jazz: The Rough Guide*, 817.
13. Kirchner, *Oxford Companion to Jazz*, 385.

and Fats Navarro. He had a fat, crisp tone and he played with immense expressiveness and urgency; his style was rooted in the blues, with slurred and bent notes, funky phrases, and great rhythmic momentum.[14] Like his predecessor Clifford Brown, he too died prematurely and tragically, in his case after being shot in a New York club where his quintet was performing, following a quarrel with a jealous girlfriend.

Morgan began working professionally in Philadelphia when he was fifteen, and he joined Gillespie's orchestra in 1956, when he was barely eighteen, remaining with the group until it disbanded in 1958. He led his first Blue Note session in 1956, recording his first two classic albums for the label, *The Cooker* and *Candy*, during 1957 and 1958. From 1958 to 1961 he was a member of Art Blakey's Jazz Messengers during one of the group's greatest phases, touring and recording extensively with the band and sharing the front line with Benny Golson, Hank Mobley, and finally Wayne Shorter. Due to a heroin addiction he quit the band in 1961, maintaining a low profile in Philadelphia until 1963.

Upon his return he entered his greatest period, recording "The Sidewinder" and composing tunes such as the "Ceora" and the memorable blues "Speedball"; he also spent a second period with Blakey (1964–65). He recorded one memorable album after another, many under his own name and with Mobley, whose improvising techniques found echoes in Morgan's own style. His playing became more adventurous and by the end of the decade he was exploring modal music, using avant-garde elements and opening his playing to the influence of funk.[15] During 1970 and 1971 he was a central figure in the short-lived Jazz and People's Movement, joining with other musicians who disrupted television talk shows to protest the absence of jazz on television. By the time of his untimely death at the age of thirty-three he had recorded many albums as a sideman and leader, including twenty-five as a leader for the Blue Note label.

JULY 11—TOMASZ STANKO (1942–)

b. Rzeszow, Poland

Trumpeter; Leader; Composer

[AVANT-GARDE JAZZ; FREE JAZZ; NEO-BOP; MODERN CREATIVE]

Other jazz notables born on this day: Kimiko Itoh (1946)
Jazz notables deceased on this day: Danny Polo (1949); Shadow Wilson (1959); George Duvivier (1985); Andor Kovács (1989); Mario Bauzá (1993); Guy Lafitte (1998)

♪

An essential and fascinating aspect of European jazz that often goes unmentioned is that it thrived under two totalitarian systems: the Nazis, followed by the Eastern European Communist regimes. Indeed, some historians have argued that this historical period— roughly 1933 to 1989—constituted a golden age of sorts in continental jazz. The reason is clear. Great numbers of people listened to jazz during those years for what it represented

---

14. Carr et al., *Jazz: The Rough Guide*, 542.
15. Bogdanov, *All Music Guide to Jazz*, 910.

as much as for the music itself. "Repressed people want freedom," Mike Zwerin argues, and "jazz is about as good an artistic expression of freedom as can be found."[16] Poland, with its central geographical location, cultural heritage, and proud history of resistance, produced passionate jazz during those years of duress, and under the auspices of the Polish Jazz Society nurtured world-class players such as pianists Krzysztof Komeda and Adam Makowicz; violinists Michal Urbaniak and Zbigniew Seifert; vocalist Urszula Dudziak; and trumpeters Henryk Majewski and Tomasz Stanko.

It would be difficult to overestimate Stanko's standing in the Polish jazz community. He has been its central figure for decades, and has been voted that country's "Musician of the Decade" on multiple occasions. Classically trained as a violinist and pianist, Stanko did not take up trumpet until 1959. He developed quickly as a jazz trumpeter and formed his first group, the quartet Jazz Darings, with Makowicz in 1962. The band started out playing hard bop, but with the departure of Makowicz it took up free jazz, becoming what is considered to be the first free jazz group in Europe. Stanko then played with Komeda (1963–67) and appeared on many of Komeda's major recordings, which added to his reputation as one of Europe's free jazz pioneers.

Komeda, who died tragically in 1969 of injuries sustained in a Los Angeles car accident after scoring Roman Polanski's famed American movie debut, *Rosemary's Baby*, is credited with paving the way for jazz in Poland. A doctor by profession, he adopted the pseudonym Komeda to conceal his involvement in jazz, which during his early career was discouraged by the Polish government. In 1956 Komeda's sextet became the first Polish jazz group to play exclusively modern music, and its spectacular performances at festivals made him Poland's most popular musician. After Komeda's death, Stanko led his own groups and collaborated regularly with leading avant-garde and creative jazz artists such as Makowicz, Urbaniak, Seifert, Don Cherry, Gary Peacock, Cecil Taylor, and Finnish drummer Edward Vesala. Though Stanko's brooding style was shaped by Komeda, it is also fair to say that Stanko was there with Komeda at the beginning, and his devotion to the folk traditions of his region had an equally big impact on Komeda's career as a composer of film music. Clearly, both men were committed to the jazz idiom as the primary means of expression for their profound artistic sensibility.

JULY 12—PAUL GONSALVES (1920–1974)

b. Boston, MA; d. London, England

Tenor Saxophonist

[SWING; BOP]

Other jazz notables born on this day: Conte Candoli (1927); Big John Patton (1935); Jean-François Jenny-Clark (1944); Bernard Lubat (1945)
Jazz notables deceased on this day: Jimmie Lunceford (1947); Benny Carter (2003)

---

16. Kirchner, *Oxford Companion to Jazz*, 543.

July

♪

For most of the 1960s Duke Ellington traveled the world, pursuing two themes that mattered greatly to him, sacred music and secular travelogues. Earlier in the decade, however, he took time from his busy schedule to feature Paul Gonsalves, the critically underrated tenor saxophonist with his band for twenty-four years (1950–74), on a recording. Gonsalves, known to colleagues as "Mex" and to Ellington fans as "the hero of the Newport Jazz Festival," did not much care in promoting his own cause. Ellington was his greatest admirer, and that was enough for him. The people around him knew of his talent and besides, performing with the Ellington band was all he ever wanted from life. In May 1962 Ellington employed his entire orchestra to spotlight his tenor soloist. As was Ellington's habit, he leased a few hours of studio time to record music for his private use. But since he hadn't written any new material, as he ordinarily did for his recordings, he decided to pursue an entirely novel course of action: the album would feature Gonsalves and only Gonsalves. The resultant album, *Featuring Paul Gonsalves*, wasn't released until 1985, long after the deaths of both Gonsalves and Ellington. The reasons for the delay are uncertain but the results, according to Gary Giddins, are clear: the recording was "a triumph—the definitive Gonsalves album, and evidence of yet another ace up Ellington's capacious sleeve."[17]

As a teenager in Providence, Rhode Island, Gonsalves attended a local performance by the popular Jimmie Lunceford orchestra and heard recordings by Coleman Hawkins, which inspired him to take up the tenor. In 1946, following his discharge from the army, he joined Count Basie's band (1946–48) as replacement for Illinois Jacquet. There he acquired a reputation for his driving solos, though his playing, an extension of the swing tenor style of Hawkins and Ben Webster, was at its best when he performed ballads, which he delivered in a breathy, barely focused tone. He played briefly with the Dizzy Gillespie Orchestra (1949–50) before joining Ellington's band as Webster's replacement. His few brief absences during the next twenty-four years were associated with drug and alcohol addiction but, thanks to Ellington's tolerance and encouragement, he was musically more in control than many others were in his situation.[18]

The greatest moment of Gonsalves's musical career occurred at the 1956 Newport Jazz Festival, when Ellington urged him to take a long solo, egging him on through twenty-seven exciting choruses of "*Diminuendo and Crescendo in Blue*" that caused quite a commotion. A few weeks later Ellington made an appearance on the cover of *Time*, and his orchestra was back on top after five difficult years. For his well-publicized performance, Gonsalves earned Duke's lasting gratitude. Gonsalves remained with the band until his death just ten days before that of Ellington, frequently taking prominent roles in the bandleader's suites.

---

17. Giddins, *Visions of Jazz*, 497.
18. Carr et al., Jazz: *The Rough Guide*, 288.

BLUE NOTES

JULY 13—ALBERT AYLER (1936–1970)

b. Cleveland, OH; d. New York, NY

Tenor Saxophonist; Leader

[AVANT-GARDE JAZZ; FREE JAZZ]

Other jazz notables born on this day: George Lewis (1900); Johnny Hartman (1923); Leroy Vinnegar (1928)

Jazz notables deceased on this day: Wessel Ilcken (1957)

♪

In 1965 John Coltrane invited seven avant-garde stylists to sit in with his quartet to record *Ascension*, which employed collective improvisation much like Ornette Coleman had used in his groundbreaking 1960 album, *Free Jazz*. In *Ascension*, Coltrane took a cue from free-saxophonist Albert Ayler, including in his improvisation saxophone sounds that resembled cries and screams. Coltrane's controversial experiments attracted new fans but also alienated others, including members of his own band. During 1965 every member of his long-standing quartet quit, including the pianist McCoy Tyner, who complained, "All I could hear was noise." Even Ravi Shankar, the sitar master whose music had influenced Coltrane profoundly, found his new work disturbing: "Here was a creative person who had become a vegetarian, who was studying Yoga and reading the Bhagavad-Gita, yet in whose music I still hear much turmoil. I could not understand it."[19]

Ayler's tonal distortions and wild expressiveness spawned many imitators and disciples on the free-jazz scene, particularly in Europe. He certainly influenced Coltrane, who admired him and who, after he had recorded *Ascension*, told Ayler, "I found I was playing just like you." A giant of free jazz, Ayler was also one of the most controversial. For ten years he took lessons on alto saxophone, and by his mid-teens he was playing professionally in R&B bands. Early on he acquired the nickname "Little Bird" because of a similarity in sound to Charlie Parker. In 1956 he joined the army, and by 1958 he had changed to tenor saxophone. While stationed in France, he occasionally played in Paris clubs, and his musical style changed drastically. After his discharge he sought work in the U.S., but his style was so radical that no one would hire him.

He returned to Europe and found work in Sweden and Denmark, where he made his first recordings and played with free-jazz pioneer Cecil Taylor. Ayler returned to the U.S. in 1963; in New York he joined the Jazz Composers' Guild and the following year he formed a quartet with Don Cherry, Gary Peacock, and Sunny Murray. In 1965 he recorded one of his most influential albums, *Bells*, a live concert at Town Hall, but by this time controversy was raging about him, from assertions that he couldn't play and was a charlatan to claims that he was the new messiah of jazz.[20] He had difficulty finding a steady audience for his radical music, but he refused to clarify his music for his audiences, stressing its spiritual and social message.

19. Ward and Burns, *Jazz: A History*, 440.
20. Bogdanov et al., *All Music Guide to Jazz*, 3rd ed., 47.

Ayler was a deeply religious person, with a powerful premonition of his own imminent death. In death, as in life, he was surrounded with controversy. On November 5, 1970, he was reported missing in New York. His body was found floating in New York's East River twenty days later. Years later, his companion Mary Parks asserted that he had committed suicide, jumping off a ferry en route to the Statue of Liberty.

JULY 14—GEORGE LEWIS (1952–)

b. Chicago, IL

Trombonist; Composer

[AVANT-GARDE; STRUCTURED IMPROVISATION]

Other jazz notables born on this day: Alan Dawson (1929)
Jazz notables deceased on this day: Zutty Singleton (1975)

♪

In the mid-1970s a coterie of avant-garde musicians took much of the jazz world by storm; some were just getting started, others were past forty. Many belonged to a Chicago cooperative called the AACM (Association for the Advancement of Creative Music), an organization led by Muhal Richard Abrams. Its members included established musicians such as Lester Bowie, Roscoe Mitchell, Joseph Jarman, Leroy Jenkins, Henry Threadgill, Steve McCall, Anthony Braxton, Fred Anderson, and Leo Smith. By the late 1970s, most of the AACM musicians had relocated to New York, where they hoped to prosper. Earlier in the decade, a type of offshoot of the AACM developed in New Haven, Connecticut, where Anthony Davis and George Lewis, students at Yale University, worked with veterans Leo Smith and Fred Anderson. Gary Giddins called this generation of avant-gardists "a new breed of musician." Defying expectation, they occasionally doubled as painters, poets, and entrepreneurs. Though they made it a point of honor to write original music, they were not averse to playing standards, for to them free jazz was one style among many.[21]

Of these musicians, Lewis is one of the most representative. As a composer, performer, teacher, theorist, and historian he has opened wide frontiers in experimental music. Although associated with the avant-garde style, his talent is comprehensive, one that embraces jazz styles from early roots to bebop and free playing, as well as inventing areas of exploration for himself. Since the 1980s, his interest in electronics has led him to perform improvised duets with computers, producing performance works in which computers are programmed to respond to sounds generated by instrumentalists.

Lewis began playing trombone in 1961, and by the age of twelve he was transcribing solos by Lester Young for trombone. He played in school bands with fellow student Ray Anderson, who was to become the other leading trombonist to emerge in the 1970s. He studied theory in Chicago with Abrams under the auspices of the AACM and then attended Yale, where he graduated with a degree in philosophy (1974). In 1977 he moved to New York, where he began a long and fruitful association with Anthony Braxton's quartet,

---

21. Ward and Burns, *Jazz: A History*, 366.

his trombone fitting in perfectly with Braxton's reeds. Since then Lewis has played with most of the top avant-garde players, while simultaneously working on advanced music outside of jazz. From 1980 to 1982 he directed the Kitchen, an avant-garde cultural center, and while based in Europe from 1982 to 1987 he worked at electronic music laboratories in Paris and Amsterdam. Since 2004 he has served on the faculty of Columbia University, where he is Professor of Music. Lewis is the author of *A Power Stronger Than Itself* (2008), a history of the influential AACM, which he joined in 1971.

JULY 15—PHILLY JOE JONES (1923–1985)

b. Philadelphia, PA; d. Philadelphia, PA

Drummer

[HARD BOP]

Other jazz notables born on this day: Sadik Hakim (1919)
Jazz notables deceased on this day: Freddie Keppard (1933)

♪

In 1954 the first annual jazz festival was held at Newport, Rhode Island. George Wein, the festival's organizer, insisted on presenting a broad range of musicians, thereby hoping to appeal to different kinds of jazz fans. Overlooked in 1954, Miles Davis was eager to be included the second time around. As a result of heroin addiction, he had hardly performed in public since 1950, although he had managed to kick his habit. By 1955 he formed a quintet with a somewhat fixed personnel: twenty-year old Paul Chambers on bass, Red Garland (a former boxer, who once lost to Davis's hero, Sugar Ray Robinson) on piano, John Coltrane on saxophone, and hard-driving Philly Joe Jones (a nickname that distinguished him from the other drumming Jo Jones, of the classic Count Basie band) on drums. Relatively unknown when Davis found them, each member of the quintet would become a major figure in jazz.

The group appeared on the final night of the Newport Jazz Festival in 1955 and was an immediate triumph. Miles was under contract with Prestige, but his newfound fame led to a long-lasting contract with Columbia, a company with the resources to make him a star. However, he could not record officially for his new label until he had fulfilled a prior contract to produce four more albums for Prestige. He was so eager to move on that he managed to record all four in two marathon sessions. The results—*Cookin'*, *Relaxin'*, *Workin'*, and *Steamin'*—were masterpieces. Musicians regard these albums so highly that they consider them the equal of the classic recordings by Louis Armstrong's Hot Five and Hot Seven bands of the 1920s. That first Davis quintet lasted only a little more than two years, but it came to be regarded as the finest small jazz ensemble of its day.

Jones, a fiery drummer and gifted accompanist, is indelibly associated with that first classic Miles Davis quintet. A superb timekeeper, he masterminded Davis's rhythm section. Like all the members of the quintet, with the exception of Davis, Jones was hooked on drugs and was occasionally unreliable. Miles didn't seem to care: "I wouldn't care if he came up on the bandstand in his BVDs and with one arm, just so long as he was there. He's got the fire I want."[22]

In 1958, while with Davis, Jones established a lifelong association with pianist Bill Evans. The relationship, unfortunately, was more than musical. Jones, a pervasive drug addict, enticed Evans in that direction, and over the years the two became junk-buddies. In 1959 Davis was finally forced to dismiss Jones, replacing him with Jimmy Cobb. Jones worked briefly with Freddie Hubbard, recorded regularly as a house drummer for Blue Note and Riverside, and occasionally led his own groups. He went to Tokyo as part of an all-star drumming show early in 1965 but was arrested for marijuana possession and deported. In 1967 he settled in Europe, living in London and Paris until 1972. He eventually returned to Philadelphia, and from 1981 to 1985 led the nine-piece band Dameronia, a group dedicated to the performance of music by Tadd Dameron, who had played an important early role in advancing his career.

JULY 16—CAL TJADER (1925–1982)

b. Saint Louis, MO; d. Manila, Philippines

Vibraphonist; Leader

[Afro-Cuban Jazz; West Coast Jazz; Latin Jazz; Cool]

Other jazz notables born on this day: Bola Sete (1923); Nat Pierce (1925)
Jazz notables deceased on this day: Serge Chaloff (1957); Jo Stafford (2008)

♪

Prior to the 1960s, when Bobby Hutcherson and Gary Burton emerged to raise the bar for all future jazz vibists, three stylists—Terry Gibbs, Teddy Charles, and Cal Tjader—built on the vibraphone legacy developed by Red Norvo, Lionel Hampton, and Milt Jackson. Tjader, undoubtedly the most famous non-Latino leader of Latin jazz bands from the 1950s until his death, turned his attention toward Afro-Cuban jazz, where he vied with Tito Puente, the Latin bandleader (and occasional vibist), for top honors. His rhythmic vibraphone style established him as the point man between the worlds of Latin jazz and mainstream bop. Through numerous recordings and a long-standing presence in the San Francisco Bay Area, he eventually had a profound influence upon Carlos Santana, and thus Latin rock.[23]

Born to Swedish-American parents who performed in vaudeville shows, Tjader was a professional child dancer by the age of four. He moved to the West Coast, where his parents opened a dance studio, then played drums while in high school, working with a Dixieland band before enlisting in the navy (1943–46). While studying at San Francisco State College, he began to double as a vibraphonist. During this period he joined fellow Bay Area resident Dave Brubeck's octet on drums in 1948, staying with Brubeck's trio for the next two years and performing on drums, vibes, and bongos. After stints with Alvino

---

22. Carr et al., *Jazz: The Rough Guide*, 405.
23. Bogdanov et al., *All Music Guide to Jazz*, 1246.

Rey and as leader of his own group, in 1953 he joined George Shearing's hugely popular quintet as a vibraphonist and percussionist. It was in Shearing's band that Tjader's love affair with Latin music began, inspired by Shearing's bassist Al McKibbon and galvanized by the 1950s mambo craze.

When he left Shearing the following year, Tjader joined the house band at the Blackhawk in San Francisco, but soon formed his own quintet, which played a blend of Latin and Afro-Cuban music with mainstream jazz. In 1957 the percussionists Willie Bobo and Mongo Santamaria abruptly left Tito Puente's band and joined Tjader after Puente disapproved of their having recorded with him. With Gene Wright (then McKibbon) on bass and Vince Guaraldi for a time as pianist and composer, Tjader achieved great popularity. Although he remained based on the West Coast and held numerous residencies at the Blackhawk during the 1960s, he toured widely and recorded a long series of mostly Latin jazz albums for Fantasy. In 1961 he switched to Verve, where he expanded his stylistic boundaries and was teamed with artists like Lalo Schifrin, Anita O'Day, Kenny Burrell, and Donald Byrd. In 1965 he achieved a hit with "Soul Sauce," a reworking of a Dizzy Gillespie/Chano Pozo piece, "Guachi Guaro." Tjader continued recording successfully, introducing musicians like congero Poncho Sanchez and flautist Roger Glenn, who were key elements in the 1979 Grammy Award-winning album that launched the Concord Picante label, *La Onda Va Bien*.

JULY 17—JOE MORELLO (1928–2011)

b. Springfield, MA; d. Irvington, NJ

Drummer

[Hard Bop; Cool]

Other jazz notables born on this day: Ray Copeland (1926); Vince Guaraldi (1928); Nick Brignola (1936); Chico Freeman (1949)

Jazz notables deceased on this day: Billie Holiday (1959); John Coltrane (1967); Howard McGhee (1987)

♪

Joe Morello, one of the finest and most celebrated drummers in jazz history, began his musical studies as a violinist. Having impaired vision since birth, he devoted himself to indoor activities, and by the age of nine he was featured with the Boston Symphony Orchestra as soloist performing the Mendelssohn Violin Concerto. At the age of twelve he made a second appearance with the orchestra, but upon meeting and hearing his idol, the great Jascha Heifetz, he felt he could never achieve "that sound." By age fifteen he had switched to drums and began jamming with locals such as Phil Woods and Sal Salvador. Before long he was taking lessons with the legendary George Lawrence Stone. Morello began improvising on Stone's published concepts, and his teacher was so impressed that he incorporated Morello's ideas into his next text. But more importantly, Stone made his pupil realize that his future was in jazz.

After moving to New York in 1952 Morello began working with an impressive list of jazz musicians, including Johnny Smith, Tal Farlow, Woods, and briefly with Stan Kenton. At this time he studied with Radio City Music Hall percussionist Billy Gladstone, one of the most technically advanced drummers of all time. From 1953 to 1956 he gained a strong reputation as a member of Marian McPartland's trio. While working with McParland at the Hickory House, Morello's technical feats attracted the attention of many drummers, who would crowd around him at a back table during intermission to watch him work out with a pair of sticks on a folded napkin. Unsuspecting amateurs would try to impress him by showing off their fancy licks. Morello would listen carefully and then play them back, not only correctly, but also at twice the speed.

After leaving McParland, Morello turned down offers from bands led by Benny Goodman and Tommy Dorsey. The offer he chose to accept was a two-month temporary tour with the Dave Brubeck Quartet, which ended up lasting twelve years (1956–67). When he joined, Morello was an extremely precise player who nevertheless managed to be relaxed and to swing, enabling the pianist to experiment with unusual time signatures, such as in the quartet's recording of "Take Five," where he performed one of the most famous drum solos in jazz history. His stint with Brubeck made Morello a household name in jazz and across the world. Due to his failing eyesight (he went blind in 1976), Morello mostly worked as a drum instructor since leaving Brubeck (Danny Gottlieb was a student in the 1980s).

JULY 18—CARL FONTANA (1928–2003)

b. Monroe, LA; d. Las Vegas, NV

Trombonist

[Cool; Bop]

Other jazz notables born on this day: Joe Comfort (1917)
Jazz notables deceased on this day: Eddie Brunner (1960); Jo Stafford (2008)

♪

Though Carl Fontana is not widely known, primarily because he spent much of his career playing commercial music in Las Vegas, he was a brilliant trombonist, highly respected and greatly liked by his fellow jazz musicians. Ask jazz trombonist Bill Watrous who his favorite trombonist is and he will immediately answer, "Carl Fontana." Leonard Feather best expressed Fontana's place in the lineage of jazz trombonists when he indicated that Fontana was the most fluid, innovative trombonist since J. J. Johnson.

Fontana studied at an early age with his father, a saxophonist and bandleader, and played in his father's group from 1941 to 1945. Unlike many young musicians in the 1930s and '40s who went directly into touring musical groups after high school, Carl attended junior college before completing a musical degree at Louisiana State University. While studying for a Master's degree he joined Woody Herman's Third Herd, beginning a three-year stint with a trombone section that included brothers Urbie and Jack Green.

After work with Lionel Hampton and Hal McIntyre he joined Stan Kenton's orchestra (1955–56), known for its remarkable trombone section. Since the mid-1940s, its style initiated and set by Kai Winding, Kenton's brass section had revolutionized trombone playing stylistically, giving it a brassier sound and greater prominence in the ensemble. The Kenton trombone section's influence was still enormous and pervasive in the mid-1950s, and despite its continuous personnel changes, it retained a remarkable stylistic consistency. Fontana was well featured while with Kenton, especially on "Intermission Riff," where his inspired solo caused a sensation. During this period he also made two recordings in Paris with the Kentonians (a group drawn from Kenton's band), which demonstrate his style particularly well.

After playing in Winding's four-trombone band (1956–57) he moved to Las Vegas, where he spent much of the 1960s in house bands and studios, emerging on an occasional basis. By the end of the decade he was playing for Dick Gibson's Colorado Jazz Party, events where brilliant jazz musicians were invited to play for rich fans. On one occasion Fontana performed there in a three-trombone unit with Watrous and Frank Rosolino. During this period he joined Gibson's group, The World's Greatest Jazz Band, where his faultless technique and challenging creativity found perfect expression. He recorded with Supersax in 1973 and a few years later his work with drummer Jake Hanna further enhanced his reputation. When he stopped recording in 2000, shortly after being diagnosed with Alzheimer's, he was matched only by Urbie Green among the senior trombonists who still performed superbly. Fontana was not only a model for younger players but also an inspiration to musicians who shared the bandstand with him. Like a great actor, he raised the bar for all who performed with him.

JULY 19—BUSTER BAILEY (1902–1967)

b. Memphis, TN; d. New York, NY

Clarinetist; Soprano Saxophonist

[CLASSIC JAZZ; SWING; BIG BAND]

Other jazz notables born on this day: Al Haig (or July 22, 1922)
Jazz notables deceased on this day: Will Marion Cook (1944)

♫

Buster Bailey was a brilliant, classically trained clarinetist who, while known for his smooth and quiet playing with John Kirby's sextet, occasionally cut loose with some wild solos, such as on the 1938 recording "Man with a Horn Goes Berserk." Although best known as a clarinetist, he played soprano saxophone on some of his early recordings, during a period when his classically trained approach came under the influence of Sidney Bechet. While he rarely "swung" in the manner of the great jazz clarinetists and his playing lacked passion, his solos were always fluent and tuneful. He remained a master technician until the end of his life.

Bailey acquired his legendary lightning technique from a classical teacher, Franz Schoepp (who also taught Jimmie Noone and Benny Goodman), and by the time he was fifteen he was touring with W.C. Handy's famous show band. He joined Erskine Tate's Vendome Orchestra in 1919 and stayed in Chicago with Tate until 1923, when he made his first recordings. That year he also accompanied Mamie Smith and spent about a year working with King Oliver's Creole Jazz Band. When Louis Armstrong left Oliver's band in 1924 to join Fletcher Henderson's orchestra in New York, Bailey followed, joining one week later on Armstrong's recommendation and remaining with Henderson off and on until 1937. He quickly moved to the forefront of Henderson's technically demanding orchestra, in a select group headed by Coleman Hawkins. His technique on clarinet meant that he was featured on many recording sessions during that period, including on dozens of records by blues singers.

During 1929 and again in the early 1930s Bailey played with Noble Sissle's band and later in the decade was a member of the Mills Blue Rhythm Band (1934–35). After working briefly with Luis Russell's orchestra under Armstrong, he joined a group at the Onyx Club that by the autumn of 1937 had become the John Kirby Sextet. From 1937 to 1946 he was showcased in a perfect setting, his precise playing complemented by Charlie Shaver's intricate creations on trumpet. With Kirby's polished and phenomenally successful swing ensemble came a starry round of club work, hit records, and weekly radio broadcasts.

Having played in all-star jam sessions, after World War II Bailey was mostly employed in Dixieland settings, working with Wilbur De Paris (1947–49), Big Chief Russell Moore (1952–53), and trumpeter Henry "Red" Allen (in 1950 and 1951 and again from 1954 to 1960, when he participated in famed sessions with Allen's band at New York's Metropole club), as well as playing with the Sauter-Finegan orchestra. In the early 1950s he also played with the Ziegfeld Theater pit orchestra for performances of *Porgy and Bess* and participated in symphony concerts. From 1961 to 1963 he played with Wild Bill Davison, after which he joined the Saints and Sinners (1963–65), a classy Dixieland sextet. Bailey spent the last two years of his life (1965–67) with Armstrong's successful All-Stars sextet, playing his supporting role as well as ever.

JULY 20—JOACHIM-ERNST BERENDT (1922–2000)

b. Berlin, Germany; d. Hamburg, Germany

Writer; Record Producer

Other jazz notables born on this day: Arnold Fishkin (1919)
Jazz notables deceased on this day: Tricky Sam Nanton (1946); Milt Gabler (2001)

♪

Surprisingly, a European and not a North American wrote the ultimate single-volume work on jazz. Known as the "Pope of Jazz" in Germany, the German jazz critic Joachim-Ernst Berendt is the author of *The Jazz Book*, the all time best-selling book on jazz. In his book Berendt points out that it was the Swiss conductor Ernest Ansermet who wrote the first serious article on jazz, the Belgian Robert Goffin who wrote the first book on jazz (in 1929), and the Frenchman Charles Delaunay who published the first jazz review (in the late 1930s). So it should come as no surprise that a European has written the most comprehensive one-volume history of jazz. The book has been translated into many languages, reflecting its universal appeal. A clandestine Russian edition appeared in the former Soviet Union, and in Japan alone it has undergone three editions. Though the book seems to have disappeared from many current jazz reading lists, it is still unrivalled as a cornerstone of jazz historical criticism. The latest American edition (1992) enlists the photographic aid of Berendt protégé Gunther Huesman and adds a new American discography.

One of the most significant forces in European jazz, Berendt distinguished himself as an author (he wrote thirty-three books, which were translated into twenty-one languages), an educator, a photographer (as evident in his yearly *Calendar of Jazz and Rock*), and as a producer of both concerts and records. His father, a minister in the Evangelical Church, was active in the underground resistance movement against Hitler, which led to his imprisonment and untimely death in the concentration camp at Dachau. In 1945 Joachim founded the Southwest Radio Baden-Baden, one of Germany's major radio and television networks. Until his retirement in 1987 he headed the jazz department, directing over ten thousand broadcasts.

In 1951 he helped form the German Jazz Federation, and during the ensuing decades he organized and directed many festivals and concert series (including Jazztime Baden-Baden, the American Folk Blues Festival, and the Berliner Jazztage, later known as Jazzfest Berlin). He also organized an annual jazz concert at the Donaueschingen Festival for Contemporary Music and directed international festivals and concerts such as the World Expo Osaka, the Olympic Games Jazz Festival in Munich (1972), and the World Music Event (1982) at New York's Lincoln Center. A champion of non-Western folk music and of its fusion with jazz, Berendt founded the World Music Festival in 1965 and the German-Japanese Jazz Meeting in 1971. Having produced over 250 recordings for various labels in Germany and Japan, in 1970 he was voted Europe's best jazz producer by the American-based music publication *Jazz & Pop*. Berendt's main legacy is undoubtedly his *Jazz Book*, an accessible yet complete history of jazz that has been updated regularly since its initial publication in 1953. He died after being struck by a car as he was walking to an event to promote his new book *Only Walking*, his version of experiences with nature.

JULY 21—SONNY CLARK (1931–1963)

b. Herminie, PA; d. New York, NY

Pianist

[HARD BOP; BOP]

Other jazz notables born on this day: Omer Simeon (1902); Kay Starr (1922); Jamey Aebersold (1939)

Jazz notables deceased on this day: Honore Dutrey (1935); Snub Mosley (1981)

♪

Of the many jazz pianists performing in the 1950s and '60s, a surprising number even of the most gifted remained relatively unknown to jazz fans. One of the prime examples was Sonny Clark. During his brief moment in the limelight, from 1957 until his tragic early death in 1963 (he died of a heart attack caused by a drug overdose while playing at a nightclub in New York City), Clark was one of the most recorded pianists in jazz. Before his addiction to heroin drastically shortened his life, he was one of the top Bud Powell-inspired bop pianists, and was much admired by other pianists, including Bill Evans, who wrote an original composition called "N.Y.C.'s No Lark" in memory of Clark. The intriguing title, an anagram of Sonny Clark, was composed shortly after Sonny's death and appeared in Evans's groundbreaking solo recording, *Conversations with Myself*, recorded only three weeks after his close friend's death.

According to Paul Hofmann, a Clark aficionado, many jazz buffs who do not own a Sonny Clark album may have heard him on other recordings without realizing it, for during the late 1950s and early '60s Clark was perhaps the pianist most in demand for the Blue Note label. In this capacity he consistently appeared with some of the era's greatest players, both as a leader and as a sideman, including saxophonists Sonny Rollins, John Coltrane, Hank Mobley, Johnny Griffin, Jackie McLean, and Ike Quebec, trombonist Curtis Fuller, trumpeter Lee Morgan, and guitarist Grant Green. Sonny was also the pianist on classic Dexter Gordon sessions that produced *Go!* and *A Swingin' Affair* (both recorded in August 1962, only five months before Clark's death).

The question remains, if most jazz musicians were aware of Clark's great talent, why not the general jazz audience? One reason may be that Clark recorded exclusively on independent labels. Columbia, the most widely distributed record company in the world, had Miles Davis under contract during those years, as well as celebrated pianists like Erroll Garner, Duke Ellington, and Dave Brubeck, so players like Clark, no matter how accomplished, tended to be overlooked. In addition, great winds of change were swirling around the jazz world at this time. By 1960 avant-garde musicians like Ornette Coleman and Cecil Taylor were beginning to exert a measurable impact on the future direction of jazz, and players like Coltrane and Davis would soon follow this trend. Clark, true to his musical calling, continued to play within the relatively restricted style known as hard bop and soon great pianists saturated even this approach. As Hofmann makes clear, "there were too many great players chasing what few good gigs existed. And Sonny's refined musical approach, particularly his phrasing, was perhaps more subtle than any other pianist's. Inspiration and inventiveness don't always translate into general popularity; they surely didn't for Clark." Nevertheless, his death at age thirty-one was a major loss to jazz.

BLUE NOTES

JULY 22—AL HAIG (1922–1982)

b. Newark, NJ; d. New York, NY

Pianist

[Bop]

Other jazz notables born on this day: Lou McGarity (1917); Bill Perkins (1924); Junior Cook (1934); Al Di Meola (1954); Joshua Breakstone (1955)

Jazz notables deceased on this day: Richie Kamuca (1977); Sonny Stitt (1982); Percy Humphrey (1995); Joe Beck (2008)

♪

In the first week of December 1945 Dizzy Gillespie and Charlie Parker boarded a train for Los Angeles. Billy Berg, the proprietor of a new Hollywood nightclub, had invited Gillespie to bring a group to the West Coast to introduce the kind of music that had been causing such a sensation on New York's Fifty-Second Street. The combo's rhythm section, a who's who of the emerging bebop movement, included bassist Ray Brown, drummer Stan Levey, vibraphonist Milt Jackson, and the conservatory-trained pianist Al Haig. One of the first and finest pianists of the bop era, Haig was in demand during the early and late periods of his career but was relatively obscure in between.

Though there is uncertainty as to whether Haig was born on July 19 or 22, 1922 (some sources cite the year of birth as 1924, but that is unlikely), Haig grew up in Nutley, New Jersey, and took classical piano lessons at an early age. While in high school he became an admirer of Teddy Wilson, whose pianistic approach probably influenced the precise articulation and emotional restraint that Haig later brought to the bop setting. His exceptional technique, which allowed him to relax even while playing at very fast tempos, enabled him to become an excellent accompanist. After two years as a piano major at Oberlin Conservatory, in 1942 Haig enlisted in the Coast Guard, where he served as a musician in the New York area.

After his discharge in the spring of 1944 he heard Gillespie during a broadcast from the Onyx Club and decided to become a professional jazz musician. After freelancing around Boston, Haig began performing on Fifty-Second Street, where he was invited to join Gillespie and Parker for rehearsals. Haig became familiar with their bop repertory, including "Salt Peanuts," "Shaw 'Nuff," "Ko-Ko," Groovin' High," and "Hot House," and as a result he was invited to participate in the historic Gillespie-Parker quintet at the Three Deuces in April and May of 1945 that produced some of the first real bop recordings. Haig remained at the Three Deuces in quintets with Parker and Don Byas, and in 1946 he took part in several more important recording sessions with Gillespie on the West Coast and in New York. From 1948 to 1950 he returned to Parker's quintet, participating in the saxophonist's first trip to Europe for the May 1949 Festival International de Jazz in Paris. At this time Haig also worked with Stan Getz (1949–51), becoming Getz's favorite accompanist during the period when the tenor saxophonist played at his coolest. He also appeared on many recordings, mostly as a sideman, finding himself at the center of the jazz world. During 1951 to 1973 Haig continued playing, but he was generally overlooked.

In October 1968 his wife was found dead in their home, and the following year he was tried for her murder and then acquitted. Perhaps the resulting notoriety brought him back to the attention of the jazz world, or possibly this disastrous affair simply coincided with the start of a revival of interest in bop. He resumed recording and touring again, and by the mid-1970s he finally became recognized as a giant of the bop movement.

JULY 23—STEVE LACY (1934–2004)

b. New York, NY; d. Boston, MA

Soprano Saxophonist; Composer; Leader

[AVANT-GARDE JAZZ; FREE JAZZ; POST-BOP]

Other jazz notables born on this day: Emmett Berry (1915); Claude Luter (1923); Richie Kamuca (1930); L. Subramaniam (1947)
Jazz notables deceased on this day: Jimmy Harrison (1931); Willem Breuker (2010)

♪

When John Coltrane's album *My Favorite Things* was released in 1961, it proved to be one of his best sellers. One reason for the album's success was that it featured Coltrane on the soprano saxophone. Up to this point, with the exception of Sidney Bechet (who died in 1959), Johnny Hodges (who stopped playing it in 1940), and Steve Lacy (only narrowly known in the late 1950s), the instrument had been largely ignored in jazz. But Coltrane changed all that. He had been listening to Bechet for some time, and through his association with Thelonious Monk he had become aware of the work of Lacy, who had played soprano with Monk. In 1959 Coltrane purchased a soprano, and used that instrument to create a voluptuous sound that was appealing, modern, and novel. After Coltrane embraced the instrument and fully revealed its expressive potential, it became a prime voice for many of the younger players, including Wayne Shorter, who used the soprano prominently in the late 1960s and beyond. The work of Lacy, Coltrane, and Shorter served as a watershed for the soprano, with dozens of talented players following suit, including Bob Wilber, Dave Liebman, Jane Bunnett, Gerry Niewood, Jane Ira Bloom, Roscoe Mitchell, Julius Hemphill, Joseph Jarman, Greg Osby, Gary Bartz, Branford Marsalis, Jan Garbarek, Evan Parker, and crossover artists Grover Washington Jr., George Howard, Ronnie Laws, and Kenny G.

Steven Lackritz (he was renamed "Lacy" by cornetist Rex Stewart in the early 1950s) was considered the first "modern" musician to specialize on soprano. His entire career, a rare example of sustained artistic development, took him from total immersion in traditional jazz in the early 1950s, through bebop and the music of Monk, to the free improvisation of the 1960s and the pluralism of the 1970s and '80s.[24] Starting on piano, then clarinet, Lacy was inspired by Bechet to take up soprano sax and play Dixieland jazz.

---

24. Carr et al., Jazz: *The Rough Guide*, 440.

In the mid-1950s Lacy made a stylistic leap, performing in a quartet with Cecil Taylor (1955–57), who was beginning to embrace free jazz. In 1957 he began a concentrated study of Monk's legacy, which led to *Reflections*, the first of many albums he devoted to Monk's compositions. After working with Monk's quintet for four months in 1960, Lacy formed a quartet with trombonist Roswell Rudd (1961–64) that exclusively played Monk's music.

Lacy began to turn towards avant-garde jazz in 1965, playing in Europe with Don Cherry, Carla Bley, Enrico Rava, and others. He toured South America with a quartet that was stranded in Argentina—Lacy forever appreciated the irony of a revolutionary free-jazz group trapped in a repressive, anti-revolutionary country—then moved to Rome, where he performed with various Italian avant-garde and rock musicians. In 1970 he settled in Paris and formed a quintet with his Swiss wife, cellist/vocalist Irene Aebi. The group performed Lacy's avant-garde pieces, combining formal composition with jazz improvisation, poetry, and dance.

JULY 24—BILLY TAYLOR (1921–2010)

b. Greenville, NC; d. New York, NY

Pianist; Educator; Leader

[HARD BOP; SWING; BOP]

Other jazz notables born on this day: Charles McPherson (1939); Jon Faddis (1953)
Jazz notables deceased on this day: Dick Wellstood (1987)

♪

Billy Taylor has done as much as anyone in jazz history to foster an awareness and appreciation of jazz, and he did so not only as a performer but also as a writer, radio disk jockey, television music director, and educator. His profiles on CBS' *Sunday Morning* television program and his popular radio program *Jazz Alive* successfully introduced jazz to a wide audience and won him an Emmy Award in 1983 for a piece on Quincy Jones. His significant book, *Jazz Piano: A Jazz History* (1982), was based on his PhD thesis at the University of Massachusetts and the NPR series *Taylor Made Piano*.

For Taylor, jazz was a central musical form for telling the story of America. When asked by Len Lyons to sum up the central point of his thesis, he replied: "Jazz is America's classical music. It has been the traditional melting pot that we're so proud of. It's where the ethnic musical cultures that make up America come together. No other music does this." In 1969 Taylor broke stereotypes when he became the first African-American band director for a network television series (*The David Frost Show*). In 1994 he began hosting the NPR series "Billy Taylor's Jazz from the Kennedy Center."

Taylor was brought up in Washington, DC, where he took piano lessons at an early age. His family favored classical music, but an uncle introduced him to great jazz pianists such as Fats Waller and Teddy Wilson. As a teenager he made trips to Harlem, where he became acquainted with pianists such as Art Tatum and the young Thelonious Monk.

In high school he doubled as a tenor saxophonist, but was intimidated by his talented schoolmate Frank Wess. While studying music at Virginia State College, he performed professionally; one evening he sat in with the Count Basie Orchestra and met Jo Jones, who became a strong supporter of his career. In 1944 Taylor moved to New York and began working in Ben Webster's quartet at the Three Deuces on Fifty-Second Street, where the numerous clubs were like a second home to the founders of bebop. From time to time he played with Dizzy Gillespie and Oscar Pettiford's quintet across the street at the Onyx (as replacement for their unreliable regular pianist, Bud Powell). In 1949 he formed a quartet that was soon taken over by Artie Shaw and renamed the Gramercy Five. By 1951 Taylor was one of the house pianists at Birdland, where he worked with such major musicians as Gillespie, Charlie Parker, Miles Davis, Milt Jackson, Art Blakey, and other founders of modern styles on their instruments.

Taylor's interest in jazz education became evident during the 1950s, when he published several primers on jazz piano styles, wrote magazine articles, lectured at music schools, and held jazz workshops. Through these activities and later, through his involvement in Jazzmobile, an organization he helped establish in 1965 to take free music to inner city neighborhoods, he became a respected spokesman for the arts in general and jazz in particular.

JULY 25—JOHNNY HODGES (1907–1970)

b. Cambridge, MA; d. New York, NY

Alto and Soprano Saxophonist

[SWING; BALLADS]

Other jazz notables born on this day: Annie Ross (1910); Don Ellis (1934); Brian Blade (1970)

Jazz notables deceased on this day: Tal Farlow (1998); Johnny Griffin (2008); Albert Mangelsdorff (2005)

♪

Johnny Hodges, the most influential alto saxophonist of the swing era, was the finest alto saxophonist in jazz before Charlie Parker. A devout romantic, he was a stunningly lyrical player with a warm, soulful sound. Possessing "the most beautiful tone ever heard in jazz," Hodges's sensuous playing on ballads has never been surpassed. Signed by Duke Ellington in May 1928, Hodges became the premier soloist in Ellington's band, remaining with the bandleader until his death in 1970 (except for a five-year hiatus from 1951 to 1955).

Raised on Hammond Street, Boston, in what became a saxophonists' neighborhood (Howard Johnson, Toots Mondello, Charlie Holmes, and Harry Carney all lived nearby), Hodges played drums and piano before switching to soprano sax when he was fourteen. Very early in his career he met Sidney Bechet (who was performing in Boston), asked for lessons, and soon began worked at his teacher's Club Bechet in New York, filling in until the older man arrived, and playing duets after he turned up. His early experiences included playing with Chick Webb and Willie "The Lion" Smith, among others. However, Hodges's real career began in 1928, when he joined Ellington's orchestra. He quickly became one of the most important soloists in the band and a real pacesetter on alto—Benny Carter was his only close competition in the 1930s. In 1937 he formed a small group drawn from the band, generally a septet, which made a series of masterful recordings, including compositions Hodges wrote with Ellington. These recordings offer a final opportunity to hear Hodges playing the soprano, which he gave up in 1940, when Ellington began featuring his alto saxophone exclusively.

Hodges directed Ellington's saxophone section for twenty-two years, playing memorably on pieces such as "Never No Lament (Don't Get Around Much Anymore)," "Warm Valley," "Passion Flower," and "Day Dream"; he also collaborated on Ellington's best-selling song, "I'm Beginning to See the Light" (1944). In 1948, while Ellington was touring Britain with a variety show, Hodges accepted a residency at the Apollo Bar in Harlem with a small band of his choice. The place was always full, and on the heels of this achievement Hodges decided to tour with a band of his own in 1951. However, after four successful years he tired of the routine and returned to Ellington. Hodges's joyous reunion with his bandleader apparently gave a new impetus to Ellington's compositions—in 1966, Duke and Billy Strayhorn arranged the haunting "Isfahan" movement from the *Far East Suite* to display his unique abilities—and the saxophonist remained with Ellington to the end of his life, even when his health began to deteriorate. Three hospital stays and numerous doctors' warnings went unheeded as Hodges continued to follow Ellington's punishing schedule. Ironically, he died of a heart attack while visiting a dentist. "Because of this great loss," Ellington mourned, "our band will never sound the same."[25]

JULY 26—JOANNE BRACKEEN (1938-)

b. Ventura, CA

Pianist; Composer

[Post-Bop]

Other jazz notables born on this day: Gus Aiken (1902 or 1903); Erskine Hawkins (1914); Charli Persip (1929)

Jazz notables deceased on this day: Laurindo Almeida (1995)

♪

A brilliant pianist flexible enough to play free, modal music, and standards, JoAnne Brackeen is considered one of the most consistently inventive pianists and composers on the scene today, by jazz fans and critics alike. Described as "the Picasso of Jazz Piano," Brackeen does invite parallels to Picasso, for like the great visual artist, she has consistently defied convention, remaking herself and her art many times over. Her playing, described by Wally Shoup as "an idiosyncratic mixture of muscularity and grace," is virtuosic and

---

25. Carr et al., *Jazz: The Rough Guide*, 354.

wholly unpredictable, and her writing is "remarkable for its creativity, stylistic range, emotional depth, and whimsical spirit."

Throughout her career Brackeen has operated at full capacity in a male-dominated field, breaking through to become an icon for women and men in jazz. Indeed, male performers such as Oscar Peterson and Ornette Coleman have named her as their favorite composer. Leonard Feather once noted that she was as important to the 1980s as Bill Evans and Herbie Hancock were to the 1960s and McCoy Tyner and Keith Jarrett to the 1970s. Brackeen seems to have digested the entire jazz tradition in her work, as well as various ethnic elements, and her compositions emerge from this brew eloquently. She has said: "I prefer using my own material to standards. Different songs are like babies, and I feel better playing one that I created and nurtured than one I adopted, no matter how good it is."[26]

As an adolescent, Joanne (née Grogan) taught herself to play jazz at the age of eleven by transcribing entire piano solos from recordings. By the age of twelve she was busy performing. After moving to the Los Angeles area, and still in her teens, she had already met and played with jazz notables such as Scott LaFaro, Charlie Haden, Don Cherry, Billy Higgins, Dexter Gordon, and Art Farmer. JoAnne was awarded a scholarship to study at the Los Angeles Conservatory of Music, but left after only three days to pursue jazz on her own. After marrying saxophonist Charles Brackeen (they divorced in 1983), she took time off to bring up their four children.

She moved to New York in 1965 and began to play in public again, working with many well-known jazz musicians. From 1969 to 1977 she received her education on the road, touring with musical legends Art Blakey, Joe Henderson, and Stan Getz. She spent two years with Blakey as the first female member of his Jazz Messengers (1969–71) and three years with Henderson (1972–75) before joining Getz, who in 1975 brought her to the attention of a wider public, particularly in Europe, where she was much appreciated. By 1977 she became established as an original stylist, performing as soloist and as a leader of trios. A self-taught musician, Brackeen has developed an instinctive ability to share her musical knowledge and pass on the tradition to others. She teaches at Berklee College of Music, the world's largest music school, and hosts her own television show.

JULY 27—KARRIN ALLYSON (1964–)

b. Great Bend, KS

Vocalist

[STANDARDS; BOP]

Other jazz notables born on this day: Bob Thiele (1922); Charlie Shoemake (1937); Nnenna Freelon (1957); Jean Toussaint (1957)

Jazz notables deceased on this day: Milt Buckner (1977); Harry "Sweets" Edison (1999); Harold Land (2001)

---

26. Carr et al., *Jazz: The Rough Guide*, 85.

♪

When Karrin Allyson was lead singer of the all-girl rock and roll band Tomboy in Omaha, Nebraska, few would have predicted that one day she would become an international jazz sensation. One of the more impressive jazz singers to emerge in the 1990s, Allyson is being hailed by critics as possibly the best all-around singer in jazz today. A true original with an irresistible style, she commands a broad repertoire, which runs from jazz to "the great American songbook" to blues, pop, samba, and French cabaret. A great scat singer and a highly expressive balladeer, she is also an excellent, classically trained pianist. *The Wall Street Journal* summed up her immense appeal accurately: "She swings like a pendulum, and her slender, sunny voice makes you smile the moment you hear it."

Allyson, the youngest of three sisters, moved to Omaha when she was six, at which time she began studying piano with her mother, a classical concert pianist. Her parents divorced when Karrin was in fifth grade, and she eventually moved to the San Francisco Bay area. After graduating from high school in California, Allyson returned to the Midwest, attending the University of Nebraska on a musical scholarship. For the next few years she divided her time between her studies, her growing fascination with jazz, and her rock band. Though her band was voted the most popular band in Omaha, not everyone was impressed with Allyson's overtures into the rock and roll scene. Some of her instructors frowned at her lifestyle, playing in clubs and bars by night and attending music classes by eight in the morning.

After graduation she moved to Minneapolis, partly to launch her jazz career and partly to join her mother and sister. After three years in Minnesota honing her skills, especially her ability to scat, Allyson moved to Kansas City, where the flourishing jazz scene helped propel her into international stardom. Rave reviews greeted her debut album with the Concord Jazz label, *I Didn't Know About You* (1992), placing her in the company of jazz giants Ella Fitzgerald and Shirley Horn. This was followed by a string of excellent Kansas City albums, including *From Paris to Rio* (voted No. 1 vocal-jazz album of 1999 by *Pulse!* magazine), a vibrant and colorful musical excursion that displays her love of the Brazilian samba and French chansons. Her 2001 tribute, *Ballads: Remembering John Coltrane*, was nominated for a Grammy in 2002. All of her recordings are highly recommended, and in them she demonstrates the potential to be an important pacesetter for decades to come.[27] From her current base in New York, Karrin maintains a furious schedule of live concerts and performances internationally and across the U.S.

JULY 28—GERALD VEASLEY (1955–)

b. Philadelphia, PA

Electric Bass Guitarist

[CROSSOVER JAZZ; CONTEMPORARY JAZZ; URBAN]

Other jazz notables born on this day: Corky Corcoran (1924); Delfeayo Marsalis (1965)

Jazz notables deceased on this day: Eddie Costa (1962)

---

27. Bogdanov et al., *All Music Guide to Jazz*, 26.

♪

Born and raised in Philadelphia, Gerald Veasley was exposed to gospel and rhythm-and-blues as a child and went on to play in various R&B bands as a teenager in the late 1960s and '70s. Along the way, he discovered jazz and came to appreciate Weather Report and Return to Forever as much as Earth, Wind & Fire and Smokey Robinson. An excellent bassist who has played his share of commercial music, Veasley clearly possesses the ability to play in improvisatory settings.

Gerald started playing the bass at the age of twelve and participated in jam sessions at home with friends of his musically inclined parents. Growing up in a stable home, he was inspired by his parents' work ethic and their appreciation of education. As an outstanding high school student, he earned a complete four-year academic scholarship to the University of Pennsylvania, where he enrolled with the intention of studying law. During his third year at Penn, his father died. To deal with the loss, he focused on music, listening to jazz recordings by Charles Mingus, Wes Montgomery, Ron Carter, and others. These all-night affairs also included working on improvisatory skills, transcribing solos, and studying chord progressions. During this period he also studied classical and flamenco guitar to expand his range as a musician. When asked why he chose to become a professional musician, he points to music's beneficial role. Music "always moved me emotionally and offered me a way to express things I couldn't find words for. When my father died, I had a hard time coming to grips with the trauma, and music proved therapeutic."

In the early 1980s numerous opportunities emerged as Veasley displayed his affinity for a wide stylistic performing range. He played avant-garde music with Odean Pope's Saxophone Choir (out of that group a trio emerged with saxophonist Pope and drummer Cornell Rochester), performed orchestral dates with flutist Leslie Burns, and joined violinist John Blake's group for a U.S. tour and three recording sessions. In 1984 Veasley and Rochester formed another band, and while continuing these associations, he joined a small group led by Grover Washington Jr., with which he toured and recorded into the 1990s. Having held the music of Weather Report and electric bassist Jaco Pastorius in high regard, Veasley showed his fusion side from 1988 to 1995, when he worked with Weather Report co-founder Joe Zawinul as a sideman with the Zawinul Syndicate. Veasley received numerous accolades during the 1980s and '90s, including being voted "Talent Deserving Wider Recognition" in every *Down Beat* critic's poll from 1983 through 1992. *Jazziz* readers voted him "Best Bassist" in the magazine's 1999 poll. In addition to performing, Veasley has also taught the history and the fundamentals of the electric bass both privately and at the university level. All signs indicate Veasley will become one of the new millennium's most popular and revered bassists.

BLUE NOTES

JULY 29—CHARLIE CHRISTIAN (1916–1942)

b. Dallas, TX ; d. New York, NY

Guitarist

[SWING; BOP]

Other jazz notables born on this day: Don Redman (1900)
Jazz notables deceased on this day: Bill Green (1996); Chuck Wayne (1997)

♪

What we now think of as the jazz electric guitar—a hollow-bodied instrument that sends an amplified signal to an external speaker—didn't appear until the late 1930s. In 1937 Eddie Durham recorded the first electric-guitar solo, a few bars on a Count Basie side called "Time Out," but it took a scrawny kid from Oklahoma City named Charlie Christian to demonstrate what the electric guitar could really do. Christian played his instrument with the fluidity of a saxophonist. Despite knowing the blues and how to swing, it was his flowing lines and rhythmic grace (much like his friend and influence Lester Young) that carried him to jazz immortality. He was clearly the most brilliant soloist of his time on electric guitar. Many swing-style players emulated him, and his posthumous impact on younger bop guitarists was enormous. Had he lived longer, he doubtless would have become the first great bop guitarist, for he was a regular participant in the Harlem jam sessions at which Dizzy Gillespie, Kenny Clarke, Charlie Parker, and a few others played as they gradually developed the new idiom.

Charlie Christian's moment of fame was terribly brief. He grew up in a slum in Oklahoma City, the son of a blind guitarist. As a boy he couldn't afford even a cheap acoustic guitar, so he made his own, using a cigar box for the body. Locally he soon became an admired musician, playing an amplified acoustic guitar as early as 1937, after becoming a student of Durham. Word of his skill reached John Hammond, an executive with Columbia Records, who traveled to Oklahoma City in 1939 to hear the youngster.

Benny Goodman had been thinking of adding a guitarist to his group and Hammond, impressed with Christian's playing, arranged an audition. When Christian arrived in Los Angeles, he was wearing a ten-gallon hat, pointed yellow shoes, a bright green suit over a purple shirt, and as the *pièce de resistance*, a string bow tie. Goodman took one look at the apparition and was ready to dismiss Christian with only a cursory hearing, but Hammond and others smuggled Christian on stage during a performance, while Goodman was on break. Reluctant to make a scene, Goodman called for "Rose Room," a piece he felt Christian would not know. The results, however, surprised even Goodman, who became so entranced by Christian's playing that the band performed the piece for the next forty-eight minutes.[28] Goodman hired Christian on the spot and within weeks he was a force in the world of jazz. For the next two years he was featured with Goodman's sextet and even took solos with the full orchestra.

---

28. Collier, *Making of Jazz*, 343.

Reared in poverty, the naïve young man was ill prepared for such success. Having suffered from incipient tuberculosis for years, in 1941 his condition worsened and he was sent to a sanatorium on Staten Island. He seemed to be improving, but then friends began coming to his room with women and liquor. At times they even sneaked him out of the hospital. Tragically, Christian contracted pneumonia and died in 1942, at the age of twenty-five. He was buried in Harlem, in the cheapest coffin available.

JULY 30—DAVID SANBORN (1945–)

b. Tampa, FL

Alto Saxophonist

[SMOOTH JAZZ; CROSSOVER JAZZ; JAZZ-POP; SOUL-JAZZ]

Other jazz notables born on this day: Hilton Jefferson (1903); Vernell Fournier (1928); James Spaulding (1937); Kevin Mahogany (1958)
Jazz notables deceased on this day: Jimmy Blanton (1942); Lucky Thompson (2005)

♫

The controversy in the jazz world surrounding the jazz-rock fusion of the 1970s was accentuated by a new generation of players and groups that further embraced stylistic ideals often found in the popular music of the 1980s. Many different combinations were tried during the 1980s and '90s, and while promoters often used the phrase "contemporary jazz" to describe these fusions of jazz with elements of pop music, R&B, and world music, the word "crossover" seems more accurate. In some cases the music is quite worthwhile, from a jazz point of view, while in other instances the jazz content is minimal. The new groups gained a huge popularity, one not enjoyed by jazz musicians since the swing era.

This new interest in jazz did not necessarily spill over to the more traditional straight-ahead jazz groups. In fact, many listeners had virtually no knowledge of the earlier jazz traditions from which these groups evolved. As a result, a new dichotomy developed in the jazz community between those who, like Wynton Marsalis, held a strong allegiance to the jazz tradition and those whose music was sometimes called jazz but in reality had roots more directly tied to the rock or pop tradition. David Sanborn is an individual positioned between these two emerging definitions of jazz. Over the past twenty years he has been the most influential saxophonist in the jazz-pop/crossover vein.

When Sanborn was growing up, the popular music of his day was R&B, as performed by Little Richard, Fats Domino, and Ray Charles. In St. Louis, where he was raised, there was a strong blues sensibility—Little Milton and Albert King played there regularly. Sanborn began sitting in with blues bands and became a skilled alto saxophonist, despite battling polio in his youth. It was while combating polio (and in an iron lung) that he was advised to take up a wind instrument as physical therapy. After studying music at Northwestern University (one of the few universities to have a sax department at that time) and the University of Iowa, he moved to the West Coast, where he played and recorded with the Paul Butterfield Blues Band (1967–71). He was with Stevie Wonder in 1972 and 1973, touring with him in a Rolling Stones concert package, and then began a long association with bandleader Gil Evans in 1973.

Over the years he worked with many pop players, including Paul Simon and David Bowie, but he made his biggest impact leading his own bands. During the 1970s and into the '80s Sanborn was perhaps the most in-demand alto session player in the United States, interpreting melodies and playing solos on dozens of albums.[29] For several years in the early 1990s he hosted a jazz radio program called *The Jazz Show* and the late night television series *Night Music*, which featured an eclectic lineup of musicians (from Sonny Rollins to James Taylor), most of whom were given the unique opportunity to play together. The show displayed Sanborn's wide musical interests, even as his own recorded work offers a stylistic bridge connecting the very commercial world of pop with the jazz tradition.

JULY 31—KENNY BURRELL (1931–)

b. Detroit, MI

Guitarist

[Hard Bop; Cool; Bop]

Other jazz notables born on this day: Gap Mangione (1938)
Jazz notables deceased on this day: Teddy Wilson (1986)

♪

As Charlie Christian defined the sound of jazz guitar for the 1940s, Kenny Burrell did during the late '50s and early '60s. Though Burrell never achieved the wide popular appeal of Wes Montgomery or George Benson, he is among the most respected figures in jazz today. Benson, B.B. King, Jimi Hendrix, Dizzy Gillespie, Stevie Wonder, and Pat Metheny are among a long list of his admirers. He was Duke Ellington's favorite guitarist, and although he never recorded with the master, he began leading seminars and teaching courses during the 1970s, often featuring Ellington's music. An articulate ambassador for jazz, Burrell has been dubbed America's "guitar laureate" by the *Detroit Free Press*. Playing an unchanging style based on bop, Burrell's mellow approach might be considered the middle step between the percussive attack of Christian and the lyrical inventiveness of Montgomery. While few fans would claim that he has been an innovator, most would point to his strong bluesy feel and the fact that he has worked with most of the giants of the soulful hard-bop era.

Part of the fertile Detroit jazz scene of the early 1950s, Burrell started playing guitar when he was twelve, and he debuted on records in 1951 with a visiting Dizzy Gillespie sextet that included Milt Jackson and John Coltrane. Dizzy offered to take him on tour, but Burrell wanted to continue his music education at Wayne State University. Upon graduating, Burrell toured with the Oscar Peterson trio for six months and then moved to New York, where he freelanced and recorded prolifically. After playing for Benny Goodman

---

29. Carr et al., *Jazz: The Rough Guide*, 671.

in 1957 he formed his own small groups. Highly in demand from the start, for the next ten years Kenny was probably the busiest jazz guitarist in the business. He appeared on countless recordings over the next forty years, both as a leader and as a sideman. Among his more notable associations have been dates with Stan Getz, Billie Holiday, Jackson, Coltrane, Gil Evans, Sonny Rollins, Quincy Jones, Stanley Turrentine, and Jimmy Smith. His work with Smith made the organist a star, and it re-established the guitar as a small-group instrument (prior to 1957, guitarists usually led their own group or played rhythm parts in a big band).

In 1972 Burrell settled in Los Angeles, where he has done studio work, performed locally, and furthered his educational endeavors. In 1978 he began teaching a course on Ellington at UCLA; this was the first regular college course on Ellington taught in the U.S. This course and his interpretation of Duke's music made him a recognized Ellington expert. As founder of the Jazz Studies program at UCLA, he is currently director of that department, which has also included Harold Land, Gerald Wilson, and Airto Moreira. Burrell continues to tour and record, while devoting himself to composition. He remains one of the most popular and respected jazz guitarists of all time. "There's no finer guitar player," George Benson has stated. "There may be somebody else who is as good, but you can't play finer guitar than Kenny Burrell."

Chapter 8

August

AUGUST 1—HERSCHEL EVANS (1909–1939) [DOB unknown]
b. Denton, TX; d. New York, NY
Tenor Saxophonist
[SWING]

Other jazz notables born on this day:
Jazz notables deceased on this day: Bud Powell (1966); Sam Wooding (1985)

♪

During the Depression, Kansas City was the wildest city in America, an economic oasis for migrants and musicians in search of work. Anything you wanted to do and could afford to do you did there. Musicians like Lester Young, scrambling for work in the rest of the country, had no trouble finding it in Kansas City. It may have been a Vanity Fair for reform-minded citizens, but for the pianist Mary Lou Williams, it was "a heavenly city—musicians *everywhere*."[1] For some reason, competition between Kansas City musicians ran deep, so much so that the trumpet player Buck Clayton once compared Kansas City musicians to gunfighters.

One evening in 1933 Coleman Hawkins was in town with Fletcher Henderson's orchestra. Hawkins, undoubtedly the most important tenor saxophonist in the nation at the time, took his horn into a local club at the end of the band's show and announced he was looking for challengers. Three of Kansas City's best tenors were waiting for him: two whose styles were based on his, Ben Webster and Herschel Evans, and Young, the era's other dominant tenor and a clear alternative to Hawkins. Williams was asleep at four o'clock in the morning when Webster went to her home to awaken her, for her pianistic skills were needed. The other pianists were all exhausted and Hawkins was still in a dueling mood, even though it was obvious that he had more than met his match. "Hawkins was king," Williams recalled, "until he met those crazy Kansas City tenor men."

In 1936 Count Basie was the first bandleader to popularize a reed section with two tenors. Paired with Evans, whose style resembled Hawkins's powerful, breathy approach, Young demonstrated nightly how and why he differed from everyone else, and his fortunes

---

1. Ward and Burns, *Jazz: A History*, 196.

rose with that of the band, which by 1940 had acquired a national reputation. In Evans, one of the earliest "Texas tenors," Basie found a perfect contrast to that of the cool-toned Young, his darkly romantic tone and authoritative style complementing Young's insuperably logical flights. Heard back to back in such performances as "One O'Clock Jump" and "Georgiana," Evans and Young defined the range of the tenor in that era.[2]

Evans had started out playing with southwestern territory bands, including that of Bennie Moten (1933–35). In 1936, after a brief stint with Lionel Hampton and Clayton in Los Angeles, he began a permanent engagement with Basie, which brought him to national prominence. He became a leading tenor in the swing style, with a rich, powerful tone and forceful delivery quite unlike the light, fluent manner of Lester Young. Their playing led to a rivalry between the two that became a hallmark of Basie's performances. Sadly, Evans died of a heart attack before his thirtieth birthday, while at the height of his powers. His untimely death in 1939 set in motion a series of events that drove Young from the Basie band the following year. It was only natural that a player of his creativity would become bored with the relatively limited solo opportunities of a big band, even if it was one of the best, and seek to become a leader in his own right.

AUGUST 2—NANÁ VASCONCELOS (1944–)

b. Recife, Brazil

Percussionist

[SOUNDTRACKS; BRAZILIAN JAZZ; LATIN JAZZ; WORLD FUSION; AFRO-BRAZILIAN]

Other jazz notables born on this day: Natty Dominique (1894 or 1896)
Jazz notables deceased on this day: Joe Shulman (1957); Boyd Raeburn (1966)

♫

Naná Vasconcelos is one of a number of creative Brazilian percussionists who changed the direction and sounds of Brazilian jazz in the post-bossa nova 1970s. Like Airto Moreira, he is a master of unconventional percussion. Naná is an especially inventive virtuoso of the berimbau, the weird yet expressive instrument that resembles an archer's bow strung with steel wire, with a resonating gourd at the bottom. He has taken this instrument far beyond its traditional uses and is acknowledged as its foremost player. The subtle melodies and rhythms he creates on berimbau and cuíca transform these instruments into strikingly original solo voices. In addition to his musical talents, Vasconcelos maintains a reputation for his ongoing commitment to people with learning disabilities, in particular for his work with handicapped children.

Vasconcelos was born in Recife on the Northeast Coast of Brazil, and despite twenty years of playing around the world, his roots are apparent in everything he plays. The son of a professional guitarist, Naná got his start in his father's band at the age of twelve, playing bongos and maracas. After playing in every imaginable context in his hometown, from street bands to symphonic orchestras, he moved to Rio de Janeiro and began to play with one of Brazil's greatest singers, Milton Nascimento. Prodded by intense curiosity and an

---

2. Giddins, *Visions of Jazz*, 175.

inquisitive ear that led him from the music of Brazil's greatest composer, Villa-Lobos, to Jimi Hendrix, Vasconcelos came to learn all of the Brazilian percussion instruments, and by the early 1960s he came to specialize in the berimbau.

In 1970 the Argentinean tenor saxophonist Gato Barbieri was in Rio and invited Naná to join his band. They played in New York and then toured Europe, starting at the Montreux Jazz Festival, where Vasconcelos caused a sensation. At the end of the tour he stayed in Paris for two years, touring and working extensively with handicapped children. Naná returned to Brazil and began an eight-year collaboration with Egberto Gismonti, touring and recording three albums of duets with the Brazilian guitarist/wood flute player. In 1978, with Don Cherry and Collin Walcott, he founded the trio Codona (1978–84), which performed a style of jazz that fused characteristics of African, Asian, and South American music. During that period Vasconcelos was a guest member of the Pat Metheny Group (1980–83), helping to steer Metheny's music in the general direction of Brazil. In 1986 Vasconcelos returned to Brazil for the first time in six years, and enormous crowds enthusiastically attended his solo performances. In addition to being featured on film soundtracks, Vasconcelos has played with Cherry's group Nu, toured and recorded extensively with Norwegian saxophonist Jan Garbarek's quartet, and led his own band Bush Dance. Vasconcelos continues to demonstrate the breadth of his musical talents, playing on recording sessions with everyone from B.B. King to Jean Luc Ponty.

AUGUST 3—TONY BENNETT (1926–)

b. Queens, NY

Vocalist

[VOCAL JAZZ; TRADITIONAL POP; BALLADS; SHOW TUNES]

Other jazz notables born on this day: Lawrence Brown (1907); Charlie Shavers (1917); Roscoe Mitchell (1940); Greg Osby (1960)
Jazz notables deceased on this day: Leroy Vinnegar (1999)

♪

In the 1950s thousands of screaming bobby-soxers surrounded the Paramount Theater in New York to see their singing idol Tony Bennett. Today the children and grandchildren of those fans are paying $100 a ticket to enjoy the same performer. With over fifty million records sold worldwide, Bennett has won ten Grammy Awards, including 1995's "Album of the Year." What accounts for his magic? *The New York Times* summed up his legacy when it stated: "Artistry, certainly. The repertoire is indeed classic . . . But perhaps most important is his ability to convey a sense of joy, of utter satisfaction, in what he is doing."

Though Bennett never claimed to be a "jazz singer," he is especially significant in that he may be the last major figure to stand midway between pop and jazz. There is no doubt that he has been deeply influenced by jazz and has always felt a kinship with jazz musicians, having collaborated with them at various times over his long career. Bennett counts among his influences Art Tatum, from whom he drew ideas on phrasing and breathing;

Mildred Bailey and Billie Holiday for their relaxed delivery; and Frank Sinatra, who once proclaimed Bennett to be the best singer in the business.[3]

The son of an Italian-born immigrant, Anthony Benedetto attended the High School of Industrial Arts in Manhattan, where he nurtured his two passions: singing and painting. His childhood idols included Bing Crosby and Nat "King" Cole, both big influences on his easy, natural singing style. Tony sang while waiting tables as a teenager and then with military bands during World War II. His big break came in 1949, when comedian Bob Hope heard him at a Greenwich Village nightclub with Pearl Bailey and booked him into his show at the Paramount Theatre. It was Hope who suggested Bennett change his stage name from Joe Bari to Tony Bennett. During the 1950s Bennett occasionally experimented with jazz, including recording with the Count Basie Orchestra, Ralph Burns, Bobby Hackett, Stan Getz, and Zoot Sims. Perhaps his most successful and unusual experiment was the 1957 album called *The Beat of My Heart*, featuring the drums of Chico Hamilton, Art Blakey, and Jo Jones, but also including Nat Adderley, Herbie Mann, Al Cohn, Kai Winding, and Milt Hinton.

In the 1970s, bitter about the dominance of rock in the music business, he collaborated with jazz stars such as Ruby Braff and Marian and Jimmy McPartland and made two now-revered duet albums with Bill Evans (*The Tony Bennett-Bill Evans Album* [1975] and *Together Again* [1977]). However, once his son Danny took over his management and started to sell him to a younger audience, Bennett started to make a remarkable comeback. Bennett's resurgence to popularity in the 1990s stems from an appearance on *MTV Unplugged* in 1993, which was turned into a hit album, "and since then he has become classic American popular music's most powerful ambassador to the generations raised on rock."[4]

AUGUST 4—LOUIS ARMSTRONG [Part Two] (1901–1971)

b. New Orleans, LA; d. New York, NY

Trumpeter; Vocalist; Bandleader

[New Orleans Jazz; Classic Jazz; Vocal Jazz; Swing; Dixieland; Traditional Pop]

Other jazz notables born on this day: Herb Ellis (1921); Earl Swope (1922); Bobo Stenson (1944); Jeff Hamilton (1953); Terri Lyne Carrington (1965)
Jazz notables deceased on this day: Eddie Condon (1973);

♪

Louis Armstrong is considered the most important and influential musician in jazz history. Often called "the father of jazz," he was the only performer in jazz history equally influential as a singer and as an instrumentalist. Although he is often identified as a trumpet player more than a singer, his singing and trumpet playing are twin manifestations of a single artistic urge.

---

3. Bogdanov et al., *All Music Guide to Jazz*, 3rd ed., 83.
4. Carr et al., *Jazz: The Rough Guide*, 59.

Over the years countless admirers imitated Armstrong's unique singing style; he popularized scat singing and his phrasing affected virtually every singer to emerge after 1930, including Bing Crosby, Billie Holiday, and Frank Sinatra.[5] As an instrumentalist, Armstrong was responsible more than anyone else for changing jazz from an ensemble-oriented folk music into an art form that emphasized inventive solo improvisations. His enormous brassy tone and remarkable range, together with his superb sense of pacing and ability to build dramatic tension, made him one of the foremost musical architects in jazz history. Perhaps his most profound contribution was his innate ability to swing, his graceful syncopation of selected rhythmic figures producing the swing feeling so essential to jazz. Experts agree that every aspect of his playing may simply be at the top of the humanly possible.

By 1930 Armstrong was a star, with imitators all around him, but his business life had come to a temporary impasse. In 1935 he encountered a powerful, often ruthless Mafia operator named Joe Glaser, who would handle Armstrong's fortunes for thirty-five years. From this point, at the expense of his career as a jazz musician, he began to concentrate on his role as a popular entertainer. Under Glaser's guidance he became the first black to appear regularly in feature-length films and to have a sponsored radio show; by the late 1930s he was a nationwide star. In 1947, after working with a big band, he formed the All-Stars, an immensely successful sextet. Playing Dixieland and swing standards along with a variety of comedy numbers, Armstrong began a schedule of nonstop traveling that lasted until his death.

During the 1950s and '60s Louis had major hits in "Blueberry Hill," "Mack the Knife," and "Hello Dolly," the latter followed by a gold-selling album of the same name. It won him a Grammy for best vocal performance. This pop success was repeated internationally four years later with "What a Wonderful World," which did not gain much attention in the U.S. until 1987, when it was used in the film *Good Morning, Vietnam*, after which it became a Top 40 hit. By the mid-1950s "Satchmo" (short for "Satchel Mouth"), as he came to be known, was one of the best-known entertainers in the world. He appeared in almost fifty popular films and traveled internationally, often in the capacity of "Ambassador of Jazz" for the U.S. State Department. When he died in 1971 there was no jazz musician who could approach him in popularity.

AUGUST 5—AIRTO MOREIRA (1941–)

b. Itaiópolis, Brazil

Percussionist

[AFRO-BRAZILIAN; CROSSOVER JAZZ; FUSION; BRAZILIAN JAZZ; LATIN JAZZ]

Other jazz notables born on this day: Tiny Davis (1909 or 1910), Lenny Breau (1941)
Jazz notables deceased on this day: Otto Hardwick (1970); Mezz Mezzrow (1972); Bob Cooper (1993)

---

5. Bogdanov et al., *All Music Guide to Jazz*, 3rd ed., 37.

August

♪

The bossa nova's tremendous popularity worldwide during the early 1960s led to an increased intermingling of Brazilian musicians and jazz musicians. By the late 1960s several Brazilian musicians came to work or live in the United States, among them drummer/percussionist Airto Moreira (known generally by his first name) and his wife, vocalist Flora Purim. Purim is known for her fantastic range (her vocal range originally covered about three octaves but, under the guidance of Hermeto Pascoal, one of Brazil's most inventive instrumentalists, she gradually increased it to six octaves) and her risk-taking scat singing. Airto, the most high-profile percussionist of the 1970s, was for a time one of the most influential Brazilian musicians in the United States. Early in his career, while touring Brazil as a drummer, Airto collected and studied over 120 different indigenous percussion instruments. In the mid-1960s, as leader of the Quarteto Novo, which included Hermeto Pascoal, he began adding his collection of instruments to the conventional drum set.

Airto settled in New York and came to international attention with Miles Davis in 1970. While touring and recording with Davis, Airto's reputation—as an impressionistic colorist rather than timekeeper—spread quickly, and soon his contributions were revolutionizing the role of percussion in jazz and popular music. He became an original member of the popular fusion band Weather Report in 1971, joining Joe Zawinul, Wayne Shorter, Miroslav Vitous, and Alphonse Mouzon. In 1972, together with Chick Corea and Stanley Clarke, Airto began an engagement with tenor saxophonist Stan Getz at the Rainbow Room in New York. Recognizing that Airto was not at his best on the drum set, Getz moved him to percussion and expanded the group to a quintet, adding Tony Williams on drums. Shortly thereafter, Airto (on drums) and Clarke joined Flora Purim as founding members of Corea's quintet, Return to Forever. Later that year Airto and Corea also recorded the classic *Captain Marvel* with Getz. In these settings Airto became the best-known Latin percussionist in jazz.

In 1973 he moved to Berkeley, California with Purim, playing on her albums and also recording under his own name. Since then he has remained busy, mostly co-leading bands with his wife and recording as a leader. In 1974, solely on the strength of his creative talent in manipulating such instruments as the tambourine and bongos and his introduction to jazz of such exotica as the berimbau, cabaca, caxixi, cuíca, ganza, and reco-reco, *Down Beat* magazine added percussion as a new category in its readers' poll, a poll he routinely headed thereafter. Airto was the first of the contemporary Latin percussionists to work in the U.S. and to make the biggest reputation, having been in so many key groups at an extraordinarily dynamic time in jazz history.

AUGUST 6—CHARLIE HADEN (1937–)

b. Shenandoah, IL

Bassist; Leader

[AVANT-GARDE JAZZ; FREE JAZZ; HARD BOP; POST-BOP]

Other jazz notables born on this day: Luis Russell (1902); Vic Dickenson (1906); Norman Granz (1918); Buddy Collette (1921); Abbey Lincoln (1930); Dorothy Ashby (1932); Baden Powell (1937); Hendrik Meurkens (1957); Ravi Coltrane (1965); Regina Carter (1966)

Jazz notables deceased on this day: Bix Beiderbecke (1931); Gene Ammons (1974)

♪

In 1959 a young bassist named Charlie Haden was at the Haig in Los Angeles to hear Gerry Mulligan's quartet when a strange looking person came up to the bandstand and asked if he could sit in. Upon receiving permission, he took out a white plastic alto and began to play with the group. His style was so unorthodox that he was asked to leave immediately. For Haden, however, those few notes by free-jazz saxophonist Ornette Coleman were a revelation: "He was playing in the intervals," he recalled, "the whole tune in about three notes." Haden pursued Coleman in vain through the crowded club. Sometime later, he caught up with Coleman, who invited him to his apartment. "We started to play," Haden recalls, "and a whole new world opened up for me . . . It was like being born again." Shortly thereafter, in a Los Angeles garage, Coleman put together a quartet of like-minded musicians—Don Cherry on trumpet, Billy Higgins on drums, and Haden—that in November 1959 played music so commanding and yet so controversial at New York's Five Spot that it seemed to challenge the very premises upon which jazz had been founded. At the time Haden was probably the only jazz bassist to fully understand Coleman's radical approach.[6]

Haden's personal history was unique among jazz musicians. Born in the Ozarks, until the age of fifteen he was a member of the Haden family band, performing hillbilly music as a singer. The band, a country and western act, played for revival meetings and country fairs in the Midwest and in the late 1930s appeared on their own radio show. Haden sang with the family group until he contracted bulbar polio at the age of fifteen. The disease weakened the nerves in his face and throat, ending his singing career. So he turned to the bass, an instrument he later played in Los Angeles with Art Pepper, Paul Bley, and Hampton Hawes before he joined Coleman. Forced to leave the band in 1960 due to an addiction to narcotics, Haden underwent rehabilitation at Synanon houses in California. In 1966 he returned to New York to help establish a Synanon house and counsel addicts, while pursuing freelance work with Coleman, Keith Jarrett (1967–75), and others. He worked with the Jazz Composers' Orchestra Association in the late 1960's and then formed his avant-garde Liberation Music Orchestra from its members.

---

6. Ward and Burns, *Jazz: A History*, 414–15.

Haden gained some valuable perspective during his rehabilitation from drugs. Always outspoken against injustice and political oppression, he recorded an album of freedom songs in 1969 with his acclaimed Liberation Music Orchestra that summed up his personal philosophy: "I feel it is the responsibility of every one of us . . . to bring deeper values back to society . . . Every great musician learns that before they [sic] can become a great musician, they [sic] have to become a good human being."[7]

AUGUST 7—RAHSAAN ROLAND KIRK (1936–1977)

b. Columbus, OH; d. Bloomington, IN

Tenor Saxophonist; Flutist; Multi-Instrumentalist; Leader

[AVANT-GARDE; POST-BOP]

Other jazz notables born on this day: George Van Eps (1913); Idrees Sulieman (1923); Marcus Roberts (1963)
Jazz notables deceased on this day: Nat Gonella (1998)

♪

During the late 1930s swing music had provided some 70 percent of the profits in the recording industry. By the mid-1970s jazz yielded less than 3 percent. Things became so desperate that a group of African-American activists, known as the Jazz and People's Movement, began disrupting network television programs to protest their lack of work.[8] Rahsaan Roland Kirk, one of the most original performers in jazz history, led the group. When discussing Kirk, a great deal of attention is always paid to his eccentricities, such as playing several horns at once, making his own instruments, and clowning on stage. However, he was an immensely creative artist and one of the great improvisers. Perhaps no improvising saxophonist has ever possessed a more comprehensive technique, or been more spontaneously inventive.[9]

Kirk was born with sight but became blind at the age of two. During his childhood and youth he played numerous instruments, including the bugle, trumpet, clarinet, and C-melody sax. He began playing tenor sax professionally in R&B bands at the age of fifteen. At sixteen he dreamed he was playing three instruments at once, and the next day he went to a music shop and tried out every reed instrument. In the basement he was shown some archaic saxophones that had been used in turn-of-the century Spanish military bands, the stritch and the manzello. He began reshaping these and other instruments, using modifications and false fingerings so that they could be played simultaneously. This self-invented technique is evident on Kirk's first recording, a 1956 R&B record called *Triple Threat*. By 1960 he had begun to incorporate a siren whistle into his solos, and shortly thereafter he had mastered circular breathing, a technique that enabled him to play without pause for breath.

---

7. Gottlieb, *Reading Jazz*, 602–4.
8. Ward and Burns, *Jazz: A History*, 456.
9. Bogdanov et al., *All Music Guide to Jazz*, 715.

People accused him of gimmickry, but Kirk defended himself by responding that he did everything for a reason, that he heard sirens and such things in his head when he played. He was, in fact, rooted deeply in the whole jazz tradition, and he knew that in much of the early music sirens, whistles, car horns, and human voices figured to brilliant effect. For Kirk jazz was "black classical music," a term he preferred to "jazz," and he was steeped in its wild, untamed spirit.[10] In addition to the saxophones and whistles, Kirk brought many other instruments to jazz, including the piccolo, the harmonica, and instruments of his own design, such as the "trumpophone" (a trumpet with a soprano sax mouthpiece) and the "slidesophone" (a small trombone or slide trumpet, also with a sax mouthpiece). In 1961 he spent several months with Charles Mingus, and after this stint he began traveling overseas. From that point he mostly led his own group, the Vibration Society, recording prolifically with many sidemen. Kirk suffered a paralyzing stroke in 1975, losing movement on one side of his body, but his homemade saxophone technique allowed him to continue performing. From 1976 until his death from another stroke a year later, he played one-handed.

AUGUST 8—BENNY CARTER (1907–2003)

b. New York, NY; d. Los Angeles, CA

Alto Saxophonist; Trumpeter; Arranger; Composer; Bandleader

[East Coast Blues; Jump Blues; Swing]

Other jazz notables born on this day: Lucky Millinder (1900); Rupert Cole (1909); Urbie Green (1926); Frank Traynor (1927)
Jazz notables deceased on this day: Johnny Dodds (1940); Cannonball Adderley (1975)

♪

Benny Carter, jazz music's premier elder statesman, ranks with Duke Ellington as one of the most extraordinary musicians in American history. As a soloist Carter, along with Johnny Hodges, was the most influential alto saxophonist of the swing era. An accomplished trumpeter and clarinetist, he also recorded proficiently on piano and trombone. As an arranger, he helped chart the course of big band jazz, and several of his compositions, including "Blues in My Heart" and "When Lights are Low," became jazz standards. Carter also made major contributions to the world of film and television. He was a major figure in every decade since the 1920s, and his consistency and longevity are unprecedented.[11] Even in the 1990s, Carter was as strong an altoist as he was in the 1930s.

Essentially self-taught, Carter started on trumpet and, after a period on C-melody sax, switched to alto. By age fifteen he was already playing at Harlem nightclubs. Carter developed fast as both musician and arranger. In 1928 he joined Fetcher Henderson's seminal orchestra, assuming the arrangement duties previously handled by Don Redman. Carter's innovative scores, particularly his writing for the saxophone section, revitalized

---

10. Carr et al., *Jazz: The Rough Guide*, 425–26.
11. Bogdanov et al., *All Music Guide to Jazz*, 204.

the band and, according to scholar Gunther Schuller, "Carter was now the arranger everyone followed." That year he also formed his first big band, performing at New York's Arcadia Ballroom. Over the years, his groups (which included such top players as Ben Webster, Chu Berry, Teddy Wilson, and Sid Catlett) became a guarantee of musical excellence.

In 1935 Carter was invited to England to serve as staff arranger for the BBC dance orchestra. Over the next three years he traveled across Europe, playing with top continental jazzmen as well as with visiting American stars such as his friend Coleman Hawkins. In Holland during this period Carter also led the first international, interracial band. Upon returning home in 1938 Carter found the big band sounds, which he had helped shape, sweeping the nation. He formed another superb orchestra (1939–41), then a sextet, which in 1941 included bebop pioneers Dizzy Gillespie and Kenny Clarke.

By 1943 he relocated to California, where he moved increasingly into studio work. Beginning with *Stormy Weather* in 1943, he arranged for dozens of feature films and television productions. After 1946 he also provided arrangements for most of the leading singers of the time, including Sarah Vaughan, Ella Fitzgerald, Ray Charles, Peggy Lee, and Louis Armstrong. Since 1975 he resumed traveling overseas, and became a virtual commuter to Japan, where his popularity was unrivaled. During the 1970s and '80s he turned his talents toward education, conducting seminars and workshops at many universities. Carter's multifaceted musical gifts remained on display during the 1990s, when he appeared around the world, recorded prolifically, and racked up Grammy awards. As Carter liked to say, "My good old days are here and now."

AUGUST 9—JACK DEJOHNETTE (1942–)

b. Chicago, IL

Drummer; Pianist

[AVANT-GARDE JAZZ; POST-BOP; FUSION]

Other jazz notables born on this day:
Jazz notables deceased on this day: Don Ewell (1983); Bill Russell (1992)

♪

Widely regarded as one of the most gifted and complete musicians in jazz and as one of the greatest drummers in the history of jazz, Jack DeJohnette brings a holistic approach to his playing. A master of every style and genre from R&B to rock, ethnic, reggae, bebop, and free improvisation, he has long described his music as "multi-directional." Not surprisingly, most contemporary drummers cite him as one of their favorite drummers. Throughout his career he has collaborated with many of the major figures in jazz, including Eddie Harris, who spotted DeJohnette's natural talent on drums early on and convinced him to specialize on that instrument.

DeJohnette began playing piano at the age of four, studying with a classical teacher for about ten years. As a teenager he became interested in blues, popular music, and jazz and he started working in small groups, emulating local pianist Ahmad Jamal. He credits his uncle, Roy Wood Sr., a famous jazz DJ in the South Side of Chicago, as the person who inspired him to pursue music. As he began listening to his uncle's records, he became interested not only in Jamal but also in the work of his drummer, Vernell Fournier. While in high school, DeJohnette led a trio that played locally. The group's drummer often left his drums at Jack's house, so after listening to jazz records the pianist would frequently go to the basement and experiment on drums. Soon he was as proficient on drums as on the piano, and for a while he played both instruments professionally. When it became evident that he was a better drummer, he made that his main instrument.

He moved to New York in 1966 and joined the popular Charles Lloyd Quartet (1966–69), one of the era's earliest and most successful crossover bands. The quartet was the first jazz group to play in U.S. rock concert halls, and the group also toured Europe six times and was the first band of modern jazz musicians to play in Russia. In 1969 DeJohnette replaced Tony Williams in Miles Davis's band and participated in several seminal jazz-rock recordings, including *Live-Evil* and the best-selling *Bitches Brew*. Miles was always on the lookout for musicians that played intuitively, that would think for themselves and stimulate him to do likewise, and DeJohnette was a major asset to Davis during this period. After leaving Davis in 1972, DeJohnette continued to be active in jazz-rock groups, including his own band Compost. In the 1970s and '80s he became something like a house drummer for ECM, recording both as leader and sideman and appearing on more albums with the label than any other musician. In 1976 he formed various bands, including Special Edition, which created some of the most interesting jazz of the 1980s. Since 1983 DeJohnette has been known for his cutting-edge collaboration with Keith Jarrett and bassist Gary Peacock in a Standards trio that for over twenty years has produced brilliant interpretations of popular tunes.

AUGUST 10—CLAUDE THORNHILL (1909–1965)

b. Terre Haute, IN; d. New York, NY

Bandleader; Composer; Arranger; Pianist

[Swing; Cool]

Other jazz notables born on this day: Arnett Cobb (1918); Chuck Israels (1936); Mike Mantler (1943)
Jazz notables deceased on this day: Buster Smith (1991)

♪

The term "cool" in jazz was the continuation of a movement that had been going on in jazz for quite some time, namely the attempt to create "symphonic jazz." The concept of "symphonic jazz" had been tried in the 1920s by bandleader Paul Whiteman and composer George Gershwin, whose "Rhapsody in Blue" and "American in Paris" were attempts to create the jazz symphony. Until the 1940s, experiments with symphonic jazz were sporadic and unsystematic, but by the late 1930s many of the musicians taking up jazz were trained in European music. And they began wondering whether some of the classical procedures could be applied to jazz, particularly to the swing bands with which most of them were associated.

The most important bandleaders who featured symphonic jazz in the 1940s were Stan Kenton and Woody Herman, whose bands utilized complex arrangements and progressive sounds. A third band moving in the same direction was that of Claude Thornhill. Though the Thornhill orchestra never became as popular as the Kenton or Herman ensembles, it was respected by musicians and eventually made important contributions to the birth of "cool jazz."

Thornhill started piano lessons at the age of ten and two years later was working in dance bands. After studying piano and composition at the Cincinnati Conservatory and the prestigious Curtis Institute in Philadelphia, he played in territory bands before moving to New York in the early 1930s. He worked for various popular bands, including briefly with Whiteman and Benny Goodman (1934–35), and played and arranged for Ray Noble's American band in 1935 and 1936. While working as a musical director for Maxine Sullivan (1937–38), he arranged a lightly swinging version of "Loch Lomond" that became a hit. In 1938 he helped singer Skinnay Ennis form a West Coast band by taking over a band led by Gil Evans, who stayed on as arranger. Thornhill led his own touring big band from 1940 to 1942, with Evans as principal arranger. Characterized by a strikingly original sound, Thornhill's orchestra attracted a lot of attention in the jazz world. Though viewed as a dance band, Thornhill's arrangements were subtle and intelligent, including the moody tone poem that became the orchestra's theme song, "Snowfall."

In 1946, after service in a naval band, Thornhill re-formed his band, which briefly included Lee Konitz and Red Rodney and was highly valued by musicians for its modern, impressionistic sound. It was one of the first big bands to use French horns and other instruments associated mainly with European concert music. The band's arrangements, written by Evans and Gerry Mulligan, inspired Miles Davis to create a nine-piece version of the same sound that came to be known retrospectively as the Birth of the Cool Nonet. The effects of a nervous breakdown and alcohol consumption slowed Thornhill's career in the 1950s, but he continued to lead small or medium-sized dance bands, which served as training ground for such players as Bob Brookmeyer, Gene Quill, and Jimmy Knepper.

AUGUST 11—JESS STACY (1904–1994)

b. Bird's Point, MO; d. Los Angeles, CA

Pianist

[SWING]

Other jazz notables born on this day: Russell Procope (1908)
Jazz notables deceased on this day: Israel Crosby (1962); Gene Roland (1982); Benny Waters (1998)

BLUE NOTES

♪

In 1933 Benny Goodman formed his first band with the help of jazz patron John Hammond. As a talent scout, Hammond's finds included many outstanding stars, from Goodman, Billie Holiday, and Count Basie in the 1930s to Bob Dylan and Bruce Springsteen in the 1960s and '70s. A rich white kid connected to the Vanderbilt fortune, Hammond loved jazz and had great taste. No other non-musician, and indeed only the major instrumentalists, had as broad an effect on the music as he did. In 1933 he provided Goodman the chance to form a recording band that included trombonist Jack Teagarden and the first recorded performance by a seventeen-year-old singer named Billie Holiday.

In the mid 1930s Hammond was responsible for putting together the crucial deal in which Goodman bought song arrangements from Fletcher Henderson. These arrangements of current pop tunes contained a style and a beat that Goodman had never dared employ with his own band. According to Hammond, it was this approach to ballads that gave the Goodman band the style that made it conquer the nation in 1935. Along with Henderson, Hammond was also responsible for bringing drummer Gene Krupa, vibraphonist Lionel Hampton, pioneer electric guitarist Charlie Christian, and pianists Teddy Wilson and Jess Stacy into Goodman's ensembles.

Largely self-taught as a musician, Stacy gained early experience on Missouri riverboats before moving to Chicago in the 1920s, where he worked for a decade in countless speakeasies, clubs, and dance halls. At the instigation of Hammond, he joined Goodman's band in July 1935, on the eve of its groundbreaking cross-country tour. He worked with Goodman intermittently for nine years, in between stints with Bob Crosby (1939–42), Horace Heidt, and Tommy Dorsey. Goodman was a perfectionist, and Stacy's technically precise and rhythmically incisive style suited Goodman's needs. His greatest ability as pianist was finding the choicest notes to use in support of jazz ensembles, large and small.

Though Stacy was rarely given the opportunity to play solos, he became a star at Goodman's historic January 16, 1938 Carnegie Hall concert. At the close of Goodman's "Sing, Sing, Sing" routine, the bandleader motioned for Stacy to play an unscheduled solo (which he had never done on that piece). The pianist constructed a remarkable two-minute impressionistic improvisation that stole honors at the concert and turned Stacy into a legend. That concert, which is considered to be the high point of Goodman's success, would never have occurred without Hammond's initiative and encouragement. Stacy's career went downhill after 1945, when he formed a short-lived big band that featured his current wife, singer Lee Wiley. He became fairly obscure after moving to California in 1947, and after 1963 he retired from performance to become a salesman for Max Factor. Not until 1973, when he was persuaded to play soundtrack music for the film *The Great Gatsby*, was his piano heard again.

AUGUST 12—PAT METHENY (1954–)

b. Lee's Summit, MO

Guitarist; Composer; Leader

[Folk-Jazz; Contemporary Jazz; Post-Bop; Fusion]

Other jazz notables born on this day: Claude Hopkins (1898—or August 3 or 24, 1903)
Jazz notables deceased on this day: Lenny Breau (1984); Marty Paich (1995); Rashied Ali (2009)

♪

Pat Metheny, like David Sanborn, demonstrates wide interest in styles that fall between jazz and pop. One of the biggest name in jazz during the 1970s and '80s, Metheny gained a great deal of popularity on account of his proficiency on the guitar, but perhaps more so due to his blend of jazz, rock, and Latin influences, which enabled him to create a warm, smooth, full-bodied guitar sound that became widely imitated.

Metheny's early background was primarily jazz based. Originally influenced by Wes Montgomery, he incorporated elements of country music and the approach of Ornette Coleman in the process of developing his own unique sound. One of the most original guitarists of the past twenty years, Metheny has an extraordinary insight into the making of improvised music. He is at his best in a fusion style that brings together elements of bop, free jazz, jazz-rock, country music, folk, and Brazilian music in a manner that is accessible and yet maintains emotional and intellectual depth.[12] Metheny has been a key figure in transforming the guitar's role in jazz, helping that instrument attain a melodic status equal to that of the tenor saxophone. In the late 1990s Metheny opened concerts with his latest invention, playing the forty-two-string Pikasso guitar, an instrument so large that it had to be played on a specially constructed stand.

Metheny started on trumpet and then played French horn, but at the age of fourteen he was in need of braces for his teeth and so he took up guitar. He developed quickly, and was so proficient that during his second semester as a student at the University of Miami he was appointed a guitar instructor. In 1973, while still a teenager, he began teaching guitar at the Berklee College of Music in Boston; Mike Stern and Al Di Meola were among his students. During his first year at Berklee he joined Gary Burton, and he spent an important period (1974–77) with Burton's band, at which time he took up the 12-string electric guitar to differentiate his lines from those of Burton's other guitarist, Mick Goodrick.

In 1978 he formed a quartet with keyboardist Lyle Mays and two former classmates at Miami, Mark Egan and Danny Gottlieb, and within a short period he was the ECM label's top artist and one of the most popular of all jazz musicians, selling out stadiums. By the age of thirty Metheny had acquired a vast worldwide audience for his music while still enjoying the admiration of his jazz peers, and this puts him in a very select company of musicians, including Miles Davis, Keith Jarrett, Wayne Shorter, and Joe Zawinul.[13] By

---

12. Kernfeld, *New Grove Dictionary of Jazz*, Vol. 2, 752.
13. Carr et al., *Jazz: The Rough Guide*, 519.

1985 he had recorded twelve records, three of which received Grammy awards. That year he also recorded with Coleman, one of his idols. From his teenage years, Metheny has loved Coleman's free-jazz style, and the tremendous success of his own endeavors has allowed him to pursue free-jazz projects with such Coleman associates as Charlie Haden, Dave Holland, and Jack DeJohnette.

AUGUST 13—GEORGE SHEARING (1919–2011)

b. London, England; d. New York, NY

Pianist; Leader

[LATIN JAZZ; COOL; BOP]

Other jazz notables born on this day: Stuff Smith (1909); Joe Puma (1927); Mulgrew Miller (1955)

Jazz notables deceased on this day: King Curtis (1971); Les Paul (2009)

♪

During the 1950s and early '60s George Shearing led one of the most popular combos in jazz. His main claim to fame was the invention of a unique quintet sound known as the "Shearing sound," derived from a combination of piano, vibraphone, electric guitar, bass, and drums. Also known as "polite bop," Shearing's cool sound generally featured unison playing between vibes, guitar, and piano—the vibes doubled the upper melody note while the guitar doubled the melody an octave lower. By smoothing out some of the jarring aspects of modern jazz, his group made the music accessible to millions of fans. A natural improviser, Shearing's appeal came from his soft touch, graceful melodies, and distinctive harmonies. The success of his urbane sound obscured his other great contribution during this period, for he also pioneered small-combo Afro-Cuban jazz in the 1950s. An arranger as well as a composer of piano scores, Shearing is best known for his uniquely constructed bop standard, "Lullaby of Birdland," commissioned in 1952 by the owners of the legendary jazz club named after Charlie "Bird" Parker.

Blind from birth, Shearing began playing the piano at the age of three, when he would pick out tunes that he heard on his family radio. As a teenager he received some music training at the Linden Lodge School for the Blind in London, but his jazz influence came through Teddy Wilson and Fats Waller recordings. He started playing professionally in the late 1930s and made his first recording in 1937, at the encouragement of fellow Brit Leonard Feather. Able to absorb the musical vocabulary of jazz quickly and convincingly, he became a star in Britain, winning seven consecutive *Melody Maker* polls as the top British pianist.

In 1947 he immigrated to New York, where he quickly came under the influence of bebop, particularly the popular style of Bud Powell. He worked as an intermission pianist at the Hickory House, where he played with major jazz artists, including with Ella Fitzgerald's trio on Hank Jones's night off. He replaced Erroll Garner in the Oscar Pettiford Trio and led a quartet with clarinetist Buddy DeFranco before forming the first and most famous of his quintets in 1949, with Marjorie Hyams on vibes. Shearing settled into lucrative recording associations with MGM (1950–55) and Capitol (1955–69), but after leaving Capitol he began phasing out his by-now-predictable quintet, finally disbanding in 1978. During the 1970s his profile was lowered considerably, but upon signing with Concord in 1979, he found himself enjoying a renaissance. He made several acclaimed albums with Mel Tormé, much as he had done earlier with Nancy Wilson, Peggy Lee, and Nat Cole. In addition to duets and trios, he also recorded a number of solo piano albums. He continued to play impressively in several formats after signing with Telarc in 1992, extending what became one of the longest, most prolific recording careers in jazz history. In 2007 he was knighted by Queen Elizabeth II for his contributions to music.

AUGUST 14—FREDDIE WEBSTER (1916–1947) [DOB unknown]
b. Cleveland, OH; d. Chicago, IL

Trumpeter

[Bop]

Other jazz notables born on this day: Toots Mondello (1911); Lorez Alexandria (1929); Eddie Costa (1930)

Jazz notables deceased on this day: Joe Venuti (1978); Abbey Lincoln (2010)

♪

To understand the history of jazz trumpet, one must look at how certain players influenced successive generations. The lineage is often traced from Louis Armstrong through Roy Eldridge, Dizzy Gillespie, Fats Navarro, and Clifford Brown. But one trumpeter who had a profound influence upon his peers was Freddie Webster. Though he is hardly a household name today, due in part to his relatively few recordings (he never led a session of his own) and his early death, Webster was one of the outstanding trumpeters in jazz history. What set him apart from others was his tone—a fat, rich sound with a beautiful wide vibrato. Because of his place as one of pioneers of the bebop movement and his formative influence on Miles Davis, he has become a legendary figure.

As a teenager, Webster formed his own band, which included his friend Tadd Dameron on piano. Dameron, who later arranged for Gillespie, credited Webster with starting him on his career in jazz. Webster left Cleveland in 1938, touring with Earl Hines's popular big band before moving to New York in 1941, where he met Gillespie, pianist Bud Powell, and others who frequently talked and jammed together at Dizzy's apartment or at the Dewey Square Hotel in Harlem. Historian Leonard Feather has called these sessions the earliest steps toward the new style of jazz called bebop. Later that year Webster rejoined the Hines's orchestra, which included Gillespie, Charlie Parker, Billy Eckstine, Sarah Vaughan, and other members of the band that became known as "The Incubator of Bop." In 1942 Webster began playing with a succession of top big bands, including those led by Benny Carter, Lucky Millinder, Jimmy Lunceford, and Cab Calloway.

As a regular participant at jam sessions at Minton's Playhouse, he was a big influence on younger players such as Kenny Dorham and Davis, who remained his greatest champion. "I used to love what he did to a note," Davis recalled. "He didn't play a lot of notes, he didn't waste any. I used to try to get his sound."[14] When Gillespie formed his first big band in 1945 with Parker and drummer Max Roach, he chose Webster to play in the trumpet section, declaring that Webster had the best sound on a trumpet since the instrument's invention. By 1946 Webster began showing signs of alarming unreliability and arrogance. Shortly before Webster's death, when Count Basie was about to hire him, Basie asked Webster what his price was and Webster replied: "After you've paid the rest of those guys, you and I split 50–50!" Obviously, Webster never played with Basie. In April 1947 Webster went to Chicago to perform with saxophonist Sonny Stitt. Like many of his fellow musicians, Webster's involvement with heroin proved to be his undoing. As Davis claimed in his autobiography, Webster died of an overdose that was intended for Stitt. Someone had arranged to give Stitt some bad heroin and "Sonny gave it to Freddie who shot it and died." It was a tragic end to a brief but spectacular career.

AUGUST 15—OSCAR PETERSON (1925–2007)

b. Montreal, Canada; d. Mississauga, Ontario, Canada

Pianist; Leader

[Swing; Bop]

Other jazz notables born on this day: Joe Garland (1903); Morey Feld (1915)
Jazz notables deceased on this day: Irene Kral (1978)

♬

Often compared to his idol Art Tatum, Oscar Peterson was one of the greatest piano players of all time. A pianist with phenomenal technique, Peterson's speed, dexterity, and ability to swing at any tempo were amazing, inspiring as well as intimidating other pianists. Effective in small groups, jam sessions, and in accompanying singers, Peterson was at his best when performing unaccompanied solos. Stylistically an eclectic, like Erroll Garner and George Shearing, his distinctive playing style formed during the mid- to late 1940s and fell somewhere between swing and bop.[15]

Peterson started piano lessons when he was five, and three years later, after overcoming tuberculosis, began to study classical music. Having won an amateur talent contest, by the age of fourteen he was working on a weekly radio show in Montreal. Early trio performances (1945–49) demonstrate Peterson's love for boogie-woogie, which he soon discarded, and the swing style of Teddy Wilson and Nat King Cole. His technique was quite brilliant even then, and although he had not yet been influenced by bop, he was already an impressive player. By this time he had developed a local reputation, but for a while he refused to leave home. In 1949 jazz impresario Norman Granz persuaded him

---

14. Carr et al., *Jazz: The Rough Guide*, 814.
15. Bogdanov et al., *All Music Guide to Jazz*, 1006.

to appear in a Jazz at the Philharmonic (JATP) concert at Carnegie Hall, and from that point he began managing Peterson's career. He was an instant success with the jazz audience, winning numerous *Down Beat* polls during the 1950s, and in time, like Shearing, he developed a somewhat broader popular following. Peterson toured regularly with JATP during the early 1950s, initially working in a duo with bassist Ray Brown.

He became a household name in 1952 when he formed a trio with guitarist Barney Kessel (soon replaced by Herb Ellis) and Brown. The Peterson-Ellis-Brown trio, which often toured with JATP, was one of jazz's great combos from 1953 to 1958. In 1958 drummer Ed Thigpen replaced the guitarist, and this combination, with the pianist as the dominant soloist, became regarded as Peterson's best trio. During the 1970s Peterson concentrated on solo performances and proved to be one of the greatest piano soloists in the history of jazz. With the formation of the Pablo label by Granz in 1972, Peterson was often teamed with guitarist Joe Pass and bassist Niels Pedersen. Under Granz, Peterson probably recorded more albums than any other jazz artist, both on his own and with just about every other prominent instrumentalist.

Amazingly, he had arthritis in both hands since high school. This condition, due to heredity, sometimes caused him pain when he played and occasionally required him to cancel a performance. Since suffering a stroke in 1993, Peterson made a gradual return, although his left hand was weakened. But even when not 100 percent, Peterson remained one of the finest musicians that jazz has ever produced

AUGUST 16—BILL EVANS (1929–1980)

b. Plainfield, NJ; d. New York, NY

Pianist

[MODAL MUSIC; POST-BOP; COOL]

Other jazz notables born on this day: Mal Waldron (1925)
Jazz notables deceased on this day: Cutty Cutshall (1968); Max Roach (2007)

♫

In 1963 a fifteen-year old boy named Alan Broadbent heard piano music emanating from a store in Auckland, New Zealand. He entered the store, listened to his first Bill Evans record, and burst into tears. This event changed the youngster's life. Broadbent became one of many jazz pianists to be influenced by Evans's intensely personal style. Gene Lees, with *Down Beat* magazine in 1959, recalls his own discovery of Evans while reviewing an album titled *Everybody Digs Bill Evans*. The album had such a mesmerizing effect on him that he listened to it for seven consecutive hours, by which time he had it memorized. A day or two later he wrote a fan letter to Evans, indicating that the album sounded like love letters written to the world from some prison of the heart. "It struck me even then," he recalled, "that to anyone of the sensitivity so manifest in the music, life must be extraordinarily painful—which turned out to be all too true."[16]

---

16. Gottlieb, *Reading Jazz*, 420.

As a youngster Evans studied piano, violin, and flute. After high school he received a music scholarship to attend Southeastern Louisiana University, some fifty miles from New Orleans. In 1955, after serving in the army, he moved to New York City, uncertain whether to become a concert pianist or a jazz musician. The mid-1950s were a heady time for jazz in New York, and Evans decided to give the jazz scene a chance. His first real break came during an engagement at the Village Vanguard, where he worked solo opposite the Modern Jazz Quartet. One night, while playing, he looked up to find Miles Davis sitting near the piano, listening intently. In 1958 he was invited to join the Miles Davis sextet; though his stay was brief, the exposure he received playing with Davis and contributing to the classic *Kind of Blue* album brought him to the attention of jazz musicians and fans everywhere. Until that time Evans had been a shy, reserved individual with feelings of inferiority. Playing with the Davis band pushed him into the spotlight, but it also caused seismic emotional shifts within the young man. Vulnerable and out of his element, Evans turned to drugs—first heroin, then cocaine.

From this point on Evans began to record and perform solo and with a series of outstanding trios. Acknowledged as the most influential pianist working in jazz, Evans became legendary after accomplishing a nearly impossible feat at the Village Vanguard, when he performed a week's engagement with the use of only one hand, his left. Before starting the gig he had hit a nerve while injecting a needle into his right arm. The arm went numb and became practically useless. In desperate need of money, Evans went through with the engagement. Word of his feat spread through the jazz community, and pianists flocked to the Vanguard to watch this amazing event.

Evans's death, as his life, had a tragic nature to it. Though his death officially resulted from a hemorrhaging ulcer and bronchial pneumonia, that fatal condition arose as the result of protracted drug use and malnutrition. Though not medically verifiable, Evans's death was a slow suicide, the specter of a lifetime of inner turmoil.

AUGUST 17—IKE QUEBEC (1918–1963)

b. Newark, NJ; d. New York, NY

Tenor Saxophonist

[Hard Bop; Jump Blues; Soul-Jazz; Swing]

Other jazz notables born on this day: George Duvivier (1920)
Jazz notables deceased on this day: Tab Smith (1971); Pearl Bailey (1990); Wild Bill Davis (1995); Flip Phillips (2001)

♪

Prior to the emergence of Coleman Hawkins in the late 1920s, the saxophone was rarely heard in the early ensembles that defined the first jazz bands. Its entrance into jazz was circuitous, through the commercial dance bands that emerged in the prewar years. When Ferde Grofé began to write arrangements in the mid-teens for the Art Hickman Orchestra in San Francisco, he introduced a two-saxophone section as a complement to the trumpet and trombone sections. A few years later, when Grofé moved on to the Paul Whiteman Orchestra, the sounds that emerged—usually called symphonic jazz—produced a powerful impact upon young bandleaders such as Fletcher Henderson, Duke Ellington, and Jean Goldkette. The music that resulted from the interplay between sections of saxophones, trumpets, trombones, and rhythm provided a versatile and useful framework—so useful that it remained an essential aspect of big jazz bands[17]

By 1930 the saxophone had become an established member of jazz ensembles. The saxophone's success as a sectional instrument opened the doorway for the arrival of innovative players like Hawkins and, through them, the debut of the saxophone as a major jazz voice. Hawkins, arguably one of the instrument's seminal figures, is credited with initiating the whole process of jazz saxophone. His earliest recordings with the Henderson orchestra sounded almost comedic, but within a few years he was able to produce solos that reflected an uncommon musical imagination. Hawkins quickly became one of the most imitated performers in jazz, with players such as Chu Berry, Herschel Evans, Buddy Tate, Flip Phillips, Ike Quebec, and dozens of others following in his footsteps. With the exception of Lester Young, practically every tenor saxophonist who emerged in the 1930s was influenced by Hawkins, rhythmically, tonally, and melodically.

Ike Quebec, one of the finest swing-oriented tenors of the 1940s and '50s, had a big, breathy sound that was distinctive and quite consistent when he was playing blues, ballads, and up-tempo pieces. Originally a pianist and dancer, he switched to tenor in 1940 and played with the Barons of Rhythm. Later on he performed with various small bands in the New York area, including those led by Hawkins, Benny Carter, and Roy Eldridge. From 1944 to 1951 he worked with Cab Calloway's orchestra and in Calloway's small groups. Basically trained as an orchestral musician as well as a featured soloist, Quebec found himself less in demand as the big-band era began to fade. In the late 1940s and again in the early 1960s, he worked as an agent for Blue Note, bringing such notables as Thelonious Monk, Bud Powell, and Dexter Gordon to the label. Drug problems kept him from recording for most of the 1950s, but he made a comeback in the early 1960s, giving no indication that he was suffering from lung cancer, which took his life in 1963, at the age of forty-four.

AUGUST 18—DON LAMOND (1920–2003)

b. Oklahoma City, OK; d. Orlando, FL

Drummer

[SWING; BOP; BIG BAND]

Other jazz notables born on this day: Buster Wilson (1897—or Dec. 16); Jimmy Witherspoon (1921)
Jazz notables deceased on this day: Paul Mares (1949)

---

17. Kirchner, *Oxford Companion to Jazz*, 602.

BLUE NOTES

♪

One of the great tragedies in the musical world occurred on December 9, 1948, when Dave Tough, a leading jazz drummer, died from head injuries sustained after falling down in a Newark, New Jersey street while intoxicated. As the leading intellectual and free spirit in the Austin High School Gang in the mid-1920s, he had a formative influence on the Chicago style of white jazz. An epileptic, the brilliant drummer was plagued by inconsistencies and difficulties throughout his short life, including length periods of incapacitation due to alcoholism. Yet when he played, he energized and elevated music to an unbelievable extent. In 1936 he moved to New York, where he became a leading drummer, playing the Dixieland circuit with Bud Freeman, Jack Teagarden, and others while anchoring the big bands of Benny Goodman, Tommy Dorsey, and Artie Shaw. Later, Tough was one of the few Dixielanders able to play bop-oriented music. He made a strong impact during 1944 and 1945 as a member of Woody Herman's First Herd, where his drumming was quite influential. But he began drinking excessively and started to miss performances. He finally left the band after suffering a seizure while touring the South, and Herman replaced him with Don Lamond, a highly original and modernistic drummer who, like Tough, was skilled in both big-band and combo settings.

Lamond grew up in Washington, DC, where he took up drums, and by the time he was in high school he was playing in swing bands. After studying at the Peabody Conservatory in Baltimore, he picked up early experience working with the big bands of Sonny Dunham and Boyd Raeburn before joining Herman in October 1945. He remained with Herman until that classic band broke up in December 1946, at which point he freelanced (including recording with Charlie Parker). The following year, when Herman formed the Second Herd, the reliable Lamond rejoined, playing such classics as "Apple Honey," "Northwest Passage," "Your Father's Mustache," "Woodchopper's Ball," and the four part "Summer Sequence" with the powerhouse unit that included such major players as trumpeter-arranger Shorty Rogers, trombonist Earl Swope, guitarist Jimmy Raney, baritonist Serge Chaloff, and the tenors of Al Cohn, Stan Getz, and Zoot Sims.

When the Second Herd disbanded in 1949 due to financial pressures, Lamond joined Harry James. A few months later, when a tour was organized, he elected to leave the group and remain in the Los Angeles area, where he worked frequently in recording studios. Lamond rejoined Herman in 1959 for a brief engagement and he would return to Herman's big band for the fortieth anniversary concert of 1976 and again during the early 1980s. In 1972, after a stint with George Wein's Newport Festival All-Stars, he moved to Orlando, Florida, where he formed an orchestra of young players from the area. He would, however, forever be remembered for his association with Herman, and indirectly, with his First Herd predecessor on drums, Dave Tough.

AUGUST 19—JIMMIE ROWLES (1918–1996)

b. Spokane, WA; d. Burbank, CA

Pianist

[MAINSTREAM JAZZ; WEST COAST JAZZ; SWING; BOP]

Other jazz notables born on this day: Eddie Durham (1906); Tim Hagans (1954)
Jazz notables deceased on this day: Chris Kelly (1929); Tiny Kahn (1953); Bill Stegmeyer (1968); Brew Moore (1973); Cedric Wallace (1985)

♪

From 1945 until his death in 2002, few if any musicians in jazz knew more about pianists and singers than bassist Ray Brown. Having traveled the world, backing the greatest jazz singers (including Ella Fitzgerald, to whom he was married from 1948 to 1952) and pianists of his day, Brown had a knack for spotting talent. In the early 1980s, while he was performing in Canada, he was introduced to a teenaged pianist named Diana Krall. Admiring her musical skills, he suggested she relocate to Los Angeles to study with some of L.A.'s outstanding teachers. When she asked Brown for his recommendation, he quickly responded: "Hank Jones and Jimmie Rowles." Both were fantastic pianists with vast experience accompanying singers. Jones, like Brown, had worked with virtually every jazz artist of his era. A brilliant pianist, he was known for his beautiful sound and impeccable taste. But Jones was unavailable, so Krall approached Rowles.

Valued for his encyclopedic repertoire, Rowles had long been in demand as an accompanist. Born James Hunter, Jimmie took the name Rowles from his stepfather. In 1940, after attending Gonzaga University, he moved to Los Angeles, where he worked with bands led by saxophonists Ben Webster and Lester Young. Until he was drafted in 1942, Rowles spent the early war years working with Benny Goodman and Woody Herman. Following his discharge he returned to Herman, working with the First Herd until it was disbanded in 1946. A year later he rejoined Goodman, performing and recording in Benny's big band and small groups. He also recorded with Dexter Gordon and briefly in the orchestras of Les Brown and Tommy Dorsey. In 1952 he recorded privately with the Gerry Mulligan-Chet Baker quartet and then missed making jazz history by reportedly failing to turn up for the subsequent studio recording, which initiated Mulligan's famous pianoless quartet.[18]

He spent the 1950s and '60s in Los Angeles, working as a studio musician. During this time he participated in numerous instrumental jazz sessions with such notables as Louie Bellson, Buddy Rich, Stan Getz, Ray Brown, Benny Carter, and Webster, but it was as an accompanist to singers, particularly Peggy Lee and Billie Holiday, that he became best known. In 1973 he moved to New York, where he became established as a jazz soloist and recorded in duos or small groups with Getz, Al Cohn, Zoot Sims, and others. After touring with Fitzgerald (1981–83), he returned to California for continued playing and nightclub work. Known for his touch, precise timing, and clever imagination, Rowles may

---

18. Kernfeld, *New Grove Dictionary of Jazz*, Vol. 3, 461.

well be one of the most underrated soloists in the business. His subtle approach is typified by his composition, "The Peacocks," which became a standard thanks to tenor saxophonist Stan Getz, who tried to rescue him from obscurity by producing a duet album for Columbia in 1975. A few years later Ray Brown did the same on the Concord label.

AUGUST 20—FRANK ROSOLINO (1926–1978)

b. Detroit, MI; d. Los Angeles, CA

Trombonist

[MAINSTREAM JAZZ; BOP]

Other jazz notables born on this day: Jimmy Raney (1927); Milford Graves (1941); Enrico Rava (1943); John Clayton (1952)
Jazz notables deceased on this day: Thad Jones (1986); John Gilmore (1995)

♫

Frank Rosolino was among the best-loved musicians in jazz. One of the finest trombone players in the history of the instrument and one of the few practitioners on the instrument to adapt fully to bebop, he will always be remembered and respected for his mastery of the trombone and for his wit and capacity for comic entertainment. Prior to his tragic death, no one ever spoke or wrote about him without the mention of his unwavering sense of humor. But behind that cut-up personality was a troubled man. The horrible way that he ended his life (committing suicide after shooting his two sons, killing one) has largely overshadowed his earlier musical accomplishments.

Despite Rosolino's reputation as a "clown prince," to him playing the trombone was serious business. His musical reputation came from his general refusal to believe that the trombone was incapable of achieving the technical facility of any other instrument. With his initial musical experiences coming on guitar and accordion, Rosolino was introduced to the trombone in the sixth grade, and he devoted much of his time attempting to imitate the demanding technical etudes he heard his brother playing on the violin. He was one of a number of players who came out of Cass Tech in Detroit, a superior high school that drew its students from all over the city.

While with the military in the Philippines during World War II, he wandered into a dance and asked to sit in with the band. Hopeful of making an impression but unable to read music, he planned to fake the big band arrangement until he had a chance to play a solo. Not surprisingly, his display of technique resulted in a transfer to the Eighty-Sixth Division Band, where he became proficient at sight-reading. By 1948 he was one of several bop-influenced musicians playing in Gene Krupa's big band. Experiences with other big bands were but preludes to his high-profile association with Stan Kenton (1952–54), where his soloing garnered him near legendary status. Following his stay with Kenton, he settled in Los Angeles, where he became a prominent session musician, recording regularly as a member of the Lighthouse All Stars (1954-60).

The exact events that that transpired in the Rosolino household during the early hours of November 26, 1978, will never be known. Previously, Frank's third wife and the mother of his two sons had committed suicide by breathing car fumes in their garage, and the trombonist had mentioned the possibility of taking his own life and that of his two sons, since he could not bear the thought of leaving them behind. But those who heard him say this failed to take him seriously, for he did not seem suicidal. Pianist Roger Kellaway may have come closest to understanding Rosolino's inner turmoil when he remarked, after the funeral: "When someone cracks four jokes a minute, we should have known there was something wrong."

AUGUST 21—COUNT BASIE (1904–1984)

b. Red Bank, NJ; d. Hollywood, CA

Bandleader; Pianist

[SWING; PIANO BLUES; BIG BAND]

Other jazz notables born on this day: Art Farmer (1928)
Jazz notables deceased on this day: Bill Harris (1973)

♪

As bandleader, Count Basie was a leading figure of the swing era and with Duke Ellington, an outstanding representative of the big band style. From 1936 to 1940 his band may have included the greatest concentration of jazz talent of any orchestra in the country, with the possible exception of Ellington's group. The radio, and talent scout John Hammond, was responsible for the national popularity of the Count Basie band. Without both, Basie might have remained just another musician playing the territories in Oklahoma and around Kansas City.

Though Bill Basie got his start as a bandleader in Kansas City, he was born in Red Bank, New Jersey. His father held various odd jobs and his mother took in laundry to get by. But they had a piano, and when Basie was six, his mother was able to come up with a quarter a week for lessons. As he got older he graduated from doing odd jobs around Red Bank's Palace movie theatre to working as an occasional replacement for the piano player who accompanied the silent movies. In 1924 he went to New York at the invitation of a friend, where he met Harlem's reigning piano kings, including Fats Waller, who taught Basie how to play the organ. By the time he was twenty he was touring extensively on the vaudeville circuit. In those years he was a proficient ragtimer, playing with all the speed, power, and agility that the style demanded. In 1927 he became stranded in Kansas City and joined Walter Page's popular Blue Devils band before being hired by Bennie Moten as a member of his influential orchestra. In 1935, after Moten's death, Basie organized a group of nine musicians into a band that included former Moten band members Joe Jones, Herschel Evans, Lester Young, and singer Jimmy Rushing.

Hammond, who had been partly responsible for putting together the Benny Goodman band that had ushered in the swing era in 1935, was in Chicago that winter, recording piano players during the day and listening to the Goodman band at the

Congress Hotel at night. Basie's band had a regular gig at the Reno Club in Kansas City at the time, and from there the group's performances went out over regional radio. One cold January night, around one o'clock in the morning, the listening audience included Hammond. He was trying to find some music on his car radio and the only station he could find at that hour was W9XBY, an experimental station in Kansas City. Hammond was amazed at what he heard. It seemed to him that the Basie band—blues-based, loose but hard swinging, with plenty of room for soloing—had everything the big commercial bands lacked. Determined to sign Count Basie and bring him to New York, he eventually drove to Kansas City. At Hammond's urging, Basie moved his band to New York, where he began performing at some of the city's best clubs. With the exception of a brief period in the early 1950s, Basie led a big band from 1935 until his death almost fifty years later. This band, the most enduring unit in jazz, was considered the epitome of swing and became broadly influential.

AUGUST 22—MALACHI FAVORS (1937–2004)

b. Chicago, IL; d. Chicago, IL

Bassist

[AVANT-GARDE JAZZ; FREE JAZZ; MODERN CREATIVE]

Other jazz notables born on this day:
Jazz notables deceased on this day: Bass Edwards (1965)

♪

In 1961 the pianist Muhal Richard Abrams organized a group called the Experimental Band, a rehearsal group that explored many of the contemporary alternatives to conventional jazz improvisation. The band had no permanent membership; rather, it consisted of smaller units, which met whatever composition and performance demands were required for concerts and recordings. Out of the Experimental Band came a comprehensive musicians' collective called the Association for the Advancement of Creative Musicians (AACM). The personnel for the AACM included prominent musicians such as saxophonists Anthony Braxton and Joseph Jarman, woodwind player Roscoe Mitchell, and bassist Malachi Favors.

In 1966 trumpeter Lester Bowie joined Mitchell and Favors in a sextet that became the first AACM ensemble to record. Their first release, *Sound*, was an early free-jazz landmark. Abstract in concept and execution, the album was an in-depth examination of the interaction between sound and silence. Where most previous free jazz prized complex chord progressions and virtuoso displays of technical prowess, the ensemble offered spontaneous collective improvisation, novel textures, toy instruments, and careful use of silence. A departure from the more extroverted work of the New York-based free jazz players, the album pointed to a new manner of playing jazz-based music. In 1968 the band was renamed the Art Ensemble of Chicago; a year later its members moved to Paris, where they recorded extensively and became one of the most important groups of the 1970s and '80s.

The work of the Art Ensemble, like that of the AACM, is difficult to describe because of the variety of compositional and performance tactics its members employed, some of which have not been squarely within the jazz tradition. In their work the musicians mimic street bands of foreign countries, perform lighthearted dramatic sketches, recite poetry, wear costumes and stage makeup, and improvise without following preset progressions of chords. Some of their music is similar to that of Ornette Coleman, Don Cherry, and Albert Ayler, especially in their large assortment of tone qualities and pitch bends. They do not use piano, and since all group members play percussion instruments, many of their recordings dispense with the conventional jazz drum set. Timekeeping and a harmonic background are provided by Favors, who has outstanding technique and distinctive improvisational flexibility.

In addition to bass, Favors played a variety of miscellaneous instruments (including banjo, zither, bells, gong, harmonica, melodica, and percussion) for ensemble recordings. The group's eclectic, theatrical repertory also includes a number of his compositions. Since the band's return to Chicago in 1971, the Art Ensemble was his primary outlet, though he played with many other prominent free-jazz musicians, including Sunny Murray, Archie Shepp, and Dewey Redman.

AUGUST 23—MARTIAL SOLAL (1927–)

b. Algiers, North Africa

Pianist

[Post-Bop; Modern Creative]

Other jazz notables born on this day: John Lindsay (1894); Avery Sharpe (1954); Brad Mehldau (1970)
Jazz notables deceased on this day: Glen Gray (1963); Maynard Ferguson (2006)

♪

One of the finest European jazz pianists of all time, Solal has not received as much recognition in America as he deserves. His unique piano style, while capable of sounding momentarily like anyone from Art Tatum to Bill Evans, is characterized by a restless abundance of ideas. The technique required to execute these ideas is equally abundant, as is his harmonic knowledge, and both are perhaps best appreciated in his frequent "solalizings," as his sometimes surprising, sometimes witty reconstructions of popular standards have been called. His original compositions, which include scores for over forty films, are equally arresting.

Born in Algiers to French parents, Solal started on piano at the prompting of his mother, an opera singer. One day he heard over the radio what he believed was a solo performance by a master pianist. Solal took this as a standard, and worked hard to equal what he heard. He did so, only to learn much later that four hands, not two as he had imagined, had been used to record the piece decisive to his ambition. In addition to piano, he also learned to play various wind instruments, knowledge he later used as a big band composer and arranger. After working locally in Algiers he settled in Paris, the city often considered the jazz center of Europe, where he played with the best French jazz musicians and those famous American soloists visiting Paris during this period. Soon he was the regular piano player at the Club St. Germain and the Blue Note, the Parisian meccas of jazz, where tourists as well as the locals flocked.

He began fronting a big band of his own in 1956, and soon thereafter he formed a quartet with drummer Daniel Humair. In 1963 the American impresario George Wein arranged an American tour, presenting Solal at festivals and concerts in Canada and the U.S., including at Wein's own Newport Jazz Festival, which helped broaden Solal's international reputation. In 1968 Solal recorded with saxophonist Lee Konitz in Italy and later performed with him at various European festivals. Over the years Solal has been primarily heard with his own trios and big bands, fronting ensembles and regularly recording original compositions and arrangements. As the recipient of the Jazzpar prize in 1999, he adequately embodied the selection committee's primary criterion that the prize must be awarded to an internationally known active jazz artist who is especially deserving of further acclaim.

AUGUST 24—BUSTER SMITH (1904–1991)

b. Alfdorf, TX; d. Dallas, TX

Alto Saxophonist; Clarinetist; Arranger

[SWING]

Other jazz notables born on this day: Claude Hopkins (1903)
Jazz notables deceased on this day: Don Byas (1972); Louis Prima (1978)

♪

Remembered as having been a mentor of Charlie Parker, Buster Smith was a fixture in Kansas City during his most significant years. He was a key member of several territory bands during the 1920s and '30s, including Walter Page's Blue Devils (1925–33) and Bennie Moten's band during its final years (1933–35), before co-leading the Barons of Rhythm at the Reno Club with Count Basie in 1935 and 1936. He then led his own bands, one of which included Parker among its personnel, before he moved to New York in 1938.

Smith grew up on a farm near Ennis, Texas and then moved with his family to Dallas. Having taught himself to play clarinet, he worked around Dallas until 1925, when he joined the Blue Devils, which was rapidly becoming the era's hottest territory band. In 1930 Smith and Page were strolling past a small upstairs club in Minneapolis when they heard the sound of a tenor saxophone drifting down the stairs. The tune was familiar, but the light, effortless sound was different from anything they had ever heard. The unknown saxophonist was Lester Young, and the two musicians decided they had to incorporate his sound into their band. It wasn't easy talking the talented saxophonist into joining, for he was making a good living in Minneapolis. But Smith had recently bought a brand-new car and Young, impressed by the appearance of wealth, got his suitcase and horn and climbed aboard. By 1933, when the depressed economy forced the group to disband, he and the remaining Blue Devils headed for Kansas City.

Like most Kansas City units, the Basie band specialized in "head arrangements," worked out informally without sheet music. Basie's theme song, "One O'Clock Jump," originated one night as Basie was finishing a piano solo and motioned to Smith to start up a riff (an ad-lib musical idea that could be repeated by sectional groups within the band). Smith started the reeds off on a figure from a Don Redman tune, to which Hot Lips Page added a trumpet part, followed up by Dan Minor's invention for the trombones. That became the "head" for a piece Basie's men called "Blue Balls." The band was about to play it just before they were to go off the air one night when the announcer asked Basie for the name of his next tune. The title, too risqué to be used over the radio, clearly wouldn't do. Noticing the time on the studio clock, Basie announced the piece as *"One O'Clock Jump."* Although Basie received the credit for composing the tune, Smith had as much to do with its composition as anyone.

When Smith went to New York in 1938, his protégé, Charlie Parker, followed him to Harlem. Smith put up with him for a while until his wife got tired of having him around. He wandered the Harlem streets before taking a job washing dishes at a small club just so he could hear another of his idols, Art Tatum, play piano every night. At this early stage in Parker's career, key elements of his sound could be traced to Smith's fluid playing, so much so that when Parker's former bandleader, Jay McShann, first heard Parker on the radio, he thought he was listening to Buster Smith.[19]

AUGUST 25—WAYNE SHORTER (1933–)

b. Newark, NJ

Tenor and Soprano Saxophonist; Composer

[Modal Music; Hard Bop; Post-Bop; Fusion]

Other jazz notables born on this day: Bob Crosby (1913); Pat Martino (1944); Charles Fambrough (1950)

Jazz notables deceased on this day: Stan Kenton (1979); Rudi Blesh (1985)

♫

Although later fusion styles seemed more pop than jazz, early fusion music had its roots in bedrock jazz values—improvisation, performer interplay, and most importantly, originality of expression. That's because most of the original fusion artists had honed their skills within an acoustic context. They came up in bop and bop-derived bands and therefore had an understanding of traditional jazz theory and practice. Aside from Miles Davis, perhaps the best example of a prominent early fusion player with a solid bop background is Wayne Shorter. The saxophonist apprenticed not only with Davis but also with Art Blakey's Jazz Messengers, two of jazz history's most formidable training camps. Experts debate whether Shorter's primary impact on jazz has been as a composer or as a saxophonist, but no one disputes his overall importance as one of jazz's leading figures during the 1960s and '70s.

---

19. Carr et al., *Jazz: The Rough Guide*, 714.

One of the outstanding tenors of the 1960s, he was with Davis through six crucial years of the trumpeter's career (1964–70), and it was with him that he first played soprano on *In a Silent Way* and *Bitches Brew* (both 1969), producing a lyrical, ethereal sound that contributed significantly to the prominence of the soprano with electronic fusion groups. In addition to his work with Davis, Shorter was a leading figure with Weather Report, a fusion band of the 1970s and '80s that featured electronics and a great deal of rhythmic and tonal abstraction.

After graduating with a degree in music education from New York University, Shorter played briefly with Horace Silver before being drafted into the army (1956–58). In 1959 he joined Blakey's Jazz Messengers, ultimately serving as the band's musical director. During that period he toured extensively and recorded several albums, thereby establishing himself as one of the most gifted of the younger saxophonists. After several attempts to lure him from Blakey, Miles Davis finally convinced Shorter in 1964 to join his quintet. Miles now had the band of his dreams: drummer Tony Williams, bassist Ron Carter, pianist Herbie Hancock, and Shorter. All were conservatory trained, and all would become leading figures in jazz and in the fusion styles that emerged around 1970. It was during this period that Shorter found his own voice as both a player and composer.

In 1970 Shorter teamed up with Joe Zawinul and Miroslav Vitous to form Weather Report. After a strong start, Shorter's playing grew gradually subservient to Zawinul's concepts. In the late 1970s he revisited the past by touring with Freddie Hubbard and ex-Miles sidemen Hancock, Carter, and Williams as V.S.O.P. Shorter finally left Weather Report in 1985, but promptly went into a creative slump. Shorter seems, paradoxically, most independent and creative when functioning under a strong leader such as Blakey or Davis. His composing and playing certainly flourished with Miles. However, Shorter is incapable of shallowness, and whether as leader or sideman, playing or composing, his music retains a visionary perspective.[20]

AUGUST 26—JIMMY RUSHING (1902 or 1903–1972)

b. Oklahoma City, OK; d. New York, NY

Vocalist

[VOCAL JAZZ; EAST COAST BLUES; JUMP BLUES; SWING]

Other jazz notables born on this day: Clifford Jarvis (1941); Branford Marsalis (1960)
Jazz notables deceased on this day: Jimmy Forrest (1980); Alberto Socarras (1987)

♫

In 1925 Oklahoma City was a metropolis of a hundred thousand people, where only forty years earlier there had been prairie, with Indians camping on the buffalo grass. By the early 1930s bands came into the city from all over the "Territory," which no longer referred to the Indian Territory, but to the entire area of Missouri, Kansas, Arkansas, Oklahoma, and Texas. At that time the city's public schools were strictly segregated. Whereas music

---

20. Carr et al., *Jazz: The Rough Guide*, 702.

instruction in the white schools seemed perfunctory, in the African-American public schools music instruction included four years of harmony—beginning in the eighth grade—and a considerable amount of theory. Deep Second was the street in town where music thrived. On Deep Second was the Aldrich, a theater run by Mrs. Braux, the musical director for the African-American public school system and the genius behind its musical curriculum. Deep Second was also the location of Slaughter's Hall, where the Blue Devils, one of the Territory's top bands, held forth on Saturday nights whenever they were in town.

The future novelist, Ralph Ellison, then a schoolboy living four blocks from the club, remembered lying in bed at night and hearing the band's vocalist, Jimmy Rushing, singing the blues with a booming voice that radiated sheer joy in whatever material he sang. Known as "Mister Five-by-Five"—a reference to his height and girth—Rushing was the classic blues shouter; he could swing with anyone and dominated even the loudest of big bands.

Jimmy Rushing is a good example of the involvement of the African-American community in Oklahoma City with music of all kinds. His father played trumpet with a brass band on Sunday concerts in the park, his mother and brother were singers, and all of them participated in the operettas staged at the high school. In addition, Jimmy learned violin and then piano, which he played by ear. After a move to California in the mid-1920s he joined Walter Page's Blue Devils (1927), where his intense, high-pitched voice became familiar all over the Southwest. From 1929 until 1935 he toured with Bennie Moten's band and finally, after Moten's death in 1935, he became a member of Basie's band.

The swinging Basie rhythm section was a perfect match for Rushing. In 1938, with help from jazz promoter John Hammond, the band relocated to New York City, where it soon became recognized as one of the top units in the nation. There were three trumpets in the group, three trombones, and four reeds, in addition to the best rhythm section in the business. Out front, at the microphone, was Rushing, the singer whose joyful voice Ralph Ellison had heard from his Oklahoma City bedroom as a boy. After the Basie ensemble broke up in 1950, Rushing briefly retired, then formed his own septet, going on tour before settling into the Savoy for two years, where he often appeared opposite Basie and created a sensation.

AUGUST 27—LESTER YOUNG (1909–1959)

b. Woodville, MS; d. New York, NY

Tenor Saxophonist; Leader

[MAINSTREAM JAZZ; SWING; COOL]

Other jazz notables born on this day: Sonny Sharrock (1940)
Jazz notables deceased on this day: Lil Armstrong (1971); Teddy Stauffer (1991)

♪

If the lives of leading musicians sometimes seem tragic, Lester Young's was probably the most poignant of all. A peaceful soul who only wanted to make beautiful music, he repeatedly found himself the center of controversy. The gradual but horrific decline of his last years suggested that being at odds with the world finally got to him.

Lester Young was one of the greatest and most influential of all saxophonists. His light, graceful tone and long flowing lines were a clear alternative to the self-confident Coleman Hawkins, the other dominant tenor player of the day. Where others drove hard and bore down on the beat, Young's phrases floated on air, symbolized by the way he twisted his saxophone at a horizontal angle high above the floor. Considered revolutionary when he first recorded, Young's superb melodic gift and logical phrasing eventually became the envy of musicians on all instruments, setting the standard for all modern jazz. Reaching for a novel adjective in 1949, jazz critic Leonard Feather wrote that Young "symbolized the gradual evolution from hot jazz to 'cool' jazz."

Although he spent his earliest days in Algiers, across the river from New Orleans, his family split up when he was ten and Young moved with his brother and sister to Minneapolis to live with his father, a carnival musician, and to play in the legendary family band. As a youngster, Young was on the road every summer. At the age of eighteen, he left home rather than make a tour of the South with his father. Ever since his boyhood encounter with a white mob, he had tried to avoid the Deep South. In 1934, after a brief period with Bennie Moten and Count Basie's Kansas City-based band, he joined Fletcher Henderson's prestigious orchestra in New York as replacement for Hawkins. But Young was no replacement. To New York ears, Young's sound was foreign, disturbing, and wrong. He only lasted a few months with Henderson before leaving due to pressure for not being a Hawkins clone.

After two years of wandering Pres eventually returned to Basie, where he was accepted on his own terms. He joined the group in 1936, just in time to star with the band as they headed east on a tour arranged by John Hammond. Young made history during his years with Basie, not only with Basie's band but also through collaborations with Billie Holiday, which led to some of jazz's best small-group sessions (it was Holiday who nicknamed Young "Pres"). During World War II Young did everything he could to avoid getting drafted. Fearing racism, he ended up experiencing it fully in a Georgia barracks, where he was incarcerated on charges that he smoked marijuana. His traumatic experience in the military affected his mental state for the remainder of his life. Though he was at his musical prime in the mid-to-late 1940s, Young bore deep emotional scars. He became increasingly dependent on alcohol and nearly stopped eating. Always a loner, Pres began to withdraw even further during the 1950s. In 1959 he became severely ill and he died alone and depressed; his old friend Billie Holiday followed him a few months later.

AUGUST 28—KENNY DREW SR. (1928–1993)

b. New York, NY; d. Copenhagen, Denmark

Pianist

[HARD BOP]

Other jazz notables born on this day: Tio Lorenzo Sr. (1867); John Marshall (1941); Peter Washington (1964); Larry Goldings (1968)
Jazz notables deceased on this day: Bob Gordon (1955); Lou McGarity (1971)

♪

In 1957, having recently been dismissed by Miles Davis for his long-standing addiction to alcohol and hard drugs, John Coltrane experienced a spiritual awakening that had immediate musical consequences. Renouncing drugs and alcohol, he was now ready to lead his own band. That year, his breakthrough year, he recorded *Blue Train*, one of the most important albums of his career, significant not only for its content but also for its impressive personnel. Joining Coltrane for that influential session were trumpeter Lee Morgan, trombonist Curtis Fuller, and an outstanding rhythm section consisting of Paul Chambers, Philly Joe Jones, and Kenny Drew Sr. In January 1958 Davis rehired Coltrane, now a very different person, and the following year Coltrane moved closer to jazz immortality when he became involved in two of the most famous jazz recordings ever made, Davis's *Kind of Blue* and his own *Giant Steps*.

Kenny Drew Sr., one of the top young bop-oriented pianists to emerge in the 1950s, learned piano at an early age and gave his first recital when he was eight. Shortly after graduation from the High School of Music and Art in New York, he became featured in sessions with some of the greatest figures in jazz, including Lester Young, Charlie Parker, and Coleman Hawkins. In 1951 he performed with Davis at Birdland and recorded with Sonny Rollins, among others. For a time he was a member of Buddy DeFranco's quartet, which included Art Blakey. He settled on the West Coast for a few years, where he formed his own band and also recorded as a sideman with Zoot Sims, Clifford Brown, and Dexter Gordon. In 1956 he returned to the East Coast as an accompanist to the singer Dinah Washington. During this period he recorded the classic album *Blue Train* with Coltrane and took part in many outstanding recording sessions.

In 1961 he traveled to Europe and remained in Paris, where he was briefly imprisoned for his addiction to drugs. In 1964 he made his home in Copenhagen, where he married an SAS stewardess (the daughter of Danish bandleader Leo Mathiesen) and built up a successful recording and music publishing company. He also formed an informal partnership with the celebrated bassist Niels-Henning Orsted Pederson that continued for the remainder of his life. A masterful musician, Drew accompanied many leading soloists of his day who were resident in Copenhagen or on tour.

Kenny Drew had the potential for greatness, but he was not as fortunate as Coltrane. Despite his success in Denmark, where he became a celebrity in the jazz scene, he would remain somewhat underrated in the U.S. for his decision to permanently move abroad.

And as a parent, he was a failure. In 1958 he fathered a son, Kenny Jr., who became a talented pianist, playing jazz and classical music professionally. Despite sharing his father's name, Kenny Jr. was raised by his aunt and grandparents and never considered the father who abandoned him in his infancy to be a musical influence.

AUGUST 29—CHARLIE PARKER (1920–1955)

b. Kansas City, KS; d. New York, NY

Alto Saxophonist

[Bop]

Other jazz notables born on this day: Jack Teagarden (1905); Dinah Washington (1924); Bennie Maupin (1940); Doug Raney (1956)
Jazz notables deceased on this day: Horace Henderson (1988)

♪

According to James Lincoln Collier, there have only been two authentic geniuses in jazz, Louis Armstrong, the much-loved entertainer, and Charlie Parker, the sociopath "who managed in a short period of time to destroy his career, every relationship important to him, and finally himself."[21] Arguably the greatest saxophonist of all time, Parker (known as "Yardbird" or simply as "Bird") is one of the most brilliant—and tragic—figures of the twentieth century. Together with Dizzy Gillespie and Bud Powell, he is considered the founder of the bebop tradition. In 1949 a jazz club named Birdland opened in New York. It was named for Parker, who was only twenty-nine at the time. It was also the last place he played before his death five years later. A legendary figure during his lifetime, Parker's influence, as his persona, is still bigger than life, making the phrase "Bird Lives" (scrawled as graffiti after his death) truer than ever.

When Charlie was about ten, his father drifted away from the family, causing Parker's mother to take a night job in order to support the struggling family. Left alone at night, Parker began attending the local cabarets. His class work suffered, flaws in his personality began to emerge, and he soon dropped out of school. He was fifteen when he married a woman four years his elder; over the next twenty years he married four times. He went to New York in 1939, washing dishes in a restaurant so he could hear Art Tatum play there nightly. That exposure to Tatum was quite possibly the single most important musical influence in his life. Then came the fateful December night at a chili house where, as he jammed on "Cherokee," he discovered how to play sounds he said he had been hearing in his head for some time, perhaps sounds inspired by Tatum's piano style. In 1941 Parker was twenty-one and as good an alto saxophonist as there was in jazz.

By 1942 he was jamming with Dizzy Gillespie and other young modernists at clubs such as Clark Monroe's Uptown House and at Minton's, but he was also acquiring the habits that would destroy him. By this time he was a heroin addict, in addition to smoking pot and cigarettes, taking pills, eating huge meals, and womanizing persistently. Many

---

21. Collier, *Making of Jazz*, 362.

stories are told about Parker nodding off on the bandstand or not showing up to a gig because he was wasted. Parker's regimen would have killed most people a lot sooner than it did him. The psychological tendencies, hostility, arrogance, mental confusions, and other character disorders surfaced first; the physical deterioration was not far behind. By 1954, grossly overweight and suffering from stomach ulcers, he could no longer control his life. On one occasion he attempted suicide by drinking iodine. He began wandering aimlessly around Greenwich Village. On March 9, 1955, he stumbled into the apartment of a friend, the Baroness de Koningswater, who tried to persuade Parker to enter a hospital, but three days later he was dead. The medical examiner, misled by the ravaged body, listed Parker's age as fifty-three; he was only thirty-four.

AUGUST 30—KENNY DORHAM (1924–1972)

b. Fairfield, TX; d. New York, NY

Trumpeter; Leader

[HARD BOP]

Other jazz notables born on this day: John Surman (1944)
Jazz notables deceased on this day: Philly Joe Jones (1985)

♪

In 1955 drummer Art Blakey and pianist Horace Silver organized the Jazz Messengers, a cooperative band that came to epitomize hard bop, a brash fusion of bop and funk that over the next four decades would become the training ground for a host of great musicians. In addition to bassist Doug Watkins, who rounded out the rhythm section, the landmark quintet also included saxophonist Hank Mobley and trumpeter Kenny Dorham, one of the first bebop horn players, who had already distinguished himself performing with some of bebop's leading stylists, including Dizzy Gillespie and Charlie Parker.

Dorham was a brilliant player who "could project great lyricism even at fast tempos, producing astonishingly long lines of fluid triplets. He was also a magnificent blues player, because his fluidity of execution was accompanied by all the tonal inflections of the vocal blues tradition."[22] In his best recordings of the mid- and late 1950s, he rivaled his greatest contemporaries in technical command, tunefulness, and beauty of timbre. Though a talented bop-oriented trumpeter and an excellent composer who played in some very significant bands, he was never a major force. His harmonic inventiveness influenced and inspired countless trumpeters all over the world, but he himself never broke through to a wider audience or got the recognition he was due, since he was consistently overshadowed by Gillespie, Miles Davis, and Fats Navarro in the 1940s and by Clifford Brown, Lee Morgan, and others in the 1950s and '60s.

Dorham started on piano at age seven and took up trumpet in high school. He enrolled at Wiley College to study chemistry, but soon switched to music. He was drafted into the army in 1942 and served on the boxing team, but after his discharge he returned

---

22. Carr et al., *Jazz: The Rough Guide*, 211.

to music. In 1944 he moved to New York, where he played at bop jam sessions at Minton's Playhouse and performed at the Savoy Ballroom. He played in the innovative bop big bands of Gillespie and Billy Eckstine (1945), and then spent short periods in the big bands of Lionel Hampton and Mercer Ellington. During 1948 to 1949 Dorham replaced Miles Davis in Charlie Parker's quintet, playing with Parker at the Paris Jazz Festival in 1949. After freelancing in New York, in 1954 he was a star soloist on the great album that served as the blueprint for the Messengers, *Horace Silver and the Jazz Messengers*.

In 1956, when the first version of the Messengers disbanded, Dorham briefly led a similar group called the Jazz Prophets. From 1956 to 1958 he replaced Clifford Brown in the Max Roach quintet, and played superlatively on another classic album of the 1950s, *Max Roach 4 Plays Charlie Parker* (1957). During the late 1950s and the '60s he led various groups of his own, composed the Latin jazz standard, "Blue Bossa," and recorded several excellent Blue Note sessions. In the early 1960s he was a booster of Joe Henderson (who played with his band in 1963 and 1964 and with whom he recorded even after the saxophonist joined Silver's quintet in 1964). By the mid-1960s Dorham was suffering from high blood pressure and the kidney disease that eventually took his life.

AUGUST 31—HANK JONES (1918–2010)

b. Vicksburg, MS; d. New York, NY

Pianist

[SWING; BOP]

Other jazz notables born on this day: Edgar Sampson (1907); Gunter Hampel (1937); Paul Winter (1939)

Jazz notables deceased on this day: Booker Ervin (1970); Milt Larkin (1996)

♫

In 1953, when the enigmatic clarinetist Artie Shaw organized his final version of the Gramercy Five, he selected his sidemen with great care: Tal Farlow (later Joe Puma) on guitar, Tommy Potter on bass, Irv Kluger on drums, and Hank Jones on piano. Because of his admiration for the George Shearing sound, he added Shearing's former vibraphonist Joe Roland. The group recorded extensively during early 1954, producing some of the finest performances of Shaw's career and "among the most enchanting small band recordings in jazz history, virtually unrivaled in defining the nexus between swing and bop."[23] The music is romantic, daring, and exquisitely played, and each player seems at the pinnacle of his work. Acknowledging that these recordings represented the epitome of all he could do on his instrument, Shaw abandoned the clarinet after this project. Hank Jones simply moved on. A musician for all seasons, his subdued style was well suited to his role as responsive accompanist.

The elder brother of Thad and Elvin Jones, Hank grew up in Pontiac, Michigan. He took up piano at an early age and came under the influence of great swing pianists

---

23. Giddins, *Visions of Jazz*, 204.

such as Earl Hines, Fats Waller, Teddy Wilson, and Art Tatum. While playing with territory bands in Michigan he met Lucky Thompson, who invited him to New York in 1944 to work at the Onyx Club with Hot Lips Page. While there, leading bop musicians inspired him, and he began to master the new style. His accessible playing and flexibility put him in great demand, and he had stints with Andy Kirk, Billy Eckstine, and Coleman Hawkins. As accompanist for Ella Fitzgerald (1947–53), he developed a harmonic facility of extraordinary taste and sophistication. As a result of his association with Fitzgerald, he began touring with Norman Granz's Jazz at the Philharmonic, and he made several historically important recordings with Charlie Parker for Granz's labels. As house pianist for the Savoy label, he took part in innumerable recording sessions during the 1950s. In 1959 he joined the staff of CBS, where he remained until 1976, working on shows such as the *Ed Sullivan Show*. During those years he remained active in jazz, touring and recording with Benny Goodman, the Thad Jones-Mel Lewis Orchestra, and then with a pickup unit dubbed the Great Jazz Trio.

Known for his beautiful, deep sound, clarity, sense of economy, and impeccable taste, Jones was one of the most underrated pianists in the business. His amazing Tatum-like harmonic imagination and his creative ability continue to be cherished around the world. Shearing, the transplanted Brit, once acknowledged his indebtedness to Jones, admitting in the prime of his career that he would travel a long distance to hear him play. Acknowledged as the founder and dean of the "Detroit school" of pianists, which includes players such as Tommy Flanagan and Roland Hanna, Hank Jones remains "the dean of all the jazz pianists."[24]

---

24. Kirchner, *Oxford Companion to Jazz*, 363.

CHAPTER 9

September

SEPTEMBER 1—ART PEPPER (1925–1982)

b. Gardena, CA; d. Panorama, CA

Alto Saxophonist

[HARD BOP; COOL; BOP]

Other jazz notables born on this day: Gene Harris (1933)
Jazz notables deceased on this day: Ethel Waters (1977); Lionel Hampton (2002)

♪

An original stylist, during the 1950s Art Pepper was one of the few altoists (along with Lee Konitz and Paul Desmond) able to develop a unique sound despite the dominant influence of Charlie Parker.[1] Though associated early on with West Coast jazz, due to location as much as to his light, precise sound, his execution was clearly hotter than cool jazz. During his final years, Pepper seemed to put all of his life's experiences into his music, and he played with startling emotional intensity. When he died suddenly at the age of fifty-six, he was one of the world's greatest altoists.

By the age of seventeen Pepper was playing on Central Avenue (the Los Angeles counterpart to New York's Fifty-Second Street) with Dexter Gordon and Charles Mingus in Lee Young's otherwise all-black band. He spent a brief time in the Benny Carter and Stan Kenton orchestras before serving time in the military (1944–46), and after the war he became absorbed with the new style, bop. He rejoined Kenton and toured as the band's outstanding soloist, spending some of his happiest days there (1947–51), though he became a heroin addict during that period. Despite playing mainly for dancing, Kenton's band began acquiring a reputation for modest experimentation, particularly with the arrival of Shelly Manne in 1946 and Pepper a year later. During the early 1950s Pepper started recording under his own name and as a sideman, but his career was interrupted by repeated imprisonment (1953–54 and 1954–56) for drug offences. He was in top form during his Contemporary recordings from 1957 to 1960, which resulted in several classic albums, but the first half of his career ended abruptly with long prison sentences (1961–64 and 1965–66). His occasional gigs between jail terms found him adopting a harder, John

---

1. Bogdanov et al., *All Music Guide to Jazz*, 996.

Coltrane-influenced tone (like Coltrane, he also took up tenor sax during this time). In 1969, while playing in Buddy Rich's band, he became seriously ill and underwent rehabilitation at Synanon (1969–71). Under the guidance and inspiration of his wife, Laurie, a patient he met while undergoing treatment, Pepper began his serious comeback in 1975.

From 1977 until his sudden death in 1982 he received increased recognition and popularity due to sensational performances in Japan and in the U.S. During the remainder of his life he was much recorded and also found wider fame through his brutally honest autobiography, *Straight Life*. His final performance took place at the 1982 Kool Jazz Festival in Washington, DC. Because of the many outstanding musicians scheduled to play at that one-day affair, each act was limited to a single hour. Those who heard Pepper that day say he was in peak form, but after an hour of playing, he was required to stop. After repeated attempts to get his attention, someone finally walked on stage and told him he had to leave. Pepper cussed the guy out and stomped off. That was his final time on stage. A week later he was dead. It was almost as if Pepper knew this would be his final time on stage, and after all he had been through in his life, he didn't want it to end.

SEPTEMBER 2—HORACE SILVER (1928–)

b. Norwalk, CT

Pianist; Bandleader; Composer

[Hard Bop; Fusion; Soul-Jazz]

Other jazz notables born on this day: Phil Napoleon (1901); Laurindo Almeida (1917); Clifford Jordan (1931); John Zorn (1953)
Jazz notables deceased on this day: Darnell Howard (1966); Arne Domnerus (2008)

♪

Horace Silver, one of the biggest names in jazz, was a major force in modern jazz on several fronts. In the 1950s he was the first important pioneer of the extroverted style known as hard bop that is dominant in the contemporary mainstream. Silver showed pianists that bebop could be simplified by a deeper commitment to the blues and that good melodic improvising could aim at funkiness rather than at complexity. He also proved that pianists could fire up a band with aggressive, percussive comping. His ability to ignite soloists with staccato, rhythmic accompanying chords is legendary. Further, as hard bop's most prolific composer, he created the driving hard bop style by combining elements of rhythm-and-blues, Latin rhythms, and gospel music with jazz. The writing style he created was a backward-looking fusion that combined bop-influenced rhythm with simple swing-era phrasing. In addition, the instrumentation of Silver's quintet (trumpet, tenor saxophone, piano, bass, and drums) served as a model for small jazz groups for over a decade. Finally, Silver's ensembles proved to be an important honing ground for young players like Donald Byrd, Art Farmer, Woody Shaw, Benny Golson, and Joe Henderson, most of who later led similar groups of their own.

Silver's earliest musical influence was the folk music he heard from his Portuguese-born father. In high school he was influenced by blues singers, boogie-woogie pianists, and by boppers like Thelonious Monk and Bud Powell. In 1950 Stan Getz performed in Hartford, Connecticut with Silver's piano trio. Silver went to New York with Getz, working with the popular saxophonist for a year before freelancing with such big-time players as Coleman Hawkins, Lester Young, and Oscar Pettiford. He started recording under his own name before joining forces with Art Blakey to form a band in 1953. The group's album, *Horace Silver and the Jazz Messengers* (1954–55), was a milestone in the development of hard bop. Some of the tunes Silver composed for that recording, such as "The Preacher" and "Doodlin'," became jazz standards.

On April 29, 1954, Silver was the pianist at a recording session led by trumpeter Miles Davis, who was making a comeback from drug addiction. Only two tracks were cut that day, "Walkin'" and "Blue 'n' Boogie," but they became two of the greatest extended blues performances in jazz history. Dan Morgenstern labeled them as "among the key recordings in the history of modern jazz."[2] In 1956 Silver left the Messengers to form his own band with Art Farmer on trumpet and Hank Mobley on tenor sax. Subsequent editions of the quintet were famous for their exciting trumpet/sax front lines, such as Blue Mitchell/Junior Cook; Freddie Hubbard/Wayne Shorter; Woody Shaw/Joe Henderson; Randy Brecker/Mike Brecker; and Tom Harrell/Bob Berg. With albums like *Blowin' the Blues Away* (1959) and *Song for my Father* (1964), Silver took his composing and arranging to a level of craftsmanship as yet unsurpassed in jazz.

SEPTEMBER 3—DAVID SANCHEZ (1968–)

b. Guaynabo, Puerto Rico

Tenor and Soprano Saxophonist; Leader

[MAINSTREAM JAZZ; CONTEMPORARY JAZZ; POST-BOP; LATIN JAZZ]

Other jazz notables born on this day: Doc Cook (1891)

Jazz notables deceased on this day: Mutt Carey (1948); Albert Nicholas (1973); Jo Jones (1985)

♪

Dizzy Gillespie was one of the most important figures in the history of jazz and, like Louis Armstrong and Miles Davis, he influenced players on all instruments. The creator of bebop, Gillespie was also one of the founders of Afro-Cuban (or Latin) jazz, adding Chano Pozo's conga to his orchestra in 1947 and utilizing complex polyrhythms early on. Although his fame and importance to jazz rest primarily on his playing, Dizzy was an enthusiastic teacher who wrote down his musical innovations and was eager to explain them to the next generation. During his final years he formed and led the United Nation Orchestra (1988–93), to which he attracted numerous Latin American sidemen, including two gifted youngsters who mixed the bebop tradition with their national heritage, Panamanian pianist Danilo Pérez and Puerto Rican saxophonist David Sanchez.

2. Kirchner, *Oxford Companion to Jazz*, 377.

Trained classically in Puerto Rico, Sanchez played percussion in salsa and show bands before taking up the saxophone at age twelve. His father, who loved Cuban boleros, and his brother, a fan of Puerto Rican rhythms, shaped his eclectic appreciation at an early age, but it was his sister who changed his life when she brought home an album titled *Basic Miles*. The recording, a Miles Davis anthology, featured saxophonist John Coltrane, and Sanchez was transfixed. He enrolled at the Universidad de Puerto Rico, considering a career in psychology, "but music was in my heart." In 1988 he won a music scholarship to Rutgers University, less than forty miles from New York City, the center of the jazz universe. His percussive background gave him a cunning grasp of rhythm, and by 1989 he was freelancing in New York with many top Latin players, including Paquito D'Rivera, Claudio Roditi, and Pérez, all fellow bandmates, who led the young saxophonist to their leader, the jazz icon named Dizzy.

When Gillespie invited the student to play with his sextet, Sanchez dropped everything and hit the road. It was a crash course more important than anything he would learn at school. After that tour Dizzy invited Sanchez to join his acclaimed United Nation Orchestra. For a year, until illness ended Gillespie's playing career in 1992, Sanchez performed with the jazz legend regularly. After his stint with Gillespie, Sanchez played with such notables as Kenny Barron, Charlie Haden, Elvin Jones, McCoy Tyner, and Slide Hampton. In 1994 he debuted *Sketches of Dreams*, his first CD as a leader. Shortly thereafter, when New York Times music critic Jon Pareles wrote that Sanchez was "carrying Latin jazz toward the millennium," he proved prophetic, for the artist's next two efforts, *Obsesión* (1998) and *Melaza* (2000) were both nominated for Grammy awards for Best Latin Jazz Album.

Sanchez succeeds at keeping his jazz fresh by infusing it with the rhythms of other cultures, something he learned from Dizzy. With Gillespie as mentor, the young saxophonist solidified his command of the eclectic, post-bop Latin style, laying crucial groundwork for his rise to leadership with his own ensembles.

SEPTEMBER 4—MEADE "LUX" LEWIS (1905–1964)

b. Chicago, IL; d. Minneapolis, MN

Pianist

[BOOGIE-WOOGIE; PIANO BLUES]

Other jazz notables born on this day: Gerald Wilson (1918); Dave Liebman (1946); Lonnie Plaxico (1960)
Jazz notables deceased on this day: Charlie Barnet (1991)

♪

The Harlem stride style established by James P. Johnson, Fats Waller, and others was the dominant school in jazz piano playing during the 1920s and '30s, but it was not the only one. Running parallel to it was a system that came from different roots. This style, a primitive jazz piano style, was practiced by thousands of self-taught musicians who played in the evenings for the entertainment of poor laborers, usually in a barn or shed of some kind that had been turned into a crude cabaret where working people of both sexes could drink and dance. The pianists were not full-time entertainers; few of them could play in more than two or three keys, and many of them knew only one. Their audiences wanted a highly rhythmic music suitable for dancing.

Because these primitive pianists were more concerned with rhythm than with harmony or melody, their styles were generally formed around a medium-tempo or fast blues employing repeated eighth notes or dotted-eighths and sixteenth figures in the bass and repeated figures, sometimes interspersed with single-note runs, in the right hand. Pianists will quickly recognize this music as boogie-woogie. Although this style of piano playing was invented around the turn of the century, it reached its peak of popularity during an economic crisis—the Great Depression. Jazz again faced a situation in which a full style of piano playing was needed as a substitute for hiring a band.

Of the boogie performers of the 1930s, three stand out: Meade "Lux" Lewis, Albert Ammons, and Pete Johnson. These three worked and recorded together, sometimes in duet and at least once as a trio. In his teenage years, Lewis became a friend of Ammons, with whom he learned to play by copying the movement of player pianos and listening to groundbreaking boogie pianists such as Jimmy Yancey, a self-taught pianist, singer, and tap dancer who for many years worked as groundskeeper at Comiskey (baseball) Park in Chicago. Lewis began playing at bars and clubs in Chicago before recording his masterpiece, "Honky Tonk Train Blues," in 1927. He faded from the limelight for a time, and then began working with Ammons at the Silver Taxi Cab Company. During the early 1930s he played at whorehouses in Michigan.

Returning to Chicago, he served as a chauffeur before finding a job in a musical trio. It was in this setting (not at a car wash or the taxi company, as legend has it) that John Hammond rediscovered Lewis in 1935.[3] The height of boogie's popularity was the period from 1935 to 1939, when Hammond brought Lewis and many of the top players to New York and recorded them. In 1938 Lewis participated with Ammons and Johnson in the Hammond-organized concert at Carnegie Hall, "From Spirituals to Swing," a concert that fueled an international boogie craze. After the concert he found steady work playing with Ammons and Johnson, but it proved to be short-lived. He returned to working alone at nightclubs, first in New York and then in California, where he became a celebrity.

SEPTEMBER 5—ALBERT MANGELSDORFF (1928–2005)

b. Frankfurt, Germany; d. Frankfurt, Germany

Trombonist; Leader

[AVANT-GARDE JAZZ; FREE JAZZ]

Other jazz notables born on this day: Eddie Preston (1925); Richie Powell (1931); Charles "Bobo" Shaw (1947)

Jazz notables deceased on this day: George Barnes (1977); Lawrence Brown (1988)

---

3. Kernfeld, *New Grove Dictionary of Jazz*, Vol. 2, 585.

♪

Albert Mangelsdorff was one of the most important trombonists in jazz. The master of multiphonics (playing more than one note at a time on a wind instrument), he was a giant of the European avant-garde.[4] Like most German jazz musicians in the 1950s, he was at first influenced by the cool jazz of Lee Konitz and Lennie Tristano, particularly the latter's 1949 performance of "Intuition," the first recording of abstract jazz improvisation. Voted Europe's "Jazz Musician of the Year" more often than any other, since 1962 Mangelsdorff appeared in American polls more than any other musician living outside the U.S. (in 1980 he was voted the "world's best trombonist" by *Down Beat*). An innovator and an influential stylist, he was also a fine composer. Characterized by a prodigious work ethic—there was hardly a day in his career when he did not practice or at least play a concert—Mangelsdorff's unending commitment to perfecting his trombone technique no doubt led to his discovery of the instrument's polytonal possibilities in the early 1970s.

Mangelsdorff came from a musical family, and his brother Emil is a noted saxophonist in Germany. During the Nazi period, jazz was banned in Germany, but Albert and his brother attended secret meetings at the Hot Club in Frankfurt, and by the age of twelve he decided that jazz was the kind of music he wanted to play. He studied violin and worked as a jazz guitarist before taking up the trombone in 1948, at the age of twenty. He played bop in the 1950s and in 1955 he joined the Dance Orchestra of Hesse Radio in Frankfurt, after which he started conducting the jazz ensemble there. By the late 1950s he was already the center of musical attention in Europe. In 1958 he visited the U.S. to play with Marshall Brown's International Youth Band at the Newport Jazz Festival. On account of his fantastic technique, the Americans hailed him as the most important new European instrumentalist.

In 1961 he formed a quintet that became one of the most celebrated European combos of the 1960s. By the time he recorded the influential album *Animal Dance* (1962) with John Lewis in Germany, Mangelsdorff was starting to lean towards the avant-garde. In 1964, when his group went on a three-month tour of Asia, he began his development towards free music, particularly after playing with Indian musicians like Ravi Shankar. It was under these ethnic influences and with the development of the freer, more abstract, side of improvisation that Mangelsdorff began to arrive at his full musical identity. He continued touring with his own groups on a worldwide basis during the late 1960s and '70s and then worked with the Globe Unity Orchestra, the United Jazz & Rock Ensemble, and co-led the French/German Jazz Ensemble, made up of young players from both countries. Much admired by his European colleagues, Mangelsdorff was a world-class musician.

---

4. Bogdanov et al., *All Music Guide to Jazz*, 794.

BLUE NOTES

SEPTEMBER 6—BUDDY BOLDEN (1877–1931)

b. New Orleans, LA; d. Jackson, LA

Cornetist; Bandleader

[NEW ORLEANS JAZZ]

Other jazz notables born on this day:
Jazz notables deceased on this day: Max Kaminsky (1994); Arnold Fishkin (1999)

♪

Although no one knows exactly when jazz music originated, "a good starting point is when cornetist Buddy Bolden formed his first band in 1895."[5] The first of the New Orleans cornet "kings" and the first important name in jazz history, Bolden was highly regarded by contemporary black musicians in the city, who embroidered his life with legendary qualities and spurious anecdotes. According to folklore, Buddy Bolden used to parade the streets of New Orleans, four or five women on his arm, playing with a trumpet sound that carried clear across town. Bolden's career was long buried in legend until Donald Marquis successfully pieced together a factual and coherent biography, *In Search of Buddy Bolden, First Man of Jazz* (1978). Contemporary musicians universally praised the power of Bolden's tone, his rhythmic drive, and the emotional content of his slow blues playing. Bolden apparently did not improvise melodies freely in the manner of later jazz musicians, but found ingenious ways of ornamenting existing melodies, often with a distinctive lick that functioned as a signature. Although he left no known recordings, Bolden undoubtedly had a formative influence on Freddie Keppard, Bunk Johnson, and other New Orleans cornetists.[6]

Unlike many of his peers, Bolden apparently came to music rather late in life. He completed school in 1890 and mastered the plasterer's trade—few musicians expected to support themselves solely with music in those days. Around 1894 he began lessons on the cornet and by 1895 he took over leadership of a band that played for private dances and parties. By 1900 the gregarious Bolden was the most popular musician in New Orleans, leading five or six bands that played in saloons, dance halls, parks, and cabarets all over town. A performer of personal charisma and crowd-pleasing musical power, by 1904 he was known as "King" Bolden. His rise to fame coincided with the emergence of Storyville, the black pleasure district at South Rampart and Perdido streets, where he soon became a local celebrity.

By 1905, when his fame was at its peak, he lived in the uncomfortable knowledge that young innovators like Keppard and King Oliver were coming up fast. Bolden began to drink more and to behave eccentrically. Spells of temporary insanity, possibly due to some form of venereal disease, began to compromise his playing ability, and the following year, during a Labor Day parade, he was put under arrest for dementia. He was soon released, but his playing days were behind him. An attack by the cornetist on his mother

---

5. Bogdanov et al., *All Music Guide to Jazz*, 3rd ed., 117.
6. Kernfeld, *New Grove Dictionary of Jazz*, Vol. 1, 263.

and mother-in-law in 1907 led to his arrest once again and then admittance to Jackson Mental Institute in New Orleans, where he remained completely forgotten for his final twenty-four years.

SEPTEMBER 7—MAX KAMINSKY (1908–1994)

b. Brockton, MA; d. Castle Point, NY

Trumpeter

[DIXIELAND]

Other jazz notables born on this day: Alvin Alcorn (1912); Graeme Bell (1914); Joe Newman (1921 or 1922); Sonny Rollins (1930); Makanda Ken McIntyre (1931)
Jazz notables deceased on this day: Rex Stewart (1967)

♫

On Monday evening, September 20, 1926, an eighteen-year-old dance band cornetist from Dorchester, Massachusetts drove to a nearby dance hall named Nuttings-on-the-Charles. That night he heard Bix Beiderbecke play with the touring Goldkette Orchestra and from that moment he was under Bix's spell. No one in the crowd had ever heard anything like this music before. "I just sat there," Max Kaminsky recalled, "vibrating like a harp to the echoes of Bix's astoundingly beautiful tone. It sounded like a choirful of angels."[7] Two years later Kaminsky left Boston for Chicago. He had dropped out of high school because he could not stay awake during class after playing the night before, and because none of his schoolmates—with the exception of his friend Harry Carney, who had left school to join Duke Ellington's band—seemed to be interested in the one thing he cared about. Chicago was the place to be, he assumed, after hearing Beiderbecke and recent recordings by Louis Armstrong.

In Chicago he met a group of like-minded youngsters, some of them Chicagoans, like Gene Krupa and Muggsy Spanier, but others, recent arrivals like he. There was George Wettling, from Topeka, Kansas, Jess Stacy, from Bird's Point, Missouri, and the cornetist Wingy Manone, who had lost his right arm in a New Orleans streetcar accident. Though barely in their twenties, these men had been deeply immersed in jazz, absorbing it first-hand from New Orleans players in Chicago while developing their own style and feeling. Kaminsky landed a job with Frank Teschemacher and Wettling and he was finally happy in his musical career; every day seemed like the Fourth of July, he recalled. One day, Wettling and Manone took him to hear Armstrong play. The first number was "West End Blues," and Kaminsky was stunned by Armstrong's bravura introduction: "the combination of Louis's dazzling virtuosity and sensational brilliance of tone so overwhelmed me that I felt as if I had stared into the sun's eye" he wrote. "All I could think of doing was to run away and hide till the blindness left me."[8]

---

7. Ward and Burns, *Jazz: A History*, 139.
8. Ibid., 163.

Kaminsky moved to New York in 1929 and became a reliable Dixieland player, working in commercial bands led by Tommy Dorsey (1936) and Artie Shaw. Following a quarrel with Shaw, Kaminsky rejoined Dorsey and finally found a home in Bud Freeman's freewheeling Summa Cum Laude Orchestra (1939–40). In 1944, after his discharge from the military, Kaminsky led his own band and was featured with Eddie Condon's groups during the 1940s and '50s. This was a difficult period for classic stylists, in the face of competition from the two trends of the time, bebop and New Orleans jazz, but Kaminsky found steady work, including playing with Charlie Parker for the opening night of Birdland. Through the 1950s he carried on in big bands and small groups, and recorded steadily. He also found time to write one of the most intelligent and informative jazz autobiographies of the period, *Jazz Band: My Life in Jazz* (1963).

SEPTEMBER 8—MARION BROWN (1931 or 1935–2010)

b. Atlanta, GA; d. Hollywood, FL

Alto Saxophonist

[AVANT-GARDE JAZZ; FREE JAZZ]

Other jazz notables born on this day: Wilbur Ware (1923)
Jazz notables deceased on this day: Oscar Pettiford (1960)

♪

Given John Coltrane's character and his determination to stamp himself with greatness, it was inevitable that he pursued free jazz. He could not allow a revolutionary current to pass without comment. In the late 1950s he became interested in the music of Ornette Coleman, the most prominent figure in the free jazz movement, and this led to the album *The Avant-Garde*, which Coltrane recorded in 1960 with Coleman's band, minus Coleman. During the mid-1960s Coltrane began turning toward increasingly radical musical styles. These controversial experiments attracted large audiences, and by 1965 Coltrane's search for new sounds resulted in frequent changes of personnel within his band. On June 28, 1965, Coltrane gathered eleven musicians for a recording session that produced one of his most awesome, and daunting recordings, *Ascension*. Besides his regular quartet, and bassist Art Davis, he used two trumpeters (Freddie Hubbard and Dewey Johnson) and four additional saxophonists (including tenors Pharoah Sanders and Archie Shepp and two altos, John Tchicai and Marion Brown).

One of the brightest and most lyrical voices of the 1960s avant-garde, Brown participated in many stimulating recordings during the 1960s and '70s without ever really becoming an influential force.[9] He studied alto saxophone, clarinet, and oboe in high school and then in army bands, where he first performed jazz. Following his discharge in 1957, he studied music at Clark College, Atlanta, and then law at Howard University in Washington, DC. He moved to New York in 1961, where he met the writers LeRoi Jones and A. B. Spellman and became involved in writing projects that furthered the cause of

---

9. Bogdanov et al., *All Music Guide to Jazz*, 3rd ed., 143.

African-Americans. For a while he moved into drama, acting in Jones's play *The Dutchman*, but before long he returned to music, joining the free improvisation movement. He met and was befriended by Shepp, Coleman, Sun Ra, and Sanders, all pioneers in avant-garde jazz. Of these, the most influential was Shepp, with whom Brown recorded early in 1965 (*Fire Music*). A few months later he participated on the monumental *Ascension* album, the single recording that placed Coltrane firmly into the avant-garde.

Brown led his own group in the mid-1960s, and in 1966 he released his defining recording, *Three for Shepp*, using such sidemen as pianist Stanley Cowell, guitarist Kenny Burrell, and trombonist Grachan Moncur III. The album was a tribute to his colleague and friend Archie Shepp, who two years earlier had recorded *Four for Trane*, a lasting tribute to mentor John Coltrane. These albums, classics of the period, affirm the avant-garde lineage and continue its legacy in jazz. Like many other jazz musicians of the era who found the music industry in America to be restrictive, Brown left for Europe (1968–70), where he played and recorded with avant-gardists such as Gunter Hampel and Steve McCall and cultivated a deep interest in African music. In 1970 the under-appreciated saxophonist returned to the U.S., where he continued to study and promote African-American ethnomusicology, both musically and academically.

SEPTEMBER 9—SONNY ROLLINS (1930–)[10]

b. New York, NY

Tenor Saxophonist; Leader

[HARD BOP; POST-BOP; BOP]

Other jazz notables born on this day: Elvin Jones (1927); George Mraz (1944)
Jazz notables deceased on this day: Wilbur Ware (1979)

♫

One of the last immortals to come of age in the 1940s, Sonny Rollins established himself as the outstanding jazz saxophonist between Charlie Parker and John Coltrane and a leading figure in the hard-bop style. Next to Stan Getz, he was the most popular tenor of the 1950s. His recordings from that period constitute landmarks in the history of tenor saxophone style. Though Rollins is known today for his originality, his influence stemmed less from any innovative conception than from his powerful, natural playing, which captured the admiration of peers such as the drummer Art Blakey, who considered him the most determined person he had ever known. Best known for his 1956 album *Saxophone Colossus*, he seemed the living embodiment of that phrase.

Rollins grew up in Harlem, a neighbor of Thelonious Monk, Bud Powell, and the great Coleman Hawkins. His initial interest in the saxophone came from an attraction to the work of altoist Louis Jordan, who fronted a popular "jump band" known as the Tympany Five. Then, under the influence of Hawkins, he switched to tenor and developed the big, heavy sound for which Hawkins was known. By 1951 his reputation was

---

10. Other authorities list Rollins's date of birth as September 7. September 9 is the date given in Barry Kernfeld, *The New Grove Dictionary of Jazz*.

spreading, for he had already recorded with Fats Navarro and Powell. During the 1950s Rollins recorded with various bands, the most important being the Miles Davis quintet (1954) and the Clifford Brown–Max Roach quintet (1955–57). Despite his musical success, Sonny suffered from a severe drug dependency. Like many admirers of Parker, he had become addicted to heroin.

In 1954 he took the first of several highly publicized retirements from jazz. He left New York for Chicago, where he found professional help, and then joined the Brown–Roach quintet. In 1957, now a star in the jazz world and in heavy demand for recordings, Sonny left the Roach band. Beset by personal problems, including alcohol, and devastated by the sudden death of Brown, he took his second leave of absence from jazz in 1959. This time he was famous, and rumors abounded to the effect that he had gone mad, or was in deep trouble, or that he was inventing a new form of jazz. But he was simply getting his life in order once again. One rumor about him, however, was true. Withdrawn from public life until November 1961, he spent hours at night practicing his horn while walking on the Williamsburg Bridge, which runs across New York's East River. But he was not doing so because he was crazy. He simply liked the sound he got there, and he could play as loudly as he wanted without offending anyone. Today, after more than fifty years as a professional, Rollins remains one of the most cunning and original of jazz visionaries.

SEPTEMBER 10—ROY AYERS (1940–)

b. Los Angeles, CA

Vibraphonist

[Jazz-Pop; Fusion; Soul-Jazz; Jazz-Funk]

Other jazz notables born on this day: Raymond Scott (1908)
Jazz notables deceased on this day: Trummy Young (1984); Pepper Adams (1986)

♪

During the twentieth century no jazz instruments were more profoundly affected by technology than the guitar and the vibraphone. But whereas the guitar had only a limited impact on jazz prior to amplification, the vibraphone (vibes) didn't even exist. The vibraphone, an instrument fundamentally different from the mallet instruments it is based on (the xylophone and marimba), stems from the mid-1920s. This instrument—the name refers to the vibrato produced by small, electric-driven rotating blades placed above the resonating tubes—alters the air column within each tube, causing slight variations in the pitch. This gives the vibraphone an expressive technique, its appealing sounds casting a hypnotic spell on listeners. Red Norvo, the first stylist on the instrument, initially treated the vibraphone as a novelty, in part because a damper pedal had not yet been developed.

The most influential early mallet player, Lionel Hampton, started as a drummer and became a vibist almost by accident. His ebullient style featured showmanship and a fast vibrato. After Norvo and Hampton, the most important innovators in the instrument's history were Milt Jackson—whose flowing, relaxed style and carefully crafted improvisations made him one of the great modern soloists on any instrument—and two stylists,

Bobby Hutcherson and Gary Burton, whose arrival in the mid-1960s raised the bar for all future jazz vibists. Three additional pioneers arose during the 1960s; Karl Berger and Gunter Hampel, two Germans living in the United States, emphasized free improvising and avant-garde textures, while Roy Ayers made effective use of the vibes in soul-jazz and even disco settings, leading the way in the 1970s for the movement called Jazz-Funk. Ayers became one of the most visible jazz vibraphonists of the 1960s, a rhythm-and-blues leader in the 1970s and '80s and something of an icon in the 1990s for the "acid jazz" generation, though his own playing remained rooted in hard bop.

Described as the most influential black musician since James Brown, Ayers's musical passion began as a five-year old child. Growing up in a musical family—his father played trombone and his mother piano—Roy was playing boogie-woogie piano at five, steel guitar at nine, and in his teens experimented with flute, trumpet, and drums before settling on vibes at seventeen. After being inspired by his idol, Lionel Hampton (who gave him a set of vibraphone sticks as a child), a session with Herbie Mann at the Lighthouse in Hermosa Beach led to a four-year stint with the versatile flutist (1966–70). After being featured on Mann's hit *Memphis Underground* album, Ayers left the band in 1970 to form Ubiquity, producing dozens of albums in ensuing years. The group veered towards disco in the late 1970s and then dispensed a crowd-pleasing amalgam of jazz and smooth, danceable funk. A great showman and a firm believer in audience participation, Ayers has been in the vanguard of those bringing jazz vibes to a wider audience, both in the U.S. and around the world.[11]

SEPTEMBER 11—HARRY CONNICK JR. (1967–)

b. New Orleans, LA

Pianist; Vocalist; Composer; Arranger

[TRADITIONAL POP; SWING]

Other jazz notables born on this day: Charles Moffett (1929); Hiram Bullock (1955)
Jazz notables deceased on this day: Joe Zawinul (2007)

♪

Harry Connick Jr.'s career can be divided into two parts, the first half encompassing straightahead New Orleans jazz and stride piano, while his later career (which paralleled his rising celebrity status) alternated between more contemporary New Orleans music and pop vocals.[12] His success with the soundtrack for the movie *When Harry Met Sally* (1989) not only launched his career at the age of twenty-one but also gave a remarkable boost to the public's interest in mainstream jazz. Like Wynton and Branton Marsalis, Connick sees his own role in the revival of traditional jazz, revitalizing it and making it entertaining once again. Like Frank Sinatra—with whom he is often compared—his popularity places him in a broader musical community than just jazz. He performs often

---

11. Carr et al., *Jazz: The Rough Guide*, 27.
12. Bogdanov et al., *All Music Guide to Jazz*, 268.

in the same swing big band format as Sinatra, but he writes most of the arrangements and often joins the other musicians on the piano. Connick's piano playing is based on the New Orleans style he learned from James Booker, a New Orleans piano teacher, but also shows the influence of Thelonious Monk and Erroll Garner.

Harry Connick was born in New Orleans, the son of two lawyers who owned a record store. Beginning on keyboards at the age of three, the precocious youngster first performed publicly at six and recorded with a local jazz band at ten. While growing up Connick became immersed in the musical styles of New Orleans. As he matured, his interests gravitated from contemporary rock and jazz to the classical piano players of jazz and the styles associated with them. Connick attended the New Orleans Center for the Creative Arts, where he studied with the famous pianist Ellis Marsalis. During this time he honed his skills playing and singing in Bourbon Street clubs.

A move to New York to study at the Manhattan School of Music gave him the opportunity to debut on Columbia Records with *Harry Connick, Jr.* (1987), a set of mostly unaccompanied standards. Jazz critics praised his maturity and engaging style and soon his playing was on display at extended stays in New York hot spots. His second album, *20,* named for his age in 1988, was the first to feature him on vocals. Connick made an international tour that year, and the following year he composed the soundtrack to the popular movie *When Harry Met Sally*, which featured his individualistic piano playing and singing; the success from that recording (double-platinum status) elevated him to the ranks of a pop star. From there he quickly achieved international status with concerts (fronting a big band since 1990), television, and a string of best-selling albums, including the soundtrack to *Sleepless in Seattle*. In 1990 Connick's matinee-idol looks propelled him to an acting career; he appeared in various Hollywood films after that, including a starring role in 1995's *Copycat*, and later that year he married actress Jill Goodacre. Despite his pop-funk and romantic recordings, Connick remains a compelling performer with a serious interest in the history and development of New Orleans music.[13]

SEPTEMBER 12—SCOTT HAMILTON (1954–)

b. Providence, RI

Tenor Saxophonist

[MAINSTREAM JAZZ; SWING]

Other jazz notables born on this day: Cat Anderson (1916); Steve Turre (1948)

Jazz notables deceased on this day: Charlie Holmes (1985); Jaco Pastorius (1987); Stanley Turrentine (2000)

♪

Whereas jazz purists value innovation and deprecate predictability, traditional fans are overwhelmingly attracted to the music's more familiar side. If nostalgic listeners are unfamiliar with Scott Hamilton, they will certainly appreciate the 1940s-minded jazz for which he is known. When the big-toned tenor appeared in the mid-1970s with an appeal-

---

13. Carr et al., *Jazz: The Rough Guide*, 161.

ing swing style on tenor, he caused a minor sensation, for few other players during the fusion era were exploring pre-bop jazz at his high level.[14] Long associated with cornetist Warren Vaché, another contemporary jazz musician who chose to work in the swing style, Hamilton is known for his warmth and lovely ballads. Over the years, as he has matured and gained a greater sense of self within his instrument, his tone has richened into what may be "the perfect mainstream tenor sound."

Hamilton was born in Providence, Rhode Island, a scant ten miles from Newport, home of the famous Newport Jazz Festival. The festival was inaugurated in 1954, the same year as Scott's birth, and twenty years later Hamilton would work for George Wein, one of the festival's founders, recording and performing as a member of Wein's Newport All-Stars. In addition to Hamilton, Providence was also the birthplace of tenor saxophonist Paul Gonsalves, whose outstanding career with Duke Ellington was highlighted by a well-publicized solo at the neighboring festival in 1956 that caused a near riot at the jazz mecca. Gonsalves, together with explosive tenors Flip Phillips and Illinois Jacquet, became Hamilton's early influences.

Scott began playing saxophone when he was sixteen and developed quickly, moving to New York City in 1976. The following year he joined Benny Goodman for a concert tour. By this time he was playing with Vaché, whom he had met in a New York club. The huge publicity that followed the two stars guaranteed them a heady round of clubs, festivals, and recordings in the late 1970s and '80s. Under contract with Concord Records, Hamilton recorded a long string of albums with his own quintet of young mainstreamers, all notable for their consistency and solid swing. In addition, he has shared the spotlight with traditionalists such as Buddy Tate, Ruby Braff, Rosemary Clooney, and the Concord Jazz All-Stars. By the 1990s Hamilton became recognized as the leader of his field, with imitators such as tenor saxophonist Harry Allen acknowledging his influence.

SEPTEMBER 13—CHU BERRY (1910–1941)

b. Wheeling, WV; d. Conneaut, OH

Tenor Saxophonist

[SWING]

Other jazz notables born on this day: Larry Shields (1893); Leonard Feather (1914); Mel Tormé (1925); Douglas Ewart (1946)
Jazz notables deceased on this day: Sidney De Paris (1967); Helen Humes (1981)

♪

The rise of the saxophonists in the 1930s, and especially the dominance of Coleman Hawkins, put a premium on tenor saxophonists. Of these, the leading players in small swing bands, after Hawkins, were Lester Young, Ben Webster, and Leon "Chu" Berry. All were veterans of the Fletcher Henderson orchestra, where they succeeded one another. Particularly strong on up-tempo numbers, Berry was the only saxophonist who presented

---

14. Bogdanov et al., *All Music Guide to Jazz*, 534.

a real challenge to Hawkins on full-blown, fast-fingered terms. He was known for his well-constructed solos and was the equal of Hawkins in harmonic sophistication and superior when it came to swing and drive.

When Berry moved to New York in 1930, he arrived carrying his tenor in a red velvet bootbag and wearing a goatee beard. His appearance earned him the nickname "Chu," after Billy Stewart remarked that Berry looked like Chu Chin Chow. After star roles with several bands, including those of Benny Carter and Teddy Hill (1933–35), he joined Henderson (1935–36), despite offers from Duke Ellington. By then he had become close friends with the young trumpeter Roy Eldridge, and the two began terrorizing New York jam sessions after hours, "cutting down opposition with deadly skill."[15] In 1937 Berry was spotted at Minton's Playhouse by Cab Calloway, and he remained as the band's star soloist until his death in an auto accident at the age of thirty-one. Berry died young, without being different enough from Hawkins to be regarded as an alternative. Had he not died prematurely, he might have offset the overwhelming influence of Young on later tenor saxophonists, for Hawkins and many others considered him a musical genius.[16]

SEPTEMBER 14—JOSEPH JARMAN (1937–)

b. Pine Bluff, AR

Reed Player; Composer

[AVANT-GARDE JAZZ; FREE JAZZ]

Other jazz notables born on this day: Oliver Lake (1942)
Jazz notables deceased on this day: Lajos Martiny (1985)

♪

During the 1970s and '80s the Art Ensemble of Chicago (AEC) was probably the best-known representative of avant-garde jazz. Roscoe Mitchell, Lester Bowie, Malachi Favors, and Joseph Jarman founded the Art Ensemble, the flagship ensemble of Chicago's Association for the Advancement of Creative Musicians, in 1967. In 1969 the group moved to Paris, which at that time was both a flourishing jazz scene and a haven for African-American musicians. There they were joined by percussionist Famoudou Don Moye, and the group appended "of Chicago" to their name. After eighteen months (during which time they recorded twelve albums), they returned to the U.S., having established an international reputation. The AEC's music is pluralistic, joining traditional elements from old New Orleans with free jazz and theatricality with percussion, whistles, gongs and log drums. Art Ensemble members seem to play almost every instrument imaginable, including ones that most listeners have never seen before. The band is still in existence, although members currently focus their efforts elsewhere, and they rarely perform in Chicago anymore. Jarman withdrew from the ensemble in 1993 and currently lives in Brooklyn, where he pursues his interest in spiritual studies.

15. Carr et al., *Jazz: The Rough Guide*, 64.
16. Gottlieb, *Reading Jazz*, 855.

Jarman has always been adventurous and an utterly unpredictable player. With his striking African face paint, theatrical poetry recitations, and his ability to play fourteen different woodwind instruments in addition to percussion, he never failed to command attention onstage. Born in Arkansas, he moved to Chicago during his childhood. As a teenager he played drums at DuSable High School and didn't start on saxophones and clarinet until later, while in the army. Having played bebop in college with saxophonist Roscoe Mitchell and freely improvised music with him in Muhal Richard Abrams's Experimental Band, in 1965 he joined the AACM.

At this time he began leading a group that explored poetry and elaborate program music with a strong theatrical slant. That year he played his composition, *Imperfections in a Given Space*, with the classical avant-garde musician John Cage. The following year he recorded his first album as a leader, *Song For*, a radical statement with an unusual utilization of sound and silence, and premiered theatrical pieces. He continued in a variety of creative ventures until 1969, when two of his musicians died suddenly. He disbanded his group and devoted himself to the AEC, where his theatrical performances kept the music from ever getting too conservative or predictable. After leaving the AEC in the 1990s Jarman became a sensei at the Brooklyn Buddhist Association, where he is a practitioner of Zen therapy and a highly regarded instructor in the martial art of aikido. In addition to his religious activity he leads a trio with Myra Melford (who, incidentally, gained a black belt as Jarman's student in aikido) and Leroy Jenkins.

SEPTEMBER 15—CANNONBALL ADDERLEY (1928–1975)

b. Tampa, FL; d. Gary, IN

Alto Saxophonist; Bandleader

[Hard Bop; Soul-Jazz]

Other jazz notables born on this day: Stanley Dance (1910); Ram Ramirez (1913); Al Casey (1915); Gene Roland (1921); Arvell Shaw (1923)

Jazz notables deceased on this day: Bill Evans (1980); Willie Bobo (1983); Johnny Hartman (1983); Cootie Williams (1985); Barrett Deems (1998)

♪

One of the great alto saxophonists and the greatest to play that instrument in the hard bop style, Cannonball Adderley was called "the new Bird" because his début in 1955 occurred shortly after Charlie Parker's death. Like Parker, his style was fluid, supercharged and unpredictable, but he also displayed influences of Benny Carter and the swing era style. Rhythmically, the strutting phraseology of Eddie "Cleanhead" Vinson and Louis Jordan left its mark, as on many of Cannonball's generation.

A masterful, confident improviser, Adderley had an exuberant and happy sound that communicated immediately to listeners. He could bend his huge sound with blue notes and wails, creating an earthy, legato tone. His full tone, with vibrato, projected a warm and glowing effect. During 1957 to 1959, his creative peak, he played with Miles Davis and John Coltrane, demonstrating he could match Coltrane's virtuosity. As bandleader, he showed that he had learned a great deal from Davis. Cannonball's use of the rhythm section gave musical substance to the 1960s style of soul-jazz, with which he was especially identified. His quartet was best known for "funky hits" such as "Mercy, Mercy, Mercy," "Walk Tall," and "Country Preacher."

During his childhood years Cannonball (Julian Edwin) acquired his nickname, a corruption of "cannibal," describing his huge appetite. He had an established career as a high school band director in Florida both before and after a stint with army bands from 1950 to 1953. During a 1955 visit to New York to play with his brother, cornetist Nat Adderley, he was in the audience at the Café Bohemia when Jerome Richardson was late for an engagement with Oscar Pettiford's band. Cannonball was asked to sit in, and on a rendition of "I'll Remember April" his playing created such a sensation that he was persuaded to play jazz full-time in New York.

Signed to a recording contract, he formed an excellent quintet with his brother in 1956, but financial struggles caused its demise in 1957. Adderley then joined Davis, forming part of an extraordinary sextet with Coltrane and participating on such classic recordings as *Milestones* and *Kind of Blue*. Cannonball's second attempt to form a quintet with his brother in 1959 was much more successful. The group, with changing rhythm sections, remained intact until 1975. During its Riverside years (1959–63) the Adderley Quintet primarily played soulful renditions of hard bop, and Cannonball really excelled in the straightahead settings. During 1962 and 1963, Yusef Lateef made the group a sextet and pianist Joe Zawinul became an important new member. The collapse of Riverside Records in 1963 resulted in Adderley signing with Capitol, where his recordings became gradually more commercial. During his last year Cannonball was revisiting the past a bit, but before his music could evolve any further, he died suddenly from a stroke.

SEPTEMBER 16—JOE VENUTI (1903–1978)

b. Philadelphia, PA; d. Seattle, WA

Violinist

[CLASSIC JAZZ; SWING; DIXIELAND]

Other jazz notables born on this day: Jon Hendricks (1921); Charlie Byrd (1925); Gordon Beck (1938); Hamiet Bluiett (1940); Frank Szabo (1952); Earl Klugh (1954)
Jazz notables deceased on this day: Bernie Leighton (1994); Andrzej Trzaskowski (1998)

♪

Although renowned as one of the world's great practical jokers, Joe Venuti's significance is as the most important violinist in early jazz. He was a boyhood friend of Eddie Lang (jazz's first great guitarist), and the two teamed up in numerous settings during the second half of the 1920s, including recording influential duets.[17] There are many outrageous stories

---

17. Bogdanov et al., *All Music Guide to Jazz*, 1282.

about Venuti—pouring flour down the tuba during the filming of Paul Whiteman's *King of Jazz*, playing naked for a brothel full of madams in Philadelphia, pouring liquid Jello into a sleeping Bix Beiderbecke's bath—but perhaps the most outrageous was recorded by trumpeter Red Nichols, who was living at the Pasadena Hotel when Bix Beiderbecke came to New York in 1925. Nichols invited him to be his roommate and together they rented a piano. They also threw parties. Venuti was a regular, as was Babe Ruth and other celebrities. Nichols recalled one memorable evening when Venuti, already under the influence of bootleg gin, began wondering which key predominated on the piano. He figured if all the keys were struck at once, one should win. Bets were taken and a few nights later, at the next gathering, Venuti and a few others pushed the piano to the window, lifted it, and dropped it from the fifth floor into the alley below. Nichols remembered an enormous crash and the snapping of piano wires and then added, "There was no hint of any pitch."

Venuti claimed he was born on a ship as his parents emigrated from Italy to the U.S. He grew up in Philadelphia and by 1924 he was in Detroit, directing Jean Goldkette's Book-Cadillac orchestra. In 1925 he relocated to New York, where he and Lang were greatly in demand for recordings, studio work, and club appearances. Venuti performed with most of the top white jazz musicians during that segregated era, and in 1929 he and Lang joined Whiteman's distinguished orchestra. Lang's premature death in 1933 was a major blow to Venuti, who gradually faded away from the spotlight. His recordings with Lang were highly influential in Europe, serving as a model for the quintet led by Django Reinhardt and Stéphane Grappelli in Paris.

After visiting Europe in 1935 Venuti formed a big band (1935–43) that, while never very successful, helped introduce singer Kay Starr. After his discharge from the military during World War II, the "Mad Fiddler from Philly" (as he became known) stuck to studio work in Los Angeles. He was regularly featured on Bing Crosby's early-1950s radio show, but in reality the period from 1936 to 1966 was dismal for Venuti as he drifted into alcoholism and was largely forgotten by the jazz world. Despite a comeback in the final decade of his life, Venuti's best years were during the "Roaring Twenties," when he and his incorrigible pals advocated the myth of perpetual adolescence.

SEPTEMBER 17—BROTHER JACK MCDUFF (1926–2001)

b. Champaign, IL; d. Minneapolis, MN

Organist; Leader

[Hard Bop; Soul Jazz; Jazz-Funk]

Other jazz notables born on this day: Hubert Rostaing (1918)
Jazz notables deceased on this day: Jimmy Yancey (1951); Omer Simeon (1959); Dodo Marmarosa (2002)

♪

Pianist Fats Waller first introduced the organ to jazz, using instruments that were installed in theaters by the Wurlitzer Company to accompany silent films. Another pianist,

Count Basie, who studied organ technique with Waller and occasionally performed with his band at theaters that housed pipe organs, maintained the tradition. The inability to transport pipe organs to locations where jazz was typically performed obviously limited the instrument's use. In response, the Hammond Company developed the portable B-3 electric organ in 1935. Both Waller and Basie adopted the new instrument, though the first important soloist and its most influential performer was Jimmy Smith.

Forming his own group in the 1950s, Smith adapted bebop keyboard technique on the instrument as well as developed the use of the foot pedals to play bass lines. By omitting a bass player, he established a new instrumental configuration known as the organ trio (organ, drums, and saxophone or guitar). Jack McDuff—along with Jimmy McGriff, Bill Doggett, Don Patterson, Shirley Scott, Groove Holmes, and Charles Earland—was one of the first organists influenced by Smith's style. A talented bandleader and organist as well as a capable arranger, "Brother" McDuff had one of the most soulful styles of all time on the Hammond B-3. Initially, like all the organists of his generation, he was heavily indebted to Jimmy Smith. However, unlike some of the more excitable players of this group, he had a less grating tone and a sober, coherent approach to improvisation.

A self-taught musician, McDuff began his professional career as bassist. He taught himself organ and piano in the mid-1950s and began gaining attention while working with Willis "Gator" Jackson in the late 1950s. He made his recording debut as a leader in 1960, playing in a studio pickup band with tenor saxophonist Jimmy Forrest. McDuff organized his own band the following year. At various times his groups included Grant Green, Joe Henderson, Harold Vick, Leo Wright, Kenny Burrell, and Pat Martino, but things really took off when he hired a young guitarist named George Benson (1962–65). They formed one of the most popular combos of the mid-1960s, and made several excellent albums.

McDuff continued leading a regular group into the 1990s, featuring himself on electric piano as well as on organ. His group appeared at the Newport Jazz Festival in 1974 and 1975, and in 1986 he was reunited with his former and now famous sideman Benson at the Chicago Jazz Festival. He benefited from the widespread revival of interest in Hammond organ playing in the 1990s and continued leading groups from his base in Minneapolis. In the mid-1990s he performed and recorded as co-leader in a two-organ quintet with Joey DeFrancesco, the most important of the next generation of organists to use the B-3 in modern jazz settings.

SEPTEMBER 18—EMILY REMLER (1957–1990)

b. New York, NY; d. Sydney, Australia

Guitarist

[HARD BOP]

Other jazz notables born on this day: Frank Socolow (1923); Pia Beck (1925); Steve Marcus (1939); Steve Slagle (1951); John Fedchock (1957)
Jazz notables deceased on this day: Jimmy Witherspoon (1997)

Emily Remler's sudden death at age thirty-two from a heart attack (probably precipitated by her heroin habit) stunned the jazz world. Although she never became an innovator, albums like *This Is Me* (1990), her first—and tragically, her last—excursion into electric jazz-pop, indicates that she could have become a strong force in that area had she lived longer. While strongly marked by her appreciation of guitarist Wes Montgomery—who, coincidently, also died of a heart attack at a fairly young age—Remler was also interested in the directions pursued by Pat Metheny. Remler was equally adept at playing with and without a pick in such diverse styles as bop, jazz-rock, and Latin music. Her playing incorporated fluid eighth-note passages, doublings at the octave in the manner of Montgomery, and blues phrasing.

Remler began playing guitar when she was ten and was inspired first by folk music and by the work of rock guitarists Jimi Hendrix and Johnny Winter and later, while attending the Berklee College of Music (1974–76), by that of jazz guitarists Montgomery, Pat Martino, and Charlie Christian. She spent the next three years teaching and gigging in New Orleans, where as the house guitarist at the Fairmount Hotel, she accompanied Nancy Wilson, Michel Legrand, and popular singer Robert Goulet. Guitarist Herb Ellis aided her career when he introduced her at the Concord Jazz Festival in 1978. Encouraged by Ellis, she made her first album as leader in 1980 and appeared at international festivals the following year. She played with the Los Angeles version of the show *Sophisticated Ladies* (1981–82), and then led her own trio and quartet in New York.

During the following years she played with Astrud Gilberto (for three years in the early 1980s) and recorded an impressive album of duos with Larry Coryell (*Together*, 1985). She also appeared with the group Great Guitars (which included Ellis, Barney Kessel, and Charlie Byrd), led a quartet with Eddie Gomez, and was a member of pianist Monty Alexander's group. She married Alexander in 1982, but they were divorced in 1985. She moved to New York that year and spent the remainder of her life working primarily as a soloist. She toured Europe with Richie Cole and then the U.S. and Japan as an accompanist to Rosemary Clooney. She recorded and toured successfully with David Benoit shortly before her fatal heart attack on May 3 (or in the early hours of May 4); she was found dead in bed that morning. Equally adept at mainstream and jazz fusion, Remler was becoming one of the most respected young jazz guitarists at the time of her allegedly drug-related death while touring Australia.

SEPTEMBER 19—MUHAL RICHARD ABRAMS (1930–)

b. Chicago, IL

Pianist; Composer; Arranger

[Avant-Garde Jazz; Free Jazz; M-Base]

Other jazz notables born on this day: Helen Ward (1916)
Jazz notables deceased on this day: John Simmons (1979)

♪

In April 1989 a jury convened in Denmark through the Danish Jazz Center voted Muhal Richard Abrams the first recipient of the Jazzpar Prize, considered the most substantial and prestigious jazz award in the world. The prize carries a financial award and promotes concerts in Denmark and France. Judges from five nations selected nominees in this inaugural annual competition and unanimously chose Abrams as the first recipient. The Danish press expressed much puzzlement when the decision was announced, for Abrams was still a relatively unknown figure. The ensuing concert tour was so successful, however, that even the most skeptical of critics had to acknowledge that the committee could not have made a better choice.

Abrams, who served as a mentor to a generation of avant-gardists, is a talented composer who helped bridge the gap between hard bop, free jazz, and contemporary classical music. Despite attending the Chicago Musical College for four years, he was essentially a self-taught musician. Influenced early on by bebop pianist Bud Powell, Abrams performed at a wide variety of jobs during the 1950s, including as arranger for a jump band led by saxophonist King Fleming, and then as pianist for the hard bop group MJT + 3 (1957–59). During that period he accompanied leading soloists passing through Chicago, including Miles Davis, Max Roach, Dexter Gordon, and Sonny Rollins.

In 1961 he formed the short-lived Experimental Band, one of the earliest free-jazz groups, which in 1965 grew into the more comprehensive musicians' cooperative, the Association for the Advancement of Creative Musicians (AACM). As the association's first president, Abrams helped establish the organization as a vital force on the Chicago jazz scene. As well as organizing festivals and concerts, Abrams and the AACM exerted a profound influence on a new generation of players, setting up a school for young musicians and sponsoring local recording sessions for them. Out of this group various performing ensembles developed, the best known being the Art Ensemble of Chicago, formed in 1968 when trumpeter Lester Bowie joined forces with Joseph Jarman, Roscoe Mitchell, and Malachi Favors. When Abrams relocated to New York in 1976, his move hastened the acceptance of a music that had received little more than token support outside of Chicago (despite having made an impact in Europe).

Whether as pianist or leader of a group, Abrams's music tends to vary in quality. The reason seems clear, because for him the process of playing—spontaneous improvisation—is more important than the end product. This attitude may derive partly from his experiences as mentor, for musical experimentation was the medium through which self-discovery, self-help, and a sense of community were achieved during the early days in Chicago.[18]

---

18. Carr et al., *Jazz: The Rough Guide*, 3.

SEPTEMBER 20—STEVE COLEMAN (1956–)

b. Chicago, IL

Alto Saxophonist; Leader

[FREE FUNK, M-BASE; POST-BOP]

Other jazz notables born on this day: John Dankworth (1927); Red Mitchell (1927); Joe Temperley (1929); Billy Bang (1947)

Jazz notables deceased on this day: Ben Webster (1973); Sam Woodyard (1988); Jimmy Hamilton (1994)

♪

Although the avant-garde school of jazz reached its zenith during the 1960s, its legacy is played out today by contemporary jazz performers. Many of these composers and performers were connected to Chicago and to the Chicago-based Association for the Advancement of Creative Musicians (AACM). During the late 1980s a group of black musicians known as M-BASE (short for "macro-basic array of structured extemporization") developed in Brooklyn. Parallels have been drawn between it and the AACM. Saxophonists Greg Osby and Steve Coleman, together with pianist Geri Allen and trombonist Robin Eubanks, are among those who spearheaded the development of the organization. Although AACM and M-BASE each operate as collectives for the advancement of their ideas, the groups differ in their musical heritage. Whereas AACM has a strong alliance with the avant-garde, M-BASE works at an experimental intersection between jazz and popular music forms such as rhythm-and-blues and soul.

Steve Coleman, one of the most significant and innovative saxophonists of the 1990s, is the founder and leader of what he termed "M-Base." Growing up in Chicago's South Side, from an early age he was exposed to that city's musical heritage, including blues, soul, and jazz. He started on alto when he was fifteen and played rhythm-and-blues in his early days. Around 1978, becoming dissatisfied by what he felt was a creative dead end in the Chicago music scene, particularly after hearing musicians such as Art Blakey and Sonny Rollins come through town with bands that featured advanced musical conceptions, Coleman moved to New York, where he began working with the Thad Jones-Mel Lewis Orchestra, as well as with bands led by Cecil Taylor and Sam Rivers. At one point Coleman formed a street band with trumpeter Graham Haynes, and their music became the basis for his subsequent combo, the Five Elements (the name was taken from a kung-fu film), which he has led ever since. With this group he developed a concept of improvisation that became the basis for the M-Base concept. But Coleman was restless.

In the early 1990s, after producing a half dozen albums showcasing his tart alto against a mix of street-smart rhythms (from hip-hop and rap to funk, jazz, and soul), Coleman traveled to West Africa and then to Cuba, investigating ancient philosophy and the music of these regions for creative inspiration. Later in the decade he formed and simultaneously led several experimental bands as outlets for his immense creativity. Over the years his groups have utilized funk rhythms and some nonjazz elements in unpredictable and creative ways, exploring urban beats as much as ethnic roots, and this has led to his strikingly original alto style. His live concerts continue to be heady, almost hypnotic affairs, featuring street beats, rappers, and occasional dancers, showcasing Coleman as "one of jazz's most vital improvisers and theorizers."[19]

SEPTEMBER 21—SLAM STEWART (1914–1987)

b. Englewood, NJ; d. Binghamton, NY

Bassist; Leader

[SWING]

Other jazz notables born on this day: Papa Jack Laine (1873); Tommy Potter (1918); Chico Hamilton (1921); Sunny Murray (1937)
Jazz notables deceased on this day: Trixie Smith (1943); Bill Barron (1989)

♫

Slam Stewart, a superior swing-oriented bassist, became famous in the jazz world for his ability to bow the bass while humming the same notes an octave higher. This technique became Stewart's musical signature, heard excessively in his bass melodies over more than four decades. It appears he first encountered this device while studying at the Boston Conservatory, where he heard violinist Ray Perry humming and playing in unison, and decided to adapt that gimmick to the double bass. Though his birth name is unknown, due to his childhood adoption, Slam (Leroy Elliott) Stewart took up violin at an early age and double bass while in high school. Befriended by his adopted father's employer, he was able to study for a year at the Boston Conservatory. After playing locally in Boston, Stewart worked with Peanuts Holland in Buffalo (1936) before relocating to New York, where he started playing regularly with guitarist/comedian Slim Gaillard in a duo dubbed "Slim and Slam." "Flat Foot Floogie" became a huge hit and the group toured and recorded until Gaillard was drafted into military service in 1942.

Stewart, now a celebrity, went to Hollywood in 1943 to perform as a member of Fats Waller's group in the film *Stormy Weather*. While there, Tiny Grimes took Gaillard's place in the duo, and soon afterwards the two played at a jam session with Art Tatum, resulting in the formation of a trio. The group played mainly at the Three Deuces in New York, but after 1944, when Tatum returned to the Los Angeles area, Stewart took over leadership of the trio, with Erroll Garner serving as pianist. At this time Stewart also recorded with Lester Young, joined Johnny Guarnieri's trio, and played in Grimes's quartet. During the mid-1940s Stewart was also featured on records with Benny Goodman's quintet and sextet and with Red Norvo, including a famous session with Charlie Parker and Dizzy Gillespie.

Following his stunning duets with Don Byas in an acclaimed 1945 Town Hall concert, Stewart went on to work with Billy Taylor, Roy Eldridge, and countless other jazz greats, including further appearances with Gaillard. He even recorded two albums with bassist Major Holley, one of his many imitators (who also bowed and hummed, but in unison).

---

19. Carr et al., *Jazz: The Rough Guide*, 154.

September

In the mid-1960s Stewart moved to Binghamton, New York, where he worked in television studios and taught music at SUNY, Binghamton. After appearing with Goodman at the Newport Jazz Festival in 1973, he continued touring with the clarinetist over the years, including participating in the 1986 public television special *Benny Goodman: Let's Dance*. In 1977 he worked in New York with guitarist Bucky Pizzarelli, and the following year their duo appeared frequently on NBC's Today Show. Although best known for his original solo style, Stewart was also a skilled accompanist, as is evident from his early bop recordings with Gillespie and his saxophone and bass duos with Byas at the 1945 Town Hall concert.[20]

SEPTEMBER 22—BILL SMITH (1928–)

b. Sacramento, CA

Clarinetist; Composer

[THIRD STREAM; EARLY CREATIVE; POST-BOP]

Other jazz notables born on this day:

Jazz notables deceased on this day: Teddy Buckner (1994); Leonard Feather (1994); Willie Cook (2000)

♪

During the early 1940s, when pianist Dave Brubeck was an undergraduate at the College of the Pacific, some members of the faculty treated him with contempt for wanting to play jazz. In 1946, following his discharge from the army, he enrolled at Mills College, where he studied classical composition with the French composer Darius Milhaud. Milhaud, who had incorporated elements of jazz into his own music as early as 1923, had a very different attitude toward jazz than other classical music instructors of the era. On the first day of class, when Milhaud asked if there were any jazz musicians in the room, Brubeck was initially afraid to raise his hand, for at that time most conservatories in the U.S. would not allow students to play jazz, even in the practice rooms. After a moment's hesitation, Brubeck decided to raise his hand anyway, and so did several others. Milhaud indicated that George Gershwin and Duke Ellington were the two most important American composers, and that "if you're going to express America, you've got to have the jazz idiom in your music." Any students who wanted to write their homework in fugue and counterpoint as jazz were encouraged to do so.[21]

Inspired by Milhaud's perspective and by his support, Brubeck and several other students, including clarinetist Bill Smith, formed the Jazz Workshop Ensemble in 1946, an experimental octet that employed modernist elements borrowed from European music, including the unusual time signatures that would remain hallmarks of Brubeck's music for the next fifty years. After college Brubeck formed a trio, then a quartet, and began gathering a following on California campuses, but from 1947 to 1951 his octet, dominated by students

---

20. Kernfeld, *New Grove Dictionary of Jazz*, Vol. 3, 664.
21. Ward and Burns, *Jazz: A History*, 378–79.

of Milhaud, combined bop with modern classical music to form an interesting new blend of styles. Because the group only recorded one LP's worth of material, its life and general influence were limited. But with players such as altoist Paul Desmond, Smith on clarinet and baritone, and a rhythm section comprised of Brubeck, bassist Ron Crotty, and Cal Tjader on drums, this pioneering West Coast group performed highly original music.

By the age of fifteen the precocious William O. Smith was playing with the Oakland Symphony Orchestra. After studies at the Juilliard School in New York, he returned to the West Coast to study with Milhaud at Mills College. Unlike Brubeck, Smith became a college professor upon completing his music studies, teaching initially at the University of Southern California. In the late 1950s he recorded with Red Norvo and Shelly Manne in Los Angeles and on three occasions was Desmond's substitute with Brubeck's quartet (1959–61). After winning a Guggenheim Fellowship for composition, Smith spent six years in Italy. During this period he organized a bop quartet the American Jazz Ensemble, with which he toured and recorded. Since 1982 he has performed regularly with Brubeck's quartet. Like his mentor Milhaud, Smith has composed and performed many classical works, some of which contain elements of jazz.

SEPTEMBER 23—JOHN COLTRANE (1926–1967)

b. Hamlet, NC; d. New York, NY

Tenor and Soprano Saxophonist; Bandleader; Composer

[AVANT-GARDE JAZZ; MODAL MUSIC; FREE JAZZ; HARD BOP; POST-BOP]

Other jazz notables born on this day: Tiny Bradshaw (1905); Albert Ammons (1907); Ray Charles (1930); Les McCann (1935); Norma Winstone (1941); Jeremy Steig (1943)

Jazz notables deceased on this day: Boots Mussulli (1967)

♫

The history of jazz is filled with the names of musical personalities who have been extravagantly admired, but no jazz musician has ever received the extreme adulation visited upon John Coltrane. Not merely loved or even idolized, he came to be revered as a saint, as a mystical being on a spiritual level with the founders of the world's great religions (there is a church in San Francisco founded in his name). Leo Tolstoy once wrote: "In order to influence people, the artist must be constantly searching, so that his work is a quest. If he has discovered everything and instructs people or deliberately sets out to entertain them, he has no influence on them. Only when he is searching for the way forward, do the spectator and the listener become one with him in his quest." John Coltrane became such an artist, sharing everything he had, including his pilgrimage, with his audience. This quality clearly added to his growing mystique.

Despite a relatively brief career, Coltrane was among the most important, and most controversial, figures in jazz. No single performer has come along to dominate the succeeding decades as he dominated jazz during the 1960s. He leaped to fame during the mid-1950s while playing in the Miles Davis quintet, and it was with this band that he earned the nickname "Trane." By this time he had developed a very individualistic style, consisting of choppy, staccato pieces and filled with odd, often unrelated figures. It contained what has been described as a searching quality, and it was this searching that is perhaps the most salient characteristic of his life and work. One example was his obsessive hunt for the perfect mouthpiece. He bought hundreds of them during his career, discarding many almost immediately. Some he gave away, others he tucked away in boxes. On a more profound level, he sought for truth by rummaging endlessly among religions, hoping to find a final answer, a word to illumine his path. During the final decade of his life there was a constant experimentation with new musical forms, systems, and theories. This restlessness, this hope of finding finality, began to personify John Coltrane, and to attract followers.

Sometime in 1957 the pivotal event in his life occurred. During a stay at home, Coltrane, by now addicted to alcohol and heroin, made the decision to fast on water alone and not emerge from his room until he was free of his addiction. After several days, the experiment proved successful. In the process he experienced a spiritual awakening, which had immediate consequences on his life and music. His emotional life now in order, Coltrane was prepared to make his mark. *A Love Supreme*, the 1964 recording that made him a public figure, symbolized the enduring presence of his earlier liberation. This work became his quintessential personal statement, the recording that underscored his preeminence in the 1960s.

SEPTEMBER 24—FATS NAVARRO (1923–1950)

b. Key West, FL; d. New York, NY

Trumpeter

[Bop]

Other jazz notables born on this day: John Carter (1929)
Jazz notables deceased on this day:

♫

Despite a tragically brief career, Fats Navarro was one of the greatest jazz trumpeters of all time. His premature death did not prevent him from becoming one of the leading soloists of the bebop era, a force so pervasive and influential that his only equals during his lifetime were Dizzy Gillespie and Clifford Brown. His fat, brassy sound, which combined aspects of Roy Eldridge, Gillespie, and Howard McGhee, became the main inspiration for Brown, through whom he greatly affected the tones and styles of Lee Morgan, Freddie Hubbard, and Woody Shaw.[22] Clearly, Gillespie was one of his models, though Navarro's tone was sweeter and his style less dramatic. His melodic lines gave the impression of being carefully sculpted, and avoided the brashness of players such as Charlie Parker. For this reason,

---

22. Bogdanov et al., *All Music Guide to Jazz*, 936.

although even Parker did not outclass his inventive ability, Navarro was at home as soloist and lead trumpeter with Tadd Dameron, bop's definitive composer/arranger.

Born in Key West, Florida of mixed Latin, black, and Chinese parentage, Navarro played piano and tenor saxophone as a youth, but by the age of seventeen he was touring with dance bands as a trumpeter. He was a cousin of Charlie Shavers, who was coming into prominence as soloist with the John Kirby Sextet when Navarro was a teenager, and it is probable that Navarro took Shavers as his first model. Three years later Navarro joined Andy Kirk's nationally known jazz band, which at that time included McGhee. In 1945 Gillespie picked Navarro as his replacement in the short-lived but supremely influential Billy Eckstine Orchestra. As the group's principal trumpet soloist, Fats was among the foremost players in the new bop idiom. During the next three years he was second only to Dizzy among bop trumpeters.

In 1946, physically unequal to the heavy touring schedule and restricted musically by the big-band format, he left Eckstine. He spent the remainder of his brief career working mostly in small bop groups in New York. He recorded with Kenny Clarke, Coleman Hawkins, Illinois Jacquet, and most significantly Dameron during 1946 and 1947. He had short stints with the big bands of Lionel Hampton and Benny Goodman, worked regularly with the Dameron sextet and ten-piece band (1948–49), and made classic recordings with Powell (in a quintet with a young Sonny Rollins) and the Metronome All-Stars. His last public appearance was a 1950 Birdland appearance with Parker. Navarro was a heroin addict and that affliction led to the fatal bout with tuberculosis that ended his life at age twenty-six. His recordings with Parker in 1950 are particularly intriguing, especially when one takes into account that these excellent tracks were recorded just one week before Navarro's death, when he was emaciated and gravely ill. In 2001 the British Proper label released *The Fats Navarro Story*, a definitive four-disc set. This material, the canon from which bebop was created, is invaluable to the history of jazz.

SEPTEMBER 25—SAM RIVERS (1923–)

b. El Reno, OK

Saxophonist; Pianist; Composer

[Experimental Big Band; Avant-Garde Jazz; Free Jazz; Post-Bop]

Other jazz notables born on this day: Garvin Bushell (1902); Shadow Wilson (1919); Mike Gibbs (1937); John Taylor (1942); Barbara Dennerlein (1964)
Jazz notables deceased on this day: Stuff Smith (1967)

♪

Sam Rivers is as substantial a player as the jazz avant-garde has produced. Few free jazz saxophonists have approached music with the same degree of intellectual rigor or maintained such a high level of creativity as long as he has.[23] Though often overlooked, he has

---

23. Bogdanov et al., *All Music Guide to Jazz*, 1068.

long been one of the most original voices of the avant-garde, equally skilled on tenor, soprano, and flute.

Rivers grew up in a religious and musical family, hearing spirituals and light classics from an early age. His grandfather was a minister and a musician, his mother a pianist, and his father sang with the Fisk Jubilee Singers, a professional gospel quartet. Rivers began on piano at five and then took up the violin and alto saxophone. At twelve he played soprano in a marching band, later taking up the tenor while a student at Jarvis Christian College in Texas. In 1947 he moved to New England, where he studied composition and viola and also played violin at the Boston Conservatory of Music. By night, however, he played saxophone in Herb Pomeroy's band, which in the early 1950s also featured such players as Jaki Byard, Nat Pierce, Quincy Jones, and Serge Chaloff. From 1955 to 1957 he was in Florida, composing music and working for a variety of singers and dancers. During that time he also accompanied Billie Holiday on tour. In 1958 he returned to Boston, where he rejoined Pomeroy and also led his own quartet with pianist Hal Galper; the following year his band included the thirteen-year old Tony Williams on drums.

About this time Rivers began listening to Cecil Taylor and Ornette Coleman and became interested in the abstract music of the avant-garde. Perhaps befitting his educational background, Rivers approached free jazz from more of a classical perspective, in contrast to the style of Coleman, who came out of the blues tradition. In the early 1960s Rivers became involved with Archie Shepp, Bill Dixon, Paul Bley, and Taylor, all members of the Jazz Composers' Guild. In 1964 he moved to York, where he joined Miles Davis on a recommendation from Williams. The group toured the U.S. and played three concerts in Japan, but Rivers found Davis's musical style too conservative. From 1968 to 1970 he worked intermittently with Taylor, touring Europe with the jazz pioneer before returning to New York, where he and his wife, Bea, opened a music and dance studio in Harlem.

The studio, named Studio Rivbea, eventually relocated to a warehouse in the Soho section of New York, where it became one of the best-known venues for the presentation of new jazz. Rivers's own Rivbea Orchestra and small groups performed there, as well as guest artists. In addition to teaching at his studio, Rivers was composer-in-residence for the Harlem Opera Society and lecturer on African-American musical history at Wesleyan University (1970–73) and Connecticut College (1972). In the early 1990s, after a four-year stint with Dizzy Gillespie's legendary United Nation Orchestra, Rivers moved to Orlando, Florida, where he remains as active and creative as ever.

SEPTEMBER 26—NICHOLAS PAYTON (1973–)

b. New Orleans, LA

Trumpeter; Leader

[NEW ORLEANS JAZZ; NEO-BOP; CONTEMPORARY JAZZ]

Other jazz notables born on this day: Gary Bartz (1940

Jazz notables deceased on this day: Bessie Smith (1937); Shelly Manne (1984); Betty Carter (1998); Nick Fatool (2000)

There had been a major shortage of new trumpeters in jazz during the 1970s, but the emergence and sudden prominence of Wynton Marsalis in 1980 inspired the "young lions" movement and a new crop of mainstream brass players. In the 1990s young trumpeters like Roy Hargrove, Ryan Kisor, Marlon Jordan, and Nicholas Payton paid homage to jazz history while cautiously searching for ways to advance it.

Payton, one of the brightest trumpet stars of the 1990s, was encouraged in music by his father, bassist Walter Payton, and his mother, an operatic singer and classical pianist; by the age of eight he gigged with his father. Payton worked steadily in New Orleans while in high school, studying with Ellis Marsalis at the New Orleans Center for Creative Arts and later at the University of New Orleans. The talented youngster went on to perform and record with some of the most respected musicians in jazz, including Elvin Jones, who appointed him musical director of his Jazz Machine at the age of nineteen. In the mid-1990s he recorded with Doc Cheatham, a ninety-year old trumpeter with whom he toured until the latter's death in 1997. He then worked with important ensembles such as the Lincoln Center Jazz Orchestra and the Carnegie Hall Jazz Band. In 1996 he portrayed legendary trumpeter Hot Lips Page in Robert Altman's film *Kansas City*, and the following year he was featured in a tribute concert to Louis Armstrong, proving he could use Armstrong's music to his own advantage.

Since his professional debut at the age of eleven, Payton has displayed a keen interest in all styles of music, particularly R&B, Latin, and funk. Though he never wanted to be viewed purely as a traditionalist, he doesn't want to appear to be cutting himself off from a rich past either. After recording *Dear Louis* (a 2000 tribute to Armstrong), Payton opened a new chapter with *Sonic Trance* (2003). Utilizing groove and hip-hop, electric keyboards, and special effects for trumpet, the young artist sees his exploration as a natural progression and a timely reflection on life in the modern world. "I'm still playing jazz," he argues, "but from the perspective of a man of my age and experiences. All of the musicians I love and respect, like Ornette Coleman, John Coltrane, and Bill Evans, made statements that had not only personal, but cultural relevance to the times in which they lived." The philosophical concept underlying *Sonic Trance* hinges on self-realization, which can theoretically lead to a hopeful universal order.

SEPTEMBER 27—BUD POWELL (1924–1966)

b. New York, NY; d. New York, NY

Pianist; Leader

[Bop]

Other jazz notables born on this day: Red Rodney (1927)
Jazz notables deceased on this day: J. C. Heard (1988)

September

♪

Bud Powell seemed to epitomize everything jazz pianists were trying to achieve during the 1940s. One of bebop's most talented and influential pianists and composers, he changed the playing style of virtually every post-swing pianist. He did away with the striding technique that had been considered essential earlier, thereby reducing the role of the left hand to brief, sporadically placed dissonant chords. This "comping style" became the standard means that modern pianists would use to suggest the chords underlying their own solo lines. With his right hand he played fluid, hornlike lines, essentially transforming Charlie Parker's vocabulary to the piano. Indeed, not only his music but also his tragic life paralleled that of Parker. A flawed genius, Powell's painful personal history inspired the 1986 jazz film, *Round Midnight*.

Born to a musical family in New York City, Powell began studying piano at the age of six and quickly developed an excellent technique by playing the European classics. At fifteen he quit high school, around the same time as the experiments in modern music were beginning at Minton's Playhouse. His playing at this time was in the manner of Earl Hines, the predominant pianist of the 1930s, though it is clear that Art Tatum was also an influence. He began frequenting Minton's, where he was befriended and tutored by Thelonious Monk and with whom he helped shape the emerging bop style. He played with Cootie Williams's orchestra from 1943 to1945, before beginning to suffer nervous collapses, due in part to being beaten on the head by police during a racial incident. Powell never fully recovered and continued suffering from bad headaches and mental breakdowns, for which he was confined to sanatoriums for much of his adult life.

After nearly a year of hospitalization and several electroshock treatments in 1948, Powell emerged to find that he was looked to as a central figure of the new piano idiom. Despite his personal problems, he recorded many gems during 1947 to 1951, including compositions such as "Hallucinations," "Tempus Fugit," "Bouncing with Bud," and the remarkable "Glass Enclosure," a musical impression of his experiences in mental asylums. A breakdown in 1951 and further electroshock treatments weakened him, but Powell was still capable of playing at his best, most notably at the famous 1953 Massey Hall concert in Toronto, where he played brilliantly with Charles Mingus, Max Roach, Dizzy Gillespie, and Parker. He was in and out of institutions, including a shouting match with Parker, who was also deteriorating, on the bandstand at Birdland (Parker supposedly told Davis that he would not hire Powell because "he's even crazier than me!"). In 1959 Powell moved to Paris, where he led a trio with Kenny Clark until 1962. His warm welcome and lengthy stay in Paris extended his life a bit, but even there Powell spent part of 1962 and 1963 in the hospital. He returned to New York in 1964, disappeared after a few concerts, and died soon thereafter. But from 1945 to 1960, until the rise of Bill Evans and McCoy Tyner, Powell was the single most influential pianist in jazz.

SEPTEMBER 28—KENNY KIRKLAND (1955–1998)

b. Newport, NY; d New York, NY

Keyboardist

[Post-Bop; Latin Jazz]

Other jazz notables born on this day: Ed Thigpen (1930); John Gilmore (1931); Sirone (1940); Jay Hoggard (1954)

Jazz notables deceased on this day: Lucky Millinder (1966); Miles Davis (1991)

♪

The jazz world was stunned and saddened in 1998 to hear of the premature death of Kenny Kirkland, a gifted forty-three-year-old pianist whose technical skill, inventiveness, and versatility marked him as a player of unusual depth and promise. The exact date of his death is unknown, as he had already been dead for some time when he was discovered in his home on the morning of November 13. The cause of his death was uncertain as well, though police raised the possibility that his death was drug-related. Though he initially gained his reputation as a skillful Herbie Hancock-influenced pianist, he was eclectic and developed his own style, becoming particularly adept as an accompanist, including long-standing stints with Wynton and Branford Marsalis.

Kirkland started playing piano at the age of six and later attended Manhattan School of Music, studying classical piano performance, and then classical theory and composition. A month before his graduation he was the victim of an accident in which he broke his legs, his jaw, his wrist, and a hip. His first professional work came with Polish fusion violinist Michal Urbaniak's band (playing electric keyboards and synthesizer) during 1977, touring Europe and Scandinavia. His next high profile association was with another Eastern European jazz émigré, Miroslav Vitous (1979), the bassist who had become famous with Weather Report. By 1981 he was working in a band led by drummer Elvin Jones and moved from there to join the trumpeter Terumasa Hino, one of Japan's outstanding musicians.

He was touring Japan when he met Wynton Marsalis, also on tour, which began their long professional association (1981–85). On Marsalis's self-titled debut album, Kirkland shared the piano with Hancock, but then was the sole pianist on several of Wynton's subsequent releases. While his work with Marsalis's quintet expanded his horizons, the pianist also responded with excellent accompaniment. As opposed to many jazz pianists, Kirkland never shied from electric keyboards and synthesizers. Following a 1984 tour of Japan with Jim Hall, Eddie Gomez, and Grady Tate, Kirkland left Wynton Marsalis (to Wynton's great dismay) to play with brother Branford Marsalis before joining exotic pop/rock musician Sting, playing synthesizers with the latter and participating in an international tour. After leaving Sting in 1986 Kirkland became a studio musician, joining NBC's Tonight Show band (under the direction of Branford Marsalis) from 1992 to 1994. In 1995 he rejoined Sting and shortly before his death began working again with Branford Marsalis. During his twenty-year career Kirkland performed or recorded with varied artists such as Dizzy Gillespie, John Scofield, David Sanborn, Kenny Garrett, Carla Bley, and the rock group Crosby, Stills, and Nash, in addition to his celebrated stints with the Marsalis brothers and Sting.

SEPTEMBER 29—JEAN-LUC PONTY (1942–)

b. Avranches, France

Violinist

[CROSSOVER JAZZ; POST-BOP; FUSION]

Other jazz notables born on this day: Vic Juris (1953)
Jazz notables deceased on this day: Eddie Wilcox (1968); Barney Josephson (1988)

♪

Since the days of Django Reinhardt and Stéphane Grappelli, there have always been at least some Europeans who could compete at the highest levels of jazz. Jean-Luc Ponty, who rivals Grappelli for the title of the most prominent and influential European jazz violinist, is one of them.[24] His versatility is rare, for he is equally at home in swing, bop, free jazz, jazz-rock, and world music, playing distinguished improvisations in each style. As early as the 1960s the legendary violinist Stuff Smith said of Ponty, "He's a killer! He plays on violin like Coltrane does on saxophone." Ponty was a pioneer in the use of the electric violin, experimenting with electronic effects and at times performing on five and six-string violins that extend the lower range of the instrument. By establishing the instrument as a force in contemporary jazz, Ponty paved the way for violinists such as Jerry Goodman, Zbigniew Seifert, and Didier Lockwood.

It has been a long, fascinating odyssey for Ponty, who began as a classical violinist in the 1950s, pioneered the electric violin in jazz-rock, and by the 1990s was a leading figure in the "world music" movement. Ponty's father, a violin teacher and the director of a music school in France, got Jean-Luc started on violin at the age of five. When he was thirteen he left school to practice six hours a day in the hope of becoming a concert violinist. At fifteen, he was accepted into the Paris Conservatoire, ultimately winning the *premier prix* at age seventeen. While performing with a classical orchestra (1959–62) he became interested in jazz, thanks to the influence of Grappelli and Smith. Following military service in the French army (1962–64), he committed himself completely to jazz, leading quartets and trios in Europe, recording with Grappelli, Smith, and Svend Asmussen on *Violin Summit*, and visiting the U.S. for the first time in 1967. At first merely amplifying his violin in order to be heard, he switched over to electric violin and augmented it with devices that were associated with electric guitarists and keyboardists, like Echoplex machines, distortion boxes, and wah-wah pedals.

In 1969 Ponty returned to the U.S., performing and recording with rock star Frank Zappa's Mothers of Invention. Following a two-year period in France, where he formed the free-jazz band, Jean-Luc Ponty Experience (1970–72), he settled in the U.S., rejoin-

---

24. Bogdanov et al., *All Music Guide to Jazz*, 1025.

ing Zappa before working with John McLaughlin's Mahavishnu Orchestra (1974–75), the era's premiere rock-jazz band. At that point he set out on his own, compiling a long series of albums that pulled him toward a more lyrical, European, extension of Mahavishnu's idioms. Forming bands that played his own brand of fusion, he toured extensively and reached a large audience with his recordings. In 1983 he switched gears, using sequencers to construct electronic patterns as backdrops for his violin. Following a worldwide tour with his band in 1987 and 1988, he continued his musical odyssey through involvement in the emerging "world music" movement, recording compositions and improvisations based on traditional African music.

SEPTEMBER 30—OSCAR PETTIFORD (1922–1960)

b. Okmulgee, OK; d. Copenhagen, Denmark

Bassist; Cellist; Bandleader

[BOP]

Other jazz notables born on this day: Buddy Rich (1917)
Jazz notables deceased on this day: J. Russel Robinson (1963); Phil Napoleon (1990)

♪

In December 1943 something distinctly new was added to the rich musical mix on Manhattan's Fifty-Second Street. Dizzy Gillespie, Charlie Parker, and several other musicians had recently left Earl Hines's big band rather than undertake another tour of the Jim Crow South, and Gillespie joined forces with bassist Oscar Pettiford, co-leading a quintet at the Onyx. The nineteen-year-old Max Roach was on drums, Don Byas replaced Lester Young on tenor (followed by Budd Johnson), and George Wallington played piano. Audiences and other musicians were astonished at the group's rhythmic sense and at the furious pace with which they played. The Onyx engagement "was the thing that put [bebop] on the map," Gillespie wrote, for it was there that the new style got its name.

Pettiford was, with Charles Mingus, the top bassist of the 1945 to 1960 period. When he first appeared in New York in the early 1940s, he was accepted almost immediately as an incarnation of the recently deceased Jimmy Blanton. He was the first jazz player to adapt and elaborate Blanton's innovations within a bop context, and his ideas and discoveries had a lasting influence on the bop style as a whole. Together with Ray Brown and Mingus, who owed much to his influence, Pettiford was influential in establishing the double bass as a jazz solo instrument equal in importance to the woodwinds.

Of mixed African- and native-American extraction, Pettiford was born into a large, musical family and learned many instruments in the family's touring band, which was based in Minneapolis. Starting on piano, the youngster switched to bass when he was fourteen. He played with Charlie Barnet's band in 1942 and 1943 and traveled with the unit to New York, where he found a place in the emerging bop scene, working with Thelonious Monk at Minton's. At the Onyx he was a member of a quintet led by Roy Eldridge, where he remained as co-leader with Gillespie. Following a stint with Duke Ellington's Orchestra (1945–48), he joined Woody Herman's Second Herd (1949).

While playing baseball with Herman's men he broke his arm, and consequently his activities were greatly reduced over the next year. During this time he focused on playing cello, becoming the first musician to successfully adapt the pizzicato bass style to the cello. He went to Europe with the Jazz from Carnegie Hall show in 1958 and settled in Copenhagen, where he worked with local musicians and American jazz greats such as Stan Getz, Bud Powell, and Kenny Clarke. Despite fracturing his skull in a car crash in 1959, he continued recording until his sudden death from a stroke in September 1960. One wonders what contributions the progressive bassist might have made during the avant-garde era, had he not died unexpectedly at the movement's inception.

Chapter 10

October

OCTOBER 1—DAVE HOLLAND (1946–)
b. Wolverhampton, England
Bassist; Composer; Leader
[Avant-Garde Jazz; Free Jazz; M-Base; Post-Bop]

Other jazz notables born on this day:
Jazz notables deceased on this day: Stu Williamson (1991)

♪

By 1969 rock music was so dominant in the entertainment world that even the Newport Jazz Festival decided to include rock musicians on its program. Miles Davis and his quintet were there, together with Frank Zappa, Jethro Tull, Sly and the Family Stone, and Led Zeppelin. When Miles saw the size of the crowds in attendance—double the festival's usual size—he decided to find a way of getting in on the action. The popularity of rock and the funk music of James Brown, Jimi Hendrix, and Sly Stone had not been lost on other jazz musicians either. In 1967 saxophonist Charles Lloyd had started what would become something like a stampede of jazz musicians into the new market. With a quartet that included drummer Jack DeJohnette and pianist Keith Jarrett, he was a hit at the country's most celebrated rock venue, the Fillmore Auditorium in San Francisco.

Miles, too, faced the rock challenge head-on. In two years of furious creative activity, 1969 to 1970, he recorded over twenty LP sides, launching the jazz-rock fusion movement. The key albums that had a global influence were *In a Silent Way* and, to a greater extent, *Bitches Brew*, the electronic-filled recording that sold close to a half-million copies in its first year. The group now began to work not only in jazz clubs but at rock-oriented festivals and clubs like the Fillmore and its New York counterpart, the Fillmore East. During this period Davis's band underwent a complete change of personnel, beginning in the fall of 1968, when pianist Herbie Hancock and bassist Ron Carter left the group and were replaced by Chick Corea and Dave Holland.

While growing up in England Holland played the guitar, then the fashionable electric bass guitar. By the age of thirteen he was playing with local bands; two years later he left school to work as a musician. Having discovered jazz through recordings, he began to play double bass in 1963, and from 1964 to 1968 he attended the Guildhall School of Music and Drama in London, where he was the principal bassist in the college orchestra. During this period he played with top British players, performed with the Spontaneous Music Ensemble, and was a house player at Ronnie Scott's club, where he accompanied such visiting Americans as Coleman Hawkins, Ben Webster, and Joe Henderson. Davis heard Holland in London in the summer of 1968 and invited him to New York to join his quintet as replacement for Carter. Holland worked with Davis from 1968 to 1970; while with Davis he played increasingly on the electric bass guitar, but thereafter he reverted to his preferred instrument, the acoustic bass.

In 1970 he teamed up with Corea, Anthony Braxton, and Barry Altschul to form the outstanding free-jazz group Circle. During the 1980s he was increasingly active as a teacher, and from 1987 to 1990 he was on the faculty of the New England Conservatory. He was among the other ex-Davis musicians who joined the trumpeter for one of his last concerts in Paris (July 10, 1991), and was a member of the Miles Davis Tribute Band, with Tony Williams, Hancock, Wayne Shorter, and Wallace Roney, that toured internationally in the autumn of 1992.

OCTOBER 2—DJANGO BATES (1960–)

b. Beckenham, England

Pianist; Electronic Keyboardist; Trumpeter; Tenor Horn Player; Composer; Leader

[AVANT-GARDE; MODERN CREATIVE]

Other jazz notables born on this day: Phil Urso (1925); Howard Roberts (1929); Ronnie Ross (1933)

Jazz notables deceased on this day: George E. Lee (1958); Quentin Jackson (1976)

♪

In 1997 Django Bates became only the second non-American and the second Englishman (after Tony Coe, the previous year) to be awarded the prestigious Danish Jazzpar prize, dubbed the Nobel Prize of jazz. Bates is one of the most talented musicians Britain has produced, and his work covers the entire spectrum of jazz, from early jazz through bebop and free jazz to jazz-rock fusion. During his childhood Bates heard a lot of music, as his father collected jazz, African music, and Romanian folk music.

Django started playing the piano by ear. Later he studied piano, trumpet, and violin at the Centre for Young Musician in London, after which he studied music at Morley College, London. In 1978 he enrolled at the Royal College of Music to study composition, but he left disenchanted after only two weeks, wishing to play jazz. He did so with Borderline, a quartet led by the saxophonist Tim Whitehead. In 1979 he formed his quartet Human Chain, with which he continues to perform worldwide. In 1983 he joined Dudu Pukwana's group Zila, a band he had admired since childhood. The following year he joined Ken Stubbs's group First House, which won the third European Jazz Competition held in Leverkusen, Germany. That year Bates was a founding member of Loose Tubes, one of the most original large ensembles of the 1980s, performing and composing with the twenty-one-piece ensemble until its demise in 1990. In 1991, as a follow-up to Loose Tubes, Bates formed Delightful Precipice, a large orchestra that included the members of Human Chain as its nucleus. The orchestra's initial performances included cross-media collaborations with groups such as Snapdragon, one of Europe's leading new circus companies.

Bates is a prodigiously talented musician, adept at working as an unaccompanied soloist, in small groups, in big bands, and in a variety of media. In addition to collaborations as a duo with the concert pianist Joanna MacGregor and with international composers and bandleaders such as George Russell, George Gruntz, and Mike Gibbs, Bates has composed film soundtracks and music for drama and dance. Bates's touring and innovative compositional activity continue unabated in the new millennium, further increasing his growing international reputation.

OCTOBER 3—GEORGE WEIN (1925–)

b. Boston, MA

Pianist; Vocalist; Impresario

[MAINSTREAM MUSIC; DIXIELAND]

Other jazz notables born on this day: Von Freeman (1922
Jazz notables deceased on this day: Dave Lambert (1966); Victoria Spivey (1976) Scoville Browne (1994)

♪

Since the mid-1930s the mecca for jazz fans in New York consisted of a concentration of jazz clubs along a two-block stretch of Fifty-Second Street, between Fifth and Seventh Avenues. Never before had so much jazz been concentrated in so small a space. Fifty-Second Street was "the last time that an American street gave you a feeling of security and warmth and the excitement of musical friendship," the songwriter Alec Wilder recalled.[1] To a jazz fan like George Wein, then a teenager living in Boston, "Swing Street" was an irresistible magnet. "I was just a kid thirteen or fourteen years old and my brother was three or four years older," he recalled, "and we would come down the West Side Highway and we'd get off at Fifty-second Street, and drive. Before we checked into a hotel, we would drive straight across town down Fifty-second Street . . . It was like being in a candied heaven, and the candy was the jazz that you could grab onto. That night, we would take ten or fifteen dollars that my father had given us to go out, and I'd go into these bars where I couldn't drink and I would spend a dollar for a ginger ale. We'd go to five clubs. It was just the greatest feeling that one could have . . ."[2]

Wein never forgot that feeling, for in 1954 he founded an annual jazz festival at Newport, Rhode Island. Newport was a seaside summer retreat of some of the East

---

1. Ward and Burns, *Jazz: A History*, 317.
2. Ibid., 318.

Coast's wealthiest old families and about as far from the places where jazz began as it was possible to get. Wein's rationale was simple: festivals were important happenings and a great source of public relations for the music. Best known for his connection with the Newport Jazz Festival, Wein also established the Boston Globe Jazz & Heritage Festival in 1966, and soon thereafter became involved in the organization of several international festivals. By the 1990s his company, Festival Productions, was running several dozen festivals worldwide.

In his youth Wein studied classical piano with Margaret Chaloff (the mother of baritone saxophonist Serge Chaloff), and then formed a thirteen-piece dance band, with which he played until 1941. While a student at Boston University he performed at local nightclubs, working with many celebrated players, including Edmond Hall, Max Kaminsky, and Miff Mole. By 1951 he had opened a club in Boston name Storyville, for which he engaged well-known Dixieland and swing players. The following year he opened a second club, Mahogany Hall, and began playing as a member of its house band, the Mahogany Hall All Stars. Over the years Wein also toured and recorded with his Newport All-Stars, playing mainstream music alongside such notable performers as Ruby Braff, Pee Wee Russell, Bud Freeman, Clark Terry, Warren Vaché, Scott Hamilton, and Flip Phillips. Whether one agrees or disagrees with Wein's musical preferences, ultimately every jazz fan is indebted to his philosophy that jazz festivals are essential, and that they should feature a wide range of performers.

OCTOBER 4—STAN HASSELGARD (1922–1948)

b. Sundsvall, Sweden; d. Decatur, IL

Clarinetist

[SWING; BOP]

Other jazz notables born on this day: Chano Pozo (1915); Steve Swallow (1940); Eddie Gomez (1944)
Jazz notables deceased on this day: Bill Challis (1994); Art Farmer (1999)

♫

As early as the mid-1920s young Swedish musicians had begun to take an interest in the new sounds emanating from America. Early visits to England by The Original Dixieland Jazz Band and other musicians from the U.S. were reflected in the playing of British musicians, some of whom appeared at venues in Sweden. Many young Swedish dance band musicians were highly impressed by these presentations; some managed to work their way across the Atlantic, playing on ocean liners, and when they arrived in New York they were able to hear orchestras led by Jean Goldkette, Duke Ellington, and other outstanding bandleaders. One event, a visit to the Swedish capital by Louis Armstrong in 1933, triggered an interest in jazz that blossomed into a youth movement. By the outbreak of World War II, American swing music was the rage in Sweden. During the 1940s a revolutionary new form of jazz called bebop emerged in the United States, pushing swing out of the mainstream. In Sweden, the earliest practitioner was Stan Hasselgard, the ill-fated clarinetist who, along with Americans Buddy DeFranco and Tony Scott, was the first to fully explore bebop on that instrument.

Greatly influenced by Benny Goodman, and the only clarinetist to share the bandstand with him, Hasselgard focused on swing in the late 1930s and '40s but started exploring bebop around 1945. Known in America as Stan, Ake Hasselgard began playing the clarinet when he was sixteen. Later, while attending the University of Uppsala in Sweden, he joined the Royal Swingers, an amateur group that modeled itself after Goodman's small band. By the mid-1940s he had become well known in Swedish jazz circles but, like many other European jazz musicians, he began nurturing dreams of traveling to the homeland of jazz. In 1947 he acted on his dream, relocating to the U.S., where he quickly made an impact.

Hasselgard, whose style combined elements of swing and bebop, attracted considerable attention in New York, where he sat in with Jack Teagarden, Bud Freeman, and others on Fifty-Second Street, and also with modernists such as Charlie Parker, Dizzy Gillespie, and Miles Davis. Later that year, with the help of Barney Kessel, Red Norvo, and other American friends, he recorded four now legendary sides for Capitol, including "Swedish Pastry." In 1948 he got a chance to play and record with his idol Goodman, who employed the Swede in a two-clarinet septet that also included Teddy Wilson, Wardell Gray, and singer Patti Page. That year he headlined at a Fifty-Second-Street club called the Three Deuces with a quintet that boasted Max Roach on drums. On the opening night of his Deuces engagement (October 1948), where he was billed as "the Bebop King of Sweden," he found both Parker and Gillespie in the audience. Tragically, he died a month later, killed in an auto accident while on his way to California; he was a mere twenty-six years old.

OCTOBER 5—BILL DIXON (1925–2010)

b. Nantucket, MA; d. North Bennington, VT

Trumpeter; Composer; Teacher

[AVANT-GARDE; FREE JAZZ]

Other jazz notables born on this day: Jimmy Blanton (see Oct. 6 entry)
Jazz notables deceased on this day: Leon Roppolo (1943); Booker Little (1961)

♫

Avant-garde jazz, a minority music during the early 1960s, reflected the turmoil of that era. Expressing emotions and styles so extreme as to utterly alienate much of the traditional jazz following—itself a withering minority in the age of rock and roll, avant-garde musicians had a rough time surviving.[3] Once the novelty waned, many of the most critically admired avant-garde works sold a few thousand copies at best. And yet, as the decade progressed, the influence of the avant-garde continued to expand, and soon a host of progressive mainstream musicians such as Sonny Rollins, Jackie McLean, Charles Mingus, Roland Kirk, John Coltrane, and Miles Davis began testing its waters.

---

3. Ward and Burns, *Jazz: A History*, 364.

A pioneer in the avant-garde and one of the principal organizers of the Free Jazz movement, Bill Dixon grew up in an artistic family, his mother being a writer and blues singer. He began on trumpet while in high school and studied painting at Boston University. After military service (1944–46) he enrolled at the Hartnett School of Music in Manhattan (1946–51). By 1948 he was freelancing around New York as a trumpeter and arranger, and soon began leading his own groups. He befriended Cecil Taylor in the early 1950s, during a period when Dixon was also writing, painting, teaching art history and music, and composing. In the early 1960s he co-led an advanced quartet with Archie Shepp, and then formed the New York Contemporary Five with Shepp, John Tchicai, and Don Cherry. In 1964 Dixon organized the "October Revolution in Jazz," a four-day festival in New York's Cellar Café that brought together the most important avant-garde groups of the time. The concerts, performed by some forty groups and all before capacity audiences, marked the emergence of free jazz as a mature movement. Later that year he organized the influential but short-lived Jazz Composers' Guild, which aimed to promote free jazz and improve the working conditions of the musicians who created it. Its membership included such avant-gardists as Carla and Paul Bley, Burton Greene, Michael Mantler, Shepp, Sun Ra, and Taylor.

In 1965 Dixon began a ten-year collaboration with the dancer Judith Dunn that presented concerts of free jazz and dance at such events as the Newport Jazz Festival (1966). The performance of his composition "Pomegranate" at Newport that year led to a contract with RCA and to a highly acclaimed orchestral recording, *Intents and Purposes*. In 1968 he began teaching at Bennington College in Vermont, where he established a Black Music department. While there he created the position of Musician in Residence, an occasional post filled by free jazz performers such as Jimmy Lyons, Jimmy Garrison, and Alan Silva. During this period Dixon continued to perform jazz while exhibiting his paintings in the U.S. and Europe. He retired from Bennington in 1996, having conducted workshops and master classes around the world during his long tenure at the college.

OCTOBER 6—JIMMY BLANTON (1918–1942) [DOB uncertain]

b. Chattanooga, TN; d. Duarte, CA

Bassist

[SWING]

Other jazz notables born on this day: Sammy Price (1908); Carmen Mastren (1913); Mark Whitfield (1966)

Jazz notables deceased on this day: Jean-François Jenny-Clark (1998)

♪

In the fall of 1939 drummer Sonny Greer took bandleader Duke Ellington to a St. Louis club to hear the twenty-one year old bassist Jimmy Blanton. "All my life I'd never heard nobody like this guy," Greer said. Ellington agreed, and hired him on the spot. Blanton had a huge, warm sound, a buoyant beat, and a gift for placing the right note in the right place. But beyond that, he was more harmonically advanced than any of his predecessors and capable of melodic flights that no bassist before him had ever come close to matching. Ellington already had a good bass player named Billy Taylor and was pleased to have both men in his band, until Taylor's sudden departure one evening in Boston, humiliated by the youngster's technical superiority. Blanton would die of congenital tuberculosis within three years, but that was time enough for him to revolutionize bass playing.[4]

He could not have had such an immediate impact if he had not been discovered at the right time and by the right person, for Ellington knew immediately how to exploit Blanton's talent and took the trouble to have him well captured by the recording engineers of the period. Despite his short career, Blanton left a large recorded legacy, not only in his 130-odd recordings with Ellington's orchestra, but also in many small group performances with some of Ellington's sidemen and in a series of duos with Ellington at the piano, the most astounding of which is "Pitter Panther Patter." Blanton's playing subtly altered the Ellington sound, stabilizing the band's rhythm and greatly enhancing its swing; it also ushered in Ellington's most creative period as a composer, particularly in masterpieces such as "Ko-Ko," "Jack the Bear," and "Concerto for Cootie," where Blanton's bass part is especially prominent. Previously, John Kirby and two bassists from Chicago, Milt Hinton and Israel Crosby, had been moving towards more melodic "walking lines," while the Basie band of the late 1930s had featured Walter Page in his role as the foundation of the rhythm section. Blanton, however, combined the melodic tendencies of the first group with Page's marvelous pulse and a beautiful rounded tone to showcase his brief solo passages.[5]

Blanton started to play the bass professionally in local Chattanooga groups before moving to St. Louis, where Ellington heard him. In his tragically brief career, Blanton transformed jazz playing by contributing the earliest fully satisfying jazz solos on his instrument, and until the advent of the styles of Scott LaFaro and Charlie Haden in the 1960s, all modern bass players drew on his innovations. His legacy became the model for bass players over the next twenty years; Charles Mingus, Oscar Pettiford, and Ray Brown all reflect his influence.

OCTOBER 7—JO JONES (1911–1985)

b. Chicago, IL; d. New York, NY

Drummer

[SWING]

Other jazz notables born on this day: Larry Young (1940)
Jazz notables deceased on this day: Ed Blackwell (1992)

♪

When Count Basie uttered the words, "Even a single note can swing," he was talking from experience, because from 1935 until his death almost fifty years later, his outstanding big band was considered the epitome of swing. It gained that reputation from its celebrated rhythm section: Basie at the piano, Walter Page at bass, Jo Jones on drums, and from 1937,

---

4. Ward and Burns, *Jazz: A History*, 287.
5. Carr et al., *Jazz: The Rough Guide*, 74.

Freddie Green on guitar. Basie's All-American Rhythm Section, as he called it, was the supreme rhythmic foundation of its day. Page, one of the finest bassists of the swing era, provided the powerful "walking" 4/4 pulse that allowed Jones to keep time on the high hat and ride cymbals, thereby abandoning the heavy, thumping emphasis on the bass drum that had characterized jazz drumming up to that point. But this carefree sound, which propelled Basie to fame in the late 1930s, didn't come easily. "We worked at it," Jones said, "every day, every night. We worked alone, not with the band all the time. I didn't care what happened—one of us would be up to par. If three were down, one would carry the three. Never four were out."

"Jo Jones reminds me of the wind," said Don Lamond in a familiar quotation. "He has more class than any drummer I've ever heard . . . With Jo there's none of the damn raucous tom-tom beating or riveting-machine stuff. Jo makes sense." Musically, Jones was the finest, fastest drummer of the swing era, the pulse that powered Basie's unmatchable rhythm section. He was also among the first jazz drummers to realize the full potential of the brushes, which he used with remarkable facility. Though not given to long solos in the manner of contemporaries like Chick Webb, Gene Krupa, and Cozy Cole, Jones was an expert soloist; his avoidance of auxiliary instruments such as woodblocks and cowbells foreshadowed future developments in jazz drumming.

Jones grew up in Alabama working as a tap dancer and drummer, and on his way up he played in carnival bands, territory bands, and for such well-known leaders as Bennie Moten and Tommy Douglas. He joined Page's Blue Devils in Oklahoma City in the late 1920s, and in 1934 began his association with Count Basie. He left briefly in 1936 to join Page in the rhythm section of the Jeter-Pillars Orchestra in St. Louis, but by the end of the year both musicians had returned to Basie's group. Jones remained with the Basie band (other than 1944 to 1946, when he was in the military) until 1948, and in later years he participated in many reunions with Basie alumni. By now an established star, Jones turned freelance, working with Illinois Jacquet, Lester Young, Art Tatum, Teddy Wilson, Coleman Hawkins, Roy Eldridge, and others, and with Jazz at the Philharmonic, as well as leading his own groups in clubs and for recordings arranged by John Hammond. "I think Jo can do more things superlatively well than any drummer I ever heard," Hammond stated; "he's always been my favorite."

OCTOBER 8—PEPPER ADAMS (1930–1986)

b. Highland Park, MI; d. New York, NY

Baritone Saxophonist

[Hard Bop]

Other jazz notables born on this day: Clarence Williams (1893?); Bill Stegmeyer (1916); J.C. Heard (1917)

Jazz notables deceased on this day: Harry Carney (1974); David Izenzon (1979); Oscar Moore (1981); Edward Inge (1988); Bernie Privin (1999)

There have been few jazz musicians as consistently controversial as bandleader Stan Kenton. Loved by many but dismissed by purists, Kenton ranks with Chet Baker and Sun Ra as jazz's top cult figures. During the 1940s and '50s Kenton led a succession of highly original bands that emphasized emotion, power, and advanced harmonies over swing, and this upset listeners who were unable to think progressively.[6] Kenton was also controversial for his ideas about the origin and nature of jazz. When he read the results of the 1956 *Down Beat* critics poll, in which guitarist Tal Farlow and clarinetist Benny Goodman were the only white musicians to win, he wrote an angry telegram to the editor: JUST SAW YOUR FOURTH JAZZ CRITICS POLL. IT'S OBVIOUS THAT THERE IS A NEW MINORITY GROUP, "WHITE JAZZ MUSICIANS." THE ONLY THING I GAINED FROM STUDYING THE OPINIONS OF YOUR LITERARY GENIUSES OF JAZZ IS COMPLETE AND TOTAL DISGUST. In his essay on "Race, Jazz, and the White Jazz Musician," the African-American author Gerald Early indicates that "it came as news to Stan Kenton that for the past twenty years he had been performing a Negro art form. He thought of jazz as simply American, and he said as much in interviews over the years."[7] As a result of this controversy, some saw Kenton as a racist, which he undoubtedly was, for he was very much a product of the times.

It seems ironic that in 1956, when Kenton fired off his prejudiced remarks to the editor of *Down Beat*, he had among his sidemen Pepper Adams, a musician with a very different experience and outlook on jazz. Adams, one of the all-time great baritonists, was admired by Kenton for his virtuosity and hard-edged sound, but surprisingly, many of the stylistic devices he featured on his horn, including adventurous harmonies, a gruff tone, and a large sound, were typical of African-American players. As a child growing up in Rochester New York, Adams played tenor and clarinet with local bands, modeling his early style after that of Coleman Hawkins. Inspired by the example of Harry Carney to take up the baritone sax, he began working professionally at the age of sixteen, after relocating to Detroit, where he became an important fixture in the city's fertile jazz scene. "More often than not," he stated, "I was the only white cat in any [Detroit] band I worked in." In January 1956 he moved to New York where, while waiting for his local musicians' union card, he joined Kenton's big band on a tour of the West, becoming one of the orchestra's featured soloists. Based in New York from 1958, he played with Goodman and Charles Mingus and was a longtime member of the influential Thad Jones-Mel Lewis band (1965–78). A product of the post-bop era, Adams was one of very few players to attempt this style on the baritone, and he remained a major stylist until his death from lung cancer in 1986.

---

6. Bogdanov et al., *All Music Guide to Jazz*, 704.
7. Ward and Burns, *Jazz: A History*, 325.

OCTOBER 9—LEE WILEY (1908–1975)

b. Fort Gibson, OK; d. New York, NY

Vocalist

[VOCAL JAZZ; TRADITIONAL POP; STANDARDS; SWING]

Other jazz notables born on this day: Elmer Snowden (1900); Yusef Lateef (1920); Chucho Valdés (1941); Dave Samuels (1948); Kenny Garrett (1960)
Jazz notables deceased on this day: Sister Rosetta Tharpe (1973); Milt Jackson (1999)

♪

In his classic text, *Jazz Singing*, Will Friedwald writes that female vocalists were as essential to the big-band era as brass, reed, and rhythm sections. "They decorated the fronts of swing bands like the figureheads on a ship," he adds, "and no bandleader who wanted to fill dance halls or sell records dared go on the road without one.[8]" In the early 1930s three white female singers—Mildred Bailey, Connee Boswell, and Lee Wiley—emerged virtually simultaneously, and these three invented and defined the species of female band singers during those formative years.

Wiley, one of the first white singers to build on the stylistic advances made by Ethel Waters, developed a sophisticated, jazz-flavored approach to popular singing. Her cool-toned contralto voice, coupled with a sensuous, veiled voice, rendered strong men powerless: "I loved Lee Wiley," said critic Stanley Green, "even before I had any idea who she was, I loved her! She sang to me—just to me!" In 1939 Wiley made music history by becoming the first singer to devote an entire album to the music of one composer. Her Gershwin, Porter, Arlen, and Rodgers & Hart sessions are considered classic and the high points of her career.

According to early press reports, Wiley was born in 1915, the daughter of a Cherokee princess. Like Boswell and Bailey, she lied about her age and probably about her background. By 1930 she left Oklahoma for New York and soon began singing at the Central Park Casino with Leo Reisman's society orchestra. She also took part in broadcasts with Paul Whiteman, Willard Robison, and other leaders and was ultimately given her own program. During the 1930s she worked on the radio constantly, while also recording her own sides, backed by the Casa Loma Orchestra, the Dorsey Brothers, and Johnny Green. By mid-decade she began appearing in clubs with small jazz groups, including Eddie Condon's at the Famous Door (Condon's trumpeter, Bunny Berigan, became her lover).

Her career was affected by the threat of tuberculosis that kept her from singing for over a year, but by 1939 she began recording her great "songbook" projects (antedating Ella Fitzgerald's by more than fifteen years), utilizing the era's top hot jazz musicians, including Condon, Berigan, Pee Wee Russell, Joe Bushkin, Fats Waller, and Jess Stacy. In 1943 she married Stacy, but after five years both their big band and stormy partnership were history. She appeared at a few of Condon's Town Hall concerts during the 1940s and at an acclaimed performance with Bobby Hackett's band at the first Newport Jazz

---

8. Gottlieb, *Reading Jazz*, 960.

Festival in 1954. She produced several outstanding albums with Hackett, including *Night in Manhattan* in 1950. By the time she cut her masterpiece, *West of the Moon* (1956), audiences had come to favor newer, bebop-inflected vocal styles, and soon Wiley was forgotten to all but veteran record collectors, having made her mark decades earlier.

OCTOBER 10—THELONIOUS MONK (1917–1982)

b. Rocky Mount, NC; d. Weehawken, NJ

Pianist; Composer

[MODAL MUSIC; HARD BOP; POST-BOP; BOP]

Other jazz notables born on this day: Milt Larkin (1910); Harry "Sweets" Edison (1915); Roy Kral (19221); Ed Blackwell (1929)

Jazz notables deceased on this day: Oscar Alemán (1980); Carl Fontana (2003); Marion Brown (2010)

♪

Originality is much prized among jazz musicians, but it is not always appreciated by observers. Thelonious Monk, one of the most creative, suffered through a decade of neglect before suddenly being acclaimed as a genius. A leader of the "eccentric bop" movement, Monk was one of the most original of jazz improvisers. He played with flat, extended fingers, instead of in the accepted curved-finger position, and his percussive technique knew no bounds, leading him on occasion to strike the keys with his elbows. Despite these and other eccentricities (he wore funny hats and endured ridicule for his habit of dancing around the piano while his sidemen soloed), Monk did not seem to be affected by criticism. As his musical preferences became established, he began discarding melody and rhythm in favor of dissonance, unresolved tone clusters, and random pitches. While his most unorthodox work was probably "Brilliant Corners," compositions like "Evidence," "Misterioso," and particularly "Criss Cross" are considered his instrumental masterpieces. Some of his compositions, such as "Straight, No Chaser," and "'Round Midnight," became standards in the jazz world.

A self-taught pianist, in the early 1940s Monk became house pianist at Minton's Playhouse, a jazz supper club in Harlem where he and other jazz modernists helped formulate the emerging bop style. Monk, however, was never essentially a bop player. By the mid-1940s he was too individualistic a player to fit into any school. When the beboppers began to work and record regularly after 1945, they rarely chose Monk for their groups. It is not surprising that he had difficulty getting work, for by this time he was playing in an idiosyncratic style of which he was the only practitioner. His unusual technique and his use of space in his rhythmic solos led some people to believe that he was an inferior pianist; others assumed that he was crazy.

To make matters worse, in 1951 some narcotics were found in a car in which he and pianist Bud Powell were sitting. The narcotics belonged to Powell, but Monk would not inform on him. As a result, Monk's cabaret card was revoked, and for the next six years he was unable to work in clubs around New York City. He could, however, record; in

1956 he recorded the classic *Brilliant Corners*, a breakthrough album for him in terms of acceptance. In 1957 Monk's situation changed permanently as the result of a booking at the Five Spot, a bar that was becoming a fashionable venue for the presentation of avant-garde music. Monk assembled a quartet, using the relatively unknown John Coltrane on tenor saxophone, and the now-historic gig was the making of both men. From that time Monk became not merely an established figure in jazz, but one of its leading players.

OCTOBER 11—ART BLAKEY (1919–1990)

b.Pittsburgh, PA; d. New York, NY

Drummer; Bandleader

[HARD BOP]

Other jazz notables born on this day: Billy Higgins (1936); Lester Bowie (1941); Fred Hopkins (1947)

Jazz notables deceased on this day: Connee Boswell (1976); Johnny Costa (1996)

♪

Art Blakey, hard bop's longest-lived and most eloquent exponent, was a major figure in modern jazz for at least two reasons: as an important stylist on his instrument and as legendary leader of the Jazz Messengers. Blakey was a master teacher, and over the years the Messengers were a training ground for many great musicians. A list of the band's alumni over a thirty-year period is a who's who of straightahead jazz, and includes such notables as Clifford Brown, Freddie Hubbard, Hank Mobley, Wayne Shorter, Horace Silver, Keith Jarrett, and Wynton Marsalis. Blakey's pattern consisted in hiring relatively young but talented individualists, whose musical compositions became the basis for his repertory. At the time of his death, the Messengers' hard bop aesthetic dominated jazz, and Blakey himself had arguably become the most influential jazz musician of the past twenty years. Blakey's influence as bandleader would not have been nearly so great had he not been such a skilled instrumentalist. According to Chris Kelsey, "[n]o drummer ever drove a band harder, none could generate more sheer momentum in the course of a tune . . . and woe to the young saxophonist who couldn't keep up, for Blakey would run him over like a fullback."[9]

Starting out as a self-taught pianist, Blakey was playing professionally as a seventh grader, leading his own commercial band. He got married at the age of sixteen and was forced to seek work in the Pittsburgh steel mills to support his family. He switched to drums and began working in clubs at night. He received his big break in 1944, when he was asked to join the Billy Eckstine band. Eckstine had originally selected the drummer Shadow Wilson, but then Wilson was drafted into the service. The government had exempted Blakey from the draft on account of a silver plate in his head, the result of a beating by police. Eckstine's band, the famous "cradle of modern jazz," at that time included such pioneers of the forthcoming bebop revolution as Dizzy Gillespie and Charlie Parker.

For Blakey, performing jazz was like attending school, and it was during his time with Eckstine that he realized the need to create bands for young African-American

---

9. Bogdanov et al., *All Music Guide to Jazz*, 3rd edition, 104.

musicians, so that they could learn and grow as he had. He had put himself through every kind of experience and survived all kinds of trouble: he was so short—less than five feet—that one critic dismissed him early on as a "pygmy"; a Georgia policeman beat him so badly that he needed surgery on his skull; his first wife died; he adopted Islam; and he was an unabashed heroin addict.[10] But jazz kept him focused, upbeat, and vital, and that's the message he preached as he traveled the world for the next forty-five years. In the early 1950s Blakey began an association with Silver, a like-minded pianist, and in 1955 they formed a group called Horace Silver and the Jazz Messengers. A year later, when Silver left the band, Blakey became its leader. From then on school was in session, and Blakey was the headmaster.

OCTOBER 12—HARRY ALLEN (1966–)

b. Washington, DC

Tenor Saxophonist

[MAINSTREAM JAZZ]

Other jazz notables born on this day:
Jazz notables deceased on this day: Umberto Cesari (1992); Christian Schwindt (1992)

♪

Stan Getz was once asked for his idea of the perfect tenor saxophone soloist. He replied: "My technique, Al Cohn's ideas, and Zoot's time." Harry Allen may well be the embodiment of that ideal, for he swings hard, has great technique, and plays in a style that seems a hybrid between Zoot Sims and Getz. A revivalist in the tradition of Scott Hamilton and Ken Peplowski, Allen's work hearkens back to the pre-Coltrane age. His musical inspiration and interpretative approach come from the giants and innovators of mainstream saxophone, including Coleman Hawkins, Ben Webster, Getz, Illinois Jacquet, Lester Young, and particularly Paul Gonsalves, tenor soloist with Duke Ellington. Allen listened to Gonsalves and the Ellington band as far back as he can remember, for Allen's father, a drummer during the big band era, attended high school and played with Gonsalves.

Allen's jazz appreciation education began long before his formal schooling. His father, Maurice, played jazz records every day for Harry before the boy went off to kindergarten. Despite growing up during the rock era, the youngster became steeped in jazz and the standards before he even heard rock and roll. Allen spent his childhood in Los Angeles, starting with accordion lessons at the age of seven. When he was eleven his family moved to Rhode Island, where he took up clarinet and a year later tenor saxophone. A tenor player in Rhode Island recommended that he pick up a Scott Hamilton album, and he immediately knew what he wanted to sound like. From 1984 to 1988 Allen attended Rutgers University, studying saxophone with Sahib Shihab, Bob Mintzer, and John Purcell. He later admitted that he also attended Rutgers to be near Manhattan. His first

---

10. Ward and Burns, *Jazz: A History*, 397.

year at Rutgers was the last year of Eddie Condon's club, and that's where he went to hear such notables as Hamilton, Jacquet, Buddy Tate, and Al Klink.

While at Rutgers Allen got his first gig with the help of master bass player Major Holley, replacing Sims at a studio recording with Bucky Pizzarelli, Ruby Braff, and other likeminded players. Holley also led Allen to Oliver Jackson, whom Allen subsequently accompanied on several tours to Europe. Since 1989, when he graduated from Rutgers with a degree in jazz tenor saxophone, Allen has performed regularly with Bucky Pizzarelli and recorded frequently with Bucky's son, John, in addition to such artists as Kenny Barron, John Colliani, Warren Vaché, Jeff Hamilton, Rosemary Clooney, Flip Phillips, Scott Hamilton, and British pianist Keith Ingham. Allen's recordings have won many awards, particularly in Japan, where he has a large following. He continues to record extensively and makes frequent appearances at jazz festivals and concerts. Unlike many of his contemporaries, Allen has largely bypassed the modern, avant-garde, and impressionistic schools of jazz, choosing instead to follow in the footsteps of so many distinguished mainstream mentors.

OCTOBER 13—ART TATUM (1910–1956)

b. Toledo, OH; d. Los Angeles, CA

Pianist

[SWING]

Other jazz notables born on this day: Ray Brown (1926); Lee Konitz (1927); Johnny Lytle (1932); Pharoah Sanders (1940)
Jazz notables deceased on this day: Joe Sullivan (1971)

♪

Between December 1953 and January 1955 Art Tatum, one of the most admired pianists in jazz history, recorded over one hundred solos during four marathon sessions. The recordings were fortuitous, for by the time they were made, Tatum was seriously ill. In two years' time, he would be dead. Though not a bebopper, Tatum provided much of the harmonic foundation on which that music was based. His style was so impressive technically that he left other pianists in utter amazement. He could perform double runs and complex arpeggios at speeds no one else in jazz could approach, and do so with ease and elegance. At a 1949 concert he played "I Know That You Know" at the astonishing metronome speed of 450, meaning that at times he was playing at a rate of a thousand notes a minute.[11] What makes Tatum's piano technique doubly remarkable is that he was legally blind, having been born with cataracts on both eyes.

There has been no more complete master of the instrument, and to no other pianist does the cliché "a legend in his own time" apply more readily. Despite impaired vision, Tatum seemed to play everything twice as fast as his peers, while increasing the level of swing and harmonic variety. His influence on other pianists was profound, if not devastating. Friends delighted in taking him to cabarets and those after-hours clubs where players

---

11. Collier, *Making of Jazz*, 381.

jammed, hoping to spring him on unsuspecting musicians. Some became so nervous at his appearance that they fumbled at their specialties. Others simply refused to play in his presence. The story is told about Fats Waller who, upon discovering that Tatum was in the club where he was playing, stood up at the piano and announced, "I play piano, but God is in the house tonight." Jazz pianists idolized him, as did classical virtuosos such as Vladimir Horowitz and Walter Gieseking, who were known to go to the Onyx Club on Fifty-Second Street to marvel at his phenomenal skills.

Tatum had a superb memory for melody and an infallible sense of pitch—he rarely had to hear a tune more than once to play it back with embellishments, and an ear for pitch so uncanny he could tell the denomination of a coin dropped on a table by the sound it made—and picked up many of his ideas from piano rolls, radio broadcasts, recordings, and groups he heard in Toledo and Cleveland. One of his neighbors, the singer Jon Hendricks, claims he even mastered one lightning-fast duet, not knowing it had taken four hands to record the original. In 1932 he traveled with singer Adelaide Hall to New York, but stayed on as a soloist. According to one legend, he was challenged by the three most respected pianists in New York—James P. Johnson, Willie "The Lion" Smith, and Waller—and outplayed each in turn. From then on he was generally acknowledged as the most accomplished of all jazz pianists. "The first time I heard Art Tatum I thought I was listening to four guys," the pianist Jimmy Rowles admitted. "He was simply unbelievable."

OCTOBER 14—KAZUMI WATANABE (1953–)

b. Tokyo, Japan

Guitarist; Leader

[FUSION]

Other jazz notables born on this day: Dusko Goykovich (1931)
Jazz notables deceased on this day: Alphonso Trent (1959); Bing Crosby (1977)

♪

Though jazz originated in America and soon gained a loyal following in Europe, it eventually reached its greatest international success in Japan. Prior to the 1950s jazz was little known in Japan, and during World War II, it was banned. After the war, radio programs of the Far East Network, intended for the American occupation forces, aired the latest popular music to Japanese citizens, and jazz soon attracted a following. In 1953, visits by American jazz musicians, including Norman Granz's Jazz at the Philharmonic (JATP) show and Louis Armstrong's All Stars, created quite a stir. These visits became landmark events for Japanese jazz, and consequently George Kawaguchi formed the Big Four, modeled after saxophonist Charlie Ventura's Big Four. In 1954 the band's members were individually named Number One on their respective instruments in the *Swing Journal* (Japan's leading jazz magazine, first issued in 1947) readers' poll. The group was short-lived, but its presence created a jazz boom in Japan. In 1964 Japan held its first international jazz festival, attracting such stars as Miles Davis, and by 1978 some sixty American bands visited

Japan annually. In addition, vast numbers of American jazz records—many of which were unavailable in the U.S.—were released in Japan.

In the 1950s two creative Japanese pianists—Shotaro Moriyasu and Toshiko Akiyoshi—emerged to lead the embryonic bebop movement. With his superb skills and rich knowledge of music, Moriyasu had a great impact on the younger generation, but tragically, he committed suicide in 1955 by jumping in front of a train. Akiyoshi, Japan's "First Woman in Jazz," formed her own band in 1953 (with the gifted alto saxophonist Sadao Watanabe among her sidemen), and shortly thereafter was "discovered" by Oscar Peterson, who was in Japan with JATP. Peterson helped her set up a recording session with members of his rhythm section and encouraged her to emigrate. Three years later she enrolled at the Berklee School of Music in Boston, and became the first Japanese musician to have a significant career in America.

In the 1970s and '80s many fusion groups were formed in Japan, as in other countries, which featured synthesizers and electric bass. Sadao Watanabe and trumpeter Terumasa Hino did so and reached large markets. Other popular groups in this field were Native Son, led by tenor saxophonist Kousuke Mine; T-Square, which is still popular; and two bands—Kylyn Band (1970s) and the Mobo Club Band (1980s)—led by rock-oriented Kazumi Watanabe, arguably Japan's premiere guitarist.

Kazumi became interested in jazz at an early age and was a recording artist while still a teenager. In 1979 he formed Kylyn and in 1983 the Mobo band, which toured the U.S. and Europe and performed often in New York. Chosen "Best Jazzman" twenty-four years in a row in *Swing Journal*'s annual poll, Kazumi ranks with Al Di Meola and Scott Henderson among the pacesetters in jazz-fusion.[12] Japan currently boasts many gifted young jazz artists in Japan; only time will tell whether they will rival or even surpass the pioneering Akiyoshi, Hino, or Watanabe.

OCTOBER 15—BILL CHARLAP (1966-)

b. New York, NY

Pianist

[HARD BOP; POST-BOP; BOP]

Other jazz notables born on this day: Al Killian (1916); Freddy Cole (1931); Palle Danielsson (1946)

Jazz notables deceased on this day: Lee Blair (1966)

♪

One of the most talented, lyrically-blessed jazz pianists around, and among the most gifted interpreters of standards, pianist Bill Charlap is able to reconstruct songs with a deft touch and a sensibility that far exceeds his age and life experience. Charlap is unique among contemporary jazz players in that Richard Rodgers and Harold Arlen are as significant to him as Charlie Parker and Thelonious Monk. Insisting that the melody and lyrics of a song are just as important as improvisation, Charlap's approach to melody makes

---

12. Bogdanov et al., *All Music Guide to Jazz*, 1305.

American popular songs sound fresh and new, and when he improvises, he's endlessly inventive, in terms of coming up with original melodic lines.

Charlap grew up in a musical household, the son of Broadway songwriter "Moose" Charlap and vocalist Sandy Stewart (a well-known popular singer in the 1960s who toured, notably, with Benny Goodman) and a nephew of Dick Hyman. He began piano at an early age, and then studied at New York's High School of Performing Arts, a public school that taught talented, racially diverse students from across the city. "That kind of cultural diversity," he argues, is "the best thing that could possibly happen to a child in New York City." He enrolled at SUNY–Purchase, but dropped out of college after two years to practice and gig on his own. He moved back to New York City and rented an inexpensive apartment, then a piano. Constructing a foam-filled platform, he placed acoustical tiles on the walls (so his playing wouldn't disturb the neighbors) and began practicing—all day, every day, for a year.

In the late 1980s Bill Mays recommended the young man as his replacement in the Gerry Mulligan Quartet, where he remained for two years. During that time Charlap worked with Benny Carter, Clark Terry, Frank Wess, and others while accompanying singers such as Tony Bennett, Carol Sloane, and Sheila Jordan. In 1995 he secured the coveted piano chair with the Phil Woods Quintet. Since then Charlap has appeared at many of the world's major jazz festivals, touring and performing globally.

His current trio with bassist Peter Washington and drummer Kenny Washington (no relation) made its first release in 1997 with the highly acclaimed album, *All Through the Night*. The group had immediate rapport, creating an aesthetic based on admiration for the trios formed in the 1950s and '60s by pianists Oscar Peterson, Bill Evans, and most importantly, Ahmad Jamal. Building on ideas about the purity they like to hear in music, Charlap, Kenny, and Peter Washington embrace a common understanding and deep feeling about their type of playing. "I think we bring that knowledge to what we like to do without really talking about it," Charlap told Don Williamson in an interview for *Jazz Review*. "Our deepest conversations about music happen when we're *playing* music." With his elegant lyric sensibility and use of classic harmonies, Bill Charlap manages to suggest something at once timeless yet modern in his approach to jazz piano and small-group playing.

OCTOBER 16—ROY HARGROVE (1969–)

b. Waco, TX

Trumpeter; Flugelhorn Player; Leader

[Hard Bop]

Other jazz notables born on this day: Lenny Hambro (1923); Tim Berne (1954)
Jazz notables deceased on this day: Gene Krupa (1973); Art Blakey (1990); Etta Jones (2001)

♪

Greeted with considerable acclaim when he burst upon the scene in the late 1980s, Hargrove established himself in the following decade as one of the premiere trumpeters in jazz. A fine straightahead player known for the purity and brilliance of his tone, Hargrove's fiery solos resulted in him winning the *Down Beat* Readers' Poll in 1995. Although known as an aggressive, brilliant player on up-tempo material, his forte is the slow-burning ballad, so his work behind singers is particularly memorable. He has been in demand as a guest on dozens of discs, from legends such as Oscar Peterson and Shirley Horn to his own contemporaries. In addition to fronting quartets, quintets, and nonets, he also founded the exciting eleven-piece Cuban-American big band Crisol and toured in a trumpet summit with Wynton Marsalis, Nicholas Payton, and Jon Faddis. In 1996 he traveled to Cuba, where he recruited some of the island's finest players (including piano legend Chucho Valdés) and recorded the Grammy-winning *Habana*.

Inspired by the gospel music he heard in church and the R&B and funk music that played on the radio, Hargrove became devoted to jazz while in junior high school, when he heard David "Fathead" Newman perform at his school. From then on all he wanted to do was improvise like him. In his freshman year, while studying music at Dallas' prestigious Booker T. Washington School for the Visual and Performing Arts, he was discovered by Wynton Marsalis, who was conducting a jazz clinic at the school. With the help of Marsalis, Hargrove was soon performing with major players including Bobby Watson, Ricky Ford, Carl Allen, and in the group Superblue. Hargrove attended Berklee College of Music for a year (1988–89) and in 1990 released his first recording, *Diamond in the Rough*.

He has toured ever since with his own group, which for several years included a college colleague, altoist Antonio Hart. In his 1994 debut album with Verve, the critically acclaimed *With the Tenors of Our Time*, Hargrove shared separate songs with five great saxophonists: Joe Henderson, Stanley Turrentine, Johnny Griffin, Joshua Redman, and Branford Marsalis. Stylistically, every album he has released since then has been different from the preceding one. Most recently, he has ventured into the black pop mainstream, particularly with his 2003 release, *The RH Factor: Hard Groove*. Like a twenty-first century Quincy Jones, Hargrove has brought together a diverse array of musicians to create what has been called "an organic musical street party at the corner of hip-hop and bop," encompassing many of his musical passions. *Hard Groove* represents Hargrove's desire to move the music forward.

OCTOBER 17—COZY COLE (1909–1981)

b. East Orange, NJ; d. Columbus, OH

Drummer

[SWING]

Other jazz notables born on this day: Jimmy Harrison (1900); Lee Collins (1901); Barney Kessel (1923); Howard Alden (1958)

Jazz notables deceased on this day: Louis Cottrell Sr. (1927); Alberta Hunter (1984)

BLUE NOTES

♪

A popular performer throughout much of his career, Cozy Cole was one of the classic drummers, in the class of Sid Catlett and Zutty Singleton. Born into a musical family, Cole played drums from childhood and idolized Sonny Greer, Duke Ellington's colorful drummer, who was then performing locally. As a teenage football player he acquired the nickname Cozy, an abridgement of Colesy. He held conventional daytime jobs and performed as a tap dancer before beginning his professional career. He moved to New York in 1926, working as a barber and shipping clerk while taking lessons with Charlie Brooks, the pit drummer at the Lincoln Theater. In the late 1920s he led his own group, and in 1930 he recorded with Jelly Roll Morton, who featured the drummer on a track titled "Load of Cole."

By the early 1930s he began building a reputation with bands led by Blanche Calloway, Benny Carter, and Willie Bryant, and from 1936 he worked with Stuff Smith and Jonah Jones at the Onyx Club, the musician's hangout on Fifty-Second Street, gaining a wide range of experience that served as the basis of his later versatility. Cole also recorded dozens of titles with all-star swing groups accompanying Billie Holiday between 1935 and 1939; during this period he figured prominently on numerous recordings led by Henry "Red" Allen and Lionel Hampton. Cole achieved fame during his years with Cab Calloway's orchestra (1938–42), playing in a strong rhythm section with Bennie Payne, Danny Barker, and Milt Hinton and recording solos that feature technical aspects of drumming as well as his imaginative use of kicks, fills, and breaks; many of these routines were featured in his 1941 text, *Modern Orchestra Drum Technique*.

Even as a professional, Cole rarely missed an opportunity to study. In the 1940s he studied at the Juilliard School while working as a percussionist in studio and theater ensembles. He also led his own band at the Onyx and made important small-group recordings as a freelance. His band, which included Don Byas, the two Billy Taylors, and Tiny Grimes, replaced Benny Goodman's sextet in the show *The Seven Lively Arts* (1945), and the following year he played briefly with Goodman. When Catlett became ill in 1949, Cole replaced him and toured as a member of Louis Armstrong's All Stars for three years. During the 1950s Cole appeared in several films, played in studios, and established a drum school in New York in partnership with Gene Krupa (1954–60). In 1957 he toured Europe with Jack Teagarden and Earl Hines, and the following year he achieved great success with his recording of "Topsy." Throughout much of the 1960s he toured with his own band, and in 1969 he joined a quintet led by trumpeter Jonah Jones, his former colleague at the Onyx and in Calloway's band. During the last decade of his life he continued to work as a freelance; he played for a 1973 Calloway reunion at the Newport jazz festival and in 1976 toured Europe with another classic swing musician, alto saxophonist Benny Carter.

OCTOBER 18—WYNTON MARSALIS (1961–)

b. New Orleans, LA

Trumpeter; Leader; Composer

[CONTEMPORARY JAZZ; NEW ORLEANS JAZZ; POST-BOP; NEO-BOP; SWING; CLASSICAL]

Other jazz notables born on this day: Chris Kelly (1885, 1890, or 1891); Bobby Troup (1918); Anita O'Day (1919)
Jazz notables deceased on this day: Julie London (2000)

♪

The most famous jazz musician to emerge during the past twenty-five years, Wynton Marsalis made a major impact on jazz almost from the start. In 1984, when he was only twenty-two, he was already a superstar.[13] That year he became the first musician to win Grammy awards for both a jazz recording and a classical recording. A brilliant trumpet player, composer, and improviser, Marsalis is also a highly literate and tireless proselytizer for jazz, having spent a considerable amount of time and energy speaking in schools and conducting master classes. This resulted in a brilliant series of four films made for public television, *Marsalis on Music*, in which he explains and demonstrates the similarities and differences between jazz and European classical music. The series has been compared to Leonard Bernstein's highly successful Young People's Concerts. Marsalis's role as a communicator, as well as his musical abilities, was probably a major consideration when he was made Artistic Director of Jazz at New York's Lincoln Center in 1992.[14] At the age of thirty-five Marsalis won the Pulitzer Prize for his marathon oratorio *Blood on the Fields*, a three-hour musical depiction of slavery, becoming the first jazz composer ever to receive this distinguished award.

The son of pianist Ellis Marsalis—a New Orleans jazz pianist who is much respected by the jazz community—and one of four musical brothers, Wynton received his first trumpet at age six from Ellis's employer, trumpeter Al Hirt. He studied both classical music and jazz and played in local marching bands, funk groups, and classical orchestras. He attended Juilliard when he was eighteen and a year later joined Art Blakey's Jazz Messengers. By 1981 he was the talk of the jazz world. That year he toured in a quartet with Herbie Hancock, Ron Carter, and Tony Williams, continued working with Blakey, and recorded his first album as leader with Columbia.

In 1982 he formed his own quintet, featuring his brother Branford on saxophone, and also recorded his first classical album, with conductor Raymond Leppard in London. The award-winning recording immediately ranked him as one of the top classical trumpeters of all time. His quintet with Branford lasted until 1985, and a temporary rift developed between the brothers when Branford quit the band to tour with the pop group Sting. By that time Wynton had won countless awards and polls, including *Down Beat*'s "Best

---

13. Bogdanov et al., *All Music Guide to Jazz*, 808.
14. Carr et al., *Jazz: The Rough Guide*, 491.

Trumpeter" and "Jazz Musician of the Year." In 1985 Marsalis reacquainted himself with the earliest roots of jazz—the whole blues tradition, gospel, work songs, and particularly the early work of Louis Armstrong and the music of Duke Ellington. With the passing of so many jazz giants during the past decade, Marsalis's presence (as trumpeter, leader, writer, and spokesman for jazz) gives jazz a promising future.

OCTOBER 19—EDDIE DANIELS (1941–)
b. New York, NY

Clarinetist; Tenor Saxophonist

[HARD BOP]

Other jazz notables born on this day: Alphonse Picou (1878)
Jazz notables deceased on this day: Isham Jones (1956); Don Cherry (1995)

♪

Like Don Byron, his counterpart in more avant-garde jazz circles, Daniels is widely credited with helping to bring the clarinet into jazz prominence. A strong tenor saxophonist and one of the truly great jazz clarinetists (ranking with Benny Goodman, Artie Shaw, and Buddy DeFranco), Daniels is a virtuoso in both jazz and classical music, as demonstrated in his 1985 release, *Breakthrough*, a masterful recording with the Philharmonia Orchestra of London. Winning praise for his revolutionary blend of jazz and classical music, Daniels's overriding ambition is to enlarge the audience for both forms of music and at the same time to minimize the walls separating them.

Raised in the Brighton Beach neighborhood of Brooklyn, Daniels's interest in jazz began when as a teenager he listened to the records of Frank Sinatra and became intrigued with the singer's backing musicians, particularly their solo work. Daniels began on saxophone, having received his father's old alto, and when he was sixteen he performed in Marshall Brown's Youth Band at the Newport Jazz Festival. But he was also a talent on clarinet, and after graduating from Brooklyn College, he attained a master's degree in clarinet from Juilliard (1966).

Daniels first came to the attention of the jazz world as a tenor saxophonist with the Thad Jones/Mel Lewis Orchestra. When Thad and Mel first organized their band in 1966 to play Monday nights at the Village Vanguard, Daniels was one of the first musicians they called. Later that year he entered the International Jazz Competition in Vienna, where he won first prize as a saxophonist and made his debut recording as a leader. He continued working with the influential Jones/Lewis band for six years and toured Europe extensively with them. His clarinet solo work on the orchestra's recording, *Live at the Village Vanguard* (1967), merited sufficient attention that he won *Down Beat*'s "New Star on Clarinet" award.

Although he subsequently recorded on saxophone, Daniels did not make it big until he started specializing on clarinet in 1984. Jack Elliot, musical director of the New American Orchestra, became so impressed with Daniels's playing that he commissioned

Jorge Calandrelli to compose a major work for him. The result was "Concerto for Jazz Clarinet and Orchestra," which Daniels premiered in Los Angeles in 1984. This work became the centerpiece for his album *Breakthrough*, which Quincy Jones described as "the benchmark to judge all future recordings blending the world of classical music and jazz." At this point in his career Daniels sold his saxophones and focused solely on clarinet. After recording a tribute to Charlie Parker (*To Bird with Love*, 1987), he began collaborating with vibist Gary Burton. Their album, *Benny Rides Again* (1992), devoted to the music of Benny Goodman and Lionel Hampton, was greeted with overwhelming acclaim. The duo toured widely, playing at festivals and concerts around the world. In 1992, with his reputation on clarinet now secure, Daniels began doubling on tenor again.

OCTOBER 20—JELLY ROLL MORTON (1890–1941)

b. New Orleans, LA; d. Los Angeles, CA

Composer; Pianist

[NEW ORLEANS JAZZ; CLASSIC JAZZ]

Other jazz notables born on this day: Adelaide Hall (1901?); Carl Kress (1907); Ray Linn (1920); Eddie Harris (1934); Martin Taylor (1956)

Jazz notables deceased on this day: Budd Johnson (1984); Shirley Horn (2005)

♪

Hustler, poolshark, pimp, and bon vivant, Jelly Roll Morton was one of jazz's most legendary figures. He was proud, vain, and arrogant, boasting that he had personally invented jazz in 1902. A light-skinned Creole, he attempted to live out his life as a white man. Had he grown up with a more accepting view of himself, or been raised in a society where racial lines were less firm, he might have achieved a social position equal to his talents. But he could do neither, and as his life progressed, he increasingly fell under the sway of megalomania. By the age of fifteen, he found work in some of the high-class bordellos of Storyville. Pay was nominal, and the pianists were expected to live on tips. It helped to be on good terms with the prostitutes, who might suggest to the customer that he leave a sizable tip. From there it was a short step to pimping. During this time Jelly broke with his family. Jelly's mother had died, his father had abandoned him, and when his grandmother found out he was working as a "piano professor" in a whorehouse, she threw him out. Barely a teenager, Jelly Roll was on his own.

Though jobs for musicians were plentiful in New Orleans, by 1904 the pool-hustling ladies' man was roaming across the South. He traveled widely during his lifetime, playing in New York, and then Chicago, and from 1917 to 1922 in Los Angeles, where he also ran a club/hotel/brothel with a woman friend. By 1923 he relocated to Chicago, where for the next six years he was at his musical peak, primarily with a combo he called the Red Hot Peppers. Morton took classic small-band jazz to its artistic limits with this group, particularly in its sessions of 1926, acknowledged as his greatest.

In 1928, when the center of jazz had shifted to New York, Morton relocated once again. By this time he was publishing his songs and arrangements and making recordings as a soloist and with the different bands that he led. These records made Jelly one of the leading figures in jazz of his time, bringing him the respect and attention he had always considered his due. He began to buy Cadillacs and diamonds (hustlers of this time invested in diamonds, which were portable and easy to turn into cash, and occasionally had them set into their teeth). Following the practice, Jelly had a diamond set into one of his teeth.

In addition to being one of the first jazz pianists, Morton is often considered the first true jazz composer. During his travels he composed music that fused a variety of black musical idioms (including ragtime, blues, and spirituals) with Caribbean and white popular songs, thereby creating a style of music that began to be called "jazz." Compositions like "Grandpa's Spell" and "The Pearls" are masterpieces of his creative talent. Others, such as "King Porter Stomp," arranged by Fletcher Henderson and performed by Benny Goodman's band, are credited with ushering in the swing era.

OCTOBER 21—DIZZY GILLESPIE (1917–1993)

b. Cheraw, SC; d. Englewood, NJ

Trumpeter; Bandleader; Composer

[AFRO-CUBAN JAZZ; JUMP BLUES; BOP]

Other jazz notables born on this day: Don Byas (1912); Fred Hersch (1955)
Jazz notables deceased on this day: Dick Twardzik (1955)

♪

In the demanding world of jazz, nicknames are not easily gained; they must be earned. Genius could be acknowledged through exalted titles—King, Duke, Pres—by the simple use of proper names—Louis, Miles, Bix—or in rare cases, through epithets of uncertain origin, as in the case of Bird and Diz, two figures who dominated American popular music between 1945 and 1950. A natural comedian, Dizzy Gillespie differed from many in the bop generation by making his music seem both accessible and fun to the audience. With his puffed-out cheeks, his trademark bent trumpet (a personal design he claimed was the result of an accident in the early 1950s when a dancer tripped over his horn), his superb scat singing, and quick wit, Dizzy was a masterful showman. Like Louis Armstrong, he was accused by jazz purists of demeaning himself by his brand of humor, but humor and clowning were the natural result of his personality as well as a way of coping with an unsympathetic and sometimes hostile environment.

Gillespie's antic humor seems to have been part of his life from the beginning. His dizziness helped him survive, whether as a child coping with an abusive father or as a young man growing up in a demeaning racial environment. The youngest of nine children, Gillespie grew up in poverty in South Carolina. Inspired initially by trumpeter Roy Eldridge, Gillespie dropped out of school to become a musician. By 1939 he was a star in Cab Calloway's Orchestra, one of the highest paid black bands in New York at the time, and already his style showed some of the elements of bebop. Calloway used Dizzy as a featured instrumentalist with his big band, but regularly criticized him for some of the modern sounds he created as a soloist. In 1941 Calloway fired him over an incident that started with spitballs and ended with a backstage altercation, during which Calloway was knifed in the thigh. From then on, Dizzy followed his own inclination, leading small combos and then a series of big bands.

During the 1940s Gillespie significantly changed the face of jazz in three ways: by creating a totally original trumpet style (the trumpet had never before been played with such speed, flexibility, and drama), by helping establish bebop as the contemporary style for both small groups and big bands, and finally, by changing the way jazz musicians cooperate with one another.[15] Whereas previous generations of musicians were reluctant to share their knowledge and skills with younger players, Gillespie was an enthusiastic teacher who wrote down his musical innovations and eagerly explained them to others. For all the displays of good humor that earned him friends around the world, nobody was ever more serious about his music, when he wanted or needed to be, than this man who turned the world of jazz around. By 1993, when he died from pancreatic cancer, Dizzy, the Clown Prince of Jazz, was very much the elder statesman of jazz.

OCTOBER 22—GIORGIO GASLINI (1929–)

b. Milan, Italy

Pianist; Composer

[MODERN CREATIVE]

Other jazz notables born on this day: Clare Fischer (1928); Urszula Dudziak (1943); Jane Bunnett (1955)

Jazz notables deceased on this day: Nate Kazebier (1969); Harry Goodman (1997)

♫

Of all the European jazz scenes, the Italian may be the richest in as-yet-untapped potential, not only because of its own vast artistic heritage, but because it stands at the crossroads of so many cultures that possess their own rhythmic and melodic traditions. While Italy is known for its opera, that nation has produced more than its share of good jazz musicians, ready to perform with visiting American soloists. Chet Baker recorded with many of them, as did Don Cherry, while pursuing his gypsy life style in Europe. And Italy has no shortage of lyrical horn players, as demonstrated by Enrico Rava, the hugely popular trumpeter who "almost single-handedly brought Italian jazz to international attention."[16] Still, in terms of developing a national jazz identity, Italy lags behind Western Europe. The reason is not a lack of ambition but more a lack of national organization. During the course of his career, one musician, the consummate pianist and composer Giorgio

---

15. Carr et al., *Jazz: The Rough Guide*, 279–80.
16. Bogdanov et al., *All Music Guide to Jazz*, 1053.

Gaslini, became the catalyst for the cause of jazz in Italy, experimenting with just about every form of jazz there was to try, including bop, cool, and free jazz.

Gaslini began studying piano at seven and gave his first public performances at thirteen. He led his own orchestra before forming a trio at sixteen. He made his recording debut with the trio and appeared at the International Jazz Festival in Florence in 1948 with a large group. Gaslini then studied piano, conducting, and composition at the Conservatorio in Milan, and in the late 1950s and early '60s he directed various symphony orchestras while composing film scores and leading his own quartet. At that time he began taking his music to the people, playing with his quartet in schools, universities, factories, mental hospitals, cinemas, and concert halls, in an attempt to make jazz part of the fabric of Italian life. He also performed in the most important Italian jazz festivals and collaborated with such great soloists as Cherry, Gato Barbieri, Steve Lacy, Anthony Braxton, Jean-Luc Ponty, and Roswell Rudd. As a leader he helped develop young players, bringing them into his groups and encouraging their growth.

His first jazz opera, *Colloquio con Malcom X*, was performed in 1970 and recorded in Milan (1973–74). He also taught jazz courses in Rome (1972–73) and Milan (1979–80), bringing the subject into the conservatory for the first time in Italy. From 1976 to the present Gaslini has performed in every continent. In 1975 he was the first Italian officially invited to an American jazz festival (New Orleans), and during the early 1980s he also became the first Italian jazz musician invited to India (1982) and China (1985). In 1996 he composed and directed *Mister O*, the first "jazz melodrama" in the history of music. He has also written several books, one of which, *Technique and Art of Jazz* (1982), has become a fundamental text. All of this jazz activity makes one wonder why Gaslini stopped considering himself a jazz musician after the 1960s.

OCTOBER 23—DIANNE REEVES (1956–)

b. Detroit, MI

Vocalist

[Vocal Jazz; Traditional Pop; Standards; Vocal Pop; Urban]

Other jazz notables born on this day: Sonny Criss (1927); Gary McFarland (1933)
Jazz notables deceased on this day: Charlie Creath (1951); Johnny Williams (1998)

♪

Blessed with a rich, attractive voice and the ability to be the premier jazz singer of the 2000s, Dianne Reeves has long seemed unable to decide between jazz, R&B, world music, and pop. When she decides to sing jazz, she demonstrates the ability to reach the top, but so far she seems more comfortable in pop settings than in jazz. Her recordings, rarely reaching the heights of her exciting live performances, show an eclectic mix of folk, popular, soul, smooth jazz, and jazz styles, often on the same album.[17]

---

17. Kernfeld, *New Grove Dictionary of Jazz*, Vol. 3, 390.

Reared in a musical family—her father was a singer and her mother played trumpet—Dianne grew up in Denver, where her uncle, a classical double bass player, helped to shape her musical development. In 1973, while she was performing with her high school band at the National Association of Jazz Educators' convention in Chicago, Clark Terry discovered her. She then sang occasionally with Terry's groups, performing with him while a student at the University of Denver. In 1976, after a year of college, she moved to Los Angeles, where as a studio singer she recorded with Lenny White, Stanley Turrentine, and as a member of the fusion group Caldera. In 1980 she founded, with keyboardist Billy Childs, the fusion group Night Flight. Thereafter she participated in a heady schedule, touring worldwide with the Brazilian pop musician Sergio Mendes (1981–83) before moving to New York, where she worked and toured with Harry Belafonte (1983–86).

She started recording as a solo artist in 1982 and soon became a familiar name on the festival circuit. From 1989 she toured with the Philip Morris Superband and made several appearances with Quincy Jones at the Montreux Jazz Festival. Reeves continued to collaborate with Childs through the 1990s and led her own groups. She moved to Denver in 1992, though she remained involved in the Los Angeles area. After shifting back and forth between jazz, pop, and African music, in 1994 Reeves began to commit herself more to jazz, recording the first of several strong jazz sets for Blue Note.

Reeves enjoyed a banner year in 2002. That year her tribute recording, *The Calling: Celebrating Sarah Vaughan*, won the Grammy Award for "best jazz vocal album"; she performed at the closing ceremony of the Olympic Winter Games in Salt Lake City; she sang on the season finale of HBO's hit series *Sex and the City*; she received the Ella Fitzgerald Award at the Montreal International Jazz Festival; she was appointed the Creative Chair for Jazz of the Los Angeles Philharmonic (for which she oversees the scheduling of jazz programming at both the Hollywood Bowl and the Walt Disney Concert Hall); and she released a career-spanning compilation CD, *The Best of Dianne Reeves*. With an emotional voice that commands one's attention without needing to overpower, Reeves "has the voice and soul of a true jazz diva."[18]

OCTOBER 24—WENDELL MARSHALL (1920–2002)

b. St. Louis, MO; d. St. Louis, MO

Bassist

[SWING]

Other jazz notables born on this day: Dan Morgenstern (1929); Odean Pope (1938); Anthony Cox (1954); Rick Margitza (1961)
Jazz notables deceased on this day: Sahib Shihab (1989); Jeanne Lee (2000)

♫

During the late 1940s, following World War II, most of the big bands found they were unable to survive. In December 1948, a date that usually marks the end of the swing

---

18. Bogdanov et al., *All Music Guide to Jazz*, 1059.

era, eight of the biggest swing bands, including those of Benny Goodman, Harry James, Tommy Dorsey, Jack Teagarden, and Benny Carter, broke up. The following year even Louis Armstrong gave up on his band, moving to the smaller All Stars lineup he used for the rest of his career. By the 1950s the time of the big bands on the center stage of American popular music was over.

There were exceptions, of course, most notably Duke Ellington, whose orchestra continued to play concert and dance dates while maintaining a swinging style. In 1950 *Down Beat* presented Ellington with a special award simply for being in business. But he was struggling financially, paying many of his bills with royalties from his songs. And his orchestra no longer sounded quite the same. Drummer Sonny Greer had left, and two of the most familiar Ellington "voices," Lawrence Brown and Johnny Hodges, also went out on their own for a time. By the summer of 1955 Ellington's band had sunk to an all-time low, accompanying ice skaters at a Long Island rink. He regained his preeminence the following summer, however, at the Newport Jazz Festival, when his orchestra became a sensation after five difficult years. Ellington's orchestra during that lean period (1948–55) included Wendell Marshall, a supportive performer whose strong technique and opulent tone made him one of the finest double bass players of the 1950s. Marshall never recorded a session of his own, but some of his best solo work may be heard on the album *A Keyboard History*, recorded with pianist Mary Lou Williams in 1955.

Inspired to play bass by his cousin Jimmy Blanton, who revolutionized bass playing during his tragically brief career with Ellington (1939–42) Wendell received his first lessons from Blanton and also inherited his instrument upon the latter's premature death. After attending Lincoln University and serving in the army (1943–46), Marshall played briefly in the St. Louis area, making his first recording with violinist Stuff Smith. In 1948 he moved to New York and joined Mercer Ellington, but soon was welcomed into Ellington's band, where he helped re-establish the Blanton mystique. From 1955 he worked as a freelance, recording that year with Williams, Clark Terry, Carmen McRae, Eddie Heywood, Hank Jones, Louie Bellson, Billy Byers, and Lawrence Brown. As house bass player for Prestige from 1956 to 1963 he recorded with many notables, including Coleman Hawkins, Herbie Mann, and Pee Wee Russell. He also recorded for other labels with Art Blakey, Hodges, Mercer Ellington, Tal Farlow, and Rahsaan Roland Kirk. Sadly, he left jazz to specialize in Broadway stage work, playing in pit bands until his early retirement in 1968.

OCTOBER 25—EDDIE LANG (1902–1933)

b. Philadelphia, PA; d. New York, NY

Guitarist

[Classic Jazz]

Other jazz notables born on this day: Jimmy Heath (1926); Terumasa Hino (1942); Robin Eubanks (1955)

Jazz notables deceased on this day: Willis "Gator" Jackson; Major Holley (1990)

The importance of Eddie Lang, the founder of the jazz guitar tradition, is incalculable, "and everybody who plays guitar in popular music today owes something to him."[19] Inventor of the solo vocabulary for the guitar, Lang was highly regarded for his single-string solos and his accompaniments. As the most in-demand guitarist from 1923 to 1933, he appeared in a multitude of settings during that period. Lang's partnership with violinist Joe Venuti set the standard for chamber jazz and their recordings were highly influential in Europe, where they directly influenced the Quintet of the Hot Club of France, led by Django Reinhardt and Stéphane Grappelli. It was Lang and Reinhardt who determined the way the guitar would be played in jazz.

Born Salvatore Massaro, Lang took violin lessons for eleven years and learned guitar from his father, a guitarist and instrument maker. He switched to banjo in late adolescence and then to guitar before he turned professional. With Venuti, a boyhood friend, he established a long-lasting musical partnership. They worked as a unit, sometimes independently, sometimes under such leaders as Jean Goldkette, Roger Wolfe Kahn, and Paul Whiteman. Between 1926 and 1930 practically every important band used them on one occasion or another. During his short professional career, Lang also operated as a freelance in the New York City area. He was quickly recognized as the leading professional guitarist in America and recorded extensively. He made a number of records with Bix Beiderbecke and Frankie Trumbauer, including the classics "Singin' the Blues" and "I'm Comin' Virginia."

In that age of racial segregation, Lang helped blur the prevailing racial lines by participating in several "mixed" recording dates. On March 5, 1929, Louis Armstrong was in New York playing a one-night stand in Harlem, where a banquet was given in his honor. "I had never seen so many good musicians, white and colored, in one place at the same time," Eddie Condon recalled, and he suggested to Tommy Rockwell—the producer of Armstrong's Hot Fives and Hot Sevens—that he should take advantage of the occasion and record Armstrong immediately, before he returned to Chicago. Hesitant to record a racially mixed group, Rockwell demurred before deciding to proceed. Shortly before dawn Jack Teagarden, Joe Sullivan, and Lang joined Armstrong, Kaiser Marshall, and tenor saxophonist Happy Caldwell to record an impromptu blues.

It was a cold morning in Manhattan and the musicians had polished off a bottle of whiskey before they began to play. When the time came to name the tune, someone suggested "Knockin' a Jug." The recording became a jazz masterpiece.[20] Around that same time, Lang recorded with blues guitarist Lonnie Johnson, using the pseudonym Blind Willie Dunn to conceal interracial teamwork. In 1933, at the age of thirty-one, he died after a routine tonsillectomy. His death left a huge void, but the Gypsy guitarist Django Reinhardt carried on his legacy.

---

19. Collier, *Making of Jazz*, 324.
20. Ward and Burns, *Jazz: A History*, 165.

BLUE NOTES

OCTOBER 26—CHARLIE BARNET (1913–1991)

b. New York, NY; d. San Diego, CA

Saxophonist; Bandleader

[SWING; BIG BAND]

Other jazz notables born on this day: Tony Pastor (1907); Warne Marsh (1927); Eddie Henderson (1940)

Jazz notables deceased on this day: Burt Bales (1989)

♫

Barnet, one of the few jazz players to be born a millionaire, was somewhat of a playboy throughout his life. Although as saxophonist he was never a major improviser, he led a very popular dance band from 1939 to 1949. A fan of Duke Ellington, Barnet was a pioneer in leading integrated bands, employing black stars such as Roy Eldridge, Charlie Shavers, and Benny Carter, and he made it a habit of touring both white and African-American venues. In 1934 his group became the first white swing band to hold an engagement at the Apollo Theatre in Harlem, previously reserved for black bands. It was typical of Barnet that at his first meeting with singer Billie Holiday he insisted on breaking color-bar restrictions by drinking with her and Teddy Wilson in the whites-only area of their club.[21]

Although his family wanted him to be a lawyer, the bon vivant rebelled in his teens and dropped out of Yale University to play tenor saxophone like his idol, Coleman Hawkins. Barnet began his career in New York around 1930, making the rounds of Harlem, touring with trumpeter Jack Purvis (a wild and kindred spirit), and assembling bands, with which he began recording by 1933. His most notable early venture as bandleader was his 1934 engagement at the Apollo. His band also played on tour and for collegiate strongholds such as Glen Island Casino, where his mixed personnel received a cool reception. Glenn Miller was getting all of the attention there during those years, so the Barnet band resorted to crazy gimmicks like playing "Sunrise Serenade," one of Miller's big numbers, with Barnet blowing the melody while the rest of the band played Ellington's "Azure."

In 1939, with the hit recording of "Cherokee" and a very successful run at New York's Famous Door, Charlie Barnet soon became a household name. Bluebird records issued a new Barnet single every week during this period, and later that year the band moved back triumphantly to the Apollo. At the height of his popularity (1939–42) Barnet was continually discovering and signed new talent, including the singer Lena Horne, who was introduced by his band in 1941. In addition to singers Francis Wayne and Kay Starr, Barnet hired such emerging white players as pianist Dodo Marmarosa, clarinetist Buddy DeFranco, and guitarist Barney Kessel.

During the 1940s, as his musicians were called into the military, they were replaced by a new generation of bop-influenced performers, including trumpeters Clark Terry, Maynard Ferguson, and Doc Severinsen. When Capitol Records put pressure on Barnet to imitate Stan Kenton's sound, Barnet's reaction was exactly what might be expected

---

21. Carr et al., *Jazz: The Rough Guide*, 44.

from a Johnny Hodges fan that didn't need the money. He broke up his band and moved into hotel management, playing when and what he desired. Semi-retired throughout the remainder of his life, Barnet occasionally led swing-oriented big bands during short engagements, making his last recording in 1966. His autobiography, *Those Swinging Years* (1984), is considered one of the most attractive books written by a jazz musician.

OCTOBER 27—BOYD RAEBURN (1913–1966)

b. Faith, SD; d. Lafayette, LA

Bandleader; Tenor and Bass Saxophonist

[BOP, SWEET BANDS]

Other jazz notables born on this day: Babs Gonzales (1916 or 1919); Barre Phillips (1934); Philip Catherine (1942)

Jazz notables deceased on this day: Wellman Braud (1966); Oliver Nelson (1975); Louis Metcalf (1981); Alan Branscombe (1986)

♪

In the mid-1940s, based first in New York and then in Los Angeles, Boyd Raeburn's Orchestra was one of the most consistently interesting and progressive big bands in the business, but its music was too modernistic to survive for long. From 1945 to 1947 Raeburn's music featured some of the era's most advanced arrangements, particularly those by pianist George Handy, who utilized advanced material by composers such as Dizzy Gillespie (Raeburn's band was the first to record "A Night in Tunisia," one of Gillespie's finest pieces) and his own complex scores, influenced by Stravinsky and other modern European impressionistic composers.

Born in South Dakota, Boyd Raben (his original surname) moved to Chicago and was educated at the University of Chicago. Here he formed a commercial dance band that performed throughout the 1930s, including at the 1933 Chicago World Fair; it wasn't until 1942 that he seriously considered leading a jazz orchestra. By 1944 he had reorganized radically and began playing at New York hotels with a forward-looking swing band that included bop players-in-the-making (and future Woody Herman sidemen) Earl Swope, Sonny Berman, and Don Lamond. Initially the band demonstrated a Count Basie and Duke Ellington influence, particularly through Raeburn's main soloist, alto saxophonist Johnny Bothwell, who was called "the white Johnny Hodges." George Handy joined later that year and introduced advanced arrangements, but then left for Hollywood. In January 1945 the orchestra appeared for a week at the Apollo in Harlem, a rarity for a white group, and featured Gillespie as guest trumpeter. The band began broadcasting from New York, but when it was unable to secure a worthwhile recording contract, Raeburn left for the West Coast. Here he was rejoined by Handy, who submitted more adventurous arrangements and original compositions that marked the true beginning of the Raeburn legacy.

The band ran out of bookings in Los Angeles and temporarily disbanded, but shortly thereafter, spurred by two recording contracts, the revived ensemble spent three months recording its unusual repertoire. At this point singer Ginnie Powell (who had sung with the band in 1943 and was now Raeburn's wife) rejoined the band, recently enlarged with the addition of French horns and a harp. Presenting "concert jazz," a concept still ahead of its time, the orchestra managed to secure only a single residency, at the Club Morocco in Hollywood, but it was there that it reached its peak in the summer of 1946. Great players like Lucky Thompson, Dodo Marmarosa, Pete Candoli, and Buddy DeFranco were among many who passed through the band during its final years. Despite adulation by critics and musicians alike, the band's advanced music puzzled dance-band enthusiasts, and by 1950 Raeburn was forced to return to more commercial styles. Later in the decade he abandoned music altogether.

OCTOBER 28—CLEO LAINE (1927–)

b. Southall, Middlesex, England

Vocalist

[TRADITIONAL POP; JAZZ-POP; BALLADS; COOL; BOP]

Other jazz notables born on this day: Bill Harris (1916); Chico O'Farrill (1921); Andy Bey (1939)
Jazz notables deceased on this day: Earl Bostic (1965)

♪

With the exception of the late tenor saxophonist Ronnie Scott, owner of Ronnie Scott's, the most famous jazz club in London, Cleo Laine and her saxophonist-composer-bandleader husband, John Dankworth, are possibly the best-known English personalities in jazz. Hailed as the "Queen of Jazz," Laine is one of the most celebrated singers of our time. Like her British colleague Annie Ross, Laine often ventured beyond jazz into cabaret and musical comedy. During a career that spans fifty years she has performed opera, lieder, and pop music as well as jazz, and in the 1980s was the only singer to have been nominated for Grammy awards in the female popular, classical, and jazz categories. As a jazz singer she is both an interpreter and an improviser, and her scat singing, accompanied by husband John Dankworth on alto saxophone or clarinet, is particularly noteworthy. Known for her extraordinary four-octave range, Laine's contralto voice is also capable of great variety of color.

Laine (Clementina Dinah Campbell) was born in the Southall section of London, the daughter of a Jamaican father and English mother. Her parents sent her to vocal and dance lessons as a teenager, but when she was twenty-five she began singing professionally, after a successful audition with a band led by Dankworth. Both Laine and the band recorded during the late 1950s, and in 1958, after her marriage to Dankworth, she left the group to begin a successful stage career, though she remained active as a singer. Since 1972 she has undertaken numerous tours of the U.S., including three concert albums recorded at New York's Carnegie Hall. Her third Carnegie Hall concert, *The 10th Anniversary Concert*, in 1983 won her the first Grammy award by a Briton. She proved to be a rugged stage actress as well, winning a Theater World award, in addition to Tony and Drama Desk nominations. In 1976 she recorded a jazz version of *Porgy and Bess* with Ray Charles, and also recorded duets with James Galway and guitarist John Williams.

Laine and Dankworth continued touring through the 1990s, including with the show *Forever Ella*, a tribute to Ella Fitzgerald, and with the Duke Ellington Orchestra under Mercer Ellington; on her album *Solitude* (1994) Laine's singing and Mercer's band are overdubbed onto a piano recording made by Duke Ellington in 1941. In 1997 she received perhaps her greatest honor when she was made a Dame, becoming the first jazz artist to receive the highest British title available in the performing arts. Performing regularly with Dankworth into her seventies, Laine continues to exhibit the musical qualities that brought her fame, including her four-octave range. Whether interpreting a collection of Shakespeare's sonnets set to music, appearing in jazz festivals, operas, or singing with symphony orchestras and big bands, Laine consistently finds new forums for her talents.

OCTOBER 29—ZOOT SIMS (1925–1985)

b. Inglewood, CA; d. New York, NY

Tenor Saxophonist; Leader

[COOL; BOP]

Other jazz notables born on this day: Neal Hefti (1922)
Jazz notables deceased on this day: Woody Herman (1987); Joe Comfort (1988)

♪

Zoot Sims epitomized the swinging musician. His trademark was his unforced and naturally swinging style, together with an attractively light tone. He always sounded inspired, and although his style did not change much after the early 1950s, his enthusiasm and creativity never wavered. He joined Benny Goodman's big band for the first time in 1943, and he would be one of Goodman's favorite tenors over the next thirty years. In 1947 he gained his initial fame in Woody Herman's Second Herd, featuring one of the ablest reed sections in jazz history: Stan Getz, Herbie Stewart (then Al Cohn), and Sims on tenor and Serge Chaloff on baritone. Intensely melodic, Sims was one of several leading white tenor saxophonists whose playing was closely modeled on that of Lester Young. His sleek style transferred well to the soprano, which he took up in the 1970s.

Zoot (John Haley) Sims grew up in a family of vaudeville artists, playing drums and clarinet as a child. He took up tenor at the age of thirteen and two years later began working professionally. While with the obscure dance band of Kenny Baker he acquired his nickname, Zoot, taken from the then-current nonsense language popularized by guitarist-comedian Slim Gaillard (two other Baker bandsmen were called Scoot and Voot). In 1943 he joined Goodman in the first of several engagements, including various international tours from the 1950s through the '70s. In 1944 he played at the interracial Café Society in New York with Bill Harris. After serving in the army he rejoined Goodman (1946–47) and also played with Gene Roland.

From 1947 to 1949 he was a member of Herman's big band, where Roland's writing for four tenor saxophones led to the establishment of the famous section known as the Four Brothers. At this time Sims was one of many sidemen in Herman's band plagued by heroin addiction. Sims played briefly with Buddy Rich before replacing Wardell Gray in Goodman's bop group (1950). After a brief period with Stan Kenton's band (1953), he toured Europe and recorded with Gerry Mulligan's groups (1954–56). Sims was also a star soloist with Mulligan's Concert Jazz Band of the early 1960s, and visited the Soviet Union with Goodman in 1962. In the autumn of 1961 he became the first performer from the U.S. to play a season at Ronnie Scott's in London, returning several times between then and 1982. A freelancer throughout most of his career, Sims's trademark style seemed especially evident in groups co-led with his friend Cohn, whose forceful sound contrasted Sims's floating sound. He toured occasionally with Jazz At The Philharmonic during the 1960s and '70s and also took part in reunion concerts with Herman in 1972 and 1978. He toured Europe several times during his career, making his final tour in 1984, after hospitalization and diagnosis of his terminal cancer.

OCTOBER 30—CLIFFORD BROWN (1930–1956)

b. Wilmington, DE; d. Bedford, PA

Trumpeter; Leader

[Bop; Hard Bop]

Other jazz notables born on this day: Teo Macero (1925); Trilok Gurtu (1951); Poncho Sanchez (1951)

Jazz notables deceased on this day: Mamie Smith (1946); Pops Foster (1969); Tony Sbarbaro (1969); Steve Allen (2000)

♫

By 1956 Clifford Brown already ranked with Dizzy Gillespie and Miles Davis as one of the top trumpeters in jazz, and he was still improving.[22] On June 25 of that year he took part in a jam session at a Philadelphia instrument store called Music City. He was there as a favor for a friend, and it was past midnight when Brown, pianist Richie Powell (Bud Powell's younger brother), and Richie's wife Nancy left Philadelphia for an engagement later that day in Chicago. Forced to drive through the night, they took off in Powell's car with Nancy, an inexperienced driver, at the wheel. As rain fell during the early hours of June 26, the car skidded on a wet stretch of pavement on the Pennsylvania Turnpike and rolled over an embankment, killing all three passengers. Scott Yanow is correct in calling Brown's death at the age of twenty-five one of the great tragedies in jazz history.

Clifford Brown, a musical genius known affectionately as Brownie, accomplished a great deal in his short lifetime. By the age of twenty-two, with limited experience on the trumpet, he was already an original stylist, possessing one of the fullest and most beautiful sounds in jazz. Brown's father, an amateur musician, gave him a trumpet when

---

22. Bogdanov et al., *All Music Guide to Jazz*, 160.

he was fifteen, making his start one of the latest in jazz. His ability was such that within three years he was playing gigs in Philadelphia with musicians such as Miles Davis, Kenny Dorham, Max Roach, J.J. Johnson, and Fats Navarro. In 1950, at the age of twenty, his musical career was almost cut short by an automobile accident. For a year he was unable to play, but through the encouragement of professional musicians such as Dizzy Gillespie, he was able to work himself back into shape.

In 1954, following a European tour with the Lionel Hampton big band, he recorded some brilliant solos at Birdland with Art Blakey's quintet (a band that directly preceded the Jazz Messengers), and by mid-year he was recruited by drummer Max Roach to form a group that became known as the Clifford Brown-Max Roach Quintet. Brown made an immediate breakthrough that year, winning the New Star award on trumpet in the *Down Beat* critics' poll. The quintet, one of the most significant groups of the 1950s, had a major influence on the establishment of the style later known as hard bop. The group's live recordings, made during its two-year existence, would rank with the very best in jazz.

It is certainly ironic that while so many of his contemporaries were killing themselves with drugs, Brown, one of the few bop players who remained clean, should have died in such a meaningless way. When he died in that crash, bebop is said to have died with him. In the words of *Down Beat* editor Dan Morgenstern: "[Brown] was the last great, natural, inspirational improviser produced by the soul of Charlie Parker and his disciples, and the band in which he finished his life on earth was the last of the great bebop bands."

OCTOBER 31—ETHEL WATERS (1896–1977)

b. Chester, PA; d. Chatsworth, CA

Vocalist

[Traditional Pop; Classic Jazz; Swing; Classic Female Blues]

Other jazz notables born on this day: Illinois Jacquet (1922); Ted Nash (1922); Booker Ervin (1930)

Jazz notables deceased on this day: Tony Pastor (1969); Chauncey Morehouse (1980)

♪

More than any other performer, Ethel Waters is responsible for fusing black and white musical traditions into the hybrid art of jazz singing and, beyond that, American popular song. The impoverished daughter of a thirteen-year-old rape victim, young Ethel fantasized escape from her oppressive surroundings by imitating actors and music hall artists. Following her 1917 Baltimore stage debut, she toured southern black theaters under the billing of "Sweet Mama Stringbean." She became the first African-American woman to headline at the Palace Theater in New York, and went to Hollywood in 1929 to appear in a film in which she introduced her best-remembered song, "Am I Blue." For a time the best-paid woman in show business, black or white, she demonstrated that African-American performers could appeal to every kind of audience. Lena Horne once paid her the ultimate compliment when she called her "the Mother of us all." Her lyrical voice, polished diction, and spirited delivery of lyrics influenced generations of jazz singers, notably Ella Fitzgerald and Billie Holiday. Although her work falls short of the inventiveness and emotional intensity of some of her successors, Waters is the seminal figure in the evolution of modern jazz singing.

As ambitious as she was gifted, Waters sought to reach the more affluent white audience that supported Nora Bayes, Sophie Tucker, and other highly paid vaudeville headliners. After touring with pianist Fletcher Henderson, in 1925 she replaced the legendary Florence Mills at the Plantation Club on Broadway, where she introduced "Dinah," one of her signature pieces. Her interpretation and popularization of that song, using syncopation and rubato extensively, paved the way for the use of Tin Pan Alley material by every jazz vocalist who came after her. There was no stopping her ascent into realms previously closed to black artists.

Her 1933 Cotton Club interpretation of "Stormy Weather," backed by Duke Ellington, attracted the attention of Irving Berlin, who showcased her that year in a Broadway musical review. She made a smooth transition from a jazz singer of the 1920s to a pop music star of the 1930s, and in this respect was a strong influence on vocalists like Mildred Bailey, Lee Wiley, and Connee Boswell. Waters spent the latter half of the 1930s touring with a group headed by her husband, trumpeter Eddie Mallory, and appeared on Broadway and in the 1943 film *Cabin in the Sky*, where she introduced "Taking a Chance on Love." Waters's restless artistic quests ultimately found resolution in religious work, and after 1956 she traveled internationally on behalf of evangelist Billy Graham. Her autobiography, *His Eye is on the Sparrow* (1951), is a deeply disturbing portrait of a disadvantaged African-American woman determined to succeed.

Chapter 11

November

NOVEMBER 1—SIPPIE WALLACE (1898–1986)

b. Houston, TX; d. Detroit, MI

Vocalist

[Classic Female Blues]

Other jazz notables born on this day: Papa Joe Assunto (1905); Sam Margolis (1923); Lou Donaldson (1926); Roger Kellaway (1939); Conrad Herwig (1959)
Jazz notables deceased on this day: Sippie Wallace (1986)

♫

During the first two decades of the twentieth century, blues-singing female entertainers like Ma Rainey, Bessie Smith, Ida Cox, Victoria Spivey, Alberta Hunter, and Sippie Wallace were touring the South, working in tents, circuses, carnivals, or in the theaters on the black TOBA circuit. They were doing comedy and dramatic routines, in addition to singing, but because the blues remained their most popular drawing card and purest form of expression, they came to be known as "the Classic Blues Singers." From roughly 1920 (when the blues were first recorded) to 1933, until the depths of the Depression brought everything to a halt, the blues reigned in the market place of black music, and the women who sang them ruled as queens and empresses along with it.

The daughter of a Baptist deacon, Sippie (born Beulah Thomas) was in her mid-teens when she left Houston to pursue a musical career, singing in tent shows. In 1915 she was living in New Orleans, working with her brother Hersal, a talented blues pianist; two years later she married Matt Wallace. In 1923 she moved to Chicago, together with her brothers Hersal and George, and there she became a part of the city's jazz scene. Her first two songs for the OKeh label became hits, and soon Sippie was a star. Throughout the 1920s she produced a series of singles that were nearly all hits. Her recordings featured a number of celebrated jazz musicians, including Louis Armstrong, King Oliver, and Clarence Williams. Both Hersal and George Thomas performed on her records as well, in addition to supporting her at concerts. Between 1923 and 1927 she recorded over forty songs for OKeh, many of them originals or co-written with her brothers.

In 1926 Hersal died of food poisoning (he was only seventeen), and by 1929 Wallace had stopped performing and moved to Detroit, where she was a church organist and vocalist for the next forty years. In 1966 her cousin Victoria Spivey, who convinced Sippie to join the thriving blues and folk festival circuit, lured her out of retirement. Wallace began recording again and on the strength of her albums and her festival performances she quickly regained her popularity. In 1970 she suffered a stroke, though she was able to continue recording and performing on a limited basis. By then a fresh crop of blues singers was carrying on the tradition, including white singers like Janis Joplin, the rock star influenced by Bessie Smith, and slide guitarist Bonnie Raitt, who recorded several of Wallace's songs and performed live with her. In 1982 Raitt helped Wallace land a recording contract; the resulting album, *Sippie*, was nominated for a Grammy and won the W.C. Handy Award for best blues album of the year. The album turned out to be Wallace's last recording—she died on her birthday in 1986, at the age of eighty-eight.

NOVEMBER 2—BUNNY BERIGAN (1908–1942)

b. Hilbert, WI; d. New York, NY

Trumpeter; Bandleader

[Swing]

Other jazz notables born on this day: Rudy Van Gelder ? (1924) [see Nov. 26 entry]; Phil Woods (1931); Kurt Elling (1967)
Jazz notables deceased on this day: Carson Smith (1997)

♪

Of all the big bandleaders, the one who most typified the swing era was Bunny Berigan, the bravura trumpeter who died early of alcoholism. Like Bix Beiderbecke, he remains the trumpet tragedy of the 1930s. Berigan was a genuine romantic, perhaps the purest romantic in jazz, and the big band suited his sweeping, romantic style perfectly. Blessed with a beautiful tone and quite possibly the widest range of any trumpeter in jazz, Bunny brought excitement to every session.[1] His fine harmonic sense and uninhibited style can be heard on Tommy Dorsey's hit recordings, "Marie" and "Song of India," as well as on his own biggest hit, "I Can't Get Started" (all 1937).

Born Rowland Bernard Berigan, Bunny's short career began in the Midwest. He tried out for Hal Kemp's Orchestra unsuccessfully in 1928 but two years later he was hired for a trip to Europe and hotel work in New York. In 1931 he joined Fred Rich's CBS studio band and continued working in studios until 1935, except for a short period with Paul Whiteman's highly successful orchestra, where he was a replacement for Beiderbecke. Berigan was unhappy while with Whiteman, disliking his musical policy and the limited solo role the bandleader gave him. He soon gained a strong reputation as a hot soloist and he appeared on numerous records with studio bands, the Boswell Sisters, and the Dorsey Brothers.

---

1. Bogdanov et al., *All Music Guide to Jazz*, 102.

In 1935 he spent only a few months with Benny Goodman's Orchestra, but that was enough time to launch the swing era, for Berigan was with Goodman as he went on his historic cross-country tour, climaxing in the near-riot at the Palomar Ballroom in Los Angeles. The crowd erupted when Bunny stood to play "Sometimes I'm Happy" and "King Porter Stomp," Goodman's first hit recordings. Berigan left Goodman soon thereafter, returning to the more lucrative studio. Having leadership ideas of his own, he attempted to form his own big band, but it failed at the rehearsal stage. In 1937 he briefly joined Tommy Dorsey's band before he succeeded in putting together his own orchestra. His live appearances, with a band that featured Buddy Rich on drums, Georgie Auld on tenor, and his own unrivalled playing, were generally brilliant. By now he was the top white trumpeter in jazz.

At the end of 1940, however, he was drinking heavily and may have been suffering spells of mental imbalance. He rejoined Tommy Dorsey's band for six months, where his solos three years earlier had helped to seal Dorsey's career, but his unreliability and his own sense of despair forced Dorsey to let him go. Soon Berigan formed a new orchestra, but his health deteriorated further and on June 1, 1942, he failed to show up for an engagement with his band. Penniless and seriously ill, he was rushed to the hospital where he died the following day (Dorsey paid the funeral expenses); he was only thirty-three.

NOVEMBER 3—HENRY GRIMES (1935–)

b. Philadelphia, PA

Bassist

[Free Jazz; Hard Bop]

Other jazz notables born on this day: Billy Mitchell (1926); Andy McGhee (1927); Azar Lawrence (1953)

Jazz notables deceased on this day: Gary McFarland (1971); Eddie "Lockjaw" Davis (1986); Grachan Moncur (1996)

♫

For about a decade Henry Grimes was one of the finest bassists on the jazz scene. In 1967, at the height of the free-jazz movement, he simply walked away from the music world and disappeared. He had long been the subject of rumor and speculation: that he had died in 1971, that he had become a minister, that he had dyed his hair green and played electric bass with rock bands, that he was homeless. Until recently, a death notice in *Cadence Magazine* in 1986 seemed to have closed the book on the creative musician.

In 2002 a fan of Grimes named Marshall Marotte (a social worker living in Athens, Georgia), began doing some research into Grimes's whereabouts. If Grimes was still alive, he was likely living on the West Coast. A solid lead took him to Los Angeles, where he found Grimes sound in mind and body, though basically destitute. He had been living in a small apartment for the past twenty years, surviving on Social Security checks, which he augmented by acting, writing poetry, and various odd jobs. He had long ago sold his bass for survival needs. One of the first things Marotte did when he found Grimes was to introduce him to CDs of his former music. Grimes was amazed by what he heard, and indicated he would be interested in playing again. With Marotte's help and intervention, Grimes began his comeback. After a few gigs on the West Coast, he made a triumphant return to New York City and amazed the jazz world with his playing.

Grimes started out on violin before attending a vocational high school in Philadelphia, where he was required to take up four additional instruments: drums, English horn, tuba, and bass. In 1953, after his graduation, he commuted to New York City to attend Juilliard. After touring with Arnett Cobb and Willis "Gator" Jackson he played with the many talented young players in the Philadelphia scene of the mid-1950s, including Bobby Timmons, Lee Morgan, and Albert "Tootie" Heath. During the next decade he played brilliantly on some fifty albums with an enormous range of musicians. In 1957 he worked with Anita O'Day and Sonny Rollins, recorded with Bill Evans, and was a member of Gerry Mulligan's quartet (1957–58). At the 1958 Newport Jazz Festival he demonstrated his versatility by playing with Rollins, Benny Goodman's orchestra, Lee Konitz, and Thelonious Monk. In 1963 he recorded what he later called his favorite date, a session with Rollins and Coleman Hawkins released on LP as *Sonny Meets Hawk*.

While continuing to associate with mainstream players, in 1961 Grimes became part of the free-jazz movement, playing with clarinetist Perry Robinson, pianist Cecil Taylor (off and on during 1961–66), saxophonist Albert Ayler (1964–66), and trumpeter Don Cherry, among others, while leading only one session of his own (1965). Then, for reasons that are still unclear, he vanished for the next thirty-five years. His comeback, however, became one of the great jazz stories of 2003.

NOVEMBER 4—WILLEM BREUKER (1944–2010)

b. Amsterdam, Netherlands; d. Amsterdam, Netherlands;

Saxophonist; Clarinetist; Composer

[AVANT-GARDE; EXPERIMENTAL BIG BAND]

Other jazz notables born on this day: Joe Sullivan (1906); Peter Schilperoort (1919); Ralph Sutton (1922); Carlos "Patato" Valdez (1926)

Jazz notables deceased on this day: Buddy Bolden (1931); Ray Linn (1996); Vernel Fournier (2000)

♪

A leader in the European avant-garde and free music community, Willem Breuker was probably the best known, most prolific, and influential figure in twentieth century Dutch music.[2] In recognition of his outstanding contributions, he was awarded the Dutch National Jazz Prize in 1970, the Jazz Prize of the West German Music Critics in 1976, and in 1998 he was inducted into the order of the Lion of the Netherlands. In 1967 he helped form the Instant Composers Pool (with Misha Mengelberg and Han Bennink), a nonprofit organization that sponsors performances and recordings of music by European

---

2. Bogdanov et al., *All Music Guide to Jazz*, 151.

free players. Later on he formed the Willem Breuker Kollektief, the pioneering eclectic jazz ensemble that has been his primary vehicle since.

Born to a middle class family near the end of World War II, Breuker recalls a childhood filled with sound and music. His most important musical influence was the radio, where he heard many types of music, but what he enjoyed most was music he could not understand. He soon discovered that what really intrigued him was not listening to others play, but playing music himself. Even then he enjoyed improvising. Since his parents worked during school hours, he often skipped school to listen to music on the radio. His first music lessons were on clarinet, and later he took up saxophone. After being denied admission to Amsterdam's conservatory, he began attending night school, with plans of becoming a teacher. But before he could finish his degree, he began working professionally as a musician. Around this time he started performing at jazz competitions, sometimes winning prizes but also causing scandals for his controversial approach. By the end of the decade he was recognized as one of the most important free jazz saxophonists in Europe.

In 1974 he formed his eleven-piece Kollektief and began touring widely. In twenty-five years of performing around the world and at countless festivals, the Kollektief acquired a diverse and highly appreciative audience. Equally at home in jazz clubs or in philharmonic halls, the Kollektief played a hybrid of music that cut across traditional musical lines. Its performances combine jazz and classical music with popular genres. "Rarely has any band, inside or outside jazz, combined instrumental virtuosity and antic irreverence so thoroughly," said *The Boston Globe* of the Kollektief. "When I play," Breuker told the *Melbourne Herald Sun*, "I really want the audience to follow what we are doing, to feel that they are part of the band instead of just sitting there watching us." The group's zany collectivism presaged later cut-up artists like John Zorn, though in so doing it looked back to vaudeville and earlier New Orleans traditions.[3]

NOVEMBER 5—REGINALD VEAL (1963–)

b. Chicago, IL

Bassist

[Neo-Bop]

Other jazz notables born on this day: Jack McVea (1914)
Jazz notables deceased on this day: Hot Lips Page (1954); Art Tatum (1956); Lu Watters (1989); Eddie Harris (1996)

♪

In the 1990s a host of essential jazz artists died—Miles Davis, Stan Getz, Dizzy Gillespie, Gerry Mulligan, Art Blakey, Ella Fitzgerald, and Sarah Vaughan—leaving many longtime fans fearful for the future of the music. But one person, Wynton Marsalis, came along to change all that. His sudden prominence in 1980 started the "young lions" movement and resulted in major labels (most of which had shown no interest in jazz during the previous

---

3. Carr et al., *Jazz: The Rough Guide*, 92.

decade) suddenly signing and promoting young players. Appropriately enough, it was the great drummer Art Blakey who introduced Wynton to the jazz world. Blakey's band, the Jazz Messengers, had carried the torch for the sophisticated variant of bebop known as hard bop since the middle 1950s, along the way serving as a valuable training ground for numerous young musicians.

At first Marsalis attracted attention primarily because of his command of the trumpet, but by the end of the 1980s he emerged as the leader of a full-fledged movement. Numerous young musicians began following his path, seeking inspiration in an updated variety of bop that came to be called straightahead or neo-bop jazz. In 1990 Marsalis was the focus of a cover story in *Time* magazine titled "The New Jazz Age," which proclaimed that straightahead jazz, after having "almost died in the 1970s," was being revitalized by a whole new generation of talented musicians that was "going back to the roots."

In 1987 a Chicago-born bassist named Reginald Veal joined the movement when he became a member of Marsalis's septet. He had moved to New Orleans at an early age and there had learned piano and later electric bass guitar, which he played in his father's gospel group. After high school he attended Southern University in Baton Rouge, where he studied bass trombone. Encouraged by Wynton Marsalis to take up the acoustic bass, Veal began working with Wynton's father Ellis Marsalis, an outstanding New Orleans pianist, and then briefly played in a quintet led by Donald Harrison and Terence Blanchard before joining Wynton's band (1987–93), where his contribution was essential to the group's early success in recreating small-group swing performances. From the early 1990s Veal toured with the Lincoln Center Jazz Orchestra, and although he settled in Atlanta in 1994, he continued an intermittent association with Wynton and the Lincoln Center orchestra. In the mid-1990s he toured and recorded with saxophonist Branford Marsalis, both in the hip-hop ensemble Buckshot LeFonque and in Branford's trio.

Over the years Veal has performed in various straightahead settings with younger musicians such as Harry Connick Jr., Marcus Roberts, Nicholas Payton, and Dianne Reeves, as well as in the premiere of several commissioned works written by Marsalis, including the oratorio *Blood on the Fields*, for which Wynton won the Pulitzer Prize in 1997, thereby validating jazz's artistic stature and ensuring a promising future to the next generation of jazz players.

NOVEMBER 6—ARTURO SANDOVAL (1949–)

b. Artemisa, Cuba

Trumpeter; Pianist; Composer

[Cuban Jazz; Afro-Cuban Jazz; Latin Jazz]

Other jazz notables born on this day: Dick Cathcart (1924)
Jazz notables deceased on this day: Clarence Williams (1965)

November

♪

In 1973 a group of musicians in Havana formed the Afro-Cuban jazz ensemble Iraquere, an exciting band that continues to serve as a Latin jazz tutorial for musicians and audiences alike on the Castro-controlled island. The group had its origins in the Orquesta Cubana de Música Moderna, a name chosen in 1967 to signal the influence of jazz without specifying it. Iraquere's original aim was to further the fusion of jazz, rock, and classical with both contemporary and traditional Cuban styles. The band was highly praised in 1977 by such jazz standouts as Dizzy Gillespie and Stan Getz, who were among the first official U.S. visitors to Cuba since Castro's takeover in 1959. Iraquere toured throughout the world, signed with an American record label (the first post-Castro Cuban group to do so), and became a top-rated jazz ensemble. Forbidden to perform in the U.S., Iraquere appeared unannounced at a 1979 Carnegie Hall concert in New York, playing its first performance in the United States and capturing the attention of the Latin jazz community. Joining Iraquere at this concert were Gillespie, Getz, and many other crossover musicians who fostered Latin jazz, including the Machito orchestra, Tito Puente's band, Mongo Santamaria, and Cal Tjader. The concert signaled the Latin-jazz revival in the 1980s.

Under Chucho Valdés, its brilliant musical director, Iraquere trained such modern Afro-Cuban musicians as saxophonist Paquito D'Rivera, pianist Gonzalo Rubalcaba, and trumpeter Arturo Sandoval. D'Rivera, one of the foremost Latin bop saxophonists and the group's breakout star, defected to the U.S. in 1980 and joined Gillespie's United Nation Orchestra, a group he directed after Dizzy's death in 1993. Rubalcaba, also influenced by Gillespie, decided to stay in Cuba. The third Gillespie-inspired Cuban standout, Sandoval, an extraordinary trumpet virtuoso with an exceptional range, longed to leave Cuba as well and finally found his opportunity in 1990, defecting while his wife and child were safely out of Cuba.

The son of an auto mechanic, Sandoval dreamed of playing the trumpet. But when he approached a local trumpet player for lessons, he was told he had no talent. Undeterred, he went home and practiced "until blood came out of my mouth." He took up the classical trumpet at twelve and enrolled in the Cuban National School of the Arts. As one of the founding members of Iraquere, he met his idol Dizzy Gillespie in 1977, and Gillespie immediately became a mentor and a colleague, playing with Sandoval in concerts in Europe and Cuba. By 1981 Sandoval was leading his own band, which had great success in Europe, South America, and in his homeland, where he was voted best instrumentalist each year from 1982 to 1990. Throughout this period he considered his escape from Cuba. In 1990, while in the midst of a European concert tour, he defected to the U.S. Shortly thereafter he rejoined D'Rivera, this time as a featured member of Gillespie's orchestra. After Dizzy's death Sandoval settled in Miami, returning to live among Cuban expatriates, only this time with total freedom.

BLUE NOTES

NOVEMBER 7—AL HIRT (1922–1999)

b. New Orleans, LA; d. New Orleans, LA

Trumpeter; Bandleader; Vocalist

[DIXIELAND]

Other jazz notables born on this day: Joe Bushkin (1916); Howard Rumsey (1917); Alvin Batiste (1932); David S. Ware (1949)

Jazz notables deceased on this day: Adelaide Hall (1993); Shorty Rogers (1994)

♪

During the mid-1960s, when he recorded his pop hits "Java" (1963), "Sugar Lips" (1964) and "Cotton Candy" (1964), Al Hirt was the best known trumpeter in the U.S. Praised for his wide range and his startling bravura style, the physically imposing trumpeter (six feet two inches tall and nearly three hundred lbs.) was often dismissed by jazz critics for selling out to commercial success. But Hirt was always comfortable staying close to home—musically and professionally. For most of the 1950s he played in the Dixieland idiom, often performing with clarinet player Pete Fountain, who achieved nearly the same level of national fame, and the two remained close friends and colleagues until Hirt's death. Despite recording a number of Dixieland albums in the late 1950s, Hirt never claimed to be a jazz trumpeter. He resumed playing in a more jazz-oriented style during the late 1960s, when he opened a club on Bourbon Street in New Orleans. During this period he performed regularly at the popular New Orleans Jazz and Heritage Festival. Jazz critics and fans consider Hirt's Audio Fidelity recordings (1958–60) and his collaborations with Fountain the most rewarding of his career.

At the age of sixteen, while sitting enthralled through Benny Goodman's 1938 Carnegie Hall concert in New York City, Hirt decided to pursue a career in music. After studying classical trumpet at the Cincinnati Conservatory (1940–43) and playing with army bands during World War II, he landed stints with Benny Goodman's orchestra and in the swing bands of both Tommy and Jimmy Dorsey. Influenced by the playing of Harry James as well as by his own classical training, Hirt returned to New Orleans, where he led Dixieland bands while working with the New Orleans Symphony. In 1950 he competed in Horace Heidt's national youth contest and got his first big break touring as a soloist in Heidt's band. National fame came in 1960, when his Dixieland Six booked into a luxury hotel in Las Vegas. As much a showman as a musician, Hirt caught the attention of singer Dinah Shore, who featured him on her television variety show.

Al Hirt's many accomplishments include a return visit to Carnegie Hall in 1965, this time for his own "standing room only" concert; winning a Grammy for "Java"; playing for eight U.S. presidents—including at the inauguration of President John F. Kennedy—and for Pope John Paul II's 1987 visit to New Orleans; and appearing in five Super Bowl programs, including headlining the half-time show at the first Super Bowl game in 1967. His weight and lifestyle eventually took its toll, and in later years he was forced to perform in a wheelchair. He closed his Bourbon Street club in 1983, upset with the deterioration of the French Quarter, but he continued to play, mostly at Fountain's club, until a few months before his death.

NOVEMBER 8—DON BYRON (1958–)

b. New York, NY

Clarinetist and Bass Clarinetist; Leader

[AVANT-GARDE JAZZ; KLEZMER; M-BASE; POST-BOP]

Other jazz notables born on this day: Chris Connor (1927); Russell Malone (1963)
Jazz notables deceased on this day: Shorty Baker (1966); Collin Walcott (1984); Red Mitchell (1992); Dick Cathcart (1993); Lester Bowie (1999); Dick Morrissey (2000)

♪

Don Byron, one of America's most eclectic musicians, has been called "the most intriguing new jazz clarinetist to emerge since Eddie Daniels." Since being named "Jazz Artist of the Year" by *Down Beat* in 1992, he has been consistently voted "Best Clarinetist" by critics and readers in leading international music journals. As clarinetist, composer, arranger, and social critic, Byron redefines every genre of music he plays, be it classical, salsa, hip-hop, funk, klezmer, or any style of jazz. Byron embraces ethnicities, which for him exist as flavors, to be appreciated and shared without social or ideological stigma. He first attained notoriety for playing klezmer (Jewish street music from Eastern Europe), specifically the music of the late Mickey Katz. While the novelty of a black man playing Jewish music grabbed the attention of critics, it was Byron's jazz related work that ultimately made him a major figure.[4] As a vital member of New York's cultural community, he has served as the director of jazz for the Brooklyn Academy of Music and has participated in such diverse projects as composing music for silent film, scores for television, and a commissioned work for the Kronos Quartet.

Born and raised in the South Bronx, a diverse neighborhood with sizeable Jewish and Hispanic populations, Byron was exposed to a wide variety of music by his father, a mailman who played bass in calypso bands, and his pianist mother, who took him to both jazz clubs and the symphony. When he developed asthma as a child, his doctor suggested he take up a wind instrument as therapy, so Byron chose clarinet. He took as models Tony Scott, Artie Shaw, and especially Jimmy Hamilton, and he learned improvisation by listening to saxophonist Joe Henderson. In high school, while studying classical clarinet, he played and arranged salsa numbers for local bands. Later, as a jazz student with George Russell at the New England Conservatory of Music, he performed with Latin and jazz bands and led the Klezmer Conservatory Band (1980–87).

He eventually moved back to New York, where he began playing with several of the city's more prominent jazz avant-gardists, including David Murray and Hamiet Bluiett. For a while he doubled on the baritone saxophone, performing with the Duke Ellington Orchestra, Mario Bauzá, and Murray's big band. Since then, Byron has played with dozens of groups, ranging from a contemporary classical chamber ensemble to the rock band Living Colour. He continues to lead the Existential Dred band (which includes as one of its members Sadiq Bey, a poet/rapper) and his long-standing group, Music for Six

---

4. Bogdanov et al., *All Music Guide to Jazz*, 191.

Musicians, which performs the Latin and Afro-Caribbean rhythms at his musical roots. An exceptional musician and a stalwart of the New York contemporary jazz scene, Byron is notable for having expanded the range of the clarinet, in the process helping to reestablish that instrument's prominence in jazz.

NOVEMBER 9—MEZZ MEZZROW (1899–1972)

b. Chicago, IL; d. Paris, France

Clarinetist; Tenor Saxophonist

[DIXIELAND]

Other jazz notables born on this day: Muggsy Spanier (1901)
Jazz notables deceased on this day: Jan Johansson (1968); Joe Roccisano (1997)

♪

In the 1920s no white parents anywhere in the United States would encourage their child to enter the field of jazz. Most white families, and certainly white middle-class families, considered popular music of any sort as a generally unacceptable profession. And jazz, associated with African Americans, liquor, and sexuality, was anathema. This social isolation of blacks from whites inevitably placed limits on cultural and musical cross-fertilization between the races.

One person growing up in Chicago at this time disagreed with these conventions. Mezz Mezzrow (his real name was Milton Mesirow) loved black music and black culture to such an extent that he spent much of his life renouncing his own culture and race. During various stints in jail (in the 1930s and '40s he was a reliable supplier of marijuana for Louis Armstrong and a good many other musicians), he passed as a light-skinned black so he would be placed in the black cellblocks, where he felt more at home. In 1942 his draft card read RACE: NEGRO. Like Armstrong, he learned to play music in reform school, having gotten into trouble with the law at the age of fifteen, when as a member of a tough Jewish gang he was caught in a stolen car in front of a police station. A passionate propagandist for Chicago-style and New Orleans jazz and the rights of African-Americans, by the mid-1920s he began associating with young Chicago-style musicians, playing occasionally with the Austin High Gang and visiting some of the famous South Side clubs where Armstrong, King Oliver, and other top African-Americans displayed their musical prowess. Mezzrow began working with a group of musicians that formed guitarist Eddie Condon's circle, but his constant preoccupation with black players and his determination to identify with them made him an outsider even there.

As his career progressed, Mezzrow increasingly sought projects that included African-American players. Following a brief trip to Europe in 1929, he worked as a freelance musician in New York, where he organized numerous all-star recording sessions that featured integrated bands as early as 1933; he also formed one of the earliest inter-racial jazz bands in 1937. The French critic Hughes Panassié was a big supporter of Mezzrow's playing, and by 1938, with the comeback of New Orleans jazz, sponsored excellent sessions featuring the clarinetist with jazz luminaries James P. Johnson, Tommy Ladnier, and Sidney Bechet, including a near-classic recording of "Really the Blues." In 1945 Mezzrow became a co-founder and the president of the King Jazz label, for which he made many of his best recordings in partnership with Bechet. During the early 1950s he moved to France, where he remained for the rest of his life, organizing all-star touring bands and making guest appearances. Mezzrow is best known for his autobiography, *Really the Blues*, one of the great jazz books, a colorful but rather fanciful account of a middle-class white kid from Chicago's Northwest Side who used the means at his disposable, however questionable, to further the rights of African Americans.

NOVEMBER 10—PAUL BLEY (1932–)

b. Montreal, Canada

Pianist

[AVANT-GARDE JAZZ; FREE JAZZ]

Other jazz notables born on this day: Houston Person (1934); Andrew Cyrille (1939); Hubert Laws (1939)

Jazz notables deceased on this day: Ida Cox (1967); Harlan Leonard (1983); Carmen McRae (1994)

♫

An early leader and one of the pioneering figures in the avant-garde jazz movement of the late 1950s and early '60s, Paul Bley is one of the twentieth century's most influential jazz pianists and composers. A key link between Bill Evans and Keith Jarrett, Bley's bold yet thoughtful playing has long offered pianists an alternative approach to improvising. Having played straightforward bop in his earlier years, he became one of the most singular stylists to emerge during the 1960s. His trio work during the early and mid-1960s set the direction that many other explorative trios would take in that decade.

A "musical adventurer of the highest order,"[5] Bley sought out vitally creative collaborators from his youth. By the age of thirteen he was leading groups in Montreal and began touring Canada. While still in his teens he organized a fundraising concert in Montreal, brought Charlie Parker up from New York as the main attraction, and accompanied the master saxophonist on piano. He attended Juilliard during 1950 and 1952, where he studied composition and conducting. Established musicians quickly recognized his extraordinary talents, and by 1951 he had recorded an album with the great bass player Oscar Pettiford. By the age of twenty Bley was leading his own trio in New York. Charles Mingus championed his cause and got him his first released album, *Introducing Paul Bley* (1953), an impressive debut with Mingus and Art Blakey as his rhythm section. In 1957 he moved to the Los Angeles area, where he played with musicians associated with the emerging avant-garde movement, including Ornette Coleman, Don Cherry, Charlie Haden, and Billy Higgins.

---

5. Carr et al., *Jazz: The Rough Guide*, 77.

Following his marriage to pianist/composer Carla Bley (1957–67), he returned to the East Coast to help promote her innovative miniature free-jazz compositions. In 1961 he joined Jimmy Giuffre's groundbreaking chamber jazz trio. Unfortunately, the trio's music was too advanced to gain much of a reception, and it disbanded in 1962, after recording *Free Fall*, one of the most revolutionary recordings to come out of the 1960s. During the following year, with his own trio, he recorded the album *Footloose*, which influenced many, including Jarrett, who said it was "a record I've listened to thousands of times." In 1964 Bley participated in the famous October Revolution in Jazz and was a founder of the Jazz Composers Guild, whose aim was to further the jazz avant-garde. He recorded frequently with his trios, and then when electronic instruments became more portable, he and his second wife, vocalist Annette Peacock, presented in 1969 what was reportedly the world's first synthesizer concert. In 1974, with his third wife, the artist Carol Gross, he formed his short-lived Improvising Artists label to release records of his own and of innovators such as Sam Rivers, Dave Holland, Gary Peacock, Ran Blake, Jaco Pastorius, and Sun Ra.

NOVEMBER 11—GUNTHER SCHULLER (1925–)[6]

b. New York, NY

French Horn Player; Composer; Conductor; Writer

[THIRD STREAM; CLASSICAL; RAGTIME]

Other jazz notables born on this day: Dick Wilson (1911); Mose Allison (1927); Hannibal Peterson (1948)

Jazz notables deceased on this day: Erskine Hawkins (1993); Kenny Kirkland (date uncertain); Panama Francis (2001)

♪

During the 1950s the influence of the Modern Jazz Quartet was considerable, both in America and overseas. The group's attempts to apply European classical forms to jazz greatly appealed to many conservative-trained players coming into jazz. The improvised solo in a small-group context was, according to these musicians, a limited musical form that had been thoroughly explored. It was time to find ways of fitting the music into more spacious frameworks, and during that decade a number of composers attempted to combine jazz bands and concert orchestras in various ways. Gunther Schuller heralded these experiments as representing a "Third Stream" in music, a term he coined at Brandeis University in 1957, where he founded an annual jazz festival.

Schuller is considered the jazz world's greatest classical friend.[7] The son of a violinist with the New York Philharmonic, Schuller was a French horn player with the Metropolitan Opera in New York from 1945 to 1959. Although brought up and educated in classical

---

6. Though Gunther Schuller's birthdate is now acknowledged as November 22, I am using November 11, the date established by Leonard Feather and Ira Gitler in their *Biographical Encyclopedia of Jazz*.

7. Bogdanov et al., *All Music Guide to Jazz*, 1122.

music, from the beginning he had a great understanding and appreciation of jazz. He became an early admirer of pianist/composer John Lewis and composer George Russell, working closely with both musicians on a number of occasions. He first attracted attention in jazz by playing French horn on four tracks of Miles Davis's seminal *Birth of the Cool* sessions in 1950 and also appeared in Gil Evans's orchestra on Miles's *Porgy and Bess* (1958). In 1955 Schuller and Lewis co-founded the Jazz and Classical Music Society (originally the Modern Jazz Society), which recorded *Music for Brass* (1956) and *Modern Jazz Concert* (1957) with a mixed ensemble of jazz and classical instrumentalists led by Schuller. The recorded material became the subject of intense debate in the jazz community, and numerous composers began to experiment with related ideas.

With Lewis, Schuller organized summer music schools of jazz in Lenox, Massachusetts and presented the first jazz concert ever held at Tanglewood, in 1963. From 1967 to 1977 Schuller was president of the New England Conservatory at Boston, where he created a jazz department. As the first to offer a full four-year degree in jazz, the Conservatory set a model for many music schools including Berklee, which got its own degree course a few years later. The Third Stream movement continues to this day under the guidance of Schuller and Ran Blake, who chaired the third stream department of the New England Conservatory from 1973. While remaining active in third-stream musical activity, Schuller has found the time to write essays on jazz, including two brilliant tomes: *Early Jazz: Its Roots and Musical Development* (1968) and *The Swing Era: The Development of Jazz 1930–1945* (1989). He is currently working on Volume 3, which will take readers from bebop to the present.

NOVEMBER 12—BUCK CLAYTON (1911–1991)

b. Parsons, KS; d. New York, NY

Trumpeter; Arranger

[MAINSTREAM JAZZ; SWING]

Other jazz notables born on this day: Jo Stafford (1920); Charlie Mariano (1923); Sam Jones (1924)

Jazz notables deceased on this day: Dicky Wells (1985)

♪

One cold January night in 1936 John Hammond stepped out of the Congress Hotel in Chicago and went to his car, where he had a twelve-tube Motorola radio with a large speaker. He was in town on business, and spent so much time on the road that he installed a superior instrument to keep in touch with music around the country. That night he heard Count Basie's band for the first time, broadcasting live from the Reno Club in Kansas City. His enthusiasm for the band's novel sound was immediate and he determined to sign the orchestra to a recording contract and bring it to New York. "Count Bill Basie has by far and away the finest dance orchestra in the country," he wrote in *Down*

Beat. "He has excellent soloists. . . and a driving rhythm section more exciting than any in American orchestral history."

Enthusiasm like that inevitably attracted the interest of others. Before Hammond could sign Basie for Columbia, Dave Kapp, a representative for Decca Records, came to Kansas City, and on the pretext of being Hammond's friend, signed Basie to a contract. Joe Glaser, Louis Armstrong's manager, also came to town, and hired away trumpeter Hot Lips Page, afraid he might challenge Armstrong's supremacy. Basie, about to head east and in need of a replacement for Page, found him in Buck Clayton, a master melodist who was a native of Kansas but had honed his skills in California and in a two-year stint with a hotel dance band in Shanghai, China. A valued soloist with Basie's orchestra until 1943, when he left for army service, Clayton became a celebrated studio and jam session player, writer, and arranger.

By 1937 Basie's band was a big hit in New York. The recordings made by this band, featuring the contrasting tenors of Lester Young and Herschel Evans and the twosome of Clayton and Harry "Sweets" Edison on trumpet, rank historically alongside the recordings of Armstrong's Hot Five and Hot Seven. Clayton was Basie's chief trumpeter during the band's classic period, but he is heard to better advantage on excellent recordings cut with small groups made up of musicians from the Basie band or put together by pianist Teddy Wilson, often to accompany Billie Holiday. Clayton's sensitive style and attractive tone made him an ideal accompanist for singers such as Holiday. During the late 1930s these sessions resulted in some of jazz history's finest small-group recordings.

After discharge from the army, Clayton became one of the leading figures of mainstream jazz, arranging for Basie, Benny Goodman, and Harry James and joining Norman Granz's newly formed Jazz at the Philharmonic show. He is best remembered during this period for a set of outstanding recordings for Columbia under the title *Buck Clayton Jam Sessions* (1953–56), in which he and kindred musicians cemented the mainstream jazz boom through extended performances of jazz standards. In later life his lip failed him, and he turned more and more to arranging.

NOVEMBER 13—BENNIE MOTEN (1894–1935)

b. Kansas City, MO; d. Kansas City, MO

Pianist; Bandleader

[CLASSIC JAZZ; BIG BAND]

Other jazz notables born on this day: Hampton Hawes (1928); Idris Muhammad (1939)

Jazz notables deceased on this day: Harold Vick (1987); Bill Doggett (1996)

♪

During the late 1920s and early '30s when the swing band movement was experiencing its birth pangs, there was occurring in the American Southwest a local form of music that eventually became part of the swing band phenomenon, though the music forming in this part of the country was built upon a tradition significantly different from that in the East.

The area had seen a large influx of African-Americans after the Civil War, and these growing communities were still closely connected to the black folk music tradition through work songs and gospel church music. The area was especially rich in the blues, and the region's musicians were far more inclined to use a blues approach to jazz than were their counterparts in the East. Consequently, the Southwestern players tended to think less in terms of complicated written scores, which many could not read, working instead from relatively simple "head" arrangements, which they harmonized by ear and memorized. Though some of the top Southwestern bands, such as the Bennie Moten group, did at times use relatively difficult arrangements, these two factors—the feeling for the blues and the limitation in technique—produced in that region a simpler big band style, one that utilized riffs over worked-out melodies. Whereas Eastern bands were using complex arrangements and rich harmonies, the emphasis in the Southwestern territories was on ability to swing, good soloing, and on rhythm created by the piano. The bands that were developing this style became known as "territory" bands. Each had a home base, and each sought a monopoly in the surrounding area. By the late 1920s the Moten band was acknowledged to be the top territory band.

Though this band was the Southwest's most prestigious, it was not considered by everyone to be the hottest band. That title, many felt, belonged to the Blue Devils, a band organized in Oklahoma City by a local bass player named Walter Page. The Blue Devils eventually included saxophonist Lester Young, trumpeter "Hot Lips" Page (no relation to Walter), pianist Count Basie, and vocalist Jimmy Rushing. After the group disbanded for financial reasons, Moten was able to lure several of the former Blue Devils into his band, including Basie, Hot Lips, Rushing, and Young. Tenor saxophonist Ben Webster, drummer Jo Jones, and eventually Walter Page, also joined.

These musicians helped establish the Kansas City or southwest style of orchestral jazz, characterized by a well-integrated rhythm section and the frequent use of instrumental riffs and blues chord sequences. The group's arrangements effectively blended solo and ensemble passages into organic compositions. Except for Ellington's, they were the most advanced arrangements of their time. The group was doing well in the territories until 1935, when Moten died suddenly, during a routine tonsillectomy. After Moten's death, the group's personnel and style continued through the Count Basie orchestra.

NOVEMBER 14—ART HODES (1904?–1993)

b. Nikoliev, Ukraine; d. Harvey, IL

Pianist; Broadcaster; Writer

[DIXIELAND]

Other jazz notables born on this day: Clancy Hayes (1908); Billy Bauer (1915); Don Ewell (1916); Ellis Marsalis (1934)
Jazz notables deceased on this day: Hilton Jefferson (1968); Wild Bill Davison (1989)

BLUE NOTES

♪

Chicago was a hot town in the 1920s. The North Side had its famous clubs—the Green Mill, College Inn, Blackhawk, Kelly's Stables, and Friar's Inn—but the hottest music could be found on the South Side "Stroll." Starting with the Pekin Inn at Twenty-Seventh Street, the Stroll's clubs, speakeasies, theaters, and ballrooms sat practically door-to-door along State Street. Some of the most famous spots were the Lincoln Gardens and the Dreamland, where Louis Armstrong debuted with King Oliver, and the Plantation and Sunset cafés, where they played in rival bands. There was also the De Luxe Café, where Jelly Roll Morton and Freddie Keppard played, the Grand Terrace and Regal Theater, where Earl Hines appeared, Jimmie Noone's Apex Club, and the Vendome Theater, one of several venues used by Erskine Tate's elegant orchestra.

Among those who came to Chicago's South Side clubs was a ragtag crew of jazz-mad young white musicians whose version of New Orleans music would eventually be labeled "Chicago-style jazz." Some came from comfortable suburban homes, others from the slums, but together they represented the next generation of Chicago jazzmen. The first wave included Bix Beiderbecke, Eddie Condon, Benny Goodman, and members of the Austin High Gang (particularly Jimmy McPartland, Frank Teschemacher, Bud Freeman, and Dave Tough). Within a few years Muggsy Spanier, George Wettling, Gene Krupa, Wingy Manone, Art Hodes, and others would follow their example.

Hodes, who came with his family from the Ukraine to the U.S. when he was six months old, was unsure of the year of his birth: "somewhere between 1904 and 1906," he recalled. "We left hurriedly, and we had no papers." His arrival in the 1920's was fortuitous, however, for he had the opportunity to witness Chicago jazz during its prime years in the 1920s, where he soaked up the music of barroom piano professors and other jazz pioneers in gangster-controlled South Side clubs. Throughout his long career he championed traditional jazz, whether through his distinctive piano playing, his writings (which included many articles and liner notes), or his work on radio and educational television.

Renowned for the feeling he put into blues, Hodes was particularly effective on up-tempo tunes. Having taken piano lessons at Hull House (others who studied at this institution for deprived youth included Goodman and Milt Hinton) from 1916 to 1920, Hodes made his recording debut with Manone in 1928. He worked mainly in Chicago until 1938, when he moved to New York to play with fellow Chicagoans Joe Marsala (1939) and Mezz Mezzrow (1940) before forming his own band in 1941. During 1943 to 1947 Hodes edited the important magazine *The Jazz Record*, presented a weekly radio show, founded his own record label, and made a significant impression with his up-tempo Dixieland recordings (1944–45). In 1950 he returned to Chicago, where he remained active in jazz. During the 1960s he hosted the television series *Jazz Alley*, wrote for *Down Beat*, and was a jazz educator. Hodes recorded frequently after that and was widely recognized as one of the last survivors of Chicago jazz.[8]

---

8. Bogdanov et al., *All Music Guide to Jazz*, 602.

NOVEMBER 15—KEVIN EUBANKS (1957–)

b. Philadelphia, PA

Guitarist; Leader

[Post-Bop]

Other jazz notables born on this day: Gus Johnson (1913); Jerome Richardson (1920)
Jazz notables deceased on this day: Toots Mondello (1992)

♪

Though Kevin Eubanks became a familiar name to millions of Americans in 1995 when he began leading Jay Leno's *Tonight Show* Band, his reputation as a jazz guitarist had been well established for over a decade. A versatile guitarist who plays both acoustic and electric guitars in bop, free-jazz, and jazz-rock styles, Eubanks comes from a musical family that includes older brother, trombonist Robin, uncle Ray Bryant (a jazz pianist), and his mother Vera, a music teacher. Eubanks grew up in Philadelphia, where he began studying the violin at the age of seven and later became proficient on the piano and trumpet as well.

At the age of twelve he fell in love with the guitar at a memorable James Brown concert. When he told his parents he would like to add guitar to his repertoire, they were unsupportive and turned down his request for lessons. Undaunted, he acquired a guitar and began teaching himself. By the age of thirteen, inspired initially by John McLaughlin and Jimmy Hendrix, the prodigy was playing rock and funk in Philadelphia jazz clubs. In 1976, after listening to Wes Montgomery, he enrolled at Berklee, where he met saxophonist Branford Marsalis, older brother of the legendary trumpeter Wynton Marsalis. At Berklee he came under fire from his more traditional-minded instructors for playing without using a guitar pick, an unusual technique he borrowed from Montgomery who, like Eubanks, was self-taught.

After studying at Berklee, Eubanks joined Art Blakey's Jazz Messengers (1980–81), touring Europe with the famed outfit. Upon his return to the U.S. he moved to New York, where he began to establish a reputation, honing his skills in jazz clubs around Manhattan. In 1982 he toured with Sam Rivers, whose free-improvising concepts radically altered Eubanks's ideas about music, and recorded with Paquito D'Rivera, Chico Freeman, James Newton, Wynton Marsalis, and Bobby McFerrin. The following year he toured Great Britain with the Mike Gibbs band. Over the next few years he recorded a number of albums, including a series of fusion albums for GRP. While these albums brought him a wider public, they also branded him a commercial artist in the eyes of more traditional-minded purists.

In 1989 Eubanks began leading a touring band that included his brother Robin, Dave Holland, and Marvin "Smitty" Smith. It disbanded in 1992, when Eubanks moved to Los Angeles to join Branford Marsalis's new group, which was appearing on *The Tonight Show*. The invitation to join his old friend would change his life, for in 1995, when Marsalis left to pursue other projects, he was asked to take over as bandleader and music director. In his fifteen years in that late-night role (he left in 2010 to pursue his career as performer and composer), Eubanks arranged for and accompanied probably every big name in the music. In 1995 he co-authored, with J. Amaral, the how-to book, *Kevin Eubanks: Creative Guitarist*.

NOVEMBER 16—DIANA KRALL (1964–)

b. Nanaimo, British Columbia, Canada

Vocalist; Pianist; Leader

[VOCAL JAZZ; TRADITIONAL POP; CONTEMPORARY JAZZ; NEO-BOP; SWING]

Other jazz notables born on this day: W. C. Handy (1873); Jesse Stone (1901); Eddie Condon (1905); Ben Thigpen (1908); Al Lucas (1916)

Jazz notables deceased on this day: Al Haig (1982); Vic Dickenson (1984); Lee Castle (1990); Tommy Flanagan (2001)

♪

Only rarely does an artist emerge to master a musical idiom and translate it to the masses. For modern jazz, that artist is undoubtedly Diana Krall. Blessed with a natural beauty and with pianistic and vocal talent, her greatest attribute may be her choice of material. She has an uncanny ability to find the perfect song and make it her own. Whether it be Nat King Cole, George Gershwin, Cole Porter, or her wonderful rendition of David Frishberg's "Peel Me a Grape," she possesses the ability to create music that speaks personally to every listener. Following in the footsteps of jazz greats like Ella Fitzgerald and Peggy Lee, Krall has won fans and critics alike with her contemporary style and mellow vocals. Because of her talent and intuition, she has become the new female superstar of jazz and its best-selling vocalist.

Diana's love affair with classic jazz ballads began when she was an infant. She got much of her musical education from her father, a stride pianist with an extensive record collection, particularly of pianists from the 1920s and '30s. Fats Waller, Nat King Cole, Bill Evans, Frank Sinatra, opera, and the music of old radio shows helped form her musical taste. Krall attended the Berklee College of Music on a music scholarship in the early 1980s, and then moved to Los Angeles. After a three year stay (studying piano privately with Alan Broadbent and Jimmie Rowles) she settled in Toronto, but by 1990 she was based in New York, where she formed a trio with guitarist Russell Malone and a succession of bass players. After releasing her first album (*Stepping Out*, 1993) on the Montreal-based Justin Time label, she signed to GRP and then transferred to its Impulse! division for possibly her best jazz-based recording, a Nat King Cole tribute called *All for You* (1995).

Krall's recordings document her development from a relatively bold singer in the manner of Carmen McRae to a subtler and more slyly confident stylist after the manner of Shirley Horn. Later albums, including the Grammy-winning *When I Look in Your Eyes* (1999) and particularly *The Look of Love*, released in 2001 on Verve, are attempts to push Krall to a wider pop/smooth-jazz audience. Krall performed extensively in North America, Europe, and Japan during the late 1990s, appearing at major festivals and leading club and concert venues, notably Carnegie Hall, where she performed tributes to Fitzgerald (1996) and Cole (1997). Krall's *Live in Paris* album (2002) affirms her as a crossover phenomenon who has remained faithful to her bop and swing roots.

NOVEMBER 17—ROSWELL RUDD (1935–)

b. Sharon, CT

Trombonist

[AVANT-GARDE; FREE JAZZ]

Other jazz notables born on this day: Shorty Sherock (1915)
Jazz notables deceased on this day: James P. Johnson (1955)

♪

During the 1950s a group of revolutionary players in America were all simultaneously coming upon a similar set of ideas. But unlike their bebop predecessors, they had no Minton's and no Billy Eckstein band, where they could share their ideas and provide the necessary emotional support that would ensure momentum and continuity. Cecil Taylor was in Boston, hammering away at an old piano in a ruined practice studio; Ornette Coleman was practicing in a garage in Los Angeles; and Steve Lacy, Herbie Nichols, and Roswell Rudd were playing in Dixieland bands for their living. These individuals came from diverse musical and social backgrounds, and their approaches to music were often diametrically opposed. But they were all motivated by the same idea: to "free" jazz from what they saw as restrictions of chords, ordinary harmony, bar lines, and even the scale, all staples on which Western music, including jazz, had largely been based.[9]

It is no coincidence that Roswell Rudd, free jazz's most acclaimed trombonist, bypassed bebop altogether. While the blockish rhythms and rough-hewn sonorities of early jazz were tailor-made for the trombone, the technical requirements of modern jazz just about put it out of business. Over the years a number of very fine players (such as J.J. Johnson and Frank Rosolino) managed to adapt the instrument to bop, but not without sacrificing the peculiar tonal expressivity that sets the trombone apart from other jazz instruments. It wasn't until the advent of free jazz that trombonists reclaimed the slides, smears, growls, and groans that had virtually disappeared from the current of jazz's development for some twenty-plus years. Rudd exploited the trombone's natural proclivities to the fullest, bringing to free jazz many of the qualities often associated with the early jazz trombone, including a large, warm tone, an earthy vocal sound, and a deeply felt sense of rhythm.[10]

Rudd studied French horn from age eleven, and then began teaching himself to play the trombone while in his teens, influenced by the work of Woody Herman's star trombonist, Bill Harris. From 1954 to 1959 he played with traditional jazz groups, including Eli's Chosen Six, a Dixieland group he joined while attending Yale University.

---

9. Collier, *Making of Jazz*, 454.
10. Kernfeld, *New Grove Dictionary of Jazz*, Vol. 3, 467.

In the early 1960s he began working with the avant-garde, including with Taylor (1960), Nichols (1960–62, who became something of a mentor to him), and Lacy, in a quartet that exclusively played the music of Thelonious Monk. In 1964 he was a founding member of the New York Art Quartet, for which he also wrote compositions and arrangements, and later that year he took part in the October Revolution in Jazz, an early free jazz festival organized by Bill Dixon in New York City. Rudd faded from visibility during the 1970s and '80s, but he resumed recording during the 1990s, when he regained his reputation as "the father of free jazz trombone."

NOVEMBER 18—DON CHERRY (1936–1995)

b. Oklahoma City, OK; d. Malaga, Spain

Cornetist; Bandleader

[AVANT-GARDE JAZZ; FREE JAZZ; WORLD FUSION]

Other jazz notables born on this day: Boots Mussulli (1917); Claude Williamson (1926); Sheila Jordan (1928); Cindy Blackman (1959)

Jazz notables deceased on this day: Ted Heath (1969); Lennie Tristano (1978); Cab Calloway (1994)

♪

Don Cherry was a major force in two areas: in free jazz and as a pioneer of the movement in jazz to absorb and fuse vital elements of ethnic music.[11] He first came to public attention as a regular member of Ornette Coleman's groups (1957–61), playing a pocket (miniature) cornet. Lacking the speed, agility, and range of the average modern jazz trumpeter, Cherry instead explored the tone qualities of his instrument. Like Coleman, Cherry's sound came as close to the expressive qualities of the human voice as was instrumentally possible.[12] Since the mid-1960s he became progressively involved in ethnic music, studying techniques and instruments from cultures as different as Tibet, China, Africa, and India. Considering himself a "world musician," he began calling his music "primal music."

When he was four years old Cherry moved to Los Angeles. He became fascinated with brass instruments and traveled daily to study with the respected music teacher Samuel Brown; among his fellow students was drummer Billy Higgins. As a teenager he played the piano in a rhythm-and-blues band with Higgins, and in 1956 they met Coleman. Cherry became impressed with the eccentric saxophonist and joined a small group of dedicated musicians who practiced in a garage. In 1959 he and Coleman spent the summer at the Lenox School of Music, at the invitation of John Lewis and Gunther Schuller, where jazz critics Nat Hentoff and Martin Williams championed them. Later that year they made their controversial New York debut, playing free jazz in a quartet with Charlie Haden and Higgins. That Five Spot engagement threw the jazz world into

---

11. Carr et al., *Jazz: The Rough Guide*, 134.
12. Bogdanov et al., *All Music Guide to Jazz*, 220.

turmoil. It did not help that Coleman was playing a plastic alto and that Cherry was using a pocket trumpet. It looked as if they were playing on toys. But all the musicians, supporters and detractors alike, had the uneasy feeling that just as Charlie Parker and Dizzy Gillespie had thrown the swing players into obsolescence, so Coleman and Cherry might represent the future of jazz.[13]

Cherry stayed with Coleman through the early 1960s and then moved to Europe, where he led a band with Gato Barbieri (1964–66). The rest of the 1960s he spent gypsy-fashion, wandering the world, playing and absorbing its music. During the early 1970s Cherry settled in Sweden, working an organic farm and teaching world music and culture to children on radio, television, and through workshops. By the end of the decade he began an association with Collin Walcott, who was also steeped in the ethnic musics of the world. In 1982 Cherry received a grant to work with school children in Watts, where he had been brought up, introducing them to jazz. He continued to tour during the 1980s and into the '90s, including a 1993 tour with Coleman, but by this time his health had deteriorated from the effects of a drug addiction that had plagued him throughout his career.

NOVEMBER 19—KENNY WERNER (1951–)

b. Brooklyn, NY

Pianist

[POST-BOP]

Other jazz notables born on this day: Vincent Herring (1964)
Jazz notables deceased on this day: Georg Brunis (1974); Sonny Criss (1977)

♫

Kenny Werner, an iconoclastic thinker and renegade spirit, is one of the most astounding small-group pianists on the scene today. His empathy for a given musical situation makes him highly valued as a sideman, especially with singers (notably Roseanna Vitro) and horn players, including frequent associates Joe Lovano and Tom Harrell. The award-winning pianist got an early start in life, joining a children's song-and-dance group at the age of four and playing stride piano on television at the age of eleven. He attended Manhattan School of Music while still in high school, and then became a concert piano major upon graduation. His emotional need to improvise gradually pulled him away from the classical world and into the realm of jazz. In 1970 he transferred to Berklee, where he began to find his creative direction. In Boston he came under the influence of piano teacher Madame Chaloff (saxophonist Serge Chaloff's mother), who became his spiritual guide. "She was the first person I met who pulled together spiritual and musical aspects," Werner recalls. She ignited in him a concept that was furthered by his next teacher, Juao Assis Brasil, a concert pianist who demonstrated to Werner effortless piano playing with a self-loving attitude. Brasil's ideology blossomed in Werner and constitutes his approach to music and creativity.

---

13. Collier, *Making of Jazz*, 465.

Werner worked in Brazil and Bermuda and upon his return began playing and recording with Charles Mingus, Archie Shepp, the Mel Lewis Orchestra, and saxophonist Joe Lovano, with whom he established a particularly strong musical alliance. He freelanced with jazz greats such as Bob Brookmeyer, Ron Carter, and Dizzie Gillespie before forming a long-lasting trio with Ratzo Harris and Tom Rainey (1981–95). The band only recorded twice, though the members continued as colleagues on the faculty of the New School in New York. Their final recording, the trio's only live recording in its fifteen-year history (*Live at Visiones*, 1995), allowed listeners to witness the intensity that happened regularly when the members played gigs.

In 2000, after several years of experimenting with various combinations, Werner settled on a trio with Ari Hoening (drums) and Johannes Weidenmuller (bass). With these young and talented sidemen he formed a unique relationship, and after their first recording in November 2000, a live date from the Sunset Café in Paris, he made a decision never to record a trio in the studio again. "It just doesn't tell the story of the kind of great things that happen spontaneously on the bandstand when we have the resonance of people listening and watching," he explained. Werner expanded his thoughts on the interplay between performers and listeners in his 1997 book *Effortless Mastery: Liberating the Master Musician Within*, a text that changed conceptions not only about how to practice, play, and listen, but also about the role of music. Arguing that music can be a divine tool for inducing mystical ecstasy, Werner states: "I want to continue to lose myself more and more in the bliss of music. In this way, the music wakes us all to who we really are."

NOVEMBER 20—JUNE CHRISTY (1925–1990)

b. Springfield, IL; d. Los Angeles, CA

Vocalist

[VOCAL JAZZ; TRADITIONAL POP; COOL]

Other jazz notables born on this day: Don Braden (1963)
Jazz notables deceased on this day: Don Stovall (1970); Bobby Plater (1982)

♪

The bop revolution of the 1940s left the jazz world in disarray. Some ignored the new music while others attempted an accommodation with bop. By 1950 at least four identifiable factions vied with one another to determine the future of jazz: swing players, Dixielanders (who insisted that only New Orleans jazz and derivatives was the true jazz), beboppers, and a fourth group, which for a time threatened to push the rest into its shadow. This mode, known as the "cool school," was a reaction, not so much to bop, but to hot music in general.

The term "cool" in jazz was the continuation of a movement that had been going on in jazz for quite some time, namely the attempt to create "symphonic jazz." From its earliest days, jazz had felt a pull exerted by the European symphonic tradition. In 1941 the pianist/arranger Stan Kenton formed a popular band that began applying European forms to jazz. By 1943 the fourteen-piece orchestra began attracting attention, particularly after recording "Artistry in Rhythm," a hit that led the band to fame. In 1944 the band acquired vocalist Anita O'Day, a masterful scat singer and improviser. A year later, when she decided that Kenton's progressive jazz did not suit her, she recommended a nineteen-year-old singer, June Christy, as her successor.

Born Shirley Luster, Christy began her career in 1938, singing with local bands. She moved to Chicago in the early 1940s, changed her name to Sharon Leslie, and sang with a group led by Boyd Raeburn. In 1945, after hearing that O'Day had just left Kenton's Orchestra, she auditioned for the role and won. Despite a resemblance to O'Day, the singer—renamed June Christy—soon found her own style, contributing significantly to Kenton's repertoire. In 1945 she recorded the best-selling "Tampico" with the band and her fame spread rapidly. *Down Beat* named her "Best Female Vocalist with a Big Band" in 1946, 1947, 1948, and 1950.

After the band broke up in 1948 Christy worked the nightclub circuit before reuniting with Kenton in 1950 for his Innovations in Modern Music Orchestra, an ultra-modern forty-piece ensemble. She had already debuted as a solo act the year before, recording for Capitol with a group led by her husband, Kenton tenor saxophonist Bob Cooper. Her debut album for Capitol, *Something Cool* (1953–55), launched the vocal cool movement and hit the Top 20 album charts in America, as did a follow-up, *The Misty Miss Christy* (1955–56). These albums became the first of nine collaborations between Christy and an orchestra led by the superb arranger, Pete Rugolo. Christy had occasional reunions with Kenton, and despite her retirement in 1965, she appeared with the bandleader at the 1972 Newport Jazz Festival. She ceased performing altogether after a European festival tour with Shorty Rogers's West Coast Giants in 1985. Christy's breathy, husky sound and narrow vibrato were ideally suited to "cool" jazz. Although she was criticized for faulty intonation and for a weak sense of swing, she achieved considerable popular success, epitomizing the vocal "cool" movement of the 1950s.

NOVEMBER 21—COLEMAN HAWKINS (1904–1969)

b. St. Joseph, MO; d. New York, NY

Tenor Saxophonist; Leader

[MAINSTREAM JAZZ; CLASSIC JAZZ; SWING; BOP]

Other jazz notables born on this day: Geoff Keezer (1970)
Jazz notables deceased on this day: Larry Shields (1953); Ralph Burns (2001)

♫

For many people today, tenor saxophone symbolizes jazz. Coleman Hawkins, the first important tenor saxophonist and one of the three most influential tenor saxophonists in jazz history (together with Lester Young and John Coltrane), was once introduced as "the man for whom Adolphe Sax invented the saxophone," which is one way of saying that Hawkins was not only "the indomitable emperor of the tenor, to a degree that no other jazz musicians has ever dominated an instrument . . . but that he established its legitimacy in contemporary music."[14] A consistently modern improviser whose knowledge of chords and harmonics was encyclopedic, Hawkins had a forty-year prime (1925–65), during which time he held his own with any competitor.[15] He was only bested once, by twenty-four-year-old Lester Young, at a famous all-night cutting contest in Kansas City in 1933, a defeat Hawkins never forgot. Prior to the arrival of Hawkins the saxophone was seen as little more than a novelty instrument, but Hawkins's super-charged playing brought it recognition. His deep-toned, husky command of the tenor set the pace for future tenors, and the tenor sax became one of the most popular instruments in jazz.

A professional when he was twelve, Hawkins started performing for school audiences in St. Joseph, Missouri, and in his early teens he was playing regularly in Kansas City. In 1923 he moved to New York, where he became bandleader Fletcher Henderson's star tenor for ten years (1924–34). By 1925 he was a major soloist; with his roller-coaster speed, expensive clothes, and fast cars, he quickly established himself as "king of the saxophone," ruthlessly cutting down anyone rash enough to challenge him. By 1934 he tired of the struggling Henderson Orchestra and moved to Europe, spending five years (1934–39) overseas. He quickly became a celebrity, and appreciative audiences treated him more like a concert artist than an entertainer. As World War II approached, Hawkins returned to the U.S. Although Young had emerged with a totally new style on tenor, Hawkins showed that he was still a dominant force by winning heated jam sessions.

At the end of a studio session in 1939, while he was re-establishing his saxophone supremacy, Hawkins recorded "Body and Soul," the side forever associated with his name. The recording, comparable to Armstrong's seminal "West End Blues," became a jazz classic. According to legend, Hawkins had finished the recording session when the producer induced him to play "Body and Soul," a tune that had been recorded earlier that year by Chu Berry—another supposed rival. Hawkins had no arrangement and was reluctant to play the piece, but he agreed to a single take, without rehearsal. After two measures something happened: "Body and Soul" all but disappeared. Lifted on a surge of inspiration, Hawkins extended the song's initial phrase through two full choruses and a coda, never touching down on the melody. The record became a smash hit and one of the single most acclaimed improvisations in jazz.

NOVEMBER 22—HOAGY CARMICHAEL (1899–1981)

b. Bloomington, IN; d. Rancho Mirage, CA

Songwriter; Vocalist; Pianist; Bandleader

[Tin Pan Alley; Traditional Pop; Standards; Classic Jazz; American Popular Song]

Other jazz notables born on this day: Horace Henderson (1904); Ernie Caceres (1911); Gunther Schuller (1925); Jimmy Knepper (1927)
Jazz notables deceased on this day: Fred Guy (1971); Norman Granz (2001)

14. Giddins, *Visions of Jazz*, 119.
15. Bogdanov et al., *All Music Guide to Jazz*, 564–65.

♪

John Lewis, the pianist and music director of the Modern Jazz Quartet, noted that jazz had evolved in a symbiotic relationship with the American popular song: "Jazz developed while the great popular music was being turned out. It was a golden age for songs. They had a classic quality in length and shape and form and flexibility of harmony. The jazz musicians were drawn to this music as a source of [improvisational] material."[16] One of the great composers of the American popular song, Hoagy Carmichael differed from most of the others in that he was also a fine vocalist and pianist. Such Carmichael songs as "Georgia on My Mind," "Up the Lazy River," "Rockin' Chair," "The Nearness of You," "In the Cool, Cool, Cool of the Evening," "Skylark," and particularly "Stardust," one of the most-recorded tunes in history, have long been standards, each flexible enough to receive definitive treatment by jazz instrumentalists and singers alike.

Hoagy studied piano at home with his mother, a professional pianist, and then attended Indiana University, where he organized a college band while aspiring to practice law. In 1924 he formed a friendship with his idol Bix Beiderbecke, and the same year Beiderbecke and the Wolverines recorded one of his early compositions, "Riverboat Shuffle." Bix was in Cincinnati around that time, playing in a dingy third-floor ballroom called Doyle's Dancing Academy, when he received a letter from Hoagy proposing to arrange a full season of weekend dances for him and the Wolverines if the band could get to the Indiana University campus on its own. The band agreed to the proposal, but the manager of Doyle's refused to let them go. They had signed a contract that still had weeks to run, and as insurance against their leaving, he locked their instruments in his ballroom. The following night, Bix and his friends managed to slip into the building and, using some clothesline, carefully lowered their tuba, string bass, and bass drum from the third-floor window into a waiting car below. The band was a sensation on the campus and then played at dances all over Indiana and Michigan.[17]

That summer the Wolverines got the offer they had been hoping for: a thirty-day engagement at New York's Cinderella Ballroom, on Broadway. Like his friends, young Carmichael also set out in a new direction, abandoning law and moving into jazz circles. In 1929 he moved to New York to pursue a career as a successful songwriter. There he performed and recorded with Louis Armstrong, Mildred Bailey, the Dorsey Brothers, Benny Goodman, Eddie Lang, and many others. By 1935 he moved to Hollywood and found work in the film industry, playing effective cameo roles in films such as *To Have and Have Not* (1944), *The Best Years of Our Lives* (1946), and *Young Man with a Horn* (1950), the latter film ostensibly based on the life of Beiderbecke.

---

16. Kirchner, *Oxford Companion to Jazz*, 250.
17. Ward and Burns, *Jazz: A History*, 101.

BLUE NOTES

NOVEMBER 23—TYREE GLENN (1912–1974)

b. Corsicana, TX; d. Englewood, NJ

Trombonist; Vibraphonist

[SWING]

Other jazz notables born on this day: Ray Drummond (1946)
Jazz notables deceased on this day: Stan Hasselgard (1948)

♪

Tyree Glenn, who performed the unusual double of trombone and vibes, played with some of the most important bandleaders in jazz, including Benny Carter, Cab Calloway, Duke Ellington, and Louis Armstrong. He played in local bands during his teenage years and then worked in territory bands in Virginia before moving to the West Coast, where he played with groups headed by Charlie Echols (1936) and Eddie Barefield. As a member of the ensemble led by the trumpeter and saxophonist Eddie Mallory, he accompanied singer Ethel Waters on tour. In 1939 he was injured in a tour bus crash but recovered quickly to play most of that year with Carter at the Savoy in Harlem.

Following a stint with Lionel Hampton at the Paradise nightclub in Los Angeles, the much traveled sideman became a longtime member of Cab Calloway's big band (1939–46), leading a trombone section in what was clearly the best band of Cab's career. Calloway was a stickler for polished performance, and the men who played for him over the years were some of the best in the business. Dizzy Gillespie, by now developing his revolutionary bebop style, was a member of the band at this time (1939–41), but was fired in 1941 after a spitball was mischievously thrown at Calloway (he accused Gillespie but the culprit was actually trumpeter Jonah Jones).

After World War II Glenn toured Europe in Don Redman's band (along with Don Byas) and then stayed briefly to work as a freelance in a small group that included pianist Billy Taylor. After his return to the U.S. in 1947 he joined Ellington, playing trombonist "Tricky Sam" Nanton's role to perfection for four years and occasionally playing vibes, becoming Ellington's only vibraphonist. During the 1950s Glenn was active in studio work, playing vibes. He also led his own quartet, freelanced in swing and Dixieland settings, and took up acting part-time. His small combos, which performed in New York during the late 1950s and then in Chicago around 1961, featured many distinguished players, including Lester Young (whom Glenn befriended and offered a job when the famous tenor saxophonist was out of work), Buster Bailey, Shorty Baker, Hank Jones, Tommy Flanagan, Milt Hinton, Tommy Potter, Elvin Jones, and Jo Jones.

During the early 1960s jazz suffered a deep decline in public support. Blacks returned to rhythm-and-blues, white kids began buying rock albums and jamming the rock venues, and older people seemed content to simply stay home and watch television. Desperate jazz musicians took jobs wherever they could find them—in cocktail lounges, studio orchestras, or backing rock and roll performers on records. While some musicians left for Europe or simply abandoned music altogether, Glenn was able to supplement his musical career by acting for television. In 1965 he joined Louis Armstrong's All-Stars, playing vibes and trombone until 1968. After Armstrong's death he led his own small group, working briefly with Ellington in 1971. He died on May 18, 1974, six days before Ellington, and was laid to rest in the same funeral home as the bandleader.

NOVEMBER 24—TEDDY WILSON (1912–1986)

b. Austin, TX; d. New Britain, CT

Pianist

[SWING]

Other jazz notables born on this day: Scott Joplin (1868); Rosa Henderson (1896); Wild Bill Davis (1918); Serge Chaloff (1923); Al Cohn (1925)
Jazz notables deceased on this day: Dick Wilson (1941); Joe Turner (1985)

♪

During the first few years of the swing era, when Benny Goodman's band was by far the most popular of America's big bands, racism was so intense that black and white musicians rarely performed together. Studio work was almost completely restricted to white musicians. African-American musicians complained about the discrimination, but the white musicians rarely attempted to help them; only a few, notably Goodman, dared to buck the trend. As one of the first bandleaders to feature black jazz players, Goodman brought a new audience and a new level of recognition to jazz. Goodman himself learned jazz from musicians, many of them black, which had left New Orleans for Chicago during the 1910s and early '20s. His borrowings from jazz, while the music was still unacceptable to whites on cultural and social grounds, and his contributions to integration, required great courage in an age of segregation.

If Goodman was primarily a popularizer of big bands, he was also an innovator of small ones. Shortly before he began the 1935 cross-country tour that is said to have initiated the swing era, Goodman attended a dinner engagement at Mildred Bailey's house in Forest Hills, New York. An urbane young African-American pianist by the name of Teddy Wilson was also present, and after the guests had finished eating, Bailey suggested that Wilson and Goodman perform together. The results were exhilarating, as if the two had been working together for years. Wilson's style—poised but inventive, succinct but swinging—was an ideal match for Goodman's clarinet. Joined by drummer Gene Krupa, the two recorded soon thereafter, and that was the birth of the Benny Goodman Trio.

In 1936, with the addition of vibraphonist Lionel Hampton, a quartet was formed whose public appearances helped break significant ground in the long struggle against segregation. Wilson played with Goodman's small ensembles from 1935 to 1939, but his greatest fame came from studio sessions he led during that time and immediately thereafter. Those small John Hammond-arranged groups featured Billie Holiday and virtually every important jazz player of the period and made Wilson the definitive swing pianist.

BLUE NOTES

Despite their respect for one another, Goodman and Wilson never became personal friends. The reasons were not racial, but due to personality and class. Wilson's parents were academics—his father was head of English at Tuskegee University and his mother head librarian—whereas Goodman's were penniless immigrants from Russia; Goodman's mother could not even read. "I'm sure Teddy must have sized Benny up and found him lacking in many ways," wrote Helen Oakley, writer for *Down Beat* and the organizer of jazz concerts in Chicago during 1936. "Benny . . . was unpolished and sometimes quite coarse . . . Teddy's own background was so different."[18] Both men demonstrated, through their music and their actions, that racism was baseless.

NOVEMBER 25—WILLIE "THE LION" SMITH (1897–1973)

b. Goshen, NY; d. New York, NY

Pianist, Composer

[CLASSIC JAZZ; STRIDE; PIANO BLUES]

Other jazz notables born on this day: Willie Smith (1910); Paul Desmond (1924); Dick Wellstood (1927); Etta Jones (1928); Nat Adderley (1931)
Jazz notables deceased on this day: Bill Robinson (1949); Waymon Reed (1983)

♪

Born to a Jewish father and an African-American mother, William Henry Joseph Bonaparte Betholoff became one of the most illustrious proponents of the stride or Harlem ragtime style. He grew up in Newark, New Jersey, where his mother's keyboard playing in a black Baptist church sparked his early interest in music, and he took the surname Smith from his stepfather. He adopted Judaism in his youth and sometimes said he had been named "The Lion of Judea" because of his early desire to be a rabbi, although the closest he got was serving as a cantor in Harlem. According to another version popularized by Smith, he earned his nickname during World War I through his heroism at the front, where he was cited for his courageous service with an artillery battery. Whatever the origins of his title, it suited his pianistic prowess, for no one enjoyed piano combat more or fared better at it than "The Lion." He was a strong-willed man, and if he didn't like an audience, he refused to play.

Following his discharge from the service he became a star attraction at Harlem's nightly "rent parties"—all-night dances, held in crowded apartments, where the cost of admission helped pay the rent—where he held genial combat with James P. Johnson, young Fats Waller, and other rivals. He and Johnson customarily fought to a draw. Taking his style from the ragtime pianists who preceded him, Smith dressed impeccably, carried a cane, and quickly became identified with stylish clothes and his regal manner. Sporting his ever-present cigar and a Homburg hat, whenever he walked into a club he would announce grandly, "The Lion is here." Among Smith's ardent admirers at the rent parties

---

18. Ward and Burns, *Jazz: A History*, 237.

was Duke Ellington, whose piano solos often revealed Smith's direct influence (and who in 1939 composed "Portrait of the Lion" in Smith's honor).

Although he toured with singer Mamie Smith for a while and played on her pioneering 1920 blues record "Crazy Blues," Willie freelanced most of his life. He improvised charming impressionistic melodies, formalized in compositions such as "Morning Air" and "Echoes of Spring." Using the higher tones of the scale (such as ninths and elevenths), his harmonies were bold and ahead of their time. Smith's chords also inspired the magnificent harmonic imagination of the great keyboard virtuoso, Art Tatum. Smith's solo recordings with the Commodore label in 1939 cemented his place in history. These recordings show Smith to be the equal of the earlier work of Johnson and Waller; they also demonstrate Smith's interest in classical music. From then on he led bands, toured widely as a soloist, and starred at jazz festivals. In 1965 he published his larger-than-life memoirs, *Music on My Mind*.

NOVEMBER 26—RUDY VAN GELDER (1924–)
[DOB previously uncertain—now acknowledged to be Nov. 2, 1924]

b. Jersey City, NJ

Recording Engineer

[HARD BOP; SOUL JAZZ]

Other jazz notables born on this day: Kiane Zawadi (1932); Mark Dresser (1952)
Jazz notables deceased on this day: Tommy Dorsey (1956); Tiny Bradshaw (1958); Frank Rosolino (1978); Clifford Jarvis (1999)

♪

For the past six decades the name Rudy Van Gelder has been synonymous with recorded jazz. The number of sessions he has recorded from his studio in Englewood Cliffs, New Jersey, across the Hudson River from Manhattan, easily numbers in the tens of thousands. From 1953 to 1967 Van Gelder engineered practically every recording for the Blue Note label, including some of jazz's most enduring classics. In fact he mastered many of the major jazz recordings of the 1950s and '60s, not only for Blue Note, but for dozens of other labels, including Prestige, CTI, Impulse!, Riverside, and Verve. Known for its superior sound and balance, Blue Note later commissioned Van Gelder to remaster the cream of its collection, recreating the classic "Blue Note sound" that he produced in the 1950s and '60s. The reason is quite simple: Van Gelder is considered "the greatest recording engineer in jazz history."

A one-time ham radio operator and optometrist, in the late 1940s Van Gelder created a recording studio in the living room of his parents' home in Hackensack, New Jersey and began recording local jazz musicians as a hobby. In 1953 Blue Note founder Alfred Lion became so impressed with the quality of Van Gelder's recordings that he began an exclusive association with him. Rudy's skill at achieving a proper mix of instruments directly onto the master tape (long before multiple-channel recording existed) was exemplary, and his crisp, well-balanced drum-kit sounds were especially attractive. His fame rested upon his knack of capturing textures that supported whatever mood the producers and musicians were seeking. How he did it all is somewhat of a mystery, for he was extremely protective of his techniques.

Everyone who had ever recorded in his studio knew his quirks, one of which was that you never touched his equipment. At a 1989 session involving Art Farmer, Phil Woods, and Dizzy Gillespie, among others, jazz writer Gene Lees recalls driving to the studio that Van Gelder had built thirty years earlier, its high-peaked roof and cement-block walls built to capture the acoustic qualities of a church. A sign near the door advised all who entered that there was to be no smoking or drinking within the studio. Seeing Rudy wearing cotton gloves reminded Farmer of a story he had heard about Red Mitchell, who was at Van Gelder's studio with Jim Hall for a duo recording. Mitchell had attended high school with Rudy and was in the control room with him when he inadvertently touched one of the fader controls, whereupon Van Gelder said, "That's it. You don't owe me anything. Just pack up and get out."[19] Van Gelder had professional standards that could not be compromised, even by friendship. That's why jazz producers and musicians revere this man; his results are simply the best.

NOVEMBER 27—TOMMY DORSEY (1905–1956)
b. Mahanoy Plane, PA; d. Greenwich, CT

Trombonist; Bandleader

[SWING; BIG BAND]

Other jazz notables born on this day: Eddie South (1904); Randy Brecker (1945); Lyle Mays (1953); Maria Schneider (1960); Jacky Terrasson (1966)
Jazz notables deceased on this day:

♪

Even though big-band swing was created in the 1920s by African-American bandleaders such as Fletcher Henderson and Duke Ellington in New York and Bennie Moten in the Kansas City area, the sound in the 1930s came to be dominated, at least in sheer numbers, by white bands led by Benny Goodman, Artie Shaw, Glenn Miller, Harry James, and the Dorsey brothers. By 1939 there were hundreds of swing bands, but over the entire course of the swing era, from 1935 to 1945, Tommy Dorsey's band consistently ranked among the top two or three orchestras in the U.S. Billed as "The Sentimental Gentleman of Swing" (though there was nothing sentimental about the man, who was combative and ruthlessly ambitious), his remarkable melodic trombone playing was perfectly suited to the ballads in which his band specialized.

As bandleader, Dorsey provided showcases to vocalists such as Frank Sinatra, Dick Haymes, and Jo Stafford, and he employed inventive arrangers such as Sy Oliver and Bill Finegan. Over the years his sidemen numbered some of the era's best white musicians,

---

19. Gottlieb, *Reading Jazz*, 582.

including such major jazz instrumentalists as Bunny Berigan, Buddy Rich, and Bud Freeman. The definitive ballad player of the swing era, Dorsey was the biggest selling artist in the history of RCA Victor Records until the arrival of Elvis Presley, who was first given national exposure in 1956 on a television show Tommy hosted with his brother Jimmy called *Stage Show*.

Tommy, twenty-one months younger than Jimmy, received musical instruction from his father, a music teacher and band director. After playing in local groups and with their own band, the brothers moved to New York in 1924, where they joined the California Ramblers, a very popular dance band. During the mid-1920s Tommy worked as a freelance with leading New York bands such as those of Paul Whiteman and John Goldkette, recording with them as well as with leading midwestern white jazz pioneers like Bix Beiderbecke and Red Nichols. In 1927 he and Jimmy began recording under their own name, using pickup bands.

Organized as a full-time band in 1934, the Dorsey Brothers Orchestra was poised to become the most influential band in the country and might have been remembered for launching the swing era, had the quarrelsome brothers not parted company in May 1935. Jimmy continued to lead the band and Tommy took over the remnants of the Joe Haymes band, beginning his rise to fame later that year. Tommy brought in star instrumentalists, top arrangers, and a succession of great singers, and the result was a highly versatile, well-drilled jazz orchestra. He remained successful throughout the 1940s, both in films and in the studios. In 1953 Jimmy rejoined his brother and the band became known once again as the Dorsey Brothers Orchestra. On the eve of his fifty-first birthday, following a heavy meal and sedated by sleeping pills, Tommy accidentally choked to death. Jimmy led the band briefly before passing away from cancer just six months later.

NOVEMBER 28—GATO BARBIERI (1934–)

b. Rosario, Argentina

Tenor Saxophonist; Composer

[JAZZ-POP; LATIN JAZZ; AVANT-GARDE JAZZ]

Other jazz notables born on this day: George Wettling (1907); Gigi Gryce (1925)
Jazz notables deceased on this day: Jack Washington (1964); Jimmy Lytell (1972)

♪

"Mystical yet fiery, passionately romantic yet supremely cool," these paradoxes characterize the musical world of Gato Barbieri, the second Argentinean to make a significant impact upon jazz (the first being Lalo Schifrin, in whose band Barbieri played early on). Beginning professionally as a teenager, Barbieri's five-decade career has covered virtually the entire jazz landscape, from free jazz and avant-garde in the mid-1960s to film scores and Latin music during the 1970s and '80s. Regardless of his idiom, Barbieri has always been one of the most overtly emotional tenor saxophonists on record. Though early influences were Charlie Parker and John Coltrane, Barbieri achieved his own style, characterized by a wide, romantic vibrato. However, it was a composition, his sensuous theme and score for the controversial Bertolucci film *Last Tango in Paris* (1972), that made Barbieri an international star and a draw at jazz festivals everywhere.

Although Barbieri's family was musical, Gato did not take up an instrument until the age of twelve, when a hearing of Parker's "Now's the Time" encouraged him to study the clarinet. Upon moving to Buenos Aires in 1947, he picked up the saxophone and became first alto with Schifrin's orchestra. Later, when he formed his own quartet, he changed to the tenor instrument. During that time Juan Peron was in power and jazz-oriented bands were limited in what they could play. Nevertheless, Barbieri began sitting in with visiting jazz musicians such as Coleman Hawkins, Herbie Mann, and Dizzy Gillespie and he soon became Argentina's leading jazz musician. After a brief stay in Brazil, he and his Italian-born wife Michelle moved to Rome in 1962, where he began collaborating with Don Cherry, recording albums that are considered classics of the jazz avant-garde. Other associations during his free-jazz days included working with Charlie Haden, Carla Bley, and with Mike Mantler's Jazz Composers' Orchestra.

Barbieri launched his career as a leader in 1969, and he gradually began moving away from abstraction in a desire to explore his own neglected cultural roots. During the early 1970s his recordings brought him plenty of acclaim in the jazz world and gained him a following on American college campuses. He returned to South America in the mid-1970s and began to work in popular and more commercial styles, translating his *Last Tango* success into a career as a film composer. In 1997, after years of musical inactivity due to bereavement over the death of his wife, who was his closest musical confidant, and his subsequent triple bypass surgery, Barbieri returned to the studios stronger than ever, recording one of the year's most successful jazz releases. In 2002 he recorded *The Shadow of the Cat*, his fiftieth album overall, a CD that resonates with the unmistakable feeling of sensual celebration. Now in his seventies, Gato has remarried and rekindled his passion for life.

NOVEMBER 29—BILLY STRAYHORN (1915–1967)

b. Dayton, OH; d. New York, NY

Composer; Arranger; Pianist

[SWING]

Other jazz notables born on this day: Tony Coe (1934); Chuck Mangione (1940); Adam Nussbaum (1955)

Jazz notables deceased on this day: George Van Eps (1998)

♫

During Duke Ellington's fifty-year bandleading career, scores of musicians appeared with his orchestra, and some stayed with him for much of that time. But none was allowed to get too close, with the possible exception of Billy Strayhorn. A gifted composer, arranger, and pianist, Strayhorn spent almost three decades (1939–67) in the shadow of his employer, collaborator, and friend. The two seemed unlikely partners: Strayhorn was short, modest, and openly homosexual; Ellington was tall, handsome, flamboyant, and a ladies' man. Despite their differences, they complemented one another so strongly and their styles were so similar that at times even the composers themselves could not identify their specific contributions. He was "my right arm, my left arm, all the eyes in the back of my head; my brainwaves are in his head, and his in mine," Ellington explained, trying to make comprehensible their musical symbiosis. They collaborated on over two hundred compositions, including large-scale suites, musicals, and the score for the film *Anatomy of a Murder*.

With the publication of David Hajdu's excellent Strayhorn biography, *Lush Life* (1996), it became clear that Strayhorn's contribution to the Ellington legacy was even more extensive than once thought, including instances where compositions had been registered as Ellington/Strayhorn pieces ("Day Dream"), or where collaborations between the two were listed only under Ellington's name ("Satin Doll," "C-Jam Blues"). Despite such discrepancies, Strayhorn has long been renowned for some of the most sophisticated ballads in jazz, including "Lush Life," "Passion Flower," "Chelsea Bridge," and "Blood Count."

A child prodigy, Strayhorn received extensive early training in classical music. In 1938, while gigging in the Pittsburgh area with a combo called the Mad Hatters, he met Ellington when the latter's band stopped in Pittsburgh. Strayhorn submitted a piece called "Lush Life" to the bandleader and Ellington was so impressed by the young man's talent that he invited him to visit him in New York, indicating he would find a place for him in his organization. Ellington scribbled out instructions on how to reach his Harlem apartment by subway, and by their next meeting, Strayhorn had composed a new piece based on the directions. The tune, "Take the 'A' Train," was an immediate hit and soon became Ellington's theme song.

Strayhorn joined Ellington's band as associate arranger and second pianist and began working closely with the leader. Ellington was in Nevada when he got a call from New York telling him Strayhorn had died. In his grief, Ellington prepared a memorial tribute that turned out to be one of the most sublime recording projects of his own last decade. The album, a recording of Strayhorn's compositions titled *And His Mother Called Him Bill*, was masterfully executed. The high point of the album may well have been "Blood Count," a piece Strayhorn composed and submitted to the Ellington band as he lay in the hospital dying of cancer.

NOVEMBER 30—CARTER JEFFERSON (1945–1993)

b. Washington, DC; d. Krakow, Poland

Tenor Saxophonist

[HARD BOP]

Other jazz notables born on this day: Jack Shelton (1931); Johnny Dyani (1945)
Jazz notables deceased on this day: Don Redman (1964); Charlie Rouse (1988); Connie Kay (1994)

An advanced soloist who spent most of his career as a sideman, Carter Jefferson is best remembered for his association with Woody Shaw (1977–80), one of the top trumpeters of the 1970s and '80s. Shaw was very important to the morale of mainstream jazz during the period when players like Miles Davis and Freddie Hubbard were mired in fusion. "On many nights," according to Stanley Crouch, "Shaw played as if each note was a finger in the dike holding back the deluge of commercialism." Due to a series of tragic events—an eye disease that left him legally blind, his struggle with drugs, and his premature death from injuries sustained after falling under a subway train—Shaw never achieved stardom, but his commitment to the post-bop tradition and his influence on players such as Jefferson was significant.

Jefferson started on clarinet and played alto saxophone before switching to tenor. After touring with Jimi Hendrix and Motown acts such as Little Richard, the Supremes, the Temptations, and Dionne Warwick, he played with an army band in Korea in the mid-1960s. In 1968 he moved to Manhattan to attend New York University (1968–71), studying music education. During this time he also participated at Jazzmobile workshops with prominent mainstream musicians such as Jimmy Heath, Lee Morgan, and Joe Henderson. He worked with Mongo Santamaria (1971–72) before joining Art Blakey's influential Jazz Messengers (1972–73), with whom he recorded and twice toured Japan. The Messengers were a training ground for a lot of great musicians, and Jefferson was fortunate to play with Blakey.

After his important stints with Blakey and Shaw, Jefferson worked with many top players, including Elvin Jones, Roy Haynes, and Cedar Walton. During the 1980s he held various teaching positions at schools and colleges on both the East and West coasts, while traveling regularly to Europe. At this time he also worked in groups led by Malachi Thompson, Jack Walrath, and in Jerry Gonzalez's Fort Apache band, a group that creatively Latinized hard bop music. In 1991 Jefferson was the victim of a brutal mugging that left him with both jaws broken, and for a time he worked with members of the U.S. Congress on a plan to provide freelance musicians with affordable health insurance. Jefferson, like Shaw, died tragically, succumbing to the ravages of extreme alcoholism while touring Poland.

Chapter 12

December

DECEMBER 1—JACO PASTORIUS (1951–1987)
b. Norristown, PA; d. Fort Lauderdale, FL

Electric Bass Guitarist

[FUSION; POST-BOP]

Other jazz notables born on this day: Jimmy Lytell (1904); John Bunch (1921); Lou Rawls (1935)

Jazz notables deceased on this day: Taft Jordan (1981); Stéphane Grappelli (1997)

♬

John Francis Pastorius III, a precocious figure who stormed onto the stage in the 1970s only to stumble and fall tragically in the 1980s, set the standard for the electric bass guitar in jazz fusion during that period.[1] He achieved his greatest fame with the fusion band Weather Report, with whom he had a long association (1976–81). As Eberhard Weber was doing in Europe, Pastorius redefined the role of the electric bass, giving it the tonal characteristics and articulation of both an amplified acoustic guitar and an amplified double bass and producing an immensely resonant, lyrical sound. A revolutionary performer with a natural flair for showmanship, Pastorius came to embody the idea of fusion itself. He drew rave reviews as one of the instrument's most influential practitioners and set the pace for a new generation of jazz bassists, becoming the most imitated bassist after Jimmy Blanton, Paul Chambers, and Scott LaFaro.

Growing up in Fort Lauderdale, Jaco played drums until he injured his left arm in a football game. When the injury failed to heal properly, he experimented on piano, saxophone, and guitar, and he learned by listening to local Florida musicians, including the legendary saxophone/trumpet player Ira Sullivan. At seventeen he had an operation to reset his arm, and soon it was strong enough for him to play the bass, which became his main instrument. Since there were no local cliques of young jazz musicians, he played country and western music, soul, and reggae, accompanying such stars as the Supremes, the Temptations, and Nancy Wilson. He liked the Beatles, the Rolling Stones, and other rock/pop groups—and jazz drummer Max Roach. By the early 1970s he was playing with

---

1. Bogdanov et al., *All Music Guide to Jazz*, 984.

Sullivan and also with the house band at Fort Lauderdale's Bachelors III Club. There he met and played with visiting jazz musicians such as Paul Bley and Pat Metheny, as well as the fusion group Blood Sweat and Tears.[2] In 1975 he recorded his eponymous album *Jaco Pastorius*, one of the most astonishing solo debuts in jazz history. By 1976 he was a member of the groundbreaking Weather Report, attracting widespread notice with his performances on their album *Heavy Weather*. From that time he was much in demand as a bass player in a wide variety of settings.

In the mid-1980s Pastorius became overwhelmed by mental problems, exacerbated by drugs and alcohol. This led to several embarrassing public incidents, such as the violent crackup onstage at the Hollywood Bowl, in the middle of a set at the 1984 Playboy Jazz Festival. Such episodes made him an outcast in the music business, and toward the end of his life he became a street person. Pastorius died early—at age thirty-five—from injuries sustained in a beating during a brawl at the Midnight Club in Fort Lauderdale. Though almost forgotten at the time of his death, he was immediately lauded afterwards, including by Miles Davis, who wrote the tune "Mr. Pastorius" in his honor.

DECEMBER 2—WYNTON KELLY (1931–1971)

b. Jamaica, British West Indies; d. Toronto, Canada

Pianist

[HARD BOP]

Other jazz notables born on this day: Fate Marable (1890); Eddie Sauter (1914); Charlie Ventura (1916)

Jazz notables deceased on this day: Joe "Fox" Smith (1937); Chano Pozo (1948); Albert Ammons (1949—or Dec. 3); Charlie Byrd (1999)

♪

If Miles Davis had retired in 1960, he would still have been famous in jazz history, for between 1956 and 1960 he exerted an inescapable hold on the imagination of the jazz world. During that period he released eight albums on the Columbia label that made him a legend. In March of 1959 Davis took his super sextet into the studios to record five original tunes the band members had never seen before, each built on "modes," upon which they were to improvise. That groundbreaking album, *Kind of Blue*, became Davis's most famous recording and is considered by many, if not most, critics and observers, as the most influential in jazz history. In addition to Davis, the players (on all but one track) included saxophonists John Coltrane and Cannonball Adderley, pianist Bill Evans, bassist Paul Chambers, and drummer Jimmy Cobb. The exception, a track titled "Freddie the Freeloader," featured the Jamaican-born Wynton Kelly on piano, a distinctive soloist who played with a light feeling and lots of swing.

Kelly was an exceptional accompanist who also distinguished himself with his rhythmically infectious solo style. He received high praise from Miles Davis for his superb

---

2. Carr et al., *Jazz: The Rough Guide*, 592.

skills as accompanist in his band. Kelly remained with Davis until 1963, recording such albums with Miles as *At the Blackhawk*, *Someday My Prince Will Come*, and *Miles Davis at Carnegie Hall*. The many soloists he backed on record, including Adderley, Coltrane, and Hank Mobley, prized his driving accompaniment style. Influenced by Bud Powell and Horace Silver, Kelly in turn influenced Herbie Hancock, Keith Jarrett, and Benny Green, in addition to Ellis Marsalis, a widely respected jazz pianist and educator who, in 1961, named one of his sons Wynton Marsalis, after Wynton Kelly. In 1982 that trumpet prodigy burst on the scene, focused on extending the legacy of the Miles Davis quintet.

Kelly's family moved to the U.S. when he was four years old and settled in Brooklyn, where as a youth he played professionally in rhythm-and blues bands. After recording with Eddie "Cleanhead" Vinson and Eddie "Lockjaw" Davis, he began working with vocalist Dinah Washington (1950–52). He first gained attention as a soloist while performing with Lester Young and Dizzy Gillespie during 1951 and 1952. After serving in the military he performed impressively with Washington (1955–57), with Charles Mingus (1956–57), and with the Gillespie big band (1957), though he gained his greatest notoriety as Bill Evans's replacement with Miles Davis. When he left Davis, Kelly took Miles's rhythm section (Chambers and Cobb) with him to form his own trio. The group was at its best backing Wes Montgomery (1964–65). At the end of his career Kelly worked as a freelance in New York and also as a member of Ray Nance's quartet. He suffered from epilepsy, and his early death was due to a heart attack following a seizure.

DECEMBER 3—CONNEE BOSWELL (1907–1976)

b. Kansas City, MO; d. New York, NY

Vocalist

[VOCAL JAZZ; TRADITIONAL POP; CLASSIC JAZZ; SWING]

Other jazz notables born on this day: Herbie Nichols (1919)
Jazz notables deceased on this day: Bob Haggart (1998)

♪

One of the finest jazz singers of the 1930s, Connee Boswell originally rose to fame as a member of the Boswell Sisters, one of the era's premier jazz vocal groups. Despite having to spend most of her life in a wheelchair (as a result of contracting polio as an infant), she embarked on a successful career as a soloist in 1935. Her smooth, rich voice and refined musicianship appealed equally to the public and her peers. She was able to interpret a wide range of material with warmth and subtlety, and her work influenced many singers, including Ella Fitzgerald. Boswell was the first of the microphone-based singers, and she exerted a crucial influence over the next generation of popular song stylists.

Born in Kansas City, Connee moved to New Orleans in 1914, where she and her sisters grew up comfortably, learning black music from their African-American staff. Martha played piano, Helvetia played banjo, guitar, and violin, and Connee took up saxophone, cello, trombone, and piano. Connee's finest instrument, however, was her voice, and soon the three sisters were in Los Angeles for a radio series. Due to numerous broadcasting commitments, the girls were constantly on the air, and one night they discovered their close-blended timbre when Connee, suffering from a cold, lost her high notes; singing at half-volume close to a microphone produced their unique sound. In 1931 the trio created a sensation at the Paramount Theater in New York. They were signed by Brunswick Records and appeared on the first American television transmission.

During 1931 to 1936 the Boswell Sisters became quite popular, serving as the model for dozens of "sister acts" that flourished over the next twenty years, notably the Andrews Sisters. The group achieved international fame during the early 1930s, its recordings with the Dorsey Brothers' band being notably successful. At the peak of their popularity the sisters made films, including *The Big Broadcast of 1932*, *Moulin Rouge* (1934), and *Transatlantic Merry Go Round* (1934). Most of their recordings were made late at night, between midnight and dawn, after live radio or theater shows. Connee wrote their clever arrangements, leaving plenty of room for hot solos. When Vet and Martha got married and decided to retire from singing in 1936, Connee officially launched her own solo career, including radio, television, films, and records with Bing Crosby, Bob Crosby, Victor Young, and Ben Pollack, and changed her name from Connie to Connee. Most notable of her recordings was the 1937 session with Bob Crosby's Bobcats that resulted in inventive and hard-swinging versions of "Martha" and "Home on the Range." In the 1950s she took a leading role in the short-lived television show *Pete Kelly's Blues*. She also recorded a notable 1956 jazz album with Billy Butterfield, Miff Mole, Tony Sbarbaro, and Jimmy Lytell, who came together as the Original Memphis Five. Connee worked tirelessly for charity until her husband's death in 1975, when she retired.

DECEMBER 4—CASSANDRA WILSON (1955–)

b. Jackson, MS

Vocalist; Leader

[VOCAL JAZZ; STANDARDS; FREE FUNK; CONTEMPORARY JAZZ; M-BASE; WORLD FUSION]

Other jazz notables born on this day: Eddie Heywood (1915); Jim Hall (1930)
Jazz notables deceased on this day: Edward Versala (1999)

♫

With a bluesy, sultry voice and a broad expressive range, Cassandra Wilson is one of the finest singers on the contemporary jazz scene. Her albums range from the pop inflected to all-out jazz, an eclectic taste that comes naturally to Cassandra, who began her musical career performing near her Mississippi home. "Down South, musicians have to be able to play in many different circumstances and in many contexts," she explains. "They have to play jazz, they have to integrate the blues, rhythm-and-blues, and they have to know a little country. And the lines are blurred sometimes, because that's what everybody wants to hear." But through it all, she brings originality to her material. When singing jazz, she incorporates elements from the styles of Sarah Vaughan, Carmen McRae, and notably Betty Carter; however, in her pop or folk-revivalist recordings, she is indebted to

Joni Mitchell and in particular to Nina Simone. Wilson is also deeply aware of the blues heritage, and this surfaces in the majority of her work, as may be heard on her exceptional album *Blue Light 'Til Dawn* (1993).

In 1982 Wilson moved to New York and began working with Dave Holland and Abbey Lincoln. Upon meeting saxophonist Steve Coleman in 1983, she was encouraged to break away from the standard repertory and to write her own material. She subsequently became associated with Coleman and others in the activities of the M-Base movement, a collective devoted to furthering specific elements of "creative black music." She became the main vocalist with the M-Base collective, recording regularly with Coleman between 1985 and 1992, often providing a wordless vocal accompaniment.

In 1986 she toured Europe and recorded with New Air, an avant-garde trio with Henry Threadgill. Wilson began recording with a wide variety of New York musicians at that time, establishing herself as a singer of great promise. In the 1990s, as a recording artist for the Blue Note label, she broke through to a larger audience, using a mixture of originals, standards, and rock and blues material as a vehicle for her remarkable voice. In 1994 she was a member of the ensemble that performed the premiere of Wynton Marsalis's oratorio *Blood on the Fields*, and she recorded and toured with the group until around 1997.

Wilson is recognized today as an unequaled vocalist, a fact confirmed when *Time* magazine picked her as America's Best Singer in 1991. Her distinctive style and daring approach have earned her wide recognition, including chart-topping albums, a Grammy, and countless accolades. Her recordings demonstrate her ability to interpret her own original material and create a highly distinctive approach to jazz singing. Those Mississippi roots continue to run deep.

DECEMBER 5—MARSHAL ROYAL (1912–1995)

b. Sapulpa, OK; d. Culver City, CA

Alto Saxophonist; Clarinetist

[SWING]

Other jazz notables born on this day: Egberto Gismonti (1947)
Jazz notables deceased on this day: Kenny Dorham (1972); Rahsaan Roland Kirk (1977); Arvell Shaw (2002)

♪

With the exception of a brief period in the early 1950s, Count Basie led a big band from 1935 until his death in 1984. Like all bands in the Kansas City tradition, Basie's orchestra was organized around its rhythm section, which supported the interplay of brass and reeds and served as a backdrop for solos. During the band's heyday in the late 1930s Basie preferred light, expandable arrangements which were notable for their use of riffs (patterns which might have developed in rehearsal and then played by rote as a "head" arrangement). This sort of ensemble accompaniment gave full freedom to outstanding soloists such as Harry "Sweets" Edison, Herschel Evans, Dicky Wells, and Lester Young.

In 1950 financial considerations forced Basie to disband, and for the next two years he led smaller bands. After reorganizing a big band in 1952, he undertook a series of tours and recording sessions that established his band as a permanent jazz institution and training ground for young musicians. In his bands of the 1950s and '60s Basie retained his swing-style rhythm section but chose soloists with more modern leanings, particularly Thad Jones, Eddie "Lockjaw" Davis, Frank Foster, Frank Wess, and Marshal Royal. Despite the band's changing sound during this period (due to a succession of different arrangers), its relaxed precision and control of dynamics remained unequalled in jazz. For close to twenty years (from the early 1950s until 1970) the characteristic sax sound of Basie's big band was led by Marshal Royal's clear lead alto.

As a youngster Marshal (his name is often misspelled as Marshall, and his birth date appears incorrectly in various reference texts as May 12) played violin, guitar, and various reed instruments. Older brother of trumpeter Ernie Royal, Marshal began performing at the age of thirteen, and for four years he often appeared with his family's band. He spent most of the 1930s on the West Coast with Les Hite's band (1931–39) before joining Lionel Hampton (1940–42), who had just left Benny Goodman to create a band of his own. After military service with a navy band, Royal played in New York with Eddie Heywood before moving to Los Angeles, where he worked as a musician in the film studios.

In 1951 he joined the septet Count Basie had formed following the demise of his big band, replacing Buddy DeFranco on clarinet. When Basie reorganized his big band the following year, Royal remained as lead altoist and music director. Though he seldom soloed, except on ballad features, he drilled his section members into an unbeatable unit that phrased and breathed as one. After leaving Basie, Royal settled for good in Los Angeles, playing and recording in a variety of settings, including dates under his own name.

DECEMBER 6—DAVE BRUBECK (1920–)

b. Concord, CA

Pianist; Composer; Bandleader

[West Coast Jazz; Cool]

Other jazz notables born on this day: Bob Cooper (1925); Jay Leonhart (1940); Miroslav Vitous (1947)

Jazz notables deceased on this day: Danny Alvin (1958)

♪

Dance bands had visited colleges since the early days of jazz, but students who wanted to listen rather than dance often had to go far afield. Beginning in the 1950s, musicians like Dave Brubeck decided to take jazz to the students. On Monday evening, March 2, 1953, as students filed through the doors of the chapel at Oberlin College, neither they nor the musicians waiting nervously backstage were sure how the concert would go. Though Brubeck had begun gathering a following on California campuses, jazz concerts at Eastern colleges were still relatively rare, and Brubeck had been told he might find the audience at Oberlin unresponsive, since it was sure to include students from the college's prestigious music conservatory. Brubeck had himself been put down for wanting to play jazz while an undergraduate at the College of the Pacific, where he had majored in music. But the concert at Oberlin that evening was a huge success, as the audience—including the conservatory students—responded with multiple ovations. The concert was recorded, and the album that resulted, together with future concerts by the Brubeck quartet, helped introduce jazz to thousands of young people. Beginning in 1959 with the release of *Time Out*—jazz's first million-selling record—the band enjoyed worldwide success. Over the next three decades, Brubeck ranked second in record sales among all jazz-recording artists, proving that creative jazz and popular success can go together.

Brubeck received early training in classical music from his mother, but fooled her for a long time by memorizing his lessons and not learning to read music. Trouble with his eyesight from the age of two made reading music both difficult and unappealing. His father, a rancher, hoped the youngster would follow in his footsteps, so Brubeck enrolled at the College of the Pacific in 1938 for pre-veterinary studies, but the following year he followed his heart and changed his major to music. He led a service band in Europe during World War II and then in 1946 studied at Mills College with Darius Milhaud, who encouraged his students to play jazz. In 1946 Brubeck founded the Experimental Jazz Workshop Ensemble, a group mostly consisting of fellow classmates, which recorded in 1949 as the David Brubeck Octet. The octet was too radical to get much work, so Brubeck formed a trio, whose recordings of 1949 to 1951 were quite popular in the San Francisco Bay area.

In 1951 Brubeck was persuaded by altoist Paul Desmond to make the group a quartet, and by 1954, riding a wave of unexpected popularity, Brubeck appeared on the cover of *Time* magazine. The "classic" quartet traveled around the world until its breakup in 1967, when Brubeck disbanded the group to concentrate on composition. Brubeck organized several new quartets after that, and in 1999 he announced plans to found an institute for the study of jazz at the University of the Pacific, where sixty years earlier he had found little more than contempt for his beloved jazz.

DECEMBER 7—TEDDY HILL (1909–1978)

b. Birmingham, AL; d. Cleveland, OH

Tenor Saxophonist; Bandleader

[SWING]

Other jazz notables born on this day: Louis Prima (1911); Ronnie Boykins (1932); Matthew Shipp (1960)
Jazz notables deceased on this day: Kenny Baker (1999); Jay McShann (2006)

♫

In his chapter "The Bop Rebellion," James Lincoln Collier displays a photograph taken outside Minton's Playhouse, the bar where young modernists gathered in the early 1940s to create a music that came to be known as "bop." Standing by the club's canopy are four smiling, sharply dressed figures, which Collier calls "some of the heroes of the time." I have always been intrigued by that photo, not only because it captures three of the era's great jazz musicians (Thelonious Monk, Howard McGee, and Roy Eldridge) in an attractive pose, but because it contains an unknown fourth figure, described as "probably Teddy Hill, manager of the club, who brought the new men in."[3] Who was Teddy Hill, I wondered, that he was able to attract some of the most adventurous jazz musicians of his day to Minton's on 118th Street in Harlem, this cramped club that played such a pivotal role in the development of jazz?

Hill, I discovered, had led a moderately successful big band throughout the 1930s, a band that at one time or another included rising young stars such as Dizzy Gillespie, Chu Berry, Kenny Clarke, and Eldridge. In 1932 Hill had worked with the legendary pianist James P. Johnson before organizing his own eighteen-piece band. By 1935 his sidemen included Eldridge, Berry, and Dicky Wells, and although they left the following year, in 1937 the band attracted the young Gillespie, who recorded his first solos and toured England and France with the group. During his two-year tenure with Hill, Dizzy and his fellow sideman Kenny Clarke began to experiment with new rhythmic conceptions. Hill, a traditionalist, fired Clarke for his "odd" drumming, and shortly thereafter Gillespie joined the more prestigious Cab Calloway orchestra.

In late 1940, after Hill had disbanded, he was hired to manage Minton's Playhouse, a recently renovated club that had served as the dining room of the Hotel Cecil. Hill put together a series of celebrity nights, making Monday evening (the musician's traditional night off) an open house, with free food and drink for any musician willing to play without pay. Minton's was about music, not dancing or entertainment, and the club soon became the hotspot of jazz. Strangely enough, Hill asked his recently fired drummer to organize and front a house band. Clarke recruited Monk on piano, Nick Fenton on bass, and Joe Guy on trumpet. At first the music was mainstream, except for Clarke's drumming and Monk's unusual piano playing. Every Monday night musicians, black and white, came to experiment and to hear the latest in jazz. Gillespie, Bud Powell, Charlie Christian, Charlie Parker and other young visionaries began turning up regularly. Minton's prospered, and the new music rocked the jazz world. Probably never before in history had a complete art movement been created in a single room. The importance of Minton's, "the birthplace of bebop," waned after World War II, but during the movement's inception, Teddy Hill was its unlikely midwife.

DECEMBER 8—JIMMY SMITH (1925–2005)

b. Norristown, PA; d. Scottsdale, AZ

Organist; Leader

[Hard Bop; Soul-Jazz]

Other jazz notables born on this day: Sol Yaged (1922)
Jazz notables deceased on this day: Hugues Panassié (1974); Gene Ramey (1984); Gene Quill (1988); Buck Clayton (1991); Antonio Carlos Jobim (1994)

---

3. Collier, *Making of Jazz*, 349.

♪

As the 1950s drew to a close, a number of musicians began turning out albums of "soul-jazz"; its simple, funky melodies, and danceable, blues-infused rhythms became the most popular jazz style of the 1960s. With titles such as "Home Cookin'," "Cornbread," "Grits 'n Gravy," and "Back at the Chicken Shack," soul-jazz was a celebration of the down-home aspects of African-American culture. No one was more influential in popularizing this music than Jimmy Smith, the Philadelphia pianist who began experimenting with the organ in 1951, reportedly as a result of his frustration with badly out-of-tune pianos in jazz clubs. He switched permanently in 1953, after hearing Wild Bill Davis, the first important soloist on the Hammond instrument. By 1956 Smith had mastered his sophisticated combination of bebop and rhythm-and-blues, establishing the model for the "organ trio" in jazz, featuring a drummer, either a guitarist or saxophonist, and the organ. An appearance at Birdland and a highly acclaimed performance at the Newport Jazz Festival in 1957 launched his career as the first important jazz player on his instrument.

Known simply as "Incredible," Jimmy Smith "ruled" the Hammond organ in the 1950s and '60s. There had been other organists before him—pioneers like Fats Waller and Count Basie and pianists like Wild Bill Davis and Milt Buckner—who had switched keyboards without mastering the instrument's full jazz potential. Smith was different. The photographer Francis Wolf recalled seeing him for the first time at a club in Harlem: "A man in convulsions, face contorted, crouched over in apparent agony, his fingers flying, his foot dancing over the pedals. The air was filled with waves of sound I had never heard before."[4] Smith was the first to make the organ sound like a band, providing walking bass lines with his feet, chordal accompaniment in his left hand, and a solo line in his right.

His punchy sound, punctuated with a distinct blues phrasing, helped define the "soul-jazz" that emerged in the late 1950s. Smith turned a fusion of influences and styles (R&B, blues, gospel, bebop) into an attractive sound that influenced virtually every later jazz organist. Soul-jazz was good-time music, and it worked for a while. Jimmy Smith had ten albums reach the top-40 charts during the 1960s; artists like Cannonball Adderley, Ramsey Lewis, Horace Silver, Lee Morgan, and Bobby Timmons also found considerable success with the genre. But it was short-lived, for by the end of the decade an arsenal of other electric instruments began taking over—electric basses, electric keyboards, synthesizers—and Jimmy Smith and his Hammond B-3, along with most other jazz musicians, found themselves drowned out by rock music and a new amalgam called fusion.

DECEMBER 9—DONALD BYRD (1932–)

b. Detroit, MI

Trumpeter; Flugelhorn Player; Teacher

[SMOOTH SOUL; CROSSOVER JAZZ; HARD BOP; FUSION; JAZZ-FUNK; FUNK]

Other jazz notables born on this day: Bob Scobey (1916)
Jazz notables deceased on this day: Dave Tough (1948); Carter Jefferson (1993); James Moody (2010)

---

4. Ward and Burns, *Jazz; A History*, 456.

♪

In the aftermath of Clifford Brown's tragic death in 1956, jazz observers looked for likely successors, just as they had done when Charlie Parker had died the previous year. Donald Byrd, then twenty-four years old and arguably the finest hard-bop trumpeter at the time, seemed the most likely candidate. Influenced by Dizzy Gillespie, Miles Davis, and Brown, his work in the 1950s and '60s revealed immense assurance and lyricism. In the early 1960s he broke new ground in the field of education, introducing jazz courses, which at that time were virtually unknown in most U.S. universities and conservatories. He also pursued education as a composer, which took him to Europe, where he completed a course with the classical teacher and composer Nadia Boulanger. Over the years he pursued numerous degrees in music and education, receiving a PhD from Columbia Teachers College in 1982.

Having graduated from Wayne State University (1954), Byrd moved to New York the following year to complete a master's degree at the Manhattan School of Music. His elegant musical imagination and his beautiful tone brought him to the attention of established jazz performers and recording companies. After working with leading modernists such as Sonny Rollins, Max Roach, and Thelonious Monk, Byrd came to national and international prominence when he joined Art Blakey's Jazz Messengers in 1956. At this time he was the favorite studio trumpeter for the bop label Prestige, though he also recorded frequently for Riverside and Blue Note. From 1958 to 1961 he co-led a band with baritone saxophonist Pepper Adams, while also teaching at jazz clinics and touring internationally. In January 1961 Byrd invited the promising youngster Herbie Hancock to join his quintet. Two years later, when the pianist left to join Miles Davis's groundbreaking quintet, Byrd went to Paris to study composition with Boulanger.

Upon his return to the U.S. he began a career in music education, gradually becoming one of the most respected authorities on American music studies. In the 1970s his music took a decidedly commercial turn as he recorded a number of pop-oriented albums. His album *Black Byrd*, which became the best selling LP in Blue Note's history, helped launch the jazz/funk era and led to the formation of the Blackbyrds, a combo composed of musicians he taught at Howard University in the early 1970s. Art Blakey tells the story about Byrd coming to him backstage around this time and telling him how difficult it was to maintain commercial success. Blakey, a firm believer in sticking to the style one loved and developing from there, knew that Byrd had a lot of money, but he looked stressed and unhealthy, and so he told him, "Donald, I never saw an armored car following a hearse."[5] In the early 1980s Byrd suffered a stroke but, heeding Blakey's advice, he reverted to his jazz roots, bouncing back later in the decade to record mainstream music with peers such as Joe Henderson and Bobby Hutcherson and with younger musicians like Kenny Garrett and Mulgrew Miller.

---

5. Ward and Burns, *Jazz: A History*, 448.

December

DECEMBER 10—RAY NANCE (1913–1976)

b. Chicago, IL; d. New York, NY

Trumpeter; Cornetist; Violinist; Singer; Dancer

[SWING]

Other jazz notables born on this day: Irving Fazola (1912); George Tucker (1927); Bob Cranshaw (1932); Franco Ambrosetti (1941); Diane Schurr (1955)
Jazz notables deceased on this day: Charlie Teagarden (1984); Slam Stewart (1987)

♪

The history of the Duke Ellington band involves an astonishing array of musicians, most of whom were unknown when they joined. In 1924 Ellington hired James "Bubber" Miley, a brilliant mute specialist who largely founded the "jungle sound" that made Duke's group sound different than any other. Miley, a handsome, fun-loving youngster, taught his effects to trombonist Joe "Tricky Sam" Nanton, and the two created a sound later dubbed "the Ellington effect." Miley occupied a central role in the band, but by 1929 he was drinking heavily and becoming unreliable and Ellington sadly had to let him go.

His replacement was an eighteen-year-old named "Cootie" Williams, from Mobile, Alabama. Like Miley, Williams was also a master of the growl technique. Having been influenced by the bluesy New Orleans style that emphasized altering the quality of instrumental sounds to achieve a vast range of musical effects, he achieved a range of tone and shading on his instrument that was unsurpassed in his day. Williams served as Ellington's main trumpet soloist from 1929 to 1940, adding greatly to Ellington's growing success. His playing inspired Ellington to compose one of his greatest masterpieces, the "Concerto for Cootie" (1940), in which Williams may be heard using straight mute, plunger mute, and open trumpet. In 1940, in a much-publicized move, Benny Goodman lured Williams to his band. Ellington, unruffled, actually helped Williams negotiate the contract with Goodman, thinking he would be back within a year. As it turned out, Williams did return, but not until 1962.

The band survived his departure, for within weeks Ellington discovered a remarkable replacement in the multi-talented trumpeter Ray Nance who, in addition to being one of the best jazz violinists around, was also an excellent jazz singer and even a dancer. After a few years in the orchestras of Earl Hines and Horace Henderson, Nance had tired of the road and was working as a solo act in a club in Chicago, where an impressed Ellington heard him and immediately hired him. His first night on the job was the band's legendary November 6, 1940, concert in Fargo, North Dakota. A young fan named Jack Towers, who later became a master audio engineer, tested his portable disc cutter that evening with Ellington's approval, providing posterity with the music from that live two-and-a-half-hour dance outing. The band, overflowing with distinctive and unique soloists, was at one of its peaks during this period, and Nance did his best to fit in, endowing the "plunger" position in the band with his own personality.

With Ellington, who nicknamed him "Floorshow," Nance's talents were fully featured. Teamed with Nanton for the growling role originated by Miley, he often performed as a singer and dancer, and his violin was the highlight of many of the band's recordings. In 1963, when the returning Williams had taken some of his glory, Nance left for a relatively insignificant solo career.

DECEMBER 11—MCCOY TYNER (1938–)

b. Philadelphia, PA

Pianist; Composer; Leader

[HARD BOP; POST-BOP]

Other jazz notables born on this day:
Jazz notables deceased on this day: Luis Russell (1963); Dave Barbour (1965); Lee Wiley (1975); Andy Kirk (1992); Charles Earland (1999)

♪

Together with Bill Evans, McCoy Tyner has been the most influential pianist in jazz over the past forty years. A powerful virtuoso and a true original, Tyner is often associated with John Coltrane, for it was with the Coltrane quartet that he established his own identity, developing one of the most original piano styles in jazz. As Coltrane's pianist from 1960 to 1965, his contributions were central to such memorable recordings as *My Favorite Things, Impressions, John Coltrane and Johnny Hartman, Live at Birdland, A Love Supreme*, and *Ascension*.

Tyner grew up in Philadelphia, with Bud and Richie Powell as neighbors. They did not have a piano at the time, so they visited Tyner's house regularly to practice. Coltrane, another Philadelphia resident during this period, often rehearsed with Tyner as well. In 1960 Tyner achieved international acclaim when he joined Coltrane in what became the saxophonist's classic quartet. Under Coltrane's influence, Tyner flourished. But the influence flowed both ways, for few other pianists of the period had both the power and the open-minded style to inspire Coltrane as Tyner did.

One of Coltrane's most famous performances can be heard in the title track from the album *My Favorite Things*, based on the popular Rodgers and Hammerstein show, *The Sound of Music*. It proved to be one of Coltrane's best sellers, with fifty thousand copies sold in its first year alone. This album, the debut of Coltrane's quartet, featured Tyner on piano and Elvin Jones on drums; the third member of the classic Coltrane quartet, bassist Jimmy Garrison, joined later in 1961. Together they constituted one of the most important groups in jazz history. On December 9, 1964, the Coltrane quartet made one of the best-loved jazz albums of all time, a four-part devotional suite called *A Love Supreme*. "I think that record is one of the purest jazz records ever," said the tenor saxophonist Joshua Redman. "That's one of the first records I ever heard and I hope it's the last record I ever hear."[6]

---

6. Ward and Burns, *Jazz: A History*, 436.

After leaving Coltrane, Tyner struggled for a period, although artistically his playing developed significantly. Recording contracts with Blue Note and Milestone resulted in numerous outstanding albums, including *The Real McCoy* (1967); *Echoes of a Friend* (1972; this tribute to Coltrane is considered one of the great solo piano achievements of the decade); *Sahara* (1972), voted Record of the Year by the *Down Beat* critics; and his double LP *Enlightenment* (1973), recorded live at the Montreux Jazz Festival and winner of the Montreux Jury's Diamond Prize as Record of the Year. Through his tours and recordings, Tyner's international reputation grew steadily until he became one of the most revered musicians in jazz.

DECEMBER 12—FRANK SINATRA (1915–1998)

b. Hoboken, NJ; d. Los Angeles, CA

Vocalist

[VOCAL JAZZ; TRADITIONAL POP; STANDARDS; VOCAL POP; SWING; BALLADS]

Other jazz notables born on this day: Eddie Barefield (1909); Joe Williams (1918); Bob Dorough (1923); Dodo Marmarosa (1925); Toshiko Akiyoshi (1929); Grover Washington Jr. (1943); Tony Williams (1945)
Jazz notables deceased on this day: Mildred Bailey (1951); Ronnie Ross (1991)

♪

On December 30, 1942, Benny Goodman returned to the Paramount Theater on Broadway, the same venue where, five years earlier, he had set his fans to dancing in the aisles and first came to understand how much his band—and the swing music it represented—had meant to young people. At the bottom of the bill, as an added attraction, was Tommy Dorsey's one-time singer, Frank Sinatra. He had already outpolled Bing Crosby to become the nation's number one vocalist, but Goodman evidently knew very little about him. As the slender Sinatra approached the microphone, a great shriek went up from hundreds of teenage girls who had paid to see their idol. The squealing and shouting continued for nearly five minutes, stunning Goodman. Up to that point, people paid to see a band, and they would listen occasionally to a solo or a singer; but from that day on, singers reigned over American popular music.

Despite his reputation as a movie star, celebrity of mixed reputation, and possibly the greatest singer of American popular songs of the twentieth century, Frank Sinatra is nevertheless highly respected in jazz circles, above all for his relaxed and subtle sense of swing. A child of the big-band era, Sinatra dropped out of high school in his senior year to pursue a career in music. After recording the memorable "All or Nothing at All" with Harry James's big band, Sinatra joined the Tommy Dorsey Orchestra (1940–42) where, with his new kind of natural phrasing, rich baritone, jazz inflections, and depth of feeling, he helped the band to its greatest acclaim. Backed by the vocal group The Pied Pipers, Sinatra's star rose to the point where in 1942 he left Dorsey for a solo career. His big breakthrough, as support act to Goodman at the Paramount Theatre, made him America's first real teen idol.

Though Sinatra was known mostly for his smooth, straightforward ballads during his Columbia years (1943–52), in 1953 he signed a long-term recording contract with Capitol (1953–62) that placed him in a more jazz-oriented context. There followed a long series of best-selling recordings using arrangements by Nelson Riddle and Billy May, whose expert handling of big bands drew out the many facets of Sinatra's musical personality to excellent advantage. In 1961 he moved to his own label, Reprise, working with other jazz-oriented arrangers like Johnny Mandel, Neal Hefti, and Quincy Jones. Sinatra was most free paired with a great big band like that of Count Basie's, when he would bend the rhythm, embroider the melody, and stray from the tune. Toward the end of his career he often worked with a big band, recreating vintage arrangements. In 1995 he retired unofficially, his voice and memory letting him down on occasion, though he never relinquished his exquisite control over phrasing, gained largely from jazz influences.

DECEMBER 13—SONNY GREER (1895–1982)

b. Long Branch, NJ; d. New York, NY

Drummer

[SWING]

Other jazz notables born on this day: Ben Tucker (1930)
Jazz notables deceased on this day: Charlie Johnson (1959); Marshall Brown (1983)

♪

In January 1923 Duke Ellington sat in the balcony of the Howard Theater in Washington, DC to see a traveling vaudeville revue called *How Come*. Toward the end of the performance, soprano saxophonist Sidney Bechet stepped forward to play a blues-based solo that Ellington never forgot. It was a completely new sound to him, his first encounter with the New Orleans idiom, and Ellington determined to make this soulful sound central to his own music. Still just twenty-four years old, Duke was one of the most successful dance bandleaders around, but Washington seemed too small and sedate. Longing for what he called "the whirl of New York," a few weeks later Ellington headed north to join two friends, a one-time schoolmate named Otto Hardwick, who played alto saxophone, and the drummer Sonny Greer. "Harlem, in our minds," Ellington recalled, had "the world's most glamorous atmosphere. We *had* to go there."[7]

During those years New York hosted what may have been the richest cultural life in North American history—theater, literature, art, and music flourished as never before or since. Much of the city's culture emanated from Harlem, whose nightlife attracted socialites and entertainers alike. In 1927 Ellington began a three-year residency at the Cotton Club that became the turning point in his career and gave his orchestra national exposure. Sonny Greer, Duke's first drummer and for many his greatest, moved with Ellington into the Cotton Club, basking in his leader's fortuitous limelight.

---

7. Ward and Burns, *Jazz: A History*, 94–95.

Greer was the perfect fit for Ellington's orchestra, adding color and class to the rhythm section from 1924 to 1951. Greer was working as a member of the orchestra at the Howard Theater in 1919 when he met Ellington. The following year Duke recruited Greer and several others, including Elmer Snowden, who doubling as business manager, briefly took control of the group and brought it to New York in 1923. The group, known as the Washingtonians, eventually evolved into Ellington's orchestra. The exotic effects that Greer produced from a vast array of percussion equipment (including gongs, skulls, and chimes) added greatly to the "jungle" sounds that Ellington devised for the Cotton Club's shows. Greer was more effective rhythmically later on, when working alongside bassist Jimmy Blanton (1939–41). By this time he had developed an accomplished technique that enabled him to provide subtle shadings for Ellington's orchestrations rather than dominate them.[8]

In 1950, conscious of changing fashion as well as of Greer's heavy drinking, Ellington hired a second drummer. The ensuing quarrel resulted in Greer's departure, thereby ending the long-standing partnership. For the next twenty years Greer freelanced, and in 1974 he joined Brooks Kerr's trio for a hugely successful tour in tribute to Ellington, continuing to work until shortly before his death.

DECEMBER 14—PHINEAS NEWBORN JR. (1931–1989)

b. Whiteville, TN; d. Memphis, TN

Pianist

[HARD BOP]

Other jazz notables born on this day: Budd Johnson (1910); Ted Buckner (1913); Clark Terry (1920); Cecil Payne (1922); Leo Wright (1933); Stanley Crouch (1945)
Jazz notables deceased on this day: Dinah Washington (1963); Conte Candoli (2001)

♫

In 1956 a twenty-four-year old unknown pianist from Memphis named Phineas (pronounced Fine-as) Newborn Jr. recorded *Here is Phineas*, his first album as a leader. The recording was an awe-inspiring debut for a phenom whose blazing speed and technical skills would lead critics to compare him with Art Tatum and Oscar Peterson. Writing in the liner notes to the original LP, George Wein stated that he had "never encountered a musician of such tender years who had such a fantastic command of his instrument." For a short time Newborn approximated the style of Peterson and even rivaled him technically, although he lacked Peterson's warmth of touch or emotional range. Newborn was flashy and explosive, but underneath that exterior was a troubled young man. During the early 1960s, Newborn's career declined severely. Like the bebop genius Bud Powell, Newborn was a tormented artist, unable to handle well the criticism that followed the extravagant praise of his early albums.

---

8. Kernfeld, *New Grove Dictionary of Jazz*, Vol. 2, 92.

Phineas started out working in Memphis rhythm-and-blues bands with his brother, guitarist Calvin Newborn, and recorded with local players including B.B. King in the early 1950s. Brief stints with Lionel Hampton and Willis Jackson preceded army service from 1952 to 1954. After moving to New York in 1956, Newborn astounded fans and critics alike. Although he worked briefly with Charles Mingus (1958) and Roy Haynes, he usually performed at the head of a trio or quartet. His early recordings of this period are quite outstanding.

Soon thereafter his profile dropped sharply, due to a nervous collapse from which he only partially recovered. His personal problems destroyed two marriages and led to long periods of hospitalization after he moved to Los Angeles in 1960. Despite further appearances and recordings, including two of his finest albums in 1961 and 1962, the pianist was in danger of being forgotten by the jazz world.[9] In 1971 he returned to Memphis to live with his mother. His illness and hospitalizations continued, and in 1974, while preparing a solo album, he was mugged and several of his fingers were broken. Following his recovery and partial rehabilitation, he was able to pursue a moderately active international career. Based in Memphis during his final years, he served as an inspiration to younger pianists, who after his death dedicated their work as the Contemporary Piano Ensemble to their mentor.

DECEMBER 15—JOHN HAMMOND (1910–1987)

b. New York, NY; d. New York, NY

Talent Scout; Record Producer; Critic

[CLASSIC JAZZ; SWING]

Other jazz notables born on this day: Stan Kenton (1911); Gene Quill (1927); Dannie Richmond (1931); Curtis Fuller (1934); Eddie Palmieri (1936)

Jazz notables deceased on this day: Fats Waller (1943); Glenn Miller (1944); Papa Celestin (1954); Sam Jones (1981); Ken Hanna (1982); Nat Shapiro (1983)

♪

John Hammond was the best friend jazz ever had. Blessed with an impeccable taste in jazz and a Midas touch, he was responsible for discovering or promoting the careers of numerous musicians over the years. Although he was not a musician—he never even owned a record company or ran a nightclub—and though he could be overbearing in his views (both Louis Armstrong and Duke Ellington avoided his domineering influence), few individuals played a more important role in the history of jazz.[10]

The great-grandson of Cornelius Vanderbilt, Hammond was born into a wealthy family. Like other young aristocrats, he had sufficient connections and money to indulge his personal interests. At the age of twelve he heard his first live jazz and was entranced. Soon he found himself pondering the ills of racism. "The very fact that the best jazz play-

---

9. Bogdanov et al., *All Music Guide to Jazz*, 942.
10. Ward and Burns, *Jazz: A History*, 189.

ers barely made a living and were barred from all well-paying jobs in radio and in most nightclubs enraged me," he wrote in his autobiography. "There was no white pianist to compare with Fats Waller, no white band as good as Fletcher Henderson's, no blues singer like Bessie Smith, white or black. To bring recognition to the Negro's supremacy in jazz was the most effective and constructive form of social protest I could think of." Calling himself "a social dissident," Hammond began espousing a variety of causes, but scouting and promoting talented black artists came first. As early as 1933 the twenty-two-year-old Yale dropout was active in the music business. He quickly came to know booking agents, managers, and club owners, and in short time he was a force in the music business. As a producer with Columbia Records, he was able to advance the careers of his favorites. In addition to George Benson, Aretha Franklin, Bob Dylan, and Bruce Springsteen, he was a central figure in developing the jazz careers of Benny Goodman, Billie Holiday, Count Basie, and Charlie Christian. The story of each "discovery" and Hammond's efforts on their behalf is fascinating, particularly that of Holiday.

In 1933 his search for new jazz talent led him into a Harlem club named Monette's, and there he heard an eighteen-year-old vocalist. Though embarrassed by the bawdy songs she was performing, he was dazzled by the way she looked and sang. "This month there has been a real find in the person of a singer named Billie [Holiday]," he wrote in a column for *Down Beat*. "[S]he is incredibly beautiful . . . and sings as well as anybody I ever heard. Something must be done about her for gramophone records." Hammond brought Goodman, one of his protégés, to hear her, and soon she was in a recording studio with the clarinetist. Hammond, ever the matchmaker, arranged many fruitful sessions for Holiday, backed by all-star discoveries such as Teddy Wilson and members of Basie's orchestra, including Lester Young and Buck Clayton. The interplay between them produced timeless music.

DECEMBER 16—TURK MURPHY (1915–1987)

b. Palermo, CA; d. San Francisco, CA

Trombonist; Bandleader

[DIXIELAND]

Other jazz notables born on this day: Sam Most (1930)
Jazz notables deceased on this day: Keith Christie (1980); Harry Miller (1983)

♪

Despite the popularity of the swing bands in the late 1930s and early '40s, by 1939 New Orleans jazz began making a comeback. The first consequence of the Dixieland revival, as it became known, was the rediscovery of Jelly Roll Morton, Sidney Bechet, and other representatives of the older music, who began to record again. A second consequence was a series of reissues of traditional jazz recordings. By 1940 there were enough people interested in the older music to make it possible for jazz entrepreneurs to promote it in nightclubs and concert halls. The revivalist movement soon split into two distinct schools: the formalists and the naturalists.

Older players represented the naturalists, many of them white Midwesterners, who had begun playing jazz in the 1920s and had been influenced by such groups as the Original Dixieland Jazz Band, the New Orleans Rhythm Kings, and Bix Beiderbecke and the Wolverines. These performers—Eddie Condon, Bud Freeman, Miff Mole, Jimmy McPartland, Pee Wee Russell, Max Kaminsky, Georg Brunis, and others—did not see themselves as "revivalists." They had entered jazz to play this sort of music, and they had continued playing it over the years. They did not see themselves as reviving an older form so much as continuing to play what they had always played.

The formalists, however, demanded something purer. Their preference was not for Bix or the Original Dixieland Jazz Band, but for the black bands in the New Orleans tradition—Jelly Roll Morton, King Oliver, and Louis Armstrong of the Hot Fives. This, they felt, was the real jazz. They stressed repertoire as much as improvisation. Despite the distinctions, both groups were building on the same thing: the traditional New Orleans jazz band, with its front line of cornet, trombone, and clarinet playing polyphonic music over a rhythm section.[11]

In 1940 Lu Watters, a cornetist in the formalist camp, formed a band in the San Francisco area under the name of the Yerba Buena Jazz Band. The band was devoted to the music of Morton, Oliver, and other sophisticated early composers, and its trombonist was Turk Murphy, a stalwart of traditional jazz. Murphy spent eight very successful years with the Yerba Buenas, the figurehead of San Francisco's classic jazz revival. In 1949 Murphy left to form his own band, which became even more successful than the Yerbas. His bands were lively and very musical. Murphy's trombone playing was robust and full of good humor; his consistent style is apparent on the huge number of recordings that his band made from 1947 to 1987.

Based for many years in San Francisco, Murphy's groups worked occasionally on the East Coast and toured widely, particularly in Australia and Europe. In 1960 Murphy opened Earthquake McGoon's, a San Francisco club, where he played when he was not appearing at Disneyland, at festivals, or on the road. Murphy became a spokesman for revivalist jazz, writing regularly and intelligently about his brand of jazz in books and on sleeve notes. In 1986, the year before his death, he opened his Traditional Jazz Museum in San Francisco.

DECEMBER 17—RAY NOBLE (1903–1978)

b. Brighton, England; d. London, England

Bandleader; Arranger; Composer

[DANCE BANDS; TRADITIONAL POP; SWING]

Other jazz notables born on this day: Sy Oliver (1910)
Jazz notables deceased on this day: Noble Sissle (1975); Don Ellis (1978); Erskine Tate (1978); Grover Washington Jr. (1999)

---

11. Collier, *Making of Jazz*, 281.

♪

During the Swing Era every name band was associated with at least one signature tune or theme song. Bands typically played these pieces at the beginning or ending of dances and radio broadcasts.[12] Some bands, such as Benny Goodman's orchestra, had an opening theme ("Let's Dance") and a closing theme ("Goodbye"), whereas others, like Duke Ellington's ensemble, used several themes, featuring "East St. Louis Toodle-Oo" before 1941, and then "Take the 'A' Train."

Curiously, two prominent American bandleaders, Charlie Barnet and Glenn Miller, chose as their theme songs ballads written or associated with Ray Noble, a prominent British composer. Barnet's choice, "Cherokee," came from Noble's *Red Indian Suite* (1938), a composition dedicated to the American Indian, whereas Miller's theme song, "Moonlight Serenade," was "borrowed" from Noble's band book when Miller (who worked with Noble in the mid-1930s and was strongly influenced by his approach and arranging style) left after a dispute with the bandleader.

Classically trained as a pianist, Noble began his career in dance music, after winning a big band arranging contest sponsored by *Melody Maker* magazine in England. He became music director for the important HMV label (1929–34), in which capacity he recorded hundreds of British stars, in addition to a series with his New Mayfair Dance Orchestra. In 1934 Noble moved to the U.S. where, with Glenn Miller's assistance, he organized an orchestra (1935–37) that regularly played at the Rainbow Room on top of Radio City in New York City. His band was short-lived (Miller left after a year), but it included excellent musicians such as Johnny Mince, Pee Wee Erwin, Will Bradley, Claude Thornhill, and George Van Eps (with Miller as musical director). The orchestra disbanded after disputes about overtime and other personal matters, and Noble moved to Hollywood, where he became famous as an emcee on radio and later for his depiction of a pompous Englishman in comedy routines. He occasionally led dance bands into the mid-1950s, at which time he largely retired.

In the jazz field, Noble's arrangements were generally of "sweet" dance music, and his major compositions were mostly ballads such as "Goodnight, Sweetheart" and "The Very Thought of You." His legacy will endure not only through his successful romantic ballads (and for the gift he left his widow, who received a dozen red roses every month after his death), but through his influential instrumental composition "Cherokee," for which he will forever be enshrined in the hearts of jazz lovers.

---

12. A list of the most prominent bands and their theme songs can be found in Hasse, *Jazz: First Century*, 65.

BLUE NOTES

DECEMBER 18—FLETCHER HENDERSON (1897–1952)

b. Cuthbert, GA; d. New York, NY

Bandleader; Arranger; Pianist

[CLASSIC JAZZ; SWING; BIG BAND]

Other jazz notables born on this day: Eddie "Cleanhead" Vinson (1917); Ira Gitler (1928)

Jazz notables deceased on this day: Marshall W. Stearns (1966); Warne Marsh (1987)

♪

In the first two weeks of October 1924 a jazz enthusiast visiting Manhattan could, within one evening and without walking more than four blocks, have seen and heard four of the music's best-remembered figures at the dawn of their careers. Duke Ellington and his Washingtonians were at the Hollywood Club at Forty-Ninth and Broadway; a block away, Bix Beiderbecke and the Wolverines were playing at the Cinderella Ballroom; and at the Roseland Ballroom, on Fifty-First and Broadway, was Fletcher Henderson, leader of the city's most admired black band. And sitting in its brass section was a recent arrival to New York, cornetist Louis Armstrong.[13]

Henderson, a 1920 graduate from Atlanta University, originally went to New York to pursue an advanced degree in chemistry at Columbia, but when his savings ran out, he took a job as accompanist with the Black Swan record company. He quickly became a valued musician with an eye for talent and a gift for leadership. In January 1924 he assumed leadership of a band at the Club Alabam, off Broadway on Forty-Fourth Street. The band already included outstanding performers such as tenor saxman Coleman Hawkins, cornetist Joe Smith, and trombonist Big Charlie Green, and by the summer of that year, when he was invited to play at the Roseland, he was being billed as "the Colored King of Jazz." Henderson's band remained there for a decade, using New York's largest and most opulent dance hall as a springboard to national fame. Utilizing innovative arrangements by Don Redman, a conservatory-trained musician from West Virginia, he quickly rose to the top of his field.

When Smith abruptly left for a better-paying job in a Broadway pit band, Henderson managed to lure Armstrong away from Chicago. With the addition of Armstrong, Henderson's dance orchestra emerged as the first great jazz big band. Armstrong left the band in the fall of 1925, but not before revolutionizing jazz, moving the music away from the two-beat feel made famous by the Original Dixieland Jazz Band toward the flowing 4/4 beat that would become the pulsing heart of big band swing. As Max Kaminsky wrote, "[Louis] was the heir of all that had gone before and the father of all that was to come."

Henderson's band was now the band to beat. Its arrangements, by Redman and later by Henderson himself, were among the most adventurous in jazz and helped set the pattern for the big swing bands that would shortly conquer the country. But with the departure of Redman in 1927 and increased competition from other orchestras (along with some bad business decisions and the departure of stars like Hawkins), Henderson

---

13. Ward and Burns, *Jazz: A History*, 106–8.

was forced to break up his big band in early 1935. Ironically, starting in 1934 he had begun contributing versions of his better arrangements to Benny Goodman's new orchestra, which became huge hits and helped launch the swing era. In the mid-1930s, while Henderson languished, it was Goodman who emerged as jazz's "King of Swing."

DECEMBER 19—LU WATTERS (1911–1989)

b. Santa Cruz, CA; d. Santa Rosa, CA

Bandleader; Trumpeter; Composer; Arranger

[DIXIELAND]

Other jazz notables born on this day: Erskine Tate (1895); Bob Brookmeyer (1929); Bobby Timmons (1935); Lenny White (1949)
Jazz notables deceased on this day: Milt Hinton (2000)

♪

Lu Watters was a central figure in the Dixieland revival movement. When he organized the two-trumpet Yerba Buena Jazz Band in 1939 (in imitation of the pattern established by King Oliver and Louis Armstrong in Oliver's Creole Jazz Band of the early 1920s), New Orleans-style jazz was practically extinct. That has since changed. Now there are hundreds of Dixieland bands worldwide patterned after the Watters group and over one hundred festivals celebrating the music of Oliver and Jelly Roll Morton.

Voted "most promising bugler" at St. Joseph's Military Academy in Sacramento, California, Lu Watters formed his first jazz band in 1926, when he was fifteen years old. He received a scholarship to study music at the University of San Francisco but he soon dropped out of college to work as a professional musician. During a two-month-long engagement in New Orleans in the mid-1930s, while he toured the U.S. with the little-known big band of Carol Lofner, Watters became devoted to earlier styles of jazz. A few years later he organized a series of traditional-style jam sessions at a tavern near Berkeley, California, where trombonist Turk Murphy and a group of like-minded players joined him. In 1938, at the height of the swing era, he formed a swing orchestra for a long engagement at Sweet's Ballroom in Oakland. Watters inserted traditional jazz pieces into the band's repertoire whenever he could, but eventually he was fired for not playing contemporary music exclusively.

In 1939 he formed a smaller band, the Yerba Buena Jazz Band, working with kindred musicians Murphy, trumpeter Bob Scobey, and others to revive the New Orleans small-band style. By 1940 the group was on its way to a phenomenally successful career as America's first real revivalist band, packing San Francisco's Dawn Club nightly with its stomping two-beat sound. Although other small Dixieland bands existed at this time, notably those led by Muggsy Spanier and Bob Crosby, the element of authenticity projected by Watters's group set it apart and stimulated a large-scale revival of New Orleans and Chicago jazz throughout the world. Watters spent 1942 to 1945 in the navy, leading a twenty-piece band in Hawaii. In 1946, when the Yerba Buena band regrouped, it was more successful than ever. When the Dawn Club went bankrupt late in 1946, the band opened its own cooperative club in El Cerrito, with Watters serving as both cook and leader. The eventual departure of Scobey and Murphy (who soon led important groups of their own) weakened the band, and by 1950, when business fell off, Watters disbanded and retired from music to become a geologist and a cook. He did not resume playing his trumpet until 1963, when a utility company announced plans to build a nuclear plant on an earthquake fault. Watters appeared at several protest rallies with Murphy's band and recorded one last time before retiring permanently. The power plant was never built.

DECEMBER 20—ARNE DOMNÉRUS (1924–2008)

b. Stockholm, Sweden; d. Stockholm, Sweden

Alto Saxophonist; Clarinetist; Bandleader

[SWING; BOP]

Other jazz notables born on this day:
Jazz notables deceased on this day: Walter Page (1957)

♪

Sweden is considered to be at the cutting edge of European jazz innovation. During the last sixty years, Swedish jazz has attained a remarkably high artistic standard, stimulated by domestic as well as external influences. One could perhaps say that jazz came to Sweden on October 25, 1933. That was the day that Louis Armstrong gave his first concert in Stockholm. The organizers had only planned one concert, but the demand was so overwhelming that other concerts were hastily arranged. For many people, Armstrong's six concerts in Sweden signaled the beginning of a new age, the start of the first musical revolt among young people. The audiences at those events included many musicians who would be responsible for creating the Swedish jazz of the 1930s and '40s. Of course there had been jazz in Sweden before this, but Armstrong's visit marked a decisive turning point. In November 1933 the first issue of *Orkester Journalen* was published; today it is the oldest jazz magazine in the world.

Soon a young generation of Swedish musicians emerged, producing expert improvisers whose playing was highly imaginative. It included soloists with highly personal styles, such as clarinetists Ake (Stan) Hasselgard and Putte Wickman, trumpeter Rolf Ericson, Lars Gullin (who began as a clarinetist but evolved into a leading baritone saxophonist) and saxophonist Arne Domnérus, to name a few. Hasselgard, later to make a considerable reputation in the U.S., died in an automobile accident at an early age, and it was Gullin and Domnérus who went on to dominate in the field.

Domnérus emerged in the 1940s as a jazz soloist with several Swedish dance and jazz orchestras. He then led bands that included exceptional players like Gullin, Ericson, and Wickman. In 1949 he performed at the Paris Jazz Fair, an event that brought international recognition to Swedish jazz. There he came into contact with American jazz musicians such as Charlie Parker, who admired his talent and encouraged him professionally. Domnérus won international acclaim as a soloist in the early 1950s, mainly through a large number of recordings with Swedish and international all-star groups, and he came to be regarded as a leading European alto saxophonist. He was much in demand for studio work over the years, both as a leader and as a sideman. From 1956 to 1978 he worked with the Swedish Radio Big Band and Jazz Group and wrote for films and television. Initially influenced by Parker, his playing later reflected the cool style of Lee Konitz and Paul Desmond, though he evolved into a commanding soloist who could play in a wide range of musical styles, from Dixieland and swing to free jazz. Jazz in Sweden has certainly come a long way since that day in October 1933, and Arne Domnérus remains one of its distinctive standard bearers.

DECEMBER 21—PANAMA FRANCIS (1918–2001)

b. Miami, FL; d. Orlando, FL

Drummer; Bandleader

[JUMP BLUES; SWING]

Other jazz notables born on this day: Marshall Brown (1920); David Baker (1931); Hank Crawford (1934); John Hicks (1941); Alex Blake (1951)
Jazz notables deceased on this day: Johnny Coles (1997)

♪

The Savoy, Harlem's biggest and most beautiful ballroom, was one of New York's most famous nightspots, and throughout the Swing Era it was a mecca for dancing. When the integrated hall opened in 1926, it quickly became Harlem's most popular dance venue, and many of the jazz dance crazes of the 1920s and '30s originated there. The ballroom covered a whole city block and was so popular with dancers that its floor had to be replaced every three years. The management employed two bands, which played alternate sets, and this policy led to its becoming a famous venue for battles of bands. During the 1930s and '40s a number of bandleaders formed long and influential associations with the ballroom, including Chick Webb, the diminutive drummer who could hold off all opposition. His singer from 1934 was Ella Fitzgerald, who took over leadership of the ensemble after Webb's untimely death in 1939.

Other bands, such as Lucky Millinder's big band, enjoyed a similar connection with the venue, holding extended residencies before the ballroom's demise in the 1950s. On January 9, 1942, a little over a month after the Japanese attack on Pearl Harbor, Millinder's band was comfortably established at the Savoy. When a disheveled outfit from Kansas City arrived to compete with them in a battle of the bands, Millinder's men were not worried, for they were a favorite with Harlem dancers. For two hours the groups played to a stalemate, but then the Jay McShann band, led by its sensational twenty-three-year-old alto saxophonist, Charlie Parker, set a standard the hometown boys could not match. The Savoy was connected by a landline to a New York radio station, which allowed its music to be broadcast throughout the nation. Musicians hurried to Harlem, anxious to hear the talented newcomer whose arrival would change the face of jazz forever.

David Francis, Millinder's drummer on the occasion of that memorable defeat, began playing professionally in the 1930s. He moved to New York in 1938 and worked briefly with Roy Eldridge, who gave him his nickname at a moment when he was wearing a panama hat and Eldridge could not remember his new drummer's name. From 1940 to 1946 Francis was a member of Millinder's band, which often played at the Savoy opposite the Savoy Sultans. Francis loved the Sultans, and in 1946 he tried forming his own version of the group, but had little success. After five years with Cab Calloway (1947–52), he worked for a decade as a studio musician, making many recordings in New York with R&B and rock and roll groups and singers. In danger of being forgotten, he eventually returned to jazz, forming a jazz and dance band he called the Savoy Sultans, based on the unit that used to play opposite Millinder at the Savoy. The Sultans toured and recorded with huge success and from 1980 to 1987 played regularly at the Rainbow Room high atop New York's Radio City, restoring some swing to the city's skyline.

DECEMBER 22—JOHN PATITUCCI (1959–)

b. New York, NY

Bassist

[POST-BOP; FUSION]

Other jazz notables born on this day: Frank Gambale (1958)
Jazz notables deceased on this day: Ma Rainey (1939); Beaver Harris (1991)

♪

Chick Corea was one of the top keyboard stylists to emerge after Bill Evans and McCoy Tyner. In 1968 he began a two-year stint with Miles Davis during a very important transitional period, when Davis's group was involved in an abstract form of electronic jazz-rock that initiated the fusion movement of the 1970s. During the 1970s, after leaving Davis, Corea set a high standard with his Return to Forever band, an electric, jazz-rock group with a strong Latin flavor, and one of the most delightful and original groups of the decade. In the late 1970s and early '80s he began concentrating again on acoustic piano, appearing in a variety of contexts that included separate duet tours with Gary Burton and Herbie Hancock, a quartet, trios, and even some classical music. In 1985 Corea formed a new fusion group, the Elektric Band, and a few years later he formed his Akoustic Trio. The bassist for both of these groups was John Patitucci, a versatile player skilled on both acoustic and electric bass.

One of the top bassists of the 1990s, Patitucci discovered jazz by accident—his grandfather, who worked for the New York City roads department, brought home an unwanted box of jazz records one day, including albums by Thad Jones, Art Blakey, Wes Montgomery, and Ray Charles. Encouraged to take up bass by listening to the phrasing and tone of guitarist Montgomery, Patitucci began playing rock music on electric bass guitar by his early teens, and after his parents moved to Northern California in 1972, he took up acoustic bass. He studied bass at San Francisco State University (1977–78) and Long Beach State University (1978–80) before moving to Los Angeles in 1980, where he made important contacts in the studios, working with the popular composer Henry Mancini and playing with outstanding jazz performers such as Stan Getz, David Sandborn, Wayne Shorter, and Freddie Hubbard, among others.

After playing jazz with groups led by Joe Farrell, Victor Feldman, and Hubert Laws, he came to prominence in 1985 when he joined Corea as a regular member of both the Elektric and Akoustic bands. Until he met Corea, Patitucci's most regular gig was with his brother-in-law, trumpeter Mike Fahn, with whom he played for seven years. A week after meeting Corea he was in the keyboardist's bands, staying for ten years and recording seven albums with Corea. During his time with Corea he worked occasionally with Hubbard, played the double bass in the Manhattan Jazz Quintet (1988–89), and led various small groups. In 1994, after meeting and marrying his second wife Sachi—a cellist—he moved to New York, leaving Corea and the West Coast to raise a family. Since then he has worked as a leader and as a freelance, making supremely tasteful albums under his own name and continuing to work with some of the most stellar names in jazz, including occasional work with Corea, the man who initially showcased his talent.

DECEMBER 23—CHET BAKER (1929–1988)

b. Yale, OK; d. Amsterdam, Netherlands

Trumpeter; Flugelhorn Player; Vocalist; Leader

[WEST COAST JAZZ; COOL]

Other jazz notables born on this day: Joe Harris (1926)

Jazz notables deceased on this day: Ronnie Scott (1996); Don Lamond (2003); Oscar Peterson (2007)

♪

In 1952 Gerry Mulligan put together a groundbreaking "pianoless" quartet at the Haig, a small club in Los Angeles. On trumpet was Chet Baker, a cool-toned musician who earlier in the year had been chosen at an audition to play a series of West Coast dates with Charlie Parker. The quartet's breezy, effortless style was attractive, and soon a small but enthusiastic local following developed. Then, just as had happened to Benny Goodman in 1936, a writer for *Time* magazine came by the club and wrote an appreciative report, indicating that the group's sound was "just about unique in the jazz field." Soon there were long lines outside the Haig waiting to get in, and Mulligan and Baker were stars.[14]

Baker's performances with the group, particularly his ballad rendition of "My Funny Valentine," brought him instant fame. His clear tone and subdued, lyrical manner immediately became hallmarks of West Coast cool jazz, and were widely imitated. The band lasted less than a year, folding after Mulligan was jailed for a drug charge. But critics and fans alike hailed Baker and he won a number of polls in the next few years. During the mid-1950s *Down Beat* readers voted him the best trumpet player in the country, ahead of Miles Davis, Louis Armstrong, and Dizzy Gillespie. In 1954 the trumpeter released *Chet*

---

14. Ward and Burns, *Jazz: A History*, 375–76.

Baker Sings, a vocal album that increased his popularity but alienated traditional jazz fans that deplored his fragile, limited voice. Nevertheless, he continued to sing throughout the rest of his career.

Acclaimed as a "great white hope" at the age of twenty-three, Chet could have been a movie star. Instead he became a drug addict in the mid-1950s and had an erratic lifestyle.[15] He toured the U.S. in 1957 with the Birdland All Stars and took a group to Europe later that year. He returned to Europe in 1959, settling in Italy, where he acted in an Italian film. While in Italy he was arrested for drug use and spent almost a year and a half in jail. In 1962 he was arrested in West Germany and expelled to Switzerland and then to France. He eventually moved to England to appear as himself in the film *The Stolen Hour* (1963). He was deported from England to France because of a drug offense and was arrested again in West Germany, followed by a deportation back to the U.S. in 1964.

In 1966 he suffered a severe beating in San Francisco, the result of a botched drug deal. The incident is frequently exaggerated to the point where it is said that all his teeth were knocked out, which was not the case, though one tooth was broken. The general deterioration of his teeth led to his need of dentures in the late 1960s, forcing him to retrain his embouchure. Although he never kicked his habit and maintained a nomadic lifestyle, wandering throughout Europe during his final fifteen years, his trumpet playing actually improved during the 1970s and '80s. Surprisingly, he was still in his musical prime when he died in a mysterious fall from a hotel window in Amsterdam after taking heroin and cocaine. Baker remains "one of the great cult figures of jazz."

DECEMBER 24—BABY DODDS (1898–1959)

b. New Orleans, LA; d. Chicago, IL

Drummer

[NEW ORLEANS JAZZ]

Other jazz notables born on this day: Jabbo Smith (1908); Woody Shaw (1944)
Jazz notables deceased on this day: Lorenzo Tio Jr. (1933)

♪

In the winter of 1918 to 1919 a St. Louis-based pianist named Fate Marable recruited Louis Armstrong and other key musicians from New Orleans and formed a nine-piece riverboat band to play aboard Mississippi steamers. Marable, whose group became known as "the floating conservatoire," was a disciplinarian who insisted that his musicians learn to read music as well as play it. The band members were expected to play waltzes, light classics, and the latest songs, while a cashier with a good ear kept track of any wrong notes played and docked their paychecks accordingly. But Armstrong got paid fifty dollars a week—more money than he had ever seen—and he got to play alongside some of the best young musicians in New Orleans, including the clarinetist Johnny Dodds and his younger brother Warren, known as "Baby."

---

15. Bogdanov et al., *All Music Guide to Jazz*, 3rd ed., 53.

According to Warren the band originally included white musicians, but when they began grumbling about working for a colored man, the Streckfus brothers experimented with an all-black outfit. At first whites just stared, refusing to dance; some had never seen a Negro with a tie and collar playing music. But it was just a matter of time. According to Dodds, the next time they boarded "you couldn't get them off the boat." Baby drew special attention by shimmying while playing drums: "Used to have a bunch around me packed five or six deep; and Louis Armstrong would have a bunch five or six deep. It was a wonderful thing, and we were the two sensational men on the boat, Louis and I."[16] By 1922, when Armstrong joined King Oliver's Creole Jazz Band in Chicago, the Dodds brothers were already members.

Baby Dodds, the misbehaving younger brother, bought his first set of drums at the age of sixteen. He was soon playing all over New Orleans in a showy style, including with Bunk Johnson, Oscar Celestin, and with Marable's riverboat band (1918–21). He joined Oliver in San Francisco in 1922 and then traveled with the cornetist to Chicago, where he remained for the next two decades. In addition to recording with Oliver's classic band, Dodds was an important part of the 1927 "Hot Seven" sessions, led by Jelly Roll Morton and Louis Armstrong. He remained in Chicago, often playing with his disciplinarian older brother until the latter's death in 1940.

By that time, with the revival of New Orleans jazz, Dodds was much sought after for small traditional groups led by Jimmie Noone, Johnson, Sidney Bechet, and others. His adventurous style became controversial, particularly with Dixielanders such as Johnson and musicians like Lester Young, who preferred a discreet beat. But many younger drummers learned directly from Dodds during his stay in Chicago, including Dave Tough and Gene Krupa. Late in life he set down his knowledge of jazz drumming in a remarkable series of recorded solos with explanatory commentary, which serve as unique documents of New Orleans drumming style.

DECEMBER 25—CAB CALLOWAY (1907–1994)

b. Rochester, NY; d. Hockessin, DE

Vocalist; Bandleader

[VOCAL JAZZ; JIVE; SWING]

Other jazz notables born on this day: Kid Ory (1886); Oscar Moore (1912 or 1916); Eddie Safranski (1914?); Pete Rugolo (1915); Don Alias (1939); Ronnie Cuber (1941); Don Pullen (1941)

Jazz notables deceased on this day: Dud Bascomb (1972); Gustav Brom (1995)

♪

A great entertainer and one of the most successful bandleaders of the 1930s and '40s, Cab Calloway was famous for his extroverted singing and flamboyant appearance (George Gershwin modeled the role of Sportin' Life in *Porgy and Bess* on him). A talented jazz

---

16. Ward and Burns, *Jazz: A History*, 76.

singer, Calloway's showmanship on stage at the Cotton Club sometimes overshadowed the quality of his outstanding bands. Cab composed a large number of songs for his bands; his best-known pieces combined nonsense phrases like "Hi-de-ho" with lyrics about the Harlem nightlife experiences of an imaginary character known as Minnie the Moocher. As a bandleader Calloway promoted the careers of a great many jazz musicians, among them Chu Berry, Ben Webster, Milt Hinton, Cozy Cole, Jonah Jones, and Dizzy Gillespie. Much beloved by musicians who knew him, Calloway knew how to maintain high morale among his band members. For some twenty lean years, he paid his men higher wages than any other bandleader.

Cab began his long and distinguished career as a hustler and part-time singer in Baltimore clubs. In 1927 he joined an all-male quartet in the famous black revue *Plantation Days*, and when they arrived in Chicago he stayed on to work solo for various clubs. In 1929 he took over leadership of the eleven-piece Alabamians, but once in New York, the group fared badly. By 1930 Calloway was at the Savoy Ballroom fronting the Missourians, the touring band that was to form the base for his great orchestra. At the Savoy he developed a spectacular approach to showmanship, and soon he and his group were transferred to the Cotton Club as relief band to Duke Ellington's orchestra. In 1931 the band began recording and broadcasting for network radio and became a hit; their theme song "Minnie the Moocher" became Calloway's much requested signature piece. In 1932 his ensemble replaced Ellington's band as house orchestra, and for the next eight years Calloway's extroverted band made headlines at the Cotton Club. During that period the group also toured regularly, appeared in films, and made a large number of recordings.

Perhaps the best Calloway bands came after 1940. During that decade the band spent a lot of time on the road—as much as fifty weeks a year—and by 1948 Cab's bandleading days were at an end. But Calloway was a survivor. From that point on he performed mainly in musical theater, playing the role of Sportin' Life opposite Leontyne Price (1952–54) and performing with Pearl Bailey in an all-black production of *Hello, Dolly!* He continued to perform and tour into the 1980s, appearing on television and in the film *The Blues Brothers* (1980). In 1987 he appeared with his daughter in the show *His Royal Highness of Hi-de-ho: the Legendary Cab Calloway*. In 1999 Calloway's grandson formed a memorial orchestra, using original music that he inherited from his grandfather.

DECEMBER 26—JOHN SCOFIELD (1951–)

b. Dayton, OH

Electric Guitarist

[Post-Bop]

Other jazz notables born on this day: Monty Budwig (1929)
Jazz notables deceased on this day: Vic Berton (1951)

Few musicians of the twentieth century have had such an important and influential impact on jazz as Miles Davis. Miles considered himself a modernist, and this view was reflected in his unending quest for change. And when he was not leading those changes, he did so by choosing sidemen and collaborators who forged the new directions. Among the musicians who greatly benefited from their association with Miles were guitarists John Scofield and Mike Stern, both of whom rose to fame while with Davis in the early to mid-1980s. Born a year apart, Scofield and Stern's careers developed along similar lines. Both grew up with the blues, rock, and funk, emulating guitarists such as B.B. King, Eric Clapton, and Jimi Hendrix. They were schoolmates at Berklee College of Music, studying with Gary Burton, Pat Metheny, and Mick Goodrick, and each had a stint during the late 1970s when they worked with Billy Cobham, the era's definitive fusion drummer, before meeting up professionally as members of Davis's band in the early 1980s.

Considered one of the "big three" of current jazz guitarists, along with Metheny and Bill Frisell, Scofield took up guitar at the age of twelve while growing up in Connecticut, where he became attracted to rhythm-and-blues, urban blues, and rock and roll. Playing guitar was a big deal in the 1960s when, thanks to stars like Elvis Presley, Chuck Berry, Muddy Waters, and Clapton, guitar heroes were coming of age. A teacher introduced Scofield to guitarists Wes Montgomery, Jim Hall, and Pat Martino, thereby sparking a lifelong love of jazz. In 1974, upon his graduation from Berklee (1970–73), another teacher (Goodrick) recommended Scofield for a reunion concert at Carnegie Hall led by Gerry Mulligan and Chet Baker. Shortly thereafter Scofield joined Spectrum, a jazz-rock group led by Cobham and George Duke, remaining with the ensemble for two years. His reputation took a quantum leap at the end of 1982 when he joined Stern in Davis's band, which had two guitarists until Stern left in 1983. Scofield toured the world and recorded three albums with Davis. By 1984 he was more of a collaborator than a sideman, composing several of the band's pieces. Since his departure from Davis in 1985 Scofield has led his own groups and recorded frequently as a leader.

A trailblazer of the 1980s and a perennial poll winner, Scofield regularly explores the outer edges of contemporary jazz. In 2001, after a decade of rekindling his love of R&B with blues-oriented artists, the risk-taking guitarist released *Uberjam*, an album that, like many of Davis's fusion efforts, was both cerebral and funky at the same time. "Of all the albums I've made," he says, "this is the one Miles would have enjoyed the most. Miles's spirit is in this music. He was always looking to take jazz to a new place."

DECEMBER 27—BUNK JOHNSON (1889–1949)

b. New Orleans, LA; d. New Iberia, LA

Trumpeter; Cornetist; Leader

[NEW ORLEANS JAZZ]

Other jazz notables born on this day: Eddie Wilcox (1907); Johnny Frigo (1916); T. S. Monk (1949)

Jazz notables deceased on this day: Hoagy Carmichael (1981)

Around 1912, when the clarinetist Sidney Bechet was but fifteen years old, he became a member of the hardest-driving band in New Orleans, the legendary Eagle Band, led by cornetist Willie "Bunk" Johnson. Though he was a refined Creole, Bechet loved playing with this "gut-bucket band" at rough joints such as the Funky Butt Hall, where Buddy Bolden, New Orleans' first cornet "king," once held sway. Johnson, who tended to exaggerate, claimed he was born in 1879 and that he played with Buddy Bolden in New Orleans, but Donald Marquis showed convincingly in his book, *In Search of Buddy Bolden* (1978), that Johnson was far younger than he claimed. Although not an influence on Louis Armstrong, as he maintained, Bunk was a major figure in New Orleans jazz from 1910 to 1914.

Bunk generally played second trumpet, a vital backup position in New Orleans bands, where jobs could last for six hours straight. He established a reputation for unreliability, taking jobs, disappearing with the advance, and then forgetting to show up. He left New Orleans around 1914 and toured the South with a variety of bands. One night in 1931 a friend was stabbed to death as he played alongside Bunk on the stand. The tragedy left its mark on Johnson's career, for his teeth were badly damaged in the ensuing brawl. Already suffering from dental problems, he soon settled in New Iberia, Louisiana, where he worked at various trades, including laboring in the rice fields.

In 1938 William Russell and Frederick Ramsey Jr., doing research for the book *Jazzmen* (1939), managed to track Johnson to New Iberia. The young writers began to correspond with him and eventually featured him in their book. A collection was taken to get Bunk new teeth and a new horn, and in 1942 he recorded privately for Russell in New Orleans. The following year he was in San Francisco playing with the Yerba Buena Jazz Band, a major force in launching the Dixieland revival. Between 1944 and 1945 Bunk recorded nearly one hundred sides; they created enormous interest and were hailed as a triumph for pure jazz. In 1945 Bechet recruited him for a band at the Savoy Café in Boston, but as an alcoholic, Johnson's playing tended to be erratic and he essentially drank his way out of the group. Soon thereafter he formed a group that played at the Stuyvesant Casino in New York. The band, consisting of primitive New Orleans musicians, was a disappointment to Bunk. He drank through his frustration, exhibited antisocial behavior (on one occasion he locked his men out of their living quarters), and the group soon disbanded. Working as a soloist in Louisiana, Chicago, and elsewhere, he returned to New York in 1947, where he assembled a band more to his liking. In 1948 he appeared in a Hollywood film, *New Orleans*, starring Armstrong and Billie Holiday, and then he returned to Louisiana for good. He died the following year, a figurehead of revivalism and an inspiration to younger New Orleans jazz musicians ever since.

DECEMBER 28—EARL HINES (1903-1983)

b. Duquesne, PA; d. Oakland, CA

Pianist; Bandleader; Composer

[CLASSIC JAZZ; SWING; BIG BAND]

Other jazz notables born on this day: Leonard Ware (1909); Moe Koffman (1928); Dick Sudhalter (1938); Lonnie Liston Smith (1940); Michel Petrucciani (1962)
Jazz notables deceased on this day: Ivie Anderson [or Dec. 27]; Billy Taylor (2010)

♪

Earl "Fatha" Hines, "the father of jazz piano," was one of a small number of pianists whose playing shaped the history of jazz. His playing expanded the piano's capabilities on every front: rhythmic, harmonic, and melodic. Hines invented a style of jazz piano known as "trumpet style," whereby he gave the piano a tonal color that approximated the brilliance of a trumpet. His forceful, physical style of playing was so great that he was known to have accidentally broken the large, very strong, bass strings on pianos. Most people could not break those strings even by smashing a fist down on them.

Born in Duquesne, now part of metropolitan Pittsburgh, Hines started to work in area clubs when he was thirteen, and when late hours began to interfere with his schoolwork, he dropped out of school. By 1923 he was in Chicago, working as a single in a café, where he pushed a small piano on casters from table to table to entertain the customers. His reputation spread quickly, and by the age of twenty-one he was leading a band at the Entertainer's Club. His precocious talent would make him, with Louis Armstrong, the city's most spectacular star in the 1920s. For several years Hines and Armstrong worked together, inspiring one another consistently. The year 1928 was one of Hines's most significant, for in that year alone he recorded his first piano solos, cut brilliant sides with Armstrong's Hot Five band—including such timeless gems as "West End Blues" and the highly original duet, "Weather Bird," recordings that quickly established him as the leading pianist in jazz—and on his twenty-fifth birthday he debuted with his big band at Chicago's Grand Terrace Ballroom, thereby fulfilling his ambition to be a bandleader.

Hines used Chicago as a base during the late 1920s and '30s, when he became widely known and admired as bandleader and pianist through tours and broadcasts. On these occasions the announcer introduced him by saying, "Here comes Fatha Hines through the deep forest with his little children" ("Deep Forest" was the band's theme song at the time). In 1940, after the addition of popular vocalist Billy Eckstine, Hines bought his way out of the long-running contract with the Mafia-owned Grand Terrace, and started touring regularly. By 1943 he made a second impact on jazz history when he took a group of young bebop players—including Charlie Parker, Dizzy Gillespie, and Sarah Vaughan—into his band, giving this new music its first important exposure. Unfortunately, the band went largely unrecorded, due to a recording ban imposed by the American Federation of Musicians. By the time the strike ended, the above-mentioned musicians were gone. Financial difficulties forced Hines to break up his orchestra in 1947, and from 1948 to

1951 he played with Armstrong's All-Stars. Hines eventually moved to San Francisco, where he headed a Dixieland band. Following triumphant concerts at New York's Little Theater in 1964, he had a major comeback that continued through the rest of his career. At the time of his death he was considered the greatest jazz pianist alive, second only to Art Tatum.

DECEMBER 29—JOE LOVANO (1952-)

b. Cleveland, OH

Tenor Saxophonist; Leader

[HARD BOP; POST-BOP]

Other jazz notables born on this day: Danilo Pérez (1965)

Jazz notables deceased on this day: Fletcher Henderson (1952); Paul Whiteman (1967)

♪

Will Friedwald of *The Village Voice*, speaking of tenor saxophonist Joe Lovano, wrote: "Move over Pavarotti; the greatest Italian tenor around today isn't Luciano, but Lovano." A top saxophonist of the 1990s, Joe Lovano is one of the most exciting talents currently operating in jazz. While not a major innovator, he nevertheless blends various stylistic elements into a personal and forward-seeking style. His playing exudes the sense of spontaneity that has always characterized jazz's finest improvisers. Comfortable playing both bop and free jazz, Lovano encompasses influences ranging from swing players to John Coltrane and even Ornette Coleman.

The son of Cleveland saxophonist Tony "Big T" Lovano, Joe started on alto when he was six, switching to tenor five years later. Lovano began playing with his father's band in his teens, during which time he also heard many of the prominent jazz artists who passed through town, including Dizzy Gillespie, James Moody, Sonny Stitt, and Rahsaan Roland Kirk. Though steeped in bebop, he also developed an interest in jazz experimentalism, displayed in the 1960s by such musicians as Coltrane, Coleman, and Jimmy Giuffre.[17] After high school Lovano moved to Boston and attended Berklee, where he met and began playing with future collaborators such as John Scofield, Bill Frisell, and Kenny Werner. At Berklee he discovered modal harmony and opened up to the broad areas of tonal freedom that he found so attractive in the music of Coltrane and others. "My training was all bebop, and suddenly there were these open forms with deceptive resolutions. That turned me on," he said, "I knew what I wanted to work on after that."

Lovano came to international attention as a member of Woody Herman's Thundering Herd (1976-79), which culminated in "The 40th Anniversary Concert" at Carnegie Hall, where he played with former Herman tenor stars Stan Getz, Zoot Sims, Flip Phillips, and Al Cohn. Eventually he settled in New York and soon became a regular member of the Mel Lewis big band, playing the band's Monday night gigs at the Village Vanguard until

---

17. Bogdanov et al., *All Music Guide to Jazz*, 777.

1992. In the early 1980s he gained further exposure and renown through his work in the trailblazing Paul Motian Trio, where he played alongside guitarist Bill Frisell.

From that point on Lovano increasingly led his own groups, experimenting in a wide array of styles and contexts and receiving much critical acclaim for recordings such as his 1996 album *Quartets: Live at the Village Vanguard*, named "Jazz Album of the Year" by readers of *Down Beat* magazine. In addition to his performing and recording activities, Lovano is active in music education. In 2001 he returned to Berklee as the first holder of the Gary Burton Chair in Jazz Performance, communicating his breadth of knowledge and experience to the next generation of jazz musicians.

DECEMBER 30—LEWIS NASH (1958–)

b. Phoenix, AZ

Drummer

[HARD BOP; POST-BOP]

Other jazz notables born on this day: Charlie Creath (1890)
Jazz notables deceased on this day: Art Rollini (1993); Ray Crawford (1997); Artie Shaw (2004)

♪

When jazz historian Ira Gitler called Lewis Nash "[p]erhaps the most talented drummer of his generation," jazz audiences everywhere took notice. And what they found only confirmed Gitler's evaluation. During the past two decades, Nash has been the drummer of choice for an incredible array of artist—from jazz masters to the hottest young players around—and he is equally in demand as a clinician and educator. His impressive discography (over three hundred recordings) includes projects with jazz legends Dizzy Gillespie, Oscar Peterson, Benny Carter, Hank Jones, and John Lewis, as well as new jazz stars such as Diana Krall, Joe Lovano, and Roy Hargrove. Demonstrating stylistic diversity, Nash is also featured on recordings by Natalie Cole, Bette Midler, Nancy Wilson, and Melissa Manchester, to name a few.

Nash took up drums at the age of ten and decided to become a jazz drummer after hearing Grady Tate on Quincy Jones's recording *Walking in Space*. While studying business at Arizona State University he played jazz locally, accompanying important visiting musicians such as Sonny Stitt, Red Garland, Art Pepper, and Lee Konitz. In 1985 he moved to New York and began working with Betty Carter, who for the last third of the twentieth century was one of the most dedicated promoters of young talent on the jazz scene. For nearly four years Nash toured internationally with the great vocalist's trio, honing his skills with world-class musicians like Benny Green, Stephen Scott, and Don Braden. He also appeared on many of Carter's recordings, including the Grammy Award-winning *Look What I Got* (1988).

During the remainder of the 1980s Nash also worked regularly with Ron Carter, Branford Marsalis, J.J. Johnson, Sonny Rollins, Art Farmer, and other jazz stars. In 1990 he became a member of Tommy Flanagan's trio, remaining with the late piano master until 2000. Together with Flanagan and bassist Peter Washington, the trio created some of the most memorable jazz recordings of the decade. During this period, Nash also toured and recorded with both the Carnegie Hall Jazz Band and the Lincoln Center Jazz Orchestra. In the late 1990s he formed his own group, the Lewis Nash Ensemble, with which he embarked on a two-year stint with the Jazz at the Lincoln Center Program, performing in the New York public school system. Providing inspiration and expertise to students became such an important part of Nash's career that in 2001 he joined the faculty of the prestigious Juilliard School of Music. Despite playing on hundreds of recordings, Nash has only released one recording to date as leader. Its title, *Rhythm Is My Business* (1989), seems to sum up Nash's career perfectly, for his lectures and workshops are currently as much in demand as his bandstand and studio work.

DECEMBER 31—JOHN KIRBY (1908–1952)
b. Baltimore, MD; d. Hollywood, CA

Bassist; Bandleader

[SWING]

Other jazz notables born on this day: Jonah Jones (1909); Cedric Haywood (1914); Jimmy Haslip (1951)
Jazz notables deceased on this day: George Lewis (1968)

♪

At the height of the big band era, from 1938 to 1942, John Kirby's sextet was perhaps the leading small jazz ensemble in the swing style. At its height, the band's personnel consisted of trumpeter Charlie Shavers, clarinetist Buster Bailey, altoist Russell Procope, pianist Billy Kyle, and drummer O'Neil Spencer, in addition to Kirby and, frequently, Kirby's wife Maxine Sullivan. Anticipating cool-jazz groups of the late 1940s and early '50s, the group concentrated on a "chamber" jazz style, performing intricate arrangements with a light sense of swing. The tight ensembles and brief solos brought out the best in each of the players.

According to Rex Stewart, Kirby's colleague from the Fletcher Henderson band, Kirby was abandoned during his infancy and had an unhappy childhood in an orphanage. He was originally a trombonist, but when he arrived in New York in 1924, his instrument was stolen. He then acquired a tuba and worked occasionally as a musician until becoming a regular member of Bill Brown and his Brownies (1929–30); by this time he was playing tuba and an aluminum-bodied double bass. He used both instruments with Henderson (1930–34) and made numerous recordings with the band. He also recorded in 1930 with an offshoot of the band, the Chocolate Dandies, under the direction of Benny Carter. In 1933 Kirby acquired a wooden double bass and ceased playing brass bass. He worked with Chick Webb (1934–35), led his own group for a brief period, and then spent further periods with Henderson (1935–36) and Webb (1936), all the while attracting attention with his strong pulse and walking bass lines. During the late 1930s he also participated in many of Billie Holiday's classic small group sessions.

In 1937 he established a small group at the Onyx Club in New York. Shavers supplied many of the group's arrangements, including "Undecided," which became a hit, and the band's abilities to "swing the classics" caught on. Dressed in white suits, "The Biggest Little Band in the Land" played all the best hotels in New York City and landed a regular NBC radio series, featuring Sullivan's swinging vocals. Their success lasted until the early 1940s, when Kyle was drafted, Spencer left for serious health reasons (he died in 1944), and Sullivan divorced Kirby and pursued an independent career. By 1945 (with Shavers's departure to join Tommy Dorsey) the only original members still in the group were Bailey and Kirby. The following year the ensemble disbanded and Kirby, suffering from diabetes and alcoholism, gradually fell into obscurity. Despite attempts to form another similar sextet (including a poorly attended Carnegie Hall reunion in 1950), Kirby was never able to duplicate his earlier success. He moved to Los Angeles in 1951, hoping to start a new band. Though he worked occasionally with Benny Carter, he became a forgotten figure in jazz, dying of diabetes at the age of forty-three.

Jazz Trivia Quiz

Below you will find a quiz consisting of sixty questions. The material is divided into the following categories:

- unconventional formations
- unusual facts
- uncommon feats, and
- unnatural fatalities

Write down your responses and then compare them with the answers found at the back of the questionnaire. Try taking the quiz before you read *Blue Notes* and then again after you have completed the reading. You will be surprised how much better you do the second time around. Don't be discouraged if you are unable to answer many of these questions correctly. Simply reading them will enlarge your perspective and should arouse the desire to learn more about the world of jazz and its intriguing cast of characters.

UNCONVENTIONAL FORMATIONS

1. Born in New Orleans on August 4, 1901, this influential jazz musician claimed throughout his life to have been born on July 4, 1900. The controversy was finally settled when his birth certificate was discovered in the late 1980s.

2. This trumpeter, who in the late 1940s ranked among the top young bop players, lost an eye in a childhood accident and nearly always wore dark glasses to hide his deformity.

3. Abandoned during his infancy, this drummer spent an unhappy childhood in an orphanage. Despite tragedy at the start of his life and disappointment at the end, he formed a sextet that became the leading small jazz ensemble in the swing style from 1938 to 1942, at the height of the big band era.

4. Despite impaired vision (he was blind in one eye and had only partial sight in the other), this pianist seemed to play everything twice as fast as his peers. Due to his advanced style, it is said that he intimidated many pianists into taking up other instruments.

5. This self-styled mystic pianist/bandleader claimed, always in a perfectly serious manner, that he was not born, but rather had arrived from another planet and belonged to an angel race.

Jazz Trivia Quiz

6. Born in Chicago during an influenza epidemic, which presumably affected his eyesight, this ingenious pianist became totally blind by the age of nine. One of jazz's true innovators, in 1946 he moved to New York, where he and his devoted followers first experimented with overdubbing and free collective improvisation.

7. Son of a rancher, this pianist entered college with the intention of a career in veterinary medicine. His picture appeared on the cover of the November 8, 1954 issue of *Time* magazine.

8. Considered the first jazz vibraphonist, this musician first learned drums at the Holy Rosary Academy in Kenosha, Wisconsin, where a Dominican nun taught him snare drum techniques. At a 1930 recording session with Louis Armstrong in Los Angeles, a vibraphone happened to be in the studio. When Armstrong asked the young man to play some notes behind him, he became the first jazz improviser to record on vibes.

9. This alto saxophonist, perhaps the most influential crossover saxophonist over the past twenty years, battled polio in his youth. While combating polio (and in an iron lung), he was advised to take up a wind instrument as physical therapy.

10. The son of a great African-American saxophonist and a Russian-Jewish dancer, this bop-based saxophonist graduated with highest honors from Harvard and turned down a chance to study law at Yale in order to become a professional musician.

11. The quintessential rebel, this legendary cornetist was a musical genius. Brought up in a strict family, the rebellious child found in music an escape from parental control. His colorful life made him a legend even before his premature death at the age of twenty-eight, the result of acute alcoholism.

UNUSUAL FACTS

12. This trumpeter was said to be half Native-American.

13. This well-known bandleader was married eight times, including to some of Hollywood's most glamorous stars.

14. This outstanding cornetist/bandleader, generally regarded as the first important personality in jazz history, went insane at the age of thirty and spent the last twenty-four years of his life in a mental institution.

15. This popular jazz-influenced guitarist who took part in the first Jazz at the Philharmonic concert in 1944 was seriously injured in an auto accident in 1948. As an alternative to amputation, his right arm was set at a permanent right angle suitable for guitar playing.

16. This popular vocalist took as his first name a childhood nickname from one of his favorite comic strips.

17. Generally associated with soul music, this vocalist/keyboardist grew up in a very poor family. At the age of five he contracted glaucoma, which went untreated, and

within a year he was blind. Born Ray Robinson, he changed his name to avoid confusion with the prizefighter Sugar Ray Robinson.

18. This male vocalist started his jazz career late, leaving his divinity studies at the University of Chicago, where he was planning to become a professor in the philosophy of religion.

19. One of the greatest jazz pianists of all time, this vocalist, composer, and comedian also pioneered the use of the pipe organ and Hammond organ in jazz, calling the pipe organ the "God box."

20. This gifted composer/arranger/pianist, one of the openly gay figures in jazz, composed his final piece as he lay in the hospital dying of cancer.

21. A leader of the "eccentric bop" movement, this self-taught pianist, one of the most original of all time, played church organ in his youth and had his first job touring as accompanist to a gospel-singing evangelist. In 1964 he became the subject of a cover story by *Time* magazine, an honor bestowed on only three other jazz musicians.

22. One of the most brilliant pianists in jazz during the late 1950s, this Memphis-born musician was plagued by mental and physical problems that destroyed two marriages and led to long periods of hospitalization. Bad luck also haunted him, such as the mugging he suffered in 1974 while preparing an album as an unaccompanied soloist, when several of his fingers were broken.

23. A master of the C-melody saxophone and the preeminent white saxophonist of the 1920s, this performer was a pilot since his earliest days as a musician. On one occasion, while flying his own plane to a gig in St. Louis, his plane developed engine trouble and ended up falling on the hotel where he was to play.

24. One of the most important innovators of the jazz avant-garde, this primitive, self-taught saxophonist became the most controversial musician in the history of jazz. Championed by Nat Hentoff, an eminent jazz critic, in 1959 he took his quartet into the Five Spot in New York, where the audience was filled with curious musicians who labeled him either a genius or a fraud.

25. Known as "the father of jazz tenor sax," this influential musician had a forty year prime (1925–65), during which time he held his own against any and all competitors.

26. One of the great tenors, this saxophonist became the star of Lionel Hampton's 1942 big band. His solo on "*Flying Home*," considered the first R&B sax solo, spawned a generation of younger tenor who built their careers from his style and practically from that song.

27. Beset by personal problems, including alcohol dependency, this saxophone collosus took a second leave of absence from jazz in 1959. Withdrawing from the public for several years, he spent countless hours practicing his horn while walking on the Williamsburg Bridge, which runs over New York's East River.

Jazz Trivia Quiz

28. The oldest of four musical brothers, this saxophonist left his brother's influential quintet and eventually joined Jay Leno's *Tonight Show* as the musical director, a position he held for two years.

29. This famous trumpeter was fired by bandleader Cab Calloway for an incident that started with a spitball and ended with a stabbing.

30. During the forty-six years that he was a member of Duke Ellington's orchestra, this musician achieved his goal of making the baritone saxophone indispensable in a big band.

31. Although he disliked the style, this musician was the last African-American clarinetist to make a name in jazz. Next to Pee Wee Russell, he is generally considered the finest of the Dixieland clarinetists of his time.

32. An accomplished reed player (among the finest jazz players on reeds during 1925–35) and one of the top bandleaders of the swing era, this musician co-led bands with his younger brother during the early and late periods of his career. In 1935 their successful big band came to an end over an argument about the tempo for a popular song.

33. The first celebrated bandleader of the swing era, this famous musician was an enigma. Possessing a reputation for being "difficult" and insensitive (his withering stare was known as "The Ray" by his sidemen), he was among the first make a stand for racial integration, endangering his own career by featuring African-Americans in his bands.

34. Known as "Little Jazz," this diminutive trumpeter had a combative edge that made him one of the most exciting trumpeters to emerge during the swing era.

35. One of the great trumpeters of the 1920s, this performer was a master with the plunger mute, distorting his sound in a colorful manner. The most impressive of the early Ellington soloists and the most prominent voice in Duke's "Jungle Band" of 1926 to 1928, he was largely responsible for Ellington's early success and had an effect on much of the bandleader's subsequent music.

UNCOMMON FEATS

36. One of the jazz era's most durable musicians, this self-taught ragtimer and composer played well into his 90s.

37. Known for his on-stage antics, this musician's routines included playing trombone with his foot and inviting customers to stand on his stomach during performances.

38. As a member of Stan Kenton's orchestra in 1950, this instrumentalist could play higher than any trumpeter up to that point in jazz history.

39. A limited but memorable Brazilian vocalist, this housewife had no professional musical experience when she visited New York with her vocalist/guitarist husband in

1963. Her unscheduled appearance at a bossa nova recording session led to a successful performing career that lasted into the 1990s.

40. Often called jazz's greatest female musician, this excellent pianist provided distinctive arrangements for swing bands led by Andy Kirk, Benny Goodman, Earl Hines, Tommy Dorsey, and Duke Ellington. By the mid-1940s, she was a source of inspiration for the leaders of the bebop revolution.

41. One of the most distinctive of all pianists, this musician proved that it was possible to be a sophisticated player without knowing how to read music. Able to sit at the piano without prior planning and record three albums in one day, he is best remembered for his composition "Misty."

42. This talented bop pianist sustained an injury in 1945, when he was beaten on the head by racist cops, after which he began to suffer nervous collapses from which he never fully recovered. As an adult he was institutionalized regularly and given electric shock treatments. Despite his personal problems, his playing during that period was often brilliant.

43. During the 1970s this pianist from Allentown, Pennsylvania was the enfant terrible of jazz piano, playing entire concerts of spontaneous improvisations. From 1975 to 1985, no one did more to stimulate interest in jazz piano among a broad international audience than he did. In the autumn of 1996 he was tragically stricken with chronic-fatigue syndrome, which forced him to put his career on hold.

44. A child prodigy, this alto saxophonist from West Virginia essentially invented the jazz-oriented big band in the 1920s. His arrangements for bandleader Fletcher Henderson transformed the sound of Henderson's band, the premiere black jazz orchestra in the country at the time.

45. Somewhat of a playboy throughout his life, ending up with many ex-wives and plenty of anecdotes, this saxophonist led a very popular dance band during the swing period. One of the few jazz players to be born a millionaire, he was a pioneer in leading integrated bands.

46. A longtime member of the Ellington orchestra (1951–74), this saxophonist's musical career skyrocketed at the 1956 Newport Jazz Festival when Ellington urged him to take a long solo. The solo, lasting through twenty-seven exciting choruses, nearly caused a riot.

47. A "jazz messiah" to some (he is the only jazz musician to have a church founded in his name) and an "anti-jazz" figure to others, during his relatively brief career this performer was among the most important, and most controversial, figures in jazz. By 1957 he was playing with remarkable speed and agility, as much as any other saxophonist in jazz history. This fluency, at times approaching a thousand notes a minute, came to be characterized as his "sheets-of-sound" style.

48. One of the all-time great tenor saxophonists, this musician was known as "The Sound" because of his exquisite tone.

Jazz Trivia Quiz

UNNATURAL FATALITIES

49. This trumpeter died of throat cancer two days after Louis Armstrong; his dying wish was granted when his mouthpiece was buried in Armstrong's coffin.

50. His career marred by drug addiction, this trumpeter, acclaimed at age twenty-three as "a great white hope," spent much of his career deported from one country to another. He died in Amsterdam in 1988, after falling from a second-story window.

51. Suffering from an eye disease that severely limited his sight, this trumpeter fell under a subway train in New York and died at the age of forty-four.

52. Considered by many to be the finest jazz trombonist of all time, this innovative musician fell ill with prostate cancer and tragically took his own life on February 4, 2001.

53. Distraught over his family life, this performer shot his two sons, killing one and blinding the other, and then committed suicide.

54. This popular vocalist was at the top of her field when she committed suicide on May 19, 2001, by jumping from a Manhattan hotel window.

55. This excellent bandleader of the late 1920s and early '30s formed the first of several dance bands that included such future jazz talents as Benny Goodman, Glenn Miller, and Jack Teagarden. He was plagued by personal and professional bitterness when he ended his life by hanging himself in his Palm Springs bathroom on June 7, 1971.

56. One of the most influential female singers of the mid-twentieth century, this vocalist had a distinctive, high-pitched voice. She survived seven marriages before dying of an accidental overdose of diet pills mixed with alcohol at the early age of thirty-nine.

57. The death of this extraordinary trumpeter in a car accident at the age of twenty-five ranks as one of the great tragedies in jazz history. Traveling with him that fateful night was Richie Powell (Bud Powell's younger brother) and Powell's wife, Nancy, who was at the wheel when the car skidded on a wet stretch of the Pennsylvania Turnpike and rolled over an embankment, killing all three passengers.

58. Nicknamed "Rabbit" because of his love for lettuce and tomato sandwiches, this famous and influential alto saxophonist, possessor of "the most beautiful tone ever heard in jazz," died while visiting a dentist.

59. When this brilliant altoist died at the age of thirty-four, his body was so wasted from the ravages of an abusive lifestyle that the medical examiner, required to list the age of the deceased, examined the corpse and listed the age as fifty-three.

60. Best known for his hit "*The Sidewinder*," this trumpeter was shot to death in a New York club by a jealous girlfriend; he was only thirty-three years old.

ANSWER SHEET

The grading scale for questions answered correctly is:

1–10	Poor
11–20	Fair
12–30	Good
31–40	Excellent
41–50	Outstanding
51–60	Brilliant

1. Louis Armstrong
2. Howard McGhee
3. John Kirby
4. Art Tatum
5. Sun Ra
6. Lennie Tristano
7. Dave Brubeck
8. Lionel Hampton
9. David Sanborn
10. Joshua Redman
11. Bix Beiderbecke
12. Harry "Sweets" Edison
13. Artie Shaw
14. Buddy Bolden
15. Les Paul
16. Bing Crosby
17. Ray Charles
18. Mark Murphy
19. Fats Waller
20. Billy Strayhorn
21. Thelonious Monk
22. Phineas Newborn
23. Frankie Trumbauer
24. Ornette Coleman
25. Coleman Hawkins
26. Illinois Jacquet

27. Sonny Rollins
28. Branford Marsalis
29. Dizzy Gillespie
30. Harry Carney
31. Larry Shields
32. Jimmy Dorsey
33. Benny Goodman
34. Roy Eldridge
35. Bubber Miley
36. Eubie Blake
37. Georg Brunis
38. Maynard Ferguson
39. Astrud Gilberto
40. Mary Lou Williams
41. Erroll Garner
42. Bud Powell
43. Keith Jarrett
44. Don Redman
45. Charlie Barnet
46. Paul Gonsalves
47. John Coltrane
48. Stan Getz
49. Charlie Shavers
50. Chet Baker
51. Woody Shaw
52. J. J. Johnson
53. Frank Rosolino
54. Susannah McCorkle
55. Ben Pollack
56. Dinah Washington
57. Clifford Brown
58. Johnny Hodges
59. Charlie Parker
60. Lee Morgan

Appendix I

ENTRY POINTS FOR THE ENJOYMENT OF JAZZ MUSIC: WHERE TO START?

There are many ways to enter the jazz world. The key is to keep an open mind toward different styles, since the more rewarding jazz recordings grow in interest with each listen. A good place to start is by exploring the great masters of the music, particularly with recordings from the six immortal giants who virtually invented large aspects of the music: Louis Armstrong, Duke Ellington, Charlie Parker, Dizzy Gillespie, Miles Davis, and John Coltrane.[1] From that point on, when one discovers what area of the music is most enjoyable, one can start exploring the music of contemporaries such as Jelly Roll Morton, Sidney Bechet, Bix Beiderbecke, Fats Waller, Bessie Smith, Benny Goodman, Coleman Hawkins, Lester Young, Art Tatum, Count Basie, Billie Holiday, Ella Fitzgerald, Bud Powell, Thelonious Monk, Gerry Mulligan, Dave Brubeck, Stan Getz, Lee Morgan, Cannonball Adderley, Sonny Rollins, Horace Silver, Jimmy Smith, Art Blakey, Bill Evans, Charles Mingus, Ornette Coleman, Cecil Taylor, Wynton Marsalis, Keith Jarrett, and Pat Metheny. The number of significant and colorful jazz musicians and singers is endless and learning about jazz can be a most enjoyable venture.

Scott Janow, a contributor to the *All Music Guide to Jazz*, suggests the following tips for getting started. If one is coming to jazz through rhythm and blues or pop music, try listening to Grover Washington Jr. and David Sanborn and then progress to John Coltrane and Chick Corea. Listeners who enjoy rock music should explore Weather Report, John Scofield, Jean-Luc Ponty, and fusion-era Miles Davis before reaching Coltrane and Ornette Coleman. Classical fans can enter the jazz world through Bill Evans, the Miles Davis/Gil Evans recordings of the 1950s, and the Modern Jazz Quartet. Those who enjoy current dance music with catchy melodies and funky rhythms can try Lee Morgan's *The Sidewinder*, most Horace Silver albums, and records by the Stanley Turrentine/Shirley Scott group of the 1960s. Of course, everyone can benefit from getting a few Louis Armstrong records.

---

1. Note the list of recommended entry-level recordings below. This list and other select information in the appendix is adapted from the All Music Guide to Jazz website.

Appendix II

RECOMMENDED ENTRY-LEVEL JAZZ RECORDINGS

Although no two listeners of jazz have identical musical tastes, the following recordings are on most everyone's recommended list for their entry-level appeal:

Louis Armstrong, *Plays W.C. Handy* (Columbia – 1997 version)

Count Basie, *The Atomic Mr. Basie* (Roulette)

Dave Brubeck, *Time Out* (Columbia)

John Coltrane, *My Favorite Things* (Atlantic)

Miles Davis, *Kind of Blue* (Columbia)

Duke Ellington, *Uptown* (Columbia)

Stan Getz, *Getz/Gilberto* (Verve)

Dizzy Gillespie, *At Newport* (Verve)

Benny Goodman, *Sing, Sing, Sing* (Bluebird)

Billie Holiday, *The Quintessential*, Vol. 5 (Columbia)

Wynton Marsalis, *Blue Interlude* (Columbia)

Wes Montgomery, *The Incredible Jazz Guitar* (Original Jazz Classics)

Lee Morgan, *The Sidewinder* (Blue Note)

Charlie Parker, *Yardbird Suite* (Rhino)

Art Tatum, *Piano Starts Here* (Columbia)

The Smithsonian Collection of Classic Jazz (this anthology belongs in every jazz library). In 2011 this collection, long out of print, was updated and supplanted by a definitive six-disc set titled *Jazz: The Smithsonian Anthology*.

Appendix III

HISTORICAL SUMMARY
(INCLUDING JAZZ STYLES AND TIMELINE)

Overview

The origins of jazz, like those of the universe, are shrouded in uncertainty. Though the first jazz recording, by the Original Dixieland Jazz Band, was in 1917, the music existed in some form for at least twenty years before that. Influenced by classical music, marches, spirituals, work songs, ragtime, blues, and the popular music of the period, jazz was already a distinctive form of music by the time it was first documented.

Some argue that jazz music as we know it today originated with New Orleans brass bands. Musicians performing marches and popular songs of the era lacked formal musical education, so during long parades, after playing a melody several times, they would began to improvise variations, partly to relieve boredom and often for the pure fun of it. Since the first major name in jazz, cornetist Buddy Bolden, formed his original band in 1895, that year serves as a useful starting point for jazz history. Bolden was succeeded by Freddie Keppard as the top New Orleans cornetist and Keppard was eventually surpassed by King Oliver. Although some New Orleans musicians traveled north, jazz remained a regional music until World War I.

The evolution of jazz was slow until recordings in the 1920s began to speed up its progress. During a fifty-year period the music evolved rapidly from the ensemble-oriented New Orleans jazz and Dixieland to swinging big bands, sophisticated bebop and its offshoots (cool jazz, hard bop, soul jazz), avant-garde jazz (with free improvisations), and fusion, which took some of the better elements from rock's most creative period. Since the mid-1970s, the evolution of jazz has slowed greatly. Whereas during the 1925 to 1975 period old styles were quickly discarded by modernists, during the past several decades a variety of revival movements have performed virtually all jazz styles creatively.

Jazz in the Classroom

College jazz education is often said to date back to the first jazz performance degree, offered by North Texas State in 1947. However, historically black colleges offered instruction in jazz performance long before that. Perhaps the earliest rigorous college-level syllabus dates to the fall of 1950, when Marshall W. Stearns, a professor of English literature, a contributor to *Down Beat*, and the author of the highly regarded text, *The Story of Jazz*,

Appendix III

offered a course in jazz history at New York University. In the following years, Stearns helped organize courses in jazz at other colleges and universities in the New York City area.[2] The 1950 NYU course syllabus listed the following outline:[3]

> Lecture 1: Jazz Definitions
>
> Lecture 2: Jazz Prehistory
>
> Lecture 3: New Orleans
>
> Lecture 4: Jelly Roll Morton
>
> Lecture 5: The Blues
>
> Lecture 6: Ragtime
>
> Lecture 7: North to Chicago
>
> Lecture 8: Chicago and the Jazz Age
>
> Lecture 9: Big Bands in New York
>
> Lecture 10: Swing is King
>
> Lecture 11: Kansas City and the Count [Count Basie]
>
> Lecture 12: Progressive Jazz and Bebop
>
> Lecture 13: New Orleans Revival
>
> Lecture 14: Things to Come [experimental jazz in the 1940s and '50s]
>
> Lecture 15: Standards of Criticism in Jazz [the aesthetics of jazz and its place in the fine arts]

In addition to the pioneering role of Stearns, the course was team taught by George Avakian and John Hammond, both influential jazz critics and record producers, and the syllabus promised an astonishing list of guest speakers, including such performers as Louis Armstrong, Duke Ellington, Benny Goodman, Count Basie, Dizzy Gillespie, William Russell, George Shearing, and Lennie Tristano and such authors and critics as Alan Lomax, Rudi Blesh, Ralph Ellison, and William Russell. What one would give to have been enrolled in such a course!

Musical Periods

The following brief overview of jazz eras and jazz styles focuses on jazz's first century, from the 1890s to the 1990s. The organization and content of the eras follow the outline of Stearns's syllabus where possible but differ somewhat in the understanding of the early history of jazz and expand on the unit of "things to come" by exploring the radical innovations of the period from 1950 to the mid-'70s that Stearns had anticipated. Note that the

---

2. In 1952 Stearns founded the Institute of Jazz Studies at Rutgers University, which has become perhaps the single most important archive for jazz researchers.

3. Walser, *Keeping Time*, 196–99.

Appendix III

dates for the jazz periods serve as approximations. The musical styles listed are iconic in that they often defined an era.

The Ragtime Era (1900–1910)

The piano-based music of this style is classically derived and rhythmically bouncy. Although lacking the improvisation or blues feeling inherent in jazz, ragtime was a strong influence on the earlier forms of jazz.

Narrative: At its prime from 1899 to 1915, ragtime emerged from the saloons, honky-tonks, and houses of entertainment in the wide-open cities of the American Midwest. There, ragtime's founder, Scott Joplin, turned syncopated tunes into formal compositions.

Major proponents: Scott Joplin, Joe Lamb, Eubie Blake.

New Orleans Traditional (1910–1920)

This ensemble-oriented music, a direct descendant of marching brass bands, de-emphasizes solos in favor of ensembles.

Narrative: Often called "classic jazz" because it is the earliest style of jazz, this style was performed in New Orleans from 1895 until the closing of Storyville (the first legal red-light district in the Western Hemisphere) in 1917. In many respects this band music, performed for celebrations and funerals, is the most accessible style of jazz. Tuba and clarinet were prominent in the early years.

Major proponents: Johnny and Baby Dodds, Louis Armstrong, King Oliver, Preservation Hall Jazz Band(s), Papa Celestin, Sidney Bechet, Jelly Roll Morton, Jimmy Noone, Buddy Bolden.

Dixieland (1920–1930)

This happy, up-tempo riverboat music emphasized banjo and brass. Sometimes called "Chicago jazz" because it developed in Chicago in the 1920s, this style overlaps with New Orleans jazz. The front-line of trumpet, clarinet, and trombone was the accepted minimum for the Dixieland brass-band effect. The framework typically involved collective improvisation at the start, followed by individual solos with some riffing by the other horns, and a closing by the ensemble.

Narrative: The music was spread by recordings and radio broadcasts but the most effective means was by example. Riverboats out of New Orleans and bandleaders hired top musicians to entertain customers on trips up the Mississippi. In the aftermath of World War I, many jazz musicians headed to Chicago, which became the center for an active jazz scene during the 1920s. For many, the Jazz Age came alive in Chicago. King Oliver drew large crowds to the Lincoln Gardens, especially after Louis Armstrong joined him. Musicians from Bix Beiderbecke to Benny Goodman had links with Chicago, so that the city's name has come to stand for the white musicians of the 1920s. Dixieland revivals occurred in the 1950s and again in the 1970s as musicians outside the South brought a renewed interest in the music of the 1920s.

Appendix III

Major proponents: (a) *Chicago Jazz*: King Oliver, Louis Armstrong, Lil Hardin, Kid Ory, Austin High Gang, Frankie Trumbauer, Bix Beiderbecke, Earl Hines. (b) *Dixieland revivalists*: Pee Wee Russell, Edmond Hall, Barney Bigard, Matty Matlock, Bob Wilber, Ken Peplowski, George Wetling, Bob Scobey, Dick Hyman, Wilbur DeParis, Bobby Hackett, Al Hirt, Pete Fountain, Doc Cheatham, Ruby Braff, Red Nichols, Duxes of Dixieland, World's Greatest Jazz Band.

THE BLUES: VOCAL (1890S TO PRESENT)

The "blues" refers to several different kinds of music, vocal and instrumental. The blues has been played and sung in every jazz age and can be performed in a variety of styles and with many interpretations. Blues can be slow and sad, or happy and rollicking.

Narrative: Vocal blues is a folk music developed in America by African slaves and their descendents. In the beginning, blues was a form of unaccompanied solo singing. As it evolved, singers began to accompany themselves on the guitar, harmonica, or banjo. By about 1910 a rhyme scheme was adopted, characterized by a given progression of accompaniment chords. This pattern of chords, in turn, set the pace for the twentieth-century tradition of instrumental blues performance.

As a musical form the blues has never lost its importance, and is heard as frequently today as it was in all previous eras of jazz. Adaptations of the form, such as rhythm-and-blues in 1945 and rock and roll in 1955, show the durability of the form as it continues to survive through all adaptations. Many modern jazz selections still use the basic blues progression with expanded harmonies.

Major proponents: Blind Lemon Jefferson, Huddie Ledbetter, Ma Rainey, Bessie Smith.

PIANO BLUES (AND BOOGIE-WOOGIE) (1890S–1940)

This style consists of rollicking, no-holds-barred music, with train rhythms prevalent. This music later came to be called boogie-woogie. Boogie-woogie is a medium-tempo or fast blues employing repeated eighth and sixteenth figures in the bass, and repeated figures, sometimes interspersed with single-note runs, in the right hand. The left hand and the right hand operate so independently that boogie-woogie often sounds like two pianists instead of one.

Narrative: Boogie-woogie came into prominence during an economic crisis—the Great Depression of the early 1930s, when a full style of piano playing was needed as a substitute for hiring a band. Boogie-woogie became a popular fad around 1938, with recordings and concerts in such notable venues as Carnegie Hall. In time the big swing bands found it necessary to add boogie-woogie instrumentals to their repertoires: Tommy Dorsey's "Boogie-Woogie," was one of the period's biggest hits.

Major proponents: There were three fairly defined generations of boogie-woogie players. The earlier pianists were active primarily in the 1920s, including Jimmy Yancey, Cow Cow Davenport, and Clarence "Pine Top" Smith. Of the middle group, popular during the early 1930s, three stand out: Meade "Lux" Lewis, Albert Ammons, and Pete Johnson. The last group included such players as Freddie Slack, Cleo Brown, and Bob Zurke.

Harlem Stride (1920–1940)

Stride piano playing uses percussive, striding, left-hand figures in which low bass notes alternated with mid-range chords, while the right hand plays melodies and embellishments in a lively fashion. The result resembles an energetic one-man band. Stride is a style of piano jazz with roots in ragtime. However, it is more heavily rhythmic than ragtime, and more nimble.

Narrative: James P. Johnson, composer of the famous tune "Charleston," is considered to be the father of stride piano. One of the things that distinguished the Northeast, particularly New York, from other parts of the country was the presence of a large body of European-trained pianists. As a consequence, New York ragtimers were forced to learn the European system, so they played in a fuller, more orchestral style than was used elsewhere in the country. By World War I, Johnson was accepted as one of the leading pianists in his style. He went on to become one of the greatest jazz pianists of all time, influencing such future jazz giants as Art Tatum, Count Basie, Teddy Wilson, Errol Garner, and Duke Ellington. He composed some two hundred songs and pieces and collaborated with Fats Waller, a pupil who went on to become the most entertaining and exciting of all stride pianists.

Major proponents: James P. Johnson, Fats Waller, Willie "The Lion" Smith.

Swing and the Big Band Era (1930–1950)

During the big band era, most bands fell into one of two categories: sweet bands, which prized melody above all, and hot bands, which emphasized greater solo improvisation, rhythmic drive, and blues feeling. Sweet bands helped pave the way for the rise of pop singers like Frank Sinatra, Tony Bennett, and Mel Tormé. The swing style during the big band era featured American popular songs played instrumentally by jazz orchestras primarily for dancing. Musical films of the era promoted these songs and bands and the style was very popular on the radio.

Narrative: Although swing music really caught on with the masses with the emergence of Benny Goodman in 1935, the style had already existed for more than a decade. When Louis Armstrong joined the Fletcher Henderson Orchestra in 1924, his dramatic sense of swing greatly influenced Henderson's chief arranger Don Redman, and the birth of swing may be traced to this collaboration. The most significant big band of the late 1920s and one that succeeded Fletcher Henderson's as the pacesetter was that of Duke Ellington. From 1935 to 1942, swing was the popular music of the time and new stars emerged with regularity, but during World War II, many swing musicians were drafted and by the end of the war new styles had emerged, including the rise of pop singers. By 1946 many of the big bands had quit; although a few of the swing bands survived, they were rare exceptions.

Appendix III

Major proponents:

1. *Individual Instrumentalists*: Lester Young, Coleman Hawkins, Bunny Berigan, Harry James, Roy Eldridge, Cootie Williams, Buck Clayton, Jack Teagarden, Benny Goodman, Artie Shaw, Woody Herman, Chu Berry, Ben Webster, Johnny Hodges, Benny Carter, Art Tatum, Teddy Wilson, Mary Lou Williams, Lionel Hampton, Red Norvo, Django Reinhardt, Charlie Christian, Walter Page, John Kirby, Milt Hinton, Gene Krupa, Jo Jones, Big Sid Catlett, Buddy Rich, Chick Webb.

2. *Prominent Big Bands*: Fletcher Henderson, McKinney's Cotton Pickers, Casa Loma Orchestra, Luis Russell, Bennie Moten, Count Basie, Duke Ellington, Jimmie Lunceford, Ben Pollack, Andy Kirk, Bob Crosby, Benny Goodman, Tommy and Jimmy Dorsey, Glenn Miller, Artie Shaw, Charlie Barnet, Jay McShann, Boyd Raeburn, Tony Pastor, Erskine Hawkins, Cab Calloway, Billy Eckstine, Woody Herman, Stan Kenton.

3. *Vocalists*: Louis Armstrong, Bing Crosby, Jimmy Rushing, Nat King Cole, Cab Calloway, Big Joe Turner, Joe Williams, Jack Teagarden, Mel Tormé, Billy Eckstine, Bob Eberly, Frank Sinatra, Tex Beneke, Dick Haymes, Dinah Washington, Ella Fitzgerald, Mildred Bailey, Lee Wiley, Connee Boswell, Ivie Anderson, Billie Holiday, Helen Forrest, Maxine Sullivan, Martha Tilton, Helen Ward, Helen Humes, Helen O'Connell, Jo Stafford, Lena Horne, Dinah Shore, Marion Hutton, Rosemary Clooney, Doris Day, Peggy Lee, Sarah Vaughan, June Christy, Anita O'Day.

Bop (1940–1955)

Also known as bebop, bop emerged around 1940 as a reaction to big bands and swing music. Bop musicians attempted to raise the quality of jazz from dance music to the level of a chamber art form. Display of instrumental virtuosity was a high priority for bop players. Less emphasis was placed on arrangements and more on solo improvisation. When they improvised, bop musicians departed from the melodies, concentrating on harmonically intricate chord progressions instead. And as melodies and harmonies became more complex, the tempo increased. Playing at speeds that few musicians could maintain, the bop pioneers set virtuosic standards that ordinary musicians could not reach. Bop marked the departure of jazz from mainstream pop music, as many didn't like or understand it, but it was the source of (or at least an influence on) all later jazz styles.

Narrative: Somewhere around the year 1940 a new sound emerged in the jazz world, having grown from roots laid down in the 1930s by saxophonists Coleman Hawkins and Lester Young, pianists Art Tatum and Nat Cole, trumpeter Roy Eldridge, the Count Basie rhythm section, and in particular, by guitarist Charlie Christian. Whereas "early jazz" and other pre-1940 styles are sometimes referred to as the "classic period" of jazz, new styles since 1940 are classified as "modern jazz." And the first modern jazz musicians were alto saxophonist Charlie Parker, pianist Thelonius Monk, and trumpeter Dizzy Gillespie. During the mid-1940s these artists inspired numerous others, including trumpeter Miles Davis and pianist Bud Powell. By the late 1940s that influence also extended to several big bands, including that of Woody Herman.

Major proponents: Charlie Christian, Dizzy Gillespie, Thelonious Monk, Kenny Clarke, Charlie Parker, Bud Powell, Max Roach, Tadd Dameron, Miles Davis, Al Haig, J. J. Johnson, Dexter Gordon, Fats Navarro, Billy Eckstine Orchestra, Woody Herman's First Two Herds, Stan Kenton.

COOL (OR WEST COAST) JAZZ (1950S)

This mode of jazz was a reaction not so much to bop but to hot music in general. Essentially, it was a mixture of bop with certain elements of swing that emphasized a restrained feel, softer colors, and purposefully limited dynamics. Because some of the key pacesetters of the style were studio musicians centered in Los Angeles, it was nicknamed "West Coast jazz."

Narrative: The term "cool" in jazz was the continuation of a movement that had been going on in jazz for quite some time, namely the attempt to create "symphonic jazz." From its earliest days, jazz had felt a pull exerted by the European symphonic tradition, particularly by its smaller ensemble, the chamber group. By the 1940s many of the musicians taking up jazz were being trained in European music, and they began wondering whether some of the classical procedures could be applied to jazz, particularly to the swing bands with which most of them were performing. The most important of these bands were led by Stan Kenton, Woody Herman, and Claude Thornhill.

At a time when most of the big bands were calling it quits because of economic pressures and changing musical tastes, the leading edge of jazz was turning to a chamber music format, leaving its dance-band origins far behind. The move of jazz to sit-down concert style, along with the collapse of big bands, left a dance-music void in the early 1950s that would be filled by rock and roll, for teenagers needed danceable music with a good beat.

Major proponents: The Modern Jazz Quartet (John Lewis, Milt Jackson, Percy Heath, Connie Kay), Stan Getz, Lennie Tristano, Lee Konitz, Warne Marsh, Miles Davis (prior to 1960), Paul Desmond, Dave Brubeck, Chet Baker, Gerry Mulligan, Art Pepper, Kai Winding, Stan Getz, Chico Hamilton, Gil Evans, Jimmy Giuffre, Gunther Schuller, Stan Kenton, Woody Herman, Claude Thornhill, the Sauter-Finegan Orchestra. The cool sound could also be said to characterize the music of Lester Young, Count Basie, and musicians influenced by them.

HARD-BOP (1955–1970)

This style, a return to a bluesier, earthier sound than bop, while retaining and evolving its highly virtuosic instrumental styles, may be viewed as an extension of bop that largely ignored West Coast jazz. Despite the similarities between this stream of music and its foundations in bop, when the two differ, hard bop emphasized simpler improvisational lines with darker tone colors. Forms and progressions became more original and less dependent on pop tunes, and the music had a hard-driving, relentless feel, with an emphasis on consistent swing.[4]

---

4. Gridley, *Jazz Styles*, 198.

Appendix III

Narrative: By the mid-1950s many musicians began turning away from cool jazz, failing to appreciate what they considered an overly intellectual approach to jazz. But there were other factors, sociological and political, that may have been more important contributors to the dissatisfaction. During the 1950s and '60s, African-Americans began to think differently about themselves, their place in American society, and the methods for bringing about change. They began to announce that the white ways were not necessarily the best. Blacks, of course, saw jazz as their major contribution to American culture; they perceived cool jazz as essentially a white movement, based on European musical forms. If black was beautiful, why not play jazz in a black way? By way of response, a number of jazz styles emerged during the 1950s and '60s, though the majority differed only slightly from bebop. The underlying difference, however, was the conscious attempt by these players to build upon the black-American folk music tradition out of which jazz had grown.

Major proponents: Clifford Brown, Art Blakey, Horace Silver, Lee Morgan, Benny Golson, Jackie McLean, John Coltrane, Miles Davis, Sonny Rollins. Musicians playing with drummer Blakey and pianist Silver worked within this style through the 1980s, as well as groups led by Davis between 1955 and 1959.

Soul-Jazz/Original Funk (1955–1970)

Soul-jazz, considered the most popular jazz style of the 1960s, developed from hard bop. Soul-jazz differs from bebop and hard bop in placing the emphasis on the rhythmic groove. This gospel-influence music is blues-based but with modern harmonies, usually with a back beat. Organ and guitars are prevalent. As this new music developed, it came to be called "funk" or "soul" music. The term "soul" came from the church, whereas the less precise "funk" implied something earthy, with a down-home feeling. Compositions conveying this earthy, blues-drenched, gospelish feeling include Horace Silver's "The Preacher" and "Song for my Father"; Bobby Timmon's "Moanin'," Nat Adderley's "Work Song," Joe Zawinul's "Mercy, Mercy, Mercy," and Lee Morgan's "Sidewinder."

Narrative: Soul-jazz's roots, adapting the secularization of gospel music pioneered by Ray Charles, trace back to pianist Horace Silver, whose funky style infused bop with the influence of gospel music, along with the blues. With the emergence of organist Jimmy Smith in 1956, soul-jazz organ combos caught on, and soulful players became stars. Despite its eclipse by fusion and synthesizers in the 1970s, soul-jazz has made a comeback in recent years.

Major proponents: Ray Charles, Horace Silver, Jimmy Smith, Ramsey Lewis, Lee Morgan, Bobby Timmons, Gene Harris, Jack McDuff, Jimmy McGriff, Grant Green, Cannonball and Nat Adderley, Lou Donaldson, Hank Crawford, Stanley Turrentine, Shirley Scott, George Benson, Kenny Burrell, David "Fathead" Newman, Gene Ammons, Houston Person, Eddie Harris, Hank Crawford, Paul Chambers, Philly Joe Jones.

Post-Bop/Modal Jazz (late 1950s–1960s)

The term "post-bop" describes a broad range of jazz that features less reliance on popular-song forms and more on open-ended harmonies that created new possibilities for extended improvisation. In its early manifestations in the 1950s and '60s this music featured early exploration of world music influences. The expression "modal jazz" describes much of this music. A mode is essentially a scale or a collection of notes through which the improviser wanders freely. This scalar approach to music goes back to the ancient Greeks and to medieval music and is featured in Asian and primitive cultures as well.

Narrative: In a series of landmark recordings during the late 1950s and '60s, Miles Davis and his sidemen helped define this style of jazz, particularly in *Kind of Blue*, one of the pivotal albums in modern jazz. Every track on the album was modal; and the playing was spare, controlled, and moody. This album is considered by most critics and observers as the most influential in jazz history.

Between 1963 and 1970 Miles assembled a new quintet that rivaled his earlier quintets in popularity and innovation. Moving away from earlier bop formulas, the quintet exhibited lots of variety in mood and rhythmic style. Jazz-rock fusion bands of the 1970s and '80s often combined passages of chord-based improvisation with mode-based improvisation. Davis himself alternated among these approaches. The music of the so-called "new age" bands of the 1980s was largely modal. This music became the norm for jazz in the 1990s, symbolizing the eclectic scene as jazz entered its second century.

Major proponents: Miles Davis, John Coltrane, Donald Byrd, Bill Evans, Gigi Gryce, Wayne Shorter, McCoy Tyner, Kenny Dorham.

Early Free Jazz (1960s–1970s)

Free Jazz, a style that overlaps with the avant-garde jazz styles of the 1960s, derives from the practice of improvising music that is free of preset chord progressions. The original improvisers who changed the face of jazz in the late 1950s to late '60s did away with fixed harmonic and rhythmic structures in lieu of spontaneous feelings.

Narrative: By 1960 the bop movement, so creative during the late 1940s and early '50s, was in decline. Certain of the more innovative and talented jazz players, musicians such as Lennie Tristano, Charles Mingus, John Coltrane, and Miles Davis, made adjustments.

At the same time as Davis was experimenting with modal music, considerable attention was also being given to Ornette Coleman, a saxophonist whose improvisation was neither mode-based nor chord based. Instead of adhering to a single key, mode, or chord progression, Coleman's improvisations were based on shifting tone centers. What made this music so controversial, in part, was its association with black nationalism, the civil rights movement, a broadening interest in left-wing thought, and a philosophic idea basic to the "hippie" culture of the period, that everyone should be free to "do his own thing." Blacks in particular felt a commitment to the revolutionary new ideals. What became known as free jazz spread quickly outside the United States. Most countries in Europe developed their own schools of free improvisation, featuring collective improvisation over the individual solo.

Major proponents: Ornette Coleman, Cecil Taylor, Archie Shepp, Albert Ayler, Bill Dixon, Sam Rivers, Don Cherry, Eric Dolphy, Charlie Haden, Pharoah Sanders, Sun Ra, the Advancement of Creative Musicians (Muhal Richard Abrams, Anthony Braxton), the Art Ensemble of Chicago (Joseph Jarman, Roscoe Mitchell, Malachi Favors, Lester

Appendix III

Bowie), John Coltrane Quartet (1965–1967). Although the avant-garde school of jazz reached its zenith during the 1960s, its legacy continued through the World Saxophone Quartet (David Murray, Oliver Lake, Julius Hemphill, and Hamiet Bluiett), Greg Osby, Henry Threadgill, Steve Coleman and the collective M-BASE (working the experimental intersection between jazz and popular music forms such as rhythm-and-blues and soul), and the Jazz Composers Orchestra, with Carla Bley and Mike Mantler.

EARLY JAZZ/ROCK FUSION (LATE 1960S–MID 1970S)

By the late 1960s, rock had captured the attention of American listeners. It was quickly becoming the most influential musical style in the United States, perhaps even the Western world. Jazz found in this popular music yet another opportunity for the assimilation of new musical idioms, sounds, and concepts. This crossover with rock is most commonly referred to as "jazz-rock fusion" or simply "fusion," a style characterized by a melding of rock rhythms with jazz solo techniques.

Narrative: Over his fifty-year career, Miles Davis helped define jazz for several generations of listeners, and his influence remained very much a part of the jazz scene in the last decades of the twentieth century. Though Davis proved to be a central figure in the development of jazz-rock fusion, he was not the first jazz musician to pick up on the technological breakthroughs of the time, including use of synthesizers and electric keyboards. Forerunners of the jazz-rock approaches include Gary Burton's quartet of the mid-'60s and the 1966 band Free Spirits, both with Larry Coryell on guitar; Paul Bley and Sun Ra on synthesizers; and the Fourth Way, a band with pianist Mike Nock and violinist Michael White. The greatest popular acclaim did not go to these groups, however, but to high-energy rock ensembles such as Blood, Sweat & Tears; Chicago; and Ten Wheel Drive. These three groups were identified by music journalists as "jazz-rock" bands, and they were hugely popular.

It wasn't long before Davis, having taken note of such popular young musicians as guitarist Jimi Hendrix and flamboyant pop-soul bandleader Sly Stone, began to experiment with electric instrumentation. By the time he recorded *In a Silent Way* and *Bitches Brew* (both 1969), he had abandoned the acoustic quintet format in favor of sprawling electronic ensembles. With such albums as *A Tribute to Jack Johnson* and *Live-Evil* (both 1970), Davis established an entirely new persona that appealed to rock fans, many of whom may have been only marginally aware of his status as a bop icon. And with those albums, the fusion movement gained momentum, adding an impetus to the jazz-rock crossover movement that is still being felt.

Major proponents: Miles Davis, Larry Coryell, Frank Zappa, Santana, Jean-Luc Ponty, Jaco Pastorius, Billy Cobham. The list of personnel who worked with Miles Davis during the early fusion period reads like a Who's Who of jazz-rock fusion for the 1970s and '80s, among them Herbie Hancock, Chick Corea, Wayne Shorter, John McLaughlin, Joe Zawinul, and Tony Williams. These musicians later formed or participated in the most influential groups of the 1970s and early 1980s, particularly Chick Corea with Return to Forever, Joe Zawinul and Wayne Shorter with Weather Report, and John McLaughlin with the Mahavishnu Orchestra.

Neo-Bop/Post-Bop (1980–present)

A new generation of young players took bop and other influences and created traditional acoustic jazz. Sidestepping rock/fusion/electric influences, they pursued earlier styles, often with spectacular results. They may not all have be innovators, but they often tried to stretch the parameters.

Narrative: Starting with the rise of Wynton Marsalis in 1979, a whole generation of younger players chose to play an updated variety of bop that was also influenced by the mid-1960s Miles Davis Quintet. Marsalis eventually found his own sound by going back in time and exploring the music of the pre-bop masters. Many of the young players that followed Marsalis ignored fusion and even most of the innovations of the avant-garde by using hard bop as the basis for their music. It was rather unusual to have so many musicians in their twenties playing in a style that was at its prime before their birth, but by the 1990's many of these Young Lions were finally developing their own sounds and starting to build on the earlier innovations.

Major proponents: Wynton Marsalis, Kenny Garrett, Bob Berg, Terrence Blanchard, Brian Lynch, Courtney Pine, Roy Hargrove, Benny Green, Wallace Roney.

Additional Styles

The jazz styles covered in the preceding overview are the most significant in the evolution of jazz during its first century of existence. Other styles, however, both influential and popular, co-existed with the above. These include:

Progressive Big Band

This is music for listening, with denser, more modernistic arrangements than the earlier, more dance-oriented big-band styles, and more room to improvise.

Major proponents: Gil Evans, Stan Kenton, Duke Ellington, Sun Ra, Toshiko Akiyoshi, Cal Massey, Frank Foster, Carla Bley, George Gruntz, David Amram.

Latin-Jazz

This music consists of Latin rhythms melded to jazz melodies, with heavy emphasis on hot beats, horn charts, and choral lyrics in Spanish.

Major proponents: Dizzy Gillespie, Machito, Chano Pozo, Tito Rodriguez, Noro Moralez, Tito Puente, Ray Barretto, Mario Bauza, Eddie Palmieri, Poncho Sanchez, Cal Tjader, Mongo Santamaria.

World Fusion

This music combines a wide variety of world music rhythms and melodies into improvisation-based instrumental music.

Major proponents: John McLaughlina, Oregon, Airto, Flora Purim, Don Cherry, David Amram, Abdullah Ibrahim (Dollar Brand).

Appendix III

Jazz-Pop/Instrumental Pop

During the post-rock eras, several strains of fusion developed that came to be known as jazz-pop or instrumental pop. These styles were quite successful in making jazz more accessible to the average consumer. In some cases the music is quite worthwhile, from a jazz point of view, while in other instances the jazz content is minimal.

Major proponents: Herb Alpert, Chuck Mangione, Kenny G, Boots Randolph, George Benson, Acker Bilk. Two musicians whose styles fall between jazz and pop are saxophonist David Sanborn and guitarist Pat Metheny, both considered among the biggest names in jazz during the 1970s and '80s. Other jazz-pop styles of the era include the Dixieland-influenced trumpeter Al Hirt, the Latin-tinged Herb Alpert, and the funky soul-jazz style of the Ramsey Lewis Trio. In the mid-'70s pop artists like Chuck Mangione, Spyro Gyra, Bob James, and George Benson also became stars. This watered-down form of jazz has been given the inaccurate name of "contemporary jazz." Those who wish to listen to free jazz online are encouraged to visit YouTube and simply type in the name of the performer or performance you wish to hear.

Select Bibliography

Let's begin with online information on jazz. For current news articles and information, including featured stories, photos, jazz radio listening, MP3 downloads, jazz session podcasts, CD reviews, and jazz calendars, I recommend AllAboutJazz.com. This website features daily artist profiles, with links to book reviews, CD/LP track reviews, interviews, videos, and much more. Another outstanding online resource for jazz is allmusic.com. The "jazz" link on the status menu at the top of the page leads to information on jazz styles, top artists, and related topics. Additional links provide essential bibliographic and discographic information. A third website, jazz.com, provides similar information, in addition to a jazz blog. Readers interested in jazz research are encouraged to visit the website of the Institute of Jazz Studies at Rutgers, the State University of New Jersey in Newark. Those who wish to listen to free jazz online are advised to visit YouTube and then to type in the name of the performer or performance they wish to hear.

Those looking for bibliographic information should consult the exhaustive bibliography found on pages 1031 to 1079 in Volume Three of the second edition of the *New Grove Dictionary of Jazz*, edited by Barry Kernfeld (2002). The following books are recommended for jazz students at all levels of interest:

Balliett, Whitney. *American Musicians II: Seventy-one Portraits in Jazz*. New York: Oxford University Press, 1997.
Bogdanov, Vladimir, et al. *All Music Guide to Jazz*. 4th ed. San Francisco: Backbeat Books, 2002.
Carr, Ian, et al. *Jazz: The Rough Guide*. 2nd ed. London: Rough Guides, 2000.
Collier, James Lincoln. *The Making of Jazz*. New York: Delta, 1978.
Crow, Bill. *Jazz Anecdotes*. New York: Oxford University Press, 1990.
Feather, Leonard and Ira Gitler. *The Biographical Encyclopedia of Jazz*. New York: Oxford, 1999.
Giddins, Gary. *Visions of Jazz*. New York: Oxford, 1998.
Gottlieb, Robert. *Reading Jazz*. New York: Vintage Books, 1996.
Gridley, James. *Jazz Styles*. 4th ed. Englewood Cliffs, NJ: Prentice Hall, 1991.
Hasse, John Edward. *Jazz: The First Century*. New York: William Morrow, 2000.
Hentoff, Nat. *The Jazz Life*. New York: Da Capo Press, 1975.
Kernfeld, Barry. *The New Grove Dictionary of Jazz*. 2nd ed. 3 vols. New York: Macmillan, 2002.
Kirchner, Bill. *The Oxford Companion to Jazz*. New York: Oxford, 2000.
Shapiro, Nat and Nat Hentoff. *Hear Me Talkin' To Ya*. New York: Dover, 1966.
Stokes, W. Royal. *The Jazz Scene*. New York: Oxford University Press, 1991.

Select Bibliography

Walser, Robert. *Keeping Time: Readings in Jazz History*. New York: Oxford University Press, 1999.

Ward, Geoffrey C. and Ken Burns. *Jazz: A History of America's Music*. New York: Knopf, 2000.

Topical Index

JAZZ HISTORY/STYLES

Readers interested in the history of jazz, whether in its entirety or with a particular period or style, are encouraged to examine the topics listed below. When read together, the entries listed for each topic provide helpful background on that subject.

1. *The Origins of Jazz*, 41–43, 59–60, 99–100, 116–17, 169–70, 175–76, 215–17, 251–52, 266–67, 290–91, 326, 339–40, 353–54, 377

2. *New Orleans Jazz*, 23–24, 38–39, 41–42, 44–45, 64–65, 86–87, 116–17, 123–25, 130–31, 145–46, 152, 155–56, 206–7, 214–16, 221–22, 251–52, 290–91, 295–96, 312, 339–40, 360, 362–63, 403–4, 407–8, 412–13, 416

3. *The 1920s and early '30s*, 17–18, 36–37, 60–61, 63, 66–68, 79–80, 88–89, 99–100, 103–4, 121–22, 134, 137–38, 141–42, 145–46, 169–70, 171–72, 174–76, 183–85, 188–89, 191, 201–2, 208, 216–17, 256–57, 266–67, 287–88, 297–98, 300–301, 321–22, 339–40, 344–45, 351–54, 367–68, 375–77, 380–81, 400–401, 406–7, 413–14

4. *Chicago-Style Jazz*, 5–6, 16–17, 23–24, 79–80, 83, 86–87, 116–17, 119, 130–31, 135–36, 152, 201, 216–17, 221–22, 268, 291–92, 362–63, 367–68, 403–4, 417–18

5. *Kansas City-Style Jazz/Territory Bands*, 13–14, 30–31, 45–46, 98–99, 160, 171–72, 241–42, 248–49, 271–72, 274–75, 276–78, 325, 365–67, 375–76, 391–92, 409

6. *The Swing Era (1935–45)*, 16–17, 18–20, 33–34, 46–47, 67–70, 85–86, 103–4, 112, 124–29, 132–33, 157–58, 161, 165–66, 174, 183–85, 196–97, 232–33, 239–40, 251–52, 256–57, 260, 266–67, 271–72, 277–78, 297–98, 320–22, 323–25, 327–28, 335–36, 346–47, 351, 354–55, 365–66, 378, 382–83, 389–90, 397–98, 399–401, 402–3, 405–7, 409–10, 413–14, 420–21

7. *Bebop*, 2–3, 11–12, 20, 24, 34, 49–50, 54, 58–59, 65–66, 70–71, 120, 133, 139, 159, 161, 168, 194, 195, 197–98, 202, 220–21, 236, 239, 244, 262, 263–65, 270, 275, 279, 280, 281–82, 309–10, 313, 316, 322, 328, 340–41, 347–48, 350–51, 374, 393–94, 417

8. *Dixieland (Revival)*, 5–6, 12–13, 15–16, 23–24, 34–35, 42, 64, 76–77, 124–25, 135–36, 142, 156–57, 162–63, 189, 191, 201, 206–7, 214–15, 221–22, 233, 252, 291–92, 321, 360, 362–63, 367–68, 374, 390, 403–4, 407, 413, 416, 418

9. *Cool Jazz/West Coast Jazz*, 28, 111, 142–43, 151, 154–55, 168, 170, 177–78, 204–5, 258–59, 262, 278, 284, 308, 365, 374–75, 411

10. *Third Stream*, 143, 204–5, 307–8, 364–65

11. *Early Hard Bop Stylists*, 11–12, 22, 24–25, 55–56, 70, 115, 120, 129, 131–32, 138–39, 159, 161–62, 200, 222–23, 235, 246, 275, 279, 281–82, 285–86, 293, 299–300, 302, 326, 329–30, 350–51, 358, 386, 395, 396

12. *Free Jazz/Avant-Garde Jazz*, 6–7, 26–27, 32, 52, 56–57, 78–79, 89–90, 96–97, 153–54, 159, 164–65, 167, 180–82, 198–99, 205–6, 212–13, 224, 226–28, 237–38, 254, 261–62, 272, 289, 292–93, 298–99, 304, 310–11, 319, 322–23, 329, 355–57, 361, 363–64, 371–73, 383–84, 418

13. *AACM (Association for the Advancement of Creative Musicians)*, 52, 180–81, 227–28, 272–73, 304–6

14. *M-BASE*, 305–6, 391

15. *Decline of Jazz (late 1950s-early '70s)*, 26–27, 65–66, 71, 93, 106–7, 118, 167, 219, 235, 255, 293, 318, 322, 378–79

447

Topical Index

16. *Jazz-Rock Fusion*, 4–5, 47–48, 93, 101, 106–7, 118–19, 168, 189–90, 219–20, 243, 245–46, 253, 258, 275–76, 315–16, 318–19, 333, 369, 387–88, 410–11, 415

17. *Crossover Artists*, 57–58, 81–82, 84, 93, 96, 101, 110, 114–15, 118, 122–23, 141–42, 149–50, 170–71, 179–80, 192, 193, 210–11, 243, 245–46, 250–51, 252, 295, 296, 315–16, 319–20, 335, 342–43, 348–49, 351–52, 360, 370–71, 396, 399–400

18. *Latin Jazz/Afro-Cuban Jazz*, 8, 52–53, 190, 200, 229–230, 262, 286–87, 359, 361–62, 383–84

19. *Brazilian Jazz/Bossa Nova*, 27–28, 38, 102–3, 123, 149–50, 249–50, 253, 343

JAZZ-RELATED TOPICS

Drug/Alcohol Abuse, 5, 14–15, 49–50, 59, 61, 65, 80, 83, 99, 107, 108, 111, 112, 120, 148, 158–59, 163–64, 176, 179, 207, 208, 217, 223, 225, 228–29, 235, 245, 254–55, 264, 266, 267, 268, 278, 279, 280–81, 284–85, 294, 301, 303, 309, 310, 314, 328, 349, 351, 355, 373, 386, 388, 401, 411–12, 416, 421

Jazz Journalism, 20, 23–24, 64–65, 91–92, 125–26, 187–88, 233–34, 365, 368, 416

Jazz Recording, 43, 116–17, 121–22, 124, 128–29, 162–63, 169, 206–7, 209, 221, 222, 234, 381–82, 397, 403, 416

Racism in America, 11, 34, 44, 54, 55, 59–60, 87–88, 88, 119, 121, 124, 156–57, 165, 166, 169, 171–72, 179, 187, 210–11, 278, 313, 326, 339, 340, 345, 346, 362–63, 379–80, 402–3

Religion and Jazz, 3, 5, 55, 56, 81, 87, 127, 129, 163, 190, 200, 213, 214, 226–27, 234, 298–99, 308–9, 311, 352, 353–54, 380

Women in Jazz (items in this section are limited to featured artists or to entries that contain significant information on the topic), 1–2, 9–10, 22, 32–33, 38–39, 47, 57–58, 63, 74, 90–91, 102–3, 103, 109, 112–14, 121–22, 125–26, 132–34, 136–37, 140–41, 149–50, 169–71, 178–80, 198–99, 210–11, 240–42, 253, 303, 327–28, 333, 342–43, 348–49, 351–54, 364, 370–71, 374–75, 389–91, 403, 419

THE JAZZ SCENE IN SELECT U.S. CITIES

The following list of cities or regions represents only a sampling of the rich jazz expression traditionally experienced across America. Cities such as New Orleans, Chicago, and Kansas City had such a distinctive and formative role in the development of jazz that they are listed in the section on jazz history and jazz styles. Other cities—particularly New York and Los Angeles—are mentioned too frequently in the text to be cited here.

Jazz in Detroit, 3, 60–61, 88–89, 132, 180, 184, 194, 220, 246, 270, 282–83, 301, 326, 354, 396

Jazz in Philadelphia, 12, 44, 54, 101, 110, 111, 115–16, 138, 165, 167, 191, 206, 213, 223, 229, 242, 259, 301, 344, 350, 356, 369, 395, 398

Jazz in Pittsburgh, 2, 21, 33, 110, 180, 193, 208, 213–14, 329, 385, 417

Jazz in the San Francisco Bay Area, 1, 23, 56, 81, 82, 100, 109, 132, 174, 221, 229–30, 242, 253, 307–8, 318, 393, 404, 407–8, 410, 412, 413, 416, 418

Jazz in Washington, DC, 18, 21, 22, 60, 137, 140, 175, 191, 218, 220, 238, 268, 292, 400–1

JAZZ OUTSIDE THE UNITED STATES

Jazz in Canada/Canadian Artists, 50–51, 154–55, 161–62, 264–65, 269, 313, 363–64, 370–71

Jazz in Europe/European Artists, 1, 3, 4–5, 9–10, 14–15, 19–20, 21, 23, 25–26, 28–29, 31–32, 32, 33, 34, 38, 40–41, 45, 47–48, 49, 53, 54, 59–60, 66, 70, 72–73, 76–77, 84, 90–91, 96, 99, 104, 114, 117, 124–25, 136–37, 139, 143, 147, 149, 150, 151, 153, 155–56, 159, 178–79, 180, 181, 181–82, 189, 191, 194, 196, 199, 200, 203–4, 205, 207, 213, 219–20, 221–22, 223–24, 226, 229, 233–34, 238, 241, 250, 257, 258, 262–63, 272, 273–74, 279, 288–89, 293, 298, 301, 304, 307–8, 311, 313, 314, 315–16, 317, 318–20, 321–22, 331, 336, 338, 341–42, 348–49, 350, 356–57, 362, 370, 373, 374, 374–75, 376, 384, 386, 387, 396, 404, 405, 408–9, 412

Jazz in Japan/Japanese Artists, 6, 33, 114, 153–54, 162, 203, 229, 257, 285, 314, 331, 332–33, 370, 386

448

Index of Names

The following index includes all jazz-related individuals (and other prominent personalities) mentioned in the text. The index does not include references to persons listed in the daily calendar of births and deaths or in the appendix.

Abadie, Claude, 221
Abrams, Muhal Richard, 52, 92, 181, 227, 272, 299, 303–4
Adams, Pepper, 325–26, 396
Adderley, Cannonball, xxiv, 22, 53, 57, 101, 219–20, 299–300, 388–89, 395
Adderley, Nat, 23, 251, 396
Akiyoshi, Toshiko, 333
Albany, Joe, 23
Alexander, Eric, 116
Alexander, Monty, 303
Ali, Rashied, 33, 212–13
Allen, Carl, 335
Allen, Geri, 305
Allen, Harry, 41, 297, 330–31
Allen, Henry "Red," 145–46, 157, 233, 336
Allen, Woody, 78, 209
Allison, Mose, 97
Allyson, Karrin, 241–42
Altman, Robert, 62, 312
Altschul, Barry, 6–7, 154, 181, 190, 319
Ammons, Albert, 120, 160, 288
Ammons, Gene, 50, 58, 110, 120–21, 126, 220
Anderson, Andy, 15
Anderson, Fred, 227
Anderson, Roy, 227
Ansermet, Ernest, 233
Anthony, Ray, 151
Arlen, Harold, 77, 133, 327, 333
Armstrong, Lil (Hardin), 38–39, 123, 126, 152
Armstrong, Louis, xxv, xxvi, 2, 12, 19, 26, 30–31, 34–35, 38–39, 44, 57, 65, 66, 70–71, 72, 76, 78, 83, 90, 92, 95, 119, 121, 123–24, 127, 129, 130, 134, 142, 145–46, 152, 154, 157, 158, 163, 168–69, 178, 189, 191, 194, 202, 207, 208, 210, 215–16, 217, 218, 221, 228, 233, 251–52, 257, 263, 280, 286, 291, 312, 321, 332, 336, 337, 340, 343, 345, 353, 362, 366, 368, 376, 377, 378–79, 402, 404, 406, 407, 408, 411, 412–13, 416, 417–18
Asmussen, Svend, 9, 47, 315
Astaire, Fred, 40
Atkins, Chet, 187
Auld, Georgie, 161–62, 355
Ayers, Roy, 294–95
Ayler, Albert, 27, 153, 167, 213, 226–27, 273, 356

Bach, J. S., 90, 142, 204
Bailey, Buster, 85, 131, 232–33, 378, 420
Bailey, Mildred, 40, 103–4, 251, 327, 352, 377, 379
Bailey, Pearl, 22, 30, 218, 251, 414
Baker, Chet, 28, 111, 115, 140, 159, 178, 204, 269, 326, 341, 411–12, 415
Baker, Ginger, 4
Baker, Harold "Shorty," 172, 378
Baker, Kenny, 349
Baldwin, James, 167
Balliet, Whitney, 10
Bang, Billy, 47
Barbarin, Paul, 145–46
Barber, Chris, 125, 221
Barbieri, Gato, 250, 342, 373, 383–84
Barbour, Dave, 171
Barefield, Eddie, 378
Barker, Danny, 336
Barnes, Emile, 125
Barnes, George, 10
Barnet, Charlie, 14, 54, 161, 210, 316, 346–47, 405
Baron, Joey, 173
Barron, Kenny, 101, 287, 331
Bartok, Bela, 190, 204
Bartz, Gary, 237
Basie, Count, 12, 13, 15, 30–31, 40, 43, 45, 50, 54, 59, 63, 70–71, 85, 94, 105, 112, 113, 151, 158, 160, 161, 163, 171, 185, 188, 194, 198, 218, 225, 228, 239, 244, 248–49, 251, 260, 264, 271–72, 274–75, 278, 302, 324–25, 347, 365–66, 367, 391–92, 395, 400, 403

Index of Names

Basso, Guido, 51
Bates, Django, 319–20
Bauer, Billy, 90
Bauzá, Mario, 8, 52–53, 361
Bayes, Nora, 352
Bechet, Sidney, 39, 43, 66, 130–31, 145–46, 155–56, 156, 188, 189, 232, 237, 239, 363, 400, 403, 413, 416
Beck, Gordon, 41, 48
Beiderbecke, Bix, 17, 18, 34–35, 40, 60–61, 67, 79–80, 83, 86, 88–89, 100, 142, 168, 199, 217, 291, 301, 345, 354, 368, 377, 383, 404, 406
Belafonte, Harry, 195, 343
Bell, Graeme, 221
Bellson, Louie, 217–18, 269, 344
Beneke, Tex, 196–97
Bennett, Tony, 35, 250–51, 334
Bennink, Han, 182, 356
Benoit, David, 303
Benson, George, 81, 93–94, 110, 115, 150, 186, 192, 246–47, 302, 403
Berendt, Joachim-Ernst, 233–34
Berg, Billy, 326
Berg, Bob, 286
Berger, Karl, 295
Berigan, Bunny, 161, 327, 354–55, 383
Berlin, Irving, 77, 133, 352
Berman, Sonny, 347
Bernstein, Artie, 39–40
Bernstein, Leonard, 78, 337
Berry, Chu, 33, 257, 267, 297–98, 376, 394, 414
Berry, Chuck, 415
Berton, Vic, 216–17
Bertrand, Jimmy, 127
Bethune, Mary McLeod, 149
Bey, Sadiq, 361
Bickert, Ed, 51
Bigard, Barney, 18, 71–72, 105, 131
Blackman, Cindy, 9, 173
Blake, Eubie, 24, 77, 208
Blake, John, 48, 243
Blake, Ran, 32, 364, 365
Blakey, Art, 22, 54, 55, 58, 96, 109, 110, 120, 148, 159, 194, 206, 220, 223, 239, 241, 251, 275–76, 279, 281, 286, 293, 305, 329–30, 337, 344, 351, 357–58, 363, 369, 386, 396, 410
Blanchard, Terence, 358
Blanton, Jimmy, xxvi, 99, 199, 202, 316, 323–34, 344, 387, 401
Blesh, Rudi, 23–24, 64
Bley, Carla, 97, 115, 238, 315, 323, 364, 384
Bley, Paul, 7, 97, 153–54, 159, 213, 254, 311, 323, 363–64, 388
Bloom, Jane Ira, 237
Bluiett, Hamiet, 27, 33, 361
Blythe, Arthur, 56
Bobo, Willie, 230
Bolden, Buddy, 152, 290–91, 416
Bollenback, Paul, 116
Bonfa, Luiz, 27
Booker, James, 296
Bose, Stirling, 60–61
Bostic, Earl, 22, 110
Boswell, Connee, 40, 133, 142, 207, 327, 352, 354, 389–90
Bothwell, Johnny, 347
Boulanger, Nadia, 396
Bowie, David, 246
Bowie, Lester, 3, 227, 271, 304
Brackeen, JoAnne, 240–41
Braddy, Pauline, 9, 126
Braden, Don, 419
Bradford, Bobby, 56
Bradford, Perry, 169
Bradley, Will, 197, 405
Braff, Ruby, 49, 251, 297, 321, 331
Brando, Marlon, 53
Brasil, Juao Assis, 373
Braud, Wellman, 43, 105
Braxton, Anthony, 7, 32, 52, 180–81, 190, 227–28, 272, 319, 342
Brecker, Michael, 101–102, 286
Brecker, Randy, 101, 286
Breuker, Willem, 182, 356–57
Briggs, Peter, 123
Broadbent, Alan, 265, 370
Brookmeyer, Bob, 111, 151, 259, 374
Brown, Bill, 420
Brown, Clifford, 11, 55, 59, 84, 139, 222–23, 263, 279, 281–82, 293, 309, 329, 350–51, 396
Brown, James, 115, 295, 318
Brown, Lawrence, 344
Brown, Leroy, 193
Brown, Les, 16, 269
Brown, Marion, 292–93
Brown, Marshall, 289, 338
Brown Jr., Oscar, 11
Brown, Ray, 98, 109, 136, 139, 143, 236, 265, 269, 316, 324
Brown, Samuel, 372
Brown, Steve, 89
Brubeck, Dave, xxiv, 111, 193, 213, 229, 231, 235, 307–8, 392–93
Bruce, Jack, 4

Index of Names

Brunis, Georg, 6, 41–42, 48, 86–87, 162, 404
Bruno, Jimmy, 101, 116
Bryant, Ray, 369
Bryant, Willie, 336
Buckner, Milt, 115, 395
Bunnett, Jane, 33, 237
Burns, Leslie, 243
Burns, Ken, xxiii
Burns, Ralph, 37, 209–10, 251
Burnside, Vi, 125–26
Burrell, Kenny, 173, 230, 246–47, 293, 302
Bushkin, Joe, 327
Burton, Gary, 107, 229, 261, 295, 339, 410, 415, 419
Butterfield, Billy, 15–16, 19, 35, 135, 185, 390
Butterfield, Paul, 246
Byard, Jaki, 311
Byas, Don, 109, 126, 172, 195, 236, 316, 336, 378
Byers, Billy, 344
Byrd, Charlie, 28, 38, 102, 150, 303
Byrd, Donald, 132, 230, 285, 361–62, 395–96
Byron, Don, 338, 361–62

Cage, John, 182, 299
Calandrelli, Jorge, 339
Caldwell, Happy, 345
Calloway, Blanche, 126, 336
Calloway, Cab, 8, 18, 191, 202–3, 210, 263, 267, 298, 336, 340, 378, 394, 410, 413–14
Calhoun, Eddie, 214
Campbell, Eddie, 206
Candido, 8
Candoli, Conte, 177
Candoli, Pete, 209, 348
Capone, Al, 83, 86, 135
Carey, Mutt, 152
Carmichael, Hoagy, 18, 103, 376–77
Carney, Harry, 71, 105–6, 239, 291, 326
Carr, Ian, 61, 72–73
Carrington, Terri Lyne, 9
Carson, Johnny, 82
Carter, Benny, 18, 19, 24, 27, 33, 40, 49, 92, 177, 240, 256–57, 263, 267, 269, 284, 298, 299, 334, 336, 344, 346, 378, 419, 420–21
Carter, Betty, 109, 113, 173, 390, 419
Carter, James, 3–4
Carter, Regina, 47
Carter, Ron, 143–44, 243, 276, 318, 337, 374, 419
Caruso, Enrico, 207
Carver, George Washington, 171
Catlett, Sid, 18–19, 257, 336
Celestin, Oscar, 413
Challis, Bill, 89

Chaloff, Margaret, 95, 321, 373
Chaloff, Serge, 95, 147–48, 209, 268, 311, 321, 349, 373
Chambers, Dennis, 173
Chambers, Paul, 22, 228, 279, 387, 388–89
Charlap, Bill, 173, 333–34
Charlap, "Moose," 334
Charles, Ray, 62, 84, 110, 186, 245, 257, 349, 410
Charles, Teddy, 229
Cheatham, Doc, 190–91, 312
Cherry, Don, 153, 167, 213, 224, 226, 238, 241, 250, 254, 273, 322, 341–42, 356, 363, 372–73, 384
Childs, Billy, 343
Christian, Charlie, 10, 40, 63, 75, 93, 94, 161, 199, 244–45, 246, 260, 303, 394, 403
Christy, June, 74, 170, 374–75
Clapton, Eric, 4, 115, 415
Clark, Sonny, 54, 234–35
Clarke, Kenny, 2–3, 11, 22, 113–14, 139, 143, 154, 170, 244, 257, 310, 313, 317, 394
Clarke, Stanley, 253
Clarke, Terry, 173
Clay, James, 62
Clayton, Buck, 248–49, 365–66, 403
Cleveland, Jimmy, 185
Clooney, Rosemary, 297, 303, 331
Cobb, Arnett, 61, 356
Cobb, Jimmy, 22–23, 229, 388–89
Cobham, Billy, 101, 415
Coe, Tony, 319
Cohn, Al, 147–48, 209, 251, 268, 269, 330, 349–50, 418
Cole, Cozy, 17, 94, 325, 335–36, 414
Cole, Natalie, 62, 419
Cole, Nat "King," 87–88, 140, 251, 263, 264, 370
Cole, Richie, 303
Coleman, George, 173
Coleman, Ornette, 56, 78–79, 90, 165, 167, 181, 199, 226, 235, 241, 254, 261–62, 273, 292–93, 311, 312, 363, 371, 372–73, 418
Coleman, Steve, 151, 305–6, 391
Colliani, John, 331
Collier, James Lincoln, 116, 120, 280, 393
Collins, Rudy, 172
Coltrane, Alice, 206
Coltrane, John, 22, 26–27, 73, 79, 95, 101, 110, 118, 144, 146, 156, 159, 167, 194, 198–99, 202, 206, 212–13, 222, 226, 228, 235, 237, 242, 246–47, 279, 285, 287, 292–93, 293, 300, 308–9, 312, 322, 329, 375, 383, 388–89, 398, 418
Colyer, Ken, 124–25, 221

Index of Names

Condon, Eddie, 5–6, 17, 19, 35, 41, 42, 64, 83, 119, 130, 135, 142, 156–57, 162–63, 191, 292, 327, 331, 345, 362, 368, 404
Connick Jr., Harry, 295–96, 358
Conniff, Ray, 16
Connor, Chris, 170
Cook, Doc, 124, 131
Cook, Junior, 286
Cook, Will Marion, 137–38, 156
Cooper, Bob, 375
Corea, Chick, 7, 114–15, 149, 181, 189–90, 253, 318–19, 410–11
Coryell, Larry, 106–7, 146, 303
Cosby, Bill, 81
Counce, Curtis, 55
Cowell, Stanley, 293
Cox, Ida, 40, 62–63, 121, 353
Crawford, Hank, 62
Crawford, Ray, 214
Creath, Charlie, 44
Crosby, Bing, 40, 68, 92, 136, 141–42, 170, 187, 202, 251, 252, 301, 390, 399
Crosby, Bob, 15, 61, 135, 201, 260, 390, 407
Crosby, Israel, 214, 324
Crotty, Ron, 308
Crouch, Stanley, 56, 386
Crow, Bill, 91, 151
Cuber, Ronnie, 115
Cugat, Xavier, 53
Curson, Ted, 146
Curtis, King, 62
Cyrille, Andrew, 32

Dameron, Tadd, 50, 58–59, 110, 159, 161, 220, 229, 263, 310
Dance, Helen Oakley, 47, 125, 380
Daniels, Eddie, 338–39, 361
Dankworth, John, 31, 348–49
Darin, Bobby, 202
Davern, Kenny, 62
Davis, Anthony, 227
Davis, Art, 292
Davis, Eddie "Lockjaw," 21, 70–71, 113, 172, 389, 392
Davis, Ernestine "Tiny," 126
Davis, Miles, xxiv, 3, 5, 9, 11, 22, 25, 50, 59, 73, 74, 95, 98, 105, 106, 107, 111, 116, 118, 132, 139, 140–41, 144, 146, 149, 153, 154–55, 159, 168–69, 190, 192, 194, 196, 204, 213–14, 219–20, 220–21, 222, 228–29, 235, 239, 253, 258, 259, 261, 263–64, 266, 275–76, 279, 281–82, 286, 286–87, 293, 299–300, 304, 309, 311, 318–19, 322, 332, 350–51, 357, 365, 386, 388, 388–89, 396, 410, 411, 415
Davison, Wild Bill, 5–6, 42, 78, 93, 115, 189, 233, 395
Daye, Irene, 17
Dearie, Blossom, 136–37, 140
Debussy, Claude, 28
DeFrancesco, Joey, 5, 115–16, 302
DeFrancesco, "Papa" John, 116
DeFranco, Buddy, 53–54, 195, 262, 279, 322, 338, 346, 348, 392
DeJohnette, Jack, 101, 149, 153–54, 257–58, 262, 318
Delaunay, Charles, 19–20, 234
DeLucia, Paco, 5
De Moraes, Vinicius, 28
Dennerlein, Barbara, 115
De Paris, Sidney, 12
De Paris, Wilbur, 12–13, 191, 233
Desmond, Paul, 284, 308, 393, 409
Dickenson, Vic, 35
Dickerson, Carroll, 130
Dietrich, Marlene, 53
Di Meola, Al, 5, 106, 115, 186, 261, 333
Dinter, Ulli, 147
Dixon, Bill, 167, 213, 311, 322–23, 372
Dodds, Baby, 16, 64, 123, 152, 412–13
Dodds, Johnny, 38, 123, 130, 152, 412
Doggett, Bill, 302
Dolphy, Eric, 79, 144, 182, 198–99
Domino, Fats, 180, 245
Domnérus, Arne, 408–9
Donegan, Lonnie, 125
Dorham, Kenny, 22, 95, 132, 264, 281–82, 351
Dorsey, Jimmy, 37, 67–68, 69, 89, 94, 197, 360, 377, 382–83
Dorsey, Tommy, 17, 40, 54, 67–68, 69, 73–74, 84, 85, 89, 119, 148, 183, 197, 218, 231, 260, 268, 269, 292, 344, 354–55, 360, 377, 382–83, 399, 421
Douglas, Tommy, 325
Drew, Kenny, 21, 54, 279–80
Drew Jr., Kenny, 280
D'Rivera, Paquito, xxiii, 287, 359, 369
Dudziak, Urszula, 192, 224
Duhé, Lawrence, 152
Duke, George, 415
Dunham, Sonny, 184, 268
Dunn, Johnny, 169–70
Durham, Eddie, 45, 244
Dutrey, Honoré, 152
Dylan, Bob, 107, 260, 403

Index of Names

Earland, Charles, 302
Early, Gerald, 326
Eastwood, Clint, 177–78
Echols, Charlie, 378
Eckstine, Billy, 40, 49, 58–59, 65, 82, 120, 161, 170, 190, 194, 220–21, 263, 282, 283, 310, 329, 371, 417
Edison, Harry "Sweets," 71, 366, 391
Edwards, Daddy, 206
Edwards, Eddie, 117
Edwards, Teddy, 173
Egan, Mark, 261
Ehrlich, Marty, 27
Eldridge, Roy, 2, 12, 17, 33–34, 40, 63, 71, 94, 95, 97, 98, 166, 176, 263, 267, 298, 306, 309, 316, 325, 340, 346, 394, 410
Ellington, Duke, 13, 14, 15, 17–18, 25–26, 27, 37, 38, 43, 44, 46, 52, 66–67, 71, 71–72, 77, 78, 91, 98, 98–99, 105–6, 129, 133, 137–38, 142–43, 154, 157, 158, 175–76, 188, 195, 198, 210, 218, 225, 235, 239–40, 246–47, 256, 267, 271, 291, 297, 298, 307, 317, 321, 323–24, 330, 336, 338, 344, 346, 347, 349, 352, 361, 367, 378–79, 381, 382, 384–85, 397–98, 400–401, 402, 405, 406, 414
Ellington, Mercer, 25, 114, 282, 344, 349
Ellis, Don, 153
Ellis, Herb, 136, 184, 265, 303
Ellison, Ralph, 277
Elman, Ziggy, 40
Ennis, Skinnay, 154, 259
Ericson, Rolf, 408
Erskine, Peter, 173
Ertegun, Ahmet, 139
Ertegun, Nesuhi, 139
Ervin, Booker, 21, 132
Erwin, Pee Wee, 405
Eubanks, Kevin, 369–70
Eubanks, Robin, 305, 369
Europe, James Reese, 59–60
Evans, Bill, xxiv, 22, 74, 90, 96–97, 107–8, 146–47, 150, 153, 189, 195–96, 229, 235, 241, 251, 265–66, 273, 312, 313, 334, 356, 363, 370, 388, 398, 410
Evans, Gil, 9, 11, 96, 103, 111, 154–55, 204, 246, 247, 259, 365
Evans, Herschel, xxvi, 248–49, 267, 271, 366, 391

Faddis, Jon, 115, 335
Fahn, Mike, 411
Farlow, Tal, 104, 231, 282, 326, 344
Farmer, Art, 97, 144, 241, 285, 286, 382, 419
Farrell, Joe, 411
Favors, Malachi, 272–73, 298, 304
Fazola, Irving, 135–36, 215
Feather, Leonard, 78, 148, 150, 170, 218, 231, 241, 262, 263, 378
Feldman, Mark, 47
Feldman, Victor, 411
Fenton, Nick, 394
Ferguson, Maynard, 51, 219, 346
Fielding, Jerry, 178
Finegan, Bill, 382
Fitzgerald, Ella, 12, 15, 31, 47, 57, 71, 74, 98, 132–33, 139, 170, 186, 218, 242, 257, 262, 269, 283, 327, 343, 349, 352, 357, 370–71, 389, 409
Flack, Roberta, 62, 192
Flanagan, Tommy, 173, 283, 378, 420
Fleming, King, 304
Fontana, Carl, 231–32
Ford, Mary, 187
Ford, Ricky, 335
Forrest, Helen, 86, 161, 171
Forrest, Jimmy, 302
Fosse, Bob, 209
Foster, Frank, 392
Foster, Pops, 145
Fountain, Pete, 214–15
Fournier, Vernell, 214, 258
Francis, Panama, 409–10
Franklin, Aretha, 62, 115, 179, 192, 206, 403
Freed, Alan, 180
Freeman, Bud, xxiv, 10, 83, 118–19, 135, 156, 162, 201, 268, 292, 321, 322, 368, 383, 404
Freeman, Chico, 369
Friedwald, Will, 327, 418
Friesen, David, 146–47
Frisell, Bill, 97, 415, 418–19
Frishberg, Dave, 137, 370
Fuller, Curtis, 235, 279
Fuller, Gil, 8
Fulson, Lowell, 110

G, Kenny, 237
Gabler, Milt, 128, 162–63
Gadd, Steve, 114–15
Gaillard, Slim, 306, 349
Galper, Hal, 311
Galway, James, 349
Garbarek, Jan, 9, 72–73, 237, 250
Gardner, Jeff, 146
Garland, Red, 62, 101, 206, 228, 419
Garner, Erroll, 161, 192–93, 213, 235, 262, 264, 296, 306
Garrett, Kenny, 116, 151, 192, 315, 396

Index of Names

Garrison, Jimmy, 206, 323, 398
Gaslini, Giorgio, 341–42
Gaye, Marvin, 110
Geller, Herb, 177
Gershwin, George, xxiii, 28, 66, 77, 90, 100, 133, 258, 307, 327, 370, 413
Getz, Stan, xxiii, 21, 22, 28, 37–38, 74, 97, 102, 120, 139, 147, 150, 190, 209–10, 236, 241, 247, 251, 253, 268, 269–70, 286, 317, 330, 349, 357, 359, 411, 418
Gibbs, Mike, 320, 369
Gibbs, Terry, 54, 151, 153, 229
Gibson, Dick, 232
Giddins, Gary, 4, 91–92, 123, 161, 168, 209, 225, 227
Gieseking, Walter, 332
Gilberto, Astrud, xxiii, 102–3, 303
Gilberto, Joao, 28, 38, 102
Gillespie, Dizzy, xxvi, 2, 8, 11, 15, 19, 22, 24–25, 28, 31, 33–34, 35, 40, 50, 53, 58–59, 65, 77, 78, 84, 104, 111, 114–15, 120, 129, 133, 139, 143, 161, 170, 172, 173, 185, 188, 190, 192, 194, 200, 202, 220–21, 222–23, 225, 230, 236, 239, 244, 246, 257, 263–64, 280, 281–82, 286–87, 306–7, 309–10, 313, 315, 316–17, 322, 329, 340–41, 347, 350–51, 357, 359, 373, 374, 378, 382, 384, 389, 394, 396, 411, 414, 417, 418, 419
Ginsberg, Allen, 53
Gismonti, Egberto, 250
Gitler, Ira, 419
Giuffre, Jimmy, 147, 153, 364, 418
Gladstone, Billy, 231
Glaser, Joe, 30, 194, 252, 366
Gleason, Jackie, 16, 35
Gleason, Ralph J., 113
Glenn, Roger, 230
Glenn, Tyree, 378–79
Goffin, Robert, 233
Goldings, Larry, 115
Goldkette, Jean, 60–61, 67, 184, 267, 291, 301, 321, 345, 383
Golson, Benny, 22, 80, 88–89, 101, 206, 223, 285
Gomez, Eddie, 115, 303, 314
Gonella, Nat, 76–77
Gonsalves, Paul, 22, 224–25, 297, 330
Gonzales, Babs, 59
Gonzalez, Jerry, 386
Goodman, Benny, 10, 15, 16, 17, 18, 19, 23, 34–35, 37, 40, 41, 47, 48–49, 50, 51, 54, 61, 68, 69, 71, 77, 83, 85, 91, 92, 94, 104, 112, 119, 122, 127, 131, 133, 135, 143, 148, 158, 161, 162, 165–66, 171, 173, 173–74, 180, 184, 191, 201, 202, 218, 231, 233, 244, 246, 259, 260, 268, 269, 271, 283, 297, 306–7, 310, 322, 326, 334, 336, 338–39, 340, 344, 349–50, 355, 356, 360, 366, 368, 377, 379–80, 382, 392, 397, 399, 403, 405, 407, 411
Goodman, Jerry, 47–48, 315
Goodrick, Mike, 261, 413
Gordon, Dexter, 1, 21, 26, 50, 58, 65–66, 78, 120, 153, 159, 204, 220, 235, 241, 267, 269, 279, 284, 304
Gottlieb, Danny, 173, 231, 261
Goulet, Robert, 303
Grable, Betty, 86
Graham, Billy, 352
Granz, Norman, 14, 15, 54, 97–98, 133, 136, 264–65, 283, 332, 366
Grappelli, Stéphane, 10, 20, 26, 28–29, 47–48, 301, 315, 344
Gray, Glen, 35, 184–85
Gray, Jerry, 197
Gray, Wardell, 49–50, 65, 322, 350
Green, Benny, 108–9, 389, 419
Green, Big Charlie, 188, 406
Green, Freddie, 105, 325
Green, Grant, 235, 302
Green, Johnny, 327
Green, Urbie, 17, 185, 231–32
Green, Stanley, 327
Greene, Burton, 323
Greer, Sonny, 43, 137, 175, 218, 323, 336, 344, 400–401
Gridley, James, xxv
Griffin, Johnny, 21, 53, 70, 146, 173, 235, 335
Grimes, Henry, 355–56
Grimes, Tiny, 306, 336
Grofé, Ferde, 266–67
Grosz, Marty, 41
Gruntz, George, 203–4, 320
Guaraldi, Vince, 230
Guarnieri, Johnny, 94–95, 306
Gullin, Lars, 9, 408
Guy, Joe, 394

Hackett, Bobby, 1, 10, 16, 34–35, 48, 61, 156, 162, 185, 251, 327–28
Haden, Charlie, 97, 101, 241, 254–55, 262, 287, 324, 327–28, 363, 372, 384
Haggart, Bob, 16, 135
Haig, Al, 236–37
Hajdu, David, 385
Hall, Adelaide, 332
Hall, Edmond, 6, 156–57, 321
Hall, Jim, 75, 115, 314, 382, 415

Index of Names

Hamilton, Chico, 107, 144, 199, 251
Hamilton, Jeff, 173, 331
Hamilton, Jimmy, 361
Hamilton, Scott, 296–97, 321, 330–31
Hammond, John, 63, 93, 112, 157, 160, 174, 244, 260, 271–72, 277, 278, 288, 325, 365–66, 379, 402–3
Hampel, Gunter, 32, 293, 295
Hampton, Lionel, 40, 63, 65, 75, 84, 127–28, 194, 217, 229, 232, 249, 260, 282, 294–95, 310, 336, 339, 351, 378, 379, 392, 402
Hampton, Slide, 287
Hancock, Herbie, 81, 117–18, 132, 144, 189, 213, 241, 276, 314, 318–19, 337, 389, 396, 410
Handy, George, 347
Handy, John, 146
Handy, W. C., 43, 354
Hanna, Jake, 232
Hanna, Roland, 283
Hardwick, Otto, 43, 106, 174–75, 400
Hargrove, Roy, 312, 334–35, 419
Harper, Billy, 146
Harrell, Tom, 151, 286, 373
Harris, Barry, 142
Harris, Bill, 209, 349, 371
Harris, Eddie, 62, 257
Harris, Gene, 109
Harris, Ratzo, 374
Harrison, Donald, 358
Harper, Billy, 146
Harrell, Tom, 286
Hart, Antonio, 335
Hasselgard, Stan, 321–22, 408
Hawes, Hampton, 254
Hawkins, Coleman, 26, 33, 40, 43, 63, 65, 72, 95, 97, 103, 110, 119, 126, 134, 161, 163, 169–70, 188, 208, 225, 233, 248, 257, 266–67, 278, 279, 283, 286, 293, 297–98, 310, 319, 325, 326, 330, 344, 346, 356, 375–76, 384, 406
Haymes, Dick, 382
Haymes, Joe, 61, 383
Haynes, Graham, 305
Haynes, Roy, 190, 206, 386, 402
Hayton, Lennie, 211
Hazelton, David, 32
Heath, Albert "Tootie," 138, 356
Heath, Jimmy, 138–39, 386
Heath, Percy, 138–39
Heath, Ted, 87
Hefti, Neal, 400
Heidt, Horace, 260, 360
Heifetz, Jascha, 230
Hemphill, Julius, 3, 26–27, 237
Henderson, Fletcher, 18, 19, 33, 39, 46, 63, 65, 66, 89, 94, 134, 142, 165, 170, 174, 188–89, 208, 233, 248, 256, 260, 267, 278, 297–98, 340, 352, 376, 382, 403, 406–7, 420
Henderson, Horace, 397
Henderson, Joe, 109, 131–32, 146, 241, 282, 285–86, 302, 319, 335, 361, 386, 396
Henderson, Scott, 333
Hendricks, Jon, 81, 197–98, 332
Hendrix, Jimi, 48, 246, 250, 303, 318, 369, 386, 415
Hentoff, Nat, 146, 187–88, 372
Herman, Woody, 37, 74, 95, 98, 104, 120, 136, 143, 147, 150, 157–58, 185, 204, 209, 231, 259, 268, 269, 317, 347, 349–50, 371, 418
Heywood, Eddie, 191, 344, 392
Higginbotham, J. C., 145
Higgins, Billy, 241, 254, 363, 372
Hill, Chippie, 121
Hill, Teddy, 2, 33, 202, 298, 393–94
Hindenmith, Paul, 49, 190
Hines, Earl, 49, 49–50, 58, 78, 89, 94, 110, 113, 131, 178–79, 208, 220, 263, 283, 313, 316, 336, 368, 397, 417–18
Hino, Terumasa, 314, 333
Hinton, Milt, 202–3, 251, 324, 336, 368, 378, 414
Hirt, Al, 337, 360–61
Hite, Les, 127, 392
Hodes, Art, 42, 146, 367–68
Hodges, Johnny, 46, 71–72, 85, 105–6, 157, 175, 237, 239–40, 256, 344, 347
Hoening, Ari, 374
Holder, Terrence, 172
Holiday, Billie, 1, 2, 22, 33, 40, 57, 67, 94, 109, 112–13, 113, 122, 133, 159, 163, 166, 188, 191, 195–96, 210, 247, 251, 252, 260, 269, 278, 311, 336, 346, 352, 366, 379, 403, 416, 421
Holiday, Clarence, 67, 112
Holland, Dave, 7, 181, 190, 262, 318–19, 364, 369, 391
Holland, Peanuts, 306
Holley, Major, 306, 331
Holmes, Charlie, 106, 145, 239
Holmes, Groove, 302
Hope, Bob, 142, 218
Hopkins, Claude, 157
Horn, Paul, 146
Horn, Shirley, 140–41, 242, 334, 370
Horne, Lena, 40, 210–11, 346, 351
Horowitz, Vladimir, 332
Hovman, Claus, 9
Howard, George, 237

Index of Names

Hubbard, Freddie, 109, 110, 132, 229, 276, 286, 292, 309, 329, 386, 411
Hucko, Peanuts, 196–97
Hudson, George, 214
Humair, Daniel, 274
Humphrey, Bobbi, 192
Hunt, Pee Wee, 184
Hunter, Alberta, 121, 353
Hutchenrider, Clarence, 184
Hutcherson, Bobby, 55, 229, 295, 396
Hyams, Marjorie, 263
Hyman, Dick, 77–78, 334

Ingham, Keith, 1, 40–41, 331
Isaacs, Ike, 114

Jackson, Chubby, 209
Jackson, Milt, 53, 139, 143, 173, 229, 236, 239, 246-47, 294
Jackson, Michael, 84
Jackson, Oliver, 331
Jackson, Rudy, 105
Jackson, Willis "Gator," 302, 356, 402
Jacquet, Illinois, 61, 110, 225, 297, 310, 325, 330–31
Jagger, Mick, 4
Jamal, Ahmad, xxiv, 88, 140, 173, 213–14, 258, 334
James, Bob, 192
James, Harry, 85–86, 136, 148, 201, 218, 268, 344, 360, 366, 382, 399
Jarman, Joseph, 33, 52, 227, 237, 272, 298–99, 304
Jarreau, Al, 81–82, 115
Jarrett, Keith, 73, 81, 97, 147, 148–49, 153–54, 189, 241, 254, 258, 261, 318, 329, 363–64, 389
Jaspar, Bobby, 136
Jefferson, Carter, 385–86
Jenkins, Leroy, 47, 227, 299
Jobim, Antonio Carlos, 27–28, 38, 102, 132, 150
John, Elton, xxiv, 192
John Paul II, Pope, 360
Johnson, Bill, 152
Johnson, Budd, 316
Johnson, Bunk, 24, 64, 125, 189, 290, 413, 415–16
Johnson, Dewey, 292
Johnson, Howard, 239
Johnson, J.J., 24–25, 139, 154, 185, 231, 351, 371, 419
Johnson, James P., 36–37, 63, 121, 163, 287, 332, 363, 380–81, 394
Johnson, Lonnie, 44–45
Johnson, Marc, 151
Johnson, Pete, 99, 160, 288
Johnson, Robert, 44

Johnson, Will, 145
Jolson, Al, 207
Jones, Alan, 147
Jones, Elvin, 212, 282, 287, 312, 314, 378, 386, 398
Jones, Hank, 180, 194, 262, 269, 282–83, 344, 378, 419
Jones, Jo, 18, 45, 71, 136, 239, 251, 271, 324–25, 367, 378
Jones, Isham, 158
Jones, Jonah, 180, 336, 378, 414
Jones, LeRoi, 292
Jones, Philly Joe, 22, 59, 96, 101, 228–29, 279
Jones, Quincy, xxv, 84–85, 93, 115, 204, 247, 311, 335, 339, 343, 400, 419
Jones, Ralph "Shrimp," 188
Jones, Thad, 21, 92, 151, 282–83, 305, 326, 338, 392, 410
Joplin, Janice, 121–22, 354
Joplin, Scott, 43, 77
Jordan, Louis, 142, 293, 299
Jordan, Marlon, 312
Jordan, Sheila, 96, 334
Jordan, Stanley, 186
Jordan, Taft, 46

Kahn, Roger Wolfe, 217, 345
Kaminsky, Max, 19, 83, 135, 156, 291–92, 321, 404, 406
Kapp, Jack, 103
Katz, Mickey, 361
Kawaguchi, George, 332
Kay, Connie, 139, 143
Kellaway, Roger, 271
Kelly, Guy, 203
Kelly, Wynton, 22, 75, 109, 192, 213, 388–89
Kemp, Hal, 354
Kennedy, John F., xxiii, 360
Kennedy, Robert, xxiii
Kenton, Stan, 37, 53, 90, 111, 148, 150–51, 158, 177–78, 194, 204–5, 231, 232, 259, 270, 284, 326, 346, 350, 374–75
Keppard, Freddie, 39, 43, 116, 131, 145, 152, 155, 191, 203, 290, 368
Kern, Jerome, 133
Kerr, Brooks, 401
Kessel, Barney, 28, 153, 265, 303, 322, 346
Khan, Chaka, 180
Kikuchi, Masabumi, 153
King, Albert, 245
King, B. B., 246, 250, 402, 415
King Jr., Martin Luther, xxiii
King, Peter, 31
Kirby, John, 19, 76, 233, 310, 324, 420–21

Index of Names

Kirk, Andy, 70, 160, 171–72, 193, 232–33, 283, 310
Kirk, Rahsaan Roland, 4, 21, 153, 204, 255–56, 322, 344, 418
Kirkland, Kenny, 101, 314–15
Kisor, Ryan, 312
Klink, Al, 331
Kluger, Irv, 282
Knepper, Jimmy, 130, 185, 259
Koffman, Moe, 51
Koller, Hans, 153
Komeda, Krzysztof, 224
Konitz, Lee, 90, 97, 154, 173, 177, 182, 205, 259, 274, 284, 289, 356, 409, 419
Krall, Diana, 269, 370–71, 419
Kress, Carl, 10
Krog, Karin, 9
Kropinski, Uwe, 147
Krupa, Gene, 16–17, 18, 34, 47, 54, 127, 135, 151, 174, 198, 216, 218, 260, 270, 291, 325, 336, 368, 379, 413
Kuhn, Steve, 95–96
Kyle, Billy, 420

Lacy, Steve, 167, 194, 237–38, 342, 371
Ladnier, Tommy, 63, 191, 363
LaFaro, Scott, 96–97, 107–8, 195, 241, 324, 387
Laine, Cleo, 348–49
Laine, Papa Jack, 42, 207
Lake, Oliver, 27
Lambert, Dave, 81, 197–98
Lamond, Don, 267–68, 325, 347
Land, Harold, 55–56, 153, 247
Land Jr., Harold, 56
Lang, Eddie, 10, 26, 44, 89, 142, 300–301, 344–45, 377
Lanigan, Jim, xxiv, 83
Lanin, Sam, 83
LaRocca, Nick, 23, 80, 116–17, 206–7
Lateef, Yusef, 232, 206, 300
Lawrence, Elliot, 148, 151
Lawrence, Syd, 196
Laws, Hubert, 411
Laws, Ronnie, 237
Lawson, Hugh, 132
Lawson, Yank, 16, 135, 201
Lee, Jeanne, 32–33
Lee, Peggy, 41, 74, 170–71, 257, 263, 269, 370
Lees, Gene, xxiv, 108, 265, 382
Legrand, Michel, 110, 303
Lennon, John, 101, 125, 137
Leno, Jay, 369
Leppard, Raymond, 337
Levey, Stan, 236

Levy, Lou, 73–74
Lewis, George (cl), 21, 64, 125
Lewis, George (tb), 227–28
Lewis, Jerry Lee, 44
Lewis, John, 92, 142–43, 154, 289, 364, 372, 377, 419
Lewis, Meade "Lux," 160, 287–88
Lewis, Mel, 150–51, 283, 305, 326, 338, 374, 418
Lewis, Ramsey, 395
Lewis, Ted, 42
Liebman, Dave, 192, 237
Lincoln, Abbey, 11, 33, 188, 391
Linton, Charles, 133
Lion, Alfred, 128–29, 222, 381
Liston, Lonnie, 192
Liston, Melba, 126
Lloyd, Charles, 96, 148–49, 258, 318
Lockwood, Didier, 47–48, 315
Lofner, Carol, 407
London, Julie, 170
Lovano, Joe, 97, 151, 373–74, 418–19, 419
Lovano, Tony "Big T," 418
Lunceford, Jimmie, 18, 43, 59, 126, 182–83, 213, 225, 263
Luter, Claude, 221
Lyons, Jimmy, 323
Lyons, Len, 238
Lytell, Jimmy, 390
Lyttelton, Humphrey, 221

Machito, 52–53, 191, 359
Majewski, Henryk, 224
Makowicz, Adam, 224
Malcolm X, 167
Mallory, Eddie, 352, 378
Malone, Russell, 370
Manchester, Melissa, 419
Mancini, Henry, 411
Mandel, Johnny, 209, 400
Mangelsdorff, Albert, 153, 288–89
Mangione, Chuck, 115
Mangione, Gap, 115
Mann, Herbie, 53, 62, 107, 122–23, 206, 251, 295, 344, 384
Manne, Shelly, 284, 308
Manone, Wingy, 49, 291, 368
Mantler, Michael, 323, 384
Marable, Fate, 44, 124, 412–13
Mares, Paul, 42, 86–87
Maria, Tania, 149–50
Marmarosa, Dodo, 346, 348
Marotte, Marshall, 355–56
Marquis, Donald, 416

Index of Names

Marsala, Joe, 34, 131, 368
Marsalis, Branford, 237, 295, 314, 335, 337, 358, 369, 419
Marsalis, Ellis, 296, 312, 337, 358, 389
Marsalis, Wynton, 3, 81, 181, 245, 295, 312, 314, 329, 335, 337–38, 357–58, 369, 389, 391
Marsh, Warne, 90
Marshall, Kaiser, 188–89, 345
Marshall, Wendell, 343–44
Martino, Pat, 101, 186, 302, 303, 415
Mathiesen, Leo, 279
Mathis, Johnny, 82
Matlock, Matty, 135–36, 142, 201
May, Billy, 58, 136, 161, 400
Mayall, John, 48
Mays, Bill, 334
Mays, Lyle, 261
Mazur, Marilyn, 9–10
McCall, Steve, 227, 293
McCartney, Paul, 202
McConnell, Rob, 50–51
McCorkle, Susannah, 1–2, 41
McDuff, Brother Jack, 93, 133, 301–2
McFerrin, Bobby, 80–81, 82, 369
McGhee, Howard, 53, 138–39, 172, 309–10, 394
McGriff, Jimmy, 302
McIntyre, Hal, 232
McKibbon, Al, 230
McKinley, Ray, 54, 196–97
McLaughlin, John, 4–5, 116, 316, 369
McLean, Jackie, 158–59, 206, 235, 322
McPartland, Dick, 83
McPartland, Jimmy, xxiv, 83, 91, 119, 135, 156, 201, 251, 368, 404
McPartland, Marian, 41, 90–91, 126, 146, 231, 251
McRae, Carmen, 3, 113–14, 123, 344, 370, 390
McShann, Jay, 13–14, 173, 275, 409
Medeski, John, 115
Melford, Myra, 299
Mendes, Sergio, 343
Mengelberg, Misha, 181–82, 356
Mercer, Johnny, 133
Merrill, Helen, 170
Metcalf, Louis, 66–67
Metheny, Pat, 101, 246, 250, 261–62, 303, 388, 415
Mezzrow, Mezz, 23, 189, 362–63, 368
Midler, Bette, 419
Mikkelborg, Palle, 9
Miley, James "Bubber," 66–67, 169, 397
Milhaud, Darius, 307–8, 393
Miller, Eddie, 135, 201
Miller, Glenn, 35, 49, 54, 61, 69–70, 85, 135, 174, 196–97, 201, 346, 382, 405

Miller, Marcus, 191–92
Miller, Mulgrew, 396
Millinder, Lucky, 157, 263, 409
Mills, Florence, 352
Mills, Irving, 17–18
Milton, Little, 245
Mince, Johnny, 405
Mine, Kousuke, 333
Mingus, Charles, 21, 90, 104, 129–30, 159, 188, 199, 243, 256, 284, 313, 316, 322, 324, 326, 363, 374, 389, 402
Minor, Dan, 275
Mintzer, Bob, 151, 330
Mitchell, Blue, 55, 286
Mitchell, Joni, 391
Mitchell, Red, 78, 382
Mitchell, Roscoe, 227, 237, 272, 298–99, 304
Mobley, Hank, 223, 235, 281, 286, 329, 389
Mole, Miff, 156, 321, 390, 404
Moncur III, Grachan, 293
Mondello, Toots, 239
Monk, Thelonious, 58, 78, 97, 109, 113, 116, 129, 139, 159, 170, 182, 206, 237–38, 238, 267, 286, 293, 296, 313, 316, 328–29, 333, 356, 372, 394, 396
Monroe, Marilyn, 1
Monroe, Vaughan, 10
Montgomery, Buddy, 75
Montgomery, Monk, 75
Montgomery, Wes, 10, 22, 74–75, 93, 107, 243, 246, 261, 303, 369, 389, 410, 415
Moody, James, 418
Moore, Big Chief Russell, 233
Moore, Brew, 14, 53
Moore, Dudley, 193
Moore, Oscar, 187
Moreira, Airto, 247, 249, 252–53
Morello, Joe, 91, 230–31
Morgan, Lee, 132, 206, 213, 222–23, 235, 279, 281, 309, 356, 386, 395
Morgenstern, Dan, 286, 351
Moriyasu, Shotaro, 333
Morrison, George, 172
Morrow, George, 55
Morton, Jelly Roll, 13, 23, 63, 67, 77, 124, 143, 163, 172, 336, 339–40, 368, 403–4, 407, 413
Mosca, Sal, 90
Moten, Bennie, 12, 13, 30, 45, 160, 249, 271, 274, 277, 278, 325, 366–67, 382
Motian, Paul, 96–97, 108, 195, 419
Mouzon, Alphonse, 253
Moye, Famadou Don, 298

Index of Names

Mulligan, Gerry, 17, 28, 91, 101, 105, 110–11, 148, 151, 154, 159, 178, 254, 259, 269, 334, 350, 356, 357, 411, 415
Murphy, Turk, 103–4, 407–8
Murray, Albert, 160
Murray, David, 27, 56–57, 361
Murray, Don, 89
Murray, Sunny, 32, 153, 226, 273
Musso, Vido, 17

Nance, Ray, 47, 176, 389, 397–98
Nanton, Tricky Sam, 13, 105, 176, 378, 397
Nascimiento, Milton, 150, 249
Nash, Lewis, 173, 419–20
Nash, Ted, 151
Navarro, Fats, 25, 50, 58–59, 65, 139, 159, 172, 199, 220, 223, 263, 281, 294, 309–10, 351
Newborn, Calvin, 402
Newborn, Phineas, 206, 410-2
Newman, David "Fathead," 61–62, 335
Newton, James, 56, 369
Nicholas, Albert, 145
Nichols, Herbie, 182, 371
Nichols, Red, 17, 34, 40, 67, 83, 119, 142, 174, 185, 217, 301, 383
Niehaus, Lennie, 177–78
Niewood, Gerry, 237
Nimmons, Phil, 51
Noble, Ray, 259, 404–5
Noone, Jimmie, 130–31, 145, 233, 413
Noone Jr., Jimmie, 131
Norvo, Red, 40, 77, 103–4, 127, 229, 294, 306, 308, 322
Nussbaum, Adam, 173

Oakley, Helen, *see* Dance, Helen Oakley
O'Day, Anita, 17, 57, 74, 150, 170, 230, 356, 375
Oliver, King, 23, 39, 66, 71, 72, 83, 119, 124, 130, 135, 145, 151–52, 189, 233, 290, 353, 362, 368, 404, 407, 413
Oliver, Sy, 183, 382
Orsted Pedersen, Niels-Henning, 9, 48, 279
Ory, Kid, 23–24, 38, 42, 123–24, 131, 152, 215
Osby, Greg, 237, 304

Page, Hot Lips, 19, 30–31, 45, 63, 67, 166, 275, 283, 312, 366, 367
Page, Patti, 322
Page, Walter, 6, 30, 45–46, 271, 274, 277, 324, 324–25, 367
Panassié, Hugues, 20, 23, 362
Pareles, Jon, 287

Parker, Charlie, 11, 13–14, 19, 24–25, 31, 50, 52, 53, 54, 58–59, 62, 65, 71, 72, 73, 74, 77, 78, 90, 92, 93, 98, 104, 118, 120, 129, 139, 159, 168, 170, 177–78, 190, 193, 194, 195–96, 198, 206, 220–21, 226, 236, 239, 244, 262, 263–64, 268, 274–75, 279, 280–81, 281–82, 283, 284, 292, 293–94, 299, 306, 309–10, 313, 315, 322, 329, 333, 339, 340, 351, 363, 373, 383–84, 394, 396, 408–9, 409, 411, 417
Parker, Evan, 237
Parker, Leo, 22
Parlan, Horace, 21–22
Pascoal, Hermeto, 253
Pass, Joe, 14–15, 265
Pastor, Tony, 14, 161
Pastorius, Jaco, 192, 243, 364, 387–88
Patitucci, Frank, 410–11
Patterson, Don, 302
Paul, Les, 186–87
Pavarotti, Luciano, 418
Payne, Bennie, 336
Payton, Nicholas, 191, 311–12, 335, 358
Peacock, Annette, 364
Peacock, Gary, 149, 153–54, 224, 226, 258, 364
Pederson, Niels, 265
Peplowski, Ken, 330
Pepper, Art, 22, 153, 177, 254, 284–85, 419
Peraza, Armando, 53
Pérez, Danilo, 286
Perón, Juan, 384
Perry, Ray, 306
Persip, Charlie, 7
Person, Houston, 116, 180
Persson, Ake, 185
Peterson, Oscar, 15, 51, 54, 88, 91, 98, 108, 109, 110, 140, 150, 193, 213, 241, 246, 264–65, 333, 334, 335, 401, 419
Petit, Buddy, 131
Pettiford, Oscar, 239, 262, 286, 300, 316–17, 324, 363
Phillips, Esther, 179
Phillips, Flip, 53, 97–98, 209, 267, 297, 321, 331, 418
Picasso, Pablo, 240
Pierce, Nat, 311
Piron, A. J., 12
Pizzarelli, Bucky, 10, 62, 186, 307, 331
Pizzarelli, John, 10–11, 331
Pleasure, King, 136
Polanski, Roman, 224
Pollack, Ben, 15, 40, 61, 69, 83, 85, 119, 135, 174, 201–2, 389
Pollack, Jackson, 53

459

Index of Names

Pomeroy, Herb, 311
Ponty, Jean-Luc, 47–48, 250, 315–16, 342
Pope, Odean, 243
Porter, Cole, 28, 77, 133, 166, 327, 370
Porter, Randy, 147
Porter, Ray, 199
Posten, Joe, 131
Potter, Tommy, 58, 220, 282, 378
Powell, Bud, 25, 31, 65, 109, 129, 159, 168, 190, 213, 235, 239, 262, 263, 267, 280, 286, 293–94, 304, 312–13, 317, 328, 389, 394, 398, 401
Powell, Ginnie, 348
Powell, Mel, 48–49, 197
Powell, Richie, 55, 350, 398
Pozo, Chano, 7–8, 230, 286
Prado, Perez, 191
Presley, Elvis, 44, 68, 383, 415
Price, Leontyne, 414
Price, Sammy, 63
Procope, Russell, 63
Prima, Louis, 42
Procope, Russell, 420
Puente, Tito, 229–30, 359
Pukwana, Dudu, 319
Puma, Joe, 282
Purcell, John, 330
Purim, Flora, 253
Purvis, Jack, 346

Quebec, Ike, 235, 266–67
Quill, Gene, 259
Quinichette, Paul, 49

Rachmaninoff, Sergei, xxiii
Raeburn, Boyd, 194, 269, 347–48, 375
Ragas, Henry, 117
Rainey, Ma, 12, 63, 113, 121, 133–34, 191, 353
Rainey, Tom, 374
Raitt, Bonnie, 354
Ramsey Jr., Frederick, 64, 416
Raney, Doug, 22
Raney, Jimmy, 268
Rava, Enrico, 32, 238, 341
Ravel, Maurice, 131, 200
Redman, Dewey, 273
Redman, Don, 18, 19, 194, 256, 275, 378, 406
Redman, Joshua, 97, 335, 398
Reeves, Dianne, 342–43, 358
Reid, Rufus, 151
Reinhardt, Django, 10, 20, 21, 25–26, 29, 44, 49, 72, 301, 315, 345
Reisman, Leo, 327

Remler, Emily, 302–3
Rey, Alvino, 136, 147, 230
Rich, Buddy, 46, 54, 161, 218, 269, 285, 350, 355, 383
Rich, Fred, 354
Richard, Little, 245, 386
Richardson, Jerome, 300
Richman, Dannie, 173
Riddle, Nelson, 400
Rimsky-Korsakov, Nicolai, 107
Rinker, Al, 141
Rivers, Sam, 305, 310–11, 364, 369
Roach, Max, 11–12, 22, 25, 55, 110, 154, 159, 264, 282, 293, 304, 313, 316, 322, 351, 387, 396
Roberts, Marcus, 358
Robinson, Perry, 356
Robinson, Smokey, 243
Robinson, Sugar Ray, 228
Robison, Willard, 327
Rochester, Cornell, 243
Rodgers, Richard, 333
Rodgers and Hammerstein, 398
Rodgers and Hart, 327
Roditi, Claudio, 287
Rodney, Red, 159, 259
Rogers, Shorty, 268, 375
Roland, Gene, 147, 349–50
Roland, Joe, 282
Rollini, Adrian, 40
Rollins, Sonny, 25, 26, 110, 126, 139, 159, 222, 235, 246, 247, 279, 293–94, 304, 305, 310, 322, 356, 396, 419
Roney, Wallace, 319
Rongetti, Nick, 135, 156
Roppolo, Leon, 86–87
Rosolino, Frank, 17, 177, 185, 232, 270–71, 371
Ross, Annie, 136, 197–98
Ross, Diana, 113
Rouse, Charlie, 22
Rowles, Jimmie, 269–70, 332, 370
Royal, Ernie, 392
Royal, Marshal, 54, 391–92
Rubalcaba, Gonzalo, 359
Rudd, Roswell, 182, 238, 342, 371–72
Rugolo, Pete, 375
Rushing, Jimmy, 45, 271, 276–77, 367
Russell, George, 8, 72–73, 97, 153, 154, 320, 361, 364
Russell, Luis, 12–13, 67, 145, 233
Russell, Pee Wee, 34, 156, 162, 321, 327, 344, 404
Russell, William, 64–65, 204–5, 416
Russo, Bill, 204–5
Ruth, Babe, 301

Index of Names

Rypdal, Terje, 9

St. Cyr, Johnny, 38, 123–24
Salvador, Sal, 230
Sampson, Edgar, 46
Sanborn, David, 192, 245–46, 261, 315, 411
Sanchez, David, 286–87
Sanchez, Poncho, 230
Sanders, Pharoah, 213, 292–93
Sandoval, Arturo, 358–59
Santamaria, Mongo, 8, 190, 230, 359, 386
Santana, Carlos, 229
Sargent, Kenny, 184
Sauter, Eddie, 38, 103, 197, 233
Sax, Adolphe, 375
Sbarbaro, Tony, 117, 206–7, 390
Schifrin, Lalo, 199–200, 230, 383–84
Schilperoort, Peter, 221
Schoepp, Franz, 174, 233
Schuller, Gunther, 257, 364–65, 372
Schuur, Diane, 179
Scobey, Bob, 142, 407–8
Scofield, John, 315, 414–15, 418
Scorcese, Martin, 209
Scott, Raymond, 49, 94
Scott, Ronnie, 31–32, 53, 137, 319, 348, 350
Scott, Shirley, 70, 110, 302
Scott, Stephen, 419
Scott, Tony, 97, 195–96, 322, 361
Sears, Al, 172
Seifert, Zbigniew, 47, 224, 315
Severinson, Doc, 346
Shank, Bud, 147, 153, 177
Shankar, Ravi, 226, 289
Shapiro, Artie, 162
Shapiro, Nat, 188
Shavers, Charlie, 34, 238, 310, 346, 420–21
Shaw, Artie, 16, 23, 30, 34, 54, 59, 94, 143, 147–48, 158, 161–62, 165–66, 239, 268, 282, 292, 338, 361, 382
Shaw, Woody, 109, 285–86, 309, 386
Shearing, George, 15, 41, 54, 58, 70, 180, 193, 230, 262–63, 264–65, 282–83
Shepp, Archie, 22, 32, 166–67, 206, 213, 273, 292–93, 311, 322, 374
Shields, Eddie, 87
Shields, Larry, 87, 117, 206–7
Shihab, Sahib, 330
Shore, Dinah, 360
Shorter, Frank, 131–32
Shorter, Wayne, 9, 22, 219, 223, 237, 253, 261, 275–76, 286, 319, 329, 411
Silva, Alan, 323

Silver, Horace, 54, 101, 132, 139, 190, 276, 281–82, 285–86, 329–30, 389, 395
Simone, Nina, 391
Simon, George T., 48, 196
Simon, Paul, 101, 115, 246
Sims, Zoot, 10, 113, 147, 209, 251, 268, 269, 279, 330, 349–50, 418
Sinatra, Frank, 40, 74, 85, 104, 170, 186, 192, 202, 251, 252, 295–96, 338, 370, 382, 399–400
Singleton, Zutty, 16, 48, 336
Sissle, Noble, 208, 210, 233
Slack, Freddie, 197
Sloane, Carol, 334
Smith, Bessie, 12, 37, 63, 67, 113, 121–22, 155, 169, 191, 208, 353–54, 403
Smith, Bill, 307–8
Smith, Buster, 45, 62, 274–75
Smith, Charles Edward, 64
Smith, Clara, 121, 191
Smith, Jabbo, 203
Smith, Jimmy, 101, 109, 110, 115–16, 213, 247, 302, 394–95
Smith, Joe "Fox," 34, 121, 188, 207–8, 406
Smith, Johnny, 231
Smith, Leo, 227
Smith, Lonnie Liston, 192
Smith, Lovie, 63
Smith, Mamie, 121, 124, 169–70, 208, 233, 381
Smith, Marvin "Smitty," 173, 369
Smith, Stuff, 29, 47, 315, 336, 344
Smith, Willie, 183
Smith, Willie "The Lion," 66, 94, 169, 240, 332, 380–81
Smulyan, Gary, 151
Snow, Valaida, 126, 178–79
Snowden, Elmer, 18, 19, 105, 175, 401
Solal, Martial, 273–74
Sousa, John Phillip, 62, 207, 217
South, Eddie, 47, 203
Spanier, Muggsy, 42, 49, 201, 291, 368, 407
Spellman, A. B., 292
Spencer, O'Neil, 420
Spivak, Charlie, 201
Spivey, Victoria, 353–54
Springsteen, Bruce, 260, 403
Stacy, Jess, 162, 259–60, 291, 327
Stafford, Jo, 382
Stańko, Tomasz, 223–24
Starr, Kay, 170, 301, 346
Staton, Dakota, 179–80
Steely Dan, 115
Stein, Johnny, 117
Stern, Mike, 261, 415

Index of Names

Stevens, Ashton, 164
Steward, Herbie, 147–48, 177, 209, 349
Stewart, Billy, 298
Stewart, Buddy, 198
Stewart, Rex, 71, 420
Stewart, Sandy, 334
Stewart, Slam, 95, 306–7
Sting, 314–15, 337, 419
Stitt, Sonny, 21, 50, 120, 159, 194, 264, 418, 419
Stone, George Lawrence, 188, 230
Stone, Lew, 76
Stone, Sly, 318
Stowell, John, 146
Stravinsky, Igor, 107, 157, 347
Strayhorn, Billy, 38, 132, 176, 240, 384–85
Streisand, Barbra, xxiii, 202
Stryker, Dave, 116
Stubbs, Ken, 319
Sudhalter, Dick, 95
Suliemann, Idrees, 21
Sullivan, Ed, xxiii
Sullivan, Ira, 387
Sullivan, Joe, 157, 345
Sullivan, Maxine, 41, 259, 420–21
Sun Ra, 101, 164–65, 213, 293, 323, 326, 364
Sunshine, Monty, 125
Surman, John, 31
Sweatman, Wilbur, 42–43, 137
Swope, Earl, 268, 347

Tate, Buddy, 61, 172, 267, 297, 331
Tate, Erskine, 127, 233, 368
Tate, Grady, 314, 419
Tatum, Art, 77, 88, 89, 94, 238, 250, 264, 273, 275, 280, 283, 306, 313, 325, 331–32, 381, 401, 418
Taylor, Art, 146
Taylor, Billy (b) 336,
Taylor, Billy (p), 238–39, 306, 324, 336, 378
Taylor, Cecil, 32, 77, 90, 165, 167, 224, 226, 235, 238, 305, 311, 322, 356, 371–72
Taylor, Creed, 93, 102, 110
Taylor, James, 101, 246
Tchaikovsky, Pyotr Ilyich, xxiii
Tchikai, John, 167, 292, 322
Teagarden, Jack, 18, 35, 37, 40, 69, 135, 201, 222, 260, 268, 322, 336, 344, 345
Teal, Larry, 132
Tee, Richard, 115
Terrell, Pha, 172
Terry, Clark, 62, 173, 321, 334, 343, 344, 346
Teschemacher, Frank, xxiv, 5, 82–83, 174, 291, 368
Thigpen, Ed, 265

Thomas, George, 306
Thomas, George "Fathead," 208
Thompson, Lucky, 50, 194–95, 283, 348
Thompson, Malachi, 386
Thornhill, Claude, 111, 148, 151, 154–55, 258–59, 405
Threadgill, Henry, 51–52, 227, 391
Timmons, Bobby, 22, 109, 356, 395
Tio Jr., Lorenzo, 72, 131
Tizol, Juan, 52, 175
Tjader, Cal, 229–30, 308, 359
Tolstoy, Leo, 308
Tormé, Mel, 51, 57, 263
Tough, Dave, 19, 135, 209, 268, 368, 413
Towers, Jack, 397
Tristano, Lennie, 7, 89–90, 97, 204–5, 289
Trumbauer, Frank, 40, 60–61, 89, 100, 119, 142, 345
Tucker, Sophie, 169, 352
Tull, Jethro, 318
Turner, Big Joe, 159–60, 180
Turrentine, Stanley, 62, 109–10, 247, 335, 343
Turrentine, Tommy, 110
Tyner, McCoy, 95, 101, 116, 189, 206, 212–13, 226, 241, 287, 313, 398–99, 410

Ulanov, Barry, 90
Underwood, Ian, 32
Urbaniak, Michal, 47–48, 224, 314

Vaché, Warren, 297, 321, 331
Valdés, Chucho, 335, 359
Vanderbilt, Cornelius, 402
Vandross, Luther, 192
Van Eps, George, 10, 405
Van Gelder, Rudy, xxvi, 381–82
"Van" Cliburn, Harvey Lavan, xxiii
Vasconcelos, Naná, 249–50
Vaughan, Sarah, 15, 22, 32, 50, 57, 58, 74, 109, 113–14, 120, 150, 161, 170, 186, 195, 220, 257, 263, 357, 390, 417
Veal, Reginald, 357–58
Veasley, Gerald, 242–43
Ventura, Charlie, 332
Venuti, Joe, 26, 29, 47, 89, 99, 119, 300–301, 345
Vesala, Edward, 224
Vick, Harold, 302
Villa-Lobos, Heitor, 250
Vinson, Eddie "Cleanhead," 299, 389
Vitous, Miroslav, 190, 253, 276, 314
Vitro, Roseanna, 373

Walcott, Collin, 250, 373
Waldron, Mal, 33

Index of Names

Wall, Dan, 115
Wallace, Sippie, 121, 353–54
Waller, Fats, 37, 40, 77, 94, 163–64, 210, 238, 262, 271, 283, 287, 301, 306, 327, 332, 370, 380–81, 395, 403
Wallington, George, 159, 316
Walrath, Jack, 386
Walton, Cedar, 62, 386
Wanderley, Walter, 103
Waring, Fred, 186
Warlop, Michel, 47
Warwick, Dionne, 386
Washington, Dinah, 22, 57–58, 170, 179–80, 219, 279, 389
Washington Jr., Grover, 101, 192, 237, 243
Washington, Kenny, 172–73, 192, 334
Washington, Peter, 173, 334, 420
Washington, Reggie, 172
Watanabe, Kazumi, 332–33
Watanabe, Sadao, 115, 153, 333
Waters, Ethel, 12, 37, 40, 208, 210, 327, 351–52, 378
Waters, Muddy, 415
Watkins, Doug, 281
Watrous, Bill, 185–86, 231–32
Watson, Bobby, 335
Watters, Lu, 404, 407–8
Watts, Jeff "Tain," 173
Wayne, Francis, 346
Webb, Chick, 16, 40, 46–47, 52, 71, 133, 191, 240, 325, 409, 420
Weber, Eberhard, 387
Webster, Ben, 1, 98, 98–99, 126, 172, 195, 225, 239, 248, 257, 269, 297, 319, 330, 367, 414
Webster, Freddie, xxvi, 263–64
Weidenmuller, Johannes, 374
Wein, George, 228, 268, 274, 297, 320–21, 401
Welk, Lawrence, 215
Wells, Dicky, 391, 394
Wells, Henry, 183
Welsh, Alex, 221–22
Werner, Kenny, 151, 373–74, 418
Wess, Frank, 22, 239, 334, 392
Weston, Paul, 136
Wettling, George, 152, 162, 291, 368
Wheeler, Kenny, 31, 181
Whetsol, Arthur, 67, 175
Whitaker, Forrest, 178
White, Lenny, 343
Whitehead, Tim, 319
Whiteman, Paul, 61, 66, 67, 80, 89, 99–100, 103, 141–42, 217, 258–59, 267, 301, 327, 345, 354, 383
Wickman, Putte, 408

Wilber, Bob, 10, 237
Wilcox, Ed, 183
Wilder, Alec, 320
Wiley, Lee, 40, 260, 327–28, 352
Willard, Hal, 6
Williams, Clarence, 353
Williams, Cootie, 19, 40, 70, 71, 161, 313, 397
Williams, Joe, 51
Williams, John, 349
Williams, Martin, 27, 139, 372
Williams, Mary Lou, 35, 126, 172, 193, 248, 344
Williams, Pauline Braddy, *see* Braddy, Pauline
Williams, Tony, 48, 133, 253, 258, 276, 311, 319, 337
Willliamson, Don, 334
Wilson, Cassandra, 390–91
Wilson, Dick, 172
Wilson, Gerald, 55, 151, 247
Wilson, Nancy, 31, 57–58, 74, 179, 263, 303, 387, 419
Wilson, Shadow, 329
Wilson, Teddy, 19, 40, 48, 77, 85, 94, 127, 157, 191, 210, 236, 238, 257, 260, 262, 264, 283, 322, 325, 346, 366, 379–80, 403
Winburn, Anna Mae, 126
Winding, Kai, 25, 185, 232, 251
Winter, Johnny, 48, 303
Wolff, Francis, 129
Wonder, Stevie, 115, 246
Wood Sr., Roy, 258
Wooding, Sam, 191
Woods, Phil, 41, 188, 204, 230–31, 334, 382
Workman, Reggie, 33, 205–6
Wright, Gene, 230
Wright, Leo, 302
Wylie, Austin, 15
Wynn, Albert, 191

Yancey, Jimmy, 288
Yanow, Scott, 350
Young, Lee, 87, 284
Young, Lester, 19, 37, 45–46, 50, 63, 65, 67, 74, 77, 90, 94–95, 98, 99, 112, 113, 119, 123, 163, 172, 188, 196, 204, 244, 248–49, 267, 269, 271, 274, 277–78, 279, 286, 297–98, 306, 316, 325, 330, 349, 366, 367, 375–76, 378, 389, 391, 403, 413
Young, Victor, 390

Zappa, Frank, 48, 315–16, 319
Zawinul, Joe, 219–20, 243, 253, 261, 276, 300
Zoller, Attila, 153
Zorn, John, 357
Zwerin, Mike, 40, 224

www.ingramcontent.com/pod-product-compliance
Lightning Source LLC
Chambersburg PA
CBHW080531300426
44111CB00017B/2680